Karnataka's Rich Heritage
ART AND ARCHITECTURE

—··◆··—

From Prehistoric Times to the Hoysala Period

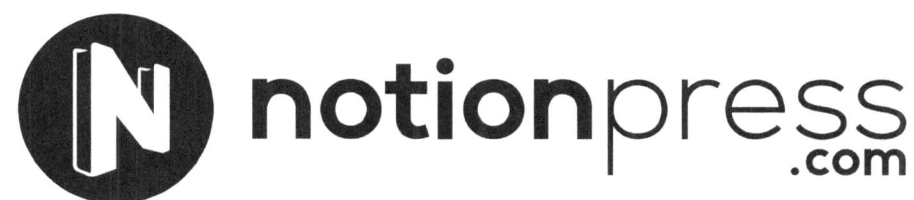

Karnataka's Rich Heritage
ART AND ARCHITECTURE

---●---

From Prehistoric Times to the Hoysala Period

LALIT CHUGH

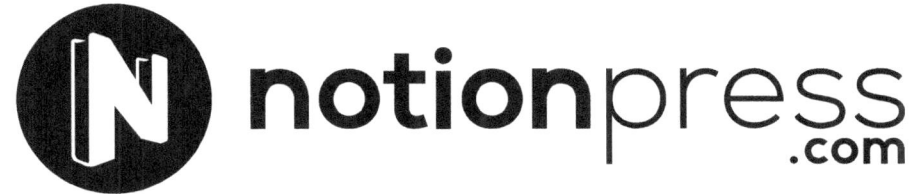

Notion Press

Old No. 38, New No. 6

McNichols Road, Chetpet

Chennai - 600 031

First Published by Notion Press 2016

Copyright © Lalit Chugh 2016

All Rights Reserved.

ISBN 978-93-5206-824-1

This book has been published in good faith that the work of the author is original. All efforts have been taken to make the material error-free. However, the author and the publisher disclaim the responsibility.

No part of the publication may be reproduced, stored in a retrieval system or transmitted in any form, electronic, mechanical or otherwise without prior permission of the publishers.

Lalit Chugh

Striving to explore and report on India's rich heritage.

While making sure that the achievements of our ancient and medieval architects and artists reach wider audiences, we will urge our readers to help in their promotion and preservation of heritage.

Published by:

Lalit Chugh
B-305, Prism sovereign Apartments,
4th Main, 12th Cross, BEML Layout,
Brookfield,
Bengaluru-560066
lalitchugh@hotmail.com
Phones: 9481908716, 9820159114, 080-25398602

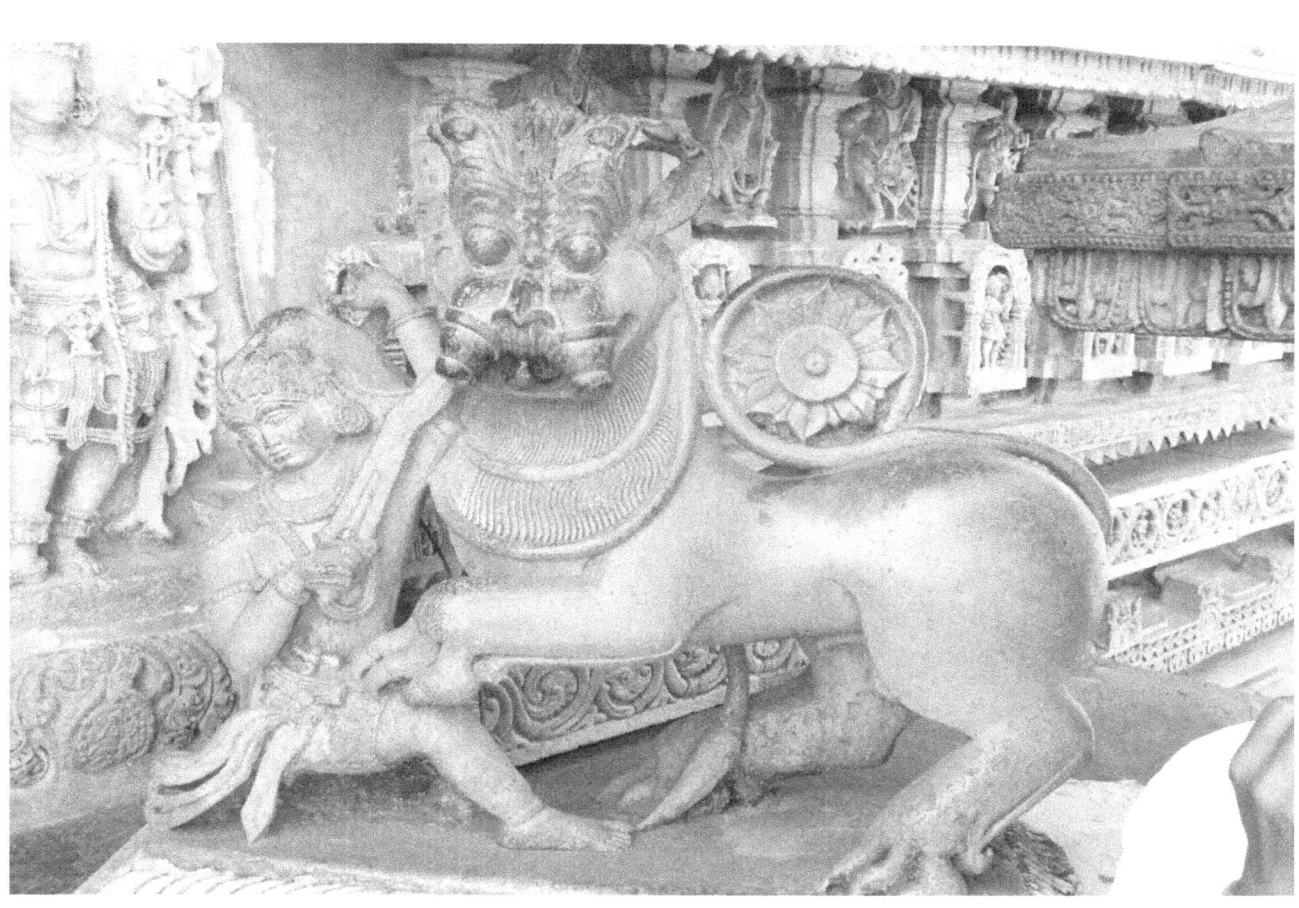

Dedicated to

My Parents and Teachers who instilled in me the Spirit of Pursuing Truth at all costs.

CONTENTS

	Preface	*xi*
1.	**INTRODUCTION**	1
	1.1 Heritage Defined	1
	1.2 Karnataka: Antiquity, Etymology, Geography and Language	2
	1.3 Purpose and Objectives of This Study	11
2.	**KARNATAKA: HISTORY AND RELIGIOUS DEVELOPMENTS**	13
	2.1 Brief History of Karnataka	13
	2.2 Growth of Religions and Various Sects	24
	2.3 Various Saints Who Influenced Karnataka's History and Culture	30
3.	**KARNATAKA'S HERITAGE AND EPIGRAPHICAL RECORDS**	39
	3.1 Karnataka's Heritage Preservation Institutions	39
	3.2 Karnataka Inscriptions	41
	3.3 Memorial Stones	54
4.	**UNDERSTANDING AND APPRECIATING TEMPLES OF KARNATAKA**	63
	4.1 Canonical Literature on Temple Architecture and Sculpture	63
	4.2 Development of Temple Architecture in Karnataka	66
	4.3 Simple Temple Architecture: Ground Plan and Different Components	70
	4.4 Vastu and Temple Designing	87
	4.5 Temples Dedicated to Different Gods and Goddesses	91
	4.6 Description of Iconography of Different Gods	102
	4.7 Patrons and Motivation for Building Temples	116
	4.8 Types of Temples in Karnataka	120
	4.9 Temple as Centres of Learning, Education and Political Institutions	126
	4.10 Temple Construction Technology and Organisation	131
	4.11 Use of Science, Mathematics, Geometry and Astronomy in Temple Design	138
5.	**HISTORY OF ART ARCHITECTURE IN KARNATAKA**	147
	5.1 Karnataka History of Architecture-Prehistoric	147
	5.2 Karnataka History of Architecture-Buddhist Influence	150
	5.3 Karnataka History of Architecture-Jaina Influence	154
	5.4 Karnataka History of Architecture-The Hindu Monuments	172
	5.5 Karnataka History of Scuplture	197
	5.6 Some of the Great Architects and Sculptors of Karnataka	214
6.	**IMPORTANT HERITAGE CIRCUITS**	217
	6.1 Banavasi and Around	217
	6.2 Gadag and Lakkundi School of Architecture	231
	6.3 The Tungabhadra Circuit	241

6.4	The Cauveri Circuit	246
6.5	The Malaprabha Valley Circuit	255
6.6	The Hoysala Circuit	271
6.7	In and Around Bengaluru	282

Lists of Temples Built During the Times of Different Dynasties   291
Glossary of Terms   307
References   313
Pictures for Chapters 5 and 6   323
Pictures for Chapter 6   345

PREFACE

STANDING in front of various Hoysala temples as a tourist in 2011, I was overawed by the creativity of the artists of those times. The symmetry and the extensive experimentation with geometrical designs; the architects carried out mesmerized me. I started wondering what kind of professional skills and what kind of management skills went into creating such highly coordinated construction and ornamentation of the constructed structure. I was involved in managing large sized projects in 2011 and a very large number of them suffered from time-overruns, cost overruns, design problems and quality issues despite the availability of high-end technology. All our computer based designing and project management would fail us at times. But what I was looking at were monuments built nearly a thousand years ago or more. What kind of project management did they have? What kind of manuals of instructions they had that the entire team of workers worked to achieve symmetry and beauty with the most ordinary technological tools at their command? I needed answers to these and many more questions and my mind was made up that I need to pursue the subject with all earnestness.

This pursuit involved extensive travel and study of the available literature on related subjects. I had to begin somewhere. Having not been trained in any related fields was proving to be daunting. I thought I should just work on the construction methodology and the canonical literature that guided the project execution of those times. As I started working it turned out that it will be an exercise in futility if I did not learn about the history of Art and Architecture in Karnataka. Not much was available by way of any comprehensive published work on their history and how these progressed over time. Though there is voluminous information available on Hoysala and Chalukya architecture, information about the monuments built during the times of other dynasties is minimal. I needed to piece together various fragments of information to reach somewhere. Moreover the changing religious preferences between the 3rd century BCE and 10th century CE and the existence of numerous sects in the religions had a very strong influence on Art and Architecture. Learning about Karnataka's history and how religious movements affected it became an essential part of my study.

Language was another handicap. I had to learn both Sanskrit and Kannada. I joined Sanskrit classes at Samskrita Bharati and simultaneously started learning Kannada from the self-learning books. Knowledge of Sanskrit was important to relate with the canonical literature and knowledge of Kannada helped me communicate with people in the field. Though I cannot speak Kannada well, I can understand if someone is explaining something to me. Most of the people who acted as my guides at various sites were Kannada speaking persons. My driver Mohan Kumar remained a valuable asset as he knows English, Hindi, Kannada, Telugu and Tamil. After a few visits to sites he had even mastered the questions that I may need to ask in the field!

Google maps come in handy when you go out looking for a village or taluk but locating an abandoned monument is another matter. I had to seek assistance from all kind of local resources. Among the people who helped in my search were postmen, policemen, school teachers, autorickshaw drivers, small shopkeepers, retired persons, revenue department officials and local farmers. Many of the monuments are not located within the precincts of villages. I needed someone to accompany me to the site which may be deep inside a forest or on top of a hill. Local people were ever willing to guide me to the right spot. Without their help it would never have been possible for me to finish my tasks.

One needs to get in touch with people who know the subject before one ventures out. A friend of over forty years, Jayanand Govindraj introduced me to three of his friends involved in temple photography and exploration. We exchanged emails and I got a direction that I needed to follow. Since one of them had conducted photography missions to temples in Karnataka, his tips came in handy. It is easier to understand Temple Architecture if you have a few books on the subject and you visit temples taking photographs of various parts and relate these with the contents of the books. Most Hindu (as also Jaina) Temples in Karnataka conform to the typical dynastic idiom and canonical literature on the subject. Understanding sculpture; however is different altogether. Firstly, not much by way of literature is available and secondly there are several Schools of Art about which you need to have some knowledge. Aparna Suresh who has studied Fine Arts gave me the initial insights into temple sculpture. She not only knows art and sculpture but is well versed in the *agamic* practices that go into temple construction and consecration. Discussions with her proved valuable for me. I have had a lot of fruitful and informative discussions with Mr. S Panchapakesan, Mr. Mohan Shenoy, Mr. Anil Kale, Mr. Jayadeva and Ms. Vidya Rao generally about temples, sects and rituals. My wife Shyamala deserves a special mention. Not only did she remain with me all these three years as support, she also visited several sites facing all the hardships of long distance travel through unfamiliar territories. She helped me in framing all the right questions that the book should answer.

The timeline for my study begins with pre-historic times, more particularly around 3500 BCE and ends at the middle of the fourteenth century CE, till the time Hoysalas were in command in larger parts of what is now known as Karnataka. Since the focus is on Art and Architecture, much of this work is related with sands, stones and sculpture. The earliest constructed structures and pieces of art relate to the times when use of bricks, terracotta and stones commenced. So much of what is contained in the book pertains to Mauryan and post-Mauryan periods though some pre-historic sites of primitive artistic, architectural and metallurgical significance have been studied.

Temples constitute the largest part of the monuments I studied. Since till the fourteenth century, Hinduism, Jainism and Buddhism were the dominant religions practiced in India, influence of these three religions on Art and Architecture constitutes a wide spectrum of this book. Canonical literature on Temple Architecture and Iconography has been written since 3rd century BCE. It includes not only ritualistic directions but also guidance involving use of sacred geometry. As I started understanding different types of Temple Architecture, I realized that extensive use of fractal geometry, mathematics, astronomy and geology was made in their design and construction. I searched for research publications pertaining to these areas related to Temple Architecture and found that a lot of work is continuing on this in various institutes in India and abroad. I have listed various publications I referred to in the List of References. Sections in Chapter 4 of the book are devoted to the canonical literature and the scientific temper that went into Temple Architecture.

Thanks to Information Technology, it is easy to get access to even the most obscure and rare publications from the archives. There are numerous organizations and institutions which provide downloading facilities for such rare works from their archives on payment of nominal fees or membership charges. This shortens substantially the time it takes to get hold of a publication and to take down notes from it. All that trouble of having to go searching for a library that stores such publication is obviated as a search on the linked networks of research institutions takes you directly to the site where the information is available. Had this facility of digital search not been available, it would have taken me several years more to write the book. A list of some of such sites is furnished at the end.

If I were to describe the book in one word, I'll call it a collage! So many scholars and professional researchers of repute have been working in related areas since the first quarter of the nineteenth century. I have learnt and taken down notes from all these works to put together in one volume. I am grateful to all these great men and women for having given me an insight into this area. I have listed them all inside the book and the List of References at the end.

To me it appears that Chapter 4 of the book will turn out to be the most useful for a layperson as it details most of the information about Temple layout, planning, components and architecture in simple and easily understandable terms, illustrated with photographs. History of Art and Architecture in Karnataka is detailed in chapter 5 describing separately the influence of Buddhism, Jainism and Hinduism on it. Chapter 6 details seven Heritage Circuits of importance in Karnataka. That should help interested persons to plan their Heritage tours. While photographs having direct contextual bearing are inserted in the main body of the book, photographs of general interest and those relating to the Heritage Circuits have been inserted separately as Plates at the end in Chapter 10. On the whole I feel that this book should be a good companion for visitors to the monuments in Karnataka.

I will be failing in my duty if I do not thank the various people who helped me in the field. The people who gave me their names and phone numbers are listed here. Mr. Hyder, Ayurvedic Practioner Hunukunda (9902961501), Mr. SR Anatharaman, Retired Postman Salgame. Mr. Venkatesh, Revenue Department Tadimalangi (9141554591), Mr. Anjani, ASI (9481823543), Mr. Sripal Jain and Mrs. Anant Lakshmi, Gommatagiri (9980614139), Mr. Vijay DS, Archaka and Mr. Someswar, Librarian Dharmapura (9880693008 and 9008383643), Mr. Srinivas, Anne Kanambi (9448592041), Mr. Jaya, Sindhaghatta (9901954544), Mr. Chamanayaka, ASI Alur (8749042835), Mr. Satyanarayana, ASI (9481207229), Mr. Ambreesh, ASI Bagali (7259804122), Mr. DB Kulkarni, Ingaleshwar (9980423325), Mr. Veerabhadra Gowda B Patil (9916112384) and Mr. Mohammad Hassan at Ron, Mr. Kiran Avadhani, Mathuru (9448839873), Mr. Lakshman Rao, Aralaguppe (7353272070), Mr. TG Ananth Rao, Ranganathaswamy Halebid (9448742370), Mr. Ashok Ishvarappa Jyoti, Halasi (8970204929), Mr. Prashant Chipragathi, Devarunda (9448470630), Mr. Revanna Kumar Librarian, Anur (8277691779), Mr. Satyanarayana, Marehalli (9964291582), Mr. Pampapathi, Hirebenkal (8151896076), Mr. Prashant Bharadwaj, Belavadi (9035041518), and Mrs. Pushpa Reddy, Kolar are the people who helped me in locating the sites and giving details about these. There are still many more who didn't wish to disclose their names and phone numbers for inclusion in a publication.

I MUST end this Note with an apology. I am not formally trained in any of the fields this book required me to comment on. I am not trained as a Historian or an Archaeologist or an Architect, or an Anthropologist or in the field of Fine Arts, yet I took the audacious decision to write a book on Art and Architecture. I know I may not have succeeded in creating a work commanding great appreciation but I am sure I have tried to explore as many dimensions relating to Karnataka's Art and Architecture as was possible within a span of three years. To that extent this work may have remained wanting in professional finesse expected in a book of this kind.

Lalit Chugh

1

INTRODUCTION

1.1 HERITAGE DEFINED

The definition and understanding of the term 'heritage' have greatly changed over decades. In addition to physical artifacts, both fixed and movable, the concept of cultural heritage today includes intangible legacies of a group of people or region. The UNESCO Charter formulated in Venice in 1964 provided guidelines for the preservation and conservation of heritage and defined it in terms of 'historic monuments.' The understanding was widened in 1965 by ICOMOS (International Council on Monuments and Sites) who defined it as 'monuments' and 'sites' and by UNESCO in 1968 calling it 'cultural property' more generally to include movable objects. In 1972 the two institutions reconciled their terminologies and agreed to include gardens, landscape and environment, more generally under the guiding principles of protection and preservation. This description was further expanded in 2003 when UNESCO published guidelines for the safeguarding of intangible cultural heritage.

Exploration and excavation at sites of archaeological and historical significance started in Karnataka over 150 years ago. Extensive field work was carried out and numerous monuments were studied from various angles. But the largest amount of work was done on temple architecture and temple building styles. It wouldn't have been possible if the inscriptions too weren't simultaneously studied, translated and their contents understood both from historical perspective and the social and economic standards of those days. Religion played a very big role in all matters social and political those days. Hence studies of religious and literary works of those days too became important. Huge amount of researched information is now available for anyone to understand and appreciate Karnataka's rich heritage.

Various scholars initiated these studies during the pre-independence era results of which were published in numerous journals, books and chronicles. A few names that come to mind from those times like BL Rice, Henry Cousens, James Furgusson, Percy Brown and others are still quoted as authorities on the subject. Indians too did tremendous amount of work in this field and their works found appreciation at various international platforms. Prominent among them are R Narasimhachar, Dr. MH Krishna, Dr. MS Nagaraja Rao, S Settar, Suryakant Kamat, Dr. KA Nilakanta Sastri, Varija R Bolar, KV Ramesh and many others.

Most of the researched articles were compiled in journals and the Mysore Archaeological Report (MAR) published every year stood out distinctively as a source of authentic information. Now that digitization has overtaken the printed matter, most past books and journals have been digitized and are available on archives. Archaeological Survey of India (ASI) was established by archaeologist Alexander Cunningham in 1856. ASI is an institution that to this day remains responsible for documentation, restoration and protection of monuments across India. ASI also publishes well researched articles in its annual reports titled Indian Archeology (year) A Review. Even these reports have been digitized for past years and are available on archives.

Numerous monographs got published of which many had specialized contents. Many of the books that are referred to were published during the pre-independence era. Many among these are available today only in the digitized form.

All these publications and Reports helped disseminate information about the heritage among wider class of people. However, a very large amount of knowledge so created was written and talked about by specialists and experts in their respective fields. As such lay person either did not have access to it or was not able to comprehend it easily. The position remains almost same even today as all archaeological research remains in the hands of the government or its appointed agencies. Government agencies invariably have a typical style of producing reports which may interest those who are connected with government work but commoners may not find them interesting with the result that most attempts at creating awareness about heritage do not yield the desired results. However, governments do invest a large amount of effort in this direction.

1.2 KARNATAKA: ANTIQUITY, ETYMOLOGY, GEOGRAPHY AND LANGUAGE

Karnataka's relationship with Mythology: According to a Hindu legend, the sage Parasurama beheaded Renuka's head with an axe on the orders of his father, the great sage Jamadagni. Parasurama tried to wash the blood stains off the axe by dipping it in various rivers, but a sesame-sized blood stain remained on his axe, until he dipped his axe in the Tunga River near Tirthahalli. This place is now called *Parasurama Tirtha* (or *Rama Tirtha*). Near *Rama Tirtha*, there is a stone *Mandapa* called *Rama Mandapa*. This legend has made Tirthahalli a holy place for Hindus and there is a belief among them that a dip in the river Tunga will cure one of all sins.

Tirthahalli has a rich archaeological history with Neolithic sites uncovered in Kundadri Hills near Agumbe and portholed burial chambers found at Arehalli near Tirthahalli. Some legends relate Tirthahalli with Ramayana too. Rameswara Temple is the main Hindu temple of Tirthahalli. It is near *Parasurama Tirtha*. The sanctum sanctorum of the temple has a Lingam which is said to have been installed by sage Parasurama himself. The day when Parasurama cleansed his axe to remove the sesame-sized blood stain, the New Moon Day of the month of Margashirsha in the Hindu calendar, is termed *Yellu Amavasya*. *Yellu* meaning sesame and *Amavasya* meaning New Moon day, and Tirthahalli has an annual festival, *Yellu Amavasya Jatre* to celebrate this.

Kishkindha is believed to be the monkey kingdom of the Vanara King Sugriva, the younger brother of Vali of Ramayana times. This was the kingdom where Sugriva ruled with assistance of his friend, Hanuman after he was installed as the chief by Rama. This kingdom is identified to be the region around the Tungabhadra river (then known as Pampa Sagar) near Hampi and is located in Koppal district of Karnataka. The mountain called Rishimukha near the river where Sugriva lived with Hanuman, during the period of his exile also is located here only.

During the time of Ramayana the whole region was dense forest called Dandaka Forest extending from Vindhyas to the South Indian peninsula. Hence this kingdom was considered to be the kingdom of *Vanaras* which in Sanskrit means forest beings (*vana* and *nara*). Hanuman was the best-known figure among the Vanaras. He was the general of the Vanara king Sugriva who was installed on the throne of Kishkindha by Rama. Sugriva's elder brother Vali was the former king of the Vanaras. He was slain by Rama.

Later during the Mahabharata times, one of the Pandavas, Sahadeva was said to have visited this kingdom during his southern military campaign to collect tribute for Yudhisthira's Rajasuya sacrifice. Sahadeva defeated the Pulindas, the hero and then marched southward. And then he beheld the celebrated caves of Kishkindha and in that region and fought for seven days with the Vanara kings Mainda and Dwivida. Those illustrious kings however, contributed to the mission of the king Yudhishthira.

The Tungabhadra and its surrounding hills and lakes are linked with ancient legends described in the *sthalapurana*, a compendium of local myths associated with Virupaksha temple at Hampi. This identifies the goddess Pampa with the village of Hampi, known as Pampakshetra in ancient times. Described as the 'mind born' daughter of Brahma, the creator god, Pampa diligently performed penances on Hemakuta hill above the Tungabhadra river, thereby attracting attention of Siva. The god was seated in meditation nearby, having destroyed Kama, the god of love who had come to distract Siva in his meditation. Siva eventually betrothed himself to Pampa and married her and he came to be known as 'Lord of Pampa' or Pampapati.

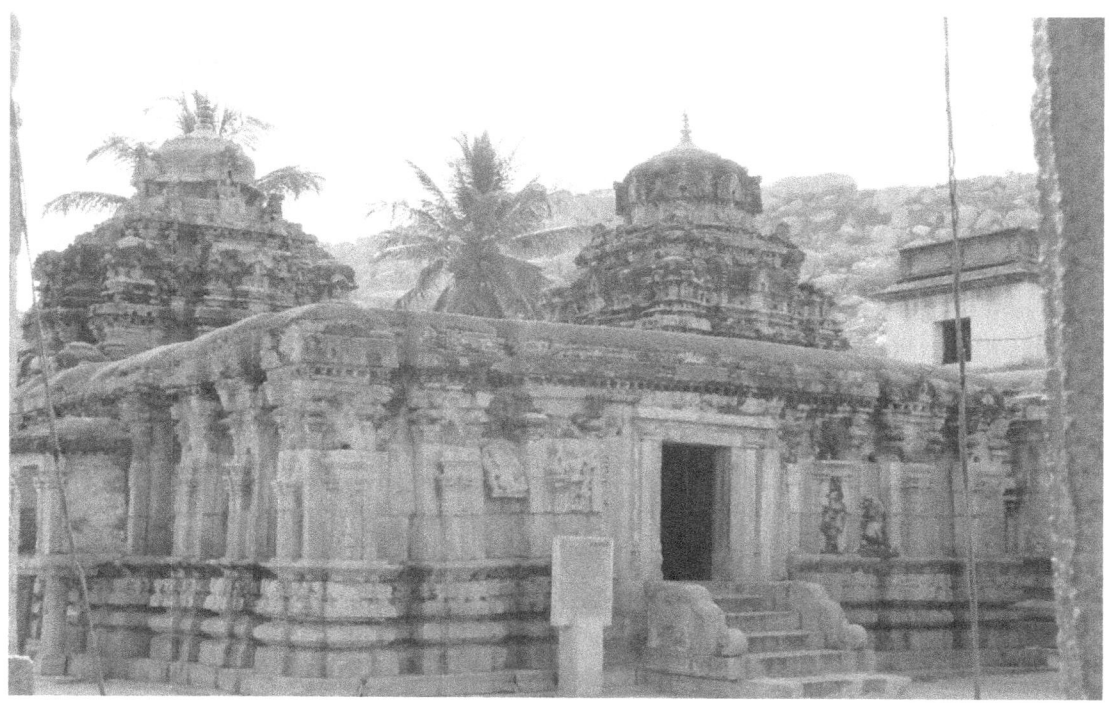

Ramalinga Group of Temples, Avani

Avani is famous for the temple dedicated to Sita situated on a hill. This temple is one of the few temples dedicated to Sitadevi in India. This hill also has the temple of Hari Shresta Adi Jambava, who gave Shyamanthak jewel to Lord Krishna. On the same occasion Krishna married Jambavati the daughter of Adi Jambav. It is also known as the Gaya of the south and has ancient temples known as the Ramalingeswara, Lakshmaneswara, Bharateswara and Shatrugneswara, dating back to the period of the Nolamba Dynasty. It is believed that Sitadevi gave birth to her twin children Lava-Kusha here.

The room in which Sita gave birth to her twin-sons is believed to exist there on the hill. This village is believed to be battleground between Rama and his sons Lava and Kusha when they held Rama's horse hostage. When Sri Narasimha Bharati IV of the Sringeri Sharada Peetham was on his *sancharas*, he camped here for a few days. During his stay here, in Avani, he found an idol of Goddess Sharada, in standing posture flanked by Srimajjagadguru Shankaracharya and the Sri Chakra. He consecrated this idol here and established a new *matha* and installed one of his *sisyas* as the head of the new *matha*. This *matha* is now known as Avani Sringeri Jagadguru Shankaracharya Sharada Peetham. There is also a belief that the sage Valmiki, the author of the epic Ramayana, was residing here during the Ramayana period.

The origin of river Cauveri too is linked to mythology. The legend goes that the Cauveri river was held in a *Kamandalu* (a container of sacred water) by Sage Agastya. Vinaayaka (Lord Ganesha) took the form of a crow and perched on the *kamandalu* of Agastya when Agastya was meditating. When Agastya realised this, he shooed away the crow. But the divine crow tipped the *kamandalu* and toppled it. Out poured Cauveri and started flowing. The crow disappeared and in its place stood a small boy. Agastya thought that the boy was playing some prank and clenching both his fists, went to pound the head of the small boy. But the boy escaped and Agastya gave chase. Finally the boy vanished and Ganesha showed himself to Agastya. Agastya was aghast at the realisation that he had just tried to knock the head of Ganesha himself. As atonement, he knocked his own head with both of his clenched fists.

It is believed that Mayura Varman, and Narasimman the Kadamba King who ruled vast areas of southern and central India in the 4th Century CE brought Brahmans from Ahi Kshetra (or Ahichatra) and put them in-charge of various temples in Tulu Nadu. Ahi Kshetra is mentioned in the Mahabharata as lying north of the Ganges, and as being the capital of northern Panchala. It is apparently the Adisadra of Ptolemy, and its remains are visible near Ramnagar in Bareilly district of Uttar Pradesh.

The Brahmans who first landed in Shivalli in Tulunadu and then spread across 31 villages came to be known as Shivalli Brahmans or Tulu Brahmans. It is from Shivalli and Tulu Brahmans that the priests of Talakaveri temple come from.

The *Puranic* story says the wicked *asura* Vatapi was killed by sage Agastya (as per Agastya-Vatapi story), the area in which the incident happened so named as *Vatapi*. As per scholar *Dr. D. P. Dikshit*, the first Chalukya king was Jayasimha (a feudatory of the Kadamba's) and in 500 CE he established the Chalukya kingdom. His grandson Pulakesin I built a fort at Vatapi. The new name of Vatapi is Badami. It thus seems that Karnataka has numerous references in the Epics, *Puranas* and local legends from ancient times. Not only that, Karnataka had close cultural exchanges with northern parts of India from ancient times. Karnataka thus stands in a unique position of being the link between the north and south from times immemorial.

Karnataka Etymology: The earliest reference to Karnataka is in Panini's work where he calls Karnadhaka as the *gotra* of a people. But allusion to it as a territory is found for the first time in the *Mahabharata*, the antiquity of whose composition is carried back to over 2000 years. In the old Sanskrit texts like *Markandeya Purana*, *Bhagavatha* and *Brihatasamhita* of Varamihira, Karnataka is pre-eminently mentioned. Similarly, ancient Tamil works *Tolkappiyam* and *Shilpakaddikaram* have also referred to the people of this land as Karunadars or Karunatakars. The Birur plates of Kadamba Vishnuvarman say that Shativarman was "the master of the entire Karnataka region. This record of 450 CE is the first inscriptional reference to the name. Sanskrit poetess Vijayanka called herself "Karnatarajapriya" and she was a Chalukyan queen. The army of the Chalukyas of Vatapi (Badami) is called Karnatabalas in the inscriptions of the Rashtrakutas. Thus, the land was known as Karnata from quite a long time, not only in the North but also to the people in the South.

The Tamil classic *Silappatikaram* of the same time period calls the people of present day Karnataka region as *Karunatakars*. The *Kalingathu parani*, a war poem written by Jayangkondar in Tamil Literature calls a people of a region called 'Karunatiyar.' In the 9th century CE, the Kannada classic *Kavirajamarga* hails the entire region between the rivers Cauveri and Godavari as *Karnata*. In the 13th century CE, Kannada poet Andayya's works use the same terminology. In the late 16th century, a Telugu work *Vasucharitamu* refers to Tirumala Deva Raya (1570 CE), the first of the Aravidu (Aravithi) line of rulers of the late Vijayanagara Empire as the reviver of the *Karnata Empire*. All this clearly shows that the name *Karnataka* has been in usage consistently since ancient times.

Some Brahmin communities have been using the word 'Karnataka' in their names for centuries to imply that they belong and originate in this land. Halenadu Karnataka Brahmins (also known as Muguru Karnataka Brahmins) have been consistently using 'Karnataka' in their community's name. The other community doing so is the Hoysala Karnataka Brahmins.

Scholars have tried to interpret Karnataka in various ways. One view is that the original Kannada which was the name of the land, has been sanskritized as Karnata. The author of *Kavirajamarga* calls this land as Kannada. So does Kannada poet Andayya. The second view is that it is because of two tribes namely *Karna* and *Nat* who inhabited the territory that the land came to be so known. According to the third view, people called *Kan* and *Kal* inhabited this land and that is why the territory came to be known as Kannada. A popular view is that the land is of black soil (*kari+nadu*) and from this is derived 'Karnadu.' But the most accepted view is that the word 'Karnata' is derived from *karu+nadu*, the big land or an elevated land. Major parts of Karnataka are situated in the Deccan Plateau and are therefore an elevated country.

Kannada Language

Kannada is among more than 20 languages of the Dravidian group. It is one of the oldest Dravidian languages. The name *Isila* found in one of the Ashokan inscriptions in Karnataka has been described as a Kannada word by Prof. D.L. Narasimhachar. According to him, it means 'throw an arrow.' Thus, Kannada was a spoken language during the 3rd century BCE itself. The next important document that helps us to prove the antiquity of Kannada is *The Geography* written by Ptolemy, a scholar from Alexandria, during the first half of the second century CE. Ptolemy speaks of many places in Karnataka such as Kalgeris (identified as Kalkeri), Modogoulla (Mudugal), Badamios (Badami) and so on. All these are not only places in Karnataka, but are also names of Kannada origin.

Kannada language and literature seem to be almost contemporaneous with Tamil though Tamil speaking people claim very high antiquity. The following dates may be assigned to existing earlier literature:

- The end of Tamil-Kannada linguistic unity: 500 BCE
- The earliest Brahmi-Tamil inscriptions: 250–150 BCE
- Pre-Tolkappiyam Tamil literature: 200–100 BCE
- Early poems of the *Sangam* literature: 50 BCE
- Other *Sangam* works: 50 BCE to 250 CE

As regards Kannada, the earliest epigraphy and literary works traced so far are:

- Halmidi stone inscription (450 CE); and
- *Kavirajamarga*, a work on rhetoric (814–872 CE)

After the *Kavirajamarga*, Kannada literature is first dominated by Jaina writers and then by *Virashaiva* writers from 11th century onwards and then comes the *Vaishnava* literature of the 14th century to 17th century CE.

However, Kannada language exists in earlier forms much before 450 CE. Pre-old Kannada (*Puruvadahale Gannada*) was the language of Banavasi in the early Common Era, the Satavahana and Kadamba periods and hence has a history of over 2000 years. The Ashoka rock edict found at Brahmagiri (dated to 230 BCE) has been suggested to contain words in identifiable Kannada. A more definite reference to Kannada was found in a play concerned with a Greek lady named Charition who is stranded on the coast of a country bordering the Indian Ocean. The king of the region and his countrymen sometimes use their own language using Kannada sentences. The play is written sometimes in the 1st or 2nd century CE.

The earliest examples of a full-length Kannada language stone inscription (*shilashasana*) containing Brahmi characters with characteristics attributed to those of proto-Kannada in *Hale Kannada* script can be found in the Halmidi inscription, dated 450 CE, indicating that Kannada had become an administrative language at that time. The Halmidi inscription provides invaluable information about the history and culture of Karnataka. The 5th century Tamatekallu inscription of Chitradurga and the Chikkamagaluru inscription of 500 CE are further examples. Recent reports indicate that the Old Kannada *Nishadi* inscription discovered on the Chandragiri hill, Shravanabelagola, is older than Halmidi inscription by about fifty to hundred years and may belong to the period 350–400 CE. The noted archaeologist and art historian S. Settar is of the opinion that an inscription of the Western Ganga King Kongunivarma (350–370 CE) is also older than the Halmidi inscription.

On the initiative of the Kannada Sahitya Academy, a memorial has been built in Halmidi village at the place where the stone inscription was discovered. While the original stone with the inscription has now been kept at the Government Museum in Bengaluru, a fibre glass replica of the same is kept at the memorial site.

Though the Halmidi inscription dates back to 450 CE, beginnings of Kannada literature may go back to a few centuries earlier than these records. The inscription is well set up in standard prose using a standard language with fully cultivated and finely finished verb forms and grammatical composition. Sentences of this type would require much linguistic ability to grasp and compose which indicates that Kannada language must have come a long way in the process of cultivating a standard literary language. Based on this it can be safely assumed that the antiquity of Kannada language may be at least two or three centuries earlier than the Halmidi inscription.

Halmidi inscription is in verse form indicating the authors of the inscription had a good sense of the language structure. The inscription is written in pre-old Kannada (*Puruvada-hale Kannada*), which later evolved into old Kannada (*Hale Kannada*), middle Kannada (*Nadu Kannada*) and eventually modern Kannada. The Halmidi inscription is the earliest evidence of the usage of Kannada as an administrative language.

Though Kannada is not spoken on the banks of Godavari today, various Kannada inscriptions found there testify to the fact that Kannada was the spoken language of people of those areas too. Kannada was also spoken in large parts of present day Maharashtra and Telengana. Kannada dynasties like the Chalukyas and Rashtrakutas had dominated the whole of the Deccan and the influence of Kannada language was felt from the Cauveri to the Godavari and even beyond.

Kannada was designated a classical language of India by the Ministry of Culture, Government of India in 2008. Kannada is one of the six languages designated as classical languages, the other five being Sanskrit, Tamil, Telugu, Malyalam and Odia.

The following criteria were laid down to determine the eligibility of languages to be considered for classification as a "Classical Language":

a) High antiquity of its early texts/recorded history over a period of 1500–2000 years;
b) a body of ancient literature/texts, which is considered a valuable heritage by generations of speakers;
c) the literary tradition be original and not borrowed from another speech community;
d) the classical language and literature being distinct from modern, there may also be a discontinuity between the classical language and its later forms or its offshoots.

Kannada fulfils all the criteria being an over 2000 years old language.

Karnataka's Geographical Description

Karnataka has a rich heritage, inspiring its people to create a bright future. With its special geographical location full of variety-its rivers, hills, valleys, plains, forests and resources-the State is known for its tourist and industrial potential. Its long history of over 2,000 years has left many beautiful forts, tanks, temples, mosques and towns of historical importance to the posterity. Karnataka has rich religious and artistic traditions. Bordered by the Western Ghats with tall peaks and lush greenery in the west, the tableland is fertile because of its black soil and river and tank irrigation facilities. The coastal strip to the west of the Ghats is renowned for its silvery beaches and rich green paddy fields.

The temples of antiquity speak of the piety of their devotees. The *agraharas* and *mathas* spread all over vouch to the scholarly pursuits to which people were attached. The hero stones strewn around all over the land speak of the heroic traits of the warrior race of antiquity. Long traditions of growing cotton are clear evidence to once flourishing rich textile industry. The ports along the coast remind one of the rich overseas trades that flourished through them. The black soil plains speak of its agricultural potential. The State's human resources with racial and religious varieties and professional skills promise to make it a hub of industriousness.

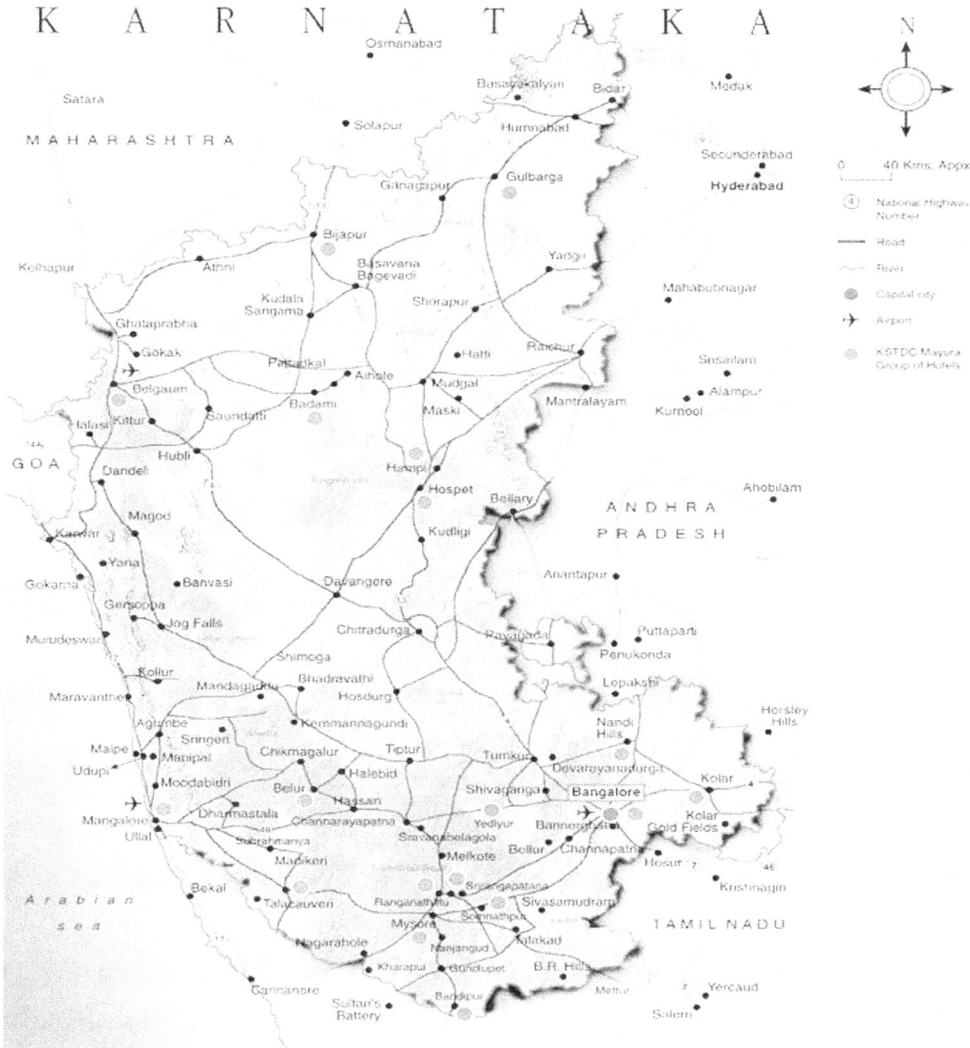

With an antiquity that dates to the Paleolithic age, Karnataka has also been home to some of the most powerful empires of ancient and medieval India. The philosophers and musical bards patronized by these empires launched socio-religious and literary movements which have endured to the present day. Karnataka has contributed significantly to both forms of Indian classical music, the Carnatic (Karnataka Music) and Hindustani traditions.

The State of Karnataka, confined roughly within 11°35' North and 18°30' North latitudes and 74°5' East and 78°35' East longitudes, is situated on a tableland where the Western and Eastern Ghat ranges converge into the Nilgiri hills. Karnataka is a state in the southern part of India. It was created on November 1, 1956, with the passing of the States Reorganization Act. Originally known as the State of Mysore, it was renamed Karnataka in 1973. Karnataka is bordered by the Arabian Sea to the west, Goa to the northwest, Maharashtra to the north, Andhra Pradesh to the east, Tamil Nadu to the southeast, and Kerala to the southwest. The state extends to about 750 km from North to South and about 400 km from East to West.

There are 30 districts in Karnataka—Bagalkot, Bengaluru Rural, Bengaluru Urban, Belagavi, Ballari, Bidar, Vijaypur, Chamarajanagar, Chikkaballapur, Chikkamagaluru, Chitradurga, Dakshina Kannada, Davanagere, Dharwad, Gadag, Kalaburgi, Hassan, Haveri, Kodagu, Kolar, Koppal, Mandya, Mysuru,

Raichur, Ramanagara, Shivamogga, Tumakuru, Udupi, Uttara Kannada and Yadgir. Yadgir is the youngest of the 30 districts having been created in December 2009. Each district is governed by a district commissioner or district magistrate.

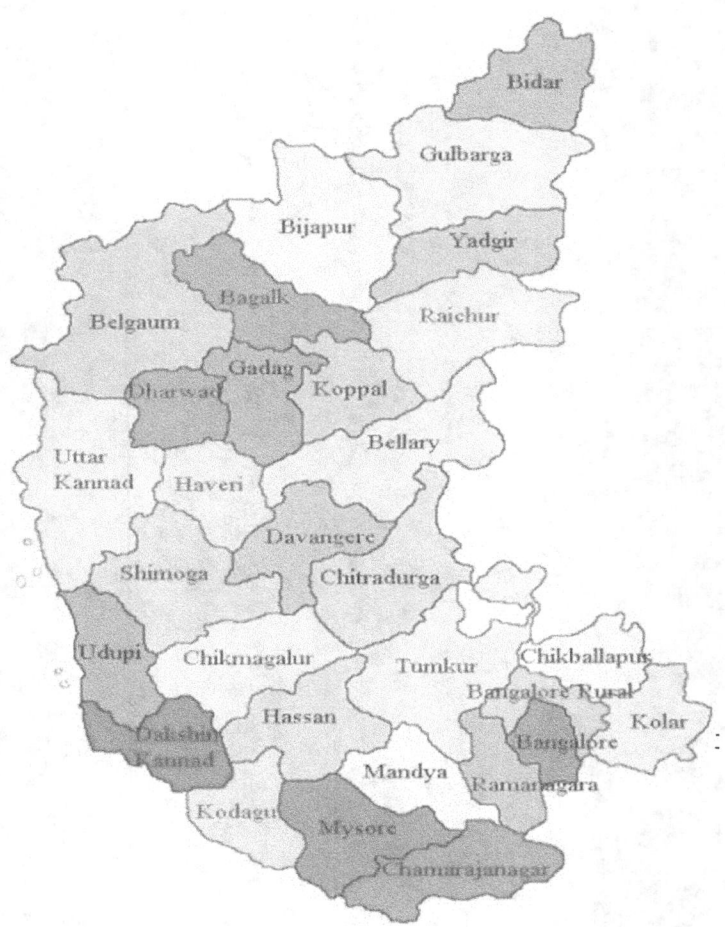

Physiography

Physiographically Karnataka State forms part of two well defined macro regions of Indian Union; the Deccan Plateau and the Coastal plains and Islands. The State has four physiographic regions as follows:

Northern Karnataka Plateau: Northern Karnataka Plateau comprises of the districts of Belagavi, Bidar, Vijaypur, Bagalkot and Kalaburgi. It is largely composed of Deccan Trap. It represents a monotonous treeless extensive plateau landscape with a general elevation of 300 to 600 metres from the mean sea level. However the river plains of the Krishna, the Bhima, the Ghataprabha and the Malaprabha with the intervening watersheds, the step like landscapes, lateritic scarpments, residual hills and ridges break the monotony of this extensive plateau. The general slope is towards east and this region is largely covered with rich black cotton soils.

Central Karnataka Plateau: Central Karnataka Plateau covers the districts of Ballari, Chikmagaluru, Chitradurga, Davanagere, Dharwad, Gadag, Haveri, Raichur, Koppal, Yadgir and Shivamogga. The region represents the transitional surface between the Northern Karnataka Plateau of Deccan Trap and Southern Karnataka Plateau with relatively higher surface. By and large, this region represents the area of Tungabhadra basin. The general elevation varies between 450 and 700 metres. However, this transitional ground is broken by several sets of parallel ridges mainly made up of Dharwar system of rocks. The height of such residual hills is about 900 metres above mean sea level. The general slope of this region is towards the east.

Southern Karnataka Plateau: The Southern Karnataka Plateau covers the districts of Begaluru, Bengaluru Rural, Hassan, Kodagu, Kolar, Mandya, Mysuru, Chamarajanagar and Tumakuru. This region largely covers the area of the Cauveri river basin lying in Karnataka. It is bounded by 600 metres contour and is characterised by a higher degree of slope. In the west and south it is enclosed by the ranges of Western Ghats and the northern part is an interrupted but clearly identifiable high plateau. In the east the valleys of the Cauveri and its tributaries open out to form undulating plains. The general elevation of the region varies from 600 to 900 metres. However residual heights of 1,500 to 1,750 metres are found in the Biligirirangan hills of Mysuru district and the Brahmagiri range of Kodagu district

Karnataka Coastal Region: The Karnataka Coastal Region, which extends between the Western Ghats edge of the Karnataka Plateau in the east and the Arabian Sea in the west, covers Dakshina Kannada, Udupi and Uttara Kannada districts. This region is traversed by several ridges and spurs of Western Ghats. It has difficult terrain full of rivers, creeks, waterfalls, peaks and ranges of hills. The coastal region consists of two broad physical units, the plains and the Western Ghats. The Coastal plains represent a narrow stretch of estuarine and marine plains. The abrupt rise at the eastern flanks forms the Western Ghats. The northern parts of the Ghats are of lower elevation (450–600 metres) as compared to Southern parts (900 to 1,500 metres). The Coastal belt with an average width of 50 to 80 km covers a distance of about 267 km. from north to south. At certain places the crest of adjoining Western Ghats reach the sea as close as 13 km near Karwar. The average height is generally 75 metres from the mean sea level.

Topography

Karnataka has representatives of all types of variations in topography -high mountains, plateaus, residual hills and coastal plains. The State is enclosed by chains of mountains to its west, east and south. It consists mainly of plateau which has higher elevation of 600 to 900 metres above mean sea level. The entire landscape is undulating broken up by mountains and deep ravines.

Plain land of elevation less than 300 metres above mean sea level is to be found only in the narrow coastal belt, facing the Arabian Sea. There are quite a few high peaks both in Western and Eastern Ghat systems with altitudes of more than 1,500 metres. A series of cross-sections drawn from west to east across the Western Ghats generally exhibit, a narrow coastal plain followed to the east by small and short plateaus at different altitudes, then suddenly rising upto great heights. Immediately after that follows the gentle east and east-north-west sloping plateau. Among the tallest peaks of Karnataka are the Mullayyana Giri (1,925 m), Bababudangiri (Chandradrona Parvata 1,894 m) and the Kudremukh (1,895 m) all in Chikamagalur district and the Pushpagiri (1,908 m) in Kodagu district There are a dozen peaks which rise above the height of 1,500 metres. The percentage of area coming under different elevations is as follows: less than 150 metres-5.16%; 150 to 300 metres-1.95%; 300 to 600 metres-43.51%; 600 to 1,350 metres-48.81% and more than 1,350 metres-0.57%.

Geology

Karnataka consists of four main types of geological formations; the Archean complex made up of Dharwad schists and granitic gneisses, the Proterozoic non-fossiliferous sedimentary formations of the Kaladgi and Bhima series, the Deccan trappean and intertrappean deposits and the tertiary and recent laterites and alluvial deposits. Significantly, about 60% of the state is composed of the Archean complex consisting of gneisses, granites and charnockite rocks. Laterite cappings that are found in many districts over the Deccan Traps were formed after the cessation of volcanic activity in the early tertiary period. Eleven groups of soil orders are found in Karnataka, viz. Entisols, Inceptisols, Mollisols, Spodosols, Alfisols, Ultisols, Oxisols, Aridisols, Vertisols, Andisols and Histosols. Depending on the agricultural capability of the soil, the soil types are divided into six types, viz. Red, lateritic, black, alluvio-colluvial, forest and coastal soils.

The geological history of Karnataka is largely confined to the two oldest eras -the Archaean and the Proterozoic. The substantial part of North Karnataka is covered by Deccan Trap. The bulk of the rocks of Karnataka are Archaean in age.

Ancient supracrustals are the oldest rocks dated so far in Karnataka. They are a group of grey gneisses giving an age of 3,400 million years. They are also described as belonging to Sargur schists.

Auriferous Schist Belts (Kolar type) are next in order of age and are a series of basic igneous rocks. They are well developed in the eastern part of the State. Older Gneissic complex consist of an extensive group of grey gneisses (3,400 to 3,000 million years) and act as the basement for an extensive belt of schists.

Younger Gneiss complex consist of a group of gneissic rocks mostly of granodioritic and granitic composition. They are found in the eastern parts of the State and range in age from 2,700 to 2,000 million years.

Younger Schist Belts (Dharwar type) are the prominent schistose rocks. They are Archaean in age and belong to the age group of 2,900 to 2,600 million years. Two main divisions in this super group are Bababudan and Chitradurga. Ranebennur group is presently classified as the top most formation within Chitradurga group.

There are seven river basins which with their tributaries drain the State. The names of river system and the area drained by them are as follows:

Krishna Basin

About 43.74 percent of the Krishna basin lies in the State. The river's course for 483 km lies in the State. The Tungabhadra which has a drainage area of 66,237 sq. km is the largest and the important of the Krishna's tributaries. Its major tributaries are the Bhima, Koyna, Panchaganga, Dudhaganga, Tungabhadra, Hiranyakeshi, Ghataprabha and the Malaprabha. This basin covers 18 districts and about 60 percent of the geographical area of the State.

The Krishna: The river Krishna rises in the Western Ghats, at an altitude of 1,336 metres near Mahabaleshwar in Maharashtra, flows from west to east for a length of about 1,400 km, through Maharashtra, Karnataka and Andhra Pradesh. The Krishna has a drainage area of about 2.59 lakh sq. km. Together with its tributaries, it flows for about 704 km length in the State

The Ghataprabha: The Ghataprabha river rises in the Western Ghats, at an altitude of 884 metres and flows eastwards for a length of 283 km before joining the Krishna. The river debouches by 53 metres at Gokak Falls in Belagavi district. The total catchment area of the river and its tributaries accounts for 8,829 sq. km in Maharashtra and Karnataka States.

The Malaprabha: The river Malaprabha also rises in Western Ghats at an altitude of 792 metres in Belagavi district, The river flows first in easterly and then in north-easterly directions and joins the Krishna at Kudalasangama, about 304 km from its source. The principal tributaries are the Bennihalla, Hirehalla and the Tas Nadi. The total catchment area of the Malaprabha and its tributaries is 11,549 sq. km., wholly in Karnataka.

The Bhima: The Bhima river also rises in Western Ghats, at an altitude of about 945 metres and flows south-eastwards through Maharashtra and Karnataka. It flows for 861 km before joining the Krishna near Kudlu in Raichur taluk. The latter 298 km of the Bhima's course is in the State. It has a drainage area of 70,614 sq. km out of which 18,315 sq. km lies in Karnataka.

The Tungabhadra: The Tungabhadra is formed north of Shivamogga at an elevation of about 610 metres by the union of twin rivers, the Tunga and the Bhadra, which rise together in the Western Ghats at an elevation of about 1,198 metres. The Varada and the Hagari are its important tributaries. It has a drainage area of 71,417 sq. km out of which 57,671 sq. km lies in the State. It flows for a distance of 293 km. in the State.

Cauveri Basin

About 42.2 percent of the area of the Cauveri basin (81,155 sq. km) lies in Karnataka. This basin covers 18 percent of the State area comprising eight districts. Its major tributaries in Karnataka are the Hemavati, Lakshmanatirtha, Harangi, Kabini, Suvarnavati, Lokapavani, Shimsha and the Arkavati.

The Cauveri: The river Cauveri has its origin in the Western Ghats in Kodagu district It flows for a length of 320 km in the State. The river flows generally in a south-east direction. The Chunchanakatte Falls (about 20 m) and the Shivasamudra Falls (about 100 m) exist in the State.

The Hemavati: The river Hemavati rises in the Western Ghats at an elevation of about 1,219 metres and joins the river Cauveri near Krishnarajasagar. The drainage area is about 5,410 sq. km and the approximate length of the river is 245 km.

The Kabini: The river Kabini has a total course of about 230 km and a catchment area of about 7,040 sq. km. It joins the Cauveri river at Tirumakudal Narasipur.

Godavari Basin

Godavari basin has a drainage are of 4,405 sq. km. Only a small part of Godavari basin lies in the State. The river Manjra is the major tributary of the Godavari and it flows for about 155 km in the State.

Pennar and Palar Basins

The North Pennar, South Pennar and the Palar rivers drain about 13,610 sq. km in the State.

West flowing Rivers: There are numerous west flowing rivers, chief among which are the Sharavati, Kali, Gangavati (Bedti), Aghanashini and the Netravati. The total catchment area of all west flowing rivers is 26,214 sq. km. They are mostly harnessed for power generation.

1.3 PURPOSE AND OBJECTIVES OF THIS STUDY

In this book heritage will include physical objects such as architectural monuments, colossal statues, large and small inscribed memorials, sculpture and artifacts, tombs, sepulchral architecture, pillars raised as memorials or religious icons, inscriptions on stone slabs and rocks/boulders as well as movable cultural property.

This publication attempts to make a significant contribution to the understanding and appreciation of heritage by providing literary references, epigraphical records and material evidence at times supported by photographs which bear witness to the changes in the political authority and control and the consequent effect on art and architecture of those times. The material in this book has largely been organized around three main themes: history, art and architecture and religions to the extent they influence art and architecture and sociological and cultural development of the region. Though the three disciplines have formally been separated, there would be numerous cross-references as the rulers of those times sought religious sanctions for most their actions including in wars and battles. Most part of the commentary here refers to literary, epigraphical, archaeological, anthropological, political, scientific and educational data to substantiate the context.

The period under study is of special significance in the history of Karnataka and south India. The political vicissitudes held sway over the social, cultural and religious life of the state, more prominently during the medieval era. Geographically the boundaries of Karnataka extended into a vast area. The mainland had spread between the rivers Cauveri in the south and Godavari in the north. The works of people in every field and walk of life were of the highest order, standards and values. Perhaps there can be no parallel to the amount of work carried out during the periods between the 10th and 13th centuries CE. Though it holds good for every field of human activity, special mention needs to be made to religions, literature, learning and art and architecture. This book will however, devote itself largely to art and architecture of these periods and draw from other fields to the extent they influence art and architecture.

Since the largest number of monuments and sites from the pre-historic times to the 14th century CE were in some or the other way related with religions and dynastic preferences, temples and religious sculpture cover a wide part of the spectrum of this study. Epigraphical records are generally found in the precincts of religious structures, tanks and sites for memorials and it becomes easy to establish direct relations between the grants recorded and the structure constructed. Epigraphical records thus help us know about the time when these structures or temples were created and also the state of evolution of technology, religions, philosophy, social, political and economic development of the time. A progressive understanding of the evolution of temple art and architecture not only lets us learn about the history of art and architecture but also of the development of the canonical literature and construction technology with time. In that sense temples do stand apart as the historians of heritage and their preservation and conservation is an important step in the preservation of heritage.

KARNATAKA: HISTORY AND RELIGIOUS DEVELOPMENTS

2.1 BRIEF HISTORY OF KARNATAKA

Geographically located on the south western part of South India, Karnataka has abundant natural resources. Its western ghats with rich forest resources, and plain valleys, is crowned with more prosperous narrow coast line. Above all, it has rich cultural tradition and connections with the *puranic* legends of historical importance. Many locations believed to be connected with the episodes from the two great epics viz, the Ramayana and the Mahabharata further lend Karnataka an important place in Hindu history. Many of the Buddhist and Jaina religious texts too were composed by the literary giants from the state.

Pre History: Karnataka has a hoary past. It is blessed with innumerable inscriptions, memorial (viz. Hero, Mahasati and Self immolation and others) stones and monuments of rich historical and cultural heritage. It has many sites of pre-historic period and most of them are found scattered in the river valleys of Krishna, Bhima, Malaprabha, Ghataprabha, Cauveri, Hemavathi, Shimsha, Tungabhadra, Manjra, Pennar, Netravati and their tributaries. It is very interesting to note that the pre-historic studies in India started with the discovery of ashmounds at Kupgal and Kudatini in 1836 CE by Cuebold, a British officer in Ballari region, which then formed part of Madras Presidency. Subsequent discoveries have revealed the existence of stone-age man with innumerable pre-historic sites in Karnataka. The pre-historic culture of Karnataka viz., the Hand-axe culture, compares favourably with the one that existed in Africa and is quite distinct from the pre-historic culture of north India. Places like Hunasagi, Gulbal, Kaladevanahalli, Tegginahalli, Budihal, Piklihal, Kibbanahalli, Nittur, Anagavadi, Kaladgi, Khyad, Nyamati, Balehonnur and Uppinangadi (Lower Palaeolithic); Herakal, Tamminahal, Savalgi, Salvadgi, Menasagi, Pattadakal, Vajjala, Naravi and Talakad (Middle Palaeolithic); Kovalli, Ingaleshwar, Yadwad and Maralabhavi (Upper Palaeolithic); Begaumpur, Vanamapurahalli, Hingani, Ingaleshwar, Tamminahal, Sringeri, Jalahalli, Kibbanahalli, Sanganakallu, Brahmagiri, Uppinangadi, Mani and Doddaguni (Mesolithic); Maski, T. Narasipur, Banahalli, Hallur, Sanganakallu, Hemmige, Kodekal, Brahmagiri, Kupgal, Tekkalkote, Kurnal, Srinivasapura, Beeramangala, Frenchrocks (Pandavapura) and Uttanur (Neolithic and Chalcolithic); Rajana Kolur, Bachigudda, Aihole, Konnur, Terdal, Hire Benkal, Kumaranahalli, Tadakanahalli, Maski, Banahalli, Badaga-Kajekaru, Belur, Borkatte, Konaje, Kakkunje, Vaddarse and Hallingali (Megalithic) are some of the important pre-historic sites in Karnataka. The *ragi* grain is found commonly in pre-historic sites of Africa and Karnataka. The early inhabitants of Karnataka knew the use of iron, far earlier than the north and iron weapons dating back to 1500 BCE have been found at Hallur in Haveri district.

Traditionally, it is believed that parts of Karnataka were subjected to the rule of the Nandas and the Mauryas. Maurya Chandragupta (either Chandragupta I, Ashoka's Grandfather or Samprati Chandragupta, Ashoka's Grandson) is believed to have visited Shravanabelagola and spent his last years there. Seventeen Ashokan (13 minor and 4 major) Rock Edicts are found in Karnataka and these testify to the extent of the Mauryan Empire. It is interesting to note that, Emperor Ashoka's name occurs for the first time in his Maski minor rock edict wherein, his familiar epithet "Devanampiya Piyadasi" is accompanied with his personal name Ashoka. Hence his Maski edict has a unique place among all his royal edicts. The language used in these Ashokan inscriptions is Prakrit and the script used therein is Brahmi. Brahmi, has been regarded as the mother of all Indian scripts, including the Devanagari script. Places like Brahmagiri, Chandravalli, Maski, Sanganakallu, Piklihall, Banavasi, Hallur, T. Narasipur, Vadagoan-Madhavapur, Banahalli, Sannati, etc., have yielded rich remnants of early (Proto) historic period, datable to 3rd Century BCE -1st Century CE.

The Satavahanas (30 BCE to 230 CE) of Paithan (also called Pratishtana) in Maharashtra have also ruled over extensive areas in northern Karnataka. Some scholars even argue that this dynasty hailed from Karnataka, as in early times, Dharwad and Ballari districts were called Satavahanihara (or the Satavahana region). Some of their rulers were called kings of Kuntala. At Sannati, Vadgaon-Madhavpur, Hampi, Brahmagiri and several other places, remains of their period have been found. Banavasi has an inscription of their queen, and at Vasana remains of a brick temple of Saiva order were found. Kanaganahalli near Sannati has the ruins of Buddhist *Stupas* of their times covered with sculptures. Among the findings at Sannati, images of Lord Buddha (both in sitting and standing postures) are significant. Moreover the images of eight Satavahana rulers were also unearthed from this place. Later, Karnataka fell into the hands of the Pallavas of Kanchi. Their feudatories, the Chutu Satakarnis, ruling from Banavasi after the fall of the Satavahanas, also seem to have accepted the overlordship of the Pallavas. Pallava domination was ended by two indigenous dynasties, namely the Kadambas of Banavasi and the Gangas of Talakad, who more or less divided Karnataka between themselves.

Kadambas of Banavasi (345–540 CE): In the 4th century, the rise to power of the Kadamba dynasty of Banavasi identified the Karnataka region as an independent political entity and Kannada as the administrative language from the middle of 5th century. The Kadambas were natives of the Talagunda region (in modern Shivamogga district) as proven by inscriptions. Mayurasharma, a Brahmin native of Talagunda who was humiliated by a Pallava guard, rose in rage against the Pallava control of the Banavasi region and declared his independence in 345 CE. After many wars, the Pallava king had to accept the sovereignty of the Kadambas and Mayurasharma, the founding king, crowned himself at Banavasi.

The fact that the Kadambas cultivated marital ties with the imperial Vakatakas and Gupta dynasties attests to their power. Kakusthavarma, the most powerful ruler of the dynasty whom inscriptions describe as "ornament of the Kadamba family" and "Sun among the kings of wide spread flame," gave one daughter in marriage to Vakataka Narendrasena and another to Skandagupta, grandson of Chandragupta II of the Gupta dynasty. Historians trace their rise to political power through the examination of the contemporaneous Sanskrit writing, *Aichitya Vichara Charcha* by Kshemendra, which quotes portions of a writing *Kunthalesvara Dautya* by the famous poet Kalidasa. Here Kalidasa describes his visit to the Kadamba kingdom as an ambassador where he was not offered a seat in the court of the Kadamba king and had to sit on the ground. Historians view this act as one of assertion by the Kadambas who considered themselves equal to the imperial Gupta dynasty.

Family feuds and conflicts ended the Kadamba rule in the middle of 6th century when the last Kadamba ruler Krishna Varma II was subdued by Pulakesin I of the Badami Chalukya feudatory, ending their sovereign rule. The Kadambas would continue to rule parts of Karnataka and Goa for many centuries to come but never again as an independent kingdom. Some historians view the Kadambas as the originators of the Karnataka architectural tradition although there were elements in common with the structures built by the contemporaneous Pallavas of Kanchi. The oldest surviving Kadamba structure is one dating to late 5th century in Halasi in modern Belagavi district. The most prominent feature of their architectural style, one that remained popular centuries later and was used by the Hoysalas and the Vijayanagar kings, is the *Kadamba Sikara* (Kadamba tower) with a *Kalasa* (pot) on top.

The earliest Kannada record found at Halmidi (450 CE) in Hassan district, was issued by this dynasty.

They also created first rock-cut shrines of Vedic tradition at Aravalem (in Goa which was then under their control) in a laterite hill range. The tanks at Chandravalli and Gudnapur are among the many irrigation tanks they built. They had Lion as their royal insignia. They were overthrown perhaps by the Chalukyas of Badami in 540 CE and at later stages, two branches of Kadamba family (one from Hangal and the other from Goa) ruled during medieval period, as subordinates of the Chalukyas of Kalyana. A branch of the Kadambas was also ruling from Odisha as subordinates of the Gangas of Kalinga in medieval times.

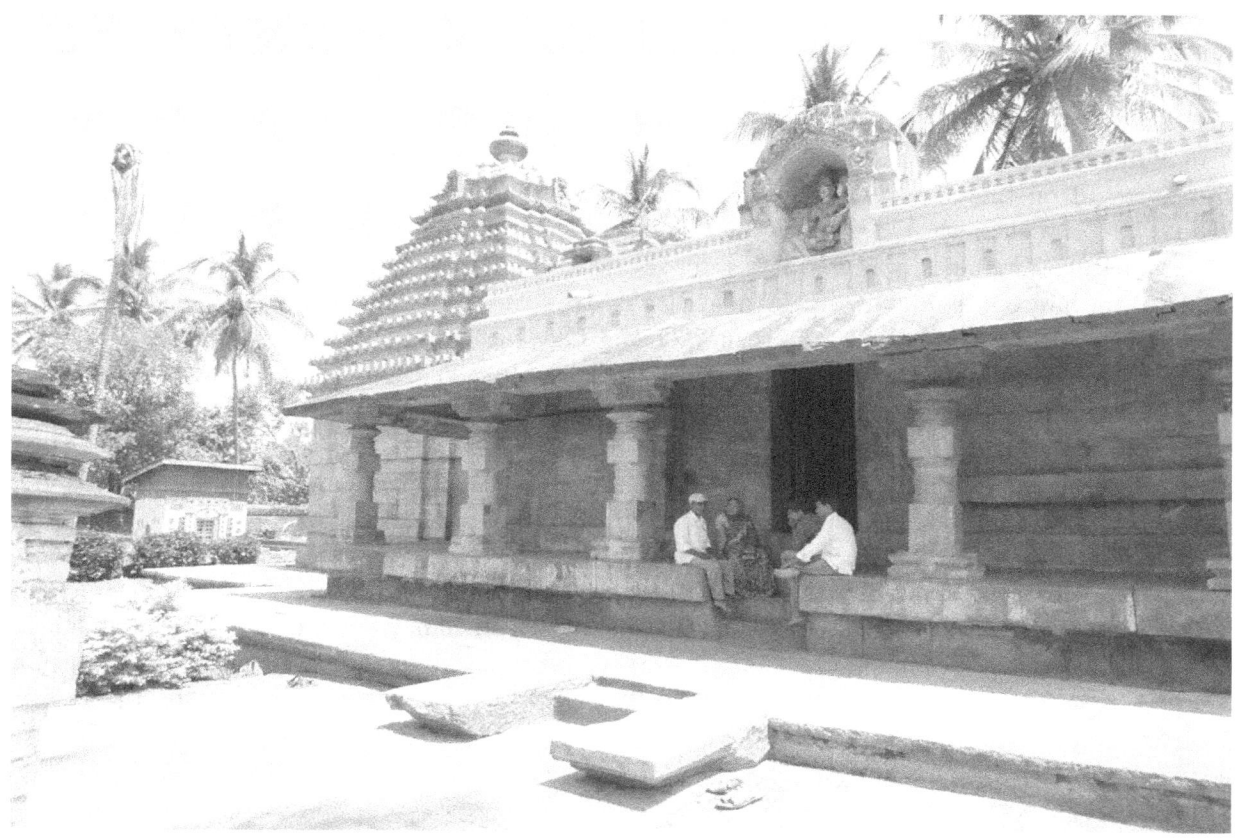

Bhu Varaha Temple at Halasi, Kadambas

Alupas of Tulunad: The Alupas who ruled over parts of coastal and adjacent region between 4th and 16th century CE with Udyavara, Mangaluru, and Barkur as their capitals, had good cultural contact with the contemporary imperial dynasties of Karnataka like the Chalukyas of Badami, Rashtrakutas, Chalukyas of Kalyana and other subsequent dynasties. Inscriptions of this dynasty found at Kadri, Someshwara, Udyavara, Barkur, Belmannu, Vaddarse etc. speak about their rule in coastal Karnataka. The metal sculpture of Avalokeswara seen in the Manjunatha temple at Kadri near Mangaluru, installed by Alupa Kundavarma in 968 CE is unique in south India.

Gangas of Talakad (350–1004 CE) also known as Western Gangas: The Western Ganga dynasty, contemporaries of the Kadambas, came to power from Kolar but in the late 4th century -early 5th century CE moved their capital to Talakad. They ruled the region historically known as Gangavadi comprising most of the modern southern districts of Karnataka acting as a buffer state between the Kannada kingdoms of Karnataka region and the Tamil kingdoms of Tamilakam. The Western Ganga architectural innovations show mixed influences. Their sovereign rule ended around the same time as the Kadambas when they came under the Badami Chalukya control. The Western Gangas continued to rule as a feudatory till the beginning of the eleventh century when they were defeated by the Cholas of Tanjavur. Important figures among the Gangas were king Durvinita and Sivamara II, admired as able warriors and scholars, and minister Chavundaraya who was a builder, a warrior and a writer in Kannada and Sanskrit. The most important architectural contributions of these Gangas are the monuments and *basadis* of Shravanabelagola, the monolith colossus of Gommateswara termed as the mightiest achievement in the field of sculpture in ancient Karnataka and the Panchakuta Basadi (five towers) at Kambadahalli. Their free standing Jaina pillars (called *Mahasthambhas* and *Brahmasthambhas*) and hero-stones (*virgal*) with sculptural detail are also considered a unique contribution.

Many Ganga princes were not only scholars and writers, but also great patrons of scholarship. Later they continued to rule over Gangavadi (which comprised major parts of south Karnataka and parts of Tamilnadu) till the close of 10th century, as subordinates of the Badami Chalukyas and the Rashtrakutas. It is the Gangas who withstood the onslaught of the Pallavas and the Cholas, who tried to subjugate south Karnataka. The Sanskrit poet Bharavi is said to have lived in the court of Durvinita for some time. The ancient Punnata Kingdom (the modern Heggadadevanakote taluk region) was merged in his Kingdom. His great grandson Bhuvikrama (654–79 CE) was a strong ally of the Chalukyas, and at the Battle of Vilande (670 CE) which was fought between the Chalukyas and the Pallavas, he helped the former to gain victory over Pallava Parameshwara Varman and bagging as a war trophy, the Pallava ruler's necklace called 'Ugrodaya' for himself. Mankunda in Channapatna taluk is said to have been his royal residence for some time. A later prince of this family, Sripurusha (725–88 CE) was not only a strong ally of the Chalukyas, but also resisted the Rashtrakutas who tried to subdue him, after the overthrow of the Chalukyas of Badami by them in 753 CE. Sripurusha, as a Chalukyan ally killed Pallava Nandi Varman II at Vilande in 731 CE and assumed the Pallava ruler's title Permanadi. This great ruler also wrote a Sanskrit work 'Gajasastra,' a treatise on theme of taming the elephants. He shifted his capital to Manne (Manyapura) in Nelamangala Taluk. His son Sivamara II (788–816 CE) and grandson Rachamalla I (816–53 CE) continued to resist Rashtrakuta power. In the end, Rashtrakuta Amoghavarsha Nrupatunga I (814–78 CE) sought reconciliation with the Gangas by marrying his daughters to the Ganga princes. At a later date, when the Cholas became strong, the Ganga king Butuga II (938–61 CE) allied himself with the Rashtrakutas against the Cholas, and helped Rashtrakuta Krishna III (939–67 CE) to humiliate the Cholas by killing the Chola crown prince Rajaditya in the battle held at Takkolam (949 CE) as elucidated in Atakur inscription.

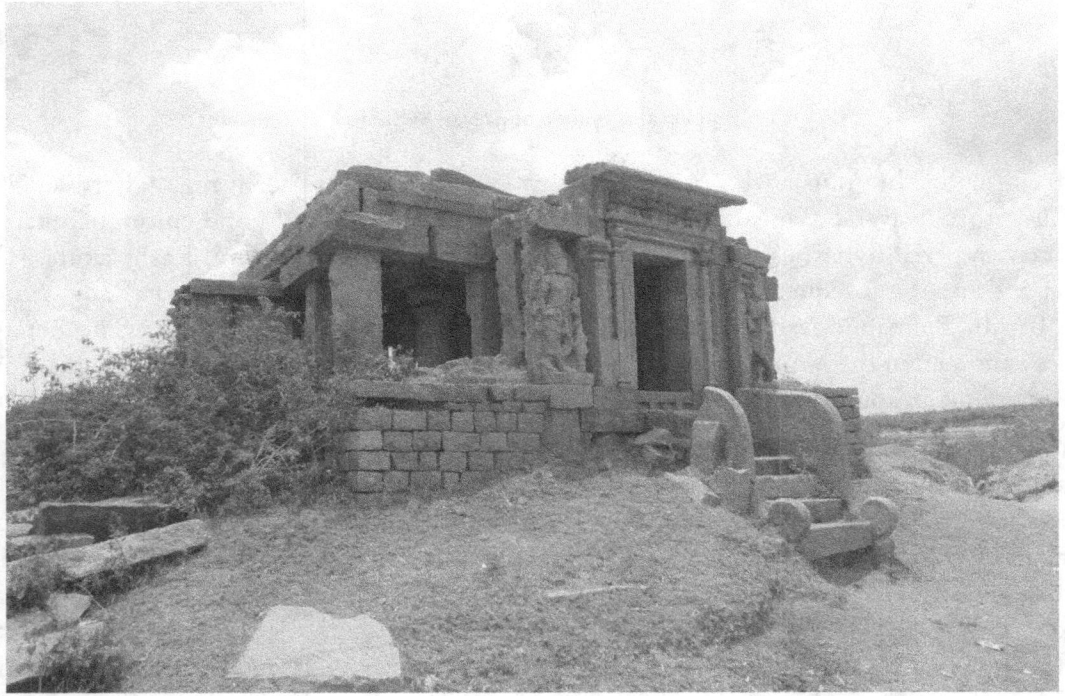

Kapileswara Temple at Manne of the Gangas

Finally their territory came to be subdued by the Cholas in 1004, and thus the Ganga rule ended. The Cholas who ruled major part of Gangavadi-96,000 with Talakad as its provincial head quarters, were ultimately expelled from Gangavadi in 1114 by Vishnuvardhana. Ganga hero-stones found at Begur,

Doddahundi etc and the masti stones (*mastikallu*) found at places like Mankunda, Seethihalli, Dodda Shivara etc. are worth mentioning. Their magnificent temples are seen at Kolar, Talakad, Begur, Nagavara, Gangavara, Nandi, Arethippur, Alur and Narasamangala. The last named has wonderful stucco figures of remarkable beauty. They also built Jaina *basadis* at Kambadahalli and Shravanabelagola. Excavations during the preceding decades at Talkad have brought to light rich remnants of the Ganga Period.

Chalukyas of Badami (540–757 CE): The Chalukya dynasty, natives of Aihole and Badami region in Karnataka, were at first a feudatory of the Kadambas. They encouraged the use of Kannada in addition to the Sanskrit language in their administration. In the middle of the 6th century the Chalukyas came into their own when Pulakesin I made the hill fortress in Badami his centre of power. During the rule of Pulakesin II a south Indian empire sent expeditions to the north past the Tapti river and Narmada river for the first time and successfully defied Harshavardhana, the King of northern India (*Uttarapatheswara*). The Aihole inscription of Pulakesin II, written in classical Sanskrit language and old Kannada script dated 634 CE proclaims his victories against the Kingdoms of Kadambas, Western Gangas, Alupas of south Kanara, Mauryas of Puri, Kingdom of Kosala, Malwa, Lata and Gurjaras of southern Rajasthan. The inscription describes how king Harsha of Kannauj lost his *Harsha* (joyful disposition) on seeing a large number of his war elephants die in battle against Pulakesin II.

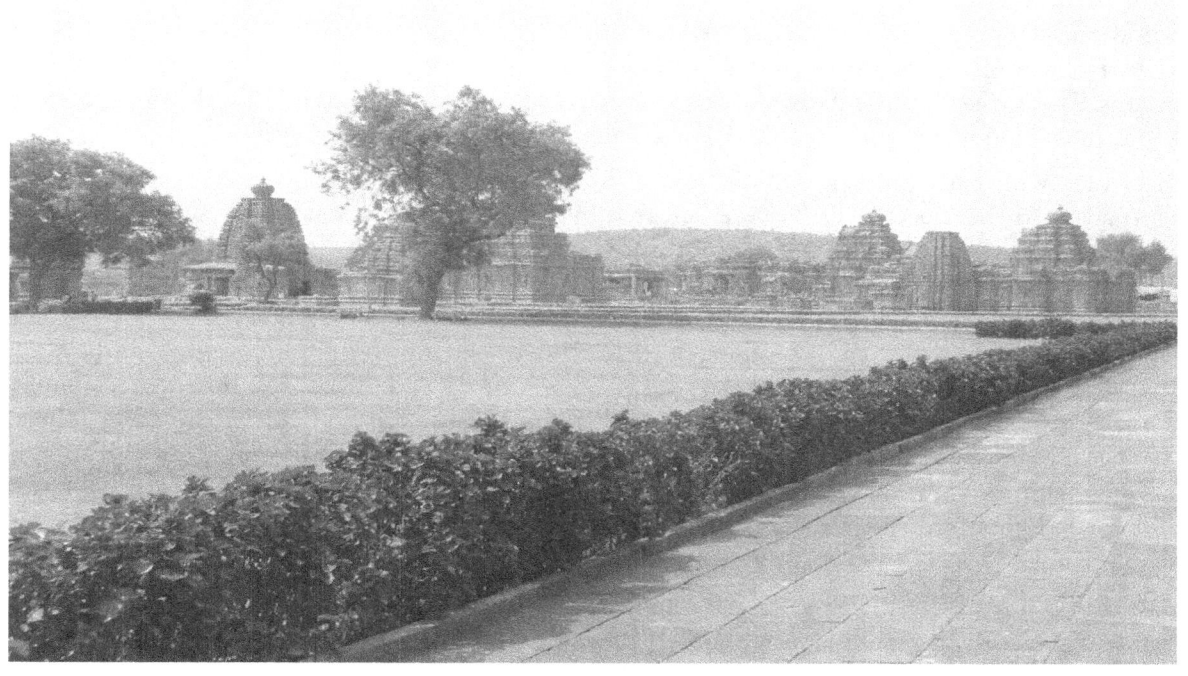

Pattadakal Group of Temples of the Badami Chalukya Period

These victories earned him the title *Dakshinapatha Prithviswamy* (lord of the south). Pulakesin II continued his conquests in the east where he conquered all kingdoms in his way and reached the Bay of Bengal in present-day Odisha. A Chalukya viceroyalty was set up in Gujarat and Vengi (coastal Andhra) and princes from the Badami family were dispatched to rule them. Having subdued the Pallavas of Kanchipuram, he accepted tributes from the Pandyas of Madurai, Chola dynasty and Cheras of the Kerala region. Pulakesin II thus became the master of India, south of the Narmada river. Pulakesin II is widely regarded as one of the great kings in Indian history. Hiuen-Tsiang, a Chinese traveller visited the court of Pulakesin II at this time and Persian emperor Khosrau II exchanged ambassadors. However, the continuous wars with Pallavas took a turn for the worse in 642 CE when the Pallava king Narasimhavarman I avenged his father's defeat, conquered and plundered the capital of Pulakesin II who may have died in battle. A century later, Badami Chalukya Vikramaditya II marched victoriously into Kanchipuram, the Pallava capital and occupied it on three occasions, the third time under the leadership of his son and crown prince Kirtivarman II. He thus avenged the earlier humiliation of the Chalukyas by the Pallavas and engraved a Kannada inscription on the victory pillar at the Kailasanatha Temple. He later overran the other traditional kingdoms of Tamil country, the Pandyas, Cholas and Keralas in addition to subduing a Kalabhra ruler.

The Kappe Arabhatta record from this period (700 CE) in *tripadi* (three line) metre is considered the earliest available record in Kannada poetics. The most enduring legacy of the Badami Chalukya dynasty is the architecture and art that they left behind. More than one hundred and fifty monuments attributed to them, built between 450 and 700 CE, have survived in the Malaprabha basin in Karnataka. All these constructions are centred in a relatively small area within the Chalukyan heartland. The structural temples at Pattadakal, a UNESCO World Heritage Site, the cave temples of Badami, the temples at Mahakuta and early experiments in temple building at Aihole are their most celebrated monuments. Two of the famous paintings at Ajanta cave no. 1, "The Temptation of the Buddha" and "The Persian Embassy" are also credited to them. Further, they influenced the architecture in far off places like Gujarat and Vengi as evidenced in the Nava Brahma temples at Alampur.

It is the Chalukyas of Badami (also called Vatapi in inscriptions) who brought the whole of Karnataka under a single rule. They are also remembered for their contributions in the field of art and architecture. Their monuments are concentrated at Badami, Nagaral, Aihole, Pattadakal, old and new Mahakuta in Karnataka and at Alampur, Gadwal, Satyavolal and Bichavolu in Andhra Pradesh. They are both rock-cut and structural, with wonderful sculptures wrought in hard red sandstone. Their Shiggaon copper plates, speak of 14 tanks in Haveri district. The Chalukyan army has been called 'Karnatabala' and described as invincible in contemporary inscriptions. The earliest representative carving of a measuring rod of 18 spans of Chalukyan period found on a rock (Kattebande) at Kurugodu in Ballari Taluk, a unique example even now visible.

The Arabs who had conquered Sindh (711 CE) under the leadership of Mohamed Kasim, tried to make inroads into the Deccan. They were defeated by the Chalukya feudatory (in south Gujarat) called Avanijashraya Pulakesin in 739 CE. The Arabs were forced to leave Sindh after this defeat. The Chalukyan empire included not only the whole of Karnataka and Maharashtra, but a greater part of Gujarat, Madhya Pradesh and Andhra, and also parts of Odisha and Tamilnadu. Vikramaditya II (733–744 CE) defeated the Pallavas and entered the Pallava capital Kanchi. But he did not loot Kanchi, like the Pallavas who had done at Badami in 642 CE. Instead after inspecting its jewels and treasures, he donated them to the Rajasimheswara temple of Kanchi, as elucidated in a Kannada inscription found carved on one of the pillars of the temple at Kanchi. His queens Lokamahadevi and Trailokyamahadevi built the Virupaksha and Mallikarjuna temples at Pattadakal to commemorate this victory. But the Chalukyan power was weakened in the long run by its frequent wars with the Pallavas and ultimately dismembered during Kirtivarma II's regime in 757 CE.

Rashtrakutas of Malkhed (753–973 CE): In the middle of 8th century the Chalukya rule was ended by their feudatory, the Rashtrakuta family rulers of Berar (in present-day Amravati district of Maharashtra). Sensing an opportunity during a weak period in the Chalukya rule, Dantidurga trounced the great Chalukyan "Karnatabala" (power of Karnata). Having overthrown the Chalukyas, the Rashtrakutas made Manyakheta their capital (modern Malkhed in Kalaburgi district). Although the origins of the early Rashtrakuta ruling families in central India and the Deccan in the 6th and 7th centuries is controversial, during the eighth through the tenth centuries they emphasised the importance of the Kannada language in conjunction with Sanskrit in their administration. Rashtrakuta inscriptions are in Kannada and Sanskrit only. They encouraged literature in both languages and thus literature flowered under their rule.

The Rashtrakutas quickly became the most powerful Deccan empire, making their initial successful forays into the Doab region of Ganges River and Jamuna River during the rule of Dhruva Dharavarsha. The rule of his son Govinda III signaled a new era with Rashtrakuta victories against the Pala Dynasty of Bengal and Gurjara Pratihara of north western India resulting in the capture of Kannauj. The Rashtrakutas held Kannauj intermittently during a period of a tripartite struggle for the resources of the rich Gangetic plains. Because of Govinda III's victories, historians have compared him to Alexander the Great and Pandava Arjuna of the Hindu epic Mahabharata. The Sanjan inscription states the horses of Govinda III drank the icy water of the Himalayan stream and his war elephants tasted the sacred waters of the Ganges River. Amoghavarsha I eulogised by contemporary Arab traveller Sulaiman as one among the four great emperors of the world, succeeded Govinda III to the throne and ruled during an important cultural period that produced landmark writings in Kannada and Sanskrit. The benevolent development of Jaina religion was a hallmark of his rule. Because of his religious temperament, his interest in the arts and literature and his peace-loving nature, he has been compared to emperor Ashoka. The rule of Indra III in the tenth century enhanced the Rashtrakuta position as an imperial power as they conquered and held Kannauj again. Krishna III followed Indra III to the throne in 939 CE. A patron of Kannada literature and a powerful warrior, his reign marked the submission of the Paramara of Ujjain in the north and Cholas in the south.

An Arabic writing *Silsilatuttavarikh* (851 CE) called the Rashtrakutas one among the four principal empires of the world. *Kitab-ul-Masalik-ul-Mumalik* (912 CE) called them the "greatest kings of India" and there were many other contemporaneous books written in their praise. The Rashtrakuta empire at its peak spread from Cape Comorin in the south to Kannauj in the north and from Banaras in the east to Broach (Bharuch) in the west. While the Rashtrakutas built many fine monuments in the Deccan, the most extensive and sumptuous of their work is the monolithic Kailasanatha temple at Ellora, the temple being a splendid achievement. In Karnataka their most famous temples are the Kashivishwanatha temple and the Jaina Narayana temple at Pattadakal. All of the monuments are designated UNESCO World Heritage Sites.

Chronologically, the history of Rashtrakutas moved in the manner described hereafter. In 753 CE, Dantidurga, a feudatory chieftain of Rashtrakuta origin overthrew the Chalukyan king Keerthivarman II, and his family inherited the fortunes of the Chalukyas. He claims that he did this by defeating the 'Karnatabala' of the Chalukyas, described as 'invincible' in those days. We owe the engraving of the celebrated monolithic Kailasa temple at Ellora (now in Maharashtra) to Dantidurga's uncle, Krishna I (756–74 CE). Krishna's son, Dhruva (780–93 CE) crossed the Narmada, and after defeating the celebrated princes like Vathsaraja of the Gurjara Pratihara family and Dharmapala, the Gouda King of Bengal extracted tribute from the ruler of Kanauj, 'the seat of India's Paramountcy.' His son Govinda III (793–814 CE) also repeated the feat when he defeated Nagabhata II, the Gurjara Pratihara, and Dharmapala of Bengal and again extracted tribute from the king of Kanauj. The achievements of the Chalukyas of Badami and Rashatrakutas by defeating the rulers of Kanauj have made the name of their era the "Age of Imperial Kanauj," a misnomer. Instead it should be called the "Age of Imperial Karnataka" as Dr. Suryantha Kamat rightly points out.

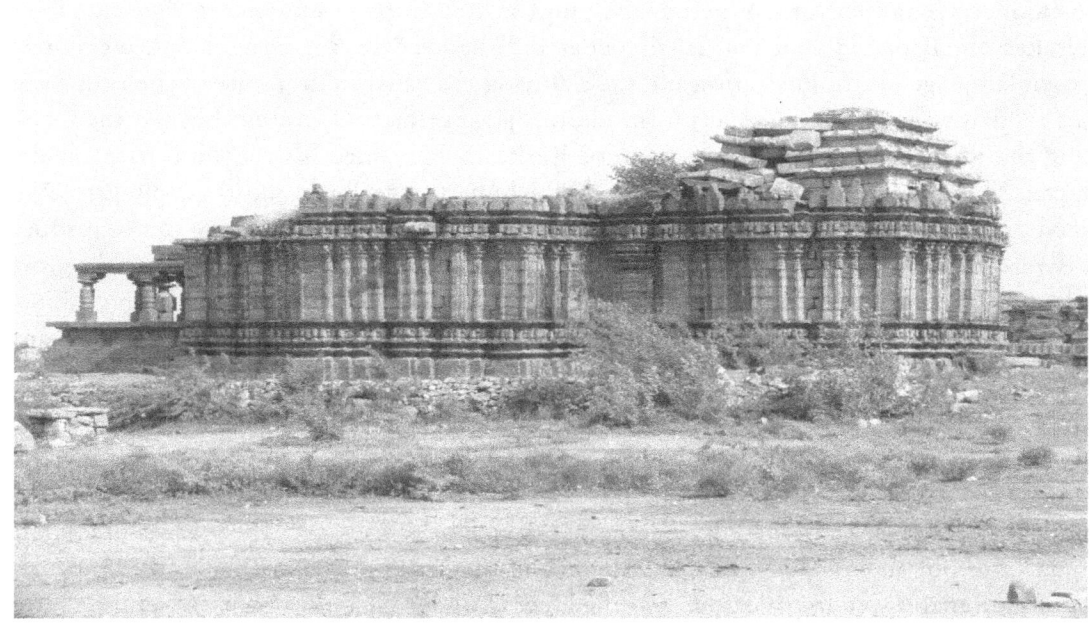

Tarakeswara Temple at Hooli of the Rashtrakutas

Amoghavarsha Nripatunga (814–78 CE), the renowned son of Govinda III, had to face the threat of the Eastern (Vengi) Chalukyas, who challenged his very existence. But he succeeded in subduing them after defeating Vengi Chalukya Vijayaditya II at Vinagavalli. He was a peace-loving monarch who used matrimony as one of the weapons in diplomacy. Although he killed as many as six contemporary political potentates who created trouble for him, he did not conduct Digvijayas like his father and grandfather. He succeeded in maintaining the Empire intact. Himself a scholar, Amoghavarsha patronized scholarship and great Jaina savants like Veerasena, Jinasena, Gunabhadra, grammarian Shaktayana and mathematician Mahaveera adorned his court. Adipurana and commentaries on the Shatkhandagamas called as Dhavala, Jayadhavala and Mahadhavala written in his court were the great Jaina works of all India importance. Kavirajamarga, the first extant Kannada work is of his times composed by his court poet Srivijaya in 850 CE. His great grandson Indra III (914–29 CE) even captured Kanauj and held it under his control for two years. One of his feudatories, Arikesari of Vemulavada patronised Sanskrit writer Somadeva (of Yashastilaka fame) and the famous early Kannada poet Pampa.

Rashtrakuta Krishna III (936–67 CE) subdued the Cholas in the South and established a pillar of victory at Rameshwaram. In fact the so-called 'Age of Imperial Kanauj' in Indian history was the Age of Imperial Karnataka, when the prowess of the Kannadiga was felt all over India. Even Rajashekhara, the celebrated Sanskrit writer, has called the Karnatas as great experts in the technique of war. Soldiers from Karnataka were employed by the Pala rulers of Bengal. One such Kannada warrior founded the Sena Dynasty of Bengal and the other Karnata Dynasty of Mithila (modern Tirhath in Bihar). The Rashtrakutas sponsored the engraving of many Hindu rock-cut temples on the Buddhist model like the Dashavatara Shrine at Ellora, the Jogeshwara near Bombay and the one at the Elephanta Island. The Rashtrakutas constructed many tanks and their temples are found at places like Sirwal, Sulepet, Gadikeshwar, Adaki, Sedam, Handarki, Mogha, Naragund, Nidagundi, Naregal, Ron, Savadi, Badami, Banashankari, Pattadakal and at Hampi. Some Rashtrakuta hero stones of exception are seen at Ron, Kaujageri, Karmadi, Belvanaki, Gadag, Betageri which need special mention. These two dynasties viz., the Chalukyas of Badami and the Rashtrakutas popularised animal husbandry by donating cows in thousands. The stones commemorating such grants (*gosasakallu*) are seen all over.

Chalukyas of Kalyana (973–1189 CE): In the late 10th century, the Western Chalukyas, also known as the Kalyani Chalukyas or 'Later' Chalukyas rose to power by overthrowing the Rashtrakutas under whom they had been serving as feudatories. Manyakheta was their capital early on before they moved it to Kalyani (modern Basavakalyan). Whether the kings of this empire belonged to the same family line as their namesakes, the Badami Chalukyas is still debated. Whatever the Western Chalukya origins, Kannada remained their language of administration and the Kannada and Sanskrit literature of their time was prolific. Tailapa II, a feudatory ruler from Tardavadi (modern Vijayapur district), re-established the Chalukya rule by defeating the Rashtrakutas during the reign of Karka II. He timed his rebellion to coincide with the confusion caused by the invading Paramara of central India to the Rashtrakutas capital in 973 CE. This era produced prolonged warfare with the Chola dynasty of Tamilakam for control of the resources of the Godavari River-Krishna River Doab region in Vengi. Someshvara I, a brave Chalukyan king, successfully curtailed the growth of the Chola Empire to the south of the Tungabhadra River region despite suffering some defeats while maintaining control over his feudatories in the Konkan, Gujarat, Malwa and Kalinga regions. For approximately 100 years, beginning in the early 11th century, the Cholas occupied large areas of south Karnataka region (Gangavadi).

In 1076, the ascent of the most famous king of this Chalukya family, Vikramaditya VI, changed the balance of power in favour of the Chalukyas. His fifty-year reign was an important period in Karnataka's history and is referred to as the "Chalukya Vikrama era." His victories over the Cholas in the late 11th and early 12th centuries put an end to the Chola influence in the Vengi region permanently. Some of the well-known contemporaneous feudatory families of the Deccan under Chalukya control were the Hoysalas, the Seuna Yadavas of Devagiri, the Kakatiya dynasty and the Southern Kalachuri. At their peak, the Western

Chalukyas ruled a vast empire stretching from the Narmada river in the north to the Cauveri river in the south. Vikramaditya VI is considered one of the most influential kings of Indian history. Important architectural works were created by these Chalukyas, especially in the Tungabhadra river valley, that served as a conceptual link between the building idioms of the early Badami Chalukyas and the later Hoysalas. With the weakening of the Kalyani Chalukyas in the decades following the death of Vikramaditya VI in 1126 CE, the feudatories of the Chalukyas gained their independence.

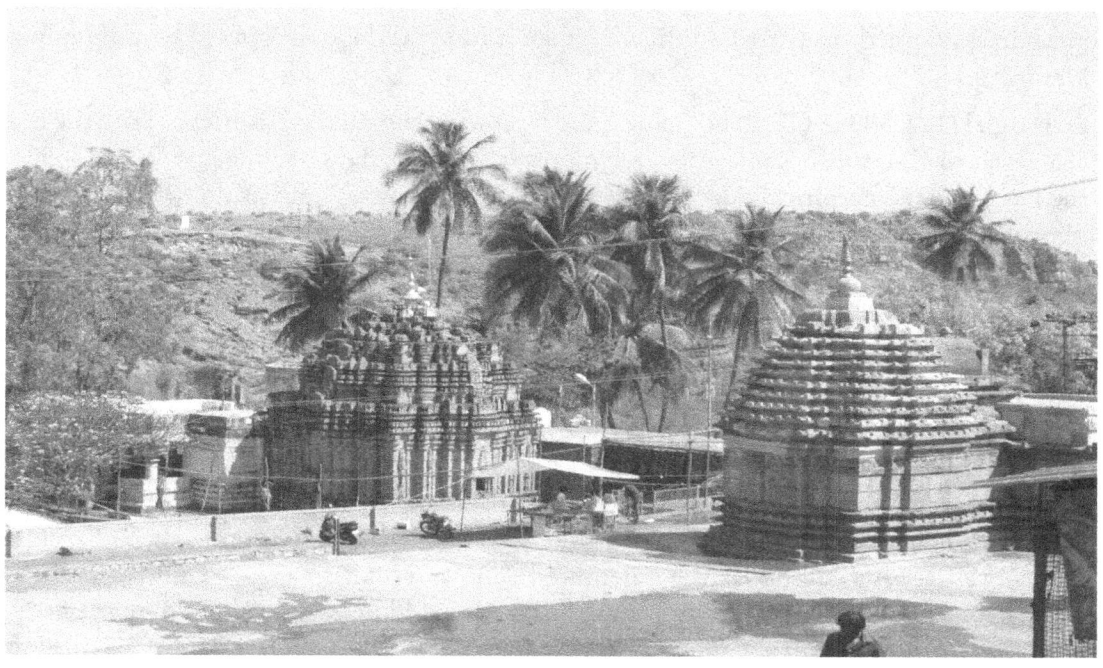

Basaveswara and Mahalingeswara Temples at Gokak of the Kalyani Chalukyas

The Kalachuris of Karnataka, whose ancestors were immigrants into the southern Deccan from central India, had ruled as a feudatory from Mangalavada (modern Mangalavedhe in Maharashtra). Bijjala II, the most powerful ruler of this dynasty, was a commander (*mahamandaleswar*) during the reign of Chalukya Vikramaditya VI. Seizing an opportune moment in the waning power of the Chalukyas, Bijjala II declared independence in 1157 CE and annexed their capital Kalyani. His rule was cut short by his assassination in 1167 CE and the ensuing civil war caused by his sons fighting over the throne ended the dynasty as the last Chalukya scion regained control of Kalyani. This victory however, was short-lived as the Chalukyas were eventually driven out by the Seuna Yadavas.

Vikramaditya VI (1076–1127 CE) proudly called as the Lord of more than 1000 inscriptions, is the king who started the Vikrama Saka Samvatsara on his coronation, celebrated in history as the patron of the great jurist Vighnaneshwara, who wrote Mithakshara, a standard work on Hindu law. The emperor has been immortalised by poet Bilhana (hailing from Kashmir) who chose his patron as the hero for his Sanskrit work, viz., Vikramankadeva Charitam. His son Someshwara III (1127–39) was a great scholar. He has compiled Manasollasa, a Sanskrit encyclopedia and Vikramankabhyudayam, a poem in which his father is the hero. Manasollasa, a great work of multi-dimensions, depicts the cultural conditions in south India, has sections on administration, medicine, architecture, painting, jewellery, cookery, dance, music, sports etc. It has 100 sections discussing various aspects of human activity.

The Chalukyas were great builders, and their beautiful temples renowned for fine and intricate engravings are found at many places like Itagi, Ron, Naregal, Gadag, Dambal, Lakkundi Lakshmeshwar, Bankapur, Hangal, Haveri, Abbaluru, Hamsabhavi, Chikkerur; Balligavi, Kuruvatti, Chaudadanapura, Unkal, Annigeri, Kundgol, Moraba, Nagavi, Adki, Yewur, Sedam, Kulageri, Kollur, Diggavi, Madiyala,

Kalgi; Saundatti, Okkunda, Halasi, Belagavi; Badami, Pattadakal, Aihole, Mahakuta, Gabbur, Devadurga; Koppal, Kuknur, Itagi, Yelburga; Kurugodu, Hadagili, Hampi, Kogali, Kadlewad, Chattaraki, Teradal, Nimbala and Muttagi. They were great patrons of scholars, and Sanskrit writers like Vadiraja and Kannada poets like Ranna, Durgasimha and Nayasena lived in their times. The Virashaiva movement saw the advent of Vachana literature in Kannada, initiated by Jedara Dasimayya and Kembhavi Bhoganna. It grew during the Kalachuri interregnum when more than 770 Sharanas including Basava, Allama, Siddarama, Channabasava, Akka Mahadevi and others lived. Virashaivism preached equality of men, tried to emancipate women, and stressed the importance of bread-labour concept by calling it as *Kayaka* for worshipping god.

Seunas of Devagiri (1173–1318 CE): The Seunas (Yadavas) who were the feudatories of both the Rastrakutas and the Chalukyas of Kalyana, became a sovereign power from the days of Bhillama V (1173–92 CE) who founded the new capital Devagiri (modern Daulatabad in Maharashtra). Earlier they ruled from Sindhinera (modern Sinnar) near Nasik. Bhillama V captured Kalyana in 1186 CE, and later clashed with Hoysala Ballala II at Soraturu in 1190 CE. Though he lost the battle, he built a vast kingdom extending from the Narmada to the Krishna river. His son Jaitugi (1192–99 CE) not only defeated Paramara Subhata Varman, but also killed Rudra and Mahadeva, the Kakatiya kings of Warangal.

Singhana II (1199–1247 CE), the greatest of the Seunas, extended the Seuna kingdom upto the Tungabhadra. But the Seunas were defeated by the army of Delhi Sultan in 1296 CE, again in 1307 CE and finally in 1318 CE, and thus the kingdom was wiped out. Their feudatory, Kumara Rama and his father Kampilaraya of Kampili also died fighting against the Muslims in 1327 CE. The Seunas have become immortal in history by the writings of the famous mathematician Bhaskaracharya, the great writer on music Sharngadeva, and of the celebrated scholar Hemadri. The Seunas and the Hoysalas drained their energy in mutual warfare, and thus the south could be easily subdued by the armies of the Delhi Sultans. Sharngadeva's work, Sangita Ratnakara, is the basis for the growth of classical music and Vidyaranya during the 14th century wrote 'Sangitasara' based on Sangita Ratnakara. The Seunas built fine temples called Hemadpanthi structures which are found all over Maharashtra. The Virabhadra temple at Yedur in Belagavi district is one of their structures. They built and renovated many temples in north Karnataka.

Hoysalas of Dwarasamudra (1052–1342 CE): The Hoysalas had become a powerful force even during their rule from Belur in the 11th century as a feudatory of the Chalukyas (in the south Karnataka region). In the early 12th century they successfully fought the Cholas in the south, convincingly defeating them in the battle of Talakad and moved their capital to nearby Halebid. Historians refer to the founders of the dynasty as natives of Malnad Karnataka, based on the numerous inscriptions calling them *Maleparolganda* or "Lord of the Male (hills) chiefs" (Malepas). With the waning of the Western Chalukya power, the Hoysalas declared their independence in the late twelfth century.

During this period of Hoysala control, distinctive Kannada literary metres such as *Ragale* (blank verse), *Sangatya* (meant to be sung to the accompaniment of a musical instrument), *Shatpadi* (seven line) etc. became widely accepted. The Hoysalas expanded the *Vesara* architecture stemming from the Chalukyas, culminating in the Hoysala architectural articulation and style as exemplified in the construction of the Chennakesava Temple at Belur and the Hoysaleswara temple at Halebid. Both these temples were built in commemoration of the victories of the Hoysala Vishnuvardhana against the Cholas in 1116 CE. Veera Ballala II, the most effective of the Hoysala rulers, defeated the aggressive Pandyas when they invaded the Chola kingdom and assumed the titles "Establisher of the Chola Kingdom" (*Cholarajyapratishtacharya*), "Emperor of the south" (*Dakshina Chakravarthi*) and "Hoysala emperor" (*Hoysala Chakravarti*). The Hoysalas extended their foothold in areas known today as Tamil Nadu around 1225 CE, making the city of Kannanur Kuppam near Srirangam a provincial capital. This gave them control over South Indian politics that began a period of Hoysala hegemony in the southern Deccan.

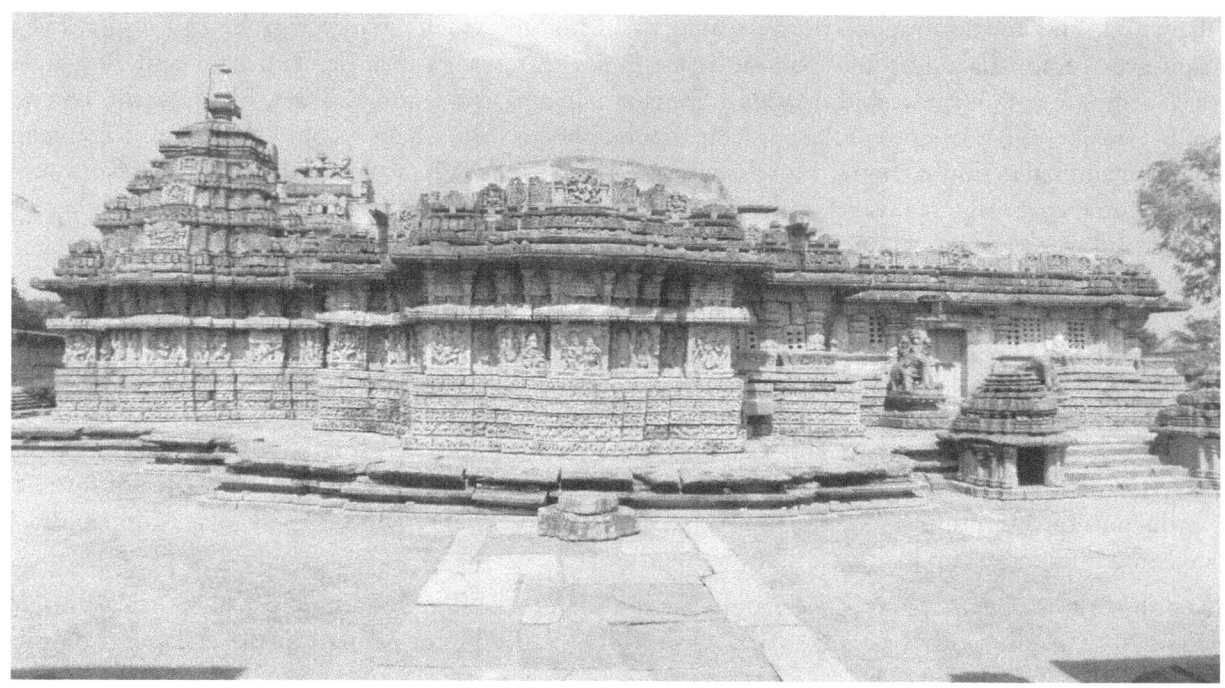

Mallikarjuna Temple at Basaralu of the Hoysalas

In the early 13th century, with the Hoysala power remaining unchallenged, the first of the Muslim incursions into south India began. After over two decades of waging war against a foreign power, the Hoysala ruler at the time, Veera Ballala III, died in the battle of Madurai in 1343. This resulted in the merger of the sovereign territories of the Hoysala empire with the areas administered by Harihara I, founder of the Vijayanagara Empire, located in the Tungabhadra region in present-day Karnataka. The new kingdom thrived for another two centuries with Vijayanagara as its capital.

The Hoysalas continued the great tradition of their art-loving overlords, viz., the Kalyana Chalukyas, and their fine temples are found at Belur, Halebid and Somanathapura. The first great ruler of the dynasty, Vishnuvardhana (1108–1152 CE) freed Gangavadi from the Cholas (who had held it since 1004 CE), in 1114 CE and in commemoration of his victory, built the celebrated Keertinarayana temple at Talakad, and Vijayanarayana (Chennakesava) Temple at Belur. His kingdom was visited by Ramanujacharya, who stayed at Saligrama, Thondanur, and Melkote in Karnataka for long. Vishnuvardhana patronised the saint and believed to have earlier influenced by Srivaishnava Chola officers in Gangavadi. He continued to patronise Jainism, as many of his commanders and his accomplished queen Shantaladevi were Jainas. His commander Ketamalla built the famous Hoysaleswara (Vishnuvardhana) temple at Halebid.

The *agraharas* in Karnataka which were numerous by then had created such a healthy intellectual atmosphere that Ramanuja, the great preacher of Srivaishnavism from Tamilnadu could get a hearing to his teachings from the intellectuals in Karnataka, which was denied to him in his own native country. Even his life was under threat there.

Though Vishnuvardhana did not fully succeed in his efforts to overthrow the Chalukya yoke his grandson Ballala (1173–1220 CE) became free. When the Cholas were attacked by the Pandyas in Tamilnadu, Ballala II drove the Pandyas back and thus assumed the title "Establisher of the Chola kingdom." Later, in the days of his son Narasimha II (1220–35), Hoysalas even secured a foothold in Tamilnadu and Kuppam near Srirangam became a second capital of the Hoysalas. As a consequence, the empire was divided among his two sons and the collateral branch continued for over six decades.

Ballala III (1291–1343), the last great Hoysala, had to struggle hard to hold his own against the invasions of the Delhi Sultans. He died while fighting against the Sultan of Madurai. It was his commanders

Harihara and Bukka, who founded the Vijayanagara Kindgom, which later grew to be an Empire. Hoysala age saw great Kannada poets like Rudrabhatta, Janna, Kereya Padmarasa, Harihara and Raghavanka. Hoysala temples at Belur, Halebid, Maddur, Somanathapur, Thondanur, Kikkeri, Bhadravathi, Banawara, Basaralu, Arasikere, Aralaguppe, Talakad, Amritapura, Hosaholalu, Melkote, Sunka Tonnur, Nagamangala, Kaidala Kurudumale, Sindhaghatta, Hosabadanur, Santhe-bachahalli, Varahanatha, Kallhalli, Koravangala, Aghalaya, Shravanabelagola, Javagal, Kaivara, Govindanahalli, Nuggehalli, Tenginaghatta, Turuvekere, etc., are wonderful works of art. The representative carving of land measuring rods used during this period are being discovered at places like, Amritapura, Mugur, and Bhairapura.

2.2 GROWTH OF RELIGIONS AND VARIOUS SECTS

Jainism had a stronghold in Karnataka in the early medieval period at Shravanabelagola as its most important centre. The first Tirthankara, Rishabha, is said to have spent his final days in Karnataka. Both Jain philosophy and literature have contributed immensely to the religious and cultural landscape of Karnataka. Jain influence on literature and philosophy is particularly evident. Shravanabelagola, Moodabidri, and Karkala are famous for Jain history and monuments.

Buddhism was once popular in Karnataka during the first millennium in places such as Kalaburgi and Banavasi. A chance discovery of edicts and several Mauryan relics at Sannati in the Kalaburgi district in 1986 has proven that the Krishna river basin was once home to both Mahayana and Theravada Buddhism. In recent times, Buddhism thrives here and calls Dzogchen monastery and the Dhondeling Tibetan refugee camps as home. A commentary on the growth of both Jainism and Buddhism in Karnataka is furnished in Chapter 5 where influence of these religions on the art and architecture of Karnataka has been detailed. However, growth of Hinduicism or Brahamanical religion needs to be treated separately on account of its extensive influence on art, architecture and culture of Karnataka.

Hindus believe gods and spirits are peripatetic and have a potential for varied manifestations. Chief deities appear in a wide variety of forms, expressing their multiple roles and moods. These forms can be iconic, that is, with a resemblance to human form; or aniconic, in other words, in an abstract symbolic form such as a pile of stones or a linga or a geometric configuration like the *yantras* or *chakras*.

Predominantly Hinduism is made up of several sects. Popular among them in Karnataka have been Saivism, Vaishnavism, Shaktism and Smartism. The discussion about the iconic forms of various gods these sects worship will thus be guided by the religious content these sects believe in.

Siva

Siva, meaning "The Auspicious One," also known as *Mahadeva* (Great God), is one of the main deities of Hinduism. He is the supreme god within Saivism, one of the three most influential denominations in contemporary Hinduism. He is one of the five primary forms of God in the Smarta tradition, and "the Destroyer" or "the Transformer" among the Trimurti, the Hindu Trinity of the primary aspects of the divine.

At the highest level, Siva is regarded as limitless, transcendent, unchanging and formless. Siva also has many benevolent and fearsome forms. In benevolent aspects, he is depicted as an omniscient Yogi who lives an ascetic life on Mount Kailasa, as well as a householder with wife Parvati and his two children, Ganesha and Kartikeya, and in fierce aspects, he is often depicted slaying demons. Siva is also regarded as the patron god of yoga and arts.

The main iconographical attributes of Siva are the third eye on his forehead, the snake Vasuki around his neck, the adorning crescent moon, the holy river Ganga flowing from his matted hair, the *trisula* as his weapon and the *damarus* his musical instrument. Siva is usually worshiped in the aniconic form of Linga.

The Sanskrit word Siva comes from Shri Rudram Chamakam of Taittiriya Samhita of Krishna Yajurveda. The root word *si* means *auspicious*. The adjective *siva*, is used as an attributive epithet for several Vedic deities, including Rudra. Siva is known by over 150 names in Karnataka and his temples are variously described from the attributes relating from these various names. However, the most common names used in naming the deity as also the temple housing the deity are Mahadeva, Mulsthaneswara, Someswara, Rameswara, Mallikarjuna, Iswara, Nandiswara, Lingeswara etc.

The Sanskrit word Saiva means "relating to the god Siva," and this term is the Sanskrit name both for one of the principal sects of Hinduism and for a member of that sect. It is used as an adjective to characterize certain beliefs and practices, such as Saivism.

Some authors associate the name with the Tamil word *sivappu* meaning "red," noting that Siva is linked to the Sun (*sivan*, "the Red one," in Tamil) and that Rudra is also called *Babhru* (brown, or red) in the Rigveda.

Siva's rise to a major position in the pantheon was facilitated by his identification with a host of Vedic deities, including Purusha, Rudra, Agni, Indra, Prajapati, Vayu, and others.

Siva as we know him today shares many features with the Vedic god Rudra, and both Siva and Rudra are viewed as the same personality in Hindu scriptures. The two names are used synonymously. Rudra, the god of the roaring storm, is usually portrayed in accordance with the element he represents as a fierce, destructive deity.

Rudra and Agni have a close relationship. The identification between Agni and Rudra in the Vedic literature was an important factor in the process of Rudra's gradual development into the later character as Rudra-Siva.

In the *Satarudriya*, some epithets of Rudra, such as Sasipanjara (Of golden red hue as of flame) and Tivaṣimati (Flaming bright), suggest a fusing of the two deities. Agni is said to be a bull, and Lord Siva possesses a bull as his vehicle, Nandi. The horns of Agni, who is sometimes characterized as a bull, are mentioned in ancient literature as an attribute of both. In medieval sculpture, both Agni and the form of Siva known as Bhairava have flaming hair as a special feature.

Rudra's transformation from an ambiguously characterized deity to a supreme being began in the Shvetashvatara Upanishad (400–200 BCE), which founded the tradition of Rudra-Siva worship. Here they are identified as the creators of the cosmos and liberators of souls from the birth-rebirth cycle. The period of 200 BCE to 100 CE also marks the beginning of the Saiva tradition focused on the worship of Siva, with references to Saiva ascetics in Patanjali's Mahabhasya and in the Mahabharata. The Siva Puranas, particularly the Siva Purana and the Linga Purana, discuss the various forms of Siva and the cosmology associated with him.

The Trimurti is a concept in Hinduism in which the cosmic functions of creation, preservation, and destruction are personified by the forms of Brahma (the creator), Visnu (the preserver) and Siva (the destroyer or transformer). These three deities have been called "the Hindu triad" or the "Great Trinity," often addressed as "Brahma-Vishnu-Maheswara."

The *Pasupata Saivism* is perhaps the most ancient of all the sects of Saivism. It is possible that the people of Indus valley practiced some form of *Pasupata Saivism*. Its founder is considered to be Siva himself who passed on the knowledge to several ancient sages. The Atharvasira Upanishad mentions *Pasupata* rite for the removal of animal bonds, probably a practice initially associated with this sect. Etymologically, *pasupata* means the herdsman's staff. Symbolically it represents the trident, the weapon of Siva with which He destroys our ignorance and impurities.

An early wave of *Pasupata Saivism* spread to the South in the 2nd century BCE after the spell of Ashoka's Buddhism. *Pasupata* sect was prevalent in South India in the Satavahana period. However, the inscriptions in Karnataka reveal references to *Pasupata* sect during the Kadamba and Kalyani Chalukya periods. The existence of this sect in Karnataka can be traced to as early as 6th century CE and later.

The sect became popular mostly through the contribution of the legendary Lakulisa (meaning lord with the club) who lived around 200 BCE in the Kathiawar peninsula of present day Gujarat. His teachings are available to us in the form of *sutras* known as *Pasupata Sutras*. He introduced a strict code of conduct and certain *yogic* practices and established a specific procedure for admitting members into the sect. According to a tradition stated in the Linga Purana, Lakulisa is considered as the 28th and the last *avatar* (incarnation) of Siva and the propounder of Yoga system. According to the same tradition, Lakulisa had four disciples, viz., Kaurushya, Garga, Mitra and Kushika. The Kurma Purana (Chap. 53), the Vayu Purana (Chap. 23), and the Linga Purana (Chap. 24) predicted that Siva (Maheswara) would appear in the form of a wandering monk called 'Lakulin' or 'Nakulisha,' and that he would have four disciples named, Kushika, Garga, Mitra, and Kanrushya, who would re-establish the cult of *Pasupati* and would therefore be called *Pasupata(s)*. Stone images of Lakulisa and his four disciples have been found in the temples built during the Badami Chalukyas' time. While Lakulisa's image is found in the Sangameswara temple at Mahakuta, the image of Lakulisa with his four disciples is found in the Cave no. 2 at Badami.

Further inscriptions also exist which refer to grants entrusted by various kings from different dynasties to the preceptors of *Lakulisa* sect. Preceptors from this sect were considered experts in Lakula-sastra. The *Kapalika* and the *Kalamukha* sects are close to *Pasupata* sect in many ways but differ in matters of practice. They follow more shocking and outrageous methods to attract public ridicule and criticism and free themselves from social conditioning and egoistic attachment to their physical selves. While externally they are encouraged to indulge in controversial behavior, internally they are advised to lead pure and austere lives.

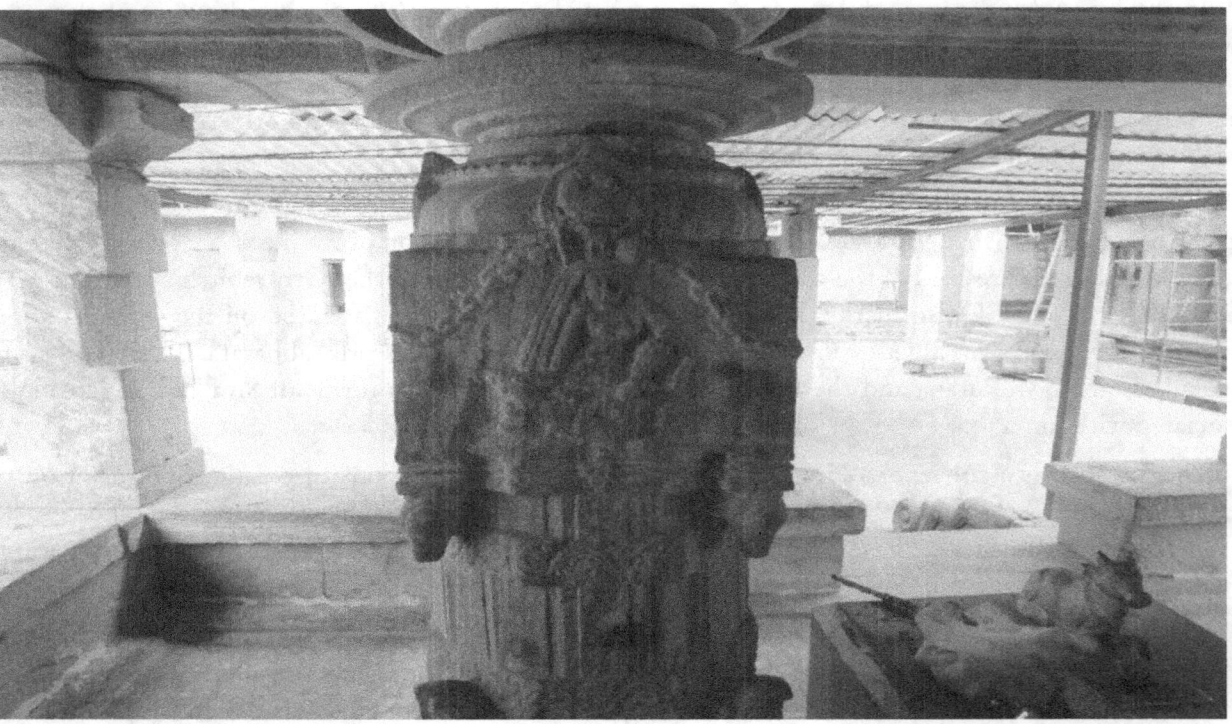

Sculpture of Matsyendranatha on the Pillar at Prasanna Rameswara Temple, Devarunda

The *Kalamukhas* who lived in parts of Karnataka enjoyed a good reputation for their asceticism, celibacy and inner purity. Preceptors of *Kalamukha* were most active and highly influential Saivites. They enjoyed liberal support from the rulers, feudatories and the people of all classes. This sect set up a tradition of famous teachers and built monumental monasteries and temples. The *Sakti-parishe* and *Simha-parishe* are the two well-known divisions of the *Kalamukha* order. Kings from nearly all dynasties in Karnataka supported the temple building activity of the *Kalamukhas*.

Natha-pantha cult was introduced in Karnataka by the Alupa kings. Bronze image of Lokeswara in Kadrika-vihara (Manjunatha temple, Kadri) was installed by the King Kundavarmarasa in 968 CE. Lokeswara represents Matsyendranatha, who is considered the spiritual son of Siva according to the *Natha-pantha* cult. The cult of Nathism is known to have developed itself into the *Vajrayana* system of the Mahayana form of Buddhism and thus was in its origin a form of Tantric Buddhism before it transformed itself into *Tantric Saivism*. An image of Matsyendranatha is also carved on one of the pillars of the Prasanna Rameshwara temple at Devarunda.

Goravas were a sect of Saivite ascetics. The word *gorava* seems to have been derived from the word guru and is also used as *guruva*. *Goravas* were respected by the society for their religious attainments, proficiency in all branches of Sanskrit and ethical standards of high order. Some *goravas* were in charge of worship and maintenance of Siva temples. *Goravas* enjoyed liberal patronage from the kings of various dynasties and were showered with grants as is evidenced by several inscriptions. Challeswara temple at Atakur of the famous Atakur Inscription was entrusted to a *gorava*.

Visnu

In Hinduism, Visnu is the Supreme God Svayam Bhagavan of Vaishnavism (one of the three principal denominations) and one of the three supreme deities (Trimurti). As one of the five primary forms of God in the Smarta tradition, he is conceived as "the Preserver or the Protector" within the Trimurti, the Hindu Trinity of the divinity (Brahma-Visnu-Maheswara).

In Hindu sacred texts, Visnu is usually described as having dark complexion of water-filled clouds and having four arms. He is depicted as a pale blue being, as are his incarnations Rama and Krishna He holds a *padma* (lotus flower) in his lower left hand, the *Kaumodaki gada* (mace) in his lower right hand, the *Panchajanya sankha* (conch) in his upper left hand and the discus weapon considered to be the most powerful weapon according to Hindu Religion, *Sudarshana Chakra* in his upper right hand.

The traditional explanation of the name *Visnu* involves the root *vis*, meaning "to settle," or also (in the Rigveda) "to enter into, to pervade," glossing the name as "the All-Pervading One." Adi Shankara in his commentary on the *Sahasranama* states derivation from *vis*, with a meaning "presence everywhere."

In the Yajur Veda, Taittiriya Aranyaka, Narayana Suktam, Narayana is mentioned as the Supreme Being. The first verse of Narayana Suktam mentions the words "*paramam padam*," which literally mean "highest position" and may be understood as the "supreme abode for all souls." This special status is not given to any deity in the Vedas apart from Visnu/Narayana. Narayana is one of the thousand names of Visnu as mentioned in the Visnu Sahasranama. It describes Visnu as the All-Pervading essence of all beings, the master of-and beyond-the past, present and future, one who supports, sustains and governs the Universe and originates and develops all elements within. This illustrates the omnipresent characteristic of Visnu. Visnu governs the aspect of preservation and sustenance of the universe, so he is called "Preserver of the Universe."

Visnu's supremacy is attested by his victories over very powerful entities. It is further attested by the accepted iconography and sculptures of Visnu in reclining position as producing Brahma emerging from his navel. Brahma the creator is thus created in turn by Visnu out of his own person. Instead Visnu reincarnates in various *avatars* to slay or defeat those demons.

Brahma

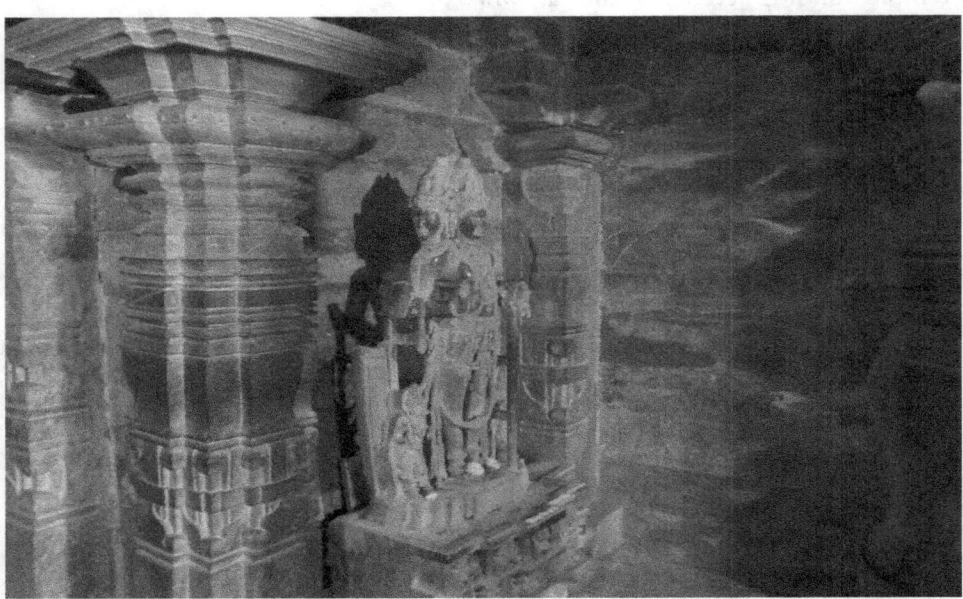

Chatur-mukha Brahma at Brahma Jinalaya, Lakkundi

According to the Brahma Purana, he is the father of Manu, and from Manu all human beings are descended. In the Ramayana and the Mahabharata, he is often referred to as the progenitor or great grandsire of all human beings. He is not to be confused with the Supreme Cosmic Spirit in Hindu Vedanta philosophy known as Brahman, which is genderless. Brahma is often identified with Prajapati, a Vedic deity. Brahma's consort is Saraswati. Being the husband of Saraswati or Vaac Devi (the Goddess of Speech), Brahma is also known as "Vaagish," meaning "Lord of Speech and Sound."

He is clad in red clothes. Brahma is traditionally depicted with four heads, four faces, and four arms. With each head, he continually recites one of the four Vedas. He is often depicted with a white beard (especially in North India), indicating the nearly eternal nature of his existence. Unlike most other Hindu gods, Brahma holds no weapons. One of his hands holds a scepter. Another of his hands holds a book. Brahma also holds a string of prayer beads called the '*akṣamala*' (literally "garland of eyes"), which he uses to keep track of the Universe's time. He is also shown holding the Vedas.

Shakti

Shakti or Devi, the goddess has been known in several popular forms -Durga, Lakshmi, Saraswati, Bhagavati, Kali, Chamundi, Uma, Kamakshi, Amba and countless more names. Thousands of temples dot the Indian landscape. "Shakti" denotes energy and is derived from the word *Sak* which means 'the ability to act.' It also refers to the cosmic energy that permeates through everything. The power is believed to preside over creation, preservation and destruction. The 'Devi Sukta' in Rig Veda, refers to Shakti as something that has no beginning and no end, something that is constant and forever.

In Karnataka, Shakti cult can be traced back to the sixth century going by the epigraphical records though worship of Shakti in one form or the other had been in vogue much earlier. Bhuvaneswari, considered the State's guardian spirit, has her shrines in Hampi's Virupaksha temple and in Bhuvanagiri (Uttara Kannada). The Bhadrakarnika at Gokarna is considered as one of the 108 Shakti Peethas in the Devi Bhagavata Purana.

Durga's Mahishasuramardini form is found in places like Aihole, Badami and Pattadakal, vouching for her superior status in the art's world during the reign of Chalukyas of Badami. Kings and dynasties who saw her as the goddess of war, started the practice of worshipping the weapons on the Vijayadashami day. Durga Parameshwari temples are also seen widely in coastal Karnataka at Katilu, Bappanadu (Mulki), and Mandarthi; the Mahishasuramardini temple at Kadiyali, Mahishasuramardini temple at Neelavar, Rajarajeshwari temple at Polali and Kali shrine at Ambalapadi in Udupi are also among the important Shakti temples in the region. Western Gangas held *Kiltabel Eretti Bhatari* i.e 'Bhatari' or 'Kali' as their family deity and worshipped her during wars. A large sized image of her is kept in the compound of the Arkeswara temple at Alur near Chamarajanagar. Cholas considered Pidari or Pattalki or Bhattarki as their family deity. Kolaramma temple in Kolar was built in honour of Pidari.

Chamundi, another incarnation of Shakti emerged as a result of slaying the demons Chanda and Munda, has been the tutelary deity of the Wodeyars. The history of Abhiseka Lakshmi or Gajalakshmi has been in existence in the State for 2,000 years and has been inscribed as a symbol in the lintels over the sanctum sanctorum of several temples. The Lakshmi temple at Sulebhavi (Belagavi) is well-known for her powers to grant wishes. Goddess Saraswati became popular in the State from 11 century CE, and has been mentioned in Kavirajamarga (8th century CE).

The 'Temple of Saraswati' at Gadag has richly carved images of this goddess. Hoysala temples with images of Saraswati in numerous forms, nonetheless reinforce her popularity from ancient times. Invocation of Saraswati during Navaratri is thought to have originated in the State during the 14th century. Renuka, the goddess of chastity has been worshiped as Yellamma from 2nd century in places like Saundatti and Chandragutti, with the rituals of a cult.

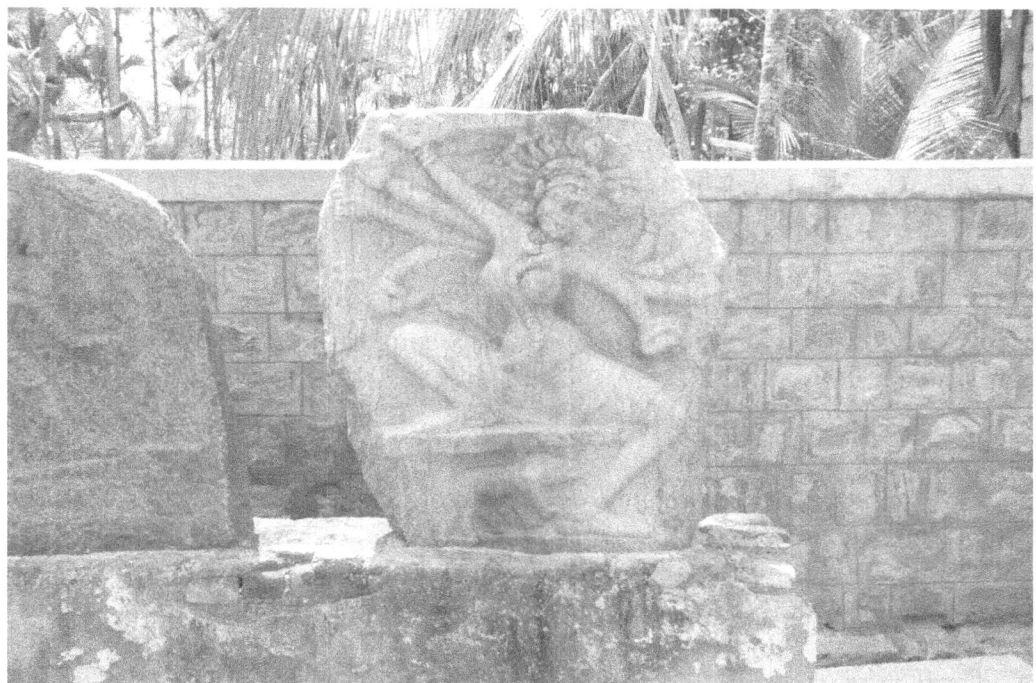

Kiltabel Eretti Bhatari, Arkeswara Temple, Alur

Sirsi's Marikamba and Huligamma at Kapala, portray a unique hybridisation of folk and vedic tradition, while Hasanamba of Hassan district is an ant-hill open to worship for a week during the Navarathri festival. Amruteswari temple at Kota may be smaller, but it is yet another evidence of people's strong faith in the goddess.

Sharadamba at Sringeri, Mookambika at Kolluru, Mangalamba at Mangaluru, Rajarajeshvari at Polali, Banashankari at Badami and Bengaluru, Annapurneswari at Horanadu, Mahalasa Narayani at Kumta and Kamakshi at Hebbur are some of the well-known Shakti temples of the State.

As the legend goes, Sala, the progenitor of the Hoysalas, was walking through a forest with his Jain Guru, Yogendra Sudatta, to worship goddess Vasantika Devi when a tiger came their way. Taking an iron rod, the teacher handed it over to Sala saying, "Poy, Sala" (Strike, Sala). Sala killed the tiger. This story is narrated in several records with a few differences in detail.

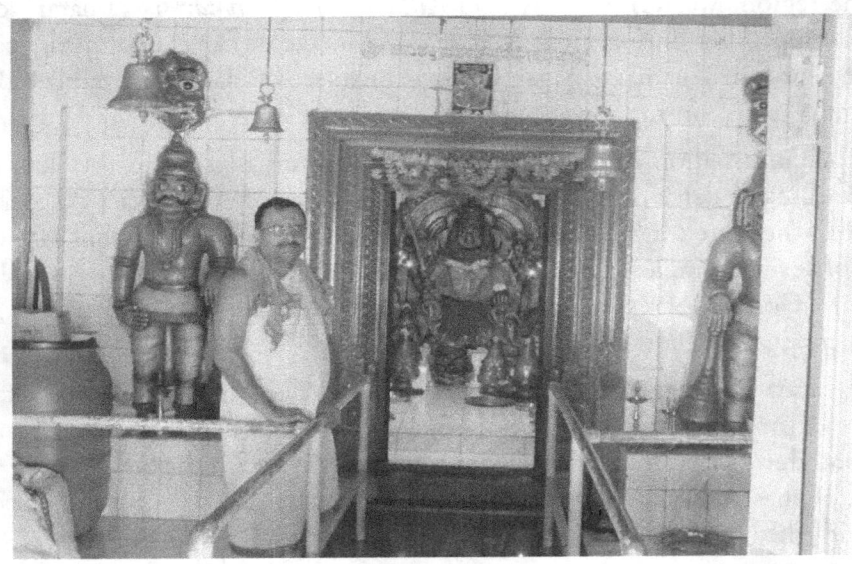

Vasantika Devi, Angadi

While the Hoysala crest in many temples depicts Sala killing a tiger, the seal on copper plates and coins shows a dead tiger and a rod. Sala was perhaps the first ruler of the dynasty. Not much is known about him but the fact that Hoysalas did worship Shakti is well established. Vasantha Parameshwari temple still stands tall in Angadi from where the Hoysalas originated.

Chandrala Parameshwari temple at Sannati has its own history. Though the temple is over 800 years old, it has a close association with Sannati and Kanganahalli *stupas* which were nearly 2000 years old. The stone slab on which king Ashoka's edict is written was used as the foundation on which the idol of the goddess was installed. The slab was recovered during excavations by ASI when the roof of a part of the temple gave way and fell on the idol. While extricating the idol, Ashoka's edict was discovered.

Cult of Shakti also influenced the performing arts of Karnataka, more notably the dance forms. The community dance, Mari Kunitha which is wide spread in Mysore and Mandya districts, display an insular flexibility in the presentation and narration. Originally belonging to the Shakti cult, these dances consist of performers standing either in rows or forming a big circle and dancing to the tune of 'Chakravaddya,' an indigenous flat percussion instrument. The dance begins at a slow pace, gathers momentum, reaches a frenzied pitch as the tempo of the beat increases and continues till the rhythm fades away. The songs are sung intermittently at each pause and hence could be heard by the audience clearly. In the dances like Kombat and Billat, which is similar to the Mari Kunitha, the artistes attired in customary 'Kodava' costume (consist of black robe, a silk waist belt and a 'Zari' bordered white turban) perform carrying deer-horns to the accompaniment of a drum and the dudi-a small drum.

2.3 VARIOUS SAINTS WHO INFLUENCED KARNATAKA'S HISTORY AND CULTURE

The three most important schools of Vedic philosophy viz. Vedanta, Advaita Vedanta, Vishishtadvaita and Dvaita blossomed in Karnataka. The Dvaita Madhvacharya was born in Karnataka. The Advaita Adi Shankara chose Sringeri in Karnataka to establish the first of his four *mathas*. The Vishishtadvaita Ramanuja, considered a saint in Sri Sampradaya, who fled persecution by the Saiva Chola dynasty of Tamil Nadu, spent the years from 1098–1122 CE in Karnataka. He first lived in Thondanur and then moved to Melukote where the Cheluvanarayana Swamy Temple and a well organised *matha* were built. He was patronized by Hoysala Vishnuvardhana. Udupi, Sringeri, Gokarna and Melukote are well known places of Sanskrit and Vedic learning. In the 12th century, Lingayatism emerged in northern Karnataka as a protest against the rigidity of the prevailing social and caste system. Leading figures of the movement such as Basava, Akka Mahadevi and Allama Prabhu established the Anubhava Mandapa where Lingayatism was preached. This was to form the basis of the Lingayat faith and today counts millions among its followers.

Under the Bhakti movement, Visnu and Siva were the main focus of devotion by both Lingayat and Brahmanical communities. Basava (1106–1167 CE), also called Basavanna, protested against caste system and was for equality among all classes. His movement was called the Bhakti Movement and it had a profound paradigm shift in the socio-cultural ethos of the state of Karnataka. The basic tenet of this philosophy, propounded from the 12th century by the Virashaiva School or Virashaivism, was opposition to the caste system, rejection of the supremacy of the Brahmans, abhorrence to ritual sacrifice, and insistence on Bhakti and the worship of the one God, Siva. His followers were called Virashaivas, meaning "stalwart Siva-worshipers." Before the start of this movement, the Bhakti tradition had taken deep roots in Tamil Nadu which permeated to Karnataka. The Ligayat or Virashaiva sect was the forerunner in this movement. They were emphatic to practice the direct interaction with god and symbolically express it through wearing small linga around their neck signifying their faith. The Saiva Siddhanta, which was practiced in Tamil Nadu and which included tantric practices also formed the base line for the Lingayat religion. But their religious ethos was not to the liking of other Hindu groups.

Allama Prabhu a poet saint in the 12th century of the Lingayat sect, was a contemporary of Basava. Allama was instrumental in prompting bhakti cult through his poems in Kannada language among Siva worshipers. This was an enlightened way of worship in which caste distinctions were discarded. It was believed that Allama was incarnate of Lord Siva and hence he was given the epithet 'Prabhu' which was suffixed to his name. His poems were totally devotional and expressed in his status of achieving detachment from rituals.

Another bhakti movement established in the 13th century was of Haridasas, a devotional group of saints who formed the group under the same name, and who were Vaishnavites of the Dviata philosophy. The founder of this movement was Naraharitirtha, a devout Madhva follower. Their worship is devoted to various forms of Visnu or Hari. This Bhakti cult's propagation was not only worship of Visnu but also to discard animal sacrifice, stop beliefs in superstitions, discourage caste system, and to end the worship of many forms of the deity. They also discouraged the practice of astrology and other rituals. Their preachings were in the Kannada language through devotional poetry, a language of the people. However, there were two sects in this group one who wanted the Sanskrit language to be followed, the Vyasakuta and the Dasakuta.

The notable Haridasa of that period were Purandardasa, Vyasaraya, Kanakadasa, Vadiraja, Vijayadasa, Vasudevadasa and Gopaladasa; many of them became heads of the religious *mathas* founded by Madhavacharya and his disciples. Haridasa are still popular and the songs scripted by many of the earlier Haridasa are very popular.

A brief description of the contribution made by these saints in promoting the Hindu culture and Virashaivism in Karnataka follows in the following paragraphs:

Shakaracharya (788–820 CE)

Adi Shankara was a philosopher and theologian who consolidated the doctrine of Advaita Vedanta. He is credited with unifying and establishing the main currents of thought in Hinduism.

His works in Sanskrit discuss the unity of the *atman* and *Nirguna Brahman* "brahman without attributes." He wrote copious commentaries on the Vedic canon (*Brahma Sutras*, Principal Upanishads and *Bhagavad Gita*) in support of his thesis. His works elaborate on ideas found in the Upanishads. He also explained the key difference between Hinduism and Buddhism, stating that Hinduism asserts "*Atman* (Soul, Self) exists," while Buddhism asserts that there is 'no Soul, no Self.'

Shankara travelled across the Indian subcontinent to propagate his philosophy through discourses and debates with other thinkers. He established the importance of monastic life as sanctioned in the Upanishads and Brahma Sutra, in a time when the Mimaṃsa school of philosophy had established strict ritualism and ridiculed monasticism. He is reputed to have founded four *mathas* (monasteries), which helped in the historical development, revival and spread of Advaita Vedanta of which he is known as the greatest revivalist. Adi Shankara is believed to be the organiser of the Dashanami monastic order and the founder of the Shanmata tradition of worship.

Shankara was most likely born in the southern Indian state of Kerala, in a village named Kaladi or Karati or Kalati according to the oldest biographies. His father died while Shankara was very young.

Shankara's hagiography describes him as someone who was attracted to the life of *Sanyasa* (hermit) from early childhood. His mother disapproved. A story, found in all hagiographies, describe Shankara at age eight going to a river with his mother, *Sivataraka*, to bathe, and where he is caught by a crocodile. Shankara called out to his mother to give him permission to become a *Sannyasin* or else the crocodile will kill him. The mother agrees, Shankara is freed and leaves his home for education. He reaches a Saivite sanctuary along a river in a north-central state of India, and becomes the disciple of a teacher named Govindapada. Several texts suggest Shankara's schooling with Govindapada happened along the river Narmada while a few other place it along river Ganges in Kashi (Varanasi) as well as Badri (Badrinath in the Himalayas).

The biographies vary in their description of where he went, who he met and debated and many other details of his life. Most mention Shankara studying the Vedas, Upanishads and Brahmasutra with Govindapada, and Shankara authoring several key works in his youth, while he was studying with his teacher. It is with his teacher Govinda that Shankara studied Gaudapadiya Karika, as Govinda was himself taught by Gaudapada.

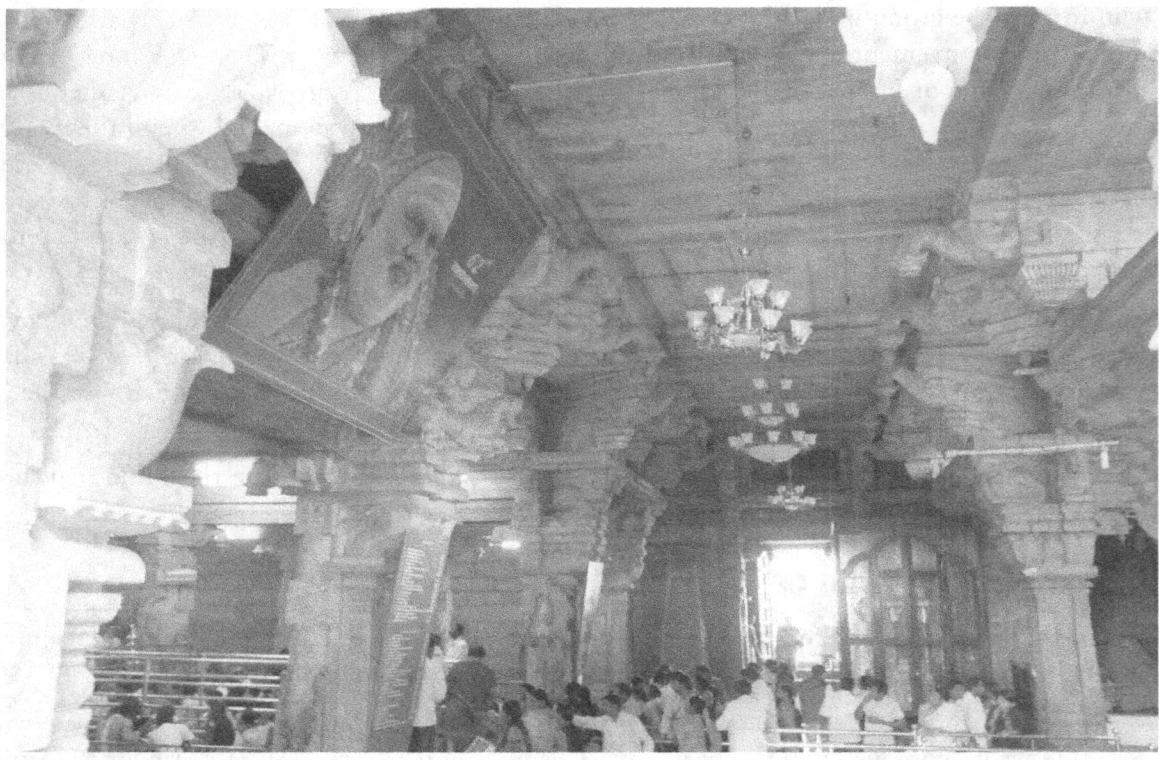

Sringeri Sharada Peetham, Sringeri

Shankara lived in the time of the so-called "Late Classical Hinduism," which lasted from 650 till 1100 CE. This era was one of political instability that followed Gupta dynasty and king Harsha of the 7th century CE. It was a time of social and cultural change as the ideas of Buddhism, Jainism and various traditions within Hinduism were competing for members. Buddhism in particular had emerged as a powerful influence in India's spiritual traditions in the first 700 years of the 1st millennium. Shankara, and his contemporaries, made a significant contribution in understanding Buddhism and the ancient Vedic traditions and then transforming the extant ideas, particularly reforming the Vedanta tradition of Hinduism, making it India's most important tradition for more than a thousand years.

Adi Shankara organised the Hindu monks of ten sects or names under four *Maṭhas* (monasteries), with the headquarters at Dwarka in the West, Jagannathpuri in the East, Sringeri in the South and Badrikashrama in the North. Each *matha* was headed by one of his four main disciples, who each continued the Vedanta Sampradaya.

Shankara was deeply involved in spreading his philosophy in Karnataka. He established the Sringeri *Matha*. It is one of the four most important seats of Hindu philosophy. Shankara's attempts at ridding the then prevalent Hinduism of the competitive religions and the aggressive competition among the various sects of Hinduism (Saivism, Vaishnavism and Shakta) among themselves bore fruits in bringing them together as one unified Hindu religion. It is in his tradition that great teachers like Vidyaranya appeared in Karnataka. Sringeri, Kudali, Shivagange, Avani and Sankheswar are some of the important *mathas* of this tradition in Karnataka.

Ramanujacharya (1017–1137 CE)

Ramanuja (1017–1137 CE) was a Hindu theologian, philosopher, and scriptural exegete, born in a Tamil family in the village of Sriperumbudur, Tamil Nadu. He is seen by Vaishnavism as the most important *acharya* (teacher) of their tradition and who was followed by Nathamuni and Yamunacharya, and by Hindus in general as the leading expounder of Vishishtadvaita, one of the classical interpretations of the dominant Vedanta school of Vedic philosophy.

According to historian Alkandavilli Govindacharya, Hoysala king Bitti Deva and his chief queen Shantala Devi had a sick daughter. She was possessed by an evil spirit and the Vaishnavite saint Ramanuja is said to have cured her. After this episode it is said that Bitti Deva embraced Vaishnavism. But from his inscriptions in the Hassan district, his daughter by one of his queens called Shantala Devi, died during his reign.

Ramanuja treated all people as equal without considering their castes. At that time low caste people were prohibited inside the temples. He led the low caste people into the temples in many places. Due to this, he is praised as a "social reformer."

In all Vaishnava temples, Ramanuja is given the foremost prominence. His blessings are invoked at the beginning of devotional services. Several temples like Venkateswara Temple at Tirumala, Parthasarathy Temple at Chennai, Cheluvanarayana Swami Temple at Melukote have exclusive shrines dedicated to him. Ramanuja stayed at Thondanur for long and after that went to Melukote where the Cheluvanarayan temple was founded and became the spiritual guide for the Hoysala kingdom. King Vishnuvardhana became his close devotee. Many Vaishnava temples like the temples at Belur and Talakad were creations under this influence. Chamapadamaswamy temple at Bannerghatta built during the Chola times has a separate pavilion where Ramanuja's image is installed along with other Alwars.

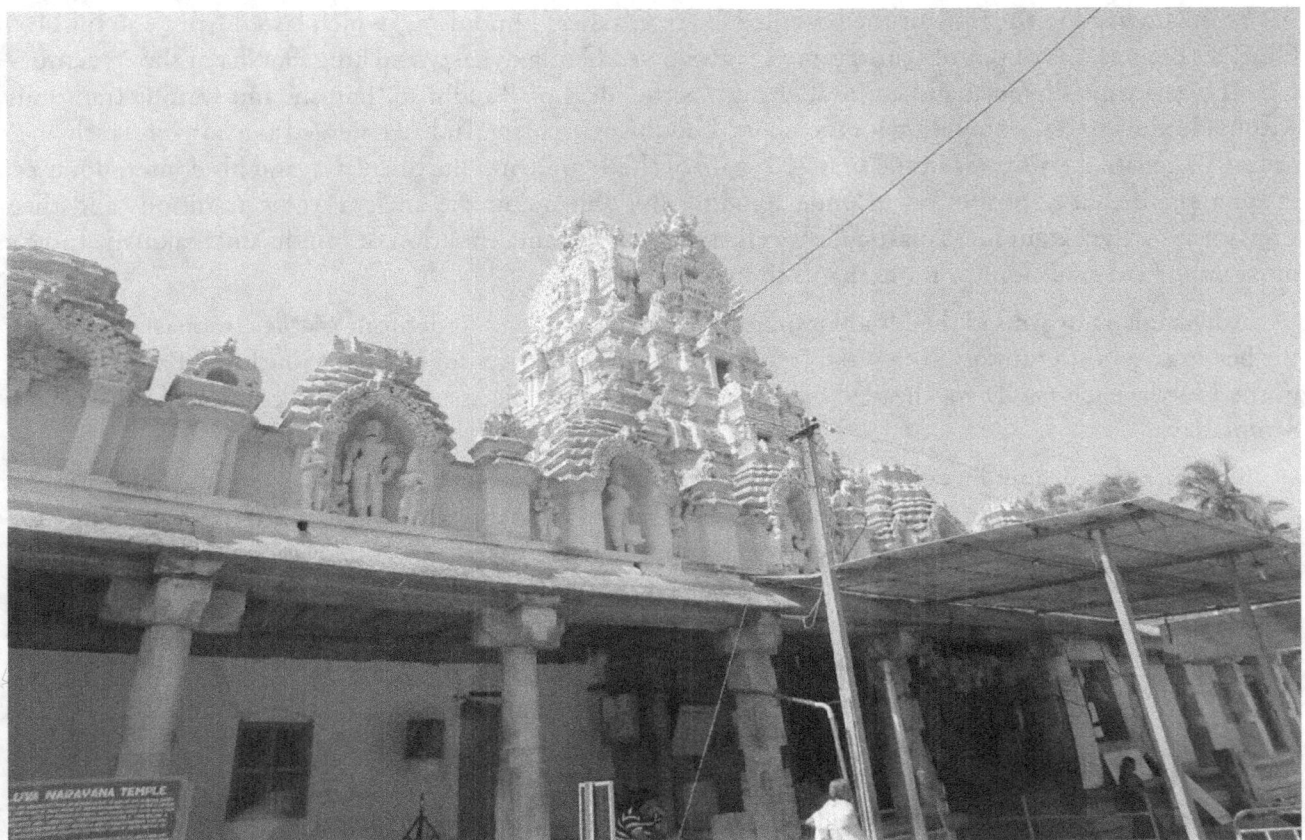

Cheluva Narayana Temple at Melkote

Basaveswara (12th century CE)

Basaveswara was an Indian philosopher, statesman, Kannada poet in Siva-focused *bhakti* movement and a social reformer during the reign of the Kalachuri-dynasty king Bijjala I in Karnataka. His life and ideas are narrated in the sacred text of the south Indian Hindu Lingayat community, the Basava Purana.

Basaveswara spread social awareness through his poetry, popularly known as *Vachanas*. Basaveswara rejected gender or social discrimination, superstitions and rituals such as the wearing of sacred thread, but introduce *Ishtalinga* necklace, with an image of the Siva Linga, to every person regardless of his or her birth as a constant reminder of one's *bhakti* (devotion) to Siva. As the chief minister of his kingdom, he introduced new public institutions such as the *Anubhava Mandapa* (or, the "hall of spiritual experience"), which welcomed men and women from all socio-economic backgrounds to discuss spiritual and mundane questions of life, in open. The traditional legends and hagiographic texts state Basaveswara to be the founder of the Lingayata tradition. However, modern scholarship relying on historical evidence such as the Kalachuri inscriptions state that Basaveswara was the poet philosopher who revived, refined and energized an already existing tradition.

Basaveswara's literary works include the Vachana Sahitya in Kannada Language. He is also known as *Bhaktibhandari* (literally, the treasurer of devotion), Basavanna (elder brother Basava) or Basaveswara (Lord Basava). Basaveswara was born about 1105 CE in the town of Bagewadi in north Karnataka, to Madiraja and Madalambike, an upper caste Brahmin family devoted to Hindu deity Siva. He was named Basava, a Kannada form of the Sanskrit *Vrishabha* in honor of Nandi bull (carrier of Siva) and the local Saivism tradition.

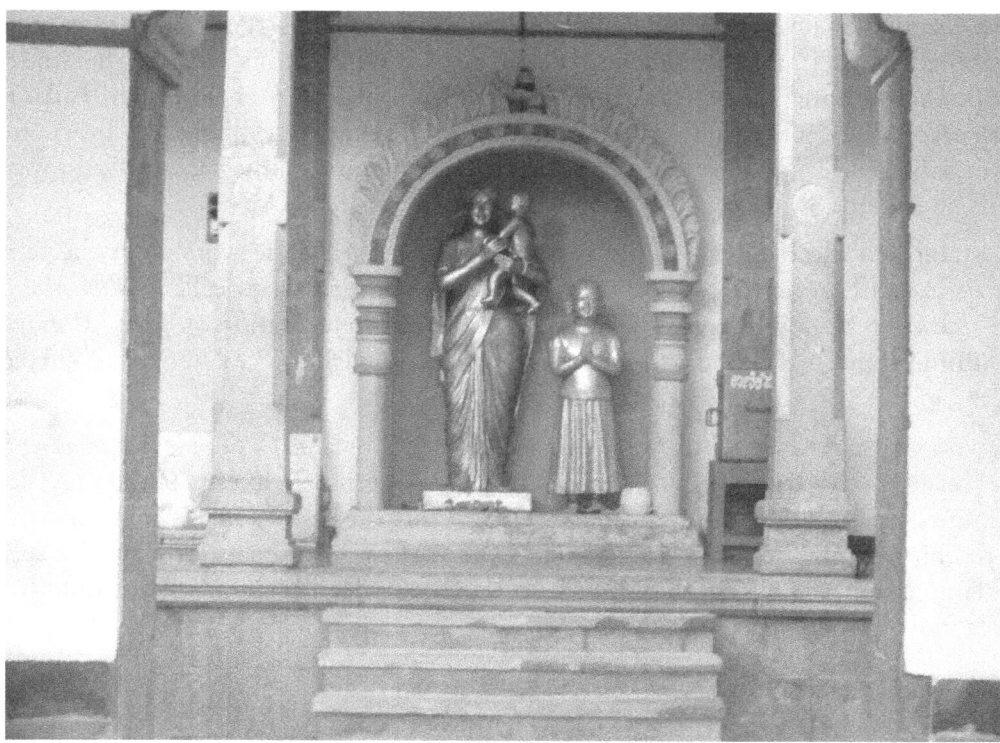
Memorial for Basaveswara's Sister and Mother in Ingaleshwar

Basaveswara grew up in Kudalasangama (northeast Karnataka), near the banks of rivers Krishna and its tributary Malaprabha. Basaveswara spent twelve years studying in a Hindu temple in the town of Kudalasangama, at Sangameswara then a Saivite school of learning, probably of the *Lakulisa-Pashupata* tradition. Jataveda Muni, also known as Eeshanya Guru, was his *guru*.

Basaveswara married a cousin from his mother side. His wife Gangambike was the daughter of the prime minister of Bijjala, the Kalachuri king. He began working as an accountant to the court of the king. When his maternal uncle died, the king invited him to be the chief minister. The king also married Basaveswara's sister named Padmavati. There is a memorial built in honour of Basaveswara's mother and sister at Ingaleshwar which was recently renovated by the Government of Karnataka.

As a leader, he developed and inspired a new devotional movement named *Virashaivas*, or "ardent, heroic worshippers of Siva." This movement shared its roots in the on-going Tamil Bhakti movement, particularly the Saiva Nayanars traditions, over the 7th to 11th century. However, Basaveswara championed devotional worship that rejected temple worship and rituals led by Brahmans, and replaced it with personalized direct worship of Siva through practices such as individually worn icons and symbols like a small linga. This approach brought Siva's presence to everyone and at all times, without gender, class or caste discrimination. Basaveswara's poems speak of strong sense of gender equality and community bond, willing to wage war for the right cause, yet being a fellow "devotee's bride" at the time of his or her need.

The Lingayats, also known as *Virashaivas* or *Veerashaivas*, traditionally believe that Basaveswara was the founder of their tradition. The community he helped form is also known as the *Sharanas*. The community is largely concentrated in Karnataka, but has migrated into other states of India as well as overseas.

Madhavacharya (1238–1317 CE)

Madhavacharya born Vasudeva (1238–1317 CE), also known as Purna Prajna and Ananda Tirtha, was a Hindu philosopher and the chief proponent of the *Dvaita* school of Vedanta. Madhva himself called his philosophy as "Tattvavada" meaning realism. It is one of the three most influential Vednta philosophies.

Madhvacharya was one of the important philosophers during the Bhakti movement. He was a pioneer in many ways, going against standard conventions and norms. While in his teenage years he was initiated as a *sanyasin* by Achyutapreksha, an ascetic of the Ekadandi order. Later he toured India several times engaging in philosophical debates and winning converts to his school of thought. Madhva composed thirty seven works in Sanskrit. His greatest is considered to be the Anu-vyakhyana, a critical exposition of the philosophy of the Brahma Sutras.

Madhva established the Krishna temple at Udupi and entrusted the worship at the temple to eight ascetic disciples each of whom were first heads of the eight monasteries called *Ashta Mathas* of Udupi According to tradition, Madhvacharya is believed to be the third incarnation of Vayu (*Mukhyaprana*) after Hanuman and Bhima and is believed to have disappeared from vision when he was seventy nine years of age.

Madhava who stayed in the environs of Udupi for some more time wrote his *bhashyas* or authoritative commentaries on all the ten Upanishads. He composed glosses on forty hymns of the Rigveda, opening up for the first time its vista of spiritual significance. He also wrote the treatise Bhagavata-tatparya highlighting the essential teachings of the Puranas. Many topical handbooks were also authored by him to suit different occasions. A large number of devotional songs too were composed by him, which could be sung by his disciples, while moving with him in groups.

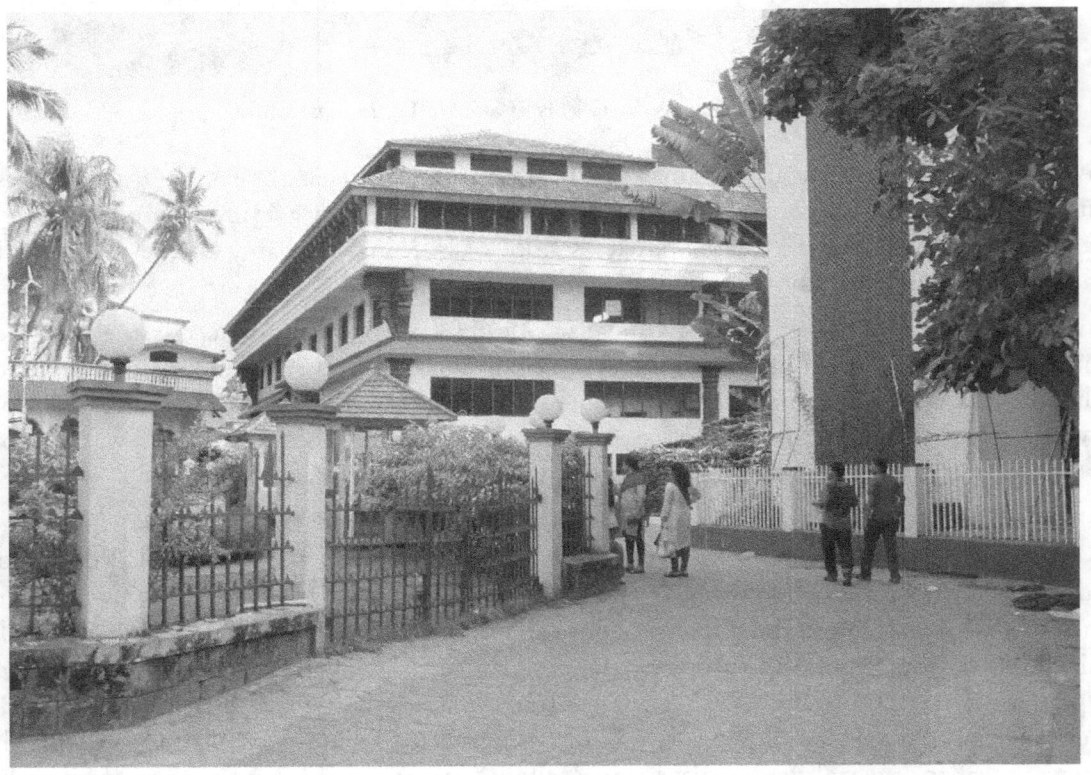

Entry Gate for Udupi Krishna Temple from Ann Brahma Side

It was during this period that Madhava installed the image of Krishna which he found in the Arabian Sea near the Udupi's coast. After sometime, he left some disciples behind for performing Krishna's worship and undertook his tour to Badri.

Once, when his party was attacked by a band of robbers on the difficult road to the Himalayas, Madhava made his pupil Upendra-tirtha silence them after a fierce fight. He used to say: "One should cultivate strength of body even like strength of mind; it is impossible for a weak body to house a strong mind." Accordingly he had made his disciples achieve strength in their body as well as in their Vedantic pursuits.

To the people of that time, Madhava's physical strength itself was something miraculous, because his body was strong and adamant. Even to this day, the huge rock-boulder lifted up and placed in the river Bhadra by Madhava, near Kalasa bears witness to his herculean strength. This incident is confirmed by the sentence inscribed on that stone.

On his return home thereafter, he wrote the treatise *Mahabharata-tatparya-nirnaya*. On his way home, he visited also Kashi. There he held a philosophical debate with an elderly Advaita ascetic, Amarendra Puri. Sri Puri had to go away silently, humbled by the dazzling genius of Madhava. Then he reached Kurukshetra. Here occurred a strange episode. Madhava got a mound there excavated and demonstrated to his disciples the buried mace of (the epic hero) Bhima therein; and once again had it buried under the ground.

Later on, Madhava arrived in Goa on his way back to Udupi. With his sweet music there he enthralled the audience. Madhava's musical genius also was as unique as his perfect physique and brilliant intellect. Writers contemporaneous with Madhava have acclaimed rapturously his musical expertise as well as his rich melody of voice.

Though Madhava considered Visnu as the supreme (*sarvottama*), he did not oppose the worship of Siva and other deities. But he considered them as gods of a lower status. He stressed *Bhaktimarga* (devotion path) rather than rituals. The vaishvanva *mathas* of the order propagated by Madhava are eight in number and located at Udupi. The Raghavendraswamy *matha* at Nanjangud also follows the philosophy originally taught by Madhavacharya.

Akka Mahadevi (1130–1160 CE)

Akka Mahadevi was one of the early female poets in the Kannada language. She was a prominent figure in the *virashaiva* Bhakti movement of the 12th century. Her Vachana poems (a form of spontaneous mystical poems), and the two short writings called *Mantrogopya* and the *Yogangatrividhi* are considered her most notable contribution to Kannada literature. She composed relatively fewer poems than other saints of the movement. Yet the term *Akka* (elder sister), which is an honorific given to her by great *Virashaiva* saints such as Basavanna, Siddharama and Allama Prabhu is an indication of her contribution to the spiritual discussions held at the "Anubhava Mandapa." She is in hindsight seen as an inspirational woman for Kannada literature and the history of Karnataka. She is known to have considered the god Siva (Chenna Mallikarjuna) as her husband, (traditionally understood as the '*madhura bhava*' or '*madhurya*' form of devotion). Akka Mahadevi was born in 1130 CE in Udutadi (or Udugani) near the ancient city of Banavasi in the modern Shivamogga district of Karnataka.

She is considered by modern scholars to be a prominent figure in the field of female emancipation. A household name in Karnataka, she had said that she was a woman only in name and that her mind, body and soul belonged to Lord Siva. During a time of strife and political uncertainty in the 12th century, she chose spiritual enlightenment and stood by her choice. It is commonly known that she took part in many gatherings of learned such as the *Anubhava mandapa* in Kalyana (now Basavakalyana) to debate about philosophy and attainment of enlightenment (or *Moksha*, termed by her as "*arivu*"). In search for her eternal soul mate, Lord Siva, she made the animals, flowers and birds her friends and companions, rejecting family life and worldly attachment.

Akka was a revelation here in that she pursued enlightenment recording her journey in *vachanas* of simple language but great cognitive rigour. Akka's poetry explores the themes of rejecting mortal love in favour of the everlasting love of God. Her *vachanas* also talk about the methods that the path of enlightenment demand of the seeker, such as killing the 'I' (ego), conquering desires and the senses and so on. She rejected her life of luxury to live as a wandering poet-saint, travelling throughout the region and singing praises to her Lord Siva.

She went in search of fellow seekers or *sharanas* because the company of the saintly or *sajjana sanga* is believed to hasten learning. She found the company of such *sharanas* in Basavakalyana. Her non-conformist ways caused a lot of consternation in a conservative society and even her eventual guru Allama Prabhu had to initially face difficulties in enlisting her in the gatherings at Anubhava mandapa. A true ascetic, Mahadevi is said to have refused to wear any clothing, a common practice among male ascetics, but shocking for a woman. Legend has it that due to her true love and devotion with God her whole body was protected by hair. A statue of Akka Mahadevi installed at her birth place Udathadi (Udutadi) is fully covered in hair.

3

KARNATAKA'S HERITAGE AND EPIGRAPHICAL RECORDS

3.1 KARNATAKA'S HERITAGE PRESERVATION INSTITUTIONS

Karnataka has the unique distinction of being a state which absorbed the art and architectural styles of both the north and south India while at the same time experimenting with own indigenous styles with perfection. All the three known temple architectural styles viz. *Nagara*, *Dravida* and *Vesara* have flourished in Karnataka. 11th century saw the peak of temple construction and architectural development in India and about half of that activity occurred in Karnataka.

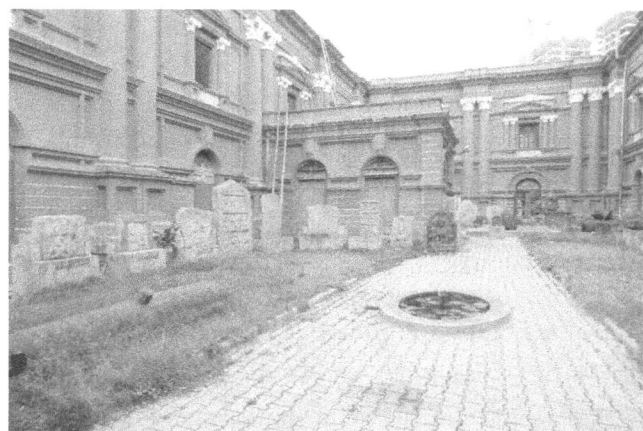
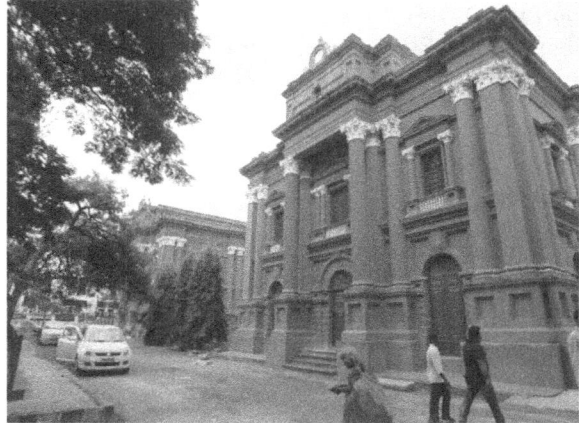
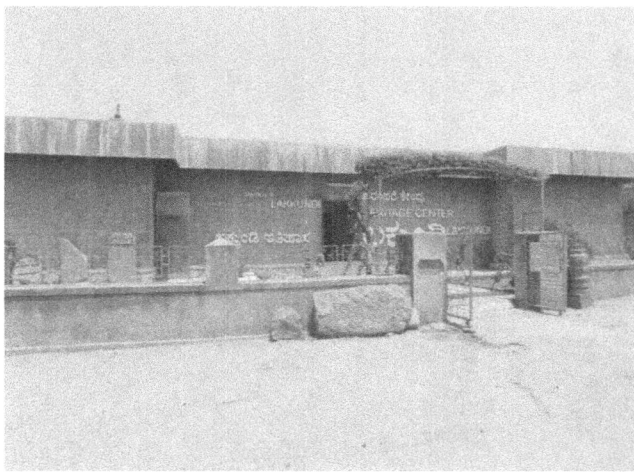
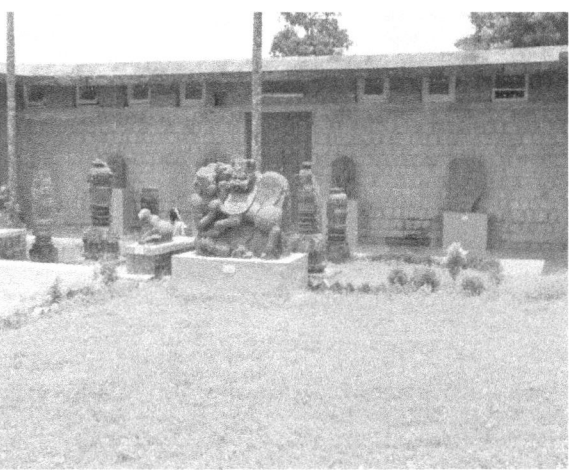

Government Museum Bengaluru, ASI Heritage Centre Lakkundi and ASI Museum Balligavi

Thus Karnataka contributed substantially to the development of Indian architectural styles and plastic art. However, outside of Karnataka not many people are aware of this rich heritage of Karnataka. Even the interest in archeological studies has been among the most vigorous in Karnataka.

The Directorate of Archaeology and Museums in Karnataka is the oldest among the departments of archaeology in Indian states. Though the department was established in January, 1885, by the erstwhile princely Mysore State, by appointing Mr. B Lewis Rice as Director, the archaeological studies had started much earlier. The first publication of the state is related to epigraphs of the region published in 1879 under the title Mysore Inscriptions. Mr. B Lewis Rice devoted himself primarily to epigraphical studies. He published 9000 inscriptions collected from eight districts of the princely state of Mysore and the province of Coorg. They were published in 12 volumes under the title Epigraphia Carnatica. A robust legislative framework for preservation and conservation of heritage exists in the state. The Karnataka Ancient and Historical Monuments and Archaeological Sites and Remains Act, 1961 is the principal legislation in this regard.

Government of Karnataka has been making concerted efforts at creating awareness about the state's heritage. There is specific Department of the state government looking after exclusively to related matters. Department of Archaeology, Museums and Heritage looks after all exploratory, maintenance, promotional and publication activities in the state. The department started a program titled *Prachya Pragne* for promoting awareness about state's heritage by including local communities in its promotion. Publication of various researched reports, information booklets and conducting awareness workshops too figures in prominently in the program. Involvement of private sector under A Public-Private Partnership for preservation and conservation of heritage has been encouraged by the Karnataka state government. The Dharmasthala Manjunatheswara Dharmasthana Trust is functioning as a strategic partner the under the guidance of the Dharmadhikari, Dr. Veerendra Hegde.

Initiative of Karnataka Itihasa Academy, an organization founded by Prof. GS Dixit and Dr. Suryanath U Kamat with the intention of bringing awareness about culture and history of Karnataka among the youth has undertaken the task of creating database of all villages, towns across Karnataka under the project titled 'Namma Ooru Namma Itihasa' – "Our Village Our History"

The objective of this project is to record for posterity a curated, visual and narrative based archive that traces the social, cultural, historical and religious significance of one's village or town. This will be a record of the history of different places as experienced and remembered by individual members of the society. Besides this initiative, the Academy is also publishing research documents both in English and Kannada.

The Department of Archaeology, Museums and Heritage has 12 museums at various locations under its superintendence and these are:

- Government Museum, Kalaburgi (Gulbarga)
- Government Museum, Basavakalyan
- Government Museum, Madikeri
- Government Museum, Chitradurga
- KRCM Government Museum, Kittur
- Government Museum and Venkatappa Art Gallery, Bengaluru
- Government Museum, Hassan
- Government Museum, Hoovina Hadagalli
- Government Museum, Gadag
- Government Museum, Raichur
- Government Museum, Mysuru
- Srimanthi Bai Memorial Government Museum, Mangaluru.

Besides the museums managed by the state government, Archaeological Survey of India too has its own museums and heritage centres in Karnataka located at Badami, Aihole, Vijayapura (Bijapur), Srirangapatnam, Halebid, Lakkundi and Balligavi. There are a total of 1360 protected monuments under the supervision of both, ASI (608) and Department of Archeology, Museums and Heritage (752) of government of Karnataka. The total number of ancient and medieval monuments; many of which are scattered unnoticed all over the state, may be several thousand in number.

Various universities too are active in this area notable being Mysuru University and Dharwad University. The universities have active research departments and collection museums. Gazetteer Department of Government of Karnataka plays a critical role in consolidation and dissemination of information on archeological sites besides the publications released by the Department of Archeology, Museums and Heritage. State gazetteer and separate district gazetteers are published by the Gazetteer Department. Each gazetteer has at least two chapters devoted to information pertaining to state's heritage. One chapter records the history and archaeology whereas one more is devoted exclusively to the places of interest, which among others includes all historical sites. Currently, the most updated document of such related subjects is the Karnataka State Handbook published in 2010.

Besides Indian universities, various universities in the western world too are conducting research on Indian heritage. Badami Chalukya, Kalyani Chalukya and Hoysala temples and sculpture have found tremendous interest among foreign scholars. Adam Hardy, Gerard Foekema, FW Bunce, Andrew Cohen, George Mitchell and many others have spent years in Karnataka to study and report on temples and sculpture of Karnataka. The Welsh School of Architecture at Cardiff University has a dedicated research centre on South Asian design and architecture called PRASADA (Practice Research and Advancement in South Asian Design and Architecture). PRASADA was founded in 1995 by Adam Hardy who has been studying the Hoysala architecture extensively. PRASADA centre is devoted to the architecture, visual arts and material culture of South Asia.

3.2 KARNATAKA INSCRIPTIONS

Much of the historical information available to us today from the past came from the inscriptions left by the people of those times. Right from the time of Mauryan Empire inscriptions in one form or the other have been left by the rulers from the past in various locations. Ashoka's seventeen edicts found in Karnataka perhaps constitute the earliest forms of inscriptions. Inscriptions can be found at many locations but most inscriptions left behind by the kings following Hinduism and Jainism have left behind numerous inscriptions in the temples built by them or Jaina *basadis*. This brief information about inscriptions details what they were made of, why they were recorded, how the content was structured and this will be useful in understanding types of inscriptions found in Karnataka.

The earliest systematic study of Kannada inscriptions was started in early nineteenth century by Colin Mackenzie, a British officer in erstwhile state of Mysore under the British rule. Then scholars like Walter Elliot, John Fleet, B Lewis Rice and many other foreigners continued the work. After Rice, R. Narasimhachar led the Department of Archaeology and continued the work in the same manner as Rice. M.H. Krishna continued the tradition and was the person who found the Halmidi inscription believed to be earliest Kannada inscription. Several other scholars have extensively studied the Kannada inscriptions and published their contents. The Department of Archaeology of the Government of Karnataka, Archaeological Survey of India, various universities, museums, Kannada Sahitya Parishat, Karnataka Itihasa Academy and many others have undertaken further research and study in this direction. Over 30000 inscriptions have been found and deciphered in Karnataka. Varija R Bolar and KV Ramesh have interesting published works to their credit on inscriptions of Karnataka. A website too has been launched on inscriptions with the primary object of spurring research in Indian history: http://www.whatisindia.com/inscriptions/

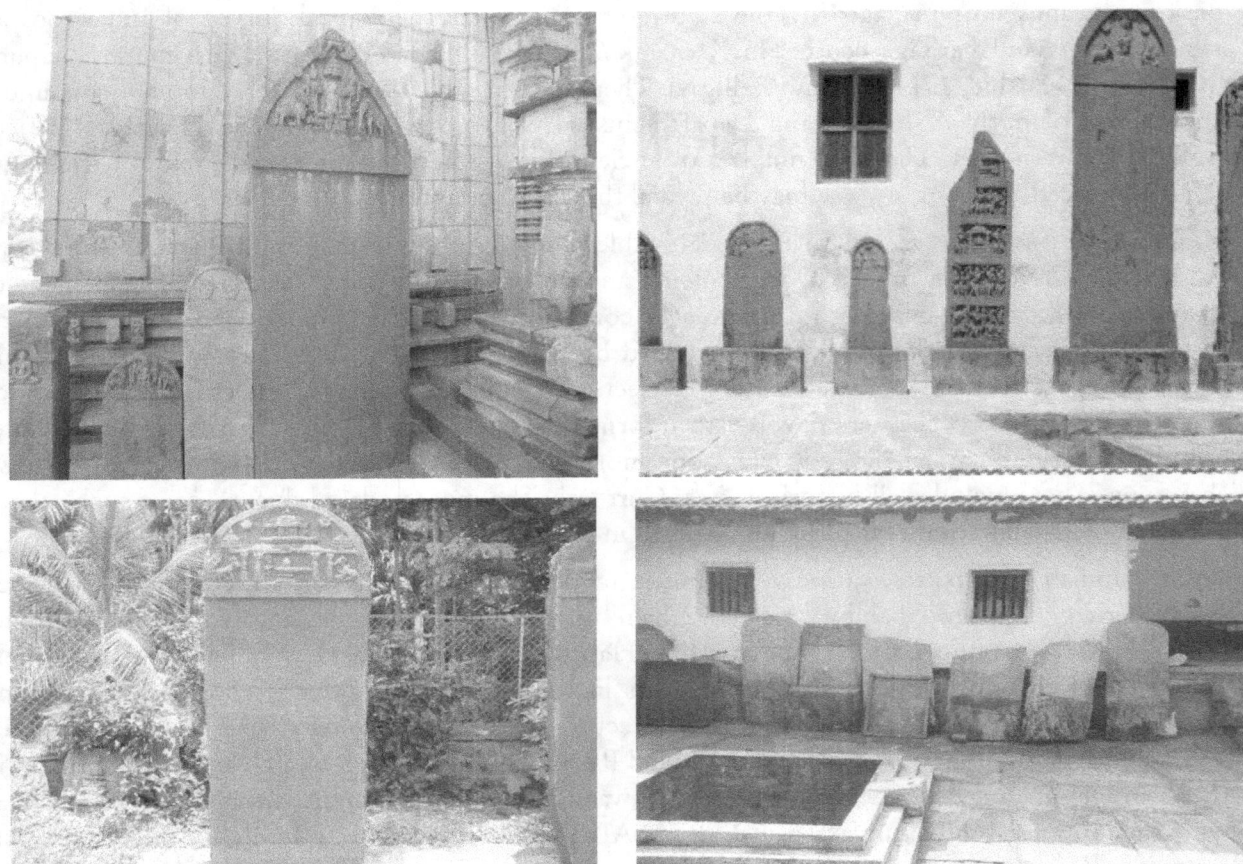

Inscription Steles from Parsvanatha Basadi Halebid, Harihareswara Temple Harihar, Balligavi Museum and Panchalingeswara Temple Barkur

Numerous publications are available where transliteration and translation of these inscriptions may be found commencing from Epigraphia Carnatica running into various volumes. Lists of such reference documents are furnished along with all other references at the end in this book.

Shasana – Inscriptions

Locally in the villages people refer to the inscriptions as Shasana, Shasanadesh or Lipi. In many villages there are people who can read *hale* Kannada and can decipher parts of these inscriptions. One can get a fairly accurate account of such inscriptions from such people though not as professionally analyzed as the scholars in the field have done.

Inscriptions are glittering source materials which throw light on the history of a place. They are documents inscribed on permanent materials like metal, conch, stones, pillars specially erected for this purpose, temple premises or boulders. The root of the word '*Shasana*' is '*Shas*,' which means an order, a punishment or a control regulation. The king usually publicized his order by heralding it and making it known that everyone has to comply with it. He would keep a copy of his order written on copper plates, or palm leaves in his treasury with the intention of preserving it for the future administrators or rulers. The orders were also inscribed on stone slabs or boulders, a simple material available. The slabs were established in places of public activity so as to be of easy access to the people for whom it was meant. Temples; of course were places where social congregations took place and hence were the much sought after locations.

Inscriptions written on stone are called '*Shila Shasanas*' or stone records. To know the ancient culture and civilization of a region, stone inscriptions play a significant part. Because they are free from the process of tampering, they are contemporary records of an incident that happened. They cannot be displaced from their original place of establishment because of their weight and difficulty in carrying them. They throw light on the places where found and neighbourhood. The orders written on them were usually issued by the king or officials, sometimes by common men. Hence they depict the true history of the local population through the language used, characters incised, and incidents described. They are the definite sources of history of a place besides the *Sthalapuranas* in which was chronicled the local history. These *sthalapuranas* were regularly updated and generally the families of the local priests were the custodians of the chronicle. *Sthalapuranas,* however were not as reliable a source of historical information as the inscriptions because these could be based on legends and might be written by an opinionated person in line with his biases, preferences and prejudices.

Script and Language Used in Inscriptions

The science of character in script writings is called Paleography. To read a record, knowledge of the script in which it is written is always of help. Kannada has undergone many stages during its development through centuries. Accordingly, the inscriptions found in various locations in Karnataka are scripted in the language and script in vogue at that time and place. Inscriptions thus help in understanding the development of languages of the place as well.

The Kannada language in inscriptions is identified as PreOld and Old Kannada. Records written in Old Kannada format correspond to the period 800 to 1000 CE. Records written in PreOld Kannada format correspond to the period 450 to 800 CE. During the times of Mauryas, Satavahanas and Chutus, inscriptions were also written in Brahmi script, Prakrit language, Pali language and Sanskrit. The inscription of 3rd century CE written around the *Nagapratima* of the times of the Chutus kept inside Madhukeswara temple in Banavasi has Brahmi labels and is in Prakrit language. The inscriptions of the Chutus at Malavalli and that of the Kadambas at Talagunda in Shivamogga district are both in Sanskrit. An inscription of the Chutus assigned to the 3rd century CE found at Banavasi refers to a Naga image. This image on a stone slab with the inscription in Brahmi script and Prakrit language is the earliest of its kind in Karnataka. The inscription records that a Chutu princess, named Sivakhanda Nagasri, got the Naga image carved and also built a tank. It can be understood that the Chutus originally belonged to the Naga clan, the tank was dedicated by Nagasri for snake worship. The Naga image is now housed in the Madhukeswara temple at Banavasi.

RS Panchmukhi in his monogram titled "Archeology of Karnatak," 1953, published by Kannada Research Institute Dharwad has made an expensive analysis of the language used in inscriptions of Karnataka over various periods of time commencing 300 BCE. According to his study, the earliest inscriptions are the edicts of Ashoka and they are written in a form of Magadhi-Prakrit. Prakrit continued to be language of nearly all inscriptions till 4th century CE. Vadgaon-Madhavpur inscription is of the 1st century CE and it is written in Prakrit. The Banavasi and Malavalli inscriptions of the 3rd century and Chandravalli rock inscription of the 4th century CE are written in Brahmi characters and Prakrit language. For the subsequent periods, Panchmukhi has prepared a chart depicting how the language of epigraphs in Karnataka changed and that also explains the slow growth of the documentary language in Karnataka. Since most inscriptions were orders and information conveyed by the rulers, the language used in them had a direct bearing on the documentary language and the language of the court of the time. The languages used in the inscriptions in Karnataka generally were Tamil, Prakrit, Sanskrit, Pre-old Kannada, Old Kannada and Telugu.

Upto the 4th century CE, the language used in inscriptions was mostly Prakrit. Thus till about 350 CE or so, Prakrit was the court language though it may not have been intelligible to common people, generally. Kannada of the 6th century CE and that of between 4th and 6th century must have been greatly influenced by Prakrit which was the recognized documentary (and literary) language of those times.

It was about the last decade of the 4th century that Prakrit was supplanted by Sanskrit. Between 4th and 6th century CE the court language was Sanskrit with an admixture of Prakrit and Kannada expressions in the grant portion of the order. The copper plates were invariably in Sanskrit while stone inscriptions were largely in Kannada (of those times). From 7th to 10th century CE, the documentary language was both Sanskrit and Kannada and very often though prose and verse was in Sanskrit, the script used was Kannada. Exceptions to these two generalizations were i) a stone inscription in Talagunda of the Kadamba king Kakusthavarman and ii) the Aihole inscription of Pulakesin II (7th century CE) which were in classical Sanskrit.

The use of Sanskrit and Kannada simultaneously continued with varying degrees upto the 13th century CE with a greater mixture of Kannada in Sanskrit portions of inscriptions. Later on Sanskrit became the conventional documentary language of the preamble, genealogy and imprecatory parts of the copper plate inscriptions (sometimes also in stone inscriptions) whereas the grant portion and description of land gifted with boundaries being invariably written in Kannada.

From 14th century onwards, Kannada started taking over mostly as the documentary language.

Types of Inscriptions

Prashathi records: They eulogize the kings and officials and are usually written by the court poet.

Dana Shasana: These are found in large numbers; they are the official documents or charter conveying the grant or gift of lands by kings, officials or common men.

Bhumi Dana -Grant of land: This is the most common of grants records found in Karnataka. In ancient times, king was owner of all the land in his territory; he liberally donated land as a welfare measure to learned Brahmans, to temples and others and such grants recorded on stones are called land grant inscriptions and such granted land was marked by boundaries with location marks. There are various types of *Bhumi-Dana Shasanas* and are classified based on the material on which they are inscribed.

Agrahara Dana -Gift of villages: In ancient and medieval south India, kings established residential quarters for learned brahmans who were well versed in four Vedas and other scriptures. King donated the ear-marked set of villages and its revenue for the upkeep and continued posterity of their knowledge. Such village(s) was under the ownership of the donee and was exempted from all types of taxes. There are references to an existing village converted into an *Agrahara*. Royal family mostly kings or queens made such grants. Most of the copper plate grants fall under this category.

Pura Dana -Gift of Town: Pura means a town, As *Agrahara* was meant for learned Brahmans, Pura was meant for non-Brahminical sects like, Veerashaiva, Priests, Jains, Bairagis, Fakirs etc,. Pura grant was made by a king or by his nobility after seeking his permission. These villages were exempted from some taxes and not all taxes. A Pura is existing village converted or newly created settlement by the ordinance of the king or by a senior official.

Umbali Dana: This land or villages grant was mainly given by king or a senior official to the non-brahman agricultural community. A person who received such grant was very much part of the administration of that village, this system prevailed in late Vijayanagara Period.

Nettaru Koduge or Grant given for Heroic Deed: Nettaru Blood Grant of land given to heroic person who participated in the war waged by the king and was instrumental for the triumph in battle field. Such persons was rewarded with grant of land for their heroic role played in the battle in subduing the enemy.

Devalaya Dana or Donation to the Temple: In the history of Karnataka we find every village consisted of a village deity and there are villages having multiple temples. After 14th century, we find every individual caste and community had a temple clearly showing the importance of temple in the community and was centre of all social activity. After the construction of a temple, king or his subordinate or village head or a brahman donated land for the newly constructed temple and for the maintenance of the temple, like offering daily worship, feeding the devotees, ascetics and students residing in temple and for the repair of the temple. Merchants and traders also donated liberally for such activities. Grants in the nature oil mills, seeds, grains, shelter and clothes too were made.

Temple grants were made not only for the traditionally recognized sects and cults but also temples dedicated to village deities or deities of a clan or community. For example, an inscription dated 968–69 CE found at Shankabasadi, Lakshmeshwar is a tablet stone reading lines 1 to 50. A reference to a temple of the Charmakaradeva is recorded while describing the boundary of south-east side of Puligere city (Lakshmeshwar). *Charmakaradeva* refers to the god of the workers in leather.

Nirmana: Construction of temples, lakes, wells

Terige Dana or Exemption of tax: This grant was given to persons who were involved in providing welfare measures for the common public, like construction of tank, well, dam or temple. King or his subordinate officers usually donated the land for such purposes. Merchants or traders were wealthy and usually such trading communities organized guilds and donated money liberally for such welfare measures. In Karnataka, we find many inscriptions in such nature with reference as charity by *vyaparis* or merchant guilds (traders). Examples of this type of inscriptions are Basavatti inscription of Sripurusha (Western Ganga) made in Saka 722 (790–791 CE) and Agara inscription of Sripurusha in 8th century CE. The latter even exempts forty persons of "forced labour."

Veeragallu-Hero Stones: Best of inscriptions found in India are Hero Stones. They depict a heroic story and are with or without inscriptions. The varieties in them are stupendous. Hero stones are memorial stones erected in memory of heroes who died in a battle field while defending kings, or defending the cattle or women in distress. Karnataka has the largest number of hero-stones scattered all over from the past.

Greed drives people to do such things as they think would entitle them to what is not rightfully theirs. Even in past ages people did resort to greed and did acts of cheating. People prepared fake inscriptions issued in the names of kings recording grant of lands to grab these lands. Such inscriptions are called *kuta-shasana*. Many such inscriptions were identified in Karnataka and no credence is given to them while recording history of the place as revealed in their contents.

Content Structure of an Inscription

Analysis of the text and contents of inscriptions shows a definite pattern in the narration. Almost all the records start with an auspicious note such as Om, Siddham, Swasthi, Shri. With this, there will be always the verse which praises the God of the respective faith of the donor. Saiva and Vaishnava records begin with their respective invocation of god. Likewise Jaina inscriptions would be in praise of a Jina or Tirthankara.

Shapashaya or Curse

To protect inscriptions from violations and destruction, the writer of inscription would include a prohibitory statement in the nature of a fear of wrong happening to the perpetrator of the act of destruction or defiling or disobeying the order contained in the inscription. They would generally mention, at the end of the order, the curse they get if anybody violates the order in the nature of a religious belief of committing sin or going to hell etc.

The top most part of Inscriptions

There are many significant carvings of architectural importance on some inscriptions. A donation record will usually have the god worshiped by the donor. Saivite records will have a Siva linga sculpture with a bull in front of it or the sculpture of a Saiva saint worshiping the linga. If it is Jaina record, the top would display a Thirthankara sculpture. A Kesava sculpture flanked by *Sankha*, *Chakra*, may be found if it is Vaishnava record. Almost all records usually have the Sun and the Moon carved at its top. It is believed that the donations as given in the record should exist as long as the existence of the Sun and the Moon.

In rare cases, sculpture of a Brahman sitting in front of a desk called *Vyasa peeta* is seen. Some of the carvings show a cow standing and feeding its calf and a sword shown by its size. They indicate that the theft of the grant is as sinful as killing a studious Brahman or a cow feeding its calf in presence of a deity.

Words of praise in honour of Donor: A king would generally be addressed as *Maharajadhiraja* – meaning king of kings. Various qualities and attributes to describe the king's benevolence and mightiness would be stated to honour him. Sometimes the king's lineage and ancestry too would be highlighted while describing his faith and belief in gods and saints. The king's knowledge of various subjects or proficiency in various arts may form part of his praise. A few examples of the contents of some inscriptions given in this chapter later should explain the complete structure.

Subject matter of grant

The inscriptions besides the usual imprecatory sentences have a subject matter of the *Shasana*. This details the purpose of the grant, details of the donee, his achievements and scholarship or deeds of valour, the property granted whether land, or revenue rights over villages and divisions, measurements of the land granted, its location and description in terms of size, directions and boundaries. Grants were also given for higher learning and pursuance of scholarship. Examples of a few inscriptions in this chapter will further elaborate on this matter.

Dates and reference to regnal year

Dates in Karnataka inscriptions are generally referred to as *Saka* era which started in 78 CE. To convert a *saka* year to the year in Christian era, one has to add number 78 to the *saka* year to get the relative CE. The examples of inscriptions in this chapter have references to dates as well.

Some prominent inscriptions from Karnataka

There are over 30000 inscriptions from Karnataka of which over 300 come from just Bengaluru and surroundings. Some of the inscriptions have left an indelible mark on the study of Karnataka's history and some contain certain unique features and have thus come to be known better than the others. A few of the prominent inscriptions are listed here in a chronological order. Though there are some labels or inscribed letters on some artifacts excavated in Banavasi from the Satavahana time and earlier, nothing much can be said about these as not much authentic work is available on these. Accordingly, the inscriptions listed here are those which have been well researched and documented.

One of the older inscriptions has this limited interpretation. Brahmi label inscription found during excavations at Banavasi is found on a bead and written in Ashokan Brahmi characters dated to third century BCE on paleographic grounds and it reads "Ra ha," or "Kha ra" in mirror image, which probably refers to the name of some artisan.

Another record is a Satavahana Chaitya motif inscription found during excavations at Banavasi which is from 2nd century CE. Its language is Prakrit and characters Brahmi. This inscription is engraved over a small terracotta Buddhist memorial panel found in an excavation and reads– "*Siddham | Rano Vasithiputasa Siva Sri Pulumavisa Mahadeviya chhaa patharo..*" and seems to be the memorial stone of the queen of the king Vasishthiputra Siva Sri Pulumavi.

The third inscription is on the *Nagapratima* from the Chutu period kept in the Madhukeswara temple in Banavasi, about which mention has already been made earlier. This inscription read thus -"To the prefect! In the year 12 of the century of the king (being) Haritiputa Satakarni, the cherisher of the Vehnukadadutu (?) family, the 7th fortnight of the winter months, 1st day, the meritorious gift of the Mahabhuvi (Mahabhoji) the king's daughter, Sivakhanda Nagasri, wife of Jivaputa, with her son – of a *naga*, a tank and a *vihara*. These three are works by the prime minister, Khadasati. Nataka, the disciple of Damoraka and son of the Acharya Jayantaka and inhabitant of Sajayataka (Sanjayanti), made the *Naga*"

Talagunda and Malavalli pillar inscriptions

Talagunda is a very small village in Shivamogga district of Karnataka. This sleepy village came into lime light on the discovery of a very important Kadamba inscription by B L Rice in 1902. The village has been referred as Sthala-Kundura, Sthana-Kundur and Sthana-kunja-pura. The antiquity of this village can be dated back to the Satavahanas as the Talagunda pillar inscription mentions that the Sivalinga here was worshiped by the Satakarnis. The presence of these Satakarnis can also be established from the nearby village of Malavalli where a pillar inscription of theirs from the Chutu line has been discovered.

The Talagunda pillar inscription revealed and clarified many mysteries surrounding the Kadambas and their origin. Lewis Rice on the discovery of this inscription in 1902 writes, "No more important or interesting inscription has been discovered in Mysore (Karnataka was known as Mysore State during those times), whether we regard its contents, its style or its execution; and it has attracted much attention in Europe." He further writes, "This learned inscription is full of interesting and important matter from beginning to end. It gives what appears to be a realistic and true account of the origin of the Kadamba line of kings, free from numerous legends that are current regarding this. In fact, the various lines of the inquiry it suggests well-nigh inexhaustible."

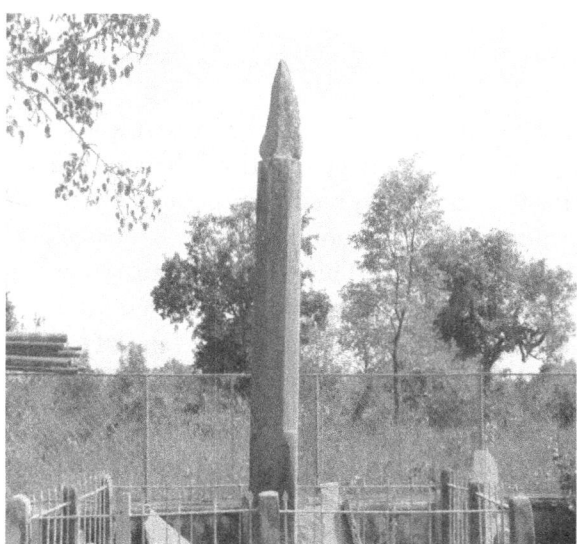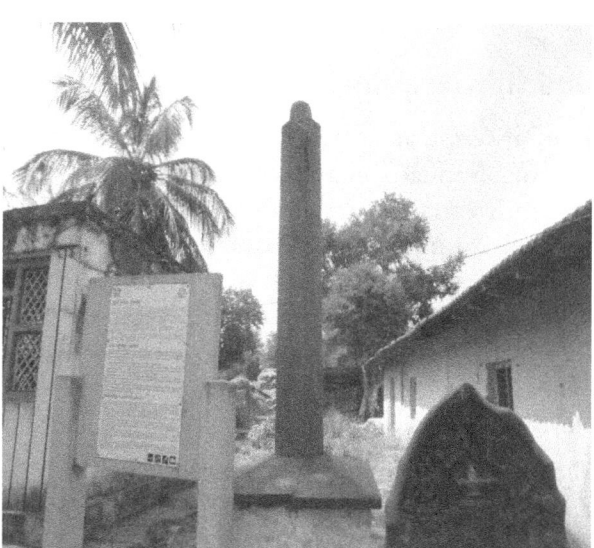

Talagunda Pillar Inscription and Malavalli Pillar Inscription

Summarised contents of the inscription read thus -"Talagunda pillar inscriptions *Epigraphia Indica vol VIII* – datable to fifth century CE on paleographic basis – language Sanskrit, characters box-headed southern alphabet – The record is written by poet Kubja, under the order of the Kadamba king Santivarman. Its immediate object is to record that Santivarman's father Kakusthavarman constructed a great tank near a Siva temple at Sthala-kundura where Satakarnis and other kings had formerly worshiped. Then the record mentions about the Kadamba family who belonged to Manavya gotra and descended from Haritiputra. It mentions that the Kadambas were a Brahmin family devoted to the study of Vedas and performer of sacrificial rites. They got their name from the fact that they carefully tended a Kadamba tree which grew near their home. Now once upon a time a member of this family, Mayurasharman, went with his *guru*, Virasimha, to the city of the Pallavas (Kanchipuram) to study sacred writings. Mayurasharman became exasperated with a Pallava horse-rider (soldier) that he abandoned his priestly vocation and took up sword. Mayursharman defeated the frontier-guards of the Pallavas and occupied the forest stretching to the gates of Sriparvata (Srisailam). He levied tribute from the Great Banas and other kings, thus caused much trouble to the Pallava kings. The Pallavas, recognizing his valor and ability, made a compact with him by which he entered in their service and eventually received a territory of his own, bounded on the west by the sea and on the east by the Prehara. Mayurasharman was anointed as a king of this territory. His son was Kangavarman, and his son was Bhagiratha. Bhagiratha's sons were Raghu and Kakusthavarman. Kakusthavarman's daughter was married to the Gupta kings."

Malavalli area was under the control of Satavahana and Chutu rulers right from the 2nd century CE. The hexagonal pillar set up in front of the Kalleswara temple has two separate inscriptions of the Satavahana and Kadamba rulers. The first inscription assignable to Vinhukada Chutukulananda Satakarni dated in 2nd century CE, is carved on three faces of the hexagonal pillar. It contains a command to his officer Mahavallabha Rajjuka informing him of the grant of the village Sahalatavi for the god of Malapali. The gift was made on the first day of the second fortnight.

The second inscription on the Malavalli pillar assignable to 3rd–4th century CE is engraved on the remaining three faces of the pillar. It refers to the rule of the Kadamba king Sivaskanda Varman and the renewal of the above earlier grant which had become defunct to Nagadatta, a *brahamana* of Kaundinya gotra in the first regnal year.

Both the inscriptions are of paramount importance to epigraphists as they record two different paleographic styles of characters of south Indian Brahmi of two different periods. While the earlier is in the typical triangular nail headed characters of 2nd and 3rd century CE, the latter is in typical Kadamba box headed characters of 3rd and 4th century CE.

Halmidi inscription

Halmidi inscription acquires a great significance as it has been considered to be the earliest known record containing Kannada characters. Scholars considered that the "Halmidi inscription" has put an end to many controversies surrounding the evolution of Kannada and they agreed to accept it as the earliest known record in Kannada characters. The 16-line inscription, which is on rectangular sandstone with a height of 2.5 feet and a width of 1 foot, has a Visnu Chakra on its top. This earliest Kannada inscription found at Halmidi in Belur taluk of Hassan district is dated 450 CE. The language is known as "Poorvada Halegannada" (primitive Kannada), with distinctive characteristics resembling those of Tamil. Halmidi was known as 'Palmidi' and 'Hanumidi' to in the past. However, the people of the village recently decided to retain the name Halmidi.

M.H. Krishna, noted archaeologist, was surprised to find the Brahmi script in the inscription, and he concluded that it was the oldest Kannada inscription available. He published the details of his study in the *Mysore Archaeological Report 1936*, and shifted the inscription to the Archaeological Museum, Mysore, and later to the Government Museum in Bengaluru where it is housed currently. A fibre glass replica of the inscription stone has been kept atop a raised platform under a canopy at Halmidi.

The inscription has become a subject of study for those who conduct research on the Kannada script, etymology, and Dravidian linguistics. The inscription is in verse form indicating the authors of the inscription had a good sense of the language structure. The inscription is written in pre-old Kannada which later evolved into old Kannada (*hale kannada*), middle Kannada and eventually modern Kannada. The Halmidi inscription is the earliest evidence of the usage of Kannada as medium for administrative use.

Dr. S. Shettar completed a detailed palaeographic study over 10 years, finding five to six inscriptions that are older than the Halmidi inscription (in Poorvada Halegannada dialect). The Tagarthi inscription is a mix of Brahmi, Kannada and Nagari scripts. It was found at Tagarthi (within the Gangavadi region in Shivamogga district) and dates to 350 CE, during the time of Western Ganga dynasty. This study pushed the date of evolution of Kannada language back by at least a century. The historian Suryanath Kamath also agrees with the findings of Dr S. Shettar.

M.G. Manjunath an epigraphist and Mysuru based scholar discovered 400 CE *Gunabhushitana Nishadi inscription* of Jainism one of the 271 inscriptions on Chandragiri hill of Shravanabelagola found near Parshwanatha Basadi. This inscription is 50 years older than the Halmidi inscription. It is mentioned in the Epigraphia Carnatica. There are Prakrit, Sanskrit and Purvada Halegannada words in it. The four lined inscription has six words. The inscription is in Satavahana Brahmi and Aadi Ganga script. M. Chidananda Murthy also agrees that *Gunabhushitana Nishadi Shasana* was a Kannada inscription (in Purvada Halegannada script).

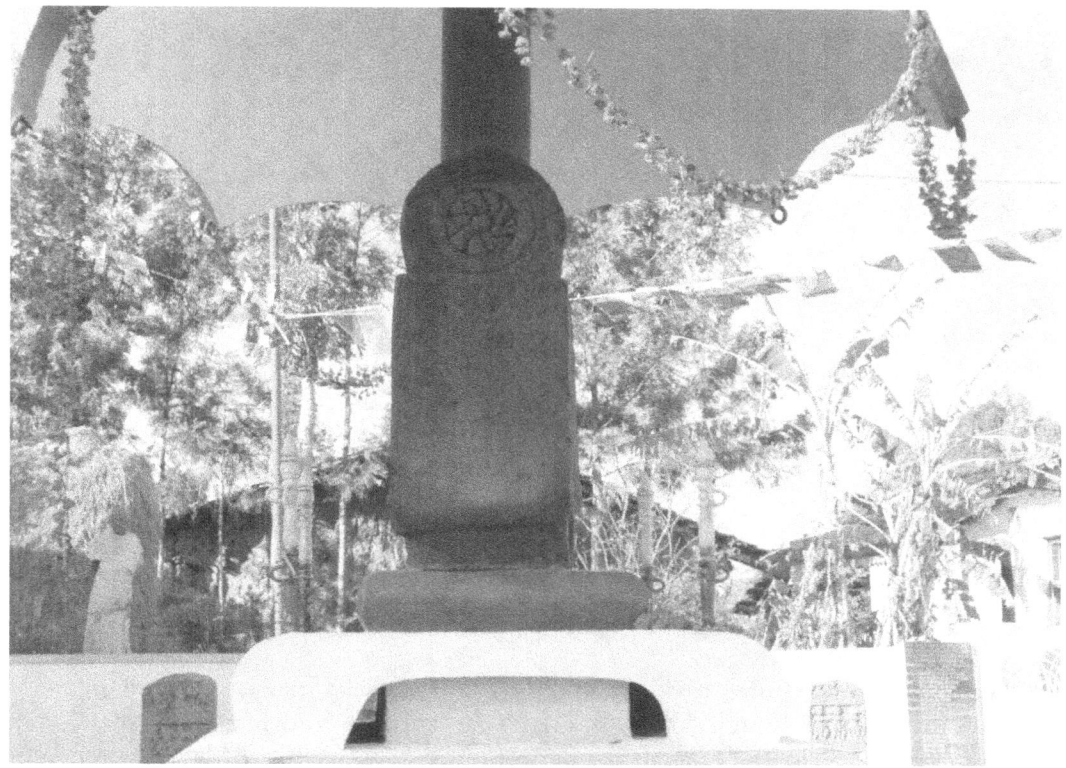

Halmidi Inscription Site

Though scholars have found inscriptions carrying Kannada characters dating back to periods earlier than the Halmidi inscription but it still continues to enjoy the status of the earliest record using Kannada characters.

Pillar inscription in Pattadakal in front of the Virupaksha temple

There are numerous Kannada language inscriptions at Pattadakal. Important among them being; at Virupaksha Temple, there is 8th century Old Kannada inscription on victory pillar, in the Sangameshvara temple, there exists a large inscription tablet (696–733 CE) describing grants made by the king Vijayaditya for the construction of the temple.

Engraved on an octagonal pillar set up in front of the Mallikarjuna temple at Pattadakal, this inscription is in the *Siddhamatrika* and Kannada–Telugu characters of the 8th century CE. It opens with invocations to Siva and Haragauri. Refers to the setting up of a *trisula*-pillar (*trisula-mudrankita saila-stambha*) by Jnanasivacharya who had come from *Mrigathanikahara-Visaya* on the northern bank of the Ganga river and was staying in the Vijayeswara temple (modern Sangameswara). This pillar was set up to the south of Vijayeswara Lokeswara (modern Virupaksha temple) temple built by Lokamata (i.e. Lokamahadevi), who was the queen of Vikramaditya Satyasraya the conqueror of Kanchipura, and to the west of Trilokeswara temple (Mallikarjuna) built by Trilokyamahadevi who was also the beloved queen of Vikramaditya and the mother of king Kirttivarman II.

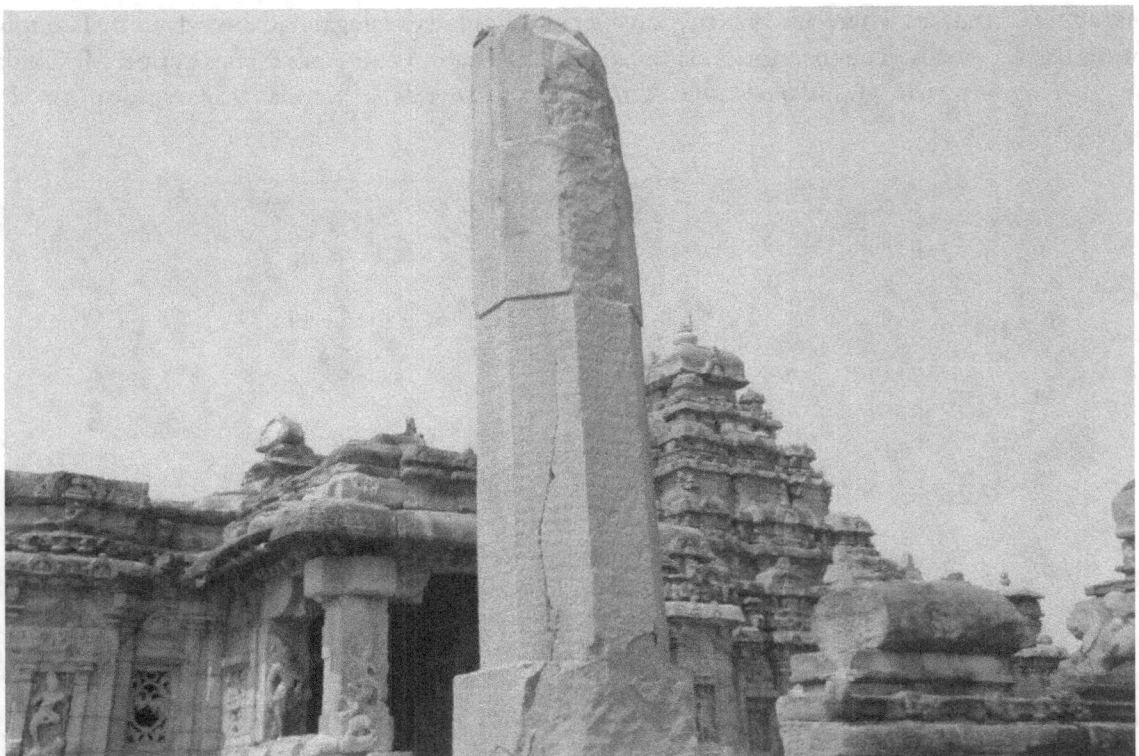

Pillar Inscription Pattadakal

A grant of 30 *navaratnas* of land near village Arapunise was made by Jnanasivacharya for the Vijayeswara temple's worship after having bought that land from Aryabhatta who had received it from the king Vijayaditya. The pillar inscription belongs to the period of the king Kirttivarman II (son of Vikramaditya II) and was set up in 755 CE.

The said octagonal pillar is the victory pillar installed after the victory of the king Vikramaditya II in his military campaigns to the Pallava territories at Kanchipuram in 745 CE.

Inscriptions as memorials of pets

One very prominent inscription of this kind is the Atakur Inscription. This inscription was in fact written to protect and honour the memorial of a pet hound. A similar inscription and memorial for a pet parrot too came into light in Goa by a Kadamba king in the 12th century CE. The parrot died on being eaten by a cat in the palace. The inscription reveals that the king was so filled with grief at the death of the parrot that he killed himself.

Atakur Inscription is about the instructions given to the *gorava* of Challeswara temple regarding the honour that had to be given to the dead hound named Kali. The inscription slab was placed in front of the Challeswara temple and the *gorava* was instructed thereby not to eat his food before offering worship to the memorial of the hound. Detailed contents of the Atakur inscription are given among the example inscriptions in the next few sections of this chapter.

Begur Inscription

Begur's most famous monument is its Panchaligeswara temples, a complex of five Siva temples. Of these, the Nageswara temple is the oldest, dating back to 890 CE. The temple shows some of the features typical of Ganga temples of that period, including the *ashtadikpalakas* (guardians of the directions) carved on the ceiling and the rows of swans carved on the outside of the structure. The remaining four shrines-

Nagareswara, Karneswara, Choleswara and Kalikamateswara-were added by later Ganga kings and during the reign of the Cholas here.

The temple abounds in inscriptions, some on the walls dating from the 12th to the 14th century CE, others in the temple compound, dating to much earlier periods. An especially elaborate hero-stone from here, in memory of the chieftain Nagattara's death in a battle in about 890 CE, was moved to the Government Museum, Bengaluru and can still be seen there. One particular inscription in the temple is of special significance to Bengaluru, for it contains the earliest known use of the name Bengaluru. In 1915, this hero-stone written in *Hale Kannada* (old Kannada), was found embedded in the floor of the Kalikamateswara shrine and mentions the death of Nagattara's son Buttana-setti and of his 'house-son' Pervona-setti in the battle of Bengaluru. Dating to about 900 CE, this effectively invests Bengaluru with a fairly ancient past.

The inscription seems to refute the popular 'Benda Kalooru' theory behind the origin of the name 'Bengaluru.' While the boiled beans anecdote relates to Hoysala king Veera Ballala's regime in 1120 CE, and modern Bengaluru was built by Kempegowda I in the 1530s, the Begur inscription indicates that a settlement called 'Bengaluru' existed much before that, as early as 890 CE.

Garuda pillar inscription at Hoysaleswara temple, Halebid

An interesting object in the Hoysaleswara temple complex is the rare *Garuda Sthamba* (Garuda pillar). Such pillars are different from *virgals* (Hero stone). *Garudas* were elite bodyguards of the kings and queens. They moved and lived with the royal family and their only purpose was to protect their master. Upon the death of their master, they committed suicide. The rare pillar on the south side depicts heroes brandishing knives and cutting their own heads. The inscription honours Kuruva Lakshma, a bodyguard of Veera Ballala II. A devoted officer, he took his life and that of his wife and other bodyguards after the death of his master. This event is narrated in an old Kannada inscription on the pillar. A 8 ft. (2.4 m) tall sculpture of Ganesha including the platform rests at the South entrance close the Garuda pillar.

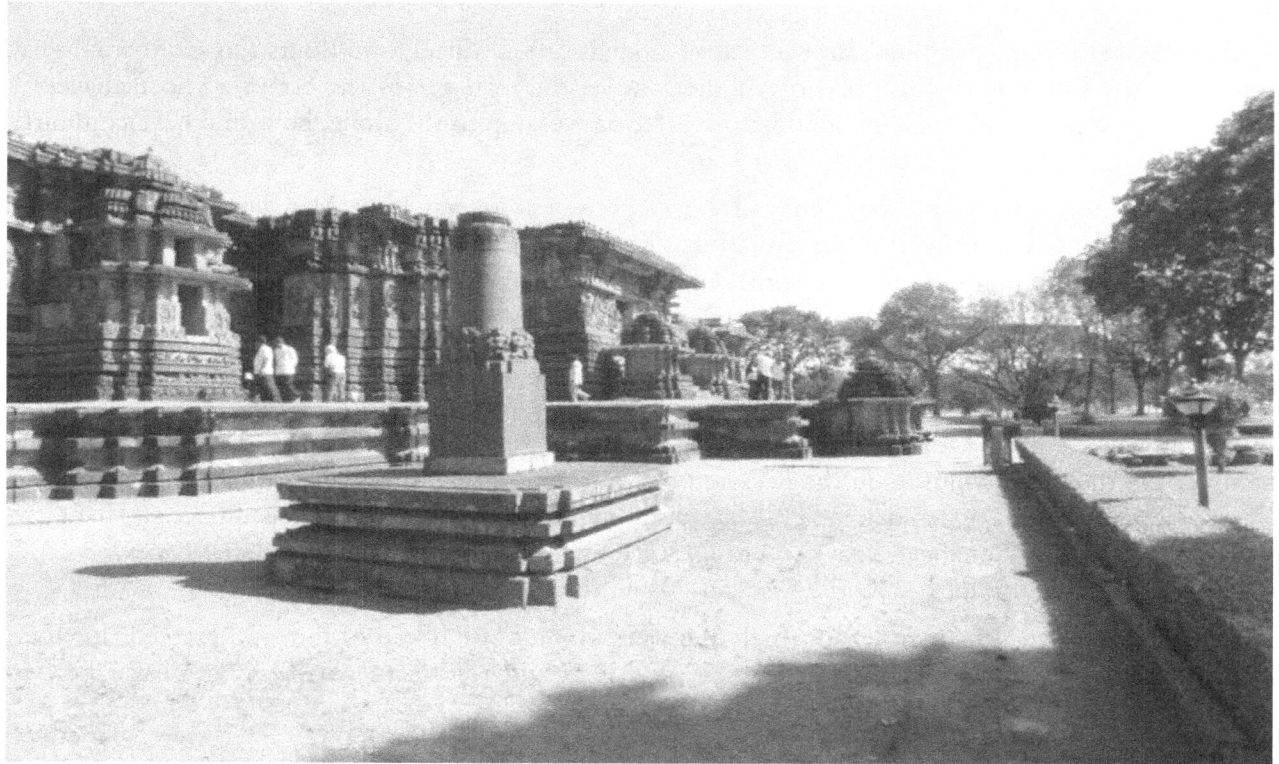

Garuda Pillar Inscription Hoysaleswara Temple Halebid Examples of some inscriptions' contents

Example 1

Atakur Inscription of Rashtrakuta king Krishna III and Western Ganga king Butuga II, Saka 872

Location: Atakur, Mandya District

Language: Kannada (prose and verse)

Script: Kannada

Date: Section A, Saka 872 falling in 949–950 CE

Translated summary of the text of the inscription:

While the Saka year eight hundred and seventy two and the cyclic year Saumya were current, when illustrious Krishna raja (alias) Kannaradeva, who was the very bee on the water-lilies that were the feet of *Sriprithavi-vallabha, Prameswara, Paramabhaktataraka* Amoghavarsadeva, who was very Trinetra (Siva) in battle, who was a marvel with elephants, a wrestler against forest-elephants, and who had taken *Kacci* having attacked Muvadi-Chola Rajaditya and having fought and killed him at Takkola was proceeding in triumph,

When *Dharma-maharajaadhiraja*, the lord of Kolalapura (Kolar), the master of Nandagiri, the truthful Ganga, the lintel of victory, the Gangeya among Gangas the Narayana among the Gangas, the illustrious Styavaka-Kongunivarma Permanadi asked, in appreciation, his servant

Manalera of the Sagara race, who was the lord of Vallabhi, who was the very Bhagiratha among noble men, who was a marvel among those who pierce, who was a very Trinetra among the Sagaras, who cut off the noses of his foes, who was a very Sudraka in war, who was the champion of Butuga (II) to make supplication, Manalera asked for Permanadi's favourite hound Kali and obtained it.

In an encounter with a mighty boar on the hill in the western quarter of Belatur in Kerenadu, Kali as well as the boar were killed. To commemorate that event the (inscribed) slab was set up in front of the Challeswara temple at Atakur and two *khandugas* (a measure of land) of land were granted below the large tank (for the maintenance of the slab).

Any cultivator or any administrator of *nadu* (subdivision) or village who flouts this grant would have committed the sin of molesting the dog. If the *gorava* (the manager of the estate), who manages the Challeswara temple should take his food before offering worship to the stone, he would have committed the sin of having molested the dog.

When the entire army and the Chola adversary himself were watching, Manalera marched ahead to meet in battle the Chola army. It is but natural that he was the subject of universal appreciation. And with king at his back and multitude of his enemies in front, this Manalera struck the forehead of the elephant that was called the fortress of the Chola so that it burst open.

Section B

While Butuga (II), having fought and killed Rachamalla, the son of illustrious Ereyappa, was ruling over the ninetysix thousand country, on the occasion of Kannaradeva fighting against the Chola, Butuga (II) having stabbed with a dagger and killed Rajaditya after converting the howdah of Rajaditya's elephant itself as the field of battle, Kannaradeva gave to Butuga, in appreciation of his valiant deed, the Banavase-12000, the Belavola-300, the Purigere-300, the Kisukad-70 and the Bagenad-70 (divisions).

Being pleased with the manner in which Manalera stood out in front of him and pierced (his foes), Butuga gave him, as *balgaccu*, the Atakur-12 (division) and the village of Kadiyur in the Belavola (division).

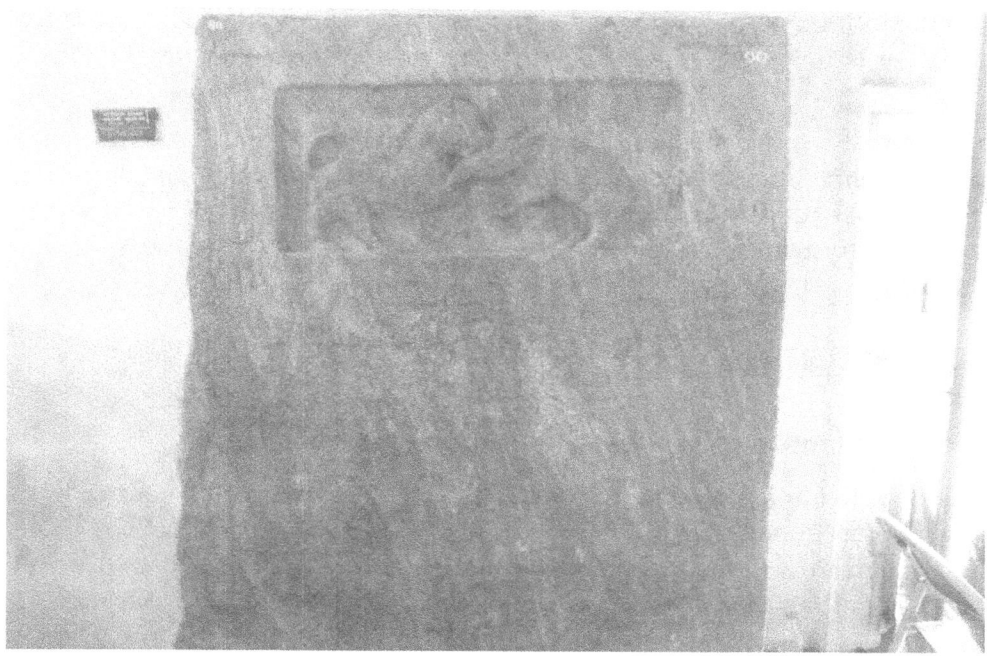

Atakur Inscription about the Hound Kali

Example 2

About existence of a dam for a reservoir: In another inscription contained in the Devarahalli Plates of Sripurusa (Western Ganga) in respect of a grant in the regnal year 50, Saka 698 (776–777 CE), there is a reference to a dam on a water reservoir while describing the boundary of the village forming part of the grant. Extracts from the inscription read thus:

"The boundaries of the gifted village were – on the eastern side, the heap (or hillock) of white rocks at Nolibela; on the south-east, the Panyangere tank; on the south, the junction of the Belagalligere tank and water course leading to Olagere tank; on the west, the heap of white rocks in the field called Kaidara-key; on the west, the tank constructed by Ponkevi Toltuvayar; on the north-west, the stone heap in *punuse* and *gottegal* localities; on the north, the big bend in the water course leading to Somagere tank; on the north-east, the Kalambratti dam."

Example 3

Bridge on a river and creation of a new village: In another inscription contained in the Hallegere Plates of Sivamara, Saka 635 (713–714 CE), there is reference to bridge caused to be built over a river for getting the land granted to rest of the division. Extracts from the inscription read thus:

"On the supplication made by Jayavriddhi and Pallavadhiraja, the beloved sons of the Pallava crown-prince,

When six hundred and thirty five years of Saka era had elapsed, in the thirty fourth year of his victorious reign, on the fifteenth day of the bright half of Jyestha,

When he was residing at the victorious camp at Talavanapura,

Was caused to be built the bridge across the Kiline river on the northern side of Keragodu in Keragodu-visaya, and having constituted a (new) village called Pallavataka comprising Kodugole and Belkere to the south of that river, and Beppampal and Punuseppatti to the north (of that river) and having divided that village into sixty six shares and given away as grant as follows:

Thity six (of the sixty six) shares were granted to the *ukthya-yajjin* Madhavasarman, son of Marasarman and grandson of Bavasarman, a resident of Mahasenapura and belonging to the Atreya-sagotra and vajasaneya-carana."

It may be noted that just like modern legal documents, these inscriptions too had a way of describing land and its appurtenants, directions, adjacent properties and locational details. Even trees were given names so that it was easy to identify lands under grant. Date of agreement or order was specified in the then prevalent calendar system. Measurements of land and produce from these were identified too for the sake of clarification as to who enjoyed the rights accruing from the lands.

3.3 MEMORIAL STONES

Various Types of Memorial stones

Best of inscriptions found in Karnataka are Memorial Stones. They are very unique to Karnataka and the varieties in them are stupendous. Memorial stones in such large numbers are found nowhere else in whole of India. Some of them are also found outside the state, in territories which were part of the territories ruled by dynasties from Karnataka.

Memorial Stones are stones dedicated to a person who sacrificed his life for the cause of king or public in war, in a battlefield; or in cattle raids and while safeguarding life and dignity of women from miscreants. These memorials present a rich variety, though not of great artistic merit. Mostly they are symbolic and invariably associated with the dead. They are simpler square or rectangular slabs out of harder rocks like granite or quartzite and also of slate stone. They are dressed neatly with sculptured panels within raised borders or frames and many among them contain inscriptions either at the terminal frame or along the borders of the sculptured scene. These may be installed in different ways. Many of them can be found covered in dolmen like chambers whereas most can be found erected in or around temple compounds, agricultural fields or water tanks. The simplest among these are the *viragals* (hero stones) like a stele set up in the open. The broad faces depict in relief the military events and the heroic personalities including ruling kings. These are meant to elevate the hero to the level of ancestors and to commemorate the heroic deed connected with the deceased.

The *prakara* (boundary wall) of Siddapa temple at Dodshivara (Dodda Shivara as in Google maps) in Kolar district comprises a veritable gallery of close to 200 hero-stones. All these come from various times but most belong to the time of the Western Ganga king Sripurusha (726–791 CE). All these were lying scattered all around in the temple compound. However, now that the temple is undergoing renovation and restoration, all these hero-stones have been lined up along the temple boundary walls covered under low stone slabs to protect them from being weather beaten. Among the hero-stones at Dodshivara there are stones sculptured with man killing a tiger rather than in a battle mode. The temple compound also has a *Mana-stambha* of the typical Jaina style. The *mana-stambha* is set up having a *dvitala* square cell with the lower chamber opening towards the cardinals. The *bhitti* (outer wall) part of this has some low relief carvings flanking the entrances and capped by a *kapota*.

A Hero stone is generally divided into three sections, the lower portion gives details of the hero and his act of sacrifice. The sculpture will have, hero fighting the enemy with a sword or a bow, or protecting his state from the army, or protecting cattle, or women in distress. This section generally depicts the reason for his /her death. The middle portion depicts the hero who sacrificed his life being carried away to heaven (*swarga*) by angels. The third portion depicts him sitting in front of a God.

These memorial stones are classified accordingly to the content of their text and narrative of the sculpture carved on them. They are found with or without inscriptions.

Viragals (Veeragallu) -Hero Stone

Hero stones are memorial stones erected in memory of heroes who died in a battle field while defending kings, or defending cattle or women in distress.

Hero stones are found all over Karnataka and about half of the hero stones found have no inscriptions on them. The largest concentration of hero stones can be found in the districts of Kolar, Shivamogga, Tumukuru, Bengaluru and Haveri. Hero stone is a unique feature of Karnataka inscriptions, other than Karnataka we can find hero stones in Tamil Nadu, Andhra Pradesh and Maharashtra, because of the proximity of these states and that the rulers from various dynasties had the boundaries of their kingdoms extending into the three states. Hero-stones may appear even while digging for a well or for laying fibre optic cables in villages.

Hero Stones can be further sub-divided based on these criteria:

Hero stones on Attack of Forts

There are many beautiful hero stones in Karnataka which depict war scenes with soldiers riding on horses and elephants. Some of them also have a fort wall etched in them. The most notable and one of a kind in whole of India is the Begur Viragal which is now housed in Bengaluru Museum. In pitched battles, expert skilled soldiers used to stay ahead to capture the fort gate. For soldiers who got killed during the attack on the fort, their king honored them by erecting memorial stones. These stones are usually ornately sculpted, and depict the soldier in the battle field and might not contain inscriptions. One such Hero stone in Lakshmeshwar, Gadag district, depicts a soldier who was killed while removing the stones of the forts, thereby causing great damage to the security of the fort.

Ooralivu – Defending Village

These hero stones were erected for the persons who died while fighting to save their village from enemy trying to capture the village in an attack. Inscriptions on some of the stones describe the scene showing how adventurous young soldiers with arms in their hands faced such attacks and died safeguarding the village.

Gograhana, Turugol or Gokals -Defending Cattle

These hero stones were erected for people who died while defending cattle theft or siege of cattle by neighboring villages. In ancient and medieval period, cattle were considered as wealth. The capture of cattle in the enemy territory was considered as an act of pride. Such attack was considered as a matter of insult to a village and they usually resisted the attack or fought to recapture the lost cattle. Hero stones were laid for village fellow men who tried to bring back their lost cattle, those people were remembered as heroes of the village.

Examples of *gograhana* were found at Hunukunda (Kolar district), Kabbalu near Shravanabelagola and Begur (Bengaluru). However, particularly interesting examples of *gograhanas* or *gokals* were found at Hebetta (4 km away from Srinivaspur in Kolar district). The earliest among them belongs to the period of Sripurusha (726–791 CE) of the Western Ganga dynasty. Another one on a bigger boulder has a *yantra* stone set up by the orders of the Ganga king Marasimha II (962–974 CE) for the benefit of cattle of the village. The broad face of the stone contains a mystic diagram with certain letters in the interstices with the syllable *hrim* repeated around while on the reverse face of the stone 32 small squares each containing a letter has been identified as a *sarvato-bhadhrika* verse. Such *gokals* were set up in front of the village and these mystic *yantras* were believed to be potent curers of animal diseases and water washed over the *yantras* was given to the cattle as medicine. In the village named Hemmige on the bank of river Cauveri opposite Talkad, there are a lot of hero-stones and loose sculpture strewn around. *Gokal-yantra* stones like the one at Hebetta (Hebatta in Google map) too were found. One such stone depicting a hero protecting cattle is kept in the compound of the Kalleswara temple at Bagali.

Pendirudeyurchu, Penbuyyall

These were hero stones installed in honour of heroes who met with death while protecting modesty of women in distress being assaulted by enemies.

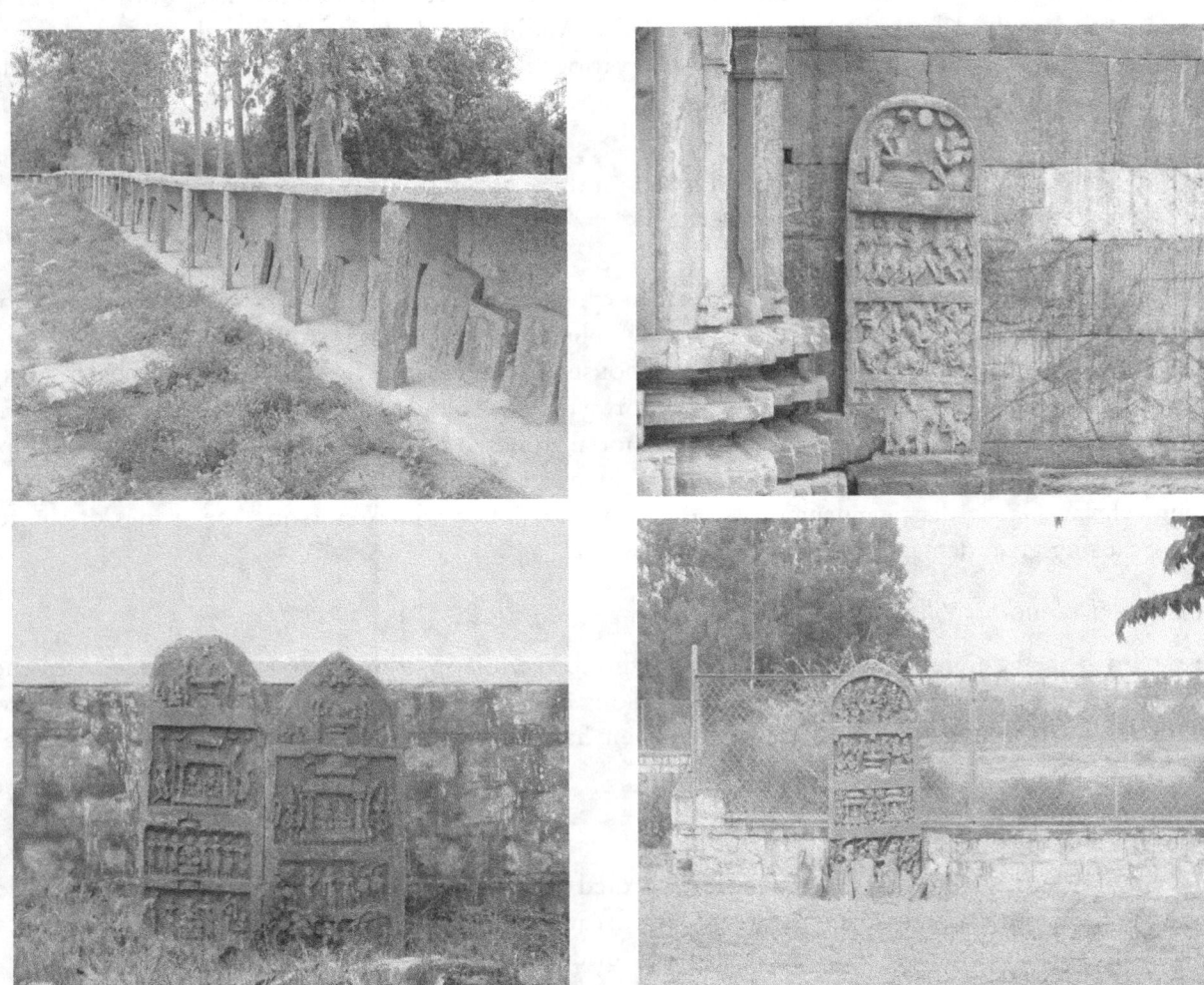

Hero-stones from Siddappa Temple Dodda Shivara, Lakshmidevi Temple Dodda Gadavalli, Iswara Temple Malali and Bucheswara Temple Koravangala

Bete -Hunting Wild Animals

These were hero stones installed in honour of valiant heroes who met their death while killing a wild beast. Since there are various varieties in this category, they have been classified based on the type of the wild beast which caused the death. Epigraphical sculptures narrate different types of boar hunting games using trained dogs. Sculptures on the epigraphs depict hunting with one or two dogs attacking or cornering the boar. Atakur inscription (dated 949.A.D) is an inscribed memorial stone erected by a grief-stricken owner in honor of his brave hound, which died while killing a wild boar; this stone erected in memory of an animal is considered a unique one. Melagani located in Kolar district, has two memorial stones of 10th century erected for heroic deeds of two hounds namely Loga and Dhalaga. Loga had attacked and killed 70 boars in its life time and Dhalaga also had attacked and killed 50 boars in its life time. Hero stones depicting killing of tiger are found in Dodashivara as well. A hero stone depicting the killing of a wild boar while simultaneously being attached by two hounds is kept in the ASI museum at Balligavi.

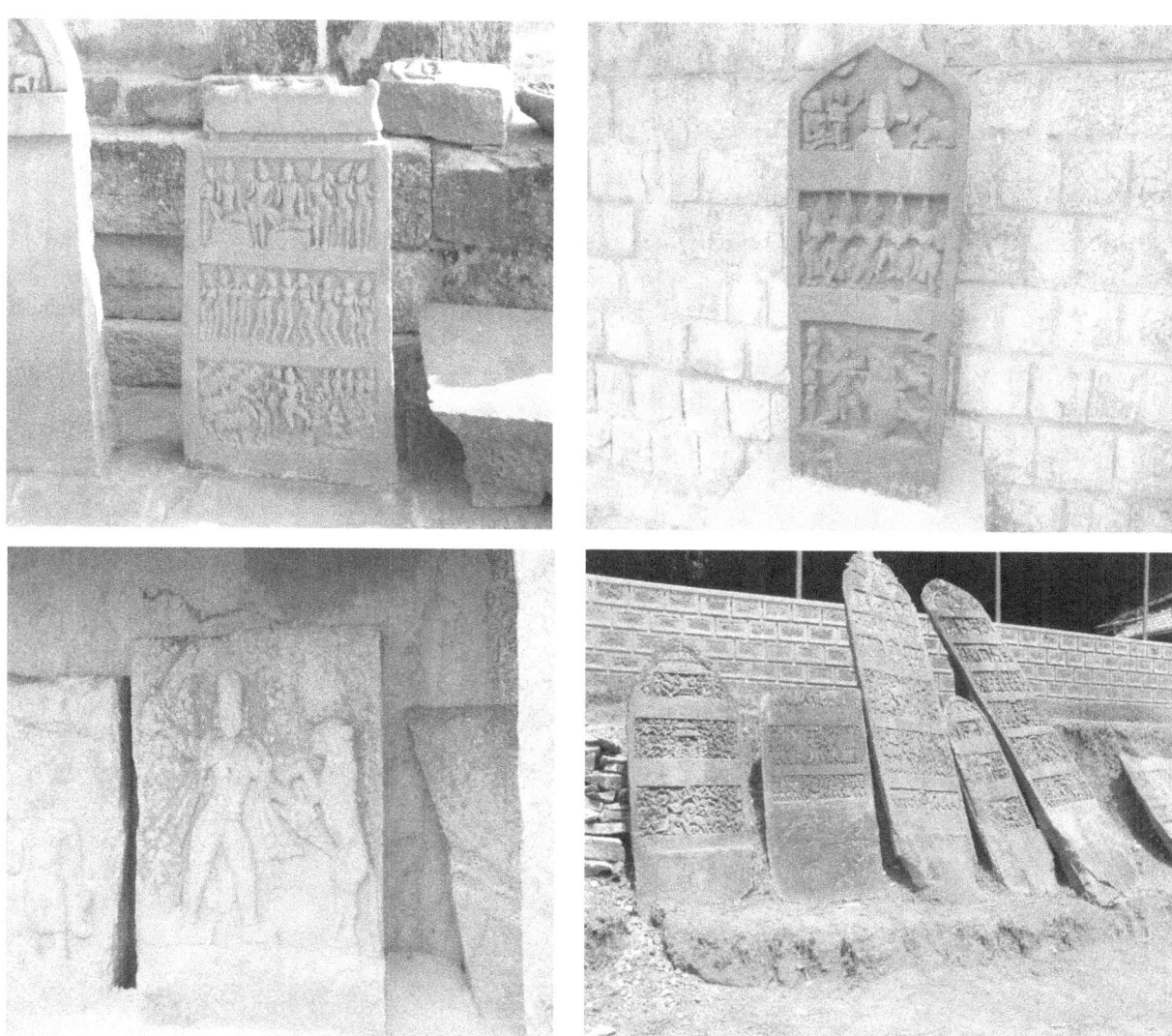

Gograhana from Kalleswara Temple Bagali, Wild Boar Killing from Balligavi Museum, Tiger Killing from Dodda Shivara and Hero-stones from Hosagunda with Battle Scenes (Sagara)

Handi Bete

These stones depict death of the hero while killing a wild boar.

Huli Bete

These stones depict death of the hero while killing a tiger.

Masti -Maha Sati – Mastikallu -Self Sacrifice on Pyre: *Mastikallu* is a memorial stone erected in memory of a lady who invited her death by self immolation after hearing the death of her husband. These stones can be seen as *Masti* and *Veera Masti*. Usually Masti stones show a right hand rising towards heaven which symbolizes blessings to all human beings and is called '*Vyasana Tholu*.' The lady who invited death this way was given divine status and was worshiped as a Goddess. *Masti* stones are unique to Karnataka. With detailed studies of these stones and other literary sources, historians note that 'Sati' ritual in Karnataka was never forced upon women, rather it was done voluntarily.

Masti

Masti stones are classified based on, whether the woman sacrificed her life along with the dead body of her husband or without.

Sahagamana

The lady entered the pyre along with body of her husband.

Anugamana

The lady entered the pyre upon hearing the death of her husband in the absence of her husband's body. The most notable and beautiful mastikallu of this type is the Dekabbe shasana belonging to 1057 CE with inscriptions which is five layered and explains the story and the events of Dekabbe's Anugamana ritual.

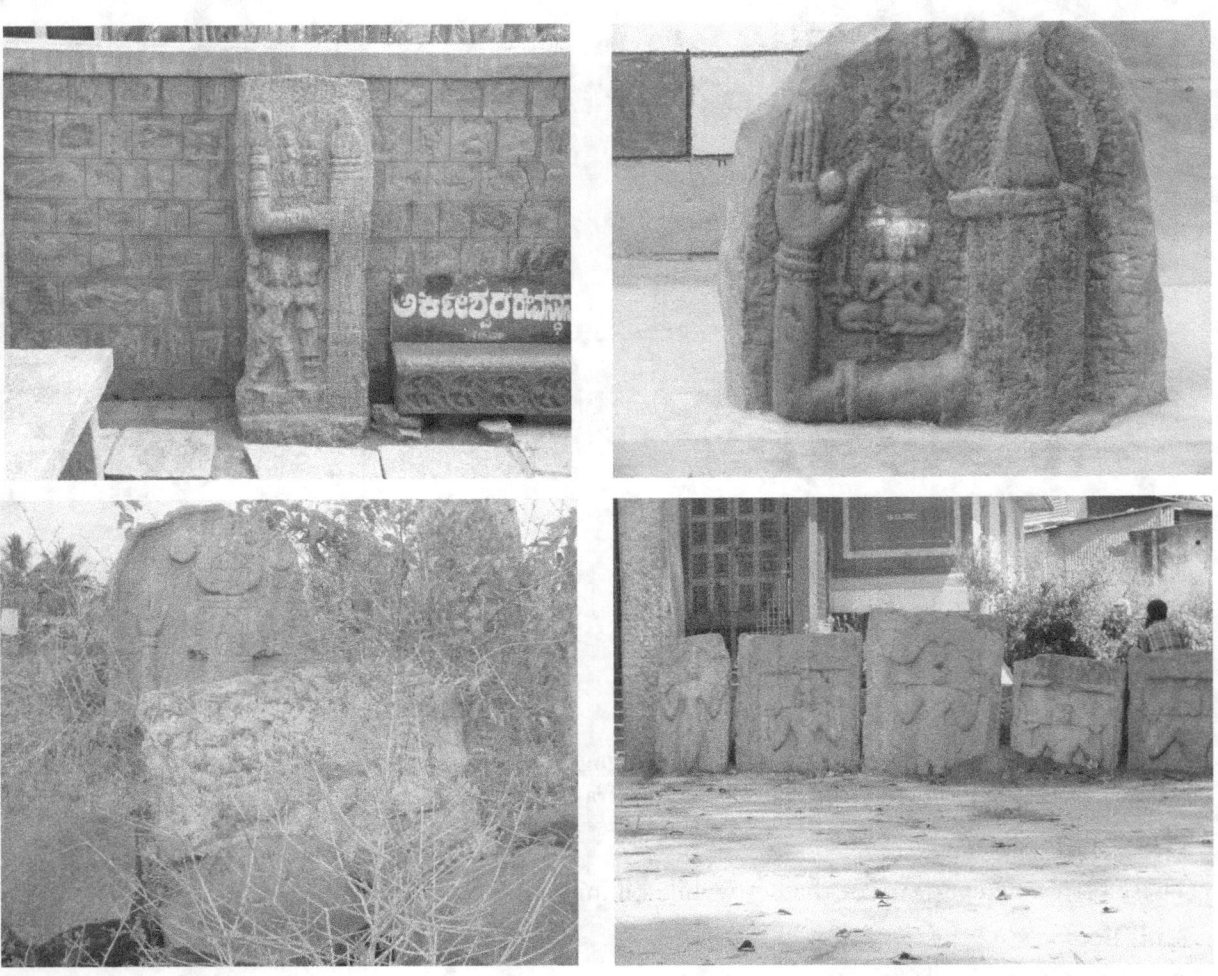

Mastikallu from Arkeswara Temple Alur, Malavalli Pillar Site, Atakur and Self-immolation Stones from Chamapakadhamaswamy Temple Bannerghatta

Veera Masti kallu

These are memorial stones with both the hero and his wife/wives being depicted in the sculpture. They are erected in memory of a hero who died a heroic death and his wife/wives who invited the death by self immolation after hearing the death of her husband.

Kilgunte – Self Burial

Kilgunte denotes live burial, plunging into pyre, falling from height and allowing oneself to be slammed, and sacrificing one's life on the demise of his master or king.

We have inscriptions along with text giving details of Kilgunte practice, but associated sculpture is rarely found. Doddahundi memorial stone (840 or 869 CE) has a unique depiction in frieze of the ritual death of the Western Ganga king Ereganga Nitimarga I. The memorial stone has its frieze set inside a square panel whose borders are etched to create the impression of flames that further accentuate the grave event. The dying king, who exudes a calm countenance, is lying on a couch with his head on a double pillow and is attended to by his personal guard Agarayya. An agitated Prince Satyavakya stands behind the king with a dagger and sword. The inscription below the frieze reads "be at the pair of lotus feet of Arhat Bhattaraka." This is typical example of Kilgunte memorial stone of type *velevali*. Some individuals may have taken an oath to sacrifice their lives in order to save their master's life as bodyguards and when the occasion demands such as death of their masters due to war, illness, etc., they follow their master in death. These individuals and the practice were called '*garuda*' (*lenka*) and '*velevali*' respectively. Doddahundi and Hemavati are fine examples of Kilgunte inscription. A Gruda pillar inscription is also found at Hoysaleswara temple in Halebid.

Sidithale

Sidi means 'blast' and *thale* means 'head.' These are memorial stones which depict self sacrifice by beheading and cutting of throat. The person is hanged to a bamboo pole which is bent. His throat is cut by knife and his head would blast off from the body as the pole gets straightened. This would tear apart his head from the body, and the head is swung away. These have been classified based on whether the person sacrificed his life for his family's welfare or for the welfare of the king.

Athmahuthi -Self Sacrifice

These are memorials in honour of the persons who invite death by cutting their throat for the welfare of his family. A row of such stones can be noticed on the way to Champakadhamaswamy temple in Bannerghatta.

Sacrifice for the welfare of the king

These are memorials of the royal servants who invite death by cutting their throat for the welfare of the family of their masters.

Dharmika Kary -Religious Ritual

There are memorials stones found in Karnataka and are erected in honour of the persons who invited death in a religious way to attain *Moksha* -freedom from the cycle of birth and death. They have been classified as follows.

Nishidi

There are memorials stone of the religious persons of Jaina sect to who invited the death in a religious way by fasting called *Sallekhana*.

Uri Uyyale -Swing on a fire

This is a ritual where in, on the day of **solar eclipse**, one sacrifices his life swinging over a religious fire.

Falling on a sharp piercing arrow

This is a ritual where in, on an auspicious day, one sacrifices his life falling on a sharp iron rods/arrows.

Shoola -Sitting on sharp objects

This is a ritual where in, on an auspicious day, one sacrifices his life sitting on a sharp object which pierces his body.

Aayaka

There are memorials stone of the religious persons of *Boudhha* (Buddhism) sect, usually depicted as part of 'Jataka' tales. Such memorial stones belonging to Mauryan and Ashokan period are found in northern Karnataka, particularly such memorial stones were found during excavations at Sannati and Kanganahalli.

Hero Stone at Begur, Bengaluru

Begur hero stone is a unique 10 century CE inscription which elucidates the techniques and strategies in a battle and gives details about sword fighting, spears throwing techniques. This is among the best hero stones available in whole of India and is now preserved in Government Museum Bengaluru. Similar and equally elaborate hero stone depicting war scenes have also been found at Kolaramma temple in Kolar, Umamaheswara temple at Hosagunda and Kameswara temple at Madigere near Chintamani.

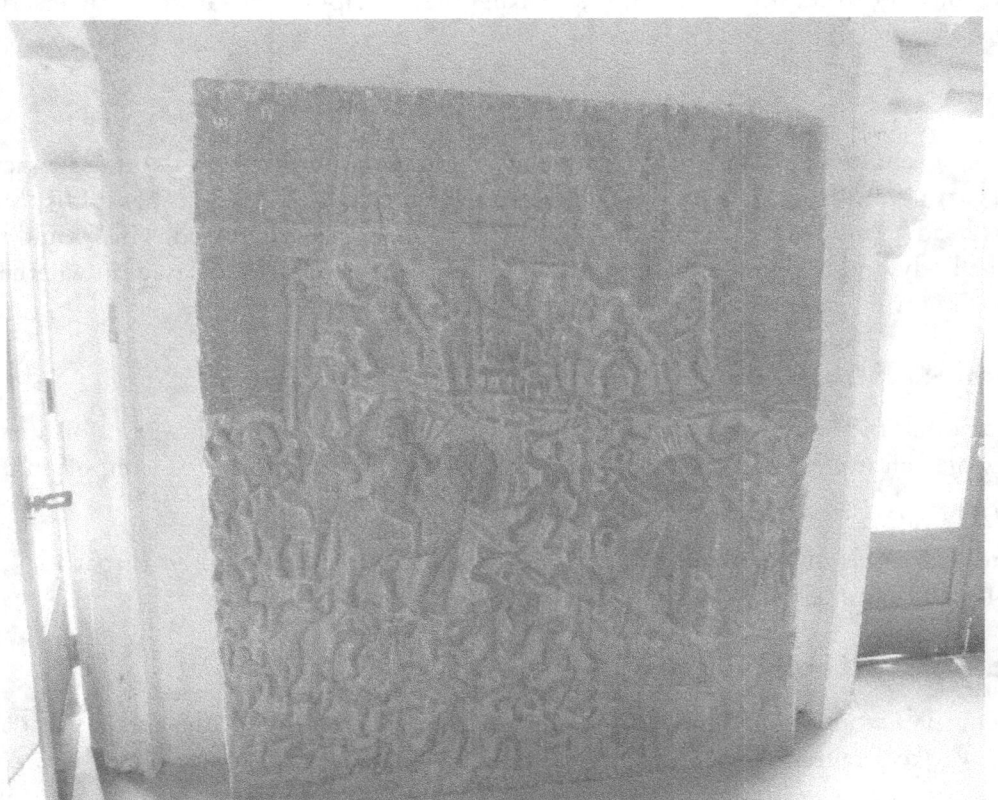

Begur Memorial Stone and Inscription, Bengaluru Museum

Begur hero stone is in two parts, the lower part depicts actual war scenes in detail. In this part, the hero warrior of this stone is seated on a fully decorated horse, holding a sword in one hand and controlling the horse with the other hand and marching towards the enemy who is on the left side of the stone. The enemy is seated on a decorated elephant with an umbrella held over his head, indicating that he is a king or an important royal dignitary. Behind this person is the depiction of 'Rana Bhairavi' (Victory Goddess), who is standing nude, holding a skull in left the hand and *damaru* (drum) in the right hand. Opposite to Rana Bhairavi, there is a lineup of musicians behind the hero warrior. Also there is a depiction of three horse riders, indicating that they too sacrificed their life in the war. The enemy is on the opposite side, seated on the elephant marching towards the hero warrior. The elephant has been stuck with arrows in its head and forehead. On its path elephant is bouncing one of soldiers from its trunk. Behind the elephant a curious image is sculpted, wounded soldiers lying on the ground in agony. The two mysterious creatures Shakini and Dhakini (devils) have come to feast on the wounded and dead soldiers.

At the bottom or the lower portion is the representation of the battle ground, fox, crows, vultures and other animals scavenging for flesh from dead bodies.

The upper part of the stone depicts, the hero, after sacrificing his life, is taken to heaven; there he is seated on a throne and *'apsaras'* (heavenly nymphs) are dancing in front of him. A similar narration of a war scene with almost same description is also carved on the pillars inside the arkeswara temple at Alur near Chamarajanagar. The pillar depiction in the temple relates to the Takkolam war of Butuga II (949–950 CE) which is also the content of the Begur inscription.

This is a very rare hero stone. No other memorial stone is found in India which can parallel this with such detailed pictorial description of the battle field. The Hero stone inscription at Kolaramma temple, Madigere and Nambihalli all in Kolar district are other three hero stones which also depict war field beautifully, but they are no match to intricate carving of the Begur Hero stone. A few more hero-stones depicting war scenes are kept in the compound of the Uma Maheswara temple at Hosagunda, Sagara (Shivamogga district). At least two of these are divided in seven portions and are carved on slabs as tall as nine feet.

4
UNDERSTANDING AND APPRECIATING TEMPLES OF KARNATAKA

4.1 CANONICAL LITERATURE ON TEMPLE ARCHITECTURE AND SCULPTURE

The word *Vastu* has been derived from *Vastoshpati* used in 'Rig Veda' and is meant to provide protection, happiness and prosperity in this life as well as after death. A *shloka* there has the meaning: "Oh God of structures and buildings, we are your devotees. Listen our prayer, make us free of disease, give wealth and prosperity, and help the well-being of all persons and animals living in the house. These houses were free from obstructions and had big compounds with great walls." Later the word *Vastu* finds mention in various *Puranas* and other Vedic texts. The Matsya Purana has eight complete chapters devoted to architecture and sculpture and in it eighteen scholars have been mentioned who were masters of *Vastu Sastra*. Their names are: Bhrigu, Atri, Vasistar, Vishwakarma, Mayan, Naradar, Nagnajit, Visalakshan, Purandaran, Brahma, Kumaraswamy, Nandikesawaran, Sounakar, Bhargavar, Vasudevar, Anirudhar, Sukran and Brahaspati. In Agni Purana there are sixteen chapters dealing with town planning.

The science of *Vastu* is considered an integral part of the Hindu architecture. This science had been developing right from the Vedic times. Being a technical subject, it was confined only to the architects and handed over verbally or in the form of hand-written monographs. The principles of construction, architecture and sculpture, as enunciated in the treatises on temple architecture, have been incorporated in the science of *Vastu*. From ancient literature, it is gathered that *Vastu* was treated as the science of construction of temples and royal palaces.

The word *Agama* generally implies a traditional doctrine or precept, a sacred writing or scripture and hence the Veda. But there is a special class of works including the mystical worship of Siva and Shakti like the Tantras which come from south India. These are sometimes known as the beginning of the *Agamas*. They are encyclopedic works like the *Puranas* whose ultimate object is also to discuss the worship of the Triad. The *Puranas*, however deal with all the three deities forming the holy Trinity, although Visnu has received preference in as much as fourteen of the *Puranas* are devoted to his worship. The *Agamas*, on the other hand initially dealt largely with Siva though *Agamas* dedicated to other deities too were evolved over time.

The *Agamas* like the *Puranas* deal with the architectural subjects too and their contribution to *Silpa sastra* are more extensive and valuable. Some of the *Agamas* deal with technical matters, which is not the case with the *Puranas*. The *Agama* named Kamilkagama devotes sixty of its seventy two chapters to architecture and sculpture. But unlike *Puranas*, Kamilkagama discusses highly technical matters such as classification of temples by architectural styles into *Nagara*, *Dravida* and *Vesara*, shapes like masculine, feminine and neuter, *Suddha*, *Misra* and *Samkirna* depending respectively on a single material, mixture of two materials and the amalgamation of many materials. The postures of the temple images like *Sthanaka* (standing), *Asana* (sitting) and *Sayana* (sleeping) too are described here.

While the *Agamas* and *Puranas* dealt with architecture and sculpture more on a philosophical and theoretical plane adding ritualistic touch to these, need for evolving knowledge for practical construction was strong too. Between 4th century CE and 11th century CE, numerous texts were written devoted exclusively to architecture, sculpture, measurements, geometry, planning, construction and civil engineering. The various texts that have led to the construction of the magnificent temples all over India during medieval times are Mayamata, Manasara, Rajavallabha, Viswakarmaprakasa, Aparajitapraccha and Samarangana Sutradhara.

Manasara is regarded as the most standard and complete treatise, rather the fountain-head of all the *Vastu* and *Silpa* texts. The very name 'Manasara' means the 'Essence of Measurement.' Of the seventy chapters of Manasara, the first eight are introductory, the next forty-two deal with architectural matters, and the last twenty are devoted to sculpture, whether sculptural details of idols of deities of the Hindus, the Buddhists and Jains, statues of great personages and images of animals and birds are all given in it.

Mayamata was written by a Tamil saint named Mamuni Mayan. He was adorned as the Vishwakarma by Veda Vyasa in Mahabharata. Mayan authored several scientific texts including the Surya Siddhanta. A memorial is being built in his honour in Mamallapuram, Tamil Nadu.

The other text that needs a special mention is Samarangana Sutradhara. This text in Sanskrit was written by the Paramara king Bhoja of Dhar in 11th century CE. Written in 83 chapters, the text deals with civil engineering, town planning and sculptural arts. It must be recognized that all this canonical literature on architecture and sculpture is still alive and in use. Extensive research both by Indians and foreigners is still on to try and understand the tenets of Hindu architecture and sculpture.

Though architecture is broadly definable as a branch of fine arts having for its object the production of edifices pleasing to a cultivated and artistic mind, it falls primarily within the realm of science. The principles of construction and engineering employed in building ancient temples and the way in which these structures were designed to support weights or counteract thrust are capable of being categorized as being scientific.

Before the replacement of the brick medium by stone, there was a short-lived phase of 'rock architecture.' The cut-in-caves and cut-out monoliths were imitations of the contemporary brick and wood architecture in all their intricate details. Since Vedic rituals needed open spaces for performing the *yagna* and wood architecture built spaces for discourse, much of Hindu architecture got planned around the wood construction. The ideas got carried down right to the age when temples started being built using stone.

Iconography, Iconometry and Canonical Literature

The cultural manifestation of Hinduism is uniquely complex. In particular, the visual arts associated with the Hindu religion are recognised as being the most complex and rich of any living religion. No serious effort to understand ancient or contemporary Indian culture can be made without a clear understanding of the visual arts and their sources in religious belief and practice. Any serious study of the subject emphasizes the ritual aspect of religious art -with reference to monumental architecture, sculpture and rural arts. The evolution of temple art over the centuries reflects on the social and anthropological roots of artistic creativity, as well as the rites, practices and beliefs of the hundreds of millions of Indians.

The branch of knowledge that deals with the representative art in the form of pictures, drawings, figures or images or icons is called iconography. Iconography, as it is understood in our context, is that branch of knowledge which deals with the representative art such as portraits, figures, artistic images or symbols, and pictures. To be precise, it is the study of religious figures or drawings of objects.

In Indian sculpture, painting, and iconography, the majority of the figures are based on the human body. This belongs to the *drista* (the visible world). All natural shapes are said to be with life. It is also the scene of the transformation of the self. In this transformed shape, the self is represented in art. The transformation results from an inner process of realization. It is not visible to the physical eye; it belongs to the *adrista* (the unseen). The world of the inner reality differs from the outer world but cannot exist without it. Therefore, art serves as the meeting ground of the two worlds and relates to the transformation of the inner world to that of the outer. The Indian understanding of the relationship of the background to the images was the transformation of a raw stony substance to an animate figure endowed with the dynamism of life with features and expression in it. The early religious images are traced back to the second millennium BCE.

The iconographic development in India has been continuous at least for about seven thousand years. The iconic specimens found in the sites of the Indus Valley Civilization, the proto-historic phase of Indian history and the descriptive hymns dealing with iconic conceptions in the Rig Veda show a continuum of sort.

The term *Silpa* designates any kind of art, a fine or mechanical art (64 such arts are enumerated in *Silpa sastras*), a skill in any art and crafts in the Indian tradition. Its origin is traced to the Vedas. *Silpa* is a pervasive term and includes within the ambit of its meaning anything creative, imitative, ideational, or skilful which in one sense or the other involves dexterity of hand or mind or both. *Silpa* also implies a technique, a ceremonial act, an artifact, indeed anything that either leads to or is a tangible product of some craft. The Aitareya Brahmaṇa regards *silpa* as the *anukaraṇa* (imitation) of *deva silpa* (divine art). By *silpa* the divine personages create and strengthen the cosmic forces, and by it a transmutation is brought about in different, disparate phenomena. It is the principle by which the non-manifested is rendered manifest, and the manifest derives its corporeality and colours.

Iconography has several integral elements in it. They include the classification of images, textual principles of making images, mode of casting, materials employed in making images, the accessories, and the characters of gods and goddesses. Strict and most elaborate rules were laid down for the measurements of the various parts of the body and their relative proportions and the different postures. In course of time, representations of gods and goddesses were made. An impression of their power and personality was created by the *sthapatis*.

In the Indian value of measurement of length there are two different kinds of units, namely, the absolute and the relative. Of these, the first is based on the length of certain natural objects, while the second is obtained from the length of a particular part or limb of the person whose measurement is under consideration.

"Iconometry" means the measurements of the icons. Iconometry is the use of relative units and in the field of image making it is the most interesting part. The measurements used for making images are the basis for perfection. Proportions of images are ruled by complex iconometrical canons. The accuracy in measurement is the criterion of perfection. The *sthapatis* have always produced their images according to prescribed measurements. In the making of the images, the *sthapati* follows two types of iconometry, the *talamana* and the *angulamana*. The word *tala* refers to the length of the palm, which is considered to be equivalent in sculptures, as in human beings, to the length of face from forehead to chin. Generally, images are made according to the *navatala* measurement. That is, the length of the image is nine times the length of its palm or face. The nine-face length is distributed thus: face, one *tala*; throat to navel, two; navel to the tip of the knee, three; lower knee to ankle, two, and the remaining one *tala* is divided among the height of foot, knee and top knot. Dwarfish figures may be made according to the *caturasratala*, or four-*tala* formula, four times the length of the image's face.

Iconometry as a science that deals with the measurements of the images may differ from region to region and period to period in the Indian context. The details regarding measurements of the *anga* "parts" (e.g. the length of nose, the breadth and width of eyes and so on) are laid down in the *silpasastra* and *agama*. The original works dealing with sculpture are *Kasyapa Silpam* and *Manasam*. Both these works deal with every branch of *Silpa*. Especially in South India the works of *Agastya*, *Kasyapa* and *Vishwakarma* are followed in carving sculpture. In *Agastya Sakaladhikara* eleven ways are specified by which the height of an image can be determined. Sri Ganpathi Sthapathi, a temple architect of international repute; in his book "Sirpa Chennool," has written the significance and elegance of making the icons using different materials and methods. This serves as the proper text book and guide for the artisans and students.

Canons of iconometry follow the ancient *"Talamana"* system in which the basic units are the *angula* and the *tala*, and the latter stands for the length of the palm. The *angula* is either a fixed length or a proportion. A span can be defined in many ways namely *Mulaberanglam, Mananglam* or *Matharangulam*. A *tala* or span is defined to be 12 *angulas* in the texts and an *angula* is approximately equivalent to 3/4th of present day inch in use. *Angula* may be defined as proportionate measure and fixed measure. The measurement of *angula* is divided into 8 *yavas*. All images in temples follow the directions from the above canonical guidelines. Subashini Venkatraman of the Department of Computer Engineering, Eritrea Institute of Technology published a paper on computerization of the *Talamana* system in the International Journal of Computer Applications in May 2011.

Different attributes, weapons, and postures that are special for each deity must be present in the image for it to be worthy of worship. Such details are described in the various *silpasastras*, treatises on sculptures, generally considered to have been compiled between the 8th and the 12th centuries CE. The popular *silpasastras* such as the *Manasara, Manasolasa, Abhilashitarthachintamaṇi, Vishwakarmiyam, Mayamata, Amsumadbhedagama, Silparatna, Rupadhyanalakṣanam,* and *Sakaladikara* provide rules for both the iconography and for the iconometry of the images. Though these *silpasastras* do not agree in all details, they do agree on the significant attributes of the more popular deities. Sculptors may show a special preference for one or another of the *silpasastras*.

This commentary may be concluded by saying that *Silpasastras* and *Silparatna* instruct the sculptors and the architect to follow the rules and formulations laid down for making images. The *Silpasastras* detail the classification of images, the mode of casting images, the attributes in the hands of images, the costumes, ornaments and headgear of images, and the characters of the gods and the goddesses.

4.2 DEVELOPMENT OF TEMPLE ARCHITECTURE IN KARNATAKA

Text and Theory of Temple Design

Sastras: The earliest evidence of the Hindu architectural theory lies in the *Sastric* texts. These oral traditions which represented theoretical recommendations rather than exact and practical prescriptions were collated and compiled from the 3rd century BCE. These outlined many ritual practices and the original *Agamic* traditions. The *Sastras* described the correct and most auspicious way to perform a large range of activities such as warfare, painting, playing music, poetry, love making (*Kamasutra*), drama and architecture. Their purpose was rather to preserve former traditions and to discuss their aesthetic contents.

The *Agamic* tradition, in general, has been dated to the pre-Mauryan period as references to the tradition are found in later Vedic literature of Atharvaveda. The *agama* or *aagama* tradition is often contrasted with the *nigama* tradition; the latter possibly a reference to the unchanging Vedic tradition. *Agama* refers to scriptures *"that which has come down."* It also means *"a traditional doctrine, or system which commands faith."*

Agamas deal with the philosophy and spiritual knowledge behind the worship of the deity, the *yoga* and mental discipline required for this worship, and the specifics of worship offered to the deity. The ritualistic pattern of worship in the *Agamic* religions differ from the Vedic form. While the Vedic form of *yajna* require no idols and shrines, the *Agamic* religions are based on idols with *puja* as means of worship. The *Agamic* deities are pinned to a specific spot and assume the territorial nature of the deity.

Each *Agama* consists of four parts:

- *Kriya pada* – consists of rules for construction of temples; for sculpting, carving, and consecration of idols of deities for worship in temples; for different forms of initiations or *diksha*.
- *Charya pada* – lays down rules for daily worship (*puja*), observances of religious rites, rituals, festivals and *prayaschittas* (penance).
- *Yoga pada* – concentrates on *yoga* and the mental discipline.
- *Jnana pada* – consists of philosophical and spiritual knowledge, knowledge of reality and liberation.

The *Aagamas* state three essential requirements for a place of pilgrimage -*Sthala*, *Tirtha* and *Murty*. *Sthala* refers to the temple, *Tirtha*, to the temple tank and *Murty* to the deity or deities worshipped. A temple may also be associated with a tree, called the *Sthala Vriksham*. For instance, the Kadamba tree at the Madurai Meenakshi Sundareswarar temple is the *Sthala Vriksham*.

Elaborate rules are laid out in the *Agamas* for *Silpa* (the art of sculpture) describing the quality requirements of the places where temples are to be built, the kind of images to be installed, the materials from which they are to be made, their dimensions, proportions, air circulation, lighting in the temple complex etc. The Manasara and Silpasastra are some of the works dealing with these rules. The rituals followed in worship services each day at the temple also follow rules laid out in the *Agamas*.

Janardana temple at Tadimalangi has the unique distinction. No worship is performed there as one of the fingers of the deity is broken. *Agamas* require perfection, symmetry and conformity with rules of *Silpa*. Even temples in ruins on restoration have to be consecrated afresh according to *sastric* and *agamic* traditions. Ranganathaswamy temple at Halebid was consecrated according to *agamas* on 11th June 2015 after its restoration as if it was a newly constructed temple.

Most commonly used *Agamas* are: Siva, Vaishnava, Shakta, Pancharatra (Centered around one diety with others surrounding), Ganapatya (Ganapati), Soura (Sun).

Manasara is a comprehensive treatise on architecture and iconography. It represents the universality of Vastu tradition and includes the iconography of Jaina and Buddhist images. The work is treated as a source book and consulted by all.

The Mayamata too occupies an important position. It is a general treatise on *Vastu sastra*; and is a text of Southern India. It is regarded a part of Saiva literature and might belong prior to the Chola period when temple architecture reached its peak. It is the best known work on *Vastu*. The work is coherent and well structured. It defines *Vastu* as the arrangement of space, anywhere, wherein immortals and mortals live.

These subjects are intertwined with Astrology. The *Vastu* Texts believe that *Vigraha* (icon or image of the deity) is closely related to *Graha* (planets). The term *Graha* literally means that which attracts or receives; and *Vigraha* is that which transmits. It is believed that the idols receive power from the planets; and transmit the power so received. It not merely is a symbolism but also one that provides logic for placement of various deities in their respective quarters and directions.

The manual relating to sculpture is called the *Silpasastra* and the text dedicated to architecture was called the *Vastusastra*. The *Vastusastra* attempted to define the ideal form of the Hindu temple. While it provided a traditional framework, its terminology was obscure and fragmentary. Further refinements occurred in the knowledge gained from the *Vastusastra* over the following centuries to give exact prescriptions for the temple architecture. One of the earliest references to temple architecture is found in the *Brihatsamhita*, an astronomical 6th century text while the science of temple building started evolving from the 4th century CE. The astronomical concerns in the text link issues of time, astronomy and astrology with architecture. Other references to buildings appear as parts of the larger Epics and *Puranas*. These texts were works of learned Brahmans who were more concerned with symbolic meanings and ritual function rather than with practical structures. Brahmans were, however consulted by the architect during construction of the building till its final completion and consecration.

Science of Temple building

Temple inscriptions indicate that temples were frequently royal donations and grants. They were dedicated at times in calendar year (a particular regnal year of a King's reign), which were traditionally associated with the movement of the sun and the moon and ritual activities such as temple solstices, equinoxes and eclipses. Astronomical and astrological calculations predicted the timing of temples' construction and orientation. Temple planning and construction invariably involved consideration of the cardinal directions with the temple usually being on the east-west axis aligned with the rising and the setting sun. The location of the sanctum (*grabhgriha*) corresponded to the sinking sun in the west so that the darkness of the womb chamber (*garbhgriha*) was mirrored by the darkness outside. The *sastras* stressed the importance of exact measurement indicating that the harmonious and correct proportioned temple had a direct bearing on the welfare of the community. These texts also provided guidelines which mathematically coordinated sections of the building or enshrined image. They indicated that only if these measurements were in correct correlation, can the temple be expected to accord with the mathematical basis of the Universe. The unit of measurement used in architecture and sculpture was the *angula* – based on a joint of a human finger.

The temple was not only constructed according to precise measurements but also according to sacred geometric designs or *mandalas* which were believed to represent the pattern of the Universe. These were first written down in the *Brihatsamhita,* an astronomical text. In this context, the temple was described as the *vastupurushamandala* which has Brahma, the all pervading formless divine principle concerned with creation, at its centre.

With the arrival of *Agamas* in Hindu religion, the details of architecture became more sophisticated in the temple and reflected the fundamental symbolism of *mandalas.* The Yoga Tattva Upanishad speaks about the symbolism in terms of the five fundamental elements that constitute the material basis of the entire cosmos. Earth elements are represented by a Square, Water with a Semicircle, fire by a Triangle, air by a Hexagonal figure and ether (sky) by a Circle. The point without dimension dot (*bindu*) is the focus of all energy. The icon in the sanctum occupies the central position and the temple represents the other necessary forms. The architectural details of a sophisticated temple reflect this fundamental symbolism. The above five forms are represented in a *Mandala* known as '*Vishwakarmamandala,*' or '*Vastupurushamandala*' which is regarded as fundamental to all temple architecture. The four sides of the *Mandala* symbolize the four main directions and the corners of the square represents four mid-directions and each of the eight quarters is presided over by a deity. The inner circle symbolizes the 'Creator' (*Brahma*), which is symbolic of activity, guarded by the eight directions. The *Mandala* is symbolic of the entire Universe. The 'all-maker' (Creator) is also the progenitor. Early temples were reputed to be built by this All-maker.

Astronomy and astrology were the determining factors in the temple's construction. The plan of the temple is strictly oriented to the cardinal directions. The architect first draws the ground plan or a diagram which forms the spiritual and actual foundation of the subsequent process of construction. Engineering principles were simple, the most common architectural form of temple construction being the combination of vertical columns and horizontal cross-beams. The stability of the building's elevation was achieved largely by sheer mass of columns and the weight of the cross-beams, and the additional supporting brackets and iron clamps.

Evolution of the Hindu Temple

Vedic religion initially did not believe in idol worship. It was all based on rituals relating to *yagna* and chanting of mantras to propitiate the Vedic gods. Later when Jainism and Buddhism were spreading fast, practitioners of Vedic or Brahamanical religion started evolving symbols and icons for worship. *Puranic* resurgence lent further impetus to the evolution of Brahamanical or Hindu iconography and its related styles of representation of anthropomorphic gods. Need for housing these icons in a building meant for the purpose of worship arose soon and hence the evolution of temples. From performing Vedic rituals in open spaces on an altar to closed temples was a gradual movement. The buildings dedicated for this purpose were constructed from perishable materials because of which no evidence of early structures exists today. Simultaneously canonical order for the practice of religion, construction of temples, rituals to be performed and exact nature of worship methods too was evolving. Various religious texts were written based on the earliest guidance from the Vedas and *Agamas* in this direction. Use of stone and bricks in the construction of temples came into being in the post-Mauryan period. References to places of pilgrimage, however can be found in the great Epics viz. The Mahabharata and Ramayana.

The planning of the temple resulted into demarcated areas for the deity, the priest and the followers. Each one of them has separate peripheries to perform their activities. This gave birth to the type of architectural planning for temple structures. Initial Brahamanical temples were simple structures with demarcated spaces for the deity, priest and followers in square or rectangular chambers with the deity being kept on a raised platform against the wall facing the main entrance to the temple. Many such chamber temples though in dilapidated condition, still exist in Karnataka. These temples generally had flat roofs and had simpler exteriors. Rock cut temples came into existence more or less at the same time as the chamber like temples. Gradually, as the skills of creating superstructures actually participating in load transfer developed there emerged tall and huge tapering towers above the main shrine. These were important owing to three reasons:

- Tapered structures/pyramidal form are more stable forms and easy to achieve;
- Great heights could be attained to mark greatness and importance of deity; and
- The tower represents the position of the cell/chamber (*garbhagriha*) housing the deity just below the tower.

All these temples had two parts – structural and non-structural. The structural solutions started from trabeated style to combinations of load bearing and non-load bearing structures. The supporting structural elements like the corbelled roofs and brackets developed during later periods and were used for both structural and aesthetic reasons. Non-structural components are generally related to the aesthetic values in overall mass of the structure. Ornamentation was done on the facade, doorways, towers etc. in the form of relief work to show the skills of the craftsmen and to create a specific idiom of architectural excellence of the period.

Various kings from different dynasties ruling over various parts of Karnataka offered their patronage to temple building activity (whether belonging to the Buddhist faith or Jainism or to the Brahamanical faith) to show their wealth, power, grace and architectural style. This has led us to follow the convention of associating temples and monuments with a particular dynasty depending upon during whose time it was built. Thus architecture started getting classified as pertaining to a particular style promoted by a dynasty such as Chalukyan architecture or Hoysala architecture.

The earliest temple buildings are, now without exception, very shaky and in more or less dilapidated state. This is chiefly due to the materials used in their construction quarried generally on the spot. Though hard stone was used, it was full of flaws and minute cracks could render it unsuitable for such parts as beams in the temple. The construction style of these buildings being trabeate necessitating long beams in most cases which were further loaded with enormous mass of material from above; naturally resulted in cracks through the middle. These may eventually collapse through the constant grinding action at the fracture thus pulverizing and chipping the surfaces unless supported by intermediate struts. Buildings were generally best preserved in places less frequented and difficult to access.

Most temples in Karnataka are of not very great size. One factor limiting the size of the temple was the length of the shafts of its loftiest pillars. The shaft or the portion of the pillar between the top of the base and under the capital was invariably a single block. Generally, the temples were rarely built using shafts of two or more stones and hence the maximum length depended upon the greatest length of the stone possible to quarry. As all parts of the temple are in strict proportion to one another, the maximum size of the temple was thus restricted by the length of the pillar shaft. Masonry work for these temples was generally dry masonry without the use of mortar or cementing. The blocks were dressed to fit one another upon level beds with their weight and that of the superincumbent masses keeping them in position thus calling gravity into play. Very little was done by way of excavating for firm foundations. Hard black earth or solid rock would generally form the foundation on which was laid a bed of rough boulders from which directly sprang the walls. Consequently any settlement or yielding of foundation caused the collapse of the walls unless provided with buttresses.

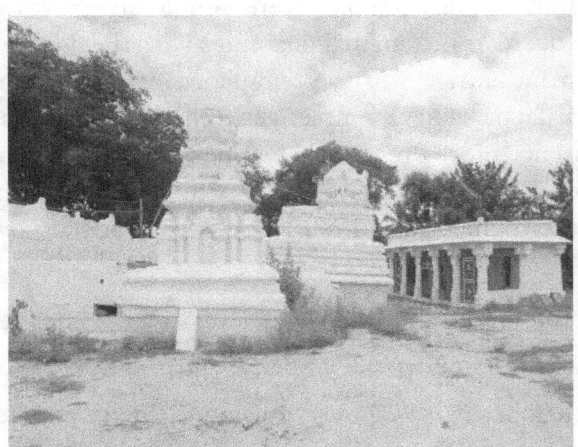 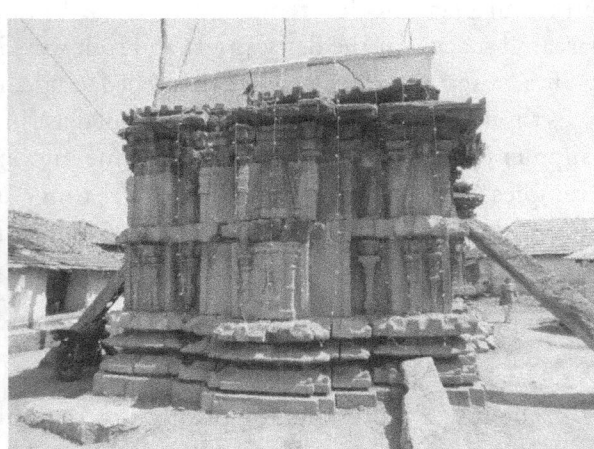

Sivarameswara Temple Kunigal and Chennakesava Temple at Dharmapura Protected by Buttresses

At many places the stone walls which were of variable thickness and far heavier than would be built at present, were run up in two shells – an outer and an inner – the space between being filled with loose boulders or dry rubble. There are many instances where the outer wall has fallen but the inner wall remaining intact and holds the roof together.

4.3 SIMPLE TEMPLE ARCHITECTURE: GROUND PLAN AND DIFFERENT COMPONENTS

A complete temple consists of a shrine containing the object of worship (*garbhaghriha*), an antechamber before it (*antarala* or *sukanasi*), a large hall in advance of this with either closed or open sides (*gudhamandapa* or *mahamandapa* or *sabhamandapa*) and one or more door or entrance with a porch in front (*mukhamandapa* or *agramandapa*). Saiva temples generally have a detached pavilion standing out in front of the main entrance in which is placed the Nandi (Siva's bull). Vaishnava temples may have a similar shelter for Varaha or boar.

The ground plans of these temples are usually square (*chaturasara*), circular (*vritta*), rectangular (*chaturasaradirgha*), apsidal (*hastiprishtha*), elliptical (*vrittayata*), hexagonal (*shadkona*), octagonal (ashtasara) and sixteen sided (shodasara). There aren't any temples with circular ground plan in Karnataka. Generally circular ground plans are used for female deities like Chausat Yogini temple in Madhya Pradesh. There are some star shaped or part star shaped temples too. The star shaped plan is arrived at by revolving a square about its centre while it may be more complicated than this if staggered patterns are added to the star shape.

The walls and wall mouldings are of four marked types and these are i) the much decorated with sculptured panels filled with an imposing array of deities and other images; ii) those equally decorated but with few images but most of the panels being filled with lozenge shaped ornament, little pilasters; iii) those decorated with running bands of pilasters; and the last iv) with plain heavy exteriors with no attempt at decoration.

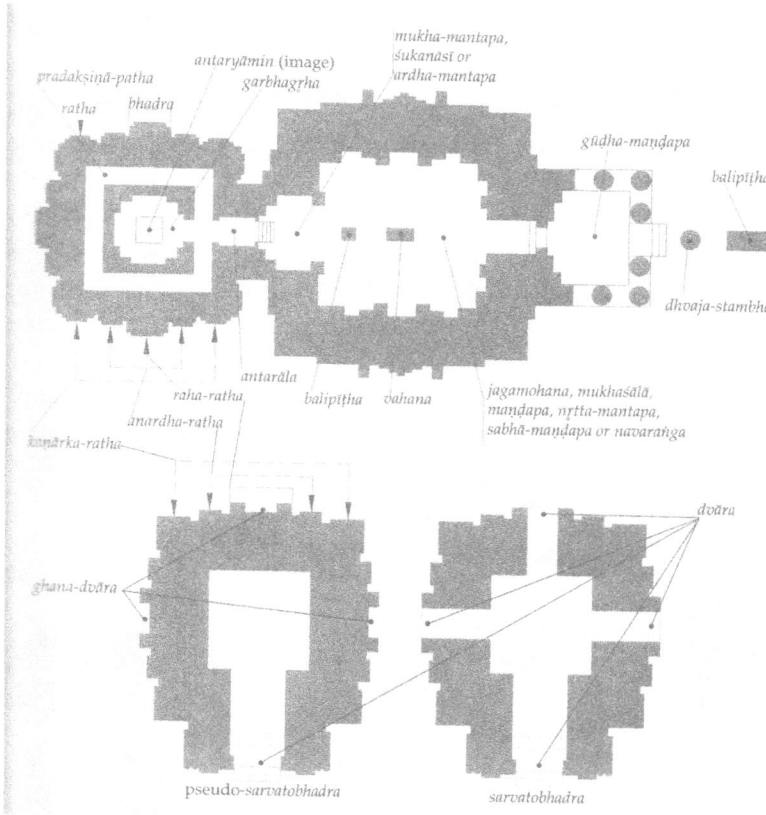

Ground Plan of a Typical Hindu Temple (FW Bunce)

Sanctum or *Garbhagriha*

The sanctum is technically known as the *garbhagriha*, the womb house. It is a very important part in the temple proper. Generally the *garbhagrihas* are square in shape. Some *garbhagrihas*, which are longer also can be seen. *Garbhagriha* used to be very small in the beginning and could admit only one worshipper at a time, though the shrine was meant for public and the basic shrine, sanctum alone constituted the real temple. This type of single cell shrines also can be seen in the present day temple architecture, which are mainly dedicated to the Mother Goddess or *gramadevata* (village deity) or *gramapurusha*. The temple should consist of a sanctum in which the icon is to be installed and housed. The structural involvements nearby the temple are also essential for the principal worship and rituals. Texts like Sri Prasna describes that the sanctum is the body of the divinity and the icon is its soul (*Jiva*). Usually it is a stone structure, square in shape and simply plain with some projected slabs in the wall or niches. There should not be any pillars in the sanctum hall. The sanctum may be provided with windows for air and light sometimes. When the arrangement of the *garbhagriha* is more than one in some temples, they are called as a *Dvikutachala*, *Trikutachala* temples and so on. In Karnataka temples with up to nine shrines too exist, most notably the Navalinga temple at Kuknur.

Sukanasi

Like the *antarala* or vestibule in front of the sanctum for the priest to stand and let worshippers look at the object of worship, a low raised structure called '*Sukanasi*' crowned *antarala*. It is erected in front of the *sikhara*, which stands on sanctum proper. Unlike the sanctum covered by flat roof stone slabs, *antarala* is also filled in the similar manner, which serves as the base (*adhisthana*) for the super structure. Architectural decoration of the *sukanasi* is not as elaborate as that of the *sikhara* as it just tapers off over the roof of the *Mahamandapa*.

Main Hall or *Mahamandapa, Gudhamandapa* or *Sabhamandapa*

The innermost shrine (*garbhagriha*) of these temples is always devoid of any decoration. Besides that since no natural light can enter this part of the temple, it remains dark and gloomy. Perhaps the idea behind keeping it that way was to let the worshippers concentrate on the deity or the object of worship rather than the peripherals. However, the ceiling of the main hall (*gudhamandapa*) is often veritable work of art. In many temples it is domical in outline. The ceiling in its simplest form is no more than one or more flat slabs laid across four beams forming a square supported by four pillars or walls. This is the case for a ceiling of the smallest span, as the span increases other means are used to cover the larger space. Triangular slabs are then laid across the corners of the square formed by the beams so as to reduce the opening to a smaller square set diagonally to that formed by the beams. If the space still remains uncovered, corner slabs are again placed above these and so on till the opening is small enough to be closed by a single square slab. These may then be carved and decorated in a lotus form or any other favourite art form.

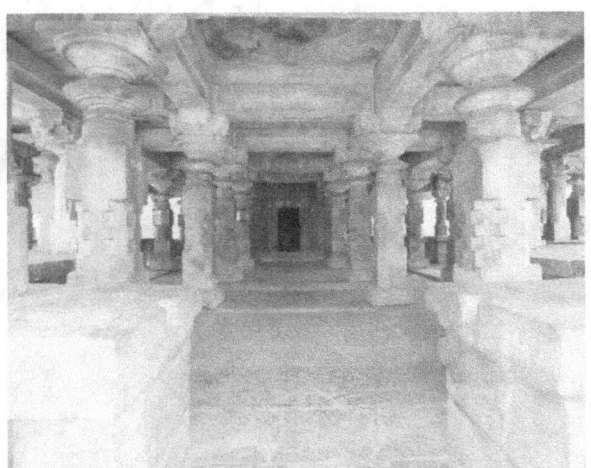 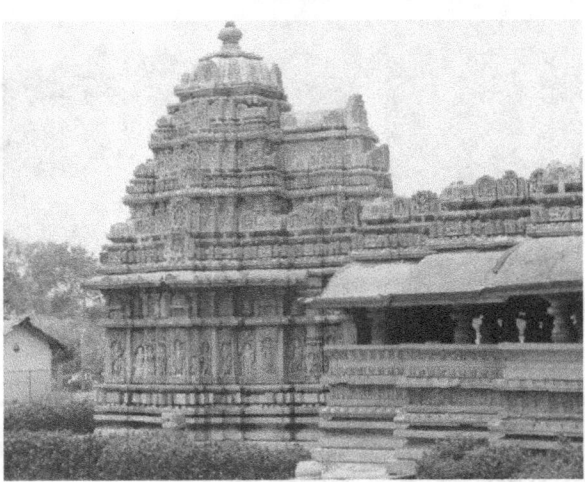

Main Hall, Garbhagriha and Antarala of Panchaligeswara Temple at Hooli and Sikhara and Sukanasi of the Northern Vimana of Veeranarayana Temple at Balevadi

In many of the temples from 8th to 11th centuries, ceilings of the *navarangas* were sculpted at the centre of a flat temple ceiling. Generally, central black schist divided by beams into nine panels will have Siva in one of his favourite *mudras* in the central panel. The eight square panels surrounding this central panel are occupied by *ashtadikpalas* (guardians of the eight directions). Positioned in their assigned directional realms, each *dikpala* is mounted on his *vahana* along with his consort. The most amazing of such *navaranga* ceilings can be seen at the Kalleswara temple at Aralaguppe. The central panel in this temple displays Siva as Natesa in his most exquisite form.

The *ashtadikpalas* are: Kubera, Yama, Indra, Varuna, Isana, Agni, Vayu and Nirrti or Rakshasa and the directions they guard respectively are: North, South, East, West, Northeast, Southeast, Northwest and Southwest. Two additional directions viz. Zenith and Nadir are guarded by Brahma and Vishnu respectively.

Much of all this fine work is hardly visible owing to poor lighting inside the temples as solid walls with hardly any windows (if at all they have anything it is some kind of perforated arabesque or latticed windows which hardly permits any light inside) do not permit enough natural light to come inside.

Ceilings of sabhamandapa

Ceilings are of different types. These are: 1) Domical ceiling 2) Flat ceiling 3) Rectangular ceiling 4) Square ceiling 5) Circular ceiling 6) Rotated squares ceiling 7) Octagonal ceiling, etc., These ceilings consist of single slab or more than one are supported by beams placed on walls and pillars. The outline of these ceilings is generally square, because the *garbhagriha, antarala* and *mukhamandapa* are square.

The entire ceiling space is divided into several *ankanas* (bays) bordered by beams and walls on four sides. In the case of large *sabhamandapas*, the central *ankana* is a large square and the remaining parts are smaller. Square ceilings are further classified into flat, rotated, circular and octagonal. Flat ceilings are generally found at the corners and on the sides of the central ceiling in the *sabhamandapas*. Two rotated squares by placing two squares, one over the other, are called trabeate system. Here the upper one is smaller and turned 45 degrees.

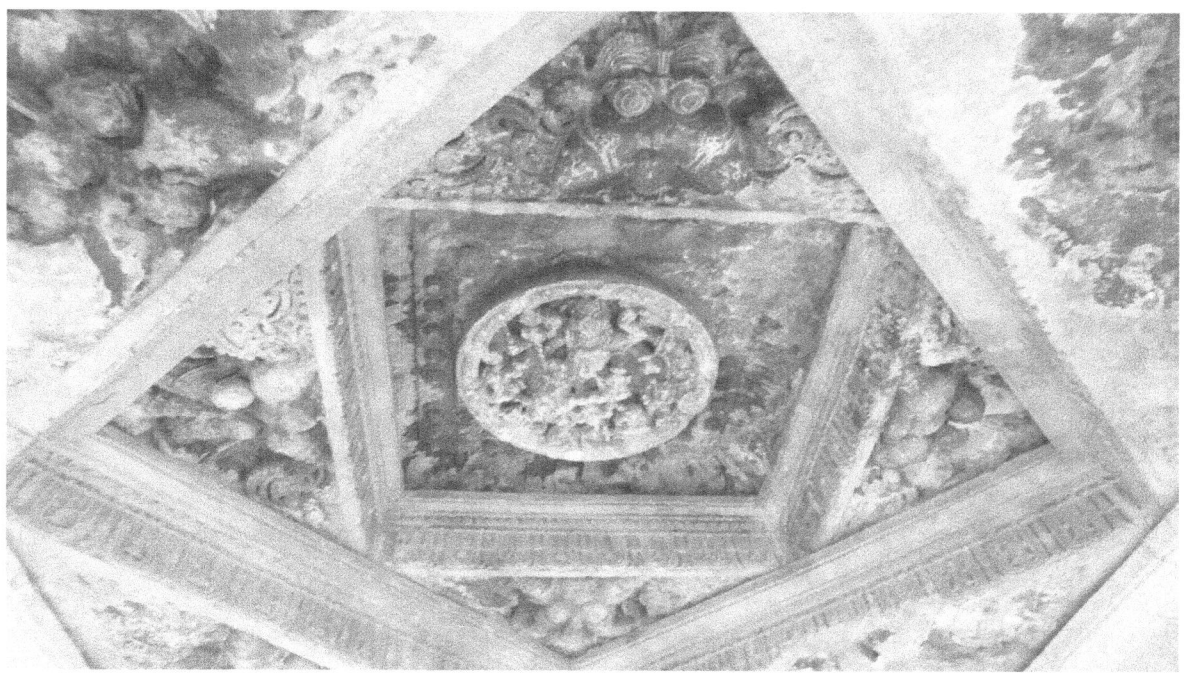

Square Slabs Placed to Cover the Celing in Trabeate Style at Lakshmidevi Temple at Dodda Gadavalli

The entire ceiling space is divided into several *ankanas* (bays) bordered by beams and walls on four sides. In the case of large *sabhamandapas*, the central *ankana* is a large square and the remaining parts are smaller. Square ceilings are further classified into flat, rotated, circular and octagonal. Flat ceilings are generally found at the corners and on the sides of the central ceiling in the *sabhamandapas*. Two rotated squares by placing two squares, one over the other, are called trabeate system. Here the upper one is smaller and turned 45 degrees over the lower. The lower square is achieved by placing four triangular slabs over the corners of the *ankana* formed by beams or walls. Placing smaller triangular slabs over the corners of the lower square forms the upper square. A flat slab is placed at the top for covering the central gap. The space of the ceiling is reduced at the top by creating these squares. The lower square is exactly half of the *ankana* and the upper square is half of that of the lower. A flat slab one-fourth of the size of the *ankana* is used at the top. The squares not only reduce the areas but also break the monotony of the comparatively plain interior.

Navaranga and Bhuvaneshvari

From 10th century CE onwards decoration styles inside and outside the temple started undergoing major transformation. Exquisite designs replaced the earlier lotus motifs and geometric figures. The central ceiling became more domical in nature with magnificent styling. This new styling called for a shift in the construction patterns too. In the largest class of domical ceilings the distance apart at which the four main pillars were set necessitated the insertion of two intermediate pillars on each side of the square and these were so placed that their points of support formed the corners of an octagon. From this triangular slabs filling in the corners, the octagon is worked up to a circle which forms the base of the dome.

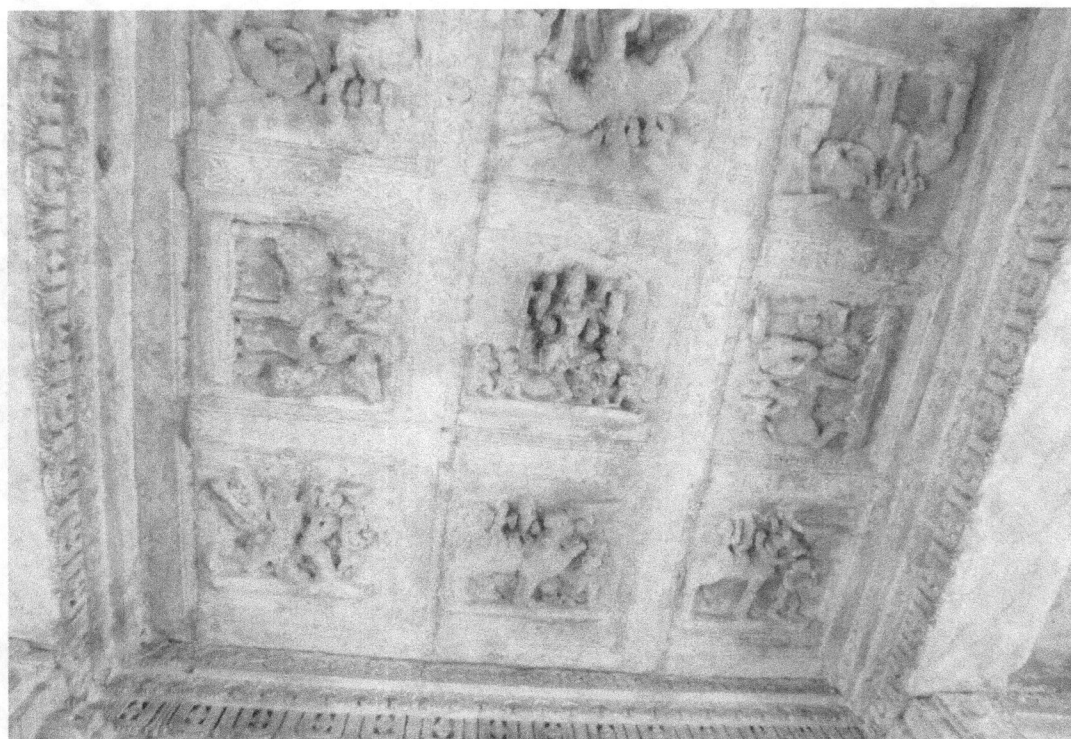

Navaranga Celing Divided into Nine Panels with Siva at the Centre and Ashtadikapalas in Other Eight, Mallikarjuna Temple, Basaralu

This is constructed on ascending concentric and diminishing rings of stones laid upon horizontal beds, each ring being corbelled forward till they meet at the crown together with one or more of the rings immediately around it forming the pendant. These rings are kept in position by being locked within the mass of fillings-in of the haunches above. The under sides of these stones were carved into rings of cusped and ribbed mouldings, each little cusp having its own small pendant. The idea recalls much elaborated earlier lotus ceiling reflecting the centrifugal growth of expression. The diminishing rings of masonry have apse-like hollows carved all around them giving a concentric, scalloped pattern. It is the overlap in the central panel and that of the projecting cusped rims of the corbelled rings that creates the opening flower effect.

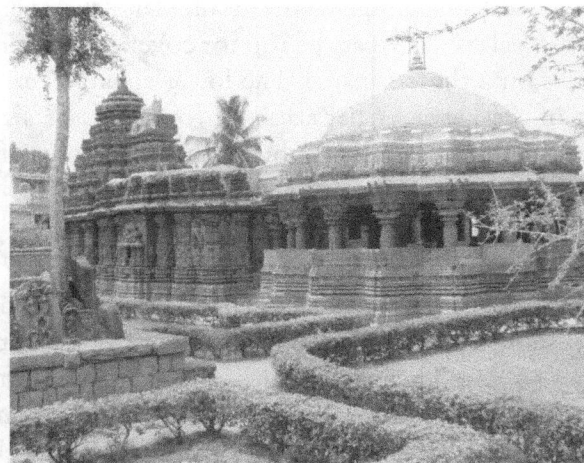 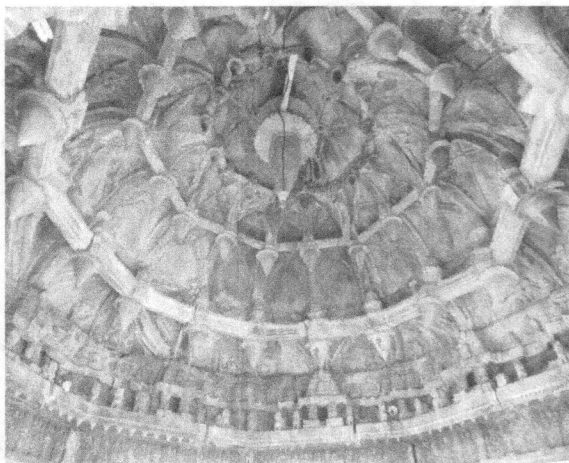

Domical Ceiling of the Outer Mandapa of the Sivalaya Temple at Arasikere

Adisthana or Temple Basement

The best way to understand and appreciate a temple's architecture is by understanding its ground plan, side elevation, front elevation and section diagram. This way one can see each component of the temple separately and understand how it connects with the rest. According to Hindu traditions and canonical instructions, the temple is also called *vastupurusha* which means an architectural piece resembling the body of a human being. "Human Being" here stands for God or Supreme Being and he is conceived in the form of a human body. As canonical texts on temple architecture and sculpture continued to evolve, this concept developed into the *vastupurushamandala*. Generally, a Hindu temple stands on a large and high platform, called *jagati* made of bricks or stones with several mouldings. It represents the feet of the man. Over this stands a smaller platform of stones called *pitha*. Over this *pitha* rises a still smaller platform called *adhisthana* or *vedi-bandha*. This is the immediate base of the temple's superstructure or the plinth. It is on this platform that the pillars and walls of the temple are raised. The top of the *adhisthana* is the floor of the temple.

The *adhisthana* or basement is the lowest member of the temple. This is the strongest, firmest and most solidly laid part and carries the weight of all other parts of the temple. The *adhisthana* is classified into different types depending on the difference in dimensions of its mouldings. The mouldings contribute to the elaboration and enrichment of the basement and stability and impressiveness of the temple. Some temples may have several and multiple mouldings in the *adhisthana*. The various mouldings are known as *Paduka, Jagati, Kumud, Gala, Anatri, Kampa, Patta, Prati* and *Vajana* and all these have different shapes and purposes. On top of the surface of the *adhisthana* of the *garbhgriha* is provided *Ambumarga*, a projection member of *pranala*, the water outlet resembling like a *gomukha* (cow's head).

Pillars or *Pada*

The pillars (*pada*) are kept above the surface of the *adhisthana* and the vertical feature provides the impression of elevation. Structurally, pillars are meant to carry the beam and load above with ease and lightness. Pillars have been used in temples from very early days. When the walls were introduced between the pillars, these produced the impression of pilasters. Pillars are of different types based on their difference in shape and ornamentation. Sometimes pillars also carry sculptural reliefs for narrating a scene or a story.

Two kinds of pillars dominate the Hindu temples, the bell pillars in *Dravida* temples and the two block pillars in *Nagara* temples. The bell pillars can have any plan, circular, square, octagonal or otherwise. Pillars may carry stylized petal motif, the lobed leaves motif or the mirror-stalks motif. Pillars also come with various types of ornamentation and sculptures. The pillar parts are called *Oma, Ghata, Mandi, Virakanda* and *Potika*.

Oma is the pedestal which extends as shaft upto the top where *Ghata* is placed. *Mandi* is the square plank above the *Ghata*. *Potika* is the corbel bracket over the pillar that supports the lintel. The *Potika* may be sculpted with figures like demons, crocodiles etc.

The length of pillars as also the height of temple ceiling has been increasing as technology for construction of temples continued to develop over time. In the initial stages, from the 3rd century to 5th century or even later, temple roofs were mounted on dwarf pillars. This made the temple ceiling low and interiors of temples dark. As the length of pillars started increasing so did the height of ceiling go up too. That made it possible to provide open halls in front of the *garbhagriha* and *antarala*. The roof of the temple rested on full length pillars in the middle of the hall but half pillars resting on raised platforms or parapet walls at the outer edges. Best examples of dwarf pillars can be seen in the city of Bengaluru itself.

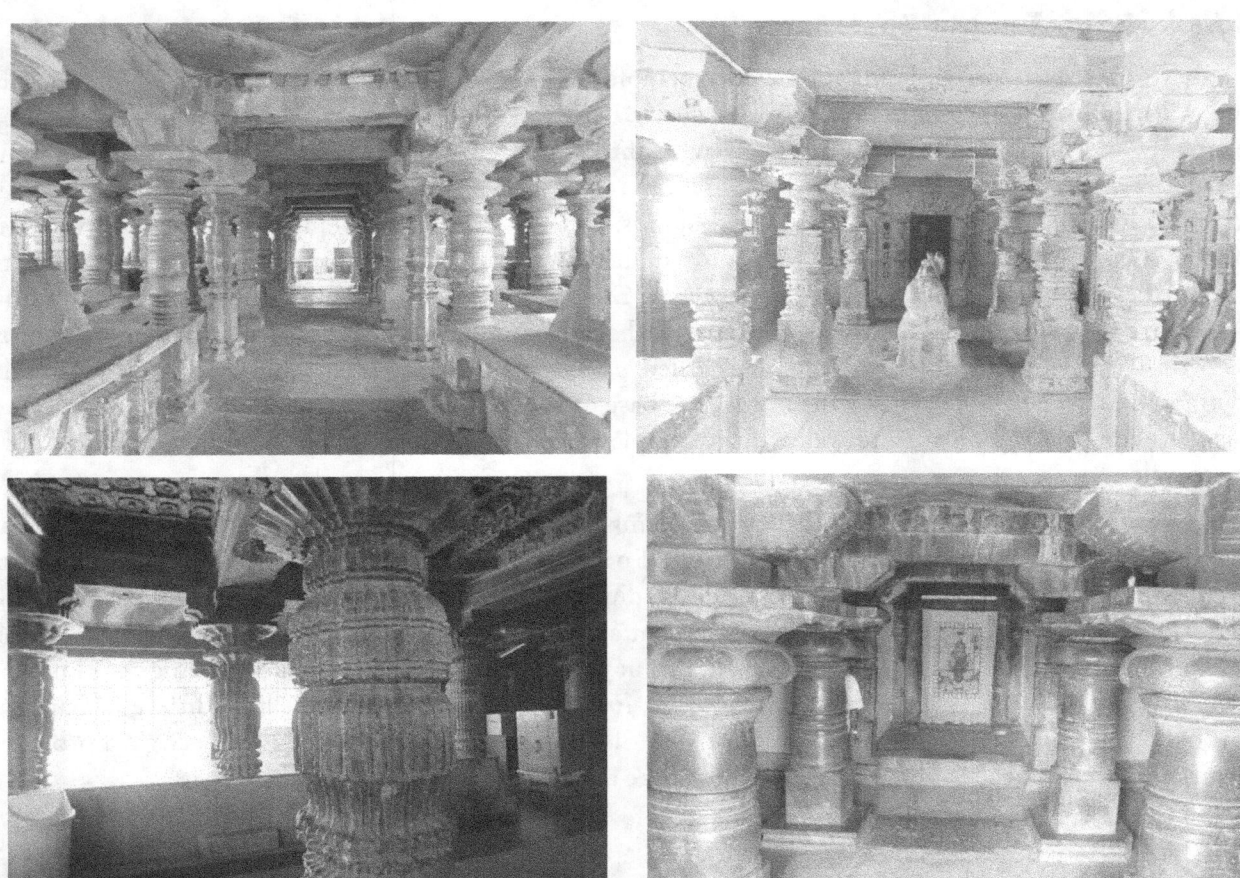

Pillars of Different Types at Kalleswara Temple Bagali, Panchalingeswara Temple Sedam, Basaveswara Temple Anekonda and Rameswara Temple Narasamangala

Nageswara temple built during the times of the Western Ganga kings Nitimarga I (830–870 CE) and Nitimarga II (904–919 CE) has very low ceiling. It is not possible for a person six feet in height to enter the temple without bending a little. The pillars used in the *agramandapa* of this temple are carved from a single shaft and are characterized by a square base, plain lower part, octagonal middle, fluted or sixteen sided shaft, topped by a square plain *phalaka*. Similar dwarf pillars are noticed in the Someswara temple at Gangavara (Chowdappanahalli). The other distinctive feature of these temples is the *gaja-pada*, elephant faced base of the pillars. That is a typical Western Ganga feature whose royal insignia was *gaja*.

Pillars supporting the corners of *garbhagriha* and *antarala* are known as canton pillars. The canton pillars are prominently shown in the rock-cut cave architecture. Pillars supporting various *mandapas* of temples are found in various shapes, such as square pillars, round pillars, projected square pillars, octagonal pillars, sixteen sided pillars, star shaped pillars, stellate pillars etc. These pillars consist of a pedestal (*oma*), shaft, capital (*ghata*), abacus (*mandi*) and corbels (*potika*).

Square Pillars: Square pillars first appeared in the rock cut cave temples. These pillars are simple massive and plain.

Round Pillars: Simple round pillars consist of a lower square block and the remaining circular portion with pot at the top. These pillars have a square base, a rectangular pedestal or *malasthana*, an octagonal and a circular shaft with a top pot and a square capital with *potikas* on its top. These pillars are simple but *kirthimukha* and lotus are adorned in it. The classical temples like those of Kalyani Chalukyas, the Hoyasalas and the Yadavas have different and more complex pillar designs including lathe turned and polished pillars. Here, the perfection is achieved in giving regular shape to the round pillars. Shafts of these pillars consist of a lower square block, a series of thin horizontal connecting bands, and upper block in the shape of a bell and the top in the shape of the upper half of a pot. Below each shaft is a base and above is a disc or cushion capital. Square abacus with circular convex base and corbels of scroll or sloping side type also are shown occasionally in it. The ornamentation in the bands may at times change from pillar to pillar. A pot (*kumbha*) and disc shape (*kalasa*) is a typical variety. Square capital of the pillar adorned with *kirthimukhas* in the corners and *potikas* may have *nagabandha* in it.

Temple doors

Brihatsamhita prescribes that the door must be located in the middle of the front wall and that it must be in the same direction as the idol. According to Agnipurana, the door must always be placed in one of the four directions and never in the corners. Texts prescribe the rules about the several aspects of door like jamb, lintel (*dvara-sakha*), door panels (*kabata*), door joints (*dvara sandhi*), door planks (*phalaka*), bolt (*kila-bhajana*), tower over the door way (*dvara gopura*) and the chamber associated with the door way (*dvara-koshtha*). *Dvara-Sakha* (door jamb) is single panelled in early temples without much ornamentation. Ornamentation developed in the later period in the door panels, and it became familiar as *Sakhas* in temple architecture such as *Lata Sakha, Patra Sakha, Pushpa Sakha*, etc. The popular simple form of door consists of only three *sakhas* in it. Sometimes the images of Gajalakshmi or Ganesh at the centre of lintel occasionally with *Purnakumbhas* on either side of the entrance and *Dvarapalas* or Ganga, Yamuna or *Purnakumbhas* at the base also can be seen in the *Dvara Sakhas* in the medieval period. During Kalyani Chalukyas period, these *dvara sakhas* were raised upto nine *sakhas* and can be seen in Karnataka.

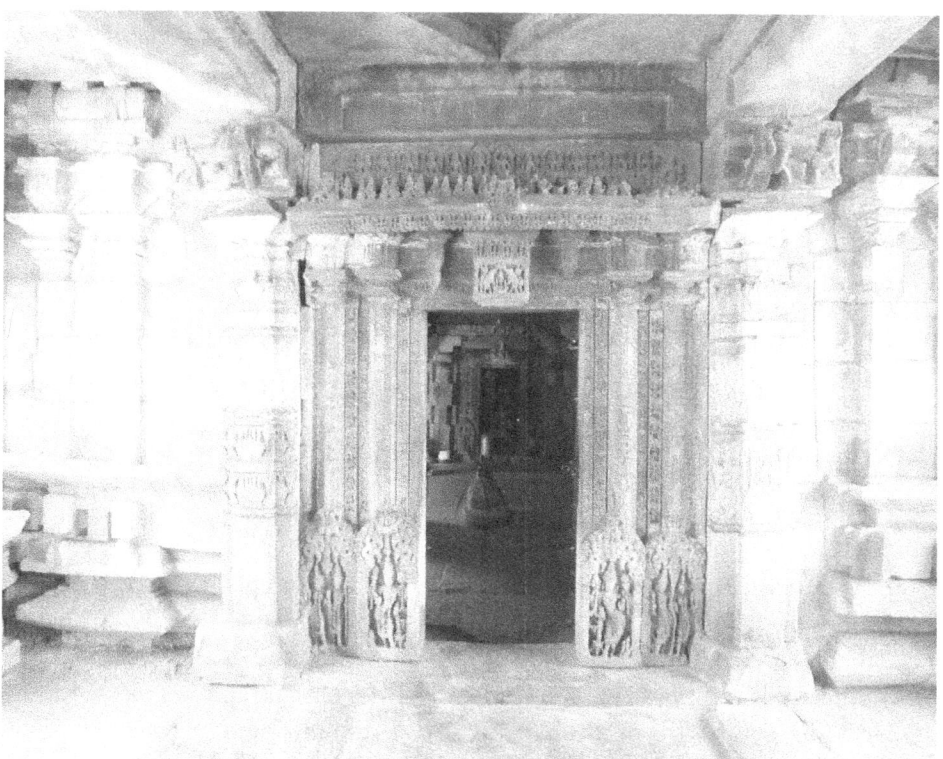

Temple Doorway Kalleswara Temple Bagali

The door ways of *garbhagriha, antarala* and *sabhamandapa* are different from each other. The *lalatabimba* (crest figure over the door) may depict Gajalakshmi, Ganesha, Garuda or Nandi which indicates the deity to whom the temple is dedicated. In front of the *antarala* and *mukhamandapa* there may be a *Torana* (ornamental foiler or festoon supported by two upright columns). Perforated door screens were incorporated in temple architecture during Kadamba period. Hattikeswara temple at Halsi in is the best example for introduction of perforated door screen in early Kadamba architecture.

Temple walls

The temple walls are decorated with *Vedika* (railing), *Panjara* (miniature apsidal shrine), *Jalandharas* (decoration with perforated screens or lattice work) separated by pilasters. There are *Kutas* (shrine with square plan of four side converging roof and single finial) which are miniature structures employed as ornamental motifs. In larger temples *Nasikas* (projected arched opening like a nose) and *Salas* (shrine with barrel vault roof) are introduced. The *Nasika* is an ornamentation designed after the shape of the nose and the *Salas* are elongated sacrificial halls. The *nasika* connects the *kuta* and *sala*. The *kuta* finds its place on the corner and the *salas* on the centre of the walls and the *Kumbha-Panjaras* come in between pillars.

Jalavatayanas (Windows)

Jalavatayanas meant for allowing light and air into temples have provided artists with a space for exhibiting their skill by carving creepers, flowers, figures and several perforations. Some *jalavatayanas* are decorated with creepers containing circular perforations. Exquisite examples of *jalavatayanas* in Karnataka can be seen in Kalleswara temple at Aralaguppe, Chennakesava temple at Belur and Kapileswara temple at Manne.

Niches

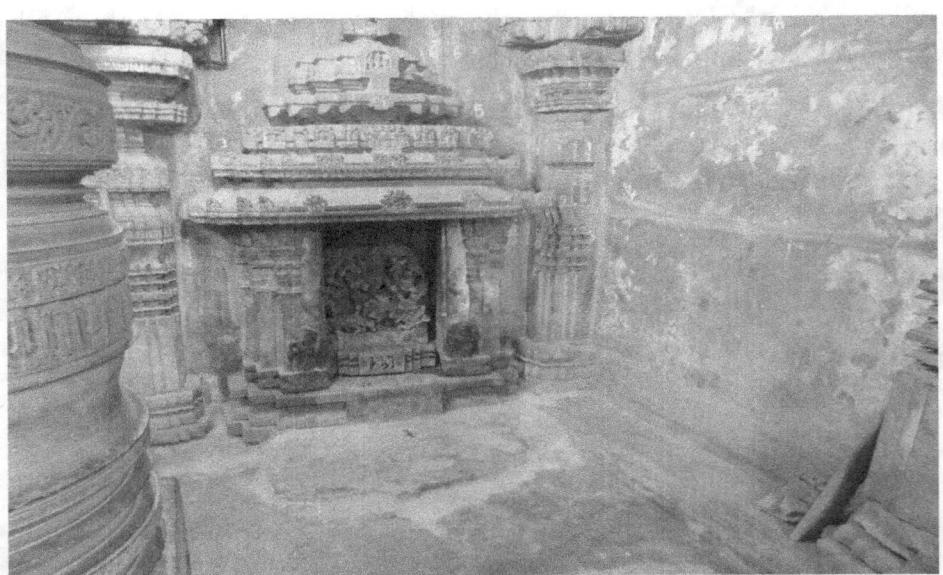

Devakoshtha on the Right of Garbhagriha Chennakesava Temple Channarayapatna

Niches may be classified into three groups, viz. simple niche, niches with pilasters, and niches with doorframes. Simple niche consists of two horizontal courses, moulded like *padma*, forming base and top, and two plain vertical courses on sides. Some niches contain three courses, viz. *padam*, lenticular *kumuda* and another *padma* at the base forming *adhisthana*, pilasters on the sides, and *kapota* surmounted by a turret. Large niche contains doorframes with multiple *sakas* and pediments similar to those of the *garbhagrihas*. The main cult deity is worshipped in the *garbhagriha* and the *parivara* or associated deities are placed in the *devakoshthas* or niches formed in the thickness of the *sabhamandapa* walls.

Vimana and Sikhara

The part of the temple that contains the cella (*garbhagriha*) is called *Vimana*. The *vimana* usually bears a tower called *Sikhara* and is therefore easily recognizable from a distance too. Its inside is simply a square plan with plain walls whereas the outside is complicated in plan and profusely decorated. The outside plan may be a star, a staggered square or a combination of a star and square and consequently the walls will show projections and recesses. Each projection of the wall may have a complete architectural articulation with many decorations. Notably the top of each projection is crowded and these tops are repeated several times in the tower. This chaos caused by numerous projections, recesses, blocks and mouldings is illusory. There is in fact a strong and logical order but difficult to perceive unless one is trained to distinguish between their various features and the geometry behind the whole.

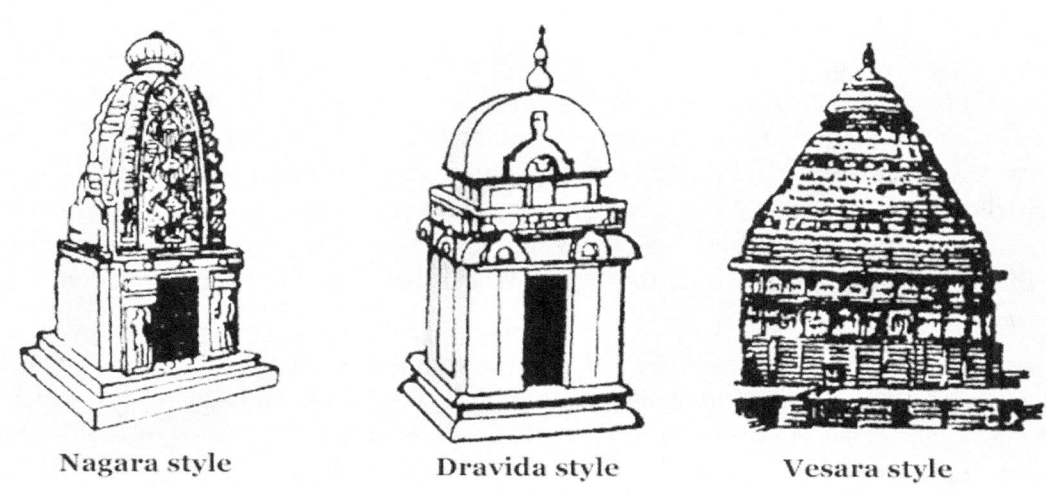

The Three Styles of Temple Vimana

The inside of the *antarala* is similar to that of the cella or sanctum. It is also square and plain and of a size equivalent to the *garbhagriha*. Its outside walls too are decorated but are only a short continuation of the walls of the shrine or *vimana*. It generally has a tower but of a low protrusion. Generally the dynastic crest or symbol would be housed on top of it like the Hoysala crest on Hoysala temples.

Sikhara

Sikhara or superstructure is the top most member of a shrine or *vimana*. A flat roof stone slab that covers the sanctum is also called as *Kapota*. Flat roof (*Kapota*) of the sanctum on which the tower rests and rises is over-laid by a single stone slab, known in the texts as '*Brahma randra sila*' (the stone). This serves as the base (*adhisthana*) for the superstructure that rises above the sanctum known as *Vimana* or *Sikhara*, which forms the important part of the temple. In early days, this vertical emphasis was laid on only one tier (*prathama tala*). Later, more number of tiers (*talas*) were added to this superstructure. It was believed that the entire area, which the *vimana* or *sikhara* overlooked was rendered holy and the area covered by the influence of this *sikhara*, would be prosperous.

Archana-Navnita, an old text classified these holy places into five types 1) *Svayam-Vyakta* (self-manifest) 2) *Daivika* (installed by Gods) 3) *Arsha* (installed by sages) 4) *Pauranika* (glorified in the *Puranas*) and 5) *Manusha* (man-made) shrines.

Various ancient texts referred to only three classifications of temple architecture, *Nagara. Dravida* and *Vesara. Nagara*: actually means squarish, cruciform in plan and its *sikhara* has a vertical emphasis. *Vesara*: is circularly emphasized horizontal aspect shape, like domical or octagonal or in the shape of vaulted roof. Another feature is storeyed towers and tall *gopuras*. It is a combination of *Dravida* and *Nagara* style of *sikhara* features. *Dravida*-Polygonal or octagonal (six or eight sided): It is circular in plan or apsidal. General conception is that *Nagara* type of temples prevails in the land between the Himalayas and Vindhya ranges. *Vesara* type of temples exists in between Vindhya ranges and Krishna river and *Dravida* type of temples prevails in between River Krishna and Kanyakumari. In that sense Karnataka has the widest range of temple architecture on display in all its splendor all over Karnataka.

The term *sikhara* meaning 'Mountain peak' may indicate that it signified 'Meru' meaning mountain or Kailasa, tall and sacred place of Siva. The North Indian (*Nagara*) *vimana* or *sikhara* is crowned by a large circular (wheel shaped) capstone block known as *'amalaka'* (ribbed disc resembling an *amalaka* fruit (Emblic Myrobalan), while its South Indian (*Dravida*) counterpart ends in a cupola (*Srnga* or *Stupi*) or Wagon roof (*khakra*). The South Indian *vimana* is generally broader and shorter than the North Indian *vimana*. The North Indian temples rise from a pedestal (*Pitha* or *Jagati*), through the wall (*tiara*) and main body (*gandi*) to the head (*mastaka*), which consists of a rib, is surmounted by a 'skull' (*khapuri*) on which is installed the *Kalasa* (finial). And on top of finial will be seen the weapon (*ayudha*) of the deity, a trident or a discus flag. The plan of the *vimana* could be round or square. It could also be six-sided or eight-sided. It could retain one form uniformly from the base to the top or combine two or more plans at different storeys, sometimes as many as sixteen. Sometimes, however it encompasses the area covered by the circumbulatory path round the sanctum as well as the rectangular *antarala* immediately in front of the sanctum. Its mass rests on a square base called support (*adhisthana* or *pitha*) and rises through stylized treatment of dormer windows in several tiers to a dome shaped tower (*sikhara*) surmounted by a cupola (*srnga* or *stupi*).

The *Dravida vimana* generally is marked by distinctly made storeys or flat floors. The lower most storey has a typical structure with *kuta vimanas* designed as mini-shrines occupying the corners with large *sala vimanas* in the middle. In between the *kuta* and *sala vimanas* are interspersed the *panjara vimanas*. Each rising storey is a replication of the series on the first storey with diminishing sizes till it reaches the *sikhara* and the *stupi*.

Closed hall and Open hall

Like the shrine or *vimana*, the closed hall has thick walls and no windows, only entrance opening. It is much larger in size and has four central pillars supporting the roof and dividing it into nine compartments or bays (*ankana*) and is called *navaranga*. Both inside and outside of the closed hall are square in plan. Not only outside but inside of the hall too is decorated. The nine ceilings of the nine *ankanas* may generally be sculpted beautifully. Pillars may be bell shaped, fluted or with square shaft and octagonal base or even lathe turned pillars. The pillars may be intricately carved and decorated with sculpture. Closed hall generally does not have more than four pillars and nine bays and consequently is of a modest size.

The other kind of hall is the open hall. Its plan is not necessarily square but may be staggered square and here the number of pillars and bays may vary. Often this plan is called "cross in square" but that name may be adequate in case of smallest form consisting of thirteen bays. The peculiar thing about open hall is that it can be larger and even much larger as the size of the stagger of the square increases. The walls of the open hall consist of a parapet wall only, resting on this parapet are half pillars supporting the outer ends of the roof. Inside are at least four full pillars. The inside of the parapet is provided with seating bench. As in the closed hall, notably the pillars and the ceilings of an open hall can be very beautiful. Since it is open sufficient day light entering the temple lets the visitor enjoy fill view of the ornamentation. On the outside the parapet is beautifully decorated with horizontal mouldings. In overall design the open hall is much more attractive than closed hall.

A bench called *kakshasana* providing a sitting place for the devotees usually surrounds the open *sabhamandapas* and the *mukhamandapas*. Many of the Karnataka temples have *kakshasana* in the *adhisthana* itself with an additional slab, set vertically for the backrest.

Mukhamandapa or Porch

The porch or *mukhamandapa* always adjoining the entrance opening of a closed hall consists of an awning supported by two or more half pillars and of two parapets on both sides. It is in fact, an open hall of only one bay. Ceiling and pillars are often beautifully decorated and a porch provides a nice entrance.

Balustrades

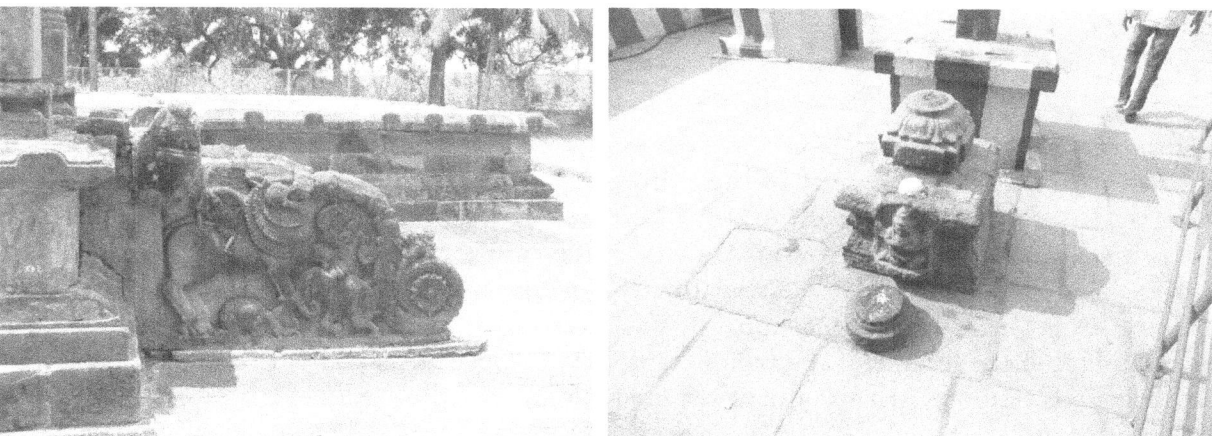

Balustrade with Yalli Carving at Tripurantakeswara Temple Balligavi and Balipitha at Gopalaswamy Temple Himavada Bette

Balustrades are guard stones flanking flights of steps with top railing. Most of the modem temples have this type of balustrades in Karnataka. The rear end of the railing top is of scroll type. Some temples have the feature of elephant balustrades in Karnataka.

Eaves or *Chadya*

The main function of eave or *chajja (chdya)* is to protect wall from rainwater. It projects forward from the ceiling level, so that water is thrown away from wall surface. The slightly projecting eaves with curved upper surface to facilitate the flow of water are found in several temples. Such eaves can be seen projecting out of the outer edges of the ceilings of the temple halls.

Torana (Ornamental arches)

Torana is an interesting feature involved in stylized temples. Kamikagama describes the *chitra torana* of the temple. Manasara gives the information regarding the measurement for the temple *torana*. Besides *chitra torana*, the texts mention two other types of *torana* 1) *Patra torana* (fashioned like the lotus leaves) and 2) *Makara torana* (arch with *makara*, a crocodile).

Pradakshinapatha or Circumambulatory

Many temples have *pradakshinapatha* or circumambulatory passage around the *garbhagriha*. Temples with such *pradakshinapatha* are called *Sandhara* and those *garbhagrihas* that do not have the *pradakshinapatha* are called *Nirandhara*. Great majority of the temples are of the *Nirandhara* type. However, most Hoysala temples stand on extended platforms providing freedom to followers to circumambulate around the temple. This not only lets the follower perform a religious ritual but also to look at the sculpture and decoration on the exterior walls of the temple.

Prakara, the Boundary wall

The area of the temple comprising of the sanctum and the halls with water tanks and gardens were enclosed by a wall (*prakara*). It looks like within the ramparts of a fort. But the enclosed wall *prakara* was a later innovation and became a special feature of South Indian temples. The texts explain that the *prakara* contributes security to the shrine, strength, protection, beauty and accommodation for attendant deities. In the South Indian temples, the *prakara* walls accommodate a series of pillared halls or pavilions, rooms for storage, resting places for pilgrims and shrines for minor deities apart from their chief purpose of protection of temple property. Although the texts prescribe that each enclosure must have doorways on all four sides, generally the wall (*prakra*) facing the sanctum alone has the opening. This door is called *mahadvara* (Main Gate) and usually it is a huge one, allowing the temple elephant or small chariot to pass through. A beautiful example here would be the Bhoganandiswara temple at Nandi.

The *prakara* in its many layers provides for a number of minor temples or shrines for the deities, connected with the presiding deity of the temple. Apart from these, the temple precincts include a *yagasala*, (a hall for occasional *yajna* or *yagas*), *kalyana-mandapa*, marriage or a general purpose hall; *asthana-mandapa*, where the processional deity holds court; *vahana mandapa*, to store the various "vehicles" used to mount the processional deity during festivals and processions like the chariot; *alankara-mandapa*, where the processional deity is dressed before being taken on procession; *vasanta-mandapa*, a hall in the middle of the temple tank used for festivals; and *utsava mandapa*, hall used on festive occasions. Temples will also usually have a treasury, a kitchen (*paka-sala*), a store room (*ugrana*), and a dining hall.

Gopura (Tower above the main door way)

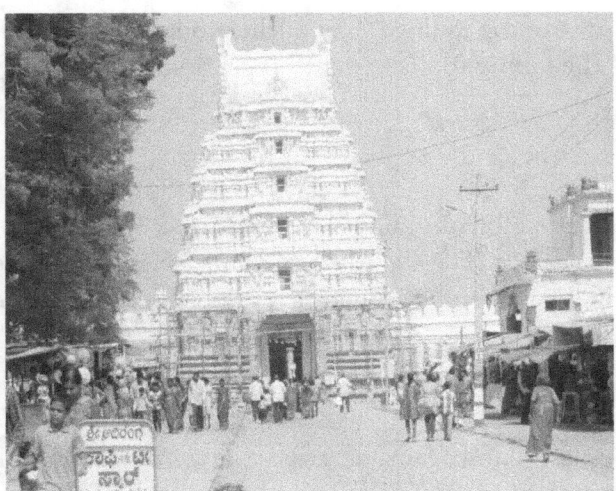 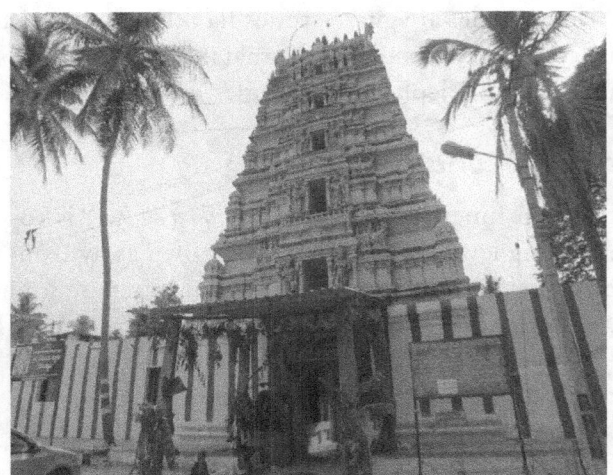

Gopura of Sriranganathaswmy Temple Srirangapatna and Narasimha Temple Maddur

The ancient texts such as Vaikhanasagama and Mayamata mention the gateway tower. *Gopura* literally means cow's pen and the term was used to denote structure that was erected at the entrance of the cow's pen. Since 10th century CE, it has become customary to have a tower above the doorway. The front portion of the *prakara* represents the tower like structure in the form of the head or face of an alligator or iguana. During later Chola period and Vijayanagara period these *gopuras* were called as *Raya Gopura*. These *gopuras* are highly ornamented and very tall. They are like multi-storeyed pyramids, oblong in plan. The texts permitted as many as 16 storeys and the height of about 200 feet for tall *gopura*. These *prakara* and *gopura* features are very common in South India, but in North India they are not so important.

Bali-Pitha (The Dispensing Seat)

The sanctum, *adytum garbhagriha*, which is the most important structural detail, is closely associated with the *Bali-Pitha* that is installed in front of the sanctum directly facing the icon. Actually there will be several 'seats' of this nature, installed in various ritualistically determined positions inside the enclosure and outside the sanctum. However, the one in front of the sanctum is the 'Chief seat' (*Pradhana-pitha*). It is a low stone altar, frequently planned in the form of a flat, relatively elaborate form with a base, cornices, wall surface and the top lotus. The canons specify that the real temple should comprise of the sanctum, the tower on top of it, the icon inside it and the dispensing seat in front of it.

Stambhas or Flag-staffs or Lamp poles

In the context of Hindu mythology, *stambha*, also spelled as *skambha*, is believed to be a cosmic column. It is believed that the *stambha* functions as a bond, which joins the heaven (*svarga*) and the earth (*prithvi*). A number of Hindu scriptures, including the *Atharva Veda*, have references to *stambha*. In the *Atharva Veda*, a celestial *stambha* has been mentioned, and that has been described as a scaffold, which supports the cosmos and material creation.

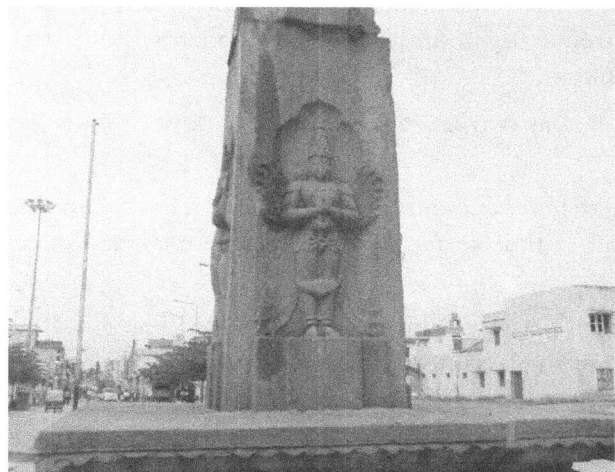
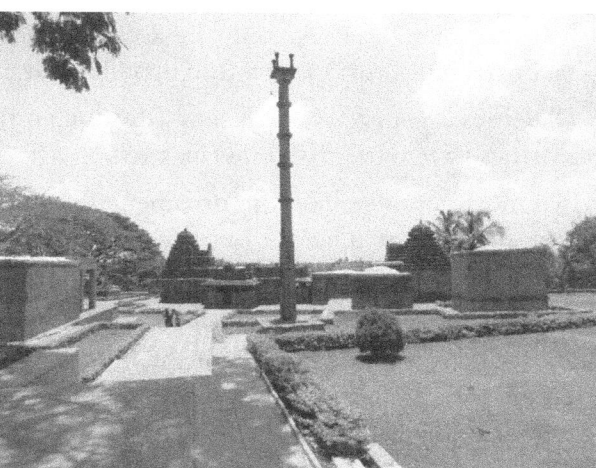

Garuda Stambha at Saumyakesava Temple Nagamangala and Dhvajastambha at Mukteswara Temple Chaudayadanapura

In Indian architecture, different types of Stambhas have been mentioned and they serve different purpose, including the following:

- Flagstaffs, called *dhvaja stamnhas*, are placed opposite the main shrine, on an axis with the main deity.
- *Kirttistambhas*, erected to commemorate victories.
- *Dipastambhas* or lamp poles are placed at a conspicuous location within the temple compound where lamps are lit at night. *Dipastambhas* may also be supplemented with a wall with groves to hold lamps so as to create a wider illuminated area in the evenings.

Water Tank (*Kalyani or Kund or Pushkarni*)

Water tank or temple *kalyani* is essential for Hindu temple. Before entering into the temple, the devotee must purify (*parishuddh*) with a dip in the tank or clean and wash hands and legs and head. Water tank is also necessary for daily requirement of water for deities and cleaning of temple.

Inside of the temple, temple sculpture

The first thing that strikes one when examining the image sculpture in the older temples is the apparent absence of drapery. Its existence is detected in most cases by an odd line here and there crossing legs at the ankles or the breasts. The sculptor was always anxious to display the form. The human figures initially were not proportionate in size and the limbs did not display a truthful extension of the body, being slimmer and too long. As times passed, the sculptor's application and finesse imparted life to sculpture. The culmination of this process is visible in the attractive Hoysala sculpture in their various temples commencing from Belur and Halebid.

Female charms were made to centre in great hips and breasts. Though faces of these female sculptures used to be expressionless, Hoysala sculptors produced some of the very enchanting beauties in the Chennakesava temple at Belur.

Another marked feature of the temple images is the amount of jewellery they are represented as wearing. This, of course, denoted wealth and prosperity of the period. The ropes of pearls and strings of precious stones are carved with a minuteness and accuracy which must have demanded endless patience from the sculptor. The range of ornaments carved on the body of these images includes necklaces, armlets, waistbands, girdles, earrings, bracelets and anklets.

Figure sculpture also embraces the modeling of gods and goddesses, *ganas*, *yakshas*, *raksasas* or demons, kings and queens and their attendants, warriors, *jogis* or mendicants, dancing girls (*apsaras*) and half animal and half human figures. Among the animals, most frequently found were the elephants, lions, tigers, horses, boars, bulls, turtles, swans, crocodiles and monkeys.

All deities except Surya or Aditya (the Sun god) who has two are represented with four or more arms. Some deities have more than one face too.

Two most notable objects in ornamental detail are the *Makara* and the *Kirtimukha*. The *makara* looks like a crocodile or an alligator but generally has no tail, it thus seems to be the fertile imagination of an artist.

The *kirtimukha* occurs alone or in conjunction with *makara*. This curious "Face of Fame" or mask is often found in repeated bands of the moulding round the basement of the temple. It is also found on the temple *sikhara* and at times is repeated nearly along a vertical line on several storeys of the *sikhara*. Description and meaning of the *Kirtimukha* (Face of Fame) is given in one of the ancient texts as a legend about the demonic character Jalandhara. When Jalandhara attempted to seduce the wife of Siva, he produced a terrible being from his third eye. The terrible being straightaway demanded something to devour. Siva commanded him to devour himself which he did all but his head. Siva being pleased with this performance declared that henceforth he should be called *Kirtimukha* and that his head will adorn the doorways of all his temples.

Rock-cut and cave temples of Karnataka

Rock-cut architecture is the creation of structures, buildings, and sculptures, by excavating solid rock where it naturally occurs. Rock-cut architecture is designed and made by man from the start to finish. However, caves and caverns, that began in natural form, are not considered to be 'rock-cut architecture' even if extensively modified. Although rock-cut structures differ from traditionally built structures in many ways, many rock-cut structures are made to replicate the facade or interior of traditional architectural forms.

Rock-cut architecture, though intensely laborious with ancient tools and methods, was presumably combined with quarrying the rock for use elsewhere; the huge amounts of stone removed have normally vanished from the site. Rock-cut architecture is also said to be cut and hewn "from the living rock." Another term sometimes associated with rock-cut architecture is monolithic architecture, which is rather applied to free-standing structures made of a single piece of material. Gommateshwara (Bahubali), the largest monolithic statue in the world is situated at Shravanabelagola. It was built in 983 CE and was carved out from a large single block of granite. There are other sites too in Karnataka where large monolithic statues of Gommateshwara have been carved like Basadi Hoskote, Gommata Giri and Arethippur.

In India, caves have long been regarded as places of sanctity. Caves that were enlarged or entirely man-made were felt to hold the same sanctity as natural caves. In fact, the sanctuary in all Indian religious structures, even free-standing ones, retains the same cave-like feeling of sacredness, being small and dark without natural light.

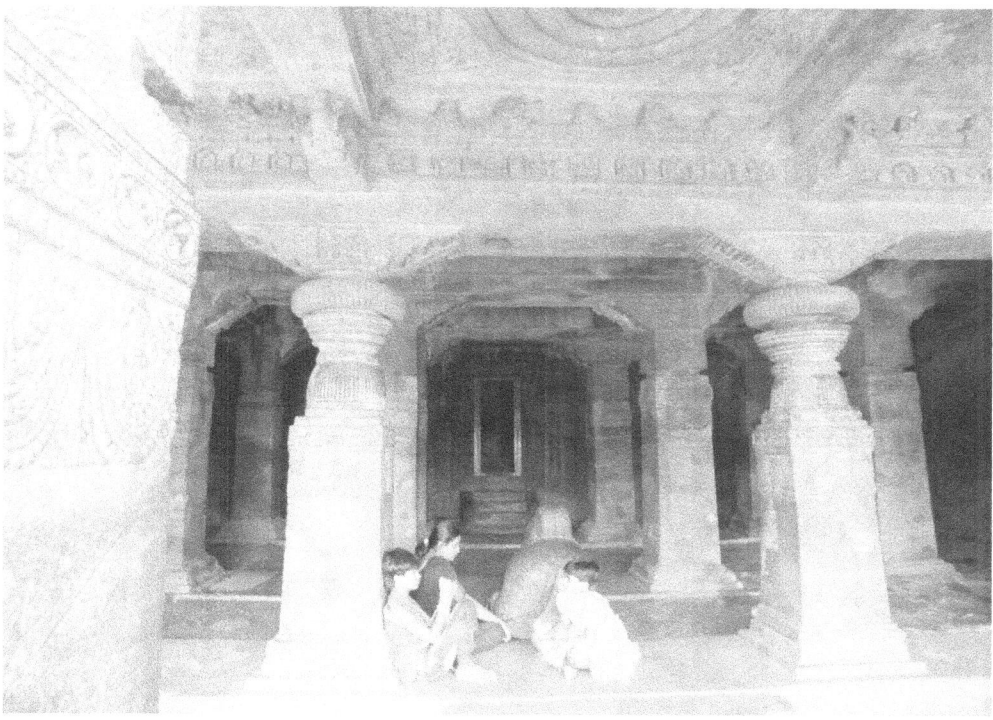

Cave 1 at Badami, Interior View

Badami is surrounded in the north and south by forts built in later times from the ramparts that crown their summits. The Badami cave temples are composed of four caves, all carved out of the soft Badami sandstone on a hill cliff in the late 6th to 7th centuries. The planning of four caves is simple. The entrance is a verandah (*mukhamandapa*) with stone columns and brackets, a distinctive feature of these caves, leading to a columned *mandapa* – main hall (also *mahamandapa*) and then to the small square shrine (sanctum sanctorum, *garbhaghriha*) cut deep into the cave. Thus Badami cave temples have rock cut halls with three basic features: pillared veranda, columned hall and a sanctum cut out deep into rock. One noteworthy feature of these cave temples is the running frieze of *Ganas* in various amusing postures carved in relief on each plinth. The Cave temples are linked by stepped path with intermediate terraces that offer spectacular views across the town and lake. Cave-temples are labeled 1 to 4 in their ascending series even though this numbering does not necessarily reflect the sequence of excavation.

Important part of historical heritage at Badami cave temples are inscriptions in old Kannada script. There is also the fifth natural cave temple in Badami – a Buddhist temple in natural cave which can be entered kneeling on all fours.

Early experiments in rock cut halls were attempted in Aihole where three cave temples were built, one each in Vedic, Buddhist and Jaina styles. Ravana Phadi cave temple in Aihole village and the Buddhist and Jaina caves on top of the Meguti hill comprise the cave architecture component at Aihole. The outside verandas of the cave temples are rather plain, but the inner hall contains rich and prolific sculptural symbolism both at Aihole and Badami.

Stepped wells or *pushkarnis* of Karnataka

The beauty of Karnataka temples is so enchanting that various other architecturally marvelous components get overlooked sometimes. The stepped wells and *pushkarnis* of equally grand architectural styles have not been studied in detail as part of Karnataka architecture. There are several such stepped wells and *pushkarnis* in Karnataka dating back from the Badami Chalukya times. Some of the more prominent among them are: Muskinabhavi at Lakkundi, Vasudeva Sarovara in the Chennakesava temple complex at Belur,

Kalyani Teertham at Melkote, Hulikere tank near Halebid, Nagakund at Sudi, Panchalinga Kalyani at Bhoganandiswara temple and the Kalyani in front of Huchchimalli gudi at Aihole.

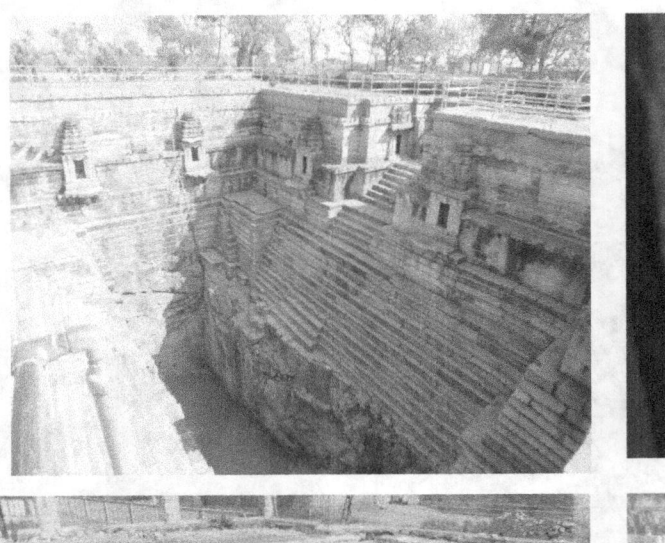
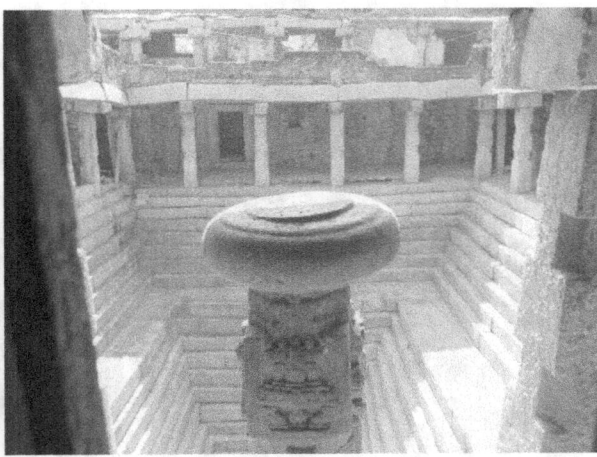
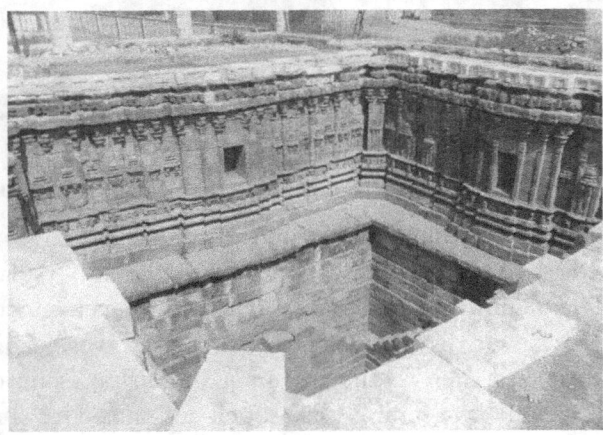
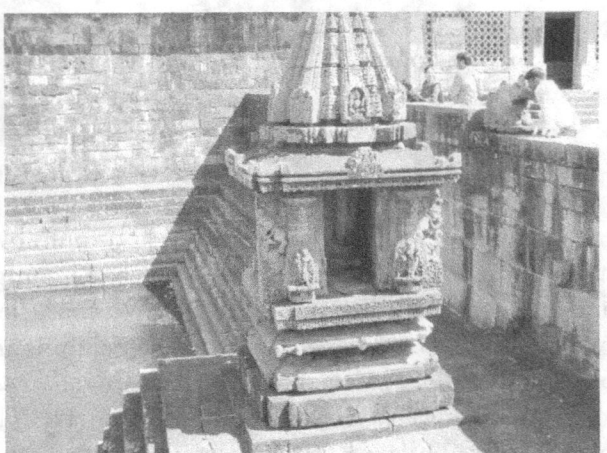

Stepped-wells or Pushkarnis-Muskinabhavi at Lakkundi, Panchalinga Kalyani at Nandi, Nagakund at Sudi and Pushkarni at Belur

Muskinabhavi is the largest stepped well in Karnataka and dates back to the early twelfth century built across the Manikeswara temple by the Kalyani Chalukyas. The well or tank has a large rectangular funnel of steps provided with small shrines and with entrances on three sides. The central entrance is wider than the others and its steps leading down to the water have an underpass. The Nagakund at Sudi too has similar features. Muskinabhavi faces the Manikeswara temple. The temple has three open bays and in front of these bays there is a flat bridge over the main stairway of the Muskinabhavi *pushkarni*. The underpass created by this bridge is really impressive because it is very lofty, much loftier than the underpass of the Nagakunda in Sudi.

Hulikere is a hamlet only 3 km south-east of Halebid reachable from Halebid by a narrow road. Here an intricate pond from the Hoysala times is found. It is an extremely attractive piece of architecture. It consists of a large funnel of steps with two galleries, the lower one running alongside eleven small shrines and sixteen niches. The small shrines are complete *vimanas* on platforms placed forwards, projecting over the walk of the lower gallery, the niches alternate with them and are positioned backwards below the walk of the upper gallery. They offer a marvelous view comparable only with a few intricate ponds from other parts of India like the Nagakund from Sudi, Muskinabhavi in Lakkundi and Kapadvanj and Modhera in Gujarat.

4.4 VASTU AND TEMPLE DESIGNING

The Hindu temples developed over two thousand years depict excellent architectural evolution which took place within the boundaries of strict models derived from religious considerations. In Hindu tradition, the temple architecture is a religious architecture which is connected to astronomy and sacred geometry. Normally, the temple is referred as a place of sanctity representing the macrocosm or the Universe and the microcosm or the inner space.

The temple architecture has kept the ancient basic proportions and rigid forms unaltered over centuries. It is very conservative and a particular form of decorative details persisted for centuries even though the original purpose and the context are lost. Even the architect and the sculptor were given a great deal of freedom in the embellishment and decoration of the prescribed underlying principles and formulae which resulted in an overwhelming wealth of architectural elements, sculptural forms and decorative exuberance.

It would be surprising for us to know that even the rudiments of Geometry, called *Rekha-Ganita* (Line Computation) in ancient India, were formulated and applied in the drafting of *Mandalas* for architectural purposes. They were also displayed in the geometric patterns used in many temple motifs. The Sulva Sutras, which literally mean 'Rule of the Chord,' give geometrical methods of constructing altars and temples. The temples layouts were called *Mandalas*.

By the 6th and 7th century CE all three organized religions in Karnataka viz. Hinduism, Jainism and Buddhism were adopting Tantric form of veneration as the means of furtherance of religiosity. Tantric form of worship included magical incantation (*mantras*), esoteric diagrams (*yantras*) and rites employed to exorcise and ward off evil spirits.

"*Yantra*" is a Sanskrit word that comes from "yam" meaning to control or subdue and "tra" meaning an "instrument" or "machine." They are machines that can "subdue" or rather contain cosmic energies and are mediums that reveal abstract universal truths. Since time immemorial, it has been believed that mystical *Yantras* reveal the inner basis of forms and shapes of the universe. No matter what the outer structure, all matter is made up of the same basic unity; the atom. (Pictures of yantras from Hangal, Bandalike and Malavalli)

Yantras are considered much more powerful than a picture or even a statue of a deity and they are used to energize the latter. In Hindu temples, the sacred inner sanctums that house the main deity, the *yantra* associated with that deity is placed under the base of the statue to initiate, energize and sanctify the space. The geometrical forms of the *Yantra* activate the right hemisphere, which is visual and nonverbal. The diagrams are essentially thought forms representing divinities or cosmic powers which exert their influence by means of sound vibrations. They can be illustrated on paper as *mandalas* or carved onto stone etc.

Mandala is a generic term in practice for any plan, chart or geometric pattern that represents the cosmos metaphysically or symbolically, more a microcosm of the Universe from a human perspective. The form of Hindu temple, according to ancient architectural traditions of the Sthapatya Veda (Indian traditional architecture) symbolized the model of cosmos. The temple was a fusion of archetypes consciously combined and skillfully crafted into structure of abstract geometry and specific numbers.

The term *Mandala* in Sanskrit means the whole world, represented as a circle (or a square) and centre in its general use. Its traditional design often utilizes circle – the symbol of cosmos in its eternity – and the square symbolizing the man-made world, relating to the earth. A *mandala* is a place in which the practitioner beholds the deities who have been invoked into it and they become an integral part of the structure. The shape and the structure used for invoking the deity in a statue is a place confined within a square or circular diagram drawn as the *mandala*. Each *mandala* in a temple represents the mystery of Universe pictorially. The worshipper imaginatively enters the *mandala* focusing successively on each of its stages and absorbing the logic of its form, while approaching the centre. Sometimes a *mandala* houses a number of deities as *abhimant devatas* who were conceived as guardians associated with the protective sphere. Regardless of the number of deities involved, the representations are arranged symmetrically.

The Hindu temple typically involves a multiple set of ideas. Perhaps Hindu traditional architecture has more symbolic meanings than other cultures. It is highly articulated. The temple is oriented to face east, the auspicious direction where the sun rises to dispel darkness. The temple design includes the archetypal image of a Cosmic Person spread out yogi-like, symmetrically filling the gridded space of the floor plan, his navel in the center, and it includes the archetype of the cosmic mountain (Meru), between earth and heaven, of fertility, planets, city of the gods, deities, etc. One encounters these simultaneous archetypal themes and meanings conveyed (and hidden) in the semi-abstract forms in many Hindu temples. There are rules of shape and proportion in the authoritative texts of Hindu tradition *(sastras* and *agamas)* which give birth to a variety of complex temple designs. The *Brihat Samhita* text *(*4th century CE*)* says the temple should reflect cosmic order.

During the medieval ages in India, no single dynastic power served as the undisputed dispenser of cultural and artistic ideas. However, despite their regional flourishes, Hindu temple designs displayed a remarkable unity of aesthetic purposes. This unified philosophy was codified into a system of rules or canons (a compendium of architectural guidelines) called the *Vastusastras*. These canons were the purview of the priestly class, and these were generally incomprehensible to even skilled building craftspeople and were seldom challenged.

Of all the canons and rules in the *Vastusastras*, the one that found the most favor with building designers from ancient times to the present day is the *Vastupurushamandala*. The *Vastupurushamandala* has been defined as "a collection of rules which attempt to facilitate the translation of theological concepts into architectural form." This law of proportions and rhythmic ordering of elements not only found full expression in temples, but extended to residential and urban planning as well.

Before we proceed further, let us briefly discuss the concept of the *Vastupurushamandala*. The faith that Earth is a living organism, throbbing with life and energy; is fundamental to the *Vastu Sastra*. That living energy is symbolized as a person; he is the *Vastu Purusha*. The site for the proposed construction is his field; *Vastupurushamandala*. The form of the temple, all that it is and signifies, stands upon the diagram of the *Vastupurusha*. It is a 'forecast' of the temple and is drawn on the leveled ground; it is the foundation from which the building arises. Whatever its actual surroundings, the place where the temple is built is occupied by the *Vastupurusha* in his diagram, the *Vastupurushamandala*. It is the place for the meeting and marriage of heaven and earth, where the whole world is present in terms of measure, and is accessible to man.

'*Vastu*' is derived from the Sanskrit root '*vas*' which encompasses a range of words related to objects that are used as a surround by human beings like clothes, house and habitation. '*Vastu*' in the context of *Vastu Sastra* means places where immortals and mortals dwell. The general meaning of '*Sastra*' is science, which makes the translation of *Vastu Sastra*, the science of places where immortals and mortals live. *Vastu Sastra* comprises of a body of knowledge that was fully developed before the advent of 1st century CE but most of the literary material between 6th century BCE and 6th century CE are lost. *Vastu Sastra* was developed and modified by a successive generation of architectural scholars through a range of Sanskrit and Tamil literary works till 15th century CE. Most of the translated and interpreted books on *Vastu Sastra* are based on six ancient Sanskrit books – *Mayamata, Manasara, Samaranganasuthradhara, Rajavallabha, Vishwakarmaprakasa* and *Aparajitapraccha*.

There is a lot of mysticism and symbolism that is associated with this *sastra*. *Vastu Sastra* is a product of Vedic science which considers humans as part of a whole. It addresses a wide range of applications like town planning, temple architecture, residential architecture, painting and sculpturing. It is important to state that *Vastu Sastra* for every site, state and country differs as per the various regional factors of that place.

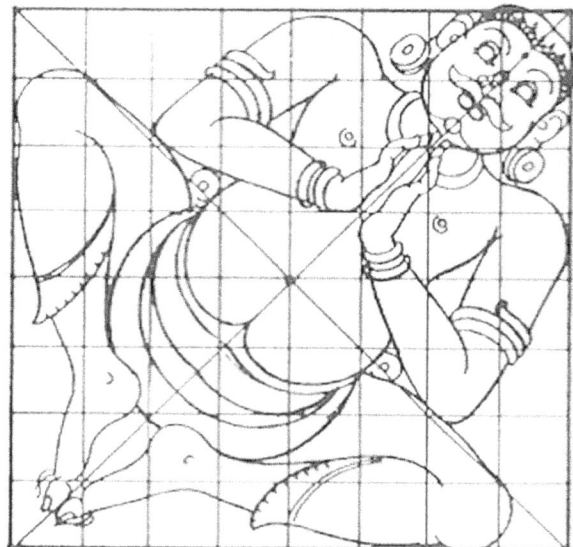
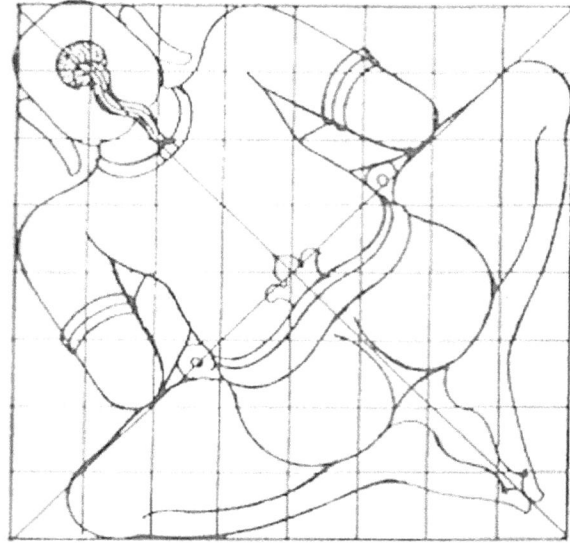

Another important aspect of *vastupurushamandala* is its fractal nature. This is embedded in the measurement system used in *Vastu Sastra*. Fredrick W. Bunce (2014) recently investigated the application of fractal geometry and *Mandala* Architecture to several temples, most of which are located in Karnataka, with the help of *vastupurushamandala*. They illustrate the complexity of the *vastupurushamandala* and relate it to the developmental plans of Hindu temples.

Vastupurushamandala illustrates space and time as inseparable and coterminous entities. The spatial aspect of *vastupurushamandala* is defined by the placement of sun, definition of directions and the institution of proportions. The oriented square form, the geometric divisions and the establishment of the 8 directions in relation to the path of the sun represents the aspect of space in *vastupurushamandala*.

The path of sun, plotted as aspects of the divinities, represents diurnal time and also dismantles different effects of sun as a spatial determinant. The rotation of the human form with in the square denotes annual cyclic repeats of time and signifies the qualities of each of the 8 directions with relation to time. The fractal geometry presented in *vastupurushamandala* denotes the expanding and iterative nature of space and time. It is this unit of measurement that transforms space and time in to tangible forms (grids).

The tangible forms are then credited with meanings as symbolic deities. For example the deity in the north-east corner is 'Isana' who is the God of creation. Isana is one of the Vedic Gods. Isana is generally regarded with positive qualities which imply meanings like open, light, receptive and interactive to the spaces constructed in the north east corner. Similarly, the south west is deity is 'Nirrti' who is the controller of destruction, decomposition and exit from life. The meanings assigned to Nirrti are heavy, closed, clean, resting and seclusion etc. The figure depicting Mandukya Mandala with 64 *padas* is taken from Wikipedia.

The design lays out a Hindu temple in a symmetrical, self-repeating structure derived from central beliefs, myths, cardinality and mathematical principles. The four cardinal directions help create the axis of a Hindu temple, around which is formed a perfect square in the space available. The circle of *mandala* circumscribes the square. The square is considered divine for its perfection and as a symbolic product of knowledge and human thought, while circle is considered earthly, human and observed in everyday life (moon, sun, horizon, water drop, rainbow). Each supports the other. The square is divided into perfect square grids. In large temples, this is often 8 × 8 or 64 grid structure. In ceremonial temple superstructures, this is an 81 sub-square grid. The squares are called *"padas".*

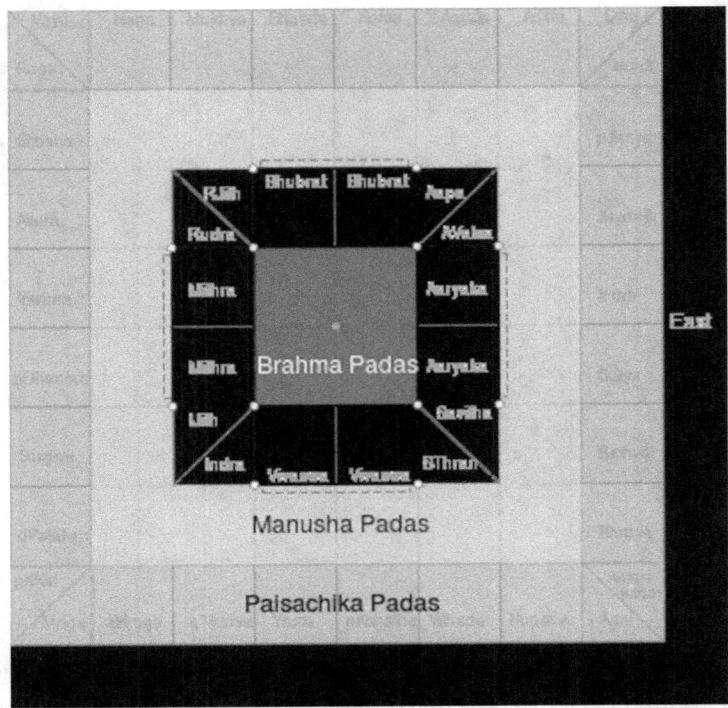

The square is symbolic and has Vedic origins from fire altar, Agni. The alignment along cardinal directions similarly is an extension of Vedic rituals of three fires. This symbolism is also found among Greek and other ancient civilizations, through the gnomon. In Hindu temple manuals, design plans are described with 1, 4, 9, 16, 25, 36, 49, 64, 81 up to 1024 squares; 1 *pada* is considered the simplest plan, as a seat for a hermit or devotee to sit and meditate on, do yoga, or make offerings with Vedic fire in front. The second design of 4 *padas* has a symbolic central core at the diagonal intersection, and is also a meditative layout. The 9 *pada* design has a sacred surrounded centre, and is the template for the smallest temple. Older Hindu temple *vastumandalas* may use the 9 through 9 *pada* series, but 64 is considered the most sacred geometric grid in Hindu temples. Bunce classifies the 64 square *mandala* as *Manduka manadala* and 81 square *mandala* as *Paramasayika mandala*. Bunce has analyzed the various temples in the both *Manduka mandala* and *Paramasayika mandala* templates. Each *pada* is conceptually assigned to a symbolic element, sometimes in the form of a deity or to a spirit or *apasara*. The central square(s) of the 64 is dedicated to the Brahma (not to be confused with Brahman), and are called *Brahma padas*.

In a Hindu temple's structure of symmetry and concentric squares, each concentric layer has significance. The outermost layer, *Paisachika padas* signify aspects of *Asuras* and evil; the next inner concentric layer is *Manusha padas* signifying human life; while *Devika padas* signify aspects of *Devas* and good. The *Manusha padas* typically houses the ambulatory. The devotees, as they walk around in clockwise fashion through this ambulatory to complete *Parikrama* (or *Pradakshina*), walk between good on inner side and evil on the outer side. In smaller temples, the *Paisachika pada* is not part of the temple superstructure, but may be on the boundary of the temple or just symbolically represented.

The *Paisachika padas*, *Manusha padas* and *Devika padas* surround *Brahma padas*, which signifies creative energy and serves as the location for temple's primary idol for *darsana*. Finally at the very centre of *Brahma padas* is *Garbhagriha* housing the *Purusha* or Space, signifying Universal Principle present in everything and every one. The spire of a Hindu temple, called *Sikhara* or *Vimana*, is perfectly aligned above the *Brahma pada(s)*.

Sikhara or *Vimana* stretches towards the sky. The vertical dimension's cupola or dome is designed as a pyramid, conical or other mountain-like shape. Scholars suggest that this shape is inspired by cosmic mountain of Meru or Himalayan Kailasa, the abode of gods according to Vedic mythology.

In larger temples, the outer three *padas* are visually decorated with carvings, paintings or images meant to inspire the devotee. In some temples, these images or wall reliefs may be stories from Hindu Epics, in others they may be Vedic tales about right and wrong or virtues and vice, in some they may be idols of minor or regional deities. The pillars, walls and ceilings typically also have highly ornate carvings or images of the four just and necessary pursuits of life -*kama, artha, dharma* and *moksa*. This walk around is called *pradakshina*.

4.5 TEMPLES DEDICATED TO DIFFERENT GODS AND GODDESSES

Temples and epigraphs form an important means to understand history and the social, cultural and economic past of the land. Temple building was one of the conspicuous practices of the people of Karnataka irrespective of the dynasty reigning at any particular time. Epigraphs left in the temple premises by the people of those times form the right guide to know about the patronage, grants, nature of activities pursued in the temples, social and cultural issues related with the temples and the motivation behind building such magnificent monuments. The temple building activity was a cultural expression of political, social, economic and religious development of those periods. Temples are the historians of heritage and they should not lose their identity. It is necessary to preserve them with due care and not allowed to become mere showpieces. They must continue to remind the society of the grandeur of the past and continue to inspire people into delivering their best.

Forms of Gods and Goddesses to whom the temples were dedicated

Worship of gods and goddesses may date back to prehistoric times. However, to know about the gods and goddesses and temples built in their honour we have to rely on supporting historical evidence besides the existence of relics of past. Any commentary on these matters would thus be based on such historical evidence. Existing monuments (whether standing or in ruins), inscriptions and epigraphical records, memorials from the past and travel records of foreign visitors constitute a reliable way to reconstruct the history associated with heritage. All comments here would be guided by the study of such records and evidences.

Since temple building activity is directly associated with the growth of religions and the proclivity of the ruling dynasties towards any given religion, a study of the religions of the land is essential. It has already been noticed in the preceding chapters how the three principal religions viz. Buddhism, Jainism and Hinduism influenced the arts and architecture, culture and social development in Karnataka in the past. However, with the emergence of Hinduism as the most dominating pantheon since the 4th century CE, its contribution to the art and architecture today is more noticeable than the other religions. By the 12th century Hinduism had become the most popular and powerful faith in Karnataka with its various sects and sub-sects and attracted the attention of the kings, nobles, officials, tradesmen, preachers, philosophers and artisans. It is observed that worship of Siva was widespread throughout the length and breadth of the state. Viewing from historically available evidence, it appears that Siva cult probably goes further back than that of Visnu. Shakti cult as such may be perhaps of the same antiquity as the Visnu cult but worship of mother goddess in one form or the other was possibly in existence as tribal and local practice much earlier than historical evidence suggests.

Siva

Siva as a popular god does not manifest himself in *avataras* (incarnations) as Visnu. He is mostly worshipped as his popular symbolic form, the Linga. Various temples do depict him in his anthropomorphic forms too but that seems to have commenced later probably in the 5th or 6th century CE. The earliest reference to Siva temple is found in an inscription from Vasana of the Satavahana period assigned to 245 CE. However, the evidence of the earliest Siva Linga is available at Talagunda in the form of Pranaveswara temple. The

Talagunda pillar inscription of the Kadambas assignable to 450 CE refers to an eternal *Sthanu* (Siva Linga) which was worshipped earlier by Satakarni, probably of the Satavahana dynasty. It is opined by scholars that the Satakarni could probably be the King Gautamiputra Satakarni. If that is to be believed then the Siva Linga at Talagunda is the earliest historically and Pranaveswara temple is the oldest in the state. Another pillar inscription found at Malavalli, a few km away from Talagunda is assignable to 3rd century CE. It refers to a command issued by the king Vinhukada Chutukulananda Satakarni I to his revenue officers (*mahavalabham-rajjukam*) relating to a grant free of all taxes to Brahman named Kondamana for enjoyment of god Malapali (Siva). Some loose sculpture lies scattered around the pillar inscription at Malavalli and a Siva temple of yore stands close to it. All these three inscriptions go into suggesting that worship of Siva was prevalent in Karnataka during the times of Satavahanas and probably earlier. Siva has been a popular Hindu god right from Satavahana period till the Hoysalas and all intervening dynasties too patronized temples of Siva.

It is evident that Karnataka has been a hub of Saivite religious activities. Saivism being one of the oldest and most widely spread Hindu cults, consisted of several sub-sects like *Pasupata, Lakulisa, Kalamukha, Kapalika, Natha-pantha* etc. *Virashaivism* too is deeply rooted in Karnataka. Siva temples in Karnataka are known by over 150 different names, the most popular among them being, Iswara, Mulsthaneswara, Mahadeva, Someswara, Chandrasekhara, Mallikarjuna, Nageswara, Siva, Kalleswara, Rameswara. Prominent temples dedicated to Siva are located at Aralaguppe (Kalleswara, Nolambas), Alur (Arkeswara and Deseswara, Gangas of Talkad), Rameswara (Narasamangala, Gangas of Talkad), Pataleswara (Talkad, Gangas of Talkad), Someswara (Madivala Bengaluru, Cholas), Someswara (Kolar, Cholas), Kamaleswara (Shiggaon, Rashtrakutas), Kalleswara (Bagali, Rashtrakutas/Kalyani Chalukyas), Kasivisveswara (Lakkundi, Kalyani Chalukyas), Navalina (Kuknur, Rashtrakutas), Mallikarjuna (Pattadakal, Chalukyas of Badami), Bhutanatha (Badami, Kalyani Chalukyas), Kedareswara (Balligavi, Hoysalas), Mallikarjuna (Basaralu, Hoysalas), Panchaligeswara (Barkur, Alupas), Bhoganandiswara (Nandi, Nolambas), Pranaveswara (Talagunda, Kadambas), Hoysaleswara (Halebid, Hoysalas) and many more places.

Visnu

Next to Saivism, Vaishnavism seems to have been the most popular Hindu sect as is evidenced by the number of temples in Karnataka and epigraphical records. Visnu in Rig Veda is sun-god. According to Vaishnavism, Visnu is the Supreme Being and He alone is the manifestation of the Universe. Vaishnavism too was patronized by all dynasties in Karnataka. However, proliferation of Visnu temples occurred only after the 10th century and Cholas and Hoysalas were responsible for the construction of the largest number of Vaishnavite temples even though temples dedicated to Visnu were built as early as 6th century by the Chalukyas of Badami.

The earliest inscriptional reference to Visnu is assignable to the Gangas of Talkad. It is assigned to the reign of king Madhava III (440–469 CE) and was found at Keregalur in Hassan district. Temples of Visnu belonging to various periods are located at Halasi (Bhoo Varaha Lakshminarasimha temple, Kadambas), Cave 3 at Badami is dedicated to Visnu (Chalukyas of Badami), Srirangapatna (Sriranganathaswamy, Gangas of Talkad), Domlur, Bengaluru (Chokkanathaswamy, Cholas), Belavadi (Veeranarayana, Hoysalas), Javagal (Lakshminarasimha, Hoysalas), Malurpatna (Narayanaswamy, Cholas), Marehalli (Lakshminarasimha, Cholas), Melukote (Cheluvanarayana, Hoysalas), Thondanur (Nambinarayana, Hoysalas) Talkad (Kirtinarayana, Hoysalas), Hangala (Varadarajaswamy, Gangas of Talkad), Narasapur (Ugranarasimha, Kalyani Chalukyas).

One temple that needs special mention for its magnificent idol is Veeranarayana temple at Ingaleshwar of 11th century CE built during the times of Kalyani Chalukyas. This temple located in an obscure location hidden among a cluster of residential units houses an amazingly beautiful image of Narayana (Visnu).

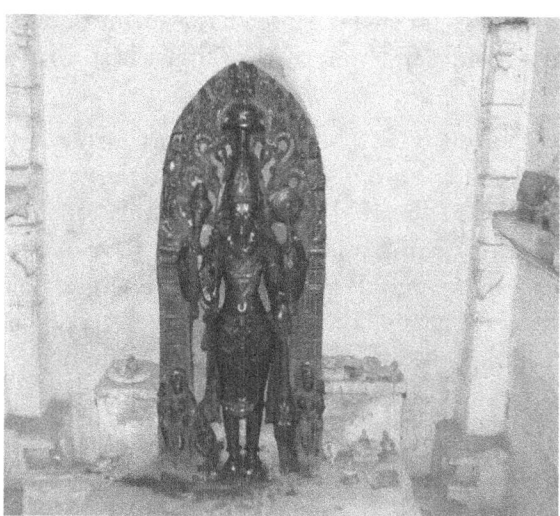 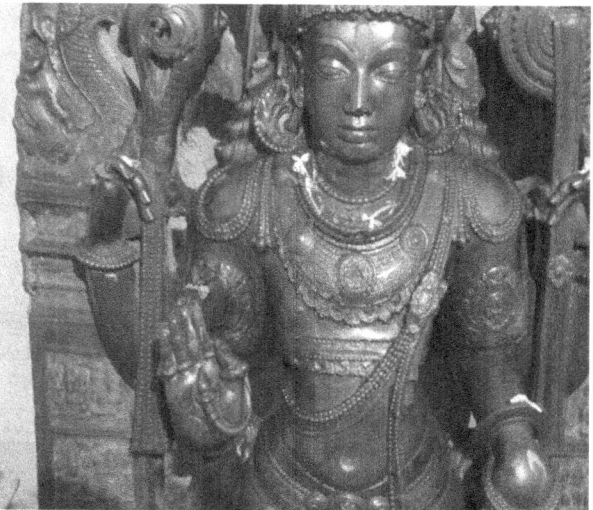

Three-feet Tall Exquisite Idol of Visnu at Veeranarayana Temple Ingaleshwar

Visnu is believed to have ten incarnations. Among them Rama and Krishna are very popular. Karnataka's mythological links with Ramayana are very well known. Temples dedicated to Rama are located at various places. However, inscriptional references to these temples are few. The important historical Rama temples in Karnataka are located at Hiremagalur (Kodandarama, Gangas of Talkad), Kudlur (Ramadevaru Sitadevi temple, Cholas), Ramanathapura (Pattabhirama, Hoysalas). Kodandarama temple at Hiremagalur perhaps is the earliest Rama temple in Karnataka. This temple is assigned to the Ganga king Madhava II (461–485 CE) which was later expanded during the times of the king Nitimarga II (904–919 CE).

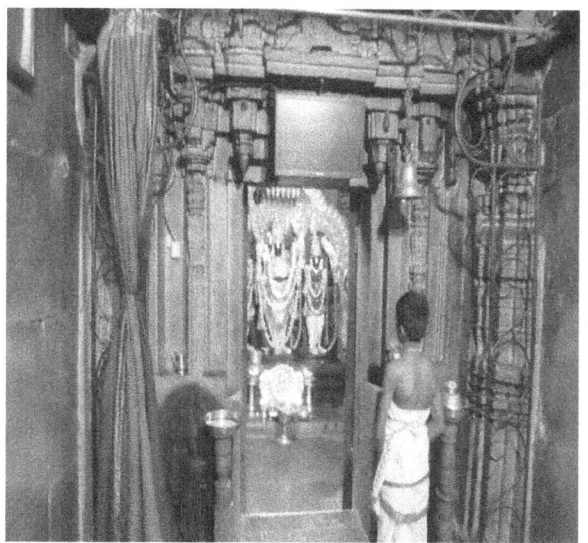 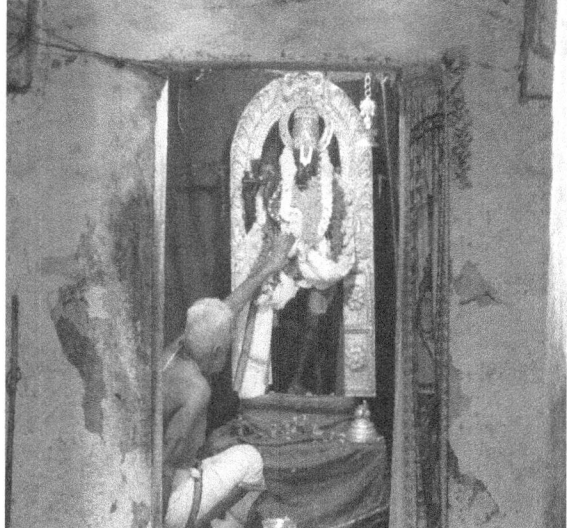

Kodandarama Temple Hiremagalur and Krishna Idol at Gopalakrishna Temple Honganur

Temples dedicated to Krishna in Karnataka are numerous with all Kesava temples built during Hoysala period being dedicated to him. The earliest reference to *Krsna* in inscriptional records is assignable to the Chola king Rajendra Chola Deva I and is dated 1013 CE and found at Honganur near Channapatna. This inscription refers to a land grant for the god Kundavai-Vinnagar-Alvar (Visnu) and is now called Gopalakrishna temple. Gopalakrishna temple in Honganur has two unique features. Krishna's idol here depicts the legs in a manner opposite to normally it is seen in Krishna's images. Instead of the right leg crossing in front of the left one as is usual, the idol here has the left leg crossed in front of the right one. And instead of the leg in front being bent to stand on the toe, it is the leg behind that is bent to be standing on the toe. Another feature of the temple is that Krishna's foster mother Yashoda has a shrine dedicated to her next to Krishna's shrine. Another temple dedicated to Krishna and built by the Cholas is the Navanitha Krishna temple at Doddamalur.

The Krishna temple at Udupi dates back to the 13th century CE. The idol here was installed by the Vaishvanite saint Madhavacharya. It is said that once Kanakadasa, a pious worshipper and devotee of Lord Krishna, was staying in a makeshift hermitage in front of Krishna *matha*. There was an earthquake in the night and the outer wall of the temple cracked leaving a wide opening for Kanakadasa to have *darshana* of the idol. Till today, devotees worship Lord Krishna by praying through the same window where Kanakadasa was seeing the offerings/Pooja from outside. It is known as Kanakana khindi, and is decorated by an arch named after him. A statue of his has also been erected. A similar window covers the immediate front of the idol and is called Navagraha khindi.

Other prominent temples dedicated to Krishna in Karnataka are located at Belur (Chennakesava, Hoysalas), Chennakesava (Somanathapura, Hoysalas), Chennakesava (Dharampura, Hoysalas), Saumyakesava (Nagamangala, Hoysalas), Kesavaswamy and Krishna temple ensemble (Hoovina Hadagali, Kalyani Chalukyas).

Shakti and her various forms

Various different manifestations of the Shakti that one can come across in Karnataka are:

Mahishasuramardini

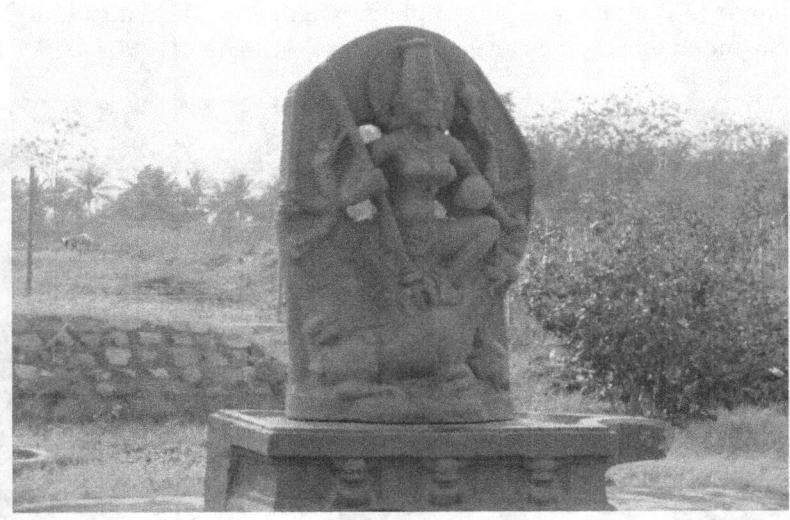

Mahishasuramardini from Rameswara Temple at Narasamangala

According to legend, Durga killed the demon Mahishasura, who was considered unconquerable. Hence, following his slaying, she was given the title Mahishasuramardini (conqueror of Mahisha). The story of this is retold in *Devimahatmyam* part of Markandeya Purana. Generally portrayal of Mahishasuramardini is that of Durga appearing with eight hands riding a fierce-looking lion. She is holding *khadga* (sword), *dhanush* (bow), *bana* (arrows), *ghanta* (bell) in her four right hands; her four left hands display *pasa*, *sankha*, and dagger. An attendant holds a *chatra* (parasol) over Durga's head. She is in the battlefield with her army of female warriors and *ganas* (dwarfs). She is shown attacking, with arrows, the demon Mahisha, causing him to retreat with his followers. Mahishasura is armed with a *gada* (club). Mahisha is a zoomorphic buffalo or the biomorphic (half animal with buffalo head on human body). Mahishasuramardini is a popular cult deity in India through the ages.

Chowdeswari

Centuries ago, it is said, that there was a kingdom called Nandavaram on the banks of the river Tunga in Karnataka. According to a legend the king of Nandavaram was a Shakti *upasaka* (devotee). With the help of Mantra Shakti, the king used to wake up at 4 O'clock in the morning, reach Kasi, bathe, in the holy Ganga and return to his kingdom before dawn and offer worship to *Devi* at Nandavarma. This was his daily practice. Maharani becoming suspicious of his absence questioned the king. The king revealed everything in detail. She having made up her mind to test the king compelled him to take her also with him. The king reluctantly accepted. The next day, he took her to Kasi along with him. Rani had her monthly course during their stay at Kasi. This affected the king and he lost his Mantra Shakti. As he was unable to return to his kingdom as usual, the King became restless and worried.

While walking along the banks of Ganga being unable to find a solution, he saw a group of Brahmans performing Chandi Homa and went near them. The Brahmans, having learnt the reasons for his restlessness promised to pass on to the king one fourth of what they had acquired as *punya* (religious merit) by offering Arghya to Surya every day at the appropriate time which would purify Rani and enable them to return to their kingdom. They asked the king what he would give them in return for their help. The king promised to give grants to them for purposes of their performing religious and charitable deeds whenever they approached him. Thus the king got the power from the Brahmans and returned to his kingdom. He did never again make use of Mantra Shakti.

Years rolled on. There came a terrible famine in Kasi. The Brahmans having remembered the king's promise went to Nandavaram and met him. They reminded him of his promise. The king had totally forgotten his promise. He abused the Brahmans and incurred their displeasure. From that day onwards all the efforts of the king started yielding negative results. The Brahmans worshipped Chowdeswari and requested her to come down to Nandavaram as the only witness for the king's promise. Devi did as they desired. The king realized his mistake. He appealed to Devi and Brahmans.

The dynasty of Brahmans thus settled at Nandavaram came to be known as Nandavariks and Chowdeswari became their *Kuladevata*, she is also the family deity of *Thogataveeras*. There still exists a beautiful temple of Chowdeswari at Nandavaram on the banks of Tungabadra and she is being worshipped on all the days of the year.

Temples dedicated to Chowdeswari exist in abundance largely in the southern districts. Western Gangas and Cholas patronized numerous temples in her honour.

Lakshmi

Lakshmi is the Hindu goddess of wealth, fortune, and prosperity (both material and spiritual), as well as the embodiment of beauty. She is the wife and active energy of Visnu. Representations of Lakshmi are also found in Jaina monuments. Lakshmi is also called *Thirumagal* because she is endowed with six auspicious and divine qualities, or *Gunas*, and also because she is the source of strength even to Visnu. When Visnu incarnated on the Earth as the *avatars* Rama and Krishna, Lakshmi incarnated as his consort: Sita (Rama's wife), and Rukmini (Krishna's wife). In the ancient scriptures of India, all women are declared to be embodiments of Lakshmi. Lakshmi's iconography and statues have also been found in Hindu temples throughout southeast Asia, estimated to be from second half of 1st millennium CE. In modern times, Lakshmi is worshiped as the goddess of wealth. She is also worshipped as the consort of Visnu in many temples.

The image, icons, and sculptures of Lakshmi are represented with symbolism. Her name is derived from Sanskrit root words for knowing the goal and understanding the objective (*lakshaya*). Her four arms are symbolic of the four goals of humanity that are considered good in Hinduism -*dharma* (pursuit of ethical, moral life), *artha* (pursuit of wealth, means of life), *kama* (pursuit of love, emotional fulfillment), and *moksha* (pursuit of self-knowledge, liberation).

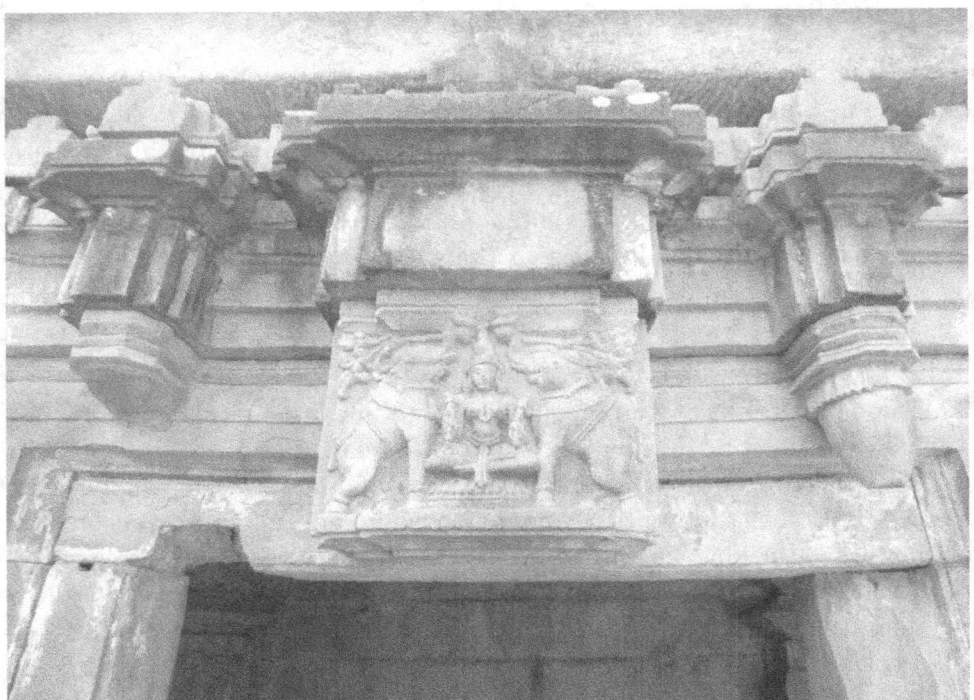

Gajalakshmi on the Lintel at Prabhulingeswara Temple Balligavi

In Lakshmi's iconography, she is either sitting or standing on a lotus and typically carrying a lotus in one or two hands. The lotus carries symbolic meanings in Hinduism and other Indian traditions. It symbolically represents reality, consciousness, and *karma* (work, deed) in the Sahasrara context, and knowledge and self-realization in other contexts. The lotus, a flower that blossoms in clean or dirty water, also symbolizes purity and beauty regardless of the good or bad circumstances in which its grows. It is a reminder that good and prosperity can bloom and not be affected by evil in one's surrounding. Below, behind, or on the sides, Lakshmi is sometimes shown with one or two elephants and occasionally with an owl. Elephants symbolize work, activity, and strength, as well as water, rain, and fertility for abundant prosperity. The owl, called *Pechaka* in eastern regions of India, signifies the patient striving to observe, see, and discover knowledge particularly when surrounded by darkness. The owl, a bird that becomes blind in daylight, is also a symbolic reminder to refrain from blindness and greed after knowledge and wealth has been acquired.

The most well known temple of goddess Lakshmi in Karnataka was built by the Hoysalas called Lakshmidevi temple at Dodda Gaddavalli near Hassan. This temple has four principal shrines dedicated to Kali, Lakshmi, Visnu and Siva as Linga. The Kali shrine is guarded by two *vetalas* showing only skin over skeletons. The shrine where cult-image of Lakshmi is housed is on the eastern side and has a closed *antarala*. The southern *garbhagriha* has Visnu image on a pedestal and the western one has a Linga. The most important shrine here is that of Lakshmi.

In the Lakshmi Narasimha temple at Marehalli near Malavalli in Mandya district, Lakshmi is seated on the left lap of Visnu. The temple doors are graced by Bhudevi and Neeladevi and these deities too are worshipped in this temple. Prominent among the beliefs here is that an *Amrutkalasa* (pot filled with nectar) lies beneath the feet of Lakshmi which when invoked with devotion fulfills all desires.

Saraswati

Saraswati is the Hindu goddess of knowledge, music, arts, wisdom and learning. She is a part of the trinity of Saraswati, Lakshmi and Parvati. All the three forms help the trinity of Brahma, Visnu and Siva to create, maintain and regenerate-recycle the Universe respectively.

The earliest known mention of Saraswati as a goddess is in Rigveda. She is also revered by believers of the Jaina religion of west and central India, as well as some Buddhist sects. The goddess Saraswati is often depicted as a beautiful woman dressed in pure white often seated on a white lotus, which symbolizes light, knowledge and truth. She not only embodies knowledge but also the experience of the highest reality. Her iconography is typically in white themes from dress to flowers to swan-the colour symbolizing *Sattwa Guna* or purity, discrimination for true knowledge, insight and wisdom. She is generally shown to have four arms, but sometimes just two. When shown with four hands, those hands symbolically mirror her husband Brahma's four heads, representing *manas* (mind, sense), *buddhi* (intellect), *citta* (imagination) and *ahamkara* (self-consciousness). Brahma represents the abstract, whereas she action and reality.

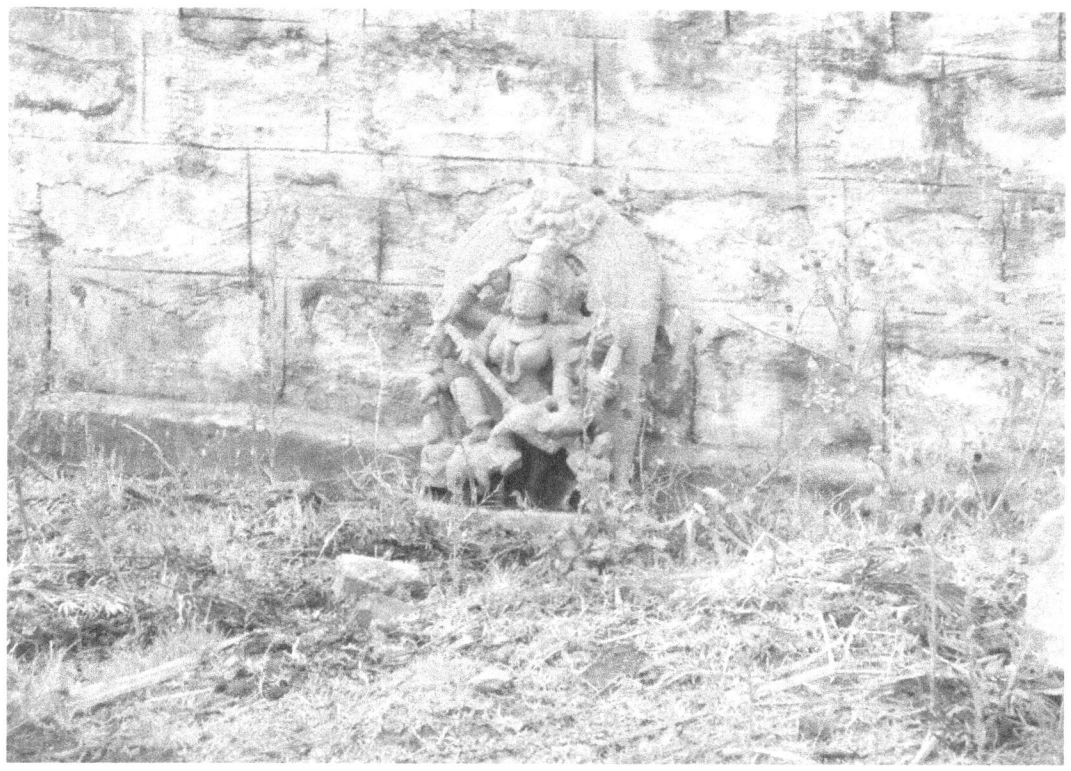

Broken Image of Saraswati from Iswara Temple Malali

The four hands hold items with symbolic meaning -a *pustaka* (book or script), a *mala* (rosary, garland), a water pot and a musical instrument (lute or *veena*). The book she holds symbolizes the Vedas representing the universal, divine, eternal, and true knowledge as well as all forms of learning. The *mala* of crystals represents the power of meditation, inner reflection and spirituality. The pot of water represents powers to purify the right from wrong, the clean from unclean, and the essence from the misleading. In some texts, the pot of water is symbolism for soma -the drink that liberates and leads to knowledge. The musical instrument, typically a *veena*, represents all creative arts and sciences, and her holding it symbolizes expressing knowledge that creates harmony. Saraswati is also associated with *anuraga*, the love for and rhythm of music, which represents all emotions and feelings expressed in speech or music.

A *hamsa* or swan is often located next to her feet. In Hindu mythology, *hamsa* is a sacred bird. It thus symbolizes discrimination between the good from the bad, the essence from the superficial, the eternal from the evanescent. Due to her association with the swan, Saraswati is also referred to as Hamsavahini, which means 'she who has a *hamsa* as her vehicle.' Sometimes a *citramekhala* (also called *mayura*, peacock) is shown beside the goddess. The peacock symbolizes colorful splendor, celebration of dance, and peacock's ability to eat poison (snakes) yet transmute from it a beautiful plumage.

Aditi or Lajja Gouri

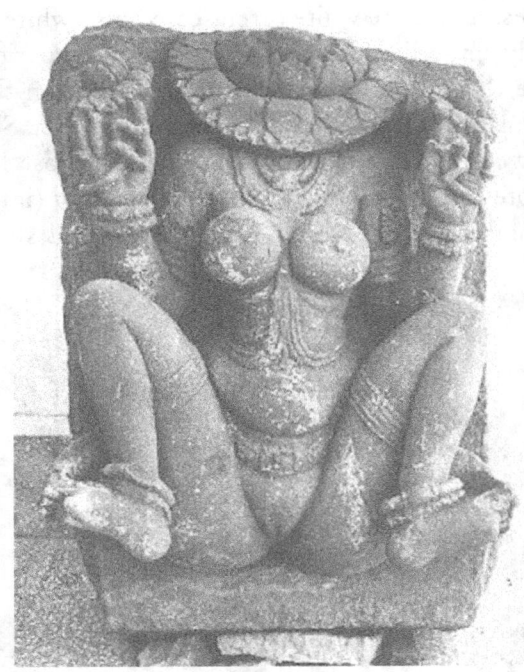

7th Century Image of Lajja-Gauri from Aihole (Wikipedia)

Lajja Gouri is one of the cult divinities whose nomenclature and iconography along with its origin and development are yet to be completely understood. Conceptually, Lajja Gouri antecedents have been traced back to Indus Valley Civilization of about 2500–1500 BCE. It is also opined that Lajja Gouri may have originated either as a tribal or local level *gramadevi* with pot serving as her original aniconic form.

Goddess in her form as Lajja Gouri is also known as Aditi, Adya Shakti, Matangi, Renuka, Yellamma, Nagna-Kabanda, Kamalamma and many other names. She is the most ancient goddess form in Hinduism. This mysterious, lotus-headed Goddess, who is always portrayed with legs opened and raised in a manner suggesting either birthing (her posture is the traditional Indian village posture for giving birth) or sexual receptivity, is most frequently referred to as Lajja Gauri. Lajja Gauri is still actively worshiped even today as a "fertility goddess" in some rural locales.

The first scriptural references to Aditi appear in no less exalted a source than the Rig Veda itself. Here, she is also referred to as *Uttanapad* because of the posture in which she is seated. Whatever Lajja Gauri's ultimate origins, she is clearly a very auspicious goddess. Everything about her suggests life, creativity, and abundance. Her images are almost always associated with springs, waterfalls and other sources of running water -vivid symbols of life-giving sustenance. Her belly usually protrudes, suggesting fullness and/or pregnancy; in earlier sculptures, her torso was often portrayed as an actual pot, another ancient symbol of wealth and abundance. Lajja Gauri's head is usually a lotus flower, an extremely powerful, elemental symbol of both material and spiritual well-being.

The legs, in *uttanapad*, are spread more naturally with the knees up, the feet are flexed with soles up, and the toes are tensed. The nude body is ornamented with necklace, *channavira* (body-encompassing jewelry that hangs from the neck, crosses between the breasts, passes around the waist and up the back), girdle, bracelets, and armlets that are like a vine tendril wrapping around the arms and actually ending in a leaf. Tassels of the anklets also seem plantlike. There is a cloth woven through the thighs.

It was John Fleet in 1881 who wrote his reaction on seeing for the first time Lajja Gouri image at Mahakuta. While Lajja Gouri's image can be seen at many temples in Karnataka, the earliest image probably dates back to 3rd–4th century CE found in Sannati. However, the most prominently known image is now housed in the museum at Badami. This stone image was taken from the Naganatha temple in Nagaral (Naganathakolla). The other image is on a mutilated slab in which the lotus head is replaced by a human one. Such images are also found in the Hucchimalli-gudi (plinth of the *agramandapa*) and Galaganatha group of temples in Aihole.

Saptamatrikas

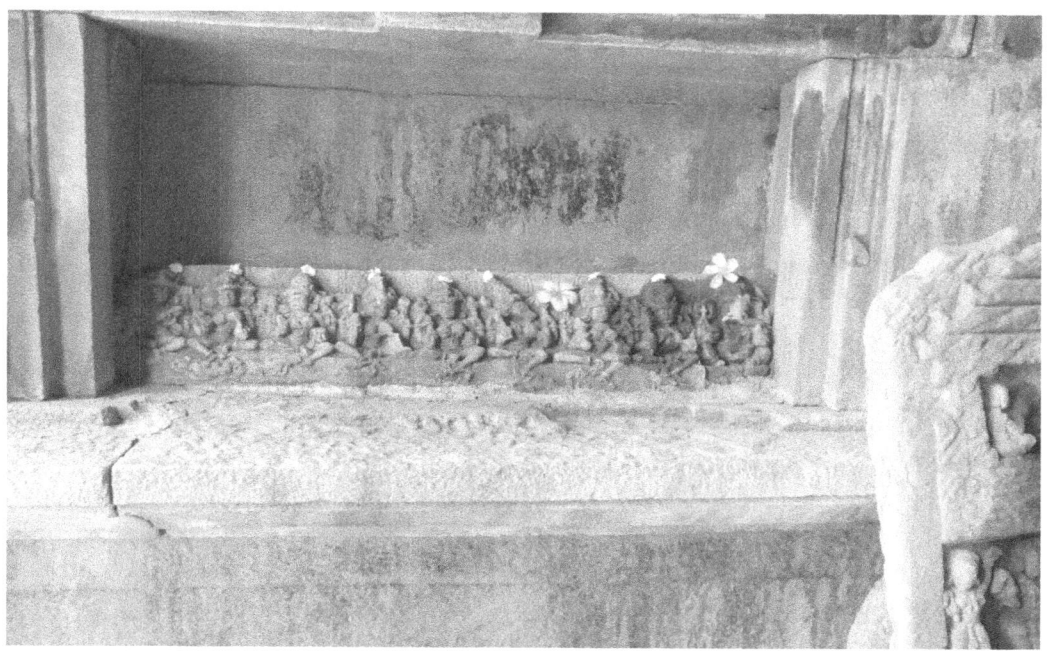

Saptamatrika Image from Kalameswara Temple Halasi of Kadamba Period

Matrikas also called *Matara* and *Matri* is a group of Hindu goddesses who are always depicted together. The word *Matrika* in Sanskrit means mother. Since they are usually depicted as a heptad, they are called Saptamatrika(s) ("seven mothers"). The *saptamatrikas* are, Brahmani, Vaishnavi, Maheswari, Indrani, Kaumari, Varahi, Chamunda and Narasimhi.

The *Matrikas* assume paramount significance in the goddess-oriented sect of Hinduism, Tantrism. In Shaktism, they are "described as assisting the great Shakta Devi (goddess) in her fight with demons." Some scholars consider them Saiva goddesses. They are also connected with the worship of warrior god Skanda. In most early references, the *Matrikas* are described as having inauspicious qualities and often described as dangerous. They come to play a protective role in later mythology, although some of their inauspicious and wild characteristics still persist in these accounts. Thus, they represent the prodigiously fecund aspect of nature as well as its destructive force aspect.

In the 6th century encyclopedia Brihat Samhita, Varahamihira says that "Mothers are to be made with cognizance of (different major Hindu) gods corresponding to their names." They are associated with these gods as their spouses or their energies (*Shaktis*). Originally believed to be a personification of the seven stars of the star cluster the Pleiades, they became quite popular by the seventh century and a standard feature of goddess temples from the ninth century onwards.

Sculpture of the *saptamatrikas* with Virabhadra on one side and Ganapati on the other and the seven *matrikas* in the middle are found in several Saivite temples in Karnataka. Saptamatrikas' sculpture can also be seen in various Hoysala temples carved on the outer walls. Large sized images of the *saptamatrikas* can be seen in Rameswara temple at Narasamangala and Arkeswara temple, Alur. Both the temples were constructed under the Western Ganga king's grants.

Lalita Tripurasundari

Tripurasundari (Beautiful Goddess of the Three Cities) also called Shodashi (Sixteen), Lalita (She Who Plays) and Rajarajeswari (Queen of Queens), is one of the group of ten goddesses of Hindu belief, collectively called *Mahavidyas* or *Dasha-Mahavidyas*. She is the foremost and the most important in *Dasha-Mahavidyas*. All other *Mahavidyas* conclude in her *vidya* i.e. Sri Vidya. Her consort is Maha Kameswara.

Tripurasundari is described as being of dusky, red, or golden in colour, depending on the meditational form, and in union with Siva. The couple is traditionally portrayed on a bed, a throne, or a pedestal that is upheld by Brahma, Vishnu, Rudra, Isana (another form of Siva, depicted in the Tantras) and Sadasiva forming the plank. She holds five arrows of flowers, a noose, a goad and sugarcane as a bow. The noose represents attachment, the goad represents repulsion, the sugarcane bow represents the mind and the arrows are the five sense objects.

Tripurasundari is also worshipped as the Sri Yantra, which is considered by practitioners of Sri Vidya to be a truer representation of the goddess. Tripurasundari combines in her being Kali's determination and Durga's charm, grace, and complexion. She has a third eye on her forehead. Usually four-armed and clad in red, the richly bejeweled Tripurasundari sits on a lotus seat laid on a golden throne. An aura of royalty characterizes her overall bearing and ambiance.

Lalita Tripurasundari is the presiding deity of the village Muguru located in the T.Narsipura taluk. There is an ancient temple of the goddess in the village. Another temple of Tripurasundari is located at Utanalli in Mysore.

Yogini cult

Yogini is the female counterpart of *Yogi*, a master practitioner of *Yoga*. In the Hindu tradition, mother is first guru (teacher) and in the Yoga tradition, proper respect of *Yoginis* is a necessary part of the path to liberation. A *Yogini* is the sacred feminine force made incarnate: the goddesses of mythology (Lakshmi, Parvati, Durga, Kali) as well as the ordinary human woman who is enlightened, both having exuberant passion, spiritual powers and deep insight, capable of giving birth to saints, peacemakers, and *Yogis*.

In some branches of *tantra Yoga*, ten wisdom goddesses (or *dakinis*) serve as models for a *Yogini's* disposition and behavior. In the mythological context, the word *Yogini* may indicate an advanced *Yoga* practitioner who is one or more of the following:

- A female who is an associate or attendant of Durga, a fierce aspect of the Divine Feminine, who slays illusion and delusion through insight and liberation.
- In several Tantric cults, the term refers to an initiated female who may take part in *maithuna* tantric rituals.

In Kolaramma temple in Kolar, Chola king Rajendra I built a new *Saptamatrika* shrine adjacent to the original shrine. In one of the inscriptions there is reference to the *Yogini* cult and is possibly related to the additional shrine. The record inscribed lists the various deities for whose worship the offerings were made included the *saptamatrikas* with Ganapati and Veerabhadra, Chamundeswari of the *Mulsthana*, Yogeswari, Kshetrapala-devatas, Maha Sasta and Surya deva. Provision was made for offering intoxicating drinks as part of worship of *Yogeswara* and *Yogini*.

Surya

Surya worship was popular among different classes of the society and even royal patronage was available for building Surya temples. In Karnataka, temples of Surya were constructed under the more popular name as Aditya. The fact that Aditya was a popular god is also reflected from the fact that many kings had -aditya as the ending part of their name such as Vikramaditya, Vijayaditya, Vinayaditya and Abhinavadiya.

Though various independent temples were built dedicated to sun god, shrines dedicated to Surya inside larger temple complexes too also existed. A shrine dedicated to Surya stands facing the Siva in Kalleswara temple at Bagali. Durga temple at Aihole is believed to have been dedicated to Surya.

Syncretistic gods

Kesavaditya, Ardhanarisvara, Sankara-narayana, Surya-narayana and Visnu Maheswara were the common syncretistic forms of gods in whose honour temples were built either as principal deity or as having a shrine dedicated to them in a larger temple complex. Temples with all three gods constituting the Hindu trinity viz. Brahma, Visnu and Maheswara too were built. Such temples were called the Traipurusha temples. An interesting aspect of Traipurusha worship was their association with *salas* (schools). In an inscription of the Rashtrakutas dated 945 CE, with reference to a Trapurusha *sala* that was located at Salotgi *agrahara* was found.

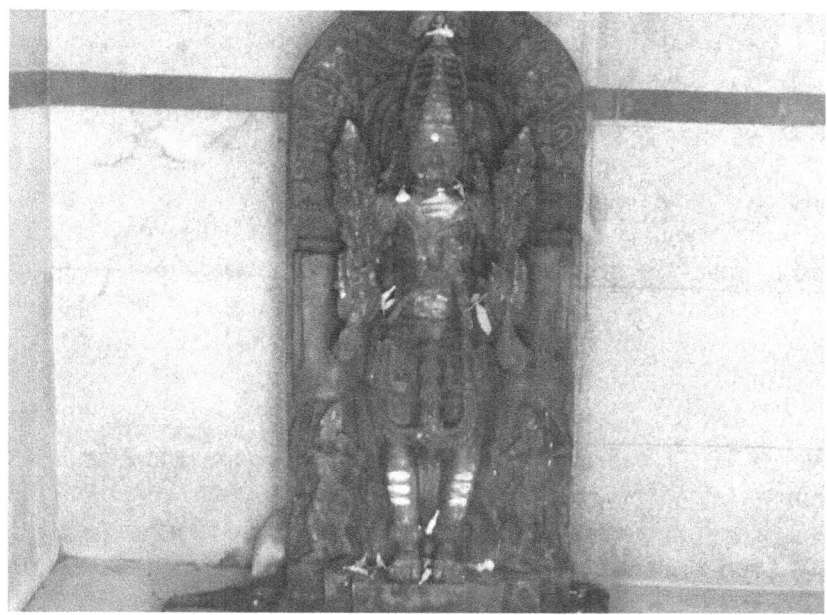

Surya Image from Kalleswara Temple Aralaguppe

Temples dedicated to Brahma are fewer in number in Karnataka. However, images of Brahma can be found in several temples. A Chaturmukha Brahma image (four-faced Brahma) is kept in front of the door to the *garbhgriha* of the Braham Jinalaya at Lakkundi.

Village deities

The worship of village deities is considered the little tradition in Hinduism. Some village deities have their origin in the tribal gods of yore. The village as a social and cultural unit very often seeks the protection of a village deity from all evils. Among the worship of village deities, the worship of female deities dominates the worship of male deities. They are worshipped as the guardian deities and are monistic with regard to ethical symbolism. These deities are believed to control weather, in particular rains, to bring and cure epidemic and animal diseases and to guard the village against natural calamities. The worship of village deities has been practiced much before the onset of *Puranic* gods. However, kings from various dynasties patronized village deities and gave grants of lands for building temples dedicated to them.

The Naga image housed in Madhukeswara temple in Banavasi given by the Chutu princess seems to have been the village deity of those times. The inscription found at Banashankari temple near Badami from the period of king Jayasimha II and dated 1019 CE records that Dwvoja (sculptor) was the servant of Banadadevi (forest goddess). Another inscription found at Banashankari issued under the same king in 1024 CE states that Ketimayya, the *maanevergade* (superintendent) erected a stone pillar in front of the temple of Banadadevi, the goddess of forest or vegetation. It seems to have been a village deity and later became popular by the name Banashankari and so did the village. Usually, the suffix *abbe* is found with the names of local goddesses, many scholars argue that Banadadevi was in fact Banadabbe.

4.6 DESCRIPTION OF ICONOGRAPHY OF DIFFERENT GODS

Hindus believe gods and spirits are peripatetic and have a potential for varied manifestations. Chief deities appear in a wide variety of forms, expressing their multiple roles and moods. These forms can be iconic, that is, with a resemblance to human form; or aniconic, in other words, in an abstract symbolic form such as a pile of stones or a linga or a geometric configuration like the *yantras* or *chakras*. Organic and inorganic matter is perceived as a potential residence for a deity or spirit, particularly the sacred images produced for veneration in a temple or domestic shrine. The image is generally required to be beautiful to encourage the deity to enter it, and the material from which it was made must be unblemished. Divine energy is believed to be infused by ritual, and the final task of the ceremony is to open the eyes of the image by means of a specific chanted *mantra* (spoken or sung religious formula) and the completion by the artist of this part of his work.

To be ritually effective and sacred an image must be given the correct preparation and invocation, after which it is perceived not only as an icon or symbol but is also believed to hold a numinous presence. The image is also said to emanate a particle of the divine whole, the divine perceived not in man's image as a separate entity but as a formless, indescribable omnipresent whole. The image allows the worshipper to catch a reflection of the deity whose effulgence transcends what the physical eye can see. This divine effulgence is beheld in man's inner vision. An image is a *murthy* not because it resembles the deity it represents but because it conforms to prescribed measurements and symbolic conventions.

Hindu images have a very distinct appearance. The deities possess human or animal characteristics but represent superhuman beings. They are portrayed sometimes with many upper limbs, sometimes with more than one head. They express mood and movement in their posture and gesture; they hold emblems and can be placed in dynamic relation to other figures or symbolic animals. They inhabit realms beyond our normal existence. This mythical world and the gods who inhabit it express the Hindu belief that 'the universe is boundlessly various, that everything occurs simultaneously and that all possibilities are not mutually exclusive.' Hindu aniconic and iconic symbols seek to represent forces and energies -aspects of a single supreme undifferentiated Iswara which is unmanifest and in real terms unrepresentable.

While iconographic description of various forms and manifestations of Shakti has already been included in Section 4.5, attributes of other principal Hindu gods and subsidiary gods follows:

Siva's attributes in Hindu iconography

Siva is recognized from the following attributes in the Hindu iconography:

- **Siva's form:** Siva has a trident in the right lower arm, and a crescent moon on his head. He is said to be fair like camphor or like an ice clad mountain. He wears five serpents and a garland of skulls as ornaments. Siva is usually depicted facing the south. His trident, like almost all other forms in Hinduism, can be understood as the symbolism of the unity of three worlds that a human faces -his inside world, his immediate world, and the broader overall world. At the base of the trident, all three forks unite. It is often not shown but Siva has 6 heads, of which only five (Isana, Tatpurusha, Vamadeva, Aghora, Sadyojata) are visible while the 6th (Adhomukh) can only be seen by the enlightened.

- **Third eye:** (Trilochana) Siva is often depicted with a third eye, with which he burned Desire (Kama) to ashes, called "Tryambakam" which occurs in many scriptural sources. In classical Sanskrit, the word *ambaka* denotes "an eye," and in the Mahabharata, Siva is depicted as three-eyed, so his name Trymbakeswara is sometimes translated as "having three eyes." However, in Vedic Sanskrit, the word *amba* or *ambika* means "mother," and this early meaning of the word is the basis for the translation "three mothers." These three mother-goddesses are collectively called the Ambikas.

- **Crescent moon:** (The epithets "Chandrasekhara/Chandramouli") Siva bears on his head the crescent moon. The epithet Chandrasekhara, "Having the moon as his crest" (*chandra* meaning "moon"; *sekhara* meaning "crest, crown") refers to this feature. The placement of the moon on his head as a standard iconographic feature dates to the period when Rudra rose to prominence and became the major deity Rudra-Siva. The origin of this linkage may be due to the identification of the moon with Soma, and there is a hymn in the Rig Veda where Soma and Rudra are jointly implored and in later literature, Soma and Rudra came to be identified with one another, as were Soma and the moon. The crescent moon is shown on the side of the Siva's head as an ornament. The waxing and waning phenomenon of the moon symbolizes the time cycle through which creation evolves from the beginning to the end.

- **Ashes:** (The epithet "Bhasmaanga Raaga") -Siva smears his body with ashes (*bhasma*). The ashes are said to represent the end of all material existence. Some forms of Siva, such as Bhairava, are associated with a very old Indian tradition of cremation-ground asceticism that was practiced by some groups who were outside the fold of brahmanic orthodoxy. These practices associated with cremation grounds are also mentioned in the Pali canon of Theravada Buddhism. One epithet for Siva is "inhabitant of the cremation ground" (Sanskrit: *smasanavasin*, also spelled *Shmashanavasin*), referring to this connection.

- **Matted hair:** (The epithet "Jataajoota Dhari/Kapardina") – Siva's distinctive hair style is noted in the epithets Jaṭin, "the one with matted hair" and Kapardin, "endowed with matted hair" or "wearing his hair wound in a braid in a shell-like (*kaparda*) fashion." A *kaparda* is a cowrie shell, or a braid of hair in the form of a shell, or, more generally, hair that is shaggy or curly.

- **Blue throat:** (Nilakaṇṭha, *nila* meaning "blue," *kaṇtha* meaning "throat") Since Siva drank the Halahala poison churned up from the Samudra Manthan to eliminate its destructive capacity. Shocked by his act, Goddess Parvati strangled his neck and hence managed to stop it in his neck itself and prevent it from spreading all over the universe, supposed to be in Siva's stomach. However the poison was so potent that it changed the color of his neck to blue.

- **Sacred Ganges:** (The epithet "Gangadhara"-Bearer of Ganga) Ganges river flows from the matted hair of Siva. The *Ganga* (Ganges), one of the major rivers of the country, is said to have made her abode in Siva's hair. The flow of the Ganges also represents the nectar of immortality.

- **Tiger skin:** (The epithet "Krittivasana") He is often shown seated upon a tiger skin, an honour reserved for the most accomplished of Hindu ascetics, the Brahmarishis.

- **Serpents:** (The epithet "Nagendra Haara" or"'Vasuki"). Siva is often shown garlanded with a snake.

- **Deer:** His holding deer on one hand indicates that He has removed the *Chanchalata* of the mind (i.e., attained maturity and firmness in thought process). A deer jumps from one place to another swiftly, similar to the mind moving from one thought to another.

- **Trident:** (*Trisula*): Siva's particular weapon is the trident. His *Trisula* that is held in His right hand represents the three *Gunas* viz. *Sattva*, *Rajas* and *Tamas*. That is the emblem of sovereignty. He rules the world through these three *Gunas*.

- **Drum:** A small drum shaped like an hourglass known as a *damaru*. This is one of the attributes of Siva in his famous dancing representation known as Nataraja. A specific hand gesture (*mudra*) called *ḍamaru-hasta* (Sanskrit for "ḍamaru-hand") is used to hold the drum. This drum is particularly used as an emblem by members of the Kapalika sect.

- **Axe:** (*Parasu*): The *parasu* is the weapon of Lord Siva who gave it to Parasurama, sixth *avatara* of Visnu, whose name means "Rama with the axe" and also taught him its mastery.

- **Nandi:** (The epithet "Nandi Vaahana") Nandi is the name of the bull that serves as Siva's mount (Sanskrit: *vahana*). Siva's association with cattle is reflected in his name Pasupati, translated as "lord of cattle." Rishabha or the bull represents *Dharma Devata*. Lord Siva rides on the bull. This denotes that Lord Siva is the protector of Dharma, is an embodiment of Dharma or righteousness.

- **Gaṇa:** The *Gaṇas* are attendants of Siva and live in Kailasa. They are often referred to as the *bhutaganas*, or ghostly hosts, on account of their nature. Generally benign, except when their lord is transgressed against, they are often invoked to intercede with the lord on behalf of the devotee. Ganesha was chosen as their leader by Siva, hence Ganesha's title *gaṇa-pati*, "lord of the *gaṇas*."

- **5 heads:** Siva is known as *panchavactra* means 5 heads which indicates 5 elements.

- **Arms:** Siva has 4 arms which signify the four Vedas.

- **Mount Kailasa:** Mount Kailasa in the Himalayas is his traditional abode. In Hindu mythology, Mount Kailasa is conceived as resembling a *Linga*, representing the centre of the universe.

Apart from anthropomorphic images of Siva, the worship of Siva in the form of a *linga*, is also important. These are depicted in various forms. One common form is the shape of a vertical rounded column. Siva means auspiciousness, and *linga* means a sign or a symbol. Hence, the *Sivalinga* is regarded as a "symbol of the great God of the universe who is all-auspiciousness." Siva also means "one in whom the whole creation sleeps after dissolution." *Linga* also means the same thing -a place where created objects get dissolved during the disintegration of the created universe.

"Lingam" is one of the most misunderstood motifs of Hinduism. Merriam-Webster dictionary defines it as a stylized phallic symbol. The expression '*linga*' in the *Agama* context signifies 'symbol' (*chinha*). Derived from the root '*ligi gatyau*,' it refers to movement, and words having been movement as their etymological meaning have also connotations of knowledge ('*sarve gatyarthah jnanarthah*'). Linga therefore means that by which the Divine is cognized or approached ('*lingyate jnayate anena iti lingam*'). Siva as Linga, his aniconic unmanifest form has a wider presence in Saivite tradition than the anthropomorphic forms.

The *Agama* texts also bring out another valid explanation for the word '*linga*': *linga* in its primary sense is broken up into '*ling*' (to dissolve, to get merged, to destroy) and '*ga*' (to emerge, to go out). Linga is so called because all phenomena are dissolved in Siva at the time of cosmic dissolution, and it emerges from Siva once again at the time of creation (Ajitagama). Traditionally, the linga is rather seen as a symbol of the energy and potential of God, Siva himself. The lingam is often represented alongside the *yoni* (Sanskrit word, literally "origin" or "source" or "womb"), a symbol of the goddess or of Shakti, female creative energy. The union of lingam and *yoni* represents the 'indivisible two-in-oneness of male and female, the passive space and active time from which all life originates.'

Linga represents Cosmic Egg ('*Brahmanda*' in Sanskrit) who has neither beginning nor end. It is believed that this changing world (*Jagat* in Sanskrit) merges or dissolves into the Formless in the end. So, the Linga is the simplest sign of emergence and mergence. Siva Lingam, therefore, symbolizes formless Lord Siva and as such is considered most sacred by Saivaites sects of Hindus.

The Hindu scripture *Siva Purana* also describes in its first section, the *Vidyeswar Samhita*, the origin of the lingam, known as Siva-linga, as the beginning-less and endless cosmic pillar (*Stambha*) of fire, the cause of all causes. Lord Siva is pictured as emerging from the Lingam -the cosmic pillar of fire -proving his superiority over gods Brahma and Visnu. This is known as Lingodbhava. The *Linga Purana* also supports this interpretation of lingam as a cosmic pillar, symbolizing the infinite nature of Siva. According to *Linga Purana*, the lingam is a complete symbolic representation of the formless Universe Bearer -the oval shaped stone resembling mark of the Universe and bottom base as the Supreme Power holding the entire Universe in it. Similar interpretation is also found in the *Skanda Purana*: "The endless sky (that great void which contains the entire Universe) is the Linga, the Earth is its base. At the end of time the entire universe and all the Gods finally merge in the Linga itself."

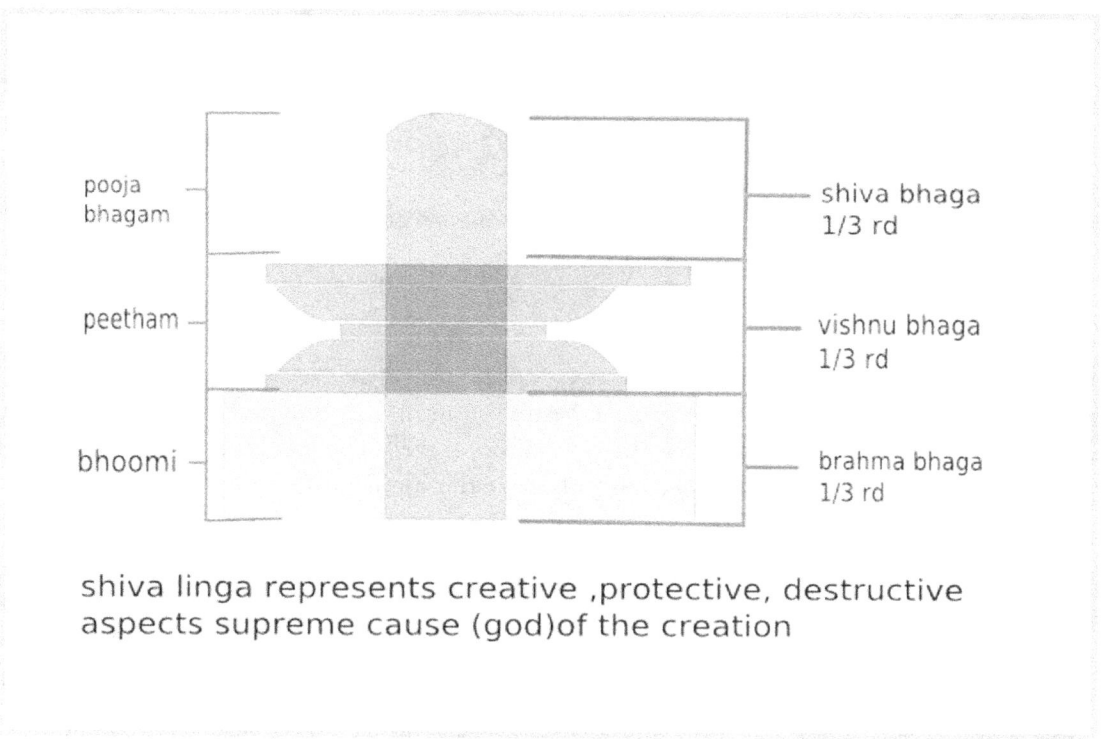

shiva linga represents creative ,protective, destructive aspects supreme cause (god)of the creation

The lingas in the temples are often formed in three parts. *Siva Purana*, in particular, has prescribed norms and standards for casting the Linga. The lowest part is the base square called the Brahmabhaga or Brahma-pitha, which represents the creator Brahma. The next part in the middle is the octagonal Visnubhaga or Visnu-pitha, which signifies Lord Visnu the sustainer. Both of these parts together form the pedestal. The top cylindrical portion is the Rudrabhaga or Siva-pitha, which is also called the Pujabhaga since this is the part that is worshipped by the devotees. The top portion is also meant to symbolize the projecting flame of fire. This flame also represents the destructive aspects as well as the preserving power of God.

Actual representation of three part structure of Siva Linga can be noticed in the picture of the Linga from Pranaveswara temple at Talagunda. The temple being under restoration, the Linga though fixed in its original spot of consecration about 2000 years ago, had been bared of the *peetham* and *yoni* parts before being reassembled to its actual form. The circular shaft, the part that is worshipped and is visible on top and the octagonal part of the shaft which constitutes the Visnu Bhaga too is clearly visible in the picture, whereas the square part is embedded in the ground and is not visible. Another picture of an abandoned Linga embedded in ground at Chowdeswari temple in Medithambihalli shows all the three parts. While the circular and octagonal parts of the shaft are fully visible, the square part is visible only in parts as much of it is inside the ground.

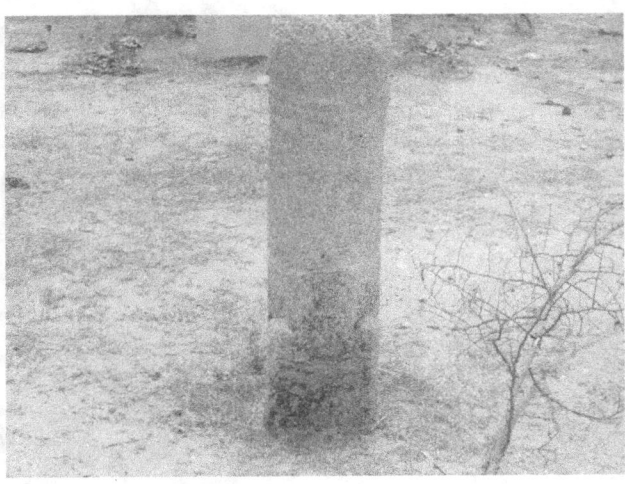 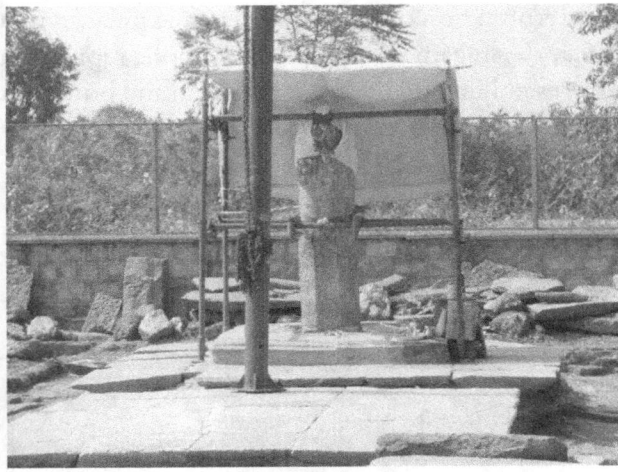

Linga Erected Outside Chowdeswari Temple Medithambihalli and Linga at Pranaveswara Temple Talagunda

Visnu

Visnu's mount *(Vahana)* is *Garuda*, the eagle. Visnu is commonly depicted as riding on his shoulders. *Garuda* is also considered as Vedas on which the Lord Visnu travels. *Garuda* is a sacred bird in Vaishnavam. In Gajendra Moksham, *Garuda* carries Lord Visnu to save the Elephant Gajendra.

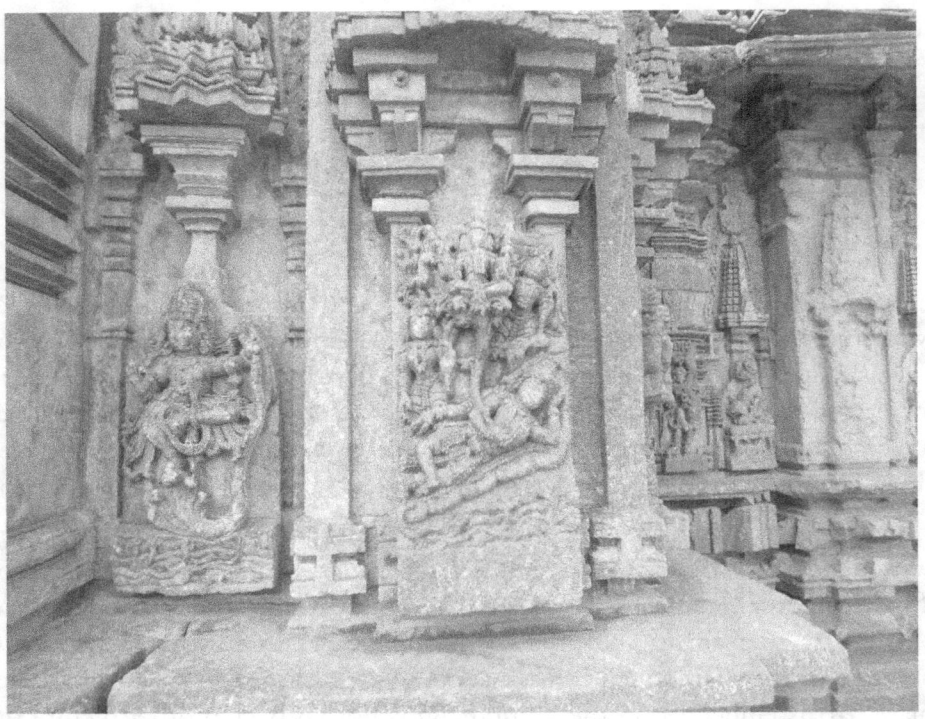

Anantasayana Visnu and Brahma Connected with His Navel at Bucheswara Temple Koravangala

Adherents of Hinduism believe Visnu's eternal and supreme abode beyond the material universe is called *Vaikuntha*, which is also known as *Paramdhama*, the realm of eternal bliss and happiness and the final or highest place for liberated souls who have attained *Moksha*. *Vaikuntha* is situated beyond the material universe and hence, cannot be perceived or measured by material science or logic. Vishnu's other abode within the material universe is *Ksheera Sagara* (the ocean of milk), where he reclines and rests on Ananta Sesha, (the king of the serpent deities, commonly shown with a thousand heads).

Anantasayi Visnu, also known as Anantasayana Visnu (both literally "sleeping on the serpent Sesha"), is the Hindu god Visnu in a reclining position (*Anantasayana* in Sanskrit, literally sleeping on the serpent Ananta). He has four arms, holding a *Chakra* in the upper right hand, a *Sankha* in his upper left hand, a *Gada* and a symbolic lotus on his lower left hand. The hoods of the serpent Sesha (Ananta) covering the head of Visnu. The Visnu image has a sharp chin, distinctive nose and wears a crown on its head, called *kiritamukuta* (a tall conical crown, typically worn by Vishnu). A lotus design shown sprouting from his navel has the creator god Brahma, sitting in meditation.

In almost all Hindu denominations, Visnu is either worshipped directly or in the form of his ten *avatars* (incarnations), the most famous of whom are Rama and Krishna.

The Puranabharati, an ancient text, describes these as the *dashavatara*, or the ten *avatars* of Vishnu. The list of *Dashavatara* varies across sects and regions but commonly it lists these names Matsya, Kurma, Varaha, Narasimha, Vamana, Parasurama, Rama, Krishna, Gautam Buddha and Kalki.

Brahma

Brahma is clad in red clothes. Brahma is traditionally depicted with four heads, four faces, and four arms. With each head, he continually recites one of the four Vedas. He is often depicted with a white beard (especially in North India), indicating the nearly eternal nature of his existence. Unlike most other Hindu gods, Brahma holds no weapons. One of his hands holds a scepter. Another of his hands holds a book. Brahma also holds a string of prayer beads called the '*akṣamala*' (literally "garland of eyes"), which he uses to keep track of the Universe's time. He is also shown holding the Vedas.

Brahma's attributes

The Four Faces – The four Vedas (Rig, Sama, Yajur and Atharva).

The Four Hands – Brahma's four arms represent the four cardinal directions: east, south, west, and north. The back right hand represents mind, the back left hand represents intellect, the front right hand is ego, and the front left hand is self-confidence.

The Prayer beads – Symbolize the substances used in the process of creation.

The Book – The book symbolizes knowledge.

The Gold – Gold symbolizes activity; the golden face of Brahma indicates that he is actively involved in the process of creating the Universe.

The Swan – The swan is the symbol of grace and discernment. Brahma uses the swan as his *vahana*, or his carrier or vehicle.

The Crown – Brahma's crown indicates his supreme authority.

The Lotus – The lotus symbolizes nature and the living essence of all things and beings in the Universe.

The Beard – Brahma's black or white beard denotes wisdom and the eternal process of creation.

Dattatreya

Dattatreya or Datta is a Hindu deity considered to be an *avatar* (incarnation) of the three Hindu gods Brahma, Visnu, and Siva, collectively known as Trimurti. The name Dattatreya is composed of two words -"Datta" (meaning *given*) and "Atreya" referring to the sage Atri, his physical father. But Dattatreya is not really a name because Lord Datta never had *Naama Samskara* (a name-giving ceremony). He was known as the "One who gave Himself" to Atri and over eons that became his name.

Various Hindu sects worship him differently, though Dattatreya is considered a form of all the three deities. He is especially considered an *avatar* of Visnu while his siblings the moon-god Chandra and the sage Durvasa are regarded forms of Brahma and Siva respectively. However, In the Natha tradition, Dattatreya is recognized as an *avatar* or incarnation of Siva and as the Adi-Guru (First Teacher) of the Adinath Sampradaya of the Nathas. Dattatreya was at first a "Lord of Yoga" exhibiting distinctly Tantric traits, he is approached more as a benevolent god than as a teacher of the highest essence of the Hindu thought. However, spiritual seekers pray to this Supreme Teacher for knowledge of the Absolute Truth. Hindu theology, credits Dattatreya as the author of the *Tripura Rahasya* given to Parasurama, a treatise on Advaita Vedanta.

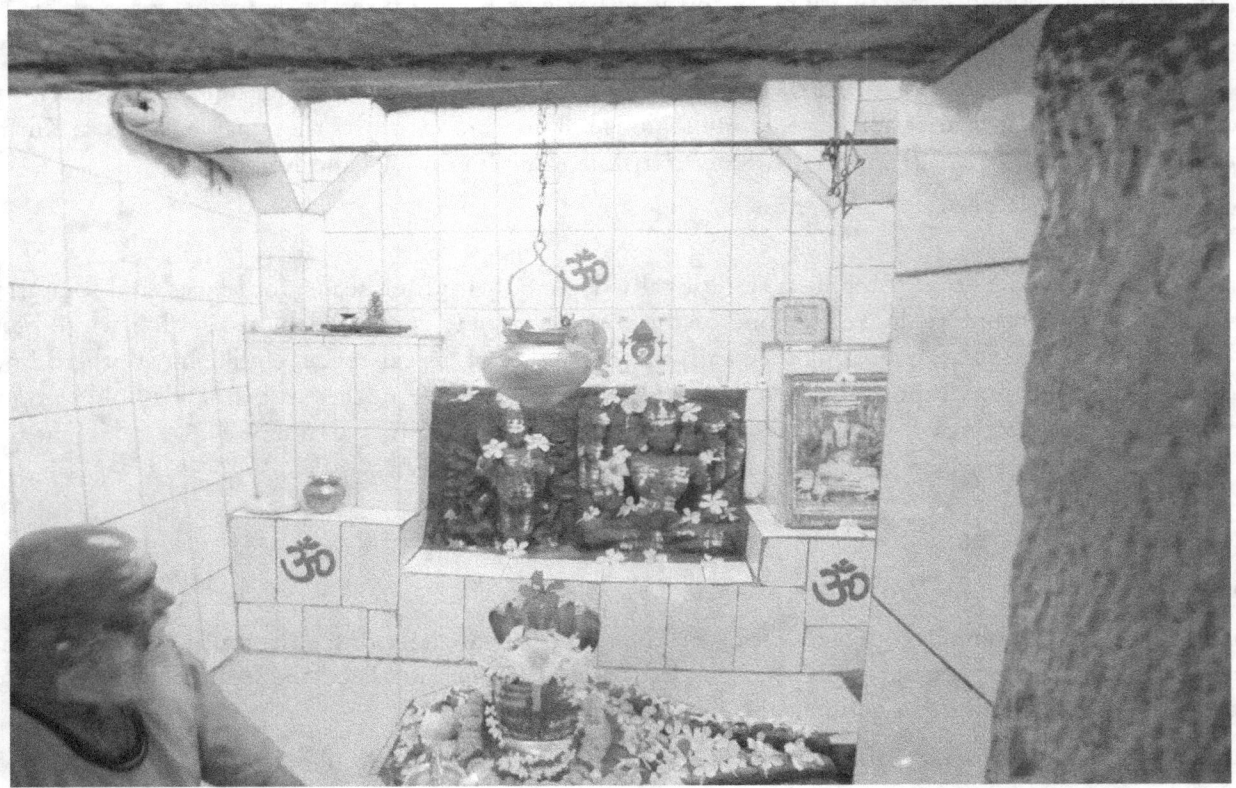

Dattatreya Temple Gokak Falls

Dattatreya is sculptured as a human being with three heads (*tri-mukha*) and six arms bearing emblems of Braham, Visnu and Siva. He is attended by dogs traditionally four in number representing the four Vedas in his hand and accompanied by a cow. Dattatreya was; however portrayed as *ek-mukha* (one faced) god too prior to 16th century CE at various temples.

Dattatreya as Hari-Hara-Pitamaha is found at Halebid on the wall of Hoysaleswara temple. Dattatreya came to be identified with a syncretistic icon at a subsequent stage.

In Badami, a stone sculpture depicts Dattatreya in this manner. He is sculptured as Visnu in the Yoga posture (*yoga-mudra*) and his triple nature is indicated by the characteristic emblems, the sawn, the *Garuda* and the bull of the three gods Brahma, Visnu and Siva being carved on the pedestal which is a *padmasana*. The figure of Visnu may be seen to have *jata-mukuta* on the head, a few of the *jattas* or ropes of matted hair hanging down from it. The *chakra* and *sankha* are in two of the hands, while the other two hands rest upon the crossed legs in the *yoga-mudra* pose. In the right ear Dattatreya wears a *sarpa-kundala* (serpent shaped earring) characteristic of Siva and in the left ear the *makara-kundala* (crocodile shaped earring) characteristic of Visnu. It is a remarkably well finished piece of sculpture. There are several temples of Dattatreya in northern Karnataka. Dattatreya temple at Chattarki is a famous temple of the Kalyani Chalukya times. At the Dattatreya temple at Gokak Falls, Dattatreya has three faces and six arms in sitting posture. The temple at Gokak too dates back to Kalyani Chalukya times.

Skanda

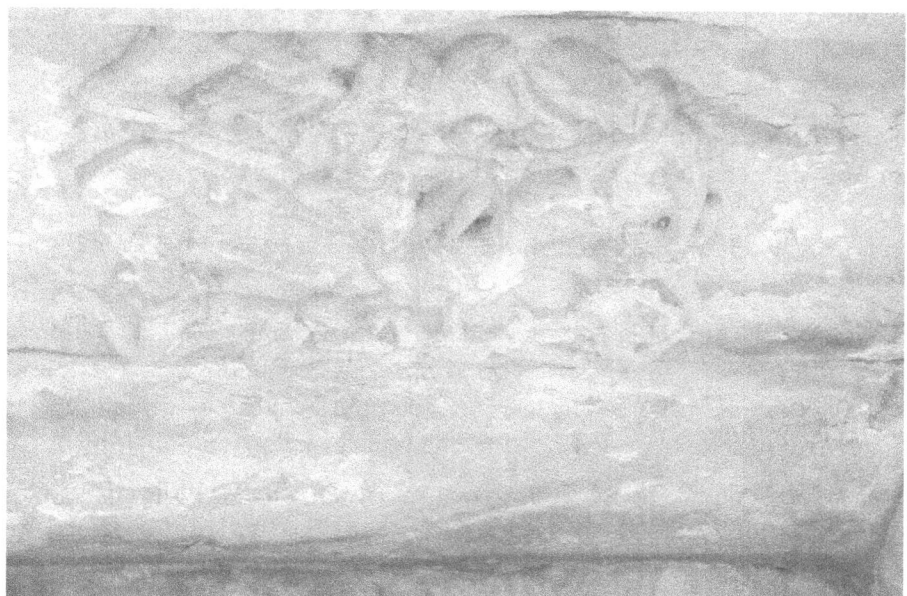

Skanda Riding a Peacock on the Ceiling of Hucchhimaligudi at Aihole

Skanda (also known as Murugan, Kartikeya and Kumaraswamy) being *Devasenapati* (war general of gods) received the attention of many dynasties and a few temples were dedicated to him in Karnataka. Skanda seated on a peacock as Mayuravahana appears on the ceiling of the porch in the Hucchimalli-gudi temple of the Chalukyas of Badami in Aihole as the earliest image in Karnataka. Generally a bird carrying a snake in its beak accompanies Skanda. Images of Skanda abound in the outer walls sculpture of many Hoysala temples.

Skanda symbols are based on the weapons-Vel, the Divine Spear or Lance that he carries and his mount the peacock.

He is sometimes depicted with many weapons including: a sword, a javelin, a mace, a discus and a bow although more usually he is depicted wielding a *sakti* or spear. This symbolizes his purification of human ills. His javelin is used to symbolize his far reaching protection, his discus symbolizes his knowledge of the truth, his mace represents his strength and his bow shows his ability to defeat all ills. His peacock mount symbolizes his destruction of the ego. His six heads represent the six *siddhis* bestowed upon yogis over the course of their spiritual development. This corresponds to his role as the *bestower of siddhis*.

Ardhanariswara

Ardhanariswara represents the synthesis of masculine and feminine energies of the universe (*Purusha* and *Prakriti*) and illustrates how Shakti, the female principle of God, is inseparable from (or the same as, according to some interpretations) Siva, the male principle of God. The union of these principles is exalted as the root and womb of all creation. Another view is that Ardhanariswara is a symbol of Siva's all-pervasive nature.

The iconographic 16th century work Silparatna, the Matsya Purana and *Agamic* texts like Amshumadbhedagama, Kamikagama, Supredagama and Karanagama (most of them of South Indian origin) describe the iconography of Ardhanariswara. The right superior side of the body usually is the male Siva and the left is the female Parvati; in rare depictions belonging to the Shaktism school, the feminine holds the dominant right side. The icon usually is prescribed to have four, three or two arms, but rarely is depicted with eight arms. In the case of three arms, the Parvati side has only one arm, suggesting a lesser role in the icon.

The male half wears a *jata-mukuta* (a headdress formed of piled, matted hair) on his head, adorned with a crescent moon. Sometimes the *jata-mukuta* is adorned with serpents and the river goddess Ganga flowing through the hair. The right ear wears a *nakra-kundala*, *sarpa-kundala* (serpent-earring) or ordinary *kundala* (earring).

In the four-armed form, a right hand holds a *parasu* (axe) and another makes an *abhaya mudra* (gesture of reassurance), or one of the right arms is slightly bent and rests on the head of Siva's bull mount, Nandi, while the other is held in the *abhaya mudra* gesture. In the Badami relief, the four-armed Ardhanariswara plays a *veena* (lute), using a left and a right arm, while other male arm holds a *parasu* and the female one a lotus.

The female half has *karanda-mukuta* (a basket-shaped crown) on her head or well-combed knotted hair or both. The left ear wears a *valika-kundala* (a type of earring). A *tilaka* or *bindu* (a round red dot) adorns her forehead, matching Shiva's third eye. The left eye is painted with black eyeliner. While the male neck is sometimes adorned with a jewelled hooded serpent, the female neck has a blue lotus matching it.

In the four-armed form, one of the left arms rests on Nandi's head, while the other is bent in *kataka* pose and holds a *nilotpala* (blue lotus) or hangs loosely at her side. In the three-armed representation, the left hand holds a flower, a mirror or a parrot. In the case of two-armed icons, the left hand rests on Nandi's head, hangs loose or holds either a flower, a mirror or a parrot. The parrot may be also perched on Parvati's wrist. Her hand(s) is/are adorned with ornaments like a *keyura* (anklet) or *kankana* (bangles).

The image of Ardhanariswara in Badami museum stands gracefully in *tribhanga* posture and similar images are there in the Mahakuta temples too.

Surya

Surya is the principal god of the Saura sect. Illustrated with seven horses, two *devis* generally in diminutive form stand close to his legs. Iconography of Surya had occupied a very important position in India. Surya has been worshipped in India from the early times. The Vedas refer to Surya and his various aspects namely Savitri, Pusan, Bhaga, Vivasvat, Mitra, Aryaman and Visnu. Most of these deities along with a few others formed the class of gods called Adityas. The various aspects of Lord Surya have been numbered as twelve. The worship of twelve Adityas along with the Navagrahas came to occupy an important place in the religious life of the people.

Surya is portrayed riding a seven horse chariot driven by **Aruna**. **Aruna** (a charioteer devoid of legs) is said to be the son of **Kasyapa** and **Vinata** and brother of *Garuda*. Surya is portrayed with two lotuses held in both his hand, and is occasionally shown with the hood of the mythical serpent **Adi Sesha** spread over his head. At the base of his image are shown his gatekeepers **Pingala** (Agni) and **Danda** (Skanda).

Usha is the foremost of **Surya's** consorts and is referred to in the Rig Veda. **Usha** is the queen of the night, and is described as dressed in gold clothing adorned with numerous stars. The second of his consorts is **Padmini** or the lotus. (The lotus blooms when the sun rises in the east). The third of Surya's consorts is **Chaya**.

Daksa

Daksa was the father of Shakti and Prajapati. He was punished by Siva's manifestation, Virabhadra by cutting the head. This was because he conducted the sacrifice without receiving Siva. Later he was fitted with the head of a goat. Images of Daksa are found at various temples in Karnataka with a goat-head. A prominent image of Daksa is found at the Rameswara temple, Narasamangala of the Western Gangas.

Naga and Nagini

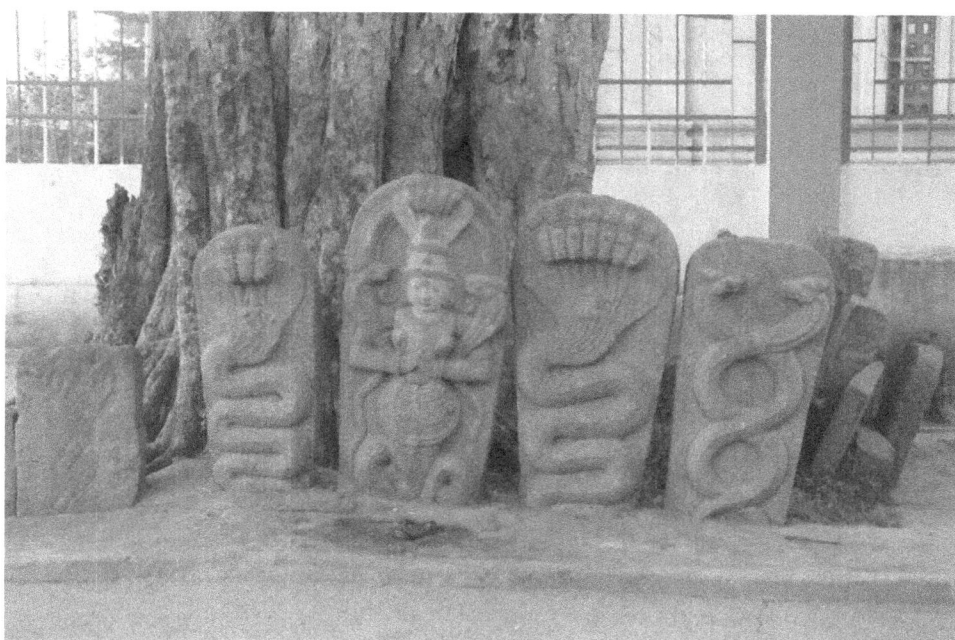

Naga-Nagini at Kashi Vishwanatha Temple Kadugodi

The Nagas were considerable population in ancient India who adorned and had for their totem the *Naga* (cobra). Even now *Naga* worship and ritual offering at anthills which inhabit snakes is practiced in various parts of Karnataka. For Siva and Ganapati, the *Naga* is an ornament while for Visnu his seat and couch. The earliest *Naga* image in any temple in Karnataka belongs to the times of the Chutus, sometime in the 2nd century CE. The *Nagapratima* of this time with an inscription is now kept in the Madhukeswara temple at Banavasi.

Finding numerous *Naga* and *Naginis* separately or entwined together in images near Siva temples is a common sight. Entwined cobras are symbolic of fertility.

Subsidiary Gods and Celestial Figures

Yalli

Yalli (also known as *Vyala* or *Vidala* in Sanskrit) is a mythical creature seen in many Hindu temples, often sculpted onto the pillars. It may be portrayed as part lion, part elephant and part horse, and in similar shapes. Also, it has been sometimes described as a *leogryph* (part lion and part griffin), with some bird-like features.

Yalli is a motif in Indian art and it has been widely used in south Indian sculpture. Descriptions of and references to *yallis* are very old, but they became prominent in south Indian sculpture in the 10th century. *Yallis* are believed to be more powerful than the lion/Tiger or the elephant.

In its iconography and image the *yalli* has a catlike graceful body, but the head of a lion with tusks of an elephant (*gaja*) and tail of a serpent. Sometimes they have been shown standing on the back of a *makara*, another mythical creature. Some images look like three-dimensional representation of *yallis*. Images or icons have been found on the entrance walls of the temples, and the graceful mythical lion is believed to protect and guard the temples and ways leading to the temple. They usually have the stylized body of a lion and the head of some other beast, most often an elephant (*gaja vyala*). Other common examples are: the lion-headed (*simha vyala*), horse (*ashva vyala*), human-(*nir vyala*) and the dog-headed (*shvana vyala*) ones.

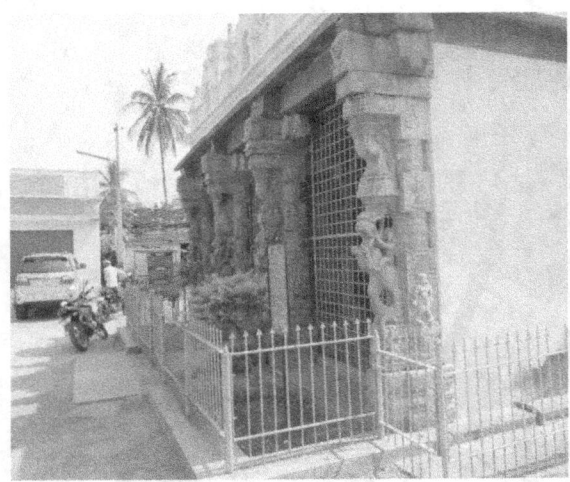 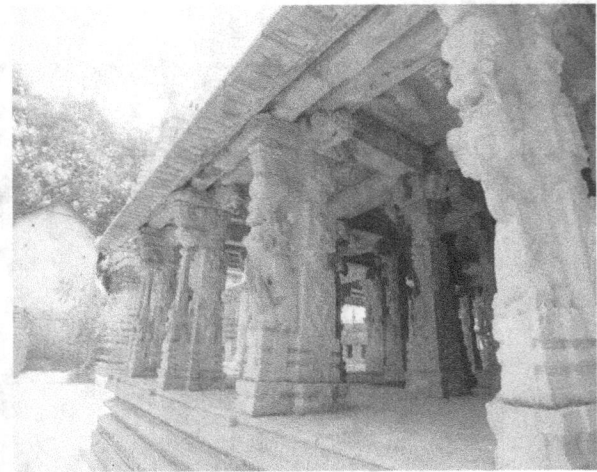

Yalli Pillars at Vijayanarayana Temple Gundulupet and Someswara Temple Kolar

Images of *yalli* are quite common in temple of Karnataka. The most prominent are visible in Hoysala temples, Kalyani Chalukya temples and Vijayanagara temples. Vijayanarayana temple at Gundulupet (Hoysala temple) has *yalli* pillars at its entrance. These beautifully carved pillars are quite striking as these are visible just when you reach the temple entrance. The other *yalli* sculpture in Karnataka can be seen on the balustrades of the Tripurakanteswara temple in Balligavi, Front pillars projecting outside of the *sabhamandapa* at Someswara temple in Kolar, *yalli* balustrades at the Mallikarjuna temple at Kuruvatti and Hoysala emblem at the Chennakesava temple Belur. *Yalli* friezes too can be seen on the *adhisthana* of many Hoysala temples among the *makara*, *hamsa* and *gaja* friezes.

Dvarapalas

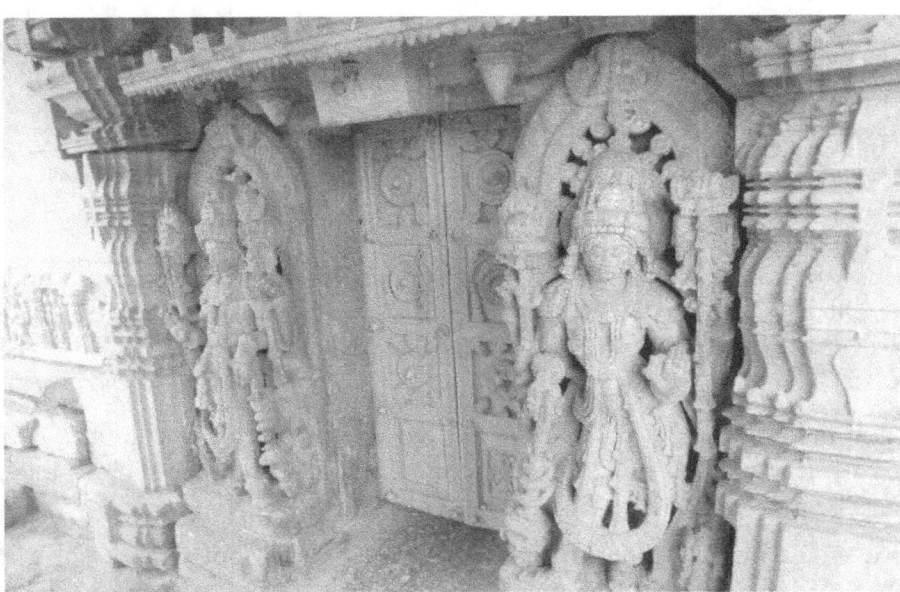

Dvarapalas at Panchalingeswara Temple Govindanahalli

Dvarapala (Sanskrit) or *dvarapalaka* is a door or gate guardian often portrayed as warrior or fearsome *asura* giant, usually armed with a weapon, the most common being *gada* (mace). The statue of *dvarapala* is a widespread architectural element in most of the Hindu temples. *Dvarapalas* as an architectural feature have their origin in tutelary deities, like *Yaksha* and warrior figures of the local popular religion.

According to *Puranic* legends and *Agamas*, Siva and Visnu temples have their typical *dvarapalas*. *Dvarapalas* of Visnu temples are generally called Bhadra-Subhadra, Chanda-Prachanda, Dhatru-Vidhatru and Jaya-Vijaya in pairs. The first named is sculpted on the right hand side of the door and the other to the left side.

Dvarapalas of Siva temples are called Nandi and Mahakala, who are stationed at the eastern gate, Heramba and Bhringi stationed at the southern gate, Durmukha and Pandura stationed at the western gate and Sita and Asita stationed at the northern gate.

According to Hindu iconometry, the *dvarapala* images are usually scaled to *sapta-tala* (seven palm lengths) or *nava-tala* (nine palm lengths).

Dikpalas

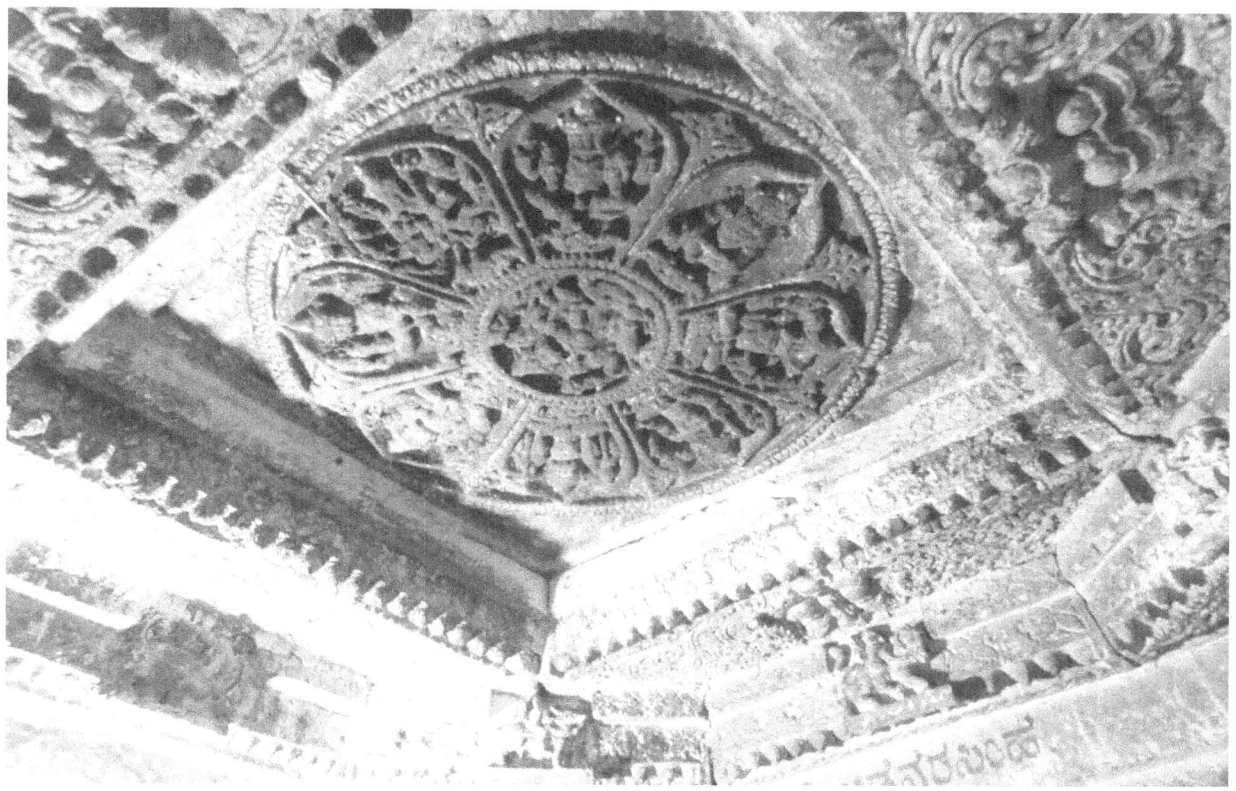

Ashtadikpalas Surrounding Visnu in the Middle at Bhoga Narasimha Temple Shantigrama

The *Dikpalas* are the Guardians of the Directions being the deities who rule the specific directions of space according to Hinduism and *Vajrayana* Buddhism. As a group of eight deities, they are called *Ashtadikpala* literally meaning guardians of eight directions. They are often augmented with two extra deities for the ten directions (the two extra directions being zenith and nadir), when they are known as the *Dasadikpala*. In Hinduism it is traditional to represent their images on the walls and ceilings of Hindu temples. The *ashtadikpalas* are: Kubera, Yama, Indra, Varuna, Isana, Agni, Vayu and Nirrti or Rakshasa and the directions they guard respectively are: North, South, East, West, Northeast, Southeast, Northwest and Southwest. Two additional directions viz. Zenith and Nadir are guarded by Brahma and Visnu respectively.

Ashtadikpalas can be seen in the sculpture on the ceilings of temples as the guardians surrounding the central deity in the *navaranga*. Among the most beautiful examples one can see the ceiling of the closed *sabhamandapa* of the Kalleswara temple in Aralaguppe. There are numerous other examples too but the Kalleswara temple ceiling occupies a special place among all the *navaranga* carvings.

Ganas

The word *gana* in Sanskrit and Pali means "flock, troop, multitude, number, tribe, series, class etc.." It can also be used to refer to a "body of attendants" and can refer to "a company, any assemblage or association of men formed for the attainment of the same aims." The word *gana* can also refer to councils or assemblies convened to discuss matters of religion or other topics.

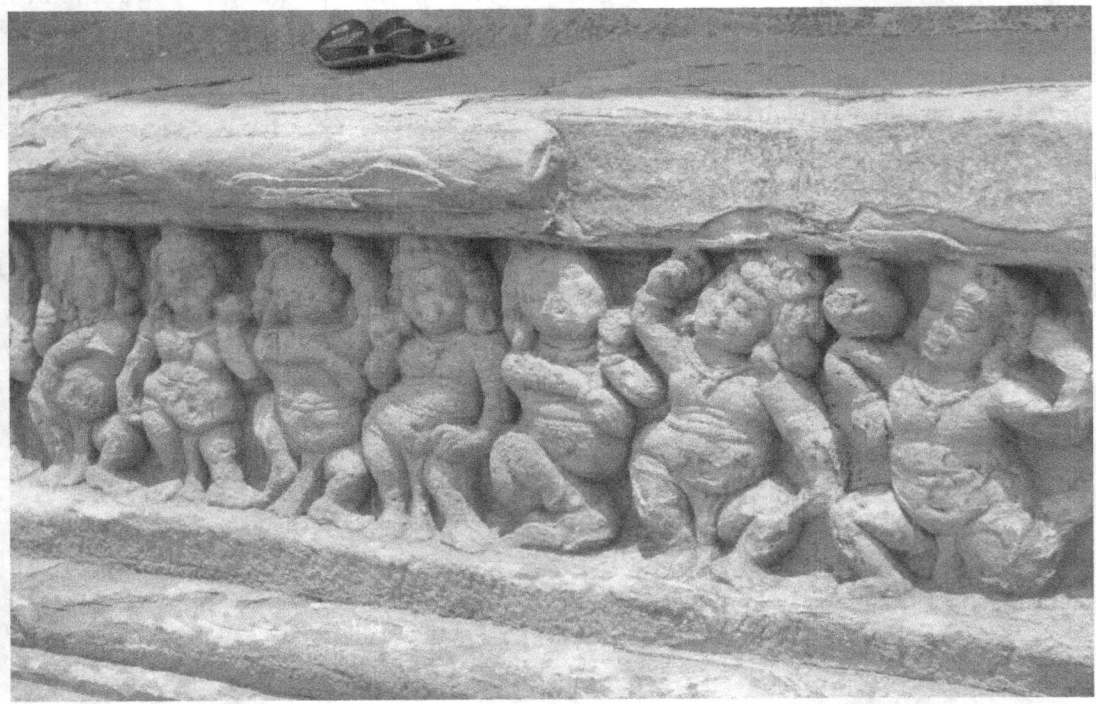

Ganas from Cave 2 at Badami

In Hinduism, the *Ganas* are attendants of Siva and live on Mount Kailasa. Ganesha was chosen as their leader by *Siva*, hence *Ganesha*'s title is *ganapati* meaning "lord of the *ganas*."

Ganas can also be seen on temple walls or basements as group of musicians and dancers. Most striking example of sculpture of *ganas* in Karnataka is in the running friezes of *ganas* in Badami caves.

Garuda

The *Garuda* is a large mythical bird-like creature, or humanoid bird that appears in both Hinduism and Buddhism. *Garuda* is the mount (*vahana*) of the Lord Visnu. *Garuda* is the Hindu name for the constellation Aquila. *Garuda* is depicted as having the golden body of a strong man with a white face, red wings, and an eagle's beak and with a crown on his head. This ancient deity was said to be massive, large enough to block out the sun.

Garuda is known as the eternal sworn enemy of the *Naga* serpent race and known for feeding exclusively on snakes, such behavior may have referred to the actual short-toed eagle of India. *Garudi Vidya* is the mantra against snake poison to remove all kinds of evil.

His stature in Hindu religion can be gauged by the fact that a dependent Upanishad, the Garudopanishad, and a Purana, the Garuda Purana, is devoted to him. Images of *Garuda* can be seen on the *Garuda Stambha* in front of nearly all Visnu temples, the most imposing ones being in front of the Saumyakesava temple (Hoysalas) at Nagamangala and Lakshmi Narasimha temple (Cholas) at Marehalli. Images of *Garuda* also figure in among the sculpture on the outer walls of many Hoysala temples.

Apsaras

An *Apsara* is a female spirit of the clouds and waters in Hindu and Buddhist mythology. They generally adorn the walls and ceilings of many Hindu temples as celestial entertainers. *Apsaras* are beautiful, supernatural female beings. They are youthful and elegant, and superb in the art of dancing. They are often wives of the *Gandharvas*, the court musicians of Indra. They dance to the music made by the *Gandharvas*, usually in the palaces of the gods, entertain and sometimes seduce gods and men. As ethereal beings who inhabit the skies, and are often depicted taking flight, or at service of a god, they may be compared to angels.

Apsaras are said to be able to change their shape at will, and rule over the fortunes of gaming and gambling. Urvasi, Menaka, Rambha, Tilottama and Ghritachi are the most famous among them. *Apsaras* are sometimes compared to the muses of ancient Greece, with each of the 26 *Apsaras* at Indra's court representing a distinct aspect of the performing arts. They are associated with fertility rites. *Gandharvas* and *Apsaras* find frequent mention in the ancient Hindu scriptures including the Epics.

Salabhanjikas or Madanikas

Salabhanjika or *Madanika* refers to the sculpture of a woman, displaying stylized feminine features, standing near a tree and grasping a branch. The name of these figures comes from the Sanskrit *salabhanjika* meaning 'breaking a branch of a *sala* tree.'

The *salabhanjika* is a standard decorative element of Indian sculpture, a graceful stone sculpture representing a young female under a stylized tree in various poses, such as dancing, grooming herself or playing a musical instrument. The *salabhanjika's* female features, like breasts and hips, are often exaggerated. Frequently these sculpted figures display complex hairdos and an abundance of jewelry.

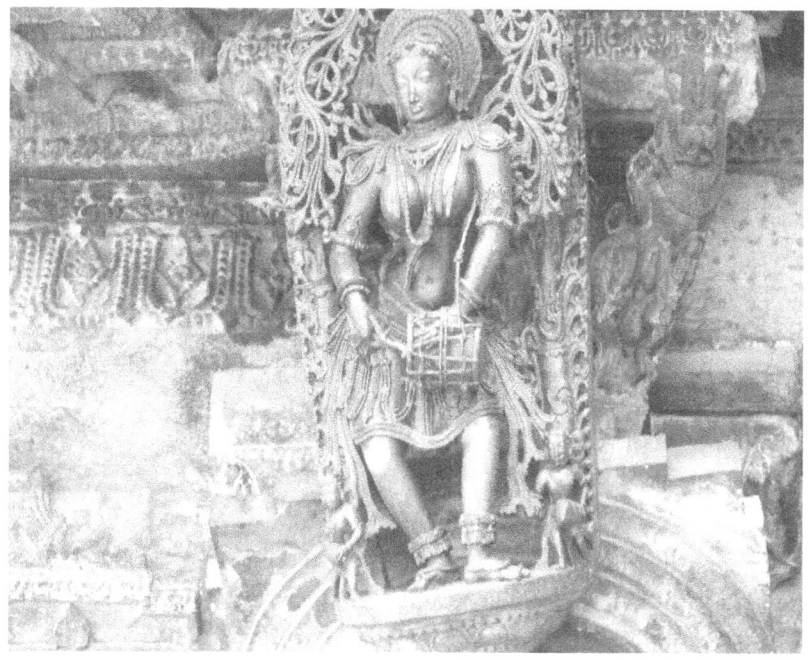

Madanika Playing Drum Chennakesava Temple Belur

The *salabhanjika* concept stems from ancient symbolism linking a chaste maiden with the *sala* tree or the *asoka* tree through the ritual called *dohada*, or the fertilisation of plants through contact with a young woman. The symbolism changed over the course of time and the *salabhanjika* became figures used as ornamental carvings, usually located in the area where worshipers engage in circumambulation, near the *garbhagriha* of many Hindu temples. Placed at an angle, *salabhanjika* figures also were used in temple architecture as a bracket figures.

Some of the most renowned *salabhanjika* sculptures are to be found in the 12th century CE Hoysala temples of Belur, Halebidu and Somanathapura, in Karnataka. Another less known location famous for its outstanding *salabhanjikas* is a Kalyani Chalukya period temple in Jalsingvi, Humnabad Taluk on the Gulbarga-Bidar state highway. Its well-endowed *Madanika* figures in seductive *tribhanga* poses are "... moon breasted, swan-waisted and elephant-hipped," according to the Indian artistic canons. These older feminine sculptures were the source of inspiration for the later Hoysala bracket-figures.

4.7 PATRONS AND MOTIVATION FOR BUILDING TEMPLES

The historical evidence provided by art and architecture from the third century BCE to the fourteenth century CE produces certain broad trends in patronage, and this gives us considerable information also on why and by whom were temples generally built. The kings and warriors invested in ritual sacrifices conducted by the Brahmans in the belief that these had the potential to give them divine empowering, sanctification and purification. Epigraphical evidence for grants made to temples was recorded by way of inscriptions on temple walls or by installing steles in the temple compound. The epigraphical records about grants given to existing temples or new temples show that the patronage was extended by people from different sections of society. The various classes of people who extended patronage to temple building or maintenance activity included the kings and queens, other members of royal family, high nobility, middle level bureaucracy, religious leaders, merchants and guilds, community groups, professional groups and individuals.

While the various dynasties followed quite similar ways of administration and revenue management under the guidance and control of several designated officials, at least three officials were always very important in the matters of taxation, treaties and records maintenance. Among the most important officials was the Minister of War and Peace (called *sandhivigrahika or mahasandhivigrahika* in the Badami Chalukya and other inscriptions). This official was literally the Defence and External Affairs Minister of the kingdom. All Treaties with neighbouring kingdoms whether for cooperation or in the event of surrender on defeat in war; were signed by this official. By virtue of this position he controlled asset and revenue flows between the victor and vanquished or partners to a treaty. The next important official was the Minister of Revenue and Records (called *akshapatalika*). This official maintained all the revenue records and responsible for collection of taxes and managing the treasury of the state. The next in importance was the Chief Secretary, Head of Clerks and General Administration (called *Divirapatti*) who was responsible for enforcement and collation of records and accounts. All grants to temples and institutions running in parallel in the temples were subject to the scrutiny of such important officials. The inscriptions issued would invariably bear the signature of such officials to ensure that the common people obeyed the orders issued therein. There were other numerous local level officials who actually carried out the instructions to create state level delivery of results.

Community patronage

Community patronage generally involved people from a certain sects or followers of a particular deity joining hands together and building their own temples dedicated to the deity they followed or the form of a god they worshipped. This also included people following a religion other than the brahamanical Hinduism, say for instance Jainism or Buddhism. In most such cases people belonging to a particular community would surrender their own lands for construction of temple and would raise contribution for construction, maintenance and management.

Kings and royal families

One of the earliest inscribed and dated temples in South India refers to king Pulakesin II, a king of the Chalukyas of Badami lineage, who was responsible for the construction of the Meguti temple in 634 CE. It is significant that this early temple was not a Hindu temple but a Jaina shrine. But even before this around

578 CE, the Viashnava Cave 3 at Badami was got excavated by Kirtivarman I, a predecessor of Pulakesin II. The inscription records the fact that this king excavated the cave and a grant was made for its upkeep on that date. The inscriptions of the Kadambas at Malavalli and Talagunda belong to even earlier periods than the above two grants. The Malavalli inscription of 3rd–4th century CE belonging to the rule of the king Siva (skanda) Varma refers to the renewal of an earlier grant effected by the Chutus for the worship of the god Malapalideva. Talagunda grant of 450 CE from the king Kakusthavarma refers to a tank got excavated by the king to serve the needs of Mahadeva (*Bhava*) temple at Talagunda. Both the grants of the Kadamba kings were for already existing temples.

Under the Pallavas in South India from the sixth century, kings claimed descent from the Puranic gods and demonstrated their kingly power by the redistribution of their booty to Brahmans, temples and lesser chiefs. The gods were brought down to earth and given a solid platform. These temples acted as the kings' powerhouses and became the focus of political and economic generation.

Impetus was given to this development by the *Puranas* which claimed that *purtadharma*, was a spiritually worthy activity held in high esteem. The conscious identification of the king as God's representative on earth reached its apogee in the mid Chola period during the reigns of Rajaraja I and Rajendra I. Kings even got their own portraits installed in the temples they built. The busts of the Chola kings can be noticed in the Bhoganandiswara temple at Nandi and Muktinatheswara temple at Binnamangala. Kings and other members of royal families from all dynasties patronized the construction, extension and maintenance of temples. Many of them even gave grants for attaching *salas*, *mathas* and *satras* to various temples.

Women patrons

The historical evidence shows the extent to which women's religious patronage has had an impact on the development and growth in the popularity of image making. Considerable evidence exists as to the importance of female patrons from as early as the second century CE. The earliest known grant is from the 3rd century where a Chutu princess gave grants for an image of Naga and excavation of a tank for a Buddhist *vihara*. The Naga image with the inscription is kept at the Madhkeswara temple in Banavasi. Women had an important ritual relationship with local cult deities, notably in the pre-Vedic worship of *yaksha* and *naga* shrines; and the terracotta votive offerings associated with these shrines may reflect the common female practice of making offerings for wish fulfillment.

The Chalukyas of Badami constructed an increasing number of small shrines and temples, many of which were built by queens. The Badami Chalukyan queen Mahadevi Khanduvula declared in an inscription that her marital happiness and offspring were due to the grace of the goddess Lajja Gauri. Early images of this goddess, who is portrayed with legs apart and the head of a lotus, are found in Aihole, Badami, Mahakuta, Siddhanakolla, and more than half a dozen survive at Ter (Osmanabad, Maharashtra), a site linked to the Chalukyas of Badami.

As has already been noted, further evidence of female patronage was the Virupaksha temple at Pattadakal, perhaps the most outstanding example of Badami Chalukya temple construction. It was built during the reign of Vikramaditya II (733–44 CE) by his chief queen Loka Mahadevi and dedicated to Siva Lokesvara. In the mid-eighth century Loka Mahadevi and another queen built temples to Siva at Pattadakal to commemorate the victory of their husband over the neighbouring Pallava ruler. The neighbouring temples Virupaksha and Mallikarjuna are almost identical. The fact that these temples were built to commemorate a victory is recorded in an inscription carved on a pillar standing opposite the two temples.

Nobility and feudatory families

Among the feudatory families who contributed considerably to the construction of temples in Karnataka were, Sendraka, Sinda, Chellaketana, Rattas of Saundatti, Bana, Nolamba and Bali families. The other people from high nobility who contributed to temple building activity were ministers, *sandhivigrahins*, *mahamandalesvaras, mahasamantas, samantas, dandanayakas, senadhipatis, sahanis* etc. The high nobility acted as an organic link between emperors and local temple institutions in their particular area of influence or control. They financed the construction of temples and they also donated for the maintenance and management of temples and rituals. They not only financed and constructed Hindu temples but also Jaina *basadis* and shrines. Most prominent name that comes to mind on this count is the Commander-in-Chief of the army of the last Western Ganga ruler who got the Gommateswara colossus installed at Vidhyagiri in Shravanabelagola in the tenth century. Many of the Hoysala temples were not actually commissioned by the kings or royal families themselves but by high nobility of their time.

Middle level bureaucracy

Officials like *heggades* or *perggades, nalgavundas, gavundas, senobovas, urodeyas, manneyas, sunkavergades* etc. contributed a lot towards the temple construction activity. The local administration was in the hands of *heggades* and they were in charge of collection of taxes on lands, tanks etc. and were assisted by *senobovas*. The *senobova*, a ubiquitous officer of the time was responsible for preparing official and legal documents including inscriptions. The *nalgavundas* and *gavundas* were the backbone of the state. As landlords and local dignitaries, the state utilized their services to collect taxes and maintain records of land ownership. They even rendered military services to the kings and overlords. Being influential locally, they also arranged resources for construction of temples and made contributions towards their maintenance too. Numerous references to *gavundas, nalgavundas* and *perggades* are found in the inscriptions of Chalukyas of Badami, Rashtrakutas and Kalyani Chalukyas.

Various taxes collected and financial terminology used in state's treasury management included *Sulka* (customs duty), *Kara* (Tribute), *Klipta* (settlement of land revenue), *Nidhi* (treasure trove), *Upanidhi* (deposit), *Uparika* (surcharge on land revenue), *Udranga* or *Parikara* (market dues), *Adityamanna* or *Unchamanna* or *Marumanna* (local land dues) and *Tere pon* (tax or tribute in gold). Besides these taxes were also collected in kind including corn, betel-leaves, oil and cattle. Taxes in kind were largely collected for supporting the temples and associated *salas, mathas* and *satras* (educational, cultural, religious institutions and hostels for students). Various revenue officials thus were connected with these grants, either by way of dedicating revenue collections or by giving exemptions in taxes.

Ascetics and religious leaders

Temples also acted as custodians and teachers of knowledge, adding to the intellectual life of the region. Ancient texts were compiled and copied and sometimes translated into regional languages. Schools with resident students were founded and maintained. Their dance performances had a vital and didactic role in the ceremonies and festivals. This process is still alive today. Ascetics and religious leaders thus had a deep interest in the running and proliferation of such religious, educational and cultural institutions. This class of patrons included priests and pontiffs who were referred to as *mahajanas*, brahmanas, *nambiyar* and ascetics. They were regular recipients of grants from various other types of patrons. They not only managed the resources gifted to the temples but also spent a considerable part of the wealth in maintaining and running the institutions. *Agraharas* played a significant role in temple patronage. Reference to *bhatara, achari, bhatta, tammadi* is noticed in various inscriptions and all these were patrons belonging to this class. A special fact to notice that a single inscription of the Nolambas from Avani in Kolar district dated 961 CE records the construction of 50 temples by Tribhuvanakartara-deva, the Kaliyuga-Rudra, who ruled the *sthana* at Avani. Krishna temple at Udupi was built at the instance of saint Madhavacharya in the 13th century CE.

Merchants and guilds

Another class of patrons was the people engaged in trade and non-agrarian pursuits. Various names of such merchants and guilds that appear in the inscriptions in Karnataka are, *settis, tisai-ayirattainnurrvar, samaya, nagaras* and *nakharas, nanadesis, gavare-gandas, ashesha kottali, telligas* etc. Merchants were present when taxes or items were donated and they took personal interest in donating gifts to temples. *Settis* also seem to have held responsible position in the administration of towns and villages. They involved themselves in temple construction as well as in gifting money. The *nanadesis* and *gavare-gandas* were a community of traders who carried goods on animals or on their own heads. The *telligas* were a guild of oil-millers. Oil was a commodity regularly needed in temples for lighting lamps. The patronage extended by *telligaraivattokkalu* and *aravattokkalu* is recorded in several inscriptions. An inscription found at Sutturu near Nanjangud dated 1032 CE belonging to the Chola kings states that land grant for the temple of Isana-Iswara-Mudaiyar and Mulsthana-Mudaiyar by the *mahajanas*, the *samaya* and *sabha*, and also by Puvina-*setti* and Chavundayya. The temple of Mulsthanadeva was constructed by Gundabbe, wife of Marayya-*setti*, who also gave land grant to it. Her son Doreyya-*setti* made a similar gift to the same gods.

Individuals

Many inscriptions record grants given by patrons whose names are mentioned in the records but their social identity is not described. Many individuals who aspired to build temples of their own which was believed to have them the highest spiritual merit gave grants for such temples.

Motivation to build temples

Temples were constructed in the past for various reasons. Most temples were constructed with devotion and also to express religious affiliations. While not many inscriptions describe the motive behind a temple grant, there are some where the purpose and objective is clearly laid down. Generally commemorative temples or sepulchral temples had well defined motivation.

One of the chief motivations for sponsorship of religious art and architecture in ancient India was the fear of death and its consequences. The desire for a favourable rebirth and ultimate escape from the circle of existence inspired the Buddhist and Jaina patrons to acquire *punya* or religious merit. The patronage of temples by Hindu kings was believed to bring political and economic benefit in state matters and also to ensure favourable status in a future birth. In medieval Hindu India the patron also had an eye to this world, with visions of the prestige attached to the funding of grand architectural monuments which helped his acquisition of power and legitimacy.

Members of royal families constructed temples to celebrate certain events, like victory in a war, supremacy over another kingdom, naming ceremonies, desire to attain abode in heaven, memorial to commemorate the death of a member of the royal family or overlords, to accure religious merit, for honour and good fortune. Mangalesa, the younger brother of Badami Chalukya king Kirtivarma I after getting the cave temple excavated and carved for Visnu wished that the accumulation of religious merit might go to his elder brother. Nolamba king Mahendra I offered his palace to construct a temple to god Mahadeva and set up the Mahendreswara temple in order to celebrate his supremacy over the kingdom as described in an inscription dated 878 CE found at Baragur near Sira. Virupaksha and Mallikarjuna temples in Pattadakal were built at the behest of two queens on the victory of Vikramaditya II over Pallava kings. Inscription dated 754 CE belonging to the reign of Badami Chalukya king Kirtivarma II is found on a monolithic pillar standing in the middle of three temples. It reads that two temples named Vijayeswara (Sngameswara) and Lokeswara were established by Vijayaditya and Lokamahadevi. It also says that another temple named Trailokyeswara was established by Trailokyamahadevi, younger queen of Vikramaditya II and younger sister of Lokamahadevi and mother of Kirtivarma II.

Reference to memorial temples during the reign of Western Gangas too was found. An inscription dated 907 CE of the reign of Nitimarga II found at Mogenahalli talks about the temples named Sivamareswara and Nitimargeswara. These two were perhaps sepulchral shrines named after the great Ganga rulers Sivamara II and Nitimarga I. The third temple found at the same spot is the Nagareswara temple mentioned in the inscription. Another temple of the Western Gangas at Alur named Arkeswara has the victory in the battle at Takkolam with the Cholas carved on the pillars of the *navaranga*. The Chola king Rajendra Chola Deva I built a temple at Honganur (Gopalakrishna temple) in the memory of his sister Kundavati.

High nobility had the ability to build temples and the power to order construction of temples. The Appirameya-Vinnagar-Alvar temple at Doddamalur named after the Chola general Aprameya was constructed to commemorate the expulsion of the Gangas of Talkad.

Intense devotion led people to construct temples. Several instances of such temples having been constructed by or at the instance of persons overwhelmed by deep devotion are there in Karnataka. A poor priest named Lingasiva-*jiya* was motivated to reconstruct a stone temple in place of an unfinished brick temple. He collected money by begging alms from public for this cause. It is recorded in the inscription of the Rashtrakutas dated 962 CE and found at Ramasagara. Temples were also constructed in the name of *gurus* by disciples. Mahendra-*bhatta* constructed a temple for his *guru*, Tribhuvanakartara-*bhatara*, and named after the *guru's* title *Kaliyuga-Rudra*. It is recorded in the inscription of the Nolamba king dated 920 CE and found at Avani in Kolar district.

Another motive for kings to patronize grand architectural projects was self aggrandizement and the potential for demonstrating his wealth. The exercise of royal power was as important as the fulfillment of expectations of his subjects in maintaining the reputation of his office. Successful kings fought military campaigns and acquired booty which had to be disposed of. Distributing wealth and booty was an expected part of a king's maintenance of the pillars of his state and consequently of his power. The Indian kings were understandably concerned to extend their territory. The temple in its sacred geometry symbolized the totality of the universe. Only if there is room can the blessings of heaven reach the earth. The kings sought to extend their boundaries and in their temples provided their philosophical expression of the Universe. The elements of kingship, including his power as a universal king over the four quarters of the Universe and all the planetary and other deities, were represented in the temple reflecting the king. Kalyani Chalukyas and Hoysalas had created vast and powerful empires during their times. Need to show that strength and prosperity of the regime was dominant during these periods. Accordingly, the temple building activity reached a peak in intensity while at the same time grandiose architectural styles too emerged. Motivation for building temples thus was powered by the need to display strength and valour.

The naming of temples after a donor, esteemed person or demon is a long established practice known from at least the fifth century, and which still continues today. All over South India and Sri Lanka there are temples and shrines erected for the dead heroes Nadukal and Viragal who as folk deities are worshipped under different names, where a ceremony is performed known as *bhutam attam*. Monuments which commemorate the dead and spirit possession serve a cathartic role, resolving the tensions and conflicts that arise from the dangerous thresholds of life. Several dolmen like sepulchral temples can be seen in Karnataka. Hunukunda, Madivala, Dodda Shivara in Kolar district have many such temples scattered all over.

The earliest portrait sculptures take two forms, both relating to service to the community. There are statues of donors or donor couples from the Buddhist sites from the second to first century BC, such as Sannati and Kanganahalli as well as hero stones. Portrait sculptures of royal patrons are however comparatively rare in India after the sixth century CE until the Chola period. Several examples exist of portrait sculptures in the Chola period, when the god-king axis was at its height. Two temples already mentioned in this regard are Bhoganandiswara temple at Nandi and Muktinatheswara temple at Binnamangala.

4.8 TYPES OF TEMPLES IN KARNATAKA

According to the Manasara and Suprabhedaagama, the three main styles of temple architecture are defined as:-*Nagara* is that in which the *vimana* was quadrangular throughout, *Vesara* in which the *vimana* was crowned by a circular *sikhara* above the neck, and *Dravida* in which the *vimana* was crowned by an octagonal or hexagonal *sikhara* above the neck, and the Manasara adds an apsidal form in the case of both *Vesara* and *Dravida* styles.

Architecture is one among the classifications of fine Arts. It is a predominant of all other fine arts. It is the principal, visible and material record through the ages. It is considered to be the matrix of civilization. It is generally classified into two main divisions. They are Secular Architecture and Religious Architecture. Secular Architecture is in no way connected with any religion, or it does not have any religious motifs. On the basis of erection, or execution or creation the architecture is again classified into two divisions as, rock-cut architecture and structural architecture. In Karnataka, exquisite examples of both rock-cut architecture and structural architecture are prevalent and these can be seen simultaneously in Badami and Aihole within a short distance of each other.

Nagara Architecture

The temples in Northern India are built according to a style known as the *Nagara* style. The *Nagara* style was developed during 5th century CE. This style is characterized by a beehive-shaped and multi-layered tower, called '*Sikhara*.' The layers of this tower are topped by a large round cushion-like element called '*amalaka*.' The plan is based on a square platform but the walls are sometimes so segmented, that the tower appears circular in shape. A study of the temples of *Nagara* style reveals two distinct features. One of the distinctions is in planning and the other one is in elevation. In plan the temple was always a square with a number of graduated projections in the middle of each side. These projections give it a cruciform shape with a number of re-entrant angles on each side. In elevation it exhibits a tower or *sikhara*, gradually inclining inwards in a convex curve.

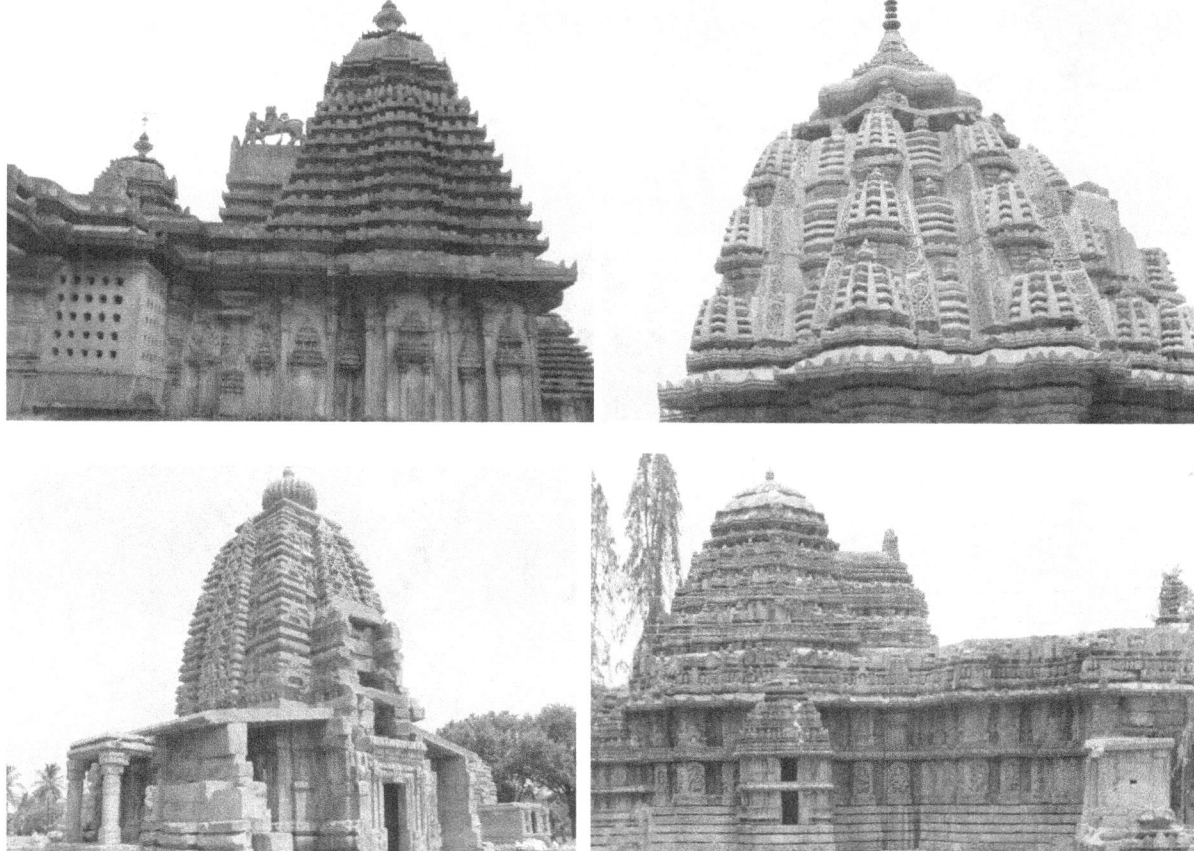

Phamsana (Nagara) Sikhara Lakshmidevi Temple Dodda Gadavalli, Bhumija (Nagara) Sikhara Sadasiva Temple Nugehalli, Latina (Nagara) Sikhara Galaganatha Temple Pattadakal and Vesara Sikhara Someswara Temple Haranahalli

The projections in the plan are also carried upwards to the top of the *sikhara*, and thus there is strong emphasis on vertical lines in elevation. On account of this and the prominence of the vigorous and unbroken outline of the tower it is also known as the *rekha sikhara*. The *Nagara* style is widely distributed over a greater part of India. It therefore, exhibits distinct verities and ramifications in different lines of evolution and elaboration that each locality chose for it. The cruciform plan and the curvilinear tower are, however, common to every medieval temple of *Nagara* style, wherever it is situated and whatever its local stamp might be. *Nagara* style of architecture largely developed in six distinct regions. These can be mentioned as Odisha, Central India, Rajputana, Gujarat and Kathiawar, Deccan and Sindhu-Ganga valleys. *Nagara* style of temple architecture influenced temple building activity in Karnataka too right from the 6th century CE.

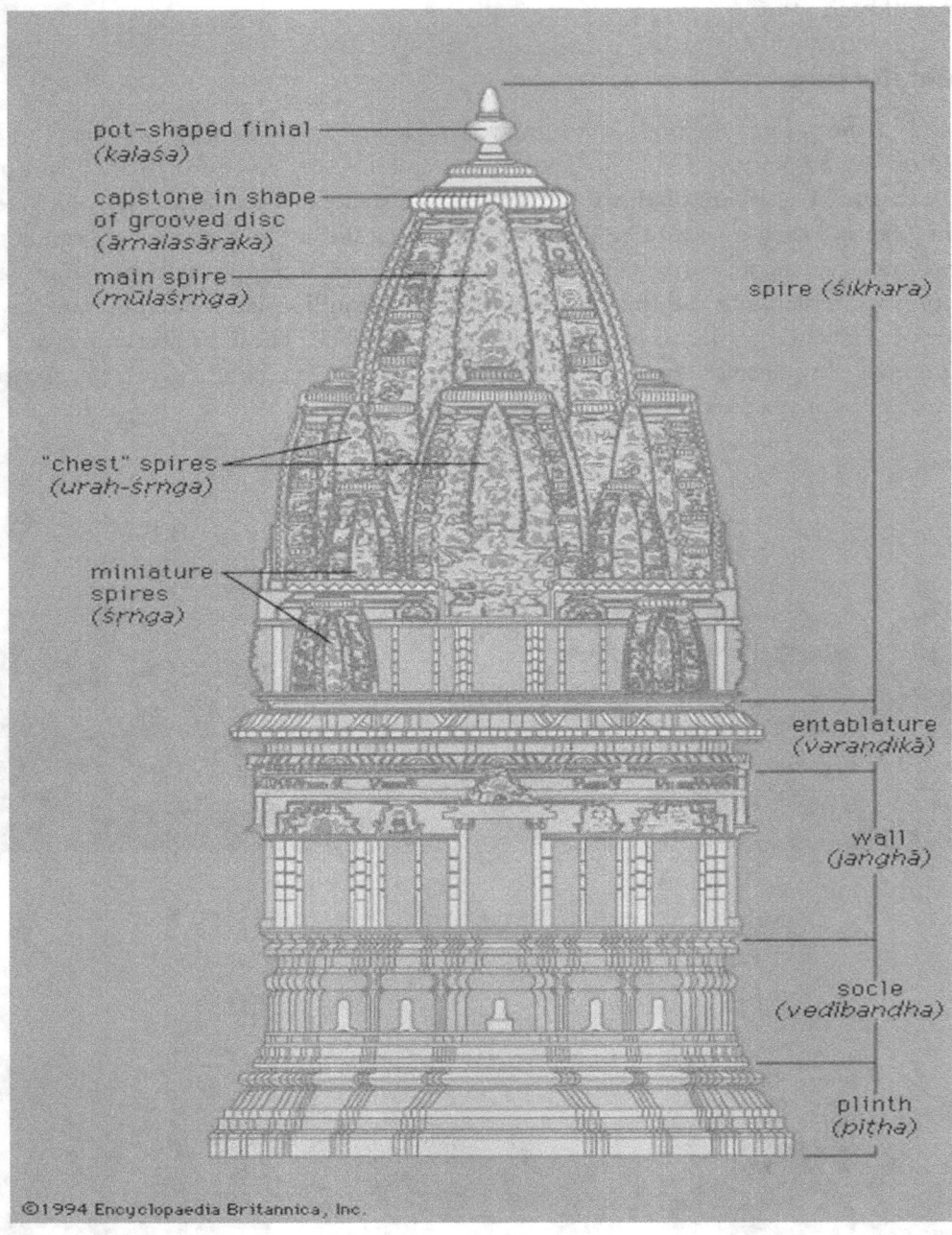

Nagara style temples can be further classified into other forms depending upon the nature of *sikhara*. Two different forms of *sikhara* common in *nagara* type temples are *latina* and *phamsana*. While the *latina sikhara* is curvilinear in outline, *phamsana sikhara* has a rectilinear outline capped by a bell-shaped member.

Important features of the *Nagara* style temples are:

- Temples belonging to the *nagara* style of architecture were largely constructed in the region between the Himalayas and the Vindhyas though the influence of *nagara* style is noticed in the Deccan and Karnataka regions too.

- These temples have sanctum which are square in plan.

- The sanctum (*garbhagriha*) is roofed by a tall curvilinear tower (*sikhara*), gradually inclining inwards and capped by an *amalaka* (a sphere shaped slab with ribs round the edge). This is crowned by a finial called *kalasa*. The *sikharas* have three, five or seven vertical projections and embellished with miniature *chaitya* window motifs (a projected horse shoe archway which is similar to those found above the entrance of a *chaitya*.) and niches and in the corners of the *sikhara* and small *amalakas*, to demarcate the division of the tower into compressed storeys.

- The outer walls of the sanctum have vertical projections called *rathas*. In the beginning there were three such projections on each side of the wall, (left, right and back) and these temples were known as *triratha* temples. In course of time the number of projections was increased to five (*pancharatha*), seven (*saptharatha*) and even nine (*navaratha*).

- In front of the *garbhagriha* there is a pavilion called *sabhamandapa* over which there is a pyramid like roof with horizontal tiers or a flat roof.

- Normally *nagara* style of temples has a closed passage for circumambulation around the *garbhagriha*, the plan being known as *sandhara*.

- Another feature found in *nagara* style of architecture is the projection in the *sikhara* over the roof of the *antarala* or *ardhamandapa* called as *sukanasi* or *mahanisika*.

- *Nagara* style of temples were largely built by the Chalukyas of Badami in Pattadakal and Aihole. The four temples built in *nagara* style in Pattadakal are Kasiviswanatha temple, Galaganatha temple, Kadasiddheswara temple and Jambulinga temple.

Dravidian architecture

Dravidian architecture was a style of architecture that emerged about two thousand years ago in the Indian subcontinent. They consist primarily of pyramid shaped temples which are dependent on intricate carved stone in order to create a step design consisting of numerous statues of deities, warriors, kings, and dancers. The majority of the existing buildings are located in the Southern Indian states of Tamil Nadu, Andhra Pradesh, Kerala, and Karnataka. Various kingdoms and empires such as the Pallavas, Cholas, Pandyan, Chera, Chalukyas of Badami, Rashtrakutas, Kalyani Chalukyas and Hoysalas amongst the many others have made a substantial contribution to the evolution of Dravidian architecture through the ages.

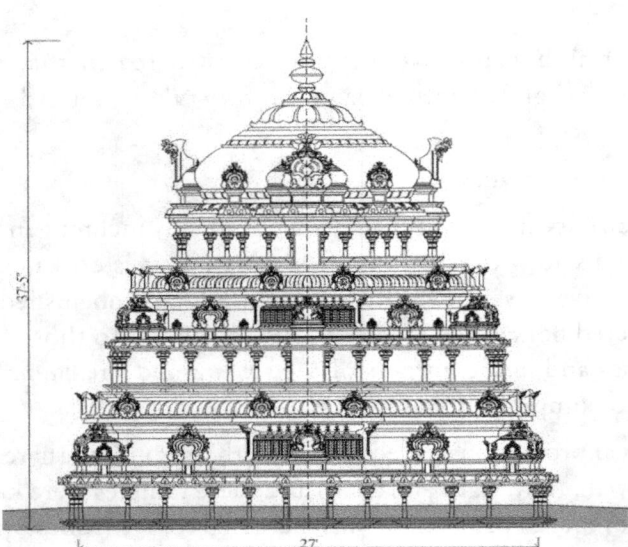
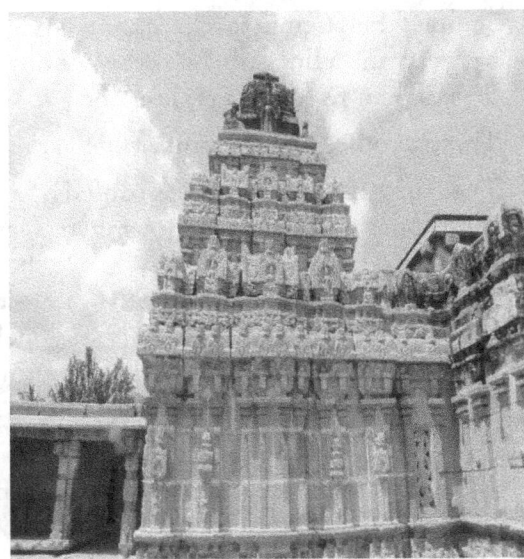

Three-storeyed Daravida Sikhara Sketch and Daravida Sikhara at Bhoganadiswara Temple Nandi

Important and distinctive features of *Dravida* architecture are:

- Temples belonging to the *dravida* style of architecture were constructed in the region between the river Krishna and Kanyakumari.
- These temples have sanctum which are rectangular in plan
- The tower over the sanctum is called *Vimana*, which is of two types, *kuta vimana* and *sala vimana*. In *kuta vimana* the tower consists of storeys (*talas*) with diminishing width as it moves up and is crowned with a square, circular, hexagonal or octagonal structure with a single finial called *stupi*. Each storey contains a *hara* or string comprising a decorative *kuta* (a miniature square, circular or octagonal shrine with domical roof and a single finial), *sala* (a miniature shrine with a barrel-vault roof and a series of *stupis* on its ridge) and *panjara* (a miniature apsidal shrine).
- Generally there will be series of *kuta*, *sala* and *panjara* in a row at each *tala*.
- In *sala vimana* the storeys are of the same pattern as in *kuta vimana* except for the crowning part which is a wagon-top, vault like or inverted boat like structure with rows of *stupis* on top along the ridge.
- Normally in *dravida* style of temples the passage for circumambulation around the *garbhagriha* is open, the plan being known as *nirandhara*.
- Another important feature of *dravida* temples generally is the construction of towers over the entrance gateway called *Gopura*. The gateway is of granite or hard stone but the superstructure, *gopura* is of brick, wood and stucco. The *gopura* has successive tiers where life-size brick and stucco figures of men and gods are placed. Atop the *gopura* there is a *salasikhara* resembling an inverted boat like structure.
- In *dravida* temples we normally find a *pushkarni* (temple tank) which is absent or optional in north Indian temples.
- Virupaksha temple, Sangameswara temple, Mallikarjuna temple and Chandrasekhara temple are good examples of temples built in *dravida* style in Pattadakal. Many of the temples built during the Chola times in southern Karnataka too are in *dravida* architectural style like Aprameyaswami temple at Dodda-malur and Lakshmi Narasimha temple at Marehalli. Hoysala temples though built under a *dravida* architectural style hide the typicality on account of the extensive ornamentation on their walls and *sikhara*.

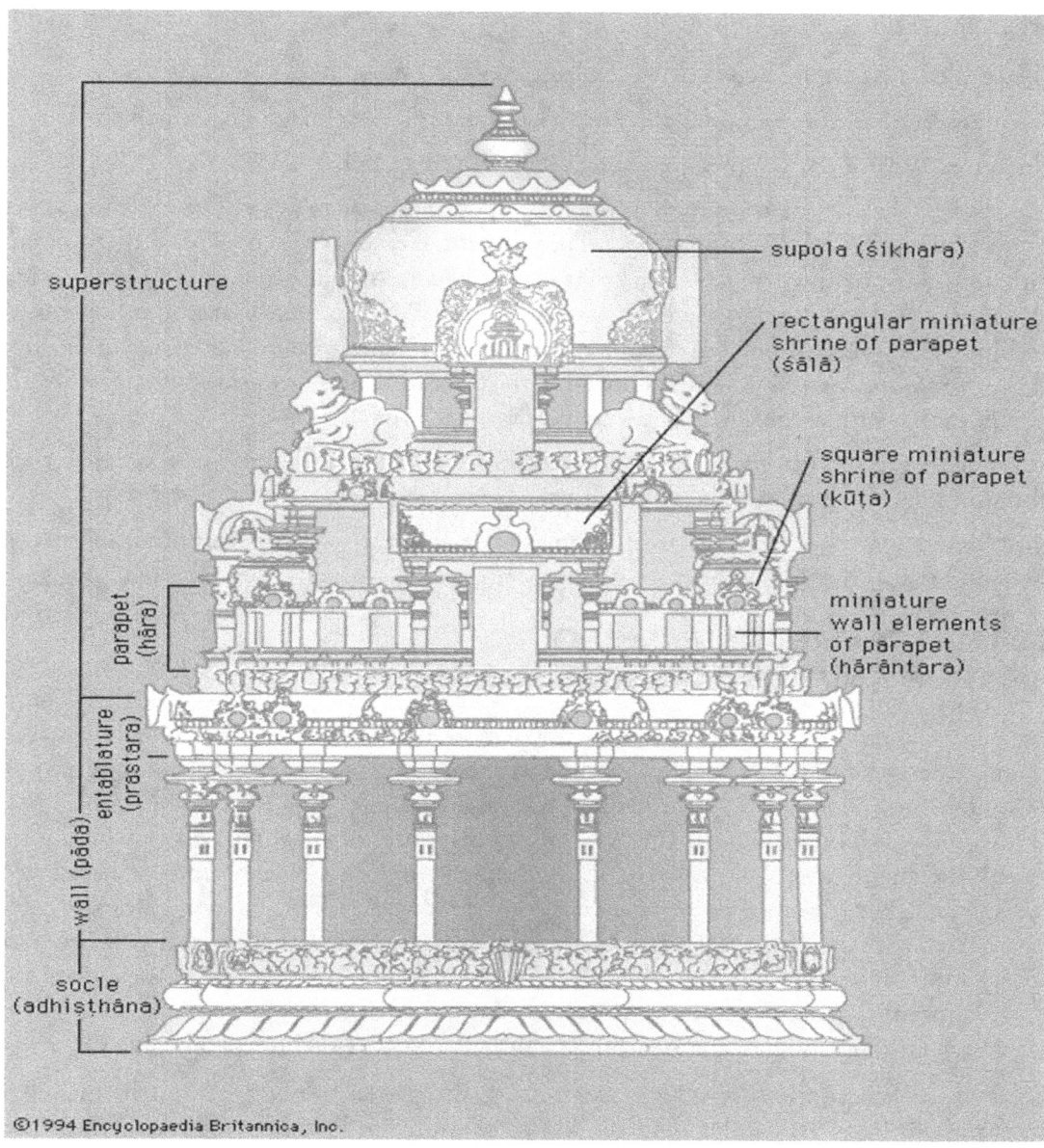

Vesara Architecture

Vesara is a combination of these two temple styles viz. the *Nagara* style and the *Dravida* style. Etymologically, the term *Vesara* is believed to have been derived from the Sanskrit word *vishra* meaning an area to take a long walk. The quarters of Buddhist and Jain monks who left urban areas to live in cave temples were called *viharas*. The prevalence of *Vesara* style of architecture is largely noticed in the Deccan and central parts of south India.

The *Vesara* style contains elements of both *Dravida* and *Nagara* styles. The *Vesara* style is also described in some texts as the 'Central Indian temple architecture style' or 'Deccan architecture.' However many historian agree that the *Vesara* style originated in what is today Karnataka. The trend was started by the Chalukyas of Badami (500–753 CE) who built temples in a style that was essentially a mixture of the *Nagara* and the *Dravida* styles, further refined by the Rashtrakutas of Manyakheta (750–983 CE), Chalukyas of Kalyani (983–1195 CE) in Lakkundi, Dambal, Gadag etc. and epitomized by the Hoysalas (1000–1330 CE). The Hoysala temples at Belur, Halebid and Somnathapura are supreme examples of this style. Papanatha temple at Pattadakal is another prominent example of *vesara* style architecture.

Important features of *vesara* type temples are:

- The plan of the temple is circular which later evolved into star-shaped.
- Temples were built over a raised platform, the surface of which is richly embellished.
- The outer walls of the temples are spaced out by means of pilasters.
- The tower (*sikhara*) of the *vesara* style developed in various stages. During the early stage the *vesara sikhara* was a blending of *nagara* and *dravida* elements and consisted of a *dravida sikhara* with a *sukanasi* or the projection in front of the *sikhara* over the *antarala*. Over a period of time we find the *vesara* tower displaying a variety of motifs and *yaksha* figures in its various tiers with a sculpture relating to the deity found in the sanctum being installed in the *sukanasi*. In the third stage, the *vesara* tower is found engraved with decorative motifs one above the other to give it a curvilinear tower like look with a low umbrella shaped finial at the apex.
- Another important feature of the *vesara* structure is the introduction of a parapet wall of *haras* along the edge of the *mukhamandapa* and *mahamandapa* roof.
- From base to the top, *vesara* type of temples are richly carved with sculptures and friezes. Inside the temples also the door frames, pillars and ceiling are luxuriantly ornamented.

4.9 TEMPLE AS CENTRES OF LEARNING, EDUCATION AND POLITICAL INSTITUTIONS

As Saivism became predominant the movement evolved a new institution known as *matha*. Initially a *matha* was an abode for the ascetics usually attached to a temple just like the Buddhist or Jaina monasteries. Over time students were lodged and boarded in the *mathas* and given free education. Soon *mathas* became centres of learning and local welfare institutions subserving various social purposes including promotion of cultural advancement. It was considered as *Vidyadana satra* and it also lent patronage to scholars engaged in spiritual knowledge. Imparting education was considered to be a religious act and people liberally patronized *mathas*. This resulted in increase in the establishment of *mathas* where education was both religious and secular. Among the subjects taught besides the religious scriptures, were astronomy, astrology, mathematics, law, strategy, warfare, arts and theatre. Apart from the *mathas*, *satras* (hostels) were also maintained where free lodging and boarding facilities were provided for people.

From a study of inscriptions, it is clear that grants were given to *mathas* for their maintenance and imparting education. Banavasi had become an important centre of learning right at the beginning of the Christian Era or Common Era. The other inscriptions dating back to the 6th century CE are from the period of the Chalukyas of Badami found at Amminabhavi in Dharwad district. The inscription dated 754 CE on the pillar at Pattadakal belonging to the King Kirtivarma II also registers a grant given for imparting education. It registers that Jnanasivacharya granted some land as a provision for discourses of the *acharya* as also for the studies of those who attend the rites. The earliest reference to *satra* attached to a Siva temple is recorded in an inscription of the Rahtrakutas and is dated 929 CE. A reference to a *satra* attached to a Visnu temple is first seen in an inscription dated 578 CE in Cave III at Badami belonging to the King Kirtivarma I of the Chalukyas of Badami.

The educational centres attached with Traipurusha temples were called *salas*. Generally these *salas* (schools) were located in *agraharas* (settlements where Brahmans lived). These Traipurusha *salas* were educational centres where students were initiated into several branches of knowledge and schools of philosophy. These were aimed at making students grow up with broad outlook. Students generally began by learning the alphabet and then began the study of five subjects like grammar, arts and crafts, medicine, logic and philosophy. This was the general scheme of studies for laymen of all sects. Other subjects of study were law (*dharmashastras*), arithmetic, ethics, art and architecture (*silpasastra*), military science (*dhanurvidya*) and performing arts.

Agraharas became the foremost educational institutions in southern India during the ancient and medieval period. They were group settlements of brahmans who formed a collective body and administered all affairs of the *agrahara*, including education. *Agraharas* were promoted by the royal houses and attracted various grants and donations. The earliest *agrahara* in ancient Karnataka is believed to be that of Talagunda or Sthanakundur (in present day Shivamogga district). An inscription mentions that Kadamba Mukanna, an ancestor of Mayuravarman, the founder of the Kadamba dynasty, brought thirty-two learned brahmans from Ahichchatra and settled them in Sthanakundur, turning it into an *agrahara* (350 CE.). This shows that kings promoted learning by inviting scholars from outside, and this practice continued in later centuries. It is said that Mayuravarman granted 144 villages to support the *agrahara*. Most of the educational activities of *agraharas* were conducted under the aegis of the local temples.

Talagunda and Banavasi continued as famous centres of education for eight centuries. Education in different subjects, such as the vedas, vedanta, prosody, *rupavatara* (grammar) and *prabhakara* (philosophy), was imparted by learned teachers to students. Besides, there were arrangements to teach Kannada at the primary level (*Kannadaksharashikshe*). The teachers, students and the temple staff were provided with clothes and other necessaries of life and there were cooks who cooked food for all inmates.

Later, the Chalukyan king Vikramaditya VI invited learned brahmans from Tamil Nadu, and turned Nirgunda into an *agrahara* (*agraharikritya*) and donated it to the brahmans.

Queens of Karnataka also took a leading role in establishing *agraharas*. Queen Kamaladevi, wife of the Kadamba king Shivachitta thought of founding an *agrahara* in Degamve (or Degaon) and told the king of her desire in the audience hall. According to an inscription, the king put the proposal before his council of ministers, which consulted one another, and finally accepted the proposal. The queen herself selected a number of Brahmans, who were well versed in different subjects. They hailed from different lands. This inscription gives an idea of how an *agrahara* came into existence and how enough care was exercised to recruit the right learned brahmans who could prove worthy of royal grants.

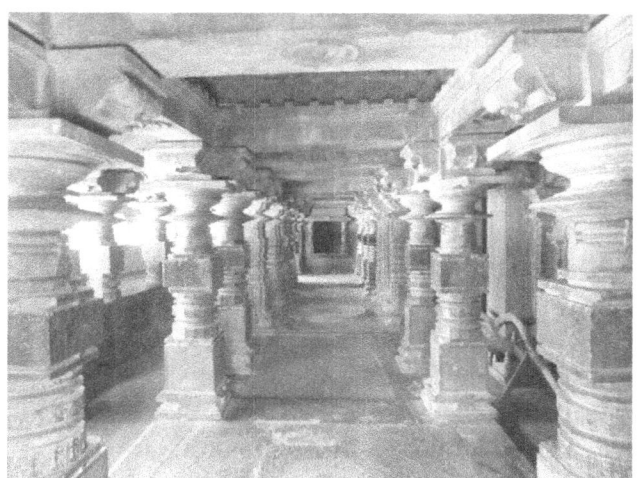 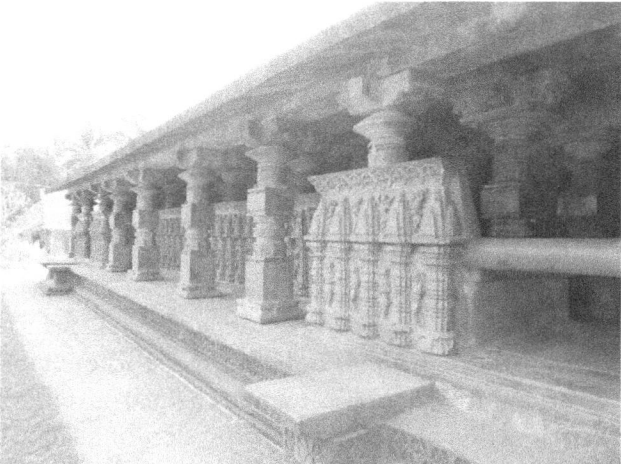

Kamalanarayana Temple Degamve

In Narasimhapura *agrahara* of Belur, boys were taught the Rigveda and the Yajurveda. Some *agraharas* taught only parts (*khandike*) of the Vedas. It is likely that the simpler prayers, invocation mantras were taught to youngsters, followed by an introduction of *padapatha* (recitation of verses), sutras, and the recitation. An *agrahara* was typically composed of different vocations such as blacksmiths (*kammara*), carpenters (*badiga*), goldsmiths (*suvarnakara*), security men (*talara*), flower-men and farmers. Youngsters of all the families in the community received elementary education locally in their families and later through guilds.

Most of the agraharas had groups of villages under them and were closely connected with other educational institutions such as *salas*, *mathas*, *brahmapuris*, and *ghatika*, and had regular exchanges among themselves.

Teaching various dance forms native to Karnataka and those based on Vedic literature too was common in these educational centres attached with temples. By the 10th century, Karnataka had evolved its own school of music, dance, and drama imbibing all the tenets of Bharata's "Natyasastra." This is quite evident from poet Pampa's famous description of Nilanjane's dance sequence in his *Adipurana*. Since music and dance were the most popular entertainment, they developed into various forms to cater to different sections of the society. Manasollasa has devoted a very long chapter containing 950 verses to music, dance, and drama. It involves scientific classification of ragas, mode of rendering them, description of various instruments, blowing and percussion, manufacturing and playing them, art of dance, qualifications of vocalists, instrumentalists and dancers. Thematic dances and operas were known. Bhulokamalla, the author was not only a great musicologist but seems to have been a good musician as well. It may be concluded that by 12th century, Karnataka was at its peak in these arts. This fact is attested by various dance postures in temple sculptures and description in *kavyas*. Methodology in music, given in Manasollasa was followed by one and all in the following centuries.

Since ancient times, people in India believed that the human body is indeed an instrument of *dharma*. Hence the body is to be properly nourished, and maintained. In medieval Karnataka people gave as much importance to physical exercise as to literary education. The principle of "a sound mind in a sound body" was not only accepted but also faithfully practiced. The system of *yoga* was the first step in spiritual training. *Yoga* comprises full-fledged toning of the body and mind. It includes the use of various body postures to control breathing and muscle movements, and to help gain control over human passions as well. It was the general belief that this balancing of the body and mind led to intellectual strength.

Physical training and sports occupied a prominent place in the life of a student. Sculpture depicting various physical exercises can be found on temple walls. Besides this, every village had one or two playgrounds, where sporting events and games were held during the annual fair of the village deity. These involved wrestling, boxing, *mallakhambha* (pillar acrobatics), archery, and demonstrations of strength such as weight lifting. Most children sports in medieval India ensured body-development. The economy and variety of indigenous games were greatly admired by visiting foreign travelers.

Besides the political, social and education role of the temples, these institutions also worked in helping the wheels of local economy working. Temples needed provisions for their day-to-day running which included food grains, oil, flowers, maintenance materials, milk and ghee, and various type of material required in the conduct of rituals. Traders and providers of these goods remained suitably occupied and employed. Temples directly employed people for the services provided such as priests, musicians, dancers, garland-makers, drummers, bell-ringers, accountant, dancing master, watchman, gardeners, *chauri* bearers and various artisans. Thus temples helped sustain the local economy besides their usual religious role for the society. Record about the provision of such services and employment of persons for various jobs is included in an inscription found in the Kolaramma temple.

Education of women in subjects relating to religions, warfare and various arts was prevalent in medieval Karnataka. Among the many girls who took to serious study in a *gurukula*, some excelled in all existing ways of learning and especially in disputations regarding the nature of Brahman. References are found in inscriptions to female ascetics of all religious sects, Buddhist, Jaina, Shakta, Vaishnava, Saiva, Ganapatya and Virashaiva mentioned in inscriptions and classics of later times.

One Gangikabbe presided over a *matha* at Potturu, received a grant from Chalukyan princess, Akkadevi in 1065 CE and ensured welfare and proper education of inmates of the *matha*. She is showered with all customary titles bestowed on male ascetics of the highest order. But the outstanding learned lady of the times appears to be Savinirmadi, whose portrait in stone was found at Margal in Kolar district. Savinirmadi's memorial dates back to the 10th century CE, and shows a young woman seated on a coach in preaching posture. Names of her parents too are inscribed in a two line inscription above her portrait describing her as one learned in all *sastras*. This indicates that she was a preceptor of eminence. The figure is neatly dressed in a sari with flowing pleats. Her thick hair is arranged in a matted top-bun, befitting a sage or *tapasvi*. In the left-hand, she is holding a palm-leaf book.

Wrestlers from Panchalingeswara Temple Sedam

Women's education and place in society

Vatsyayana (1st century CE) has listed several household chores, arts and crafts a housewife had to supervise. These included gardening, growing medicinal herbs, spinning, weaving, classification of grains, maintenance of granary, care of domesticated animals, housekeeping, accounting, reading and writing. Administering medicines, physical exercises (*vyayamiki*), painting, and tailoring besides cooking were the topics a housewife was to know.

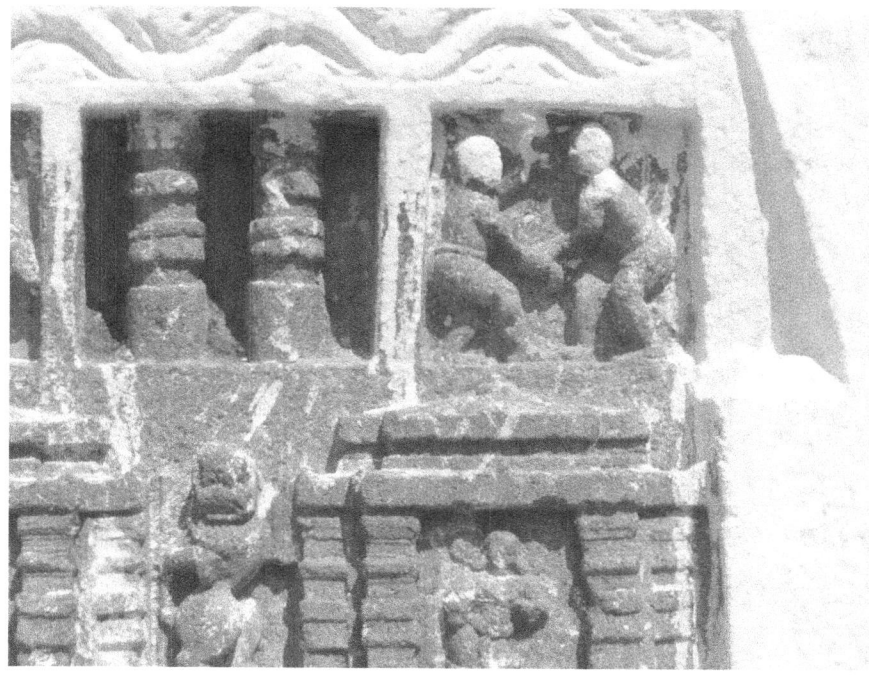

It is obvious that women of Vatsyayana's time were expected to be adept in household chores and cultivation of arts and crafts as well. He further suggests that a musician, a princess or daughters of nobles could control the household by cultivating various arts and subjects. In case of separation, death or a long journey, such ladies could spend time by learning fine arts, he advised.

Again from Vatsyayana we learn that experienced nurses, confidantes, old maids, nuns, and even aunts taught various subjects to young girls. This attests the fact that India boasts of a long and sound system of domestic system of education, which has come down to two millennia. Karnataka was no exception, and we have references in old Kannada classics of nuns, nurses and old maids teaching princesses and daughters of nobles. At times father took active interest to educate girls.

Adipurana, the Jaina classic of Pampa provides glimpses of early education for girls. Vrishabhadeva, the first Tirthankara one day sent for his two daughters Brahmi and Sundari thinking to educate them. He was convinced that education would add to their virtues. He seated them on his lap and wrote the letters "Siddham Namah" (a legacy of ancient times) for Brahmi. To Sundari he taught arithmetic. Then he proceeded with formation of words, figures of speech, literature and all arts (*samastakalasamuha*) one by one. They both were perhaps five year old and this was the age considered fit enough for schooling boys and girls in ancient times.

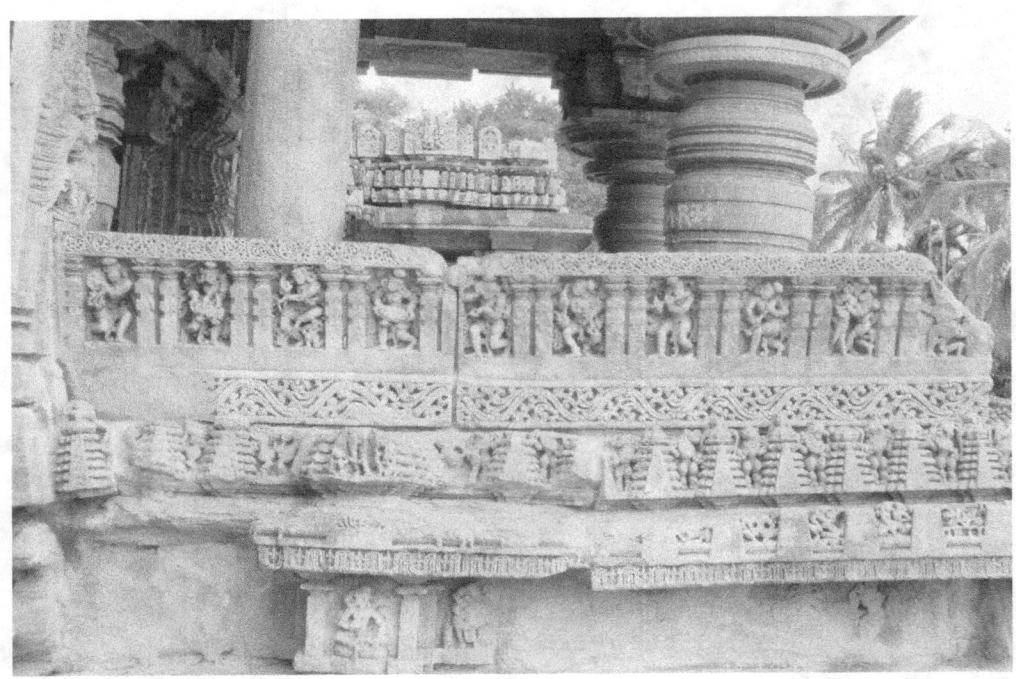

Women Playing Musical Instruments Panel on Agramandapa Nageswara Temple Mosale

Men teachers were employed to teach the princess. Bilhana was a court-poet of Chalukya king Vikramaditya VI who ruled from 1076 to 1127 C.E. He hailed from Kashmir and is credited with *Chorapanchashikha* a short work of fifty verses. Many scholars believe it is based on his personal experience. The king, his earlier patron, thought the brilliant poet would make a good teacher to his beloved daughter Champavati. But as per existing norms he dared not leave both of them alone for hours together. Hence the princess was briefed to keep her eyes closed during the lessons given to understand that the poet was suffering from leprosy. The poet was told that the princess was born blind. The lessons continued for a while. But the cat was out of the bag shortly. The guru slowly won over the disciple by pleasant conversation and love lyrics! Both fell in love and when the king came to know about it, he ordered the execution of the poet forthwith. When Bilhana was being led to the place of execution, verses broke out spontaneously and the people who had lined on both sides of the road listened and broke into tears. The anger turned to compassion; the king let Bilhana go free and married off his daughter to him.

In the higher strata, girls were taught state-craft, horse and elephant riding and wielding of various weapons. There exists a rare sculptural representation of Saviyabbe, falling in the battlefield fighting to save her husband. Princess Akkadevi, governor of Banavasi province (1024–1068 CE) defeated the rebellious chieftain of Gokage, when her military skills shone and won her the title of *Ranabhairavi* (goddess of battlefield). The tradition continued till the 17th century. Mallamma, daughter of the chieftain of Sonda was taught martial craft along with her brother Sadashiva Nayaka. This included horse riding and wielding of various weapons.

A female dancer of olden times had to be versatile. She had to learn music, acting, recitation from classics and narration as well as composing verses.

Jaina *basadis* and *mathas* continued providing spiritual training to nuns. Wandering nuns and monks imparted instruction through discourses to *shravakas* or lay-listeners. Local ladies visited *basadis* where they learnt to read sacred books of Jaina tenets (*jinagamas*) and stories of sixty-three saints. Reading of *puranas* was arranged in temples big and small, which were attended by a good number of women. They continued to prepare cotton wicks or leaf-plates while listening attentively to recitation of sacred books.

Brief mention may be made about the training of courtesans and temple girls who continued to be custodians of fine arts. They were not only tolerated but also respected in high society. In Rashtrakuta times *ganikas* or courtesans were highly accomplished in singing, dancing, and playing various musical instruments. They formed part of royal entourage and received guests at important functions. According to Manasollasa, they were present in assembly along with preceptors, courtiers and royal member. Dedicating dancing girls to temples for the service of the deity came into vogue by 6th century CE and inscriptions as well as Sanskrit and Kannada classics speak of their accomplishments.

From poet Dandin (6th century CE) to Damodaragupta (9th century); poets were familiar about the learning and accomplishment of courtesans. According to Dandin as soon as the girls were old enough, they were carefully instructed in the arts of dancing, acting, playing musical instruments, singing, painting, preparing perfumes, arranging flowers, making garlands, reading, writing, and conversation. In addition, they studied grammar, logic, and philosophy, which enabled them to participate in the assemblies of the learned.

They had to master various games. According to Damodaragupta the *ganikas* in-making, had to study science of erotica in detail, Bharata's *natyasastra*, needlework, wood and metal work, clay-modeling, cookery, and all practical training of music and dance.

Basavapurana of poet Bhima (13th century CE) speaks of various instruments played by women. They played tabor (*maddale*), blew trumpet (*kahale*), played flute, and cymbals (*tala*). Sculptures showing women playing all these instruments are replete in many Kalyani Chalukya and Hoysala temples.

It may be surmised that some system of domestic system to train women of different strata in the society prevailed. The talented among them outshone when they received proper encouragement. There were enlightened men like poet Rajashekhara (9th century CE) who declared that refinement (*samskara*) pertains to the soul and not to the gender. Many women shone as administrators of cities, towns, *agraharas*, divisions and provinces. Queens like Shantala have become immortal because of their accomplishments. Patrons like Akkadevi and Attimabbe liberally donated towards promotion of education and learning. Attimabbe outshines in encouraging poets to write books and distribute literary works free.

4.10 TEMPLE CONSTRUCTION TECHNOLOGY AND ORGANISATION

These marvels are a testimony to our ancestors' excellence in meticulous planning, accurate geometric designing, knowledge of elegant architectural proportions and their outstanding craftsmanship. Their command over architectural sciences is evident by the fact that these temples (scattered all over the country) remained intact withstanding years (sometimes centuries) of neglect, wear and tear, and sometimes even vandalism, to allow us a glimpse of our rich heritage. Their organized symmetry and exquisite geometrical configurations lead one to believe that the builders of these temples were well versed in mathematics, more particularly geometry, trigonometry, algebra and the science of accurate measurements. The positioning and directional orientation of most of these temples and particularly of those where certain astronomical events get observed year after year by way of the sun's movement and the way sunrays fall at a selected spot lead us to believe their good knowledge of astronomy too. With such scientific outlook they could achieve such amazing results even though modern scientific instruments were not available to them. Obviously then they must have used the services of highly motivated and knowledgeable teams of men to work on these grandiose projects.

They used the knowledge of geometry in other disciplines also. They derived many of the comprehensive conclusions with the help of geometry. The Indian old scripts are the evidences of those practices. The concept of progression can also be applied in the geometry. When this progression held in a proper manner or following a rule, it becomes a process, which has several names like iteration, repetition etc. However, at the end of the process, the outcome turns into a beautiful illusion. The Indians understood this beautiful illusion by practice. They were creative minds. They proved their efficiency not only in applied science but also in arts and crafts. They worshipped the nature and they were very eager to reveal the mystery of creation. Somehow they got the hints of creation; the principles of self-similarity, iteration, repetition. They observed that, in the mountains, in the trees, in ground covers, in water; everything follows those principles. Even living beings are not the exceptions. Then they followed those principles in their creations. They gave their tribute as a form of temple to the ultimate creator by following the principles of his creation.

In ancient days the sculptural art and architectural science were handed down from father to son. There are a number of Chalukyan inscriptions in support of this fact. Thus the art was practiced by the members of the same family or caste. These *silpis* or sculptors believe that they are the descendants of Vishwakarma, the divine Architect. The Vishwakarmas are able to work in different media like stone, wood, gold, iron and copper and they are called sculptor, carpenter, goldsmith, blacksmith, and coppersmith respectively. John Brower, who has done extensive study on Vishwakarmas, calls them 'the makers of the world.' Of these five groups of Vishwakarmas, mainly the names or architects and sculptors appear in the inscriptions of Badami Chalukyas and later dynasties.

Construction of a temple was always considered a sacred activity. The timely completion of these abodes, along with attention to the minutest details, required strict hierarchy of commands. On top of the hierarchy was the person who dreamt of a temple for his deity. He was *Yajmana* or *Karta* or the Patron. Most of the time, *Yajmana* was a king, a queen or a rich businessman, a guild and used to choose the *Sthapati* or the Chief Architect. *Sthapati* was expected to be the master of *Silpa Sastra*, *Vastu Sastra*, *Dharma Sastra*, *Agnipurana* and all mathematical calculations. He was the person responsible for converting *Yajmana* or *Karta's* dream into an architectural draft.

He was empowered to select his chief engineer, the *Sutragrahi*, who was responsible for converting the architectural draft into geometrical design and dimensions. In order to avoid confrontations, ego clashes and to work in perfect synchronization, *Sutragrahi* was usually the son of *Sthapati*. They were assisted in their task by *Takshaka* (the mason), *Silpi* or *Murtikar* (the sculptor) and *Vardhaki* (the carpenter).

Ancient tradition holds a mythical genealogy of the *silpis*. In the Mahabharata, Vishwakarma, the son of Prabhasa, is described as *Silpa Prajapati*, meaning the foremost among the artists. According to the Manasara, their origin was "from the four faces of Brahma, the creator of the Universe." The four faces originated in sequential order as the heavenly architect Vishwakarma, Maya, Tvashtr and Manu. Their four sons in turn were called the *sthapati, sutragrahi, vardhaki* and *takshaka*. Vishwakarma is said to be the engineer of the gods, *amaravardhaki*. It is also said that Vishwakarma wrote a treatise on art and architecture called Vishwakarmaprakasa. He was, over a period of time, deified and even today is being worshipped by artisan communities in most parts of India. The ancient texts on architecture substantially discuss the conceptual background, ethos and values of the architects and how each of them was to try and establish a relationship between the metaphysical aspects and material forms in the different structures to be built by them.

Vastuvidva, while enumerating the qualification and knowledge of the *sthapati* explains that he must be proficient in all sciences. He was to be a mathematician, historian, geologist, geographer and above all, was to possess a sound knowledge in the science of architecture. In order to select suitable wood, he was also to know botany. For testing of building materials and for combination of paints he was required to be proficient in chemistry and allied sciences. Similarly, knowledge of the climate and weather of the locality where a house, temple or any other structure was to be built was essential. In addition to these, he was to be intuitive and have foresight to calculate and decode everything very quickly. We have many references to gifts and grants of lands to the temple builders and sculptors. At times they were given a high position even in the royal service. The sculptors and architects were also honoured by royalty. It is historically known the courts of kings were adorned with intellectuals in philosophy, interpreters of law, sculptors, architects and painters.

Sthapati drew up the ground plan, elevation and sculptural ornamentation plan for the temple whereas *Sutragrahi* was responsible for delivering all these plans as the constructed temple. *Surtagrahi* interacted with the other team members viz. *Takshaka, Silpi* and *Vardhaki* and guided their resource management and work delivery. All these team members were assisted by a whole body of workers, artisans and porters. Coordination among the top five was critical for the systematic and timely delivery of functions which were planned according to a well laid down activity chart.

Just to support the points made above, a Swiss Indologist-cum-researcher-cum-artist who had lived in Benaras from 1936 till 1978 had found *olas* (palm leaf manuscripts) with considerable details of the raising of the Konarak Sun Temple (Odisha) built in 1250 CE and records about many who worked on it, from the *Sutragrahi* and *Sthapati* down to the humblest carpenter, mason and helper. A complete drawing of the temple has been done in NINE *olas!* These *olas* are in the Alice Boner Gallery of Benaras Hindu University's Bharat Kala Bhavan at present.

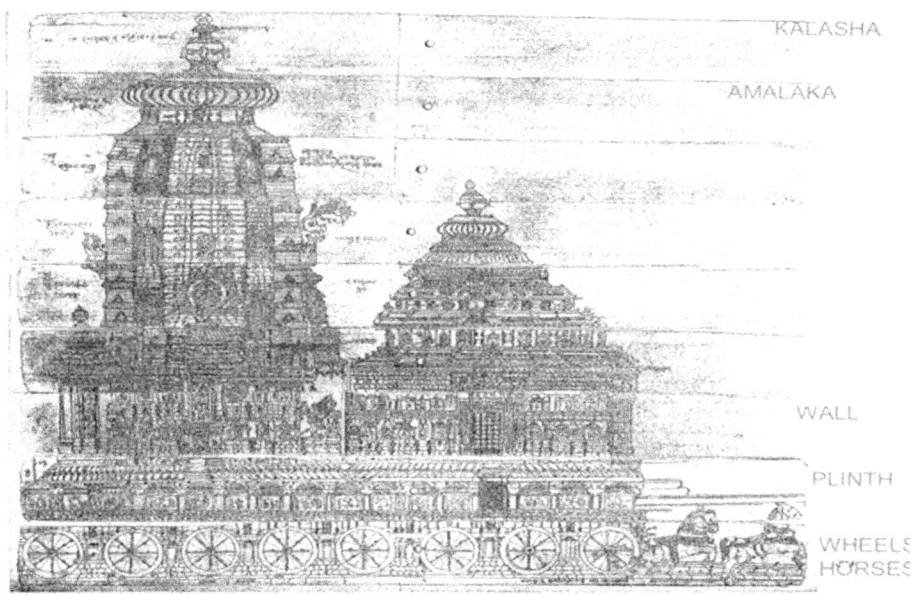

Now the question arises what happened to such drawings and plans of the so many other temples built during medieval times? Since most such drawings were recorded on perishable leaves, weather must have taken its toll on many and many may still be lying buried at various locations.

Another temple where temple ground plan and various other drawings can still be seen is the Bhojeswara temple at Bhojpur near Bhopal. The temple at Bhojpur is unique in being left unfinished, with a series of large architectural parts still located in the quarries where the stones were cut and fashioned. In addition, there are a significant number of architectural drawings engraved on the flat surfaces of the quarry showing mouldings, pillars, and temple plans. Also of note is the large earthen ramp behind the temple which shows how medieval craftsmen raised the large blocks of stone into position. Temple at Bhojpur not only depicts the temple drawings but also leaves tell-tale signs of the engineering in use in those times.

In Karnataka also area demarcations have been indicated in some temples by etching drawings of humans performing functions indicating the function or ritual performed in that part of the temple. Most notably, in Madhukeswara temple at Banavasi, the *nrittagriha* (dancing hall) and the *pujamandapa* (worshippers' ritual area) have been clearly demarcated by etchings on the floor. At the two quarries located at Shankaralingana Guddu and Motara Maradi near Pattadakal, not only iron implements of the sculptors and masons working on the temples in Pattadakal were discovered, detailed sketches of sculpture carved in the temples too were found etched on stones. The two quarries were the workshops used by the temple builders of the 7th century.

Vishwakarma community

Temple design and construction professionals generally belonged to the Vishwakarma community. Since temple building combined aesthetic, intellectual and the spiritual together, the *Sthapati* and his team members were expected to have knowledge of calligraphy, astronomy, history, music, prosody, civil engineering, mathematics, architectural planning and all such areas. Vishwakarma is the term used in India for a caste of priests, engineers, architects, sculptors, temple builders and artists. The term is also applied to five sub-castes; blacksmiths, carpenters, coppersmiths, goldsmiths and sculptors.

Two important centres where the Vishwakarma community still pursues its main activity as sculptors and artists are Swamimalai in Tamil Nadu and Sivarapatna in Karnataka. The artisans of Swamimalai are mostly involved in moulding bronze sculpture whereas the Vishwakarmas of Sivarapatna work on carving stones and rocks.

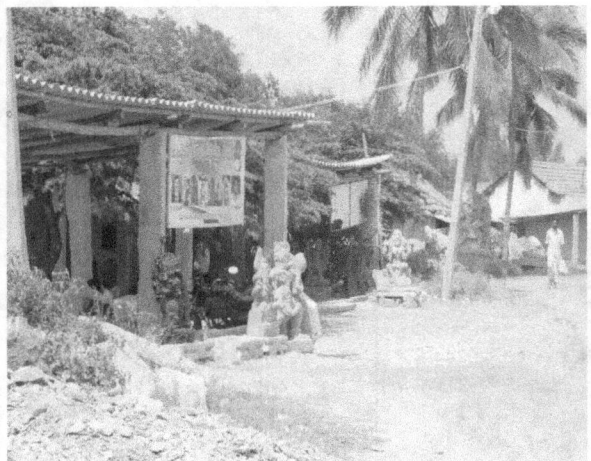
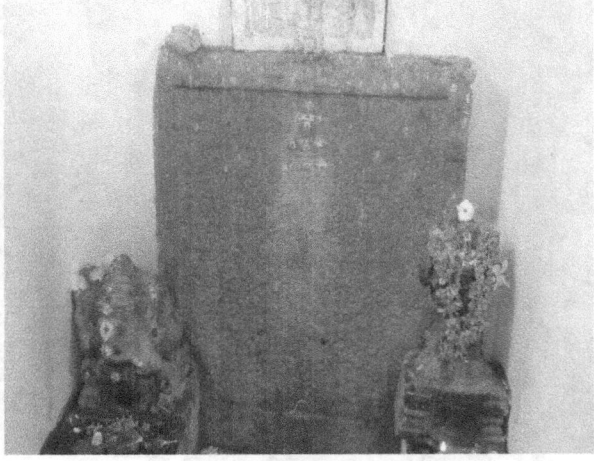

Sivarapatna Village of the Vishwakarmas

The village Sivarapatna is very well known for its intricate carvings on black and grey granite to make idols for temples. The Sivarapatna craft is popular all over India and abroad. There are myths that during the period of Ganga Dynasty a '*silpi*' (Craftsperson) named Basavalinga Acharya while traveling spent a night in a Dharmashala (inn) in the village Sivarapatna. After cooking food at night, he took some pieces of charcoal and drew a picture of a deity on the wall, which was very beautiful. Next morning when the villagers saw the line drawing they were impressed by his skills. This news spread far and wide and the king got to know about this. He came to the village to meet him and asked him to stay in the village and practice the craft and offered him land in the village to stay. There onwards the craft flourished in the village.

Jaknacharya the famous temple architect of the medieval times too belonged to the Vishwakarma community. Members of the community in Sivarapatna still practice the art of sculpture, which is taught from father to son in a traditional way. It seems that every family in the village possesses a copy of Roopadhyana Ratnavali, a Telugu book written by Ganesha Stapadi which is considered a must read on sculpting.

Temple construction process

The Hindu temple construction during the medieval period (6th–13th centuries) took place on a magnificent scale. Temple building activity really peaked in the 11th century CE in India and nearly half of this activity and temple building frenzy was found in Karnataka. A large variety of Hindu temples was constructed throughout Karnataka with distinction in scale, techniques of building and particularly the deities that were worshipped, which were the result of the differences in political, cultural, climatic, geographical and prosperity between the towns and villages.

Three distinctive architectural styles of Hindu temples developed classified into three different orders; the *Nagara* or 'northern' style, the *Dravidian* or 'southern 'style, and the *Vesara* or hybrid style. Karnataka is the only state where all the three styles of temple construction were prevalent. In fact, the *Vesara* style originated only in Karnataka.

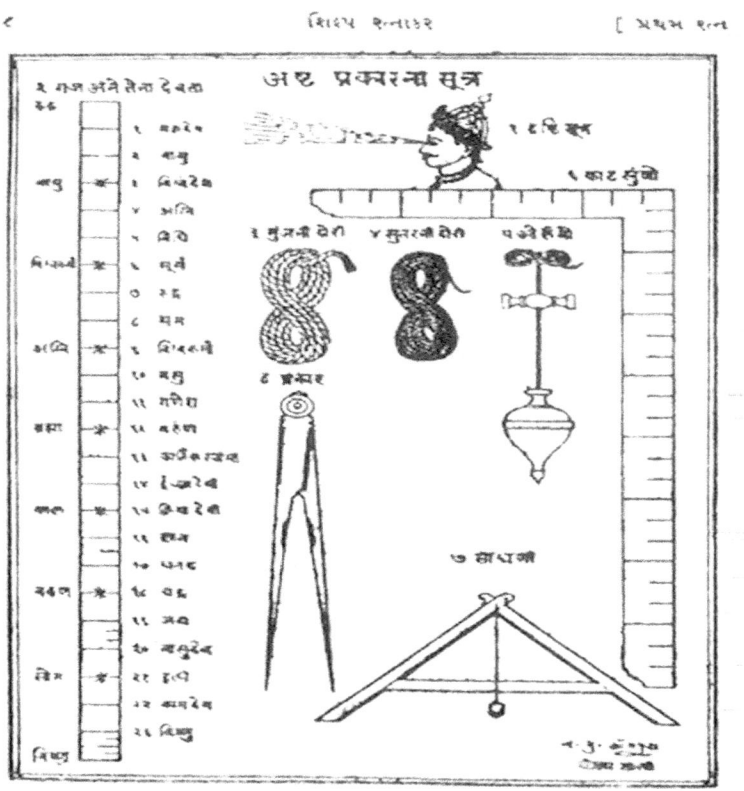

The basic construction technique used in the Hindu temple was the trabeated system or the post and lintel method which was extended by the use of corbelling techniques. This method was originally used for wooden construction in India and was later adopted for the stone structures as well. The principal tools in the hands of the *Sthapati* and *Sutragrahi* are collectively called *sutrashtaka*. The eight tools of measurement are the *sutrashtaka*: scale, rope, cord, plumb line, tri-square, compass, level and the eye. The scale and rope are of a prescribed length and are for measuring, while the rest are used for examining the site and for geometrical construction. Of the eight instruments, the eye of the geomancer is divine: "The eye is the Sun: for the Person's great dimensioned world (*matrah*) depends upon the eye, for with the eye he surverys material things, since it is with the eye that he moves about amongst dimensioned objects." *Matrah* literally means measured things, or the material world of measurable things, or whatever occupies space.

In the trabeated system only the horizontal and the vertical members are used and the stability is achieved by the massive arrangements of vertical elements such as pillars and pilasters together and heavy cross beams and lintels. The use of the spanning system to enclose the interior spaces was the most typical feature of this system. The roofing system consists of horizontally laid slabs of stone spanning from one supporting beam or wall to the other.

In the corbelling system the stones or the bricks in each horizontal course are projected out to bridge the gap between the two walls to diminish until it can be closed with a single piece of stone or brick. The corbelling system was used to create the interiors of the temple and the stone shells of the super structure that rise above the sanctum.

The construction of temple was a long process and used to last for decades. The building of the temple was divided into three stages. The first stage is the planning of the temple where *sthapati* with the *sutragrahi* and other team members did the planning to determine the overall architectural conception of the temple. The second stage was the carving of the different parts of the temple with the *takshaka* instructing the sculptors and *silpis* to carve the parts according to the drawings, specifications and guidelines. The third and the final stage was the assembling of the parts of the temple i.e. the actual construction of the temple. Even today this same process is followed with slight variations done due to the availability of modern construction technology.

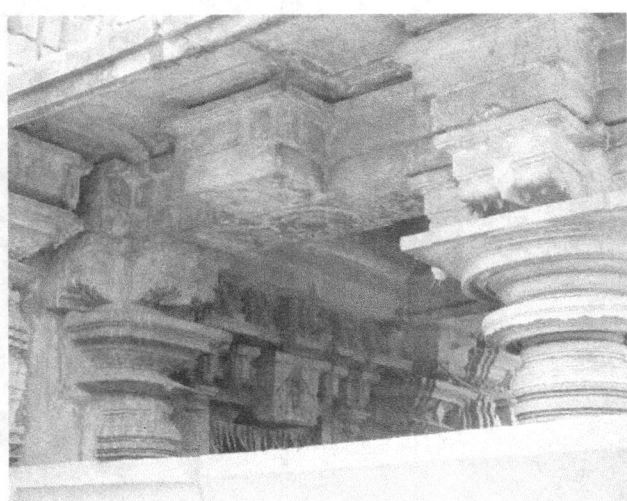 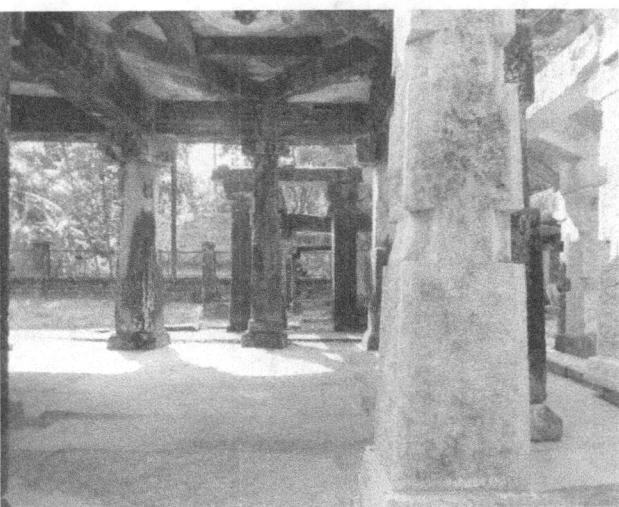

Examples of Trabeated Construction from Chennakesava Temple Anekere and Kattale Basadi Barkur

Stage I: Planning

This stage includes the **(i) Selection of the site**: Intially an auspicious land is selected for the construction of temple as mentooned in the ancient treatises. **(ii) Inspection, insemination and leveling of the site**: The probable site for the construction is first examined for the type of soil, colour, odour, form, flavour and sound by performing some simple test on site. For example, a pit is dug on the site and the soil which has been taken out is put back again and checked whether the level of the packed soil is higher, same or lower. The land with the higher and the same level of packed soil are selected for the construction. When the inspections, leveling and tilling is done, the site is ready for the laying out the divine diagram or the *vastupurashamandala*. **(iii) Orientation, measurements and layout**: The method by which orientation was undertaken was based on the 'Indian circle method' and was based on the use of an instrument known as '*shanku-yantra*' or the 'gnomon,' which is an ancient device for determining the east-west direction as well as for knowing time. This method deeply influenced the geometry of the temple plan and its development. The nature of the main deity greatly influences the orientation of the temple. **(iv) Selection of material**: stone is considered as the most sacred building material. The stones are used in temple construction according to the availability and climate of the region. The stone selected for the construction should be of even colour, hard and perfect, pleasing to touch. The hard and even stones are used for the plinth, columns, beams and slabs. The supple stones are used for the construction of sculptures, idols, carvings etc. The preferred stones for the construction were then quarried. **(v) Quarrying of stone:** In the past the stones were quarried using wooden wedges that are driven into the rocks and then wetted to cause expansion. This in turn causes the rocks to crack and are thus cut by subsequent application of pressure and dressed. **(vi) Transportation of materials:** In the past the transportation of the stones from the quarries to the building site was done on the wooden rollers drawn by the elephants or floated on the wooden barge along the rivers and the canals.

Stage II: Carving on the temple

This stage included carving different parts of the temple such as pillars, beams and brackets etc. as per the drawings and specifications decided by the *sthapati*. Each stone to be included in temple construction was carved separately and labeled to be assembled together in an interlocking system. **(i) Cutting and carving stone:** the team of the mason or *takshaka* cut stone blocks to appropriate sizes, another team of carvers would give the stone a basic shape and finally the sculptors would give these the final form desired. The joining system of each stone had to be pre-decided and rough joinery details were prepared simultaneously. **(ii) Drawing in stone:** the intricate ornate carvings on the stones depend on precise drawings and separate artists would be involved for this purpose. In earlier days, the drawings on stone were made by sharpened charcoal or natural dyes used on a sharpened bamboo shoot. While carving narrative tales from the Epics or *puranas* on stone, separate frames or panels were prepared for each episode of the tale. **(iii) Polishing the stone:** the final phase of the work involved polishing the carved stones into the final form. **(iv) Tools and equipments:** the basic tools, hammer and different type of chisels were used in cutting and carving the stone. The tools were made locally in the work yards only and were sharpened regularly to keep them work-ready.

Stage III: Process of temple building

i. **Assembly of elements:** final and most important stage for the construction of the temple was the assembly of all the parts together, at the site the carved parts of the temple were erected into their exact position by rope and pulley on the scaffoldings. Ramps were also constructed from timber and sand to ease the placing of heavy members.

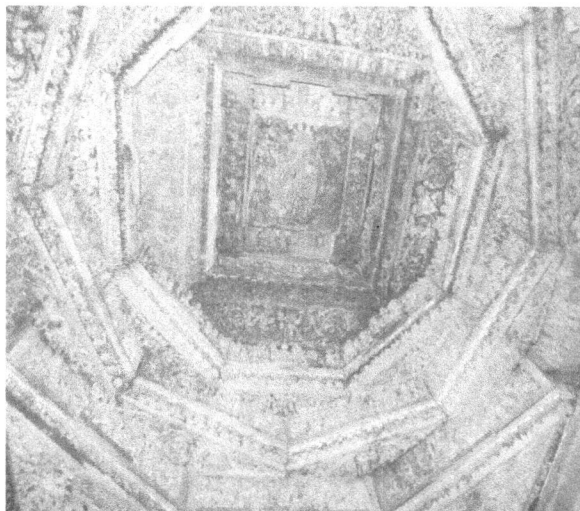 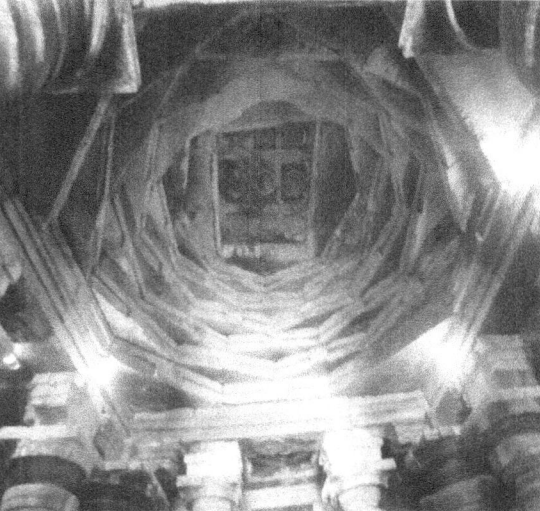

Examples of Corbelled Domical Ceilings Shantinatha Basadi and Parsvanatha Basadi at Bastihalli, Halebid

ii. **Joinery System:** In the ancient times, the traditional Hindu temples were built from the timber and bamboo using traditional *kuti* and *sala* architecture. During the period of stone construction, the architectural elements and the decorative details of the temple continued to follow the timber construction models for centuries in one form or another even though the original purpose and the context was lost. The timber joinery system was followed to assemble all the parts of the temple together. The major joining systems used were different types of mortise and tenon joint, and the lap joint. Another kind of joint similar to the mortise and tenon joint used a peg fixed between the two mortise cut out in two different stones. This joint was usually used between two courses of masonry to avoid the movement of stones due to lateral forces. In the past natural binders were used in the joints.

The final construction of the temple starts with the **(i) Laying of foundation**, a pit of was dug throughout the base which was wider than the base of the temple. The foundation was fully packed with layers of stone and rubble one layer above the other. **(ii) Plinth**, the stones placed above the foundation stones acted as the retaining wall for the rubble compacted earth with in the plinth area of the structure. The number of courses of stones at the plinth varied according to the size of the temple from 3 to 10 numbers. The top most courses on plan i.e. the stone floor of the temple, where exactly the vertical components were raised, was marked with chisel marks (mason marks) and grooves for the pillar bases without lines for rising walls and entrances. **(iii) Walls**, the main structural masonry walls are constructed as a stone composite masonry with stone, brick with lime or mud as the masonry core. The average thickness of the masonry wall varied from 800 to1200 mm. Through stones were provided at regular intervals to act as ties and thus strengthen the walls.

iii. **Columns and Beams,** are monolithic structures, extending like linear shafts. Columns were usually made up of 5 parts and all were interlocked by the mortise and tenon joints. The five parts consisted of two parts of the base one part as the shaft and two as the capital of the column. (v) *Mandapa*, may be flat roofed in the south and have pyramidical superstructure in the north. The *mandapa* ceiling is built with basic beam and slab construction method.

Were Hindu temples constructed to be earthquake proof?

Professor Vardha A. Gokhale of BN College of Architecture, Pune read a paper at the 13th World Conference on Earthquake Engineering held in Vancouver in 2004 and established that the design of the ancient and medieval Hindu temples was earthquake resistant to a very large extent.

She concluded that, "The characteristic configuration, simple geometric form of the Indian temple has increased structural strength against earthquake movements. Thoughtfully conceived design and constructional practices, which were executed with an extraordinary perfection, resulted in the creation of these everlasting, structurally sound structures, which have proved earthquake resistant to a considerable extent. The architectural heritage of India is full of possibilities which can provide the basis of inspiration for future requirements, if we can derive from them the fundamental aesthetical values constructional techniques in building design which may sometimes be valid in the very changed circumstances of today."

In support of her conclusion she dwelt on symmetry and stability of the structures by drawing from the architectural design and the construction methodology of these temples.

4.11 USE OF SCIENCE, MATHEMATICS, GEOMETRY AND ASTRONOMY IN TEMPLE DESIGN

Though architecture is broadly definable as a branch of fine arts having for its object the production of edifices pleasing to a cultivated and artistic mind, it falls primarily within the realm of science. The principles of construction and engineering employed in building ancient temples and the way in which these structures were designed to support weights or counteract thrust are capable of being categorized as scientific.

Before replacement of the brick medium by stone, there was a short-lived phase of 'rock-architecture.' The cut-in-caves and cut-out-monoliths are imitations of the contemporary brick and wood architecture in all their intricate details. With the advent of stone in temple construction, Hindus began to build huge structures involving the use of large slabs of granite for all the elevational limbs of the structure viz. *adisthana* (basement), *bhitti* and *kudyastambha* (walls and columnation), *prastara* (architrave), *griva* (clerestory), *sikhara* (roof) and *stupi* (finial). And this called for rigorous planning, resource management, skills management, organizational structuring and appropriate engineering techniques. The first signs of complex temple project management thus came into being.

The Temple is not only a home of God but his representation in the structure of temple which resembles human form. The temple design includes the archetypical image of the cosmic person spread out yogi-like, symmetrically filling the gridded space of the floor plan. The symbolism of the temple plan and elevation suggests that the *garbhagriha* represents the head and the *gopuram* the feet of the cosmic person. Other parts of the building complex are identified with other parts of the body. For instance, the *sukanasi* or *ardhamandapa* (the small enclosure in front of the *garbhagriha*) is the nose; the *antarala* (the passage next to the previous one, leading to passage next to the previous one, leading to the main *mandapa* called *sabhamandapa*, is the neck; the various *mandapas* are the body; the *prakara* (surrounding walls) are the hands and so on. Vertically, the *garbhagriha* represents the neck, the *sikhara* (superstructure over the *garbhagriha*) the head, the *kalasa* (finial) the tuft of hair (*sikha*).

Hindu cosmology, manifested in the plan of Hindu temple two dimensionally, was also manifested in its elevation and thus reflected three dimensionally and more symbolically in the whole of the temple. For the elevation too, *sthapati* took the fractal as a medium to visualize the manifested form of cosmos. To apply the fractal as a tool for constructing the temple, perhaps, *sthapati* (architect designer) used both mathematical fractal theory and formulae, but he was also influenced by the nature where God himself created mountains, trees, leaves, etc. as the examples of fractal.

In the structure of almost all Hindu temples, *sthapati* took the mountain as a model of fractal object where self-similar mounts are repeated and recurred, pointing towards the sky. They made the rising towers, *sikhara* on the temple structure by copying the form of mountain which dominates on the earth, and the replicas of soaring towers on *sikhara* depict the series of repetitive universes. Even the literal meaning of *sikhara* is mountain.

According to Hindu mythology a *Purna Vastu* or a perfect building is that which is properly oriented and constructed with carefully laid out norms to protect it from the evil forces of the nature, which include floods, storms, hurricanes and earthquakes. The 22nd chapter of Brihatsamhita, which contains 107 chapters including some on science and technology, describes earthquakes (*bhukamp*) and various aspects with reference to earthquakes resistance of the buildings. Indian temples, which were invariably built in accordance with these norms, are the living evidences of structural efficiency and technological aspects of the Indian craftsman and master builders (*sthapati*).

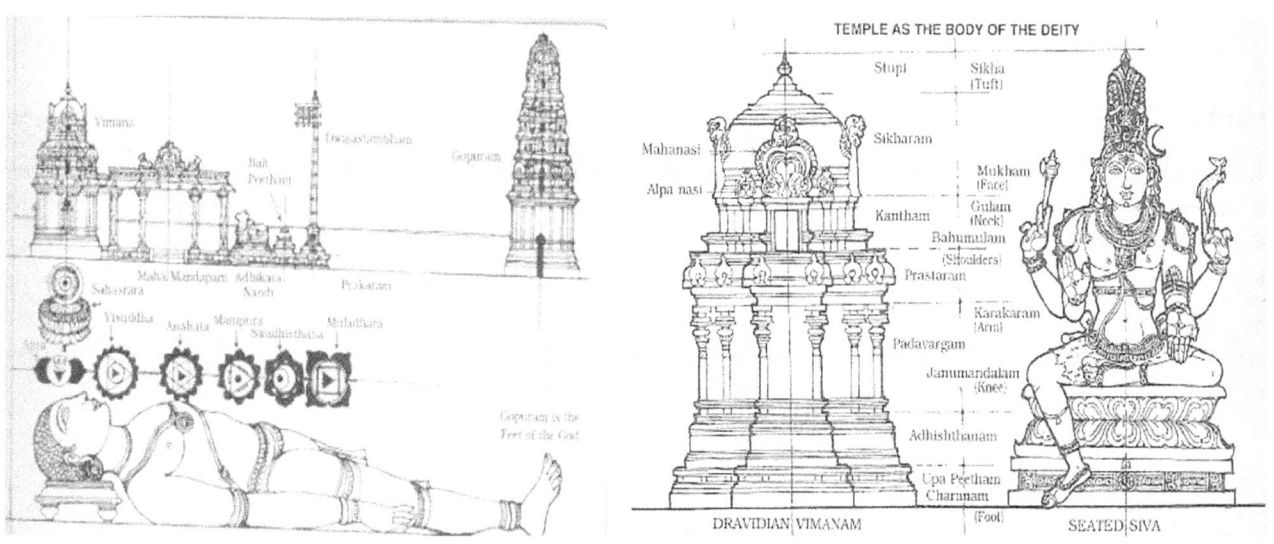

Temple Represented as Different Parts of the Body of the Cosmic Person

The concepts underlying Indian architecture can be traced back to the worldview articulated in the Vedas and the metaphysics of the Upanishads. The earth on which the temple is built must be consecrated, the water tested, and the consistency of soil examined. The chief factor that gives these temples a considerable degree of earthquake resistance is usually their configuration, for example the simple and structurally logical configuration of a *Dravida* temple particularly of the main structure (*vimana*).

The term symmetry denotes a geometrical property of building configuration. Symmetrical forms are always preferred to those configurations with non-symmetrical profile, because asymmetry tends to produce eccentricity between the center of mass and center of gravity, which result in torsion. On the other hand symmetry tends to stress the concentrations. The selection of symmetrical plan shapes and layouts is of great importance in seismic design, because symmetry about the elevational axis is of less dynamic significance than plan symmetry.

In seismic design the proportions of a building may be more important than its absolute size. The Indian doctrine of proportions is designed not only to correlate the various parts of building in an aesthetically pleasing manner but also to bring the entire building into a magical harmony with the space. In all manuscripts the proportion between the length, breadth and height of the various parts of the temple is the subject of detailed study subject to comprehensive rules. These rules which were generally strictly followed in Indian temples resulted in the proportions and seemed to be favorable for better performance against seismic forces.

Vastusastra texts are instruction manuals for the practicing architect or *sthapati* and describe in detail the construction of temple starting from selection of site, measurements and proportions and structural process to the establishment and consecration of the presiding deity. The texts generally consist of verbal instructions and formulae intended for the architect who is well versed in the basic skills of architecture and can work from these formulae. The many different forms of temples (*Samarangana sutradhara* describes 64 different kinds of temples) and the way to construct them is described in general programs. By making certain decision and following the given rules of proportions, growth and measurement, all specific details and dimensions of a temple can be worked out.

The system of measurement followed by *vastusastras* called the *Tala* system or *Talamana*, does not depend on absolute dimensions, but defines all dimensions as sets of relationships of proportions of component parts of the temple with respect to the whole. This system has the advantage that it is possible to work out the proportions of the parts irrespective of the overall size. The existence of such a general program of proportional relationships independent of absolute size enables the same procedures to be repeated in gradually diminishing sizes in correspondingly smaller grids – theoretically up to infinity! This feature was of great importance, considering that many self-similar procedures that had to be carried out in determining the forms of various parts of the temple.

Fractal Geometry and Hindu temple

In depicting an evolving cosmos of growing complexity which is self-replicating, self-generating, self-similar and dynamic, several geometrical construction procedures are followed in the designing of a Hindu temple. The growth accompanying evolution cannot be expressed merely by scaling there is also a growth of complexity of evolving shapes. The procedures used are recursive and generate visually complex shapes from simple initial shapes (like triangles, rectangles, squares, circles, ellipses etc.) through successive application of production rules that are similar to the rules of generating fractals. Some major procedures to generate complex shapes and patterns which can be identified are:

- Fractalization
- Self-similar iteration in decreasing or increasing scales
- Repetition, superimposition and juxtaposition

It will be important to have a brief discussion on what fractalization in fact means and what fractal geometry is.

The term *'Fractal'* actually comes from the Latin word *'Fractus'* which means *'broken.'* Fractal means, the recursive geometrical forms, bearing self-similarity on different scales. According to the Fractal Foundation – "A fractal is a never ending pattern. Fractals are infinitely complex patterns that are self-similar across different scales. They are created by repeating a simple process repeatedly in an ongoing feedback loop. Driven by recursion, fractals are images of dynamic systems – the pictures of Chaos. Geometrically, they exist in between our familiar dimensions. Fractal patterns are extremely familiar, since nature is full of fractals. For instance: trees, rivers, coastlines, mountains, clouds, seashells, hurricanes, etc. Abstract fractals – such as the Mandelbrot Set (a particular set of complex numbers which has a highly convoluted fractal boundary when plotted.) can be generated by a computer calculating a simple equation over and over.

"Self-similarity" is the phenomenon of each part being geometrically similar to the whole. It is the core concept of the Fractal Theory. Interestingly, self-similarity is one of the basic principles of organization in the Hindu temple architecture. The Hindu temple is designed and constructed as miniature forms of the Cosmos as envisioned in Hindu philosophy and beliefs.

Hindu Philosophy describes the cosmos as holonomic. The holonomic character implies the virtue of self-similarity, homogeneity, isotropy and symmetries of various kinds. Like a hologram, each fragment of the cosmos is considered to be whole in it and to contain information similar to the whole. The history of the evolution of the Hindu temples is a very vast field of study. Starting from the cave temples to the palatial temple complexes, all styles have followed an exhaustive path of evolution through experimentation. During Gupta period and onwards the temple architecture in India flourished in a much disciplined manner. The architects, artisans and masons gradually developed the aesthetic sense of complexity. As a result, the formation of Hindu temples became more complex and embodied an inherent sense of fractal geometry.

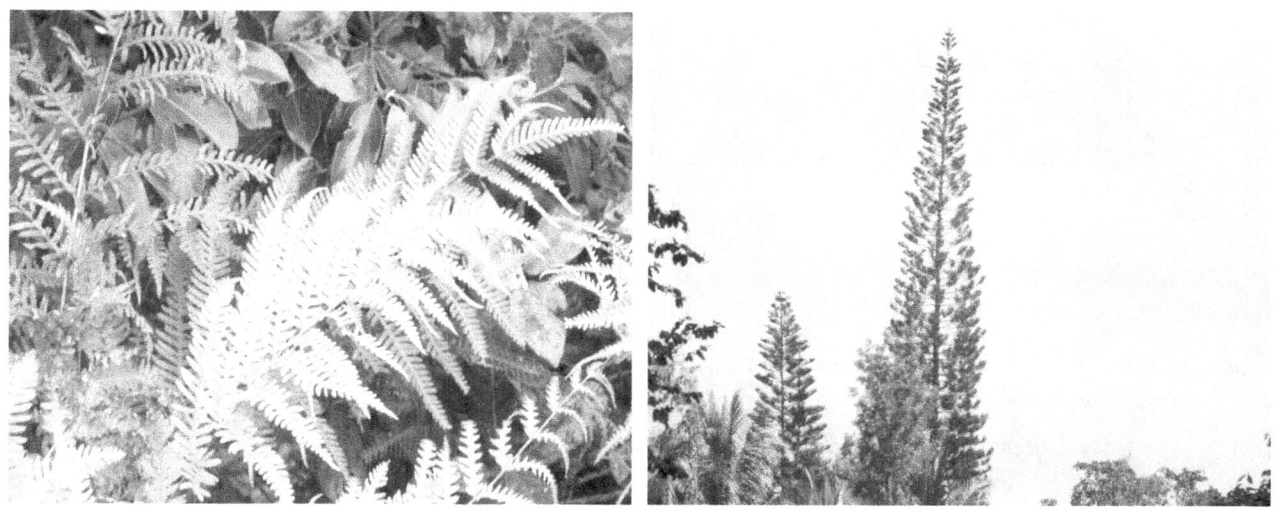

Examples of Fractals in Nature

The *Vastupurusha* (the Cosmic Person) is a key concept in Hindu temple architecture. The plan of the Hindu temple strictly follows the principles described in *Puranas* related to the *Vastupurushamandala*. It follows three basic sets of iteration and further sub-categories. Limited technical expertise exists about all the *mandalas* and their formulation through alteration and repetition of fractals. In Hindu temple architecture, geometry always plays a vital and enigmatic role. The geometry of a plan starts with a line, forming an angle, evolving a triangle, then a square and distinctly a circle and so on, ultimately deriving complex forms. As per the previous discussion, the occurrence of complexity, results into self-similarity and further it leads to the occurrence of fractal geometry. Geometry is a disciplined field and the fractals follow it. Both of them have definite paths of action. In following diagrams as shown below, the role of fractal theory in basic geometry of Hindu temple plans is exhibited.

In Sanskrit *'Vinyaasa'* means orientation and *'sutra'* means thread, line or axis. It is related with the lay out and orientation of temple plans. *Vastupurushamandala* is the base of evolution of a temple plan. *Vinyasasutra* comes into play after the initial evolution of the temple plan. During the determination of the axis and orientation of the temple and its surroundings, ancient architects used to follow the process described in Hindu scripts like *Vastusastra, Manasara* etc. However, all the plans followed geometries with fractal character. It is postulated that, some of them were made consciously and some unconsciously.

Fractal also has a great impact on temple elevations. As is the case of two-dimensional plans, fractal also controls the formation of the elevations in three dimensions. Elevation treatment of temple differs according to regions in India. Therefore, tracing out typical examples, can be exhaustive. The following divisions are almost common to all temples throughout India. Overall, the whole temple structure in three dimensions form expresses the self-similarity in the structure. On consideration of silhouettes of temple structures, a visual language of gradual progression starting from the base to the spires is prominent.

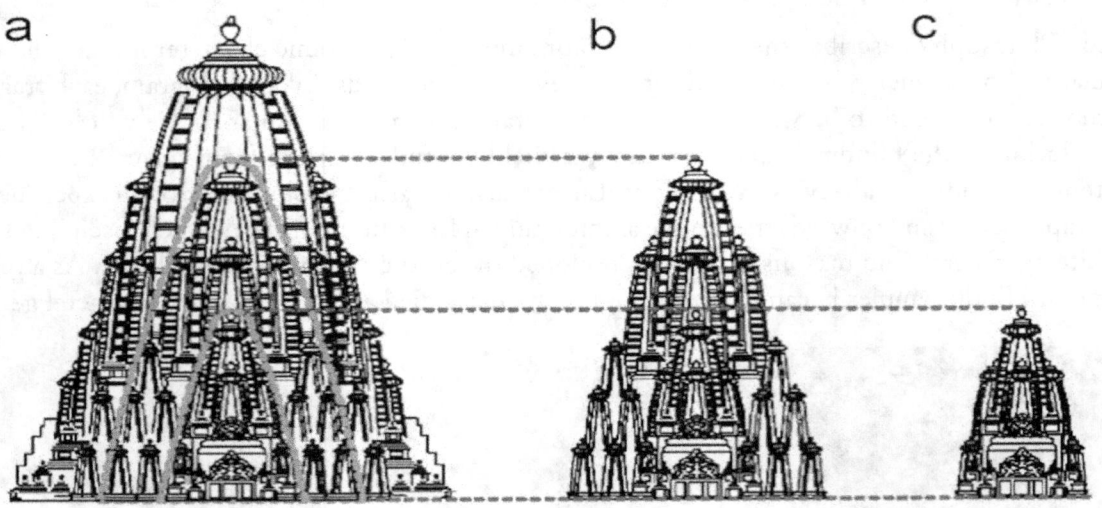

Fractals in Temple Sikhara

The following are some probable reasons behind the use of Fractal Geometry in Hindu temple architecture.

a) It can be argued that, practicing fractals is none other than the implication of the sense of completeness since the concept of fractals is that of the part to whole and whole to part.

b) The fractal theory fully supports the Hindu philosophical concept of "one among all, all is one." It brings the feeling of oneness (the concept of *Atman*).

c) It can bring a sense of strength, both structurally as well as visually.

d) Self-similar elements in the design, seek the attention of the visitors and pilgrims repeatedly and gradually entice them to think about it and create a clear state of mind with a holistic perception.

e) Self-similar repetition in structure generates an identity of elements as well as form.

f) Experimentation can also be a reason behind the evolution and realisation of fractal theory in Hindu temple architecture through the ages.

g) The term, "Self-similar" brings a sense of modularity. Therefore, it generates the same style of work using the same modules, which saves resources. Local materials, workmanship and time offer ease of execution across huge structures, such as temples within the same region.

h) Making of similar kind of elements repeatedly generates a habit and practice and practice perfects the execution.

i) From an aesthetical viewpoint, fractal geometry brings about "order in chaos" and thereby a beauty in complexity.

The use of recursive procedures involving self-similar iteration and fractalization in the designing of Hindu temples in accordance with the ancient architectural texts has given rise to a very distinct architectural style. The form of this genre of architecture results from an attempt to express certain concepts of Hindu philosophy about the cosmos, using symbolic vocabulary of forms as well as construction procedures that have a symbolic significance.

Temple design and Astronomy

Canonical texts describing the plan of the Hindu temple allude to its astronomical basis, and in this, Hindu sacred geometry is not different in conception from the sacred geometry of other ancient cultures, although it has its own unique features. If astronomical alignments characterize ancient temples of megalithic Europe, Egyptians, Maya, Aztecs, and Javanese, they also characterize Hindu temples. In some temples, the *garbhagriha* (innermost chamber) is illuminated by the setting sun only on a specific day of the year, or the temple may deviate from the canonical east-west axis and be aligned with a *nakshatra* (constellation) that has astrological significance for the patron or for the chosen deity of the temple.

A part of the astronomical knowledge coded in the temple lay-out and form is canonical or traditional, while the rest may relate to the times when the temple was erected. The astronomy of the temple provides clues relevant not only to the architecture but also the time when it was built. Numerous research projects have been undertaken by various scientific research institutions to study the relationship between the Hindu temple design and astronomical calculations. In Karnataka, there are several temples with such design configuration linked with astronomical events. While knowledge of astronomy played a vital role for the *sthapati* in deciding the axial orientation of the temple, it also became a vital tool to align rituals with astronomical events such as eclipses, equinoxes etc. The right placement of the *ashta-dikpalas* (eight guardians of the directions) in the *vastupurushamandala* and later during construction in the *navaranga* ceiling sculptures was an important consideration.

Knowledge of astronomy in India dates back to Vedic times. References to astrological and astronomical calculations exist in Vedic literature. Since the concept of temple and temple design too emanated from these texts, astronomical connections too were devised in order to relate the temple with the Cosmos as a whole.

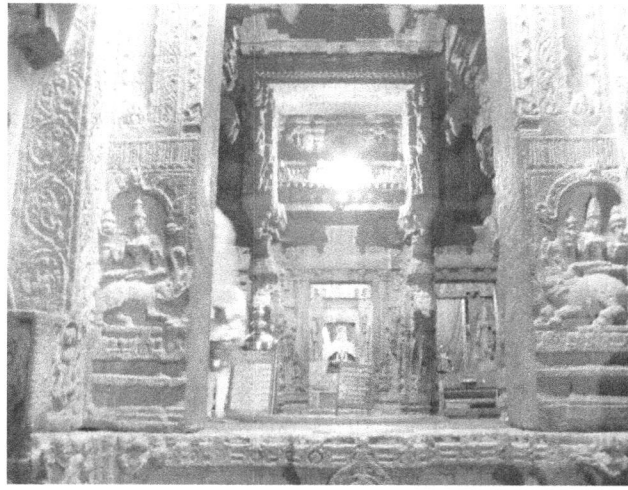
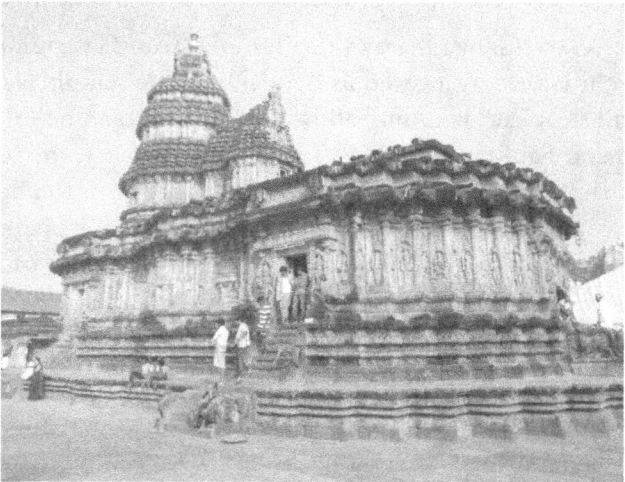

Vidyasankara Temple with Zodiac Pillars at Sringeri

In India, the Lunar Mansions, called *Nakshatras* are found from the earliest period. However, the moon no longer goes close to all the *Nakshatras*. It is generally now felt that this may be due to the precession of the equinoxes which produces subtle changes in the apparent path of the Moon in the heavens over time. Using modern astronomical software scientists have calculated the average distance of the path of the moon from all the *Nakshatras* as a function of time and found that the distance was minimum around the period close to 3000 BCE. It is therefore suggested that the *Nakshatras* were probably designed around that period, when the first large settlements were beginning to emerge in the subcontinent.

The oldest of Hindu literature is the Rig Veda which forms the basis of Hindu Religion. Its dating has been a rather controversial issue but its antiquity as the earliest Indian document has not been doubted. Rig Veda is a document of a settled community with elaborate discussions of rituals and philosophy. It however, has a separate addendum called *Vedanga Jyotisa* or the astronomical treatise of the Rig Veda that insists that "Just like the combs of peacocks and the crest jewels of serpents, so does *Jyotiṣa*." The term Megalithic period is used in general terms of prehistoric times. The specific historical time will of course be sensitive to the culture. Two scientists, Subbarayappa and Sarma have compiled the list of astronomical references in various ancient Indian literatures. From this, it is clear that the authors of Rig Veda were aware of the discrepancies between the duration of Lunar year and Solar year and the need to add intercalary month for synchronizing the two. Yajur Veda recommends 2 intercalary months in 5 years. The days are named according to the phases of the Moon. They knew that 12 lunar months amounted to 354 days. The synchronization was done using *Ekadasaratra* ceremony. This made 365 days in a year leaving an error of 0.25 days per year. But the Vedic year consisted of 12 months, each of 30 days. This gives the duration of the year as 360 days. This was synchronized to the seasons simply by adding 5 days to the calendar. Solstice days were also noted in literature.

The concept of Yuga was introduced as a more sophisticated attempt to synchronize the Solar and Lunar calendars. The 5 Yugas were, *Samvatsara, Parivatsara, Idavatsara, Anuvatsara*, and *Idvatsara*. Two intercalary months *Amhaspati* and *Samsarpa* were added to complete a Yuga. While commenting on Yuga Lagadha, the author of Vedanga Jyotisa of Yajur Veda (dated to 1350 BC) had a fairly good idea about the year being a number of full days plus fraction of a day. Even in this period, the astronomical observations are accurate enough to permit dating some of the ancient documents based on their astronomical references.

Three important temples of Karnataka believed to be linked to astronomical calculations discussed here are, Veeranarayana temple Belavadi, Gavi Gangadhareswara temple Gavipuram (Bengaluru) and Vidyasankara temple Shringeri. It is believed that the first beam of sun light falls on the principal deity of Veeranarayana on every 21st March. Obviously that relates to the design and planning of the temple layout in perfect relation with the movement of the earth around the Sun.

Gavi Gangadhareswara Temple also Gavipuram Cave Temple is an example of Indian rock-cut architecture, is located in Bengaluru. The temple is famous for its mysterious stone discs in the forecourt and the exact planning allowing the Sun to shine on shrine in certain time of the year. On the occasion of Makar Sankranti (13/14th January every year), the temple witnesses a unique phenomenon in the evening as the sunlight passes through an arc between the horns of Nandi and falls directly on the linga inside the cave and illuminating the interior idol. This is a phenomenon that is proof of the technical excellence of the ancient architects, who combined his knowledge of astronomy with great architectural skill.

Vidyasankara Temple in Shringeri is a 14th century construction famous for its twelve zodiac pillars. In the eastern half of the structure is a *mandapa* with twelve pillars, huge monoliths carrying large figures and carrying heavy projecting corbels on top. These twelve pillars are marked by the twelve signs of the zodiac in their regular order, and arranged in such a manner that the rays of the sun fall on each of them in the order of the twelve solar months. On the floor is a large circle, marked with converging lines to indicate the direction of the shadows. The central ceiling is an exquisite piece of workmanship with lotus and pecking parrots.

There are many other temples in Karnataka with astronomical considerations having gone into their construction but the three temples described above are among the most well known among them.

All this indicates that importance of astronomy, the calendar and the movements of the sun and the moon were very well understood by the ancient architects. Alice Boner writes thus while introducing *Silpaprakasa*, a treatise on Orissan temple architecture written between 9th and 13th centuries CE: "the temple must in time-space direction be established in relation to the motion of the heavenly bodies. But in as much as it incorporates in a single synthesis and unequal courses of the sun, the moon and the planets, it also symbolizes all recurrent time sequences; the day, the month, the year and the wider cycles marked by the recurrence of a complete cycle of eclipses, when the sun and the moon are readjusted in their original positions, a new cycle of creation begins."

Although the role of astronomy in Hindu temple architecture has been widely recognized, our understanding of it has remained quite imprecise and undefined.

Borromean motifs and prime knots in temples

The basic idea of a Borromean ring is that the three rings are inseparable when taken together, but if one of the rings is taken out, the other two fall apart. It is an idea where the sum is more than the parts. An idea where things that individually don't stand up to make sense, when combined not in pairs but in three, makes something meaningful. Modern mathematics classifies this object as a 'Brunnian link.' Formally a link is a collection of 'knots' that do not intersect each other, but may otherwise be linked, such as simply two interlinked rings. A 'knot' conforms to our conventional notion of a string looping around itself but mathematicians prefer that the ends of the string be joined together. A single string that is not knotted at all, and is therefore called an 'unknot' and is topologically a circle. A Brunnian link (after H Brunn, German mathematician who published his work on knot theory in the late nineteenth century) is a link such that if any one of the components is removed, the remaining ones become 'trivial' and fall apart into unlinked unknots. However the best known and simplest example of a Brunnian link is the Borromean circles, three circles interlinked in such a manner that no two of them are linked but all three are simultaneously linked. The name derives from the medieval aristocratic Borromeo family from northern Italy who used this symbol extensively, including in their coat of arms. It is presumed that it signified the inseparable union of three powerful families at that time. The symbol however has been found in several other places and predates the medieval Italian family. It appears that a version of the Brunnian links with three triangles appears on 7th century Scandinavian rune stones where the god Odin is shown with these symbols called 'valknuts,' meaning slain warriors' knots. The links found on the ceiling of Chennakesava temple in Somathapura and the ceiling of Veeranarayana temple at Belavadi, appear to be symmetrical versions of this symbol. Hinduism also created several symbols with religious connotations. Symbols like Swastika, Sri Chakra and those in the shape of *yantras* and *mandalas* also form objects of worship. One symbol called the *Anahata Chakra* has two interlinked triangles at its centre. These triangles are supported by the Brunnian links. *Anahata Chakra* can be seen carved in various temples either on the walls or at the base of pillars. *Anahata Chakra* is the fourth primary chakra according to Yogic and Shakta Tantra. It is also called the Heart Chakra. Anahata is associated with a calm, serene sound devoid of violence.

The overlapping and interlinked triangles do something more interesting. Observe how if each triangle is traced, it goes "under" or "above" the other two triangles, although it forms a coupling on the whole. Pull out one triangle from the inscription, the other two fall off. They can be taken out separately, as they lie one over the other.

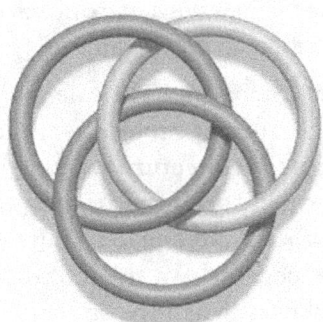

While the Borromean circles and triangles are topologically similar, they are geometrically quite different. It has been established mathematically, fairly recently, that Borromean circles of any relative sizes are impossible. However it is possible to construct Borromean configurations with ellipses of arbitrarily small eccentricities. Thus there cannot be an actual three-dimensional realization of the Borromean circles. This constraint of geometry does not forbid Borromean configurations for other shapes such as ellipses, triangles or golden rectangles. Golden rectangles are those whose sides are of the golden ratio; three such orthogonal rectangles can be inscribed in a regular icosahedron (polyhedra with 20 faces, each an equilateral triangle). There are also Brunnian links when the number of components 'n' is larger than 3. In this case there could be situations where no two components are linked, but there is a nontrivial sublink. Such links are called 'Borromean,' as opposed to Brunnian where every single sublink is trivial. Such Borromean configurations where the objects of links are not just circles and triangles may be referred to as Borromean motifs. The examples from the Veeranarayana and Chennakesava temples cited above have Borromean motifs on their ceilings.

A possible example is the model of the atom, with its usual proton, electron and the neutron. A combination of all these three forms a stable atom, while individually these components are unstable.

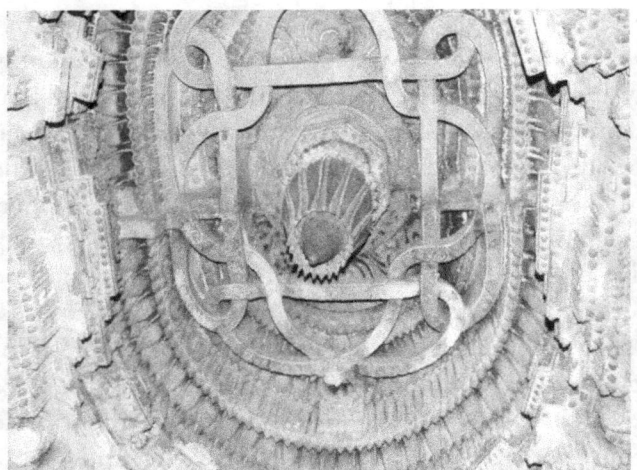 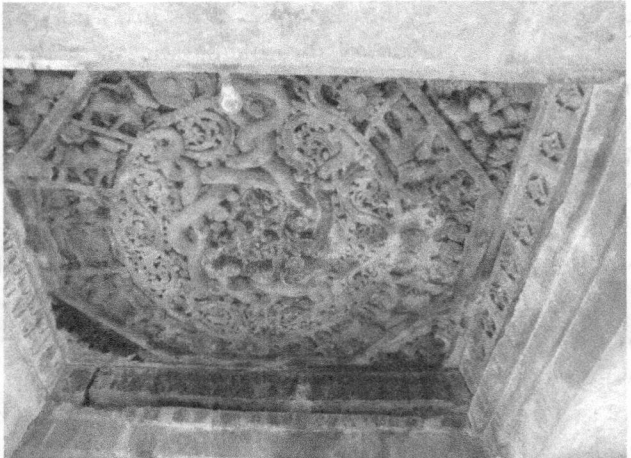

"Borromean Motif" in the Celing at Kesava Temple Somanathapura and "Prime Knots" at Veeranayana Temple Belavadi

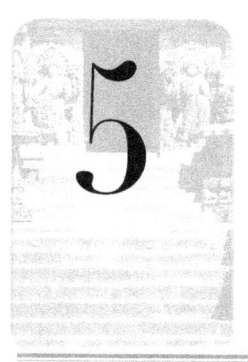

HISTORY OF ART ARCHITECTURE IN KARNATAKA

5.1 KARNATAKA HISTORY OF ARCHITECTURE-PREHISTORIC

We begin with our definition of architecture to trace its history in Karnataka. Architecture is an organized or planned usage of space created by structural design cut into stone blocks/slabs or carved out of rocky hill or of brick and mortar as a result of manual labour which symbolize the abstract or concrete utility. This form may be secular or religious and may even be product of the times and cultural development of the period to which it relates. Karnataka's architectural development may perhaps be over 5000 years old transforming from the shelter-burial-ritual ideology related structural construction to the modern day intelligent buildings. Our concern here mainly extends from the Neolithic period to 1300 CE or almost the end of the Hoysala period. Chronologically speaking, the study will first relate to the protohistoric architecture and then go into historical architecture commencing from the introduction of organized religions.

Like everywhere else during prehistoric times human beings in Karnataka too depended on forests for their supply of food primarily on hunting animals and other creatures as well as gathering forest fruits, vegetables, edible roots, honey etc. Caves and rock-shelters in the hills became their natural habitat in the process. The earliest forms of arts and architecture were all linked with wood and rocks. Rock art in the form of paintings generally depicted themes from their daily lives such as wild animals, fleeing or stationary or being hunted by men. There were certain floral representations and geometric forms too among those paintings.

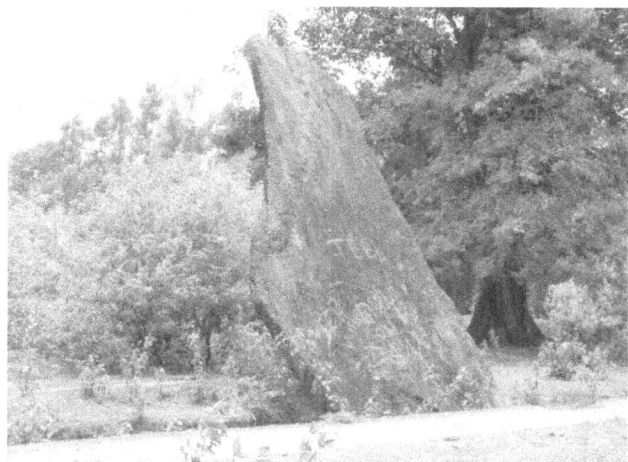
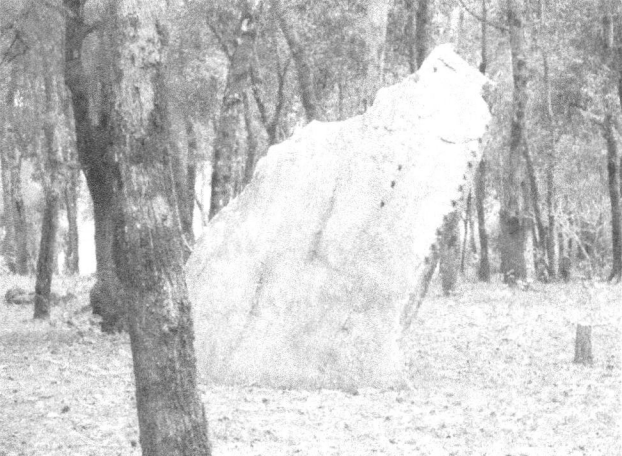

Nilskal, Menhirs from Byse

The rock-art included paintings done in caves and rock shelters, engravings etched in linear forms, peckings carried out on rock surfaces, cup-marks created on rock surfaces, carvings leading to work of art in relief or works of art on bones and ivory. Most Indian rock art works date back to periods belonging to the Mesolithic period during the times 8000–5000 BCE.

The earliest signs of construction or creating structures other than merely cave drawings in Karnataka date back to 3500 years or so. Byse, a village in Shivamogga district has Megalithic structures at a site called Nilskal Byana with menhirs standing in no particular order. However, in 2007 scientists from Manipal University and Tata Institute of Fundamental Research surveyed 26 of the menhirs in Byse and reached the conclusion that these had a certain astronomical significance the way they were erected. The menhirs which were earlier being seen as rock memorials now indicate that the site may have been an astronomical observatory more than 3000 years ago. The menhirs are speculated to date prior to 1000 BCE.

Upper or late Neolithic people constructed huts made of wattle and doab buttressed by stone boulders to make their shelters. Presumably these structures were covered by conical roofs resting on bamboo or wooden posts as revealed in archaeological excavations in sites like Brahamagiri, Sanganakallu, Tekkalakota, Piklikhal etc. From Tekkalakota excavations, it emerged that three categories of hut floors belonging to the late Neolithic phase could be described as under:

- Circular on plan, lower portion built of wattle and doab and with conical thatched roof resting on bamboo or wooden posts planted into red murrum;
- Circular with sides partially supported or buttressed against huge stone boulders;
- Square or rectangular structures built against huge boulders for support and stability.

By the time upper Neolithic age arrived, modifications in living patterns became discernible. Excavations at Piklikhal suggest well rammed houses fixed at the edge by wooden posts supporting the walls of woven reed smeared with mud. The role of structure during these times was very limited and it was perishable in nature in conformity with the semi-settled living of the people. Sanganakallu is the first established village in south India where people chose to adopt a settled life dependent on agriculture and animal husbandry rather than the old pastoral living between 3000 BCE to 2500 BCE.

Megalithic Iron age and later periods saw the appearance of high non perishable architecture that took form of different typological burials. Structures of this period like dolmens, cromlechs, rings of stones and burials have been seen at various places in Karnataka.

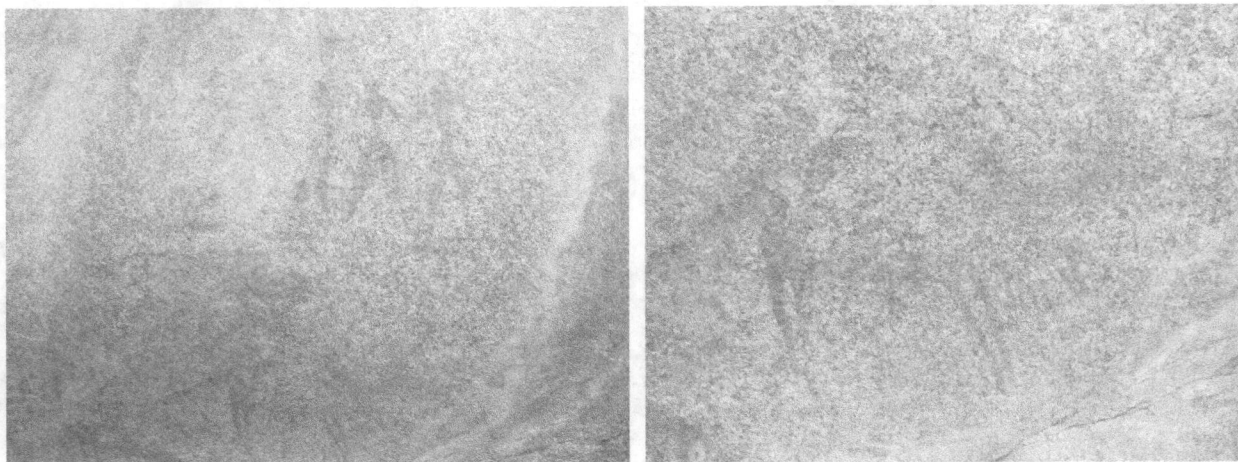

Rock Paintings from Hirebenkal

Prominent among these places with prehistoric structures are Hunukunda, Aihole, Hirebenkal, Chandravalli, Anegundi etc. Extensive use of geometric shapes is clearly visible in that many of these structures had cuttings and carvings in rectangular, square and circular shapes. Hirebenkal in particular contains nearly 400 funerary monuments dated to the transition between Neolithic and Iron Age periods. Many of the megalithic structures date back to 800–200 BCE. An old quarry site and workshop has also been discovered nearby which probably was the source of building material for the monuments. Some of the monuments are in the shape of port-holed chambers with perfect circular openings. These dolmen like monuments have been supported by stone slabs and erected perfectly without any mortar thus calling gravity into play.

Several type of such sepulchral monuments found at diverse locations included pit burials, stone circles, slabbed cist, rock-cut chambers or caves, dolmens, menhirs, umbrella stones, hood stones, port holed dolmens, stone alignments, avenues and barrows.

While construction and architecture were evolving in their initial stages in Karnataka, mining activity too was gathering momentum. Hunukunda in Kolar district is a prehistoric site where gold mining was carried out over 2000 years ago. The occurrence of cromlechs and gold husk having been found during excavations suggest that the authors of the cromlechs were ancient gold miners. The fact is also supported by the name the village bears. In ancient Tamil inscriptions the name Porkundam is mentioned. Porkundam means golden hill and perhaps Tamil rendering of the Kannada Hunukunda. Nearby is an ancient site where potsherds were discovered during excavations. Someswara temple of the Chola period is situated on this small hillock. To the west of the temple is the ancient site where there are several natural caves with remains of the prehistoric rock-cut sculptures and rock carvings.

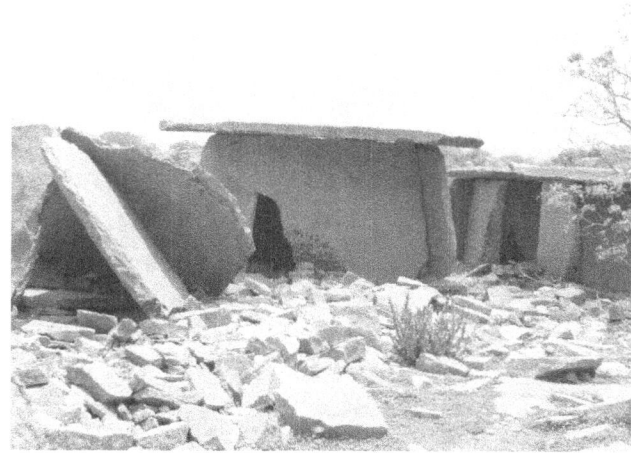
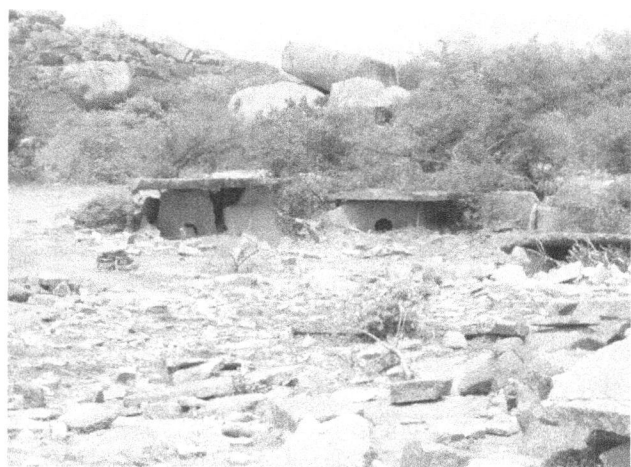

Dolmen Chambers from Hirebenkal

Iron mining and metal extraction was not new either to the people of Karnataka. The Iron Pillar at Kodachadri in the compound of the Mookambika temple is testimony to the fact that iron mining was carried out in Karnataka from ancient times. Scientists from NIT Surathkal and Indira Gandhi Centre for Atomic Research, Kalapakkam carried out studies on this pillar to establish the metallurgical heritage of the region. They concluded that the Iron Pillar was not a product of the modern iron making processes but an age old *adivasi* (tribal) and indigenous method of iron making.

Caves and rock shelters were the natural abode of men and gods through these times. During the Stone Age people started erecting walls by piling up stones or erecting stone slabs as seen in Hirebenkal. Stone walls served as protection against wind, rains and wild animals. Some kind of open air shrines too may have been in existence but no evidence of their existence has been found on archaeological grounds. Though in terms of Stone Age art there is ample data-base but in terms of stone architecture very limited evidence is available.

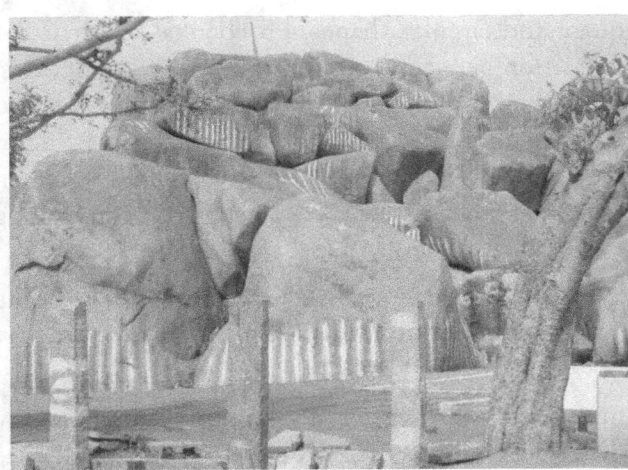 

Pre-historic Site of Hunukunda Where Ancient Gold Miners Lived

How were these prehistoric arts and architecture tied up with the classical traditions of arts and architecture of Karnataka is a difficult question to answer. There seems to be no positive evidence to support any such connection. However, the transition must have happened during the Sunga-Satavahana period as the organized religions started influencing arts and architecture. All the classical traditions were inspired by Buddhism, Jainism, Saivism, Vaishnavism, Shaktism and the traditions emanating from the local and tribal sects.

The earliest form of sacred structures or temples emerged from the hut (*kuti*) in which humans lived and rectangular huts with gable roofs called the *Sala* as shrines made from bamboos. As kingship emerged and civilization grew with evolving social systems of early eras, the concept of institutions and palace architecture developed. Bamboo was soon replaced by wood and timber. The palace was called *Prasada* and hence very often temple too is called *prasada* or palace of god. The temple architecture resulted in replacement of the open air platform shrines into structured temples with roofs and walls.

The use of stones, bricks and rock in construction probably dates back to the times of king Ashoka. Possessed of great ideals, Ashoka's policy throughout plainly indicates most earnest desire to institute permanent record of the establishment of the Buddhist faith within his widely-spread dominion. Stone and rock was thus the natural choice of medium to spread his messages. Rock edicts played a critical role in the spread of Ashoka's message across his empire. Ashoka ruled from 272 BCE to 232 BCE and accepted Buddhism in 264 BCE. Major part of Karnataka (more notably the northern parts) was under the Mauryan empire. Ashokan inscriptions do not merely indicate the boundary of the Ashokan empire but also assert that Buddhism had flourished here at that time. The principal contributions made to the art and architecture during the Ashokan times consisted of: (i) a series of edicts inscribed on the rocks, (ii) a number of tumuli or *stupas*, (iii) certain monolithic pillars, (iv) remains of a vast palace in the northern parts of India and (v) a group of rock chambers called *Chaityas* and *Viharas*.

5.2 KARNATAKA HISTORY OF ARCHITECTURE-BUDDHIST INFLUENCE

Spread of Buddhism, Jainism and Vedic Hinduism in Karnataka resulted in extensive and distinct contribution of the three religions to the progress in architecture in the region. It will be important to know a little about the way these religions contributed to the region's art and architecture.

Buddhism

It will be convenient to describe and classify various objects of Buddhist art and architecture under five following groups though at times it may really be difficult to separate them entirely from one another. Sometimes two or more of them may form parts together of one monument or shrine.

Stambha or Lat –These are pillars common to all styles of Indian architecture (be it Buddhist, Jaina or Hindu). Such pillars as part of Buddhist shrines bear inscriptions on their shafts with emblems, motifs or animals on their capital.

Stupa or Topes – These were primarily relic shrines but may be divided into two classes. First *Stupas* proper or monuments containing relics of Buddha or some other Buddhist saints; secondly the *stupas* or towers erected to commemorate some event or mark some sacred spot dear to the followers of the Buddhist faith.

Rails – These must be recognized as one of the most important features of Buddhist architecture. Generally they are found surrounding *Stupas* but they are also represented as enclosing sacred trees, temples, pillars and other objects.

Chaityas or Assembly Halls – *Chaitya* is a more general term than *Stupa* and may be applied to any building of the nature of a religious monument generally commemorating acts, miracles etc. of Buddhist saints.

Viharas or Monasteries – A *vihara* is a hall where the monks met and walked about. Sometimes these halls were also established as temples of Buddhist faith.

When it comes to spread of Buddhist architecture in Karnataka, remains of *stupas* are difficult to find even though they may have existed at various places from the times of Ashoka till about the seventh century CE. Evidence of *stupas* having been built has been found in Banavasi and Sannati during excavations. Examples of *Chaityas* and *Viharas* exist even now at some locations for example the Buddhist *Vihara* on Meguti Hill in Aihole.

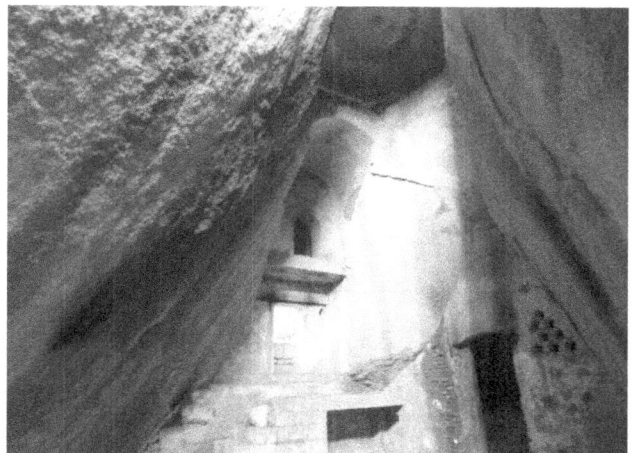 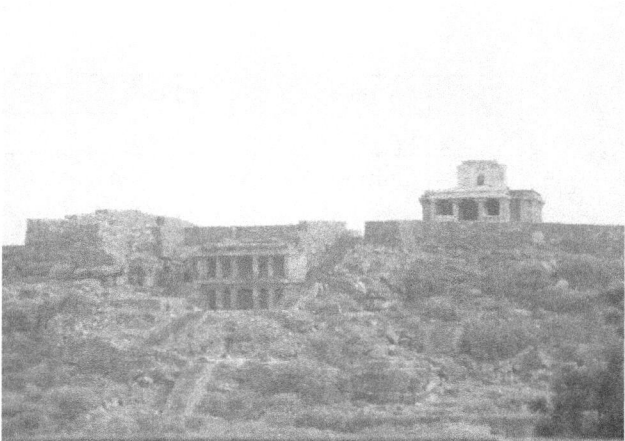

Chandravalli Cave and Meguti Hill Buddhist Chaitya Vihara and Jain Temple

Banavasi had become a place of great Buddhist tradition is evident from various Buddhist religious texts (Mahavamso). After the third Buddhist convention held at Pataliputra at the instance of Emperor Ashoka in 241 BCE, Thera Moggaliputta sent Thera Vajrantik to Banavasi to preach and spread Buddhism. Even though Buddhism existed in Karnataka prior to 241 BCE, organized thrust in spreading the religion was made at the time of Ashoka.

Four stages of spread and growth of Buddhism in Karnataka have been noticed by historians. The first stage relates to that of Mahisasana branch of the earliest Buddhism i.e. Hinayana stepping into Karnataka sometime around 400 BCE.

The second stage is during the Mauryan period because major part of Karnataka was under the Mauryan empire. During this period Buddhism struck deep roots in Karnataka.

The third stage falls during the period of Satavahanas (2nd century BCE to 2nd century CE).

The period of the Gangas, Kadambas, Chalukyas and Rashtrakutas is the fourth and the last stage. Afterwards Buddhism began to lose ground in Karnataka.

Ashoka desired that the message of Lord Buddha should reach the common man. It was with this object that he had a number of inscriptions carved. These are known as Edicts of Ashoka. The rock inscriptions are grouped as (i) major rock edicts, (ii) minor rock edicts, and (iii) cave inscriptions.

Scholars have opined that Ashokan inscriptions found in Karnataka are all minor edicts. The seventeen (17) inscriptions found in Karnataka comprising thirteen (13) Ashokan Edicts and four (4) inscriptions found at Sannati are located in various places as under.

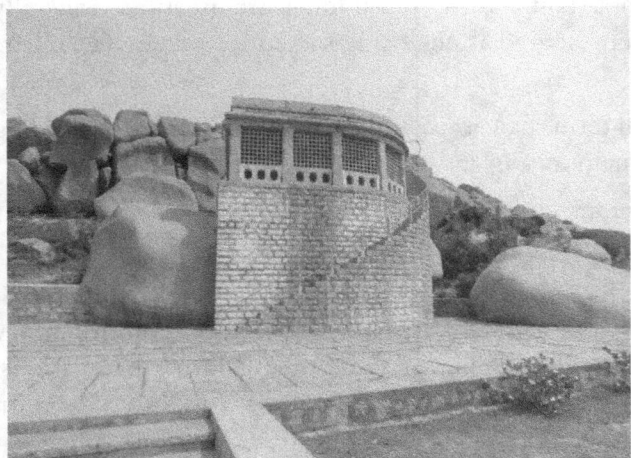

Ashoka's Edict at Ashoka Siddapura, Brahmgiri

S.No.	District	Place	No. of Inscriptions	Total
1.	Raichur	Maski	1	1
2.	Chitradurga	Brahmagiri	2	
		Siddhapur	2	
		Jatinga Rameswara	2	6
3.	Ballari	Nittur	2	
		Udegolam	2	4
4.	Kalaburgi	Sannati	4	4
5.	Koppal	Gavimath	1	
		Palkigundu	1	2

These seventeen edicts proclaim that Buddhism had taken firm roots in Karnataka.

The question arises, if Buddhism flourished before and during Ashoka's time, where are its remnants in Karnataka other than the seventeen edicts. The answer lies in that before Ashoka, there was no idol worship in Buddhism, there was no sculpture carving, no erection of *stupas* and inscriptions. Before that only rough earthen *stupas* might have been constructed. In Karnataka, it was Hinayana Buddhism then prevailed during those times. They looked upon Buddha at the human level and as the perfect man. They did not deify him. In these circumstances it has not been possible to have any remnants of Buddhism prior to Ashoka's time.

The Mauryan period was the golden age of Buddhism. The next important period in the history of Buddhism in Karnataka was the Satavahana period ranging from the 2nd century BCE to 2nd century CE. It cannot be said with certainty whether the Satavahanas accepted Buddhism as their religion but they did promote Buddhism liberally. The Satavahana family of Banavasi encouraged Mahisasana branch of Buddhism. Mahadevi Sirijantamula, wife of the king of Banavasi and sister of king Vasetti Putta Ehuvalajantamula of Iksvaku, constructed a *stambha* and *vihara* for the Mahisasaka Achrya at Nagarjunakonda.

After the Satavahanas, the Gangas and Kadambas ruled in Karnataka. The Gangas ruled from Talakad. A copper plate issued by Mahadeva II of the Ganga dynasty in 400 BCE registered a grant to a Bodhisattava. Buddhism was still alive in the Ganga territory. Though the Gangas followed the Vedic religion, they were tolerant towards Buddhism and Jainism. Likewise the Kadambas too were tolerant of Buddhism and registered grants for development of *sanghas*. A copper plate from their period states that a village called Sundarika near Karwar was given as a grant for a *vihara* and a *sangha*. Huen Tsang who visited south India during the time of Pulakesin II (640 CE) gives an account of Buddhism in Banavasi and Badami. He calls Banavasi as Konkanapura. He said that there were 400 *Baudha sangharamas* and more than ten thousand followers of Buddhism. There was Siddhartha's skull, 2 feet high, which was placed in a beautifully carved pot. They worshipped it every day. In another *vihara* near the city there was an idol of Maitreya Buddha made of sandalwood.

Likewise, in the accounts of Huen Tsang Badami was also a Buddhist centre where *sangharamas*, *viharas* and *chaityas* were found. The caves of Badami might originally have been Buddhist caves – they were Mayana basti, now called mena basadi. Mayana is a Buddhist expression derived from Mahayana Buddhism. The Buddhist *chaitya* of Aihole (on Meguti hill) belongs to a period prior to the Chalukya period. This has Mahayana influence. It was built around the 5th century CE. It is 25 feet high and on the first floor is carved an idol of Buddha.

There is some epigraphical evidence of Satavahana period too. The earliest inscription; the Vasisthiputra Sivarasi Pulumavi Rajana Mahadevi memorial stone inscription is of about 2nd century CE (latter half). This is a Prakrit inscription. Another inscription of the period says, "Nagamulika, wife of Maharathi, daughter of the Mahabhoja king of Banavasi, mother of Khanda Nagasataka, sister of Mahabhoja Ahijasena constructed a cave residence at Kanheri for Buddhist *bhikkus*."

Another Prakrit inscription of Banavasi of the 3rd century CE is also a Buddhist inscription. It informs us that Sivaskanda Nagasari, wife of Mahabhoja, daughter of the king, on an auspicious day of the 12th year of the reign of Haritaputra, Vinhukunda Chutukulananda donated along with the prince, the serpent idol (*Nagapratima*), tank and *vihara*. This *Nagapratima* is now in the premises of the Madhukeswara temple at Banavasi. Excavations near Banavasi in 1971 revealed some remnants of a *stupa*. The bricks of the *stupa* indicate the period of the *stupa* as 2nd to 3rd century CE. An idol of Maitreya Buddha has been discovered near the Madhukeswara temple. A Buddhist lamp post (*Dipastambha*) has been found at Togarsi near Banavasi.

Buddhist centres of Satavahanas and later periods in Karnataka were Chandravalli, Sannati and Banavasi. Brahamagiri belongs to the Ashokan period where two Ashokan inscriptions have been found. In Chandravalli excavations it was noticed that worship of Buddha and other deities was practiced here and coins with the engravings of a *Chaitya* and *Bodhi-tree* too were traced. Small sculptures of Buddha, *yaksha*, *gandharva* were found here.

Sannati was Buddhistic centre during the Satavahanas period and pre-Christian era. Traces of Buddhist culture have been found on both sides of the river Bhima flowing through Sannati. The finds contain remnants of a *stupa*, a holy stone pot containing holy bones and *ayaka stambhas*. The *ayaka stambhas* give symbolic representations of the birth, *pariniskramma*, enlightenment, preaching and *Nirvana* of the Buddha. Buddhist *stupas* have been carved on the stones. On another *stupa*, the feet of the Buddha are carved. ASI during excavations in Sannati has discovered a five foot tall statue of king Ashoka. The statue was found in two parts and is probably the only statue to show how king Ashoka looked and attired. The ASI, which began excavation at Sannati in 1954, has found several Buddhist monuments, including 81 scriptures and sculptures, two *stupas*, a protection wall, four scriptures engraved on stones and statues of Buddha that throw light on the influence of Buddhism and how it developed and flourished during the rule of Emperor Ashoka.

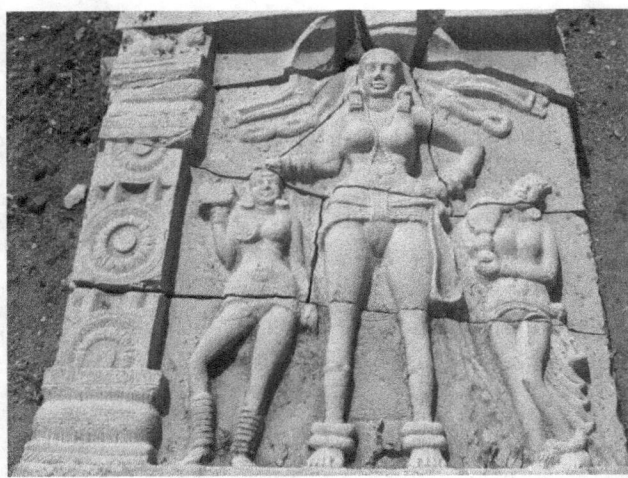 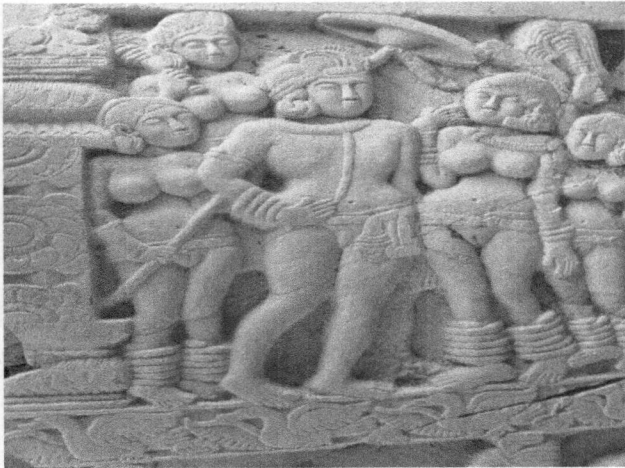

Sculpture from Sannati Excavation Site, Second Picture Depicts Emperor Ashoka

Another place of Buddhist importance is Kanganahalli barely 3 km from Sannati where the ASI carried out excavations during the years 1994–98 and 2000–2002. Numerous artifacts, remnants of shrines and sculpture have been discovered here which include the remains of a massive *stupa* with its architectural members and several brick structures in the form of *chaityas*. All these remains probably belong to the Satavahanas period. Koppal was one more centre of Buddhist importance where two Ashokan inscriptions have been found (one at Gavimath and the other at Palkigundu). At Gavimath there is a line sketch of the Buddha cut into a rock. People worship this figure as a female goddess by offering bangles. Originally, there must have been a Tara Bhagavati idol worshipped here. When the idol disappeared, people started worshipping the line sketch of the Buddha as a female deity. This is about 7 feet long.

Buddhism started declining in importance in Karnataka around 7th century CE. Avalokiteswara of Tantric Buddhism was worshipped at places in the guise of Maheswara. Evidence of Avalokiteswara being worshipped as Maheswara can still be seen in the Manjunatha temple at Kadri in Mangaluru. During the reign of Kalayana Chalukyas from 10th century onwards, in inscriptions as well as literary works, opposition to Buddhism has been noticed. Even in the southern parts of Karnataka; Buddhism was facing opposition as is evidenced by an inscriptions of 1129 CE found at Shravanabelagola. There could be several historical reasons for that. However, Tantric Buddhism seems to have continued for some time till about the end of 12th century as is evident from temples of goddess Taradevi. In the Dambal inscription the praise of Taradevi is striking. It is said that Taradevi would remove fear from the lion, elephant, fire, serpent, thieves, water, sea and spirit. Two more inscriptions of Dambal of 1098 and 1283 CE speak of gifts made to the Buddha *Viharas*.

Balligavi inscriptions of 1064 and 1067 CE are clear Tantric Buddhist records. They talk about registering a grant for land for the worship of Tara Bhagavati, Lokesa Devata and Buddhadeva. The grants were made with the approval of the Chalukya Emperor. There was a Tara Bhagavati temple in Balligavi and an idol of Tara Bhagavati was found at Dambal too. Tough Tantric Buddhism flourished for some time till the 12th century CE, as a whole Buddhism disappeared from Karnataka around that time and got assimilated in other sects of Hinduism.

5.3 KARNATAKA HISTORY OF ARCHITECTURE-JAINA INFLUENCE

Jainism, one of the oldest living faiths of India, has coexisted with Hinduism for over 2000 years in Karnataka. It is believed that Jainism entered Karnataka in about 3rd century. As tradition goes, Jainism is believed to have entered Karnataka with the migration of Chandragupta Maurya with his Jaina preceptor Bhadrabahu. After this period Jainism grew from strength to strength and heralded a glorious era, never to be witnessed in any part of India and became religion next only to Brahmanical religion in popularity and numbers. The religion enjoyed the liberal royal patronage of the Kadambas, Gangas, Chalukyas of Badami, Alupas, Rashtrakutas, Nolambas, Kalyana Chalukyas, Hoysalas, Vijayanagara rulers and their successors. The growth, spread and popularity of Jainism in Karnataka is best illustrated by the beautiful monuments that the Jainas constructed in different parts of the State. However, the Jainas had no separate architectural tradition of their own. In general the pattern of architectural and art forms, of the Jaina monuments followed the contemporary Brahmanical architectural style prevailing in Karnataka at various times and in conformity with the distinctive styles different dynasties followed during their reign.

Nearly twenty three centuries of Jaina history and their influence on art and architecture can be traced through legends, myths, inscriptions, art, architecture, sculpture, monuments and literature. Jaina monuments in Karnataka can generally be categorized in four types. These are *Basadis*, *Bettas* and Rock Shelters, *Stambhas* and *Nishidis*.

Basadis – These are monasteries or temples generally with figures of one of the Tirthankaras in a shrine at the rear of the hall, which served the needs of congregation. In many structural *basadis* there may be more than one shrine. In that case a *basadi* is called a *trikuta-basadi* or *panchakuta basadi* depending on whether it has three shrines in honour of three different Tirthankaras or five shrines for five different Tirthankaras.

The earliest construction of a Jaina monument in Karnataka is assignable to Madhava I (380–400 CE) of the Ganga dynasty. He is credited with the building of a wooden *chiatyalaya* on the hill at Mandali (Shivamogga) at the instance of his Jaina preceptor Simhanandi. The wooden *chaityalaya* or the Mandali Basadi finds mention in later inscriptions of 1060 and 1087 CE as well.

The evolution of *basadi* goes back to the stage of cave temples. In ancient times, the Jaina monks selected undisturbed and isolated places for meditation. Structural *basadis* were just an extension of the same old cave temples as the religion started expanding and need for discourse with new followers increased. The term '*basadi*' derives from the word '*vasati*' which refers to the place of residence of Jaina monks. After sometime the concept changed and the term *basadi* was taken to describe a house of god. *Basadis* were not merely centres of religious activities but in addition fulfilled a socio-political and educational role. To carry out cultural activities, *basadis* were also provided with rest houses, dining houses and drama theatres. The earliest example of a *basadi* with such additional facilities is found in the Gudnapur inscription of Kadamba Ravi Varma dating from about 485–519 CE. The engraving and worshipping of footprints of spiritual leaders and teachers too came into practice. Such footprints can be seen in Shravanabelagola. The practice of engraving Jaina idols in caves too was practiced and such places were called '*guha-jinalayas*,' meaning cave temples. Gopinatha Gutta and Arethippur are places that can be mentioned here.

The general layout or plan of the Jaina *basadi*, as can be verified from the existing Jaina monuments, generally consists of a square sanctum or *garbhagriha*, a square ante-chamber or *sukanasi*, a central hall or *gudhamandapa* (*navaranga*, closed hall) and in rare cases a small pillared porch (*mukha mandapa/mukha Chatushki*). They are generally *nirandhara* temples. No apsidal Jaina *basadi* is noticed so far. Normally the *basadis* are built inside an enclosure wall with a gateway in front, occasionally having a *dvaramandapa* without a *gopura* above it.

The structure is built above a moulded plinth. The walls of the *basadis* are filled, at regular intervals, with pilasters, having all the decorative features of the pillars found inside the temple. Pilasters support the corbels (*potika*) and architrave (*valabhi*) above. The architraves or beams sometimes contains a frieze of *hamsas* or *Ganas* or similar other decoration. The other parts of the *basadi* like doorways, the pillars, the perforated windows, the wall niches and the ceilings were all constructed in conformity with the prevailing style of architecture of the period during which these were constructed. The central part of the ceiling of the main hall, either of the *navaranga* or *mahamandapa* were often decorated with reliefs of eight guardians of space (*ashtadikpalas*) surrounding a Tirthankara or Jina in the centre. In construction of the hollow ceiling panels (*bhuvaneshvaris*) of these *basadis*, the lantern roof method (*nabhicchanda*) method too was adopted.

With the spread of Jainism and need to reach the religious tenets among wider cross-section of people, the attention was drawn to education. *Basadis* and monasteries became centres of learning where both religious and secular subjects were taught. Science, medicine, mathematics, literature and astronomy were some of the subjects which were taught here. Advancement in Kannada literature too happened through these centres of learning. Jaina canonical literature took inspiration from Hindu epics and *puranas* and that resulted in the creation of Jaina Puranas, epics and Charitres (life stories).

Bettas and Rock Shelters– *Bettas* contained hypaethral statues of Jaina Tirthankaras. These naked standing alone stone idols of super-human size raised the beliefs of the potency of adoration and perpetual rituals (*mahamastakabhisheka*). These are peculiar to Karnataka and spread to other parts of India from here only. Mostly situated over the castellated granite hillocks these are high and broad rocky outcrops with sculpted figures of Jinas and other memorial scenes. The most notable examples are the twin hills called Doddabetta (Vindhyagiri) and Chikkabetta (Chandragiri) in Shravanabelagola. Colossus of Gommateshwara stands tall on the Vindhyagiri hill since the 10th century CE.

The rock shelters and carvings of the Gangas at Arethippur are different from the *mandapa* type cut-in-cave contemporary temples of the Chalukyas of Badami. They are merely rock shelters, mostly natural ones. With little dressing of the sides and provided with flat beds or niches and lamp sockets. The Jaina figures are aligned over the granite hill overlooking a pond.

Stambhas (Manastambhas and Brahmadeva Pillars) – *Manastambhas* and *Brahmdeva* pillars are either set up within a single site or individually at various locations. Jainism took a lead over Buddhism in image worship and it reflected on settled life of Jinas rather than living like wandering monks.

Manastambhas are free standing votive columns akin to *dhvajastambha* or *dipastambha* for Hindu and Buddhist temples. The pillars indicate that a temple or sacred area is dedicated to Jaina practices and they establish a link to the Jaina mythology and are used for display of inscriptions.

Brahmadeva stambhas are pillars dedicated to Brahma or Brahmadeva. He is the *yaksha* of Shitalanatha, the tenth Tirthankara. In Karnataka, however his role is that of *kshetrapala* or guardian of the sacred temple area.

Nishidis – These are memorials raised for a Jaina who died after observance of the rituals *sallekhana* and *Samadhi* (voluntary starvation standing motionless till death). They marked such places where the ascetic breathed his last or where his body is cremated or bone relic was buried. Several *nishidigals* (stones recording the ritual of *sallekhana* and *Samadhi* by a Jina) are found on bare rocks in Shravanabelagola, Arhatpalli and Bastipura in Karnataka.

However, historically Jaina architectural development and its influence on the art and architecture progressed in the manner described below:

The Early Period (Western Ganga Period)

The chronology of the temples which come under this period is between 5th century to 10th century CE during which time most parts of southern Karnataka were ruled by the Western Gangas of Talkad and northern parts were ruled by the Kadambas, Badami Chaulkyas or Rashtrakutas. The patronage that they gave for the promotion of Jainism in their respective kingdoms is no doubt, unprecedented.

Now coming to the study of the monuments proper, we can, on definite grounds, say that the Jaina temple architecture had a very early beginning in southern Karnataka, as gleaned from the epigraphical and archeological evidences. The Halasi copper plate inscription records that Mrigeshavarma (455–80 CE) in memory of his father Santivarma (430–55 CE) got a Jinalaya constructed and gave liberal grants to Jaina ascetics. Many more records of the Kadambas of Banavasi refer to the grants made to several *sanghas* of the Jainas and to *arhadayatanas* that flourished in their kingdom.

Same was the case with southern parts of Karnataka which were under the political hold of the Gangas of Talakad. Shravanabelagola no doubt, was the nucleus of Jainism in south India even before the Gangas emerged as a political power to reckon with. Several hundred inscriptions of Shravanabelagola record the existence of many Jaina *basadis*, *sanghas* and celebrated *munis* of the creed at this centre as well as in other parts of Gangavadi.

However, it may be said, that these religious edifices of the Jainas had a very humble beginning. They were, at the best of their appearance, were not more than a simple brick and wood structure, without much show. Even these structures are in a very bad state of preservation because of the softer media used for their construction like, brick, mud and wood.

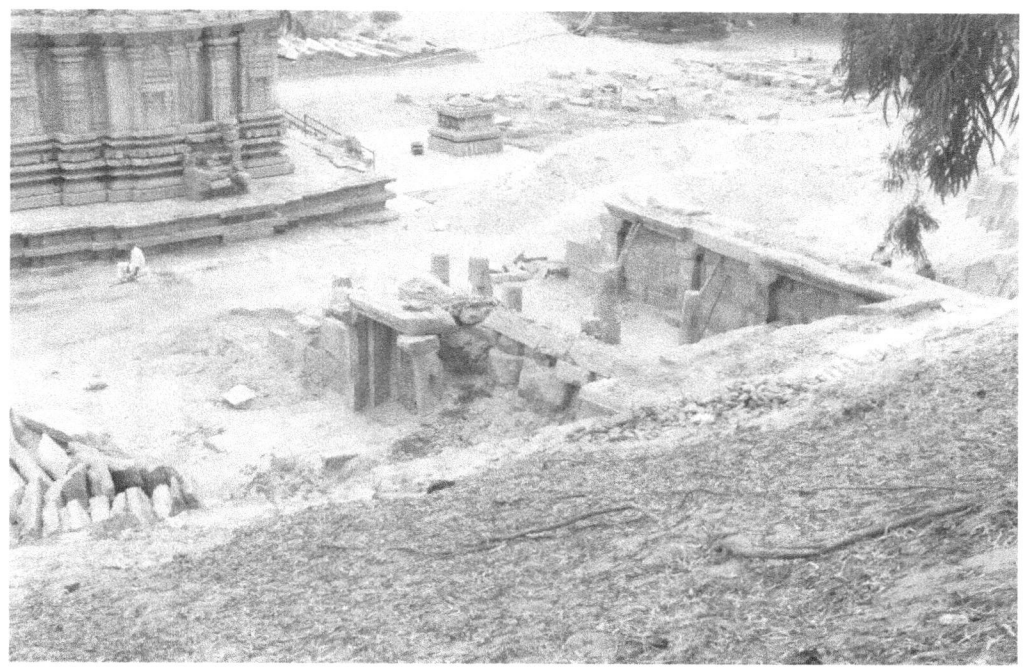

Excavation Site of Vijaya Jinalaya Basadi at Talakad

In 1897 ruins of a brick *basadi* were discovered at Nonamangala, near Malur in Kolar district. Two copper plate inscriptions and a few bronze objects were also discovered in the debris of the structure. One of the inscriptions records that the Ganga king Madhava II (461–85 CE) during his third regnal year (474 CE) at the behest of Acharya Viradeva gave a land grant to an *arhadayatana* that existed at Perbolal. The second copper plate records that during his first regnal year the king Avinita (530–70 CE), gifts to the *arhadayatana* at Uranur and Perur, affiliated to *Mulasangha* were given. These two grants no doubt refer to the *basadi* in the ruins of which were discovered. Only the basement of this brick structure is found in a field two km. west of the village and the walls were composed of a very large size bricks which were only one to two inches in thickness.

Recent excavations at Talakad have brought to light the remains of a large brick structure buried under the debris as well as the sand dune. This structure identified as a Parsvanatha Basadi is datable on stylistic ground to 7th or 8th century CE. This structure appears to have been built in two phases. The first phase consists of three cellas is a row, an early variant of a *trikuta* on plan, fronted by a common narrow *mukhamandapa*. In front of this slightly separated from the main structure, in the same axis, is another square pavillion. These two units form the first phase datable to 7th-8th century CE. The ruined stumps of the *garbhagriha* wall, brick paved flooring of the central *garbhagriha*, portions of the flooring of the left shrine and the complete structure below that level are the only remnants, of the *basadi* of the first phase. Only the shrines and the two sides of the porch appear to have had brick walls surmounting a wooden roof. The sides of the detached *mandapa* were open. Supported on the wooden pillars, there was probably a wooden roof for this pavilion also, as evidenced by the existence of several postholes. This *basadi*, particularly the roof, appears to have been destroyed in a fire accident, and was later enlarged and reconstructed.

Enlargement of the *basadi* was made by constructing a parallel wall at a distance of about one metre encompassing both the shrine and the pavilion. This second wall provided a covered circumambulatory path for the shrines, while it enlarged the pavilion in front on all the four sides, and converted the open pavilion into a large *navaranga*. The *navaranga* and the porch in front of the shrine were connected by a doorway. A well moulded stone *adhisthana*, comprising of *upana*, *jagati*, *kumuda* (round) *kantha*, *pattika* and *prati*, was provided for the structure, However It is not possible to have a clear idea of the *bhitti* and the superstructure of the *basadi*. Many decorative pieces moulded in lime mortar, *kudus*, *kirtimukha*s, burnt bricks of various shapes, sizes, and terracotta mouldings, stone pedestals of pillars have been discovered during excavations. These artistic objects indicate that a well shaped and styled *basadi* was existing at that place during 10th century CE.

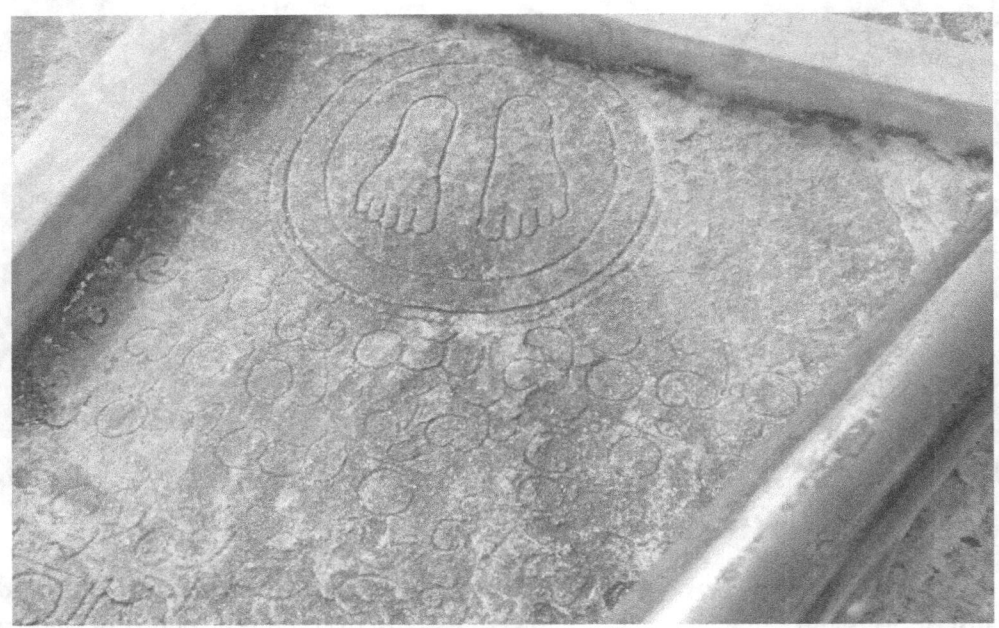

Footprints Worshipped at Shravanabelagola

The Mercara Copper plates of Avinita (469–529 CE) refers to the existence of a *basadi* at Talkad called Vijaya Jinalaya, caused by the minister of Akalavarsha Prithvivallabha at Talavananagara. It appears that this newly excavated *basadi* is perhaps, the same Jinalaya mentioned in the plates.

The plan of the I phase of this brick structure, particularly the *garbhagriha* unit bears a striking resemblance with the plan of the Chandragupta Basadi at Shravanabelagola, datable on stylistic grounds to Pallava -early Chola period (i.e., 8th–9th century CE). Three sanctums in a row, the central cella being larger than the two cellas on the sides, all the cellas having openings to a common oblong verandah or porch, closed on the two sides are features common to both the *basadis*.

The brick structures of the early period made way for the construction of *basadis* in a more permanent material like stone, which was the order of the day for the structures of the Brahmanical creed. To study and appreciate the Jaina monuments of this period one has to visit Shravanabelgola in Hassan district. Here two hillocks, 'large' (Indragiri/Vindhyagiri) and 'small' (Chandragiri) provide umpteen religious edifices, of the Jainas datable from 7th century CE, to modern period. Of these two hills the small hill contains monuments of earlier date than the large hill.

The earliest amongst the existing structures on the small hill is the Chandra Prabhanatha Basadi, built facing north. The plan of this structure consists of a *garbhagriha*, *sukanasi*, and a *navaranga* having a group of four central pillars. The *basadi* is of *misra* type, i.e., the brick structure raised over a stone plinth. It is said to have been erected by the Ganga king Sivamara II, hence called Sivamara Basadi. The next to come on the hill is the Chandragupta Basadi, a triple celled structure already cited. This *basadi* built in granite appears to have been modelled on the plan of the Talakad brick *basadi*. Three cellas arranged in a row fronted by an oblong verandah forms the core of this *basadi* even though it is covered in front by later structures. Of the three cellas, the two side ones have 'ekatala brahmachchanda vimanas,' while the *vimana* of the central shrine is missing. A sculpture of Parsvanatha is housed in the central shrine while the two side shrines house Padmavati and Kushmandini Yakshis.

The next important structure to be built on Chandragiri is the Chamundaraya basadi, a gem of Jaina architecture in the pure Dravidian style, caused to be erected by Chamundaraya, the able minister of Ganga king Marasimha II in 982 CE. The *basadi* was completed by the former's son Jinadeva in 995 CE. The *basadi* is a rectangular structure of the *sandhara* type built facing east. The plan consists of a *garbhagriha*, a *pradakshinapatha*, open *sukanasi*, *navaranga*, and a *mukhamandapa*. Above the *garbhagriha* is a *dvitala vimana* (two storeyed tower) of which the first *tala* is functional as it contains a cella and a porch with an approach staircase. The second *tala* is only conventional. The *sikhara* element is of 'Vishnuchchanda' type (octagonal) surmounted by a *stupi*.

The *garbhagriha* houses the image of Neminatha flanked by *chauri* bearers. This image bears Hoysala characteristic features hence, may be a later replacement. The cella on the first storey of the *vimana* houses the standing image of Parsvanatha installed by Chamundaraya's son Jinadeva in 985 CE.

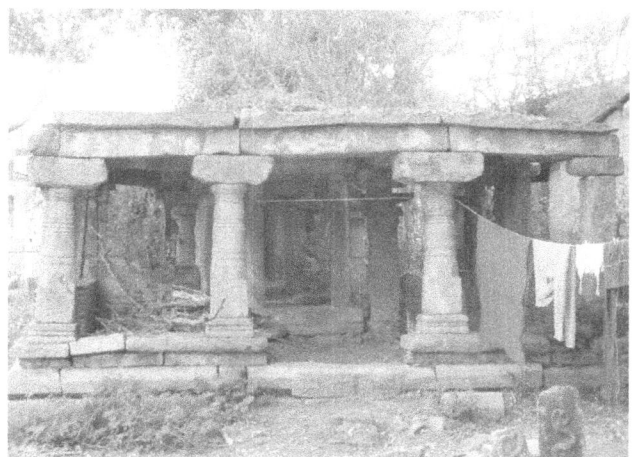 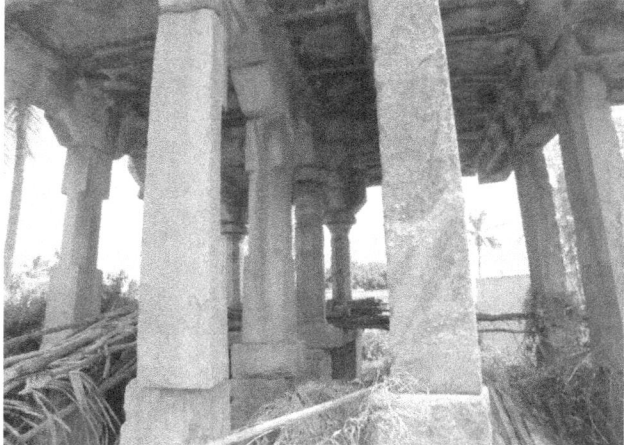

Muguru Sivalaya Basadi and Sule Devalaya at Manne

The most beautiful and splendid example of the Jaina architecture of the early period is the Panchakuta Basadi at Kambadahalli, Mandya district. Exact date of construction of this temple is not known. However, on stylistic grounds this may be placed to 10th century CE. This *basadi* facing north is built in two phases. The whole structure is enclosed by a high wall having an entrance and a porch in the north. The first phase consists of three symmetrically arranged and equally sized cellas oriented towards south, east and west. Each part has a *garbhagriha*, *sukanasi* opening to a common *navaranga* consisting of 4 central pillars. The *navaranga* has a doorway towards the north and a porch in front of it. The second phase is a *dvikuta* of a slightly later period, built just in front of the porch of first phase. It consists of two shrines built facing each other. Each shrine has a *garbhagriha*, a *sukanasi* a *navaranga* of four pillars connected to a common porch in front. In between the porches of these two phases, is a *balipitha*. This is a neatly moulded structure also sculpted on the sides. All the shrines have the images of Tirthankaras. Ekkoti Jinalaya is an interesting name given to the Panchakuta Basadi. A monastic order existed here. Both the Gangas and the

Hoysalas had maintained it as a holy centre. The emergence of resistance to Jainism in Karnataka posed a threat to the monastic order and the *basadi*. However, this *basadi* was protected by the Ekkoti Maharudras, a staunch Saiva group and they renamed it Ekkoti Jinalaya. They gave to this *basadi* a huge drum (*bheri*) and five musical instruments (*panch vadya*). They said that he who disowns and disrespects this is a sinner to god Siva.

Arethippur (earlier known as Tippur or Tippeyur in the epigraphical records) is the site where rock sculpture and *basadis* of the Ganga period thrived. While the *basadi* can be identified only from its brick remains, parts of the rock sculpture still can be seen in the hills even now. This remote village is at a distance of 22 km from Maddur (Mandya district) south-east via Rudrakhpura-Halaguru road. In the Ganjam (Srirangapatna) charters (799–800 CE) of the time of the Ganga prince Marasimha Ereyappa, son of Sivamara II (791–819 CE) is invoked *jitam bhagavata* proclaiming the faith of the ruling king and records gifts of village 'Tippuru' to Ponnadi, the chief of Arppole. Another inscribed record of Saka 838 (916–917 CE) of the time of Nitimarga Permanadi refers to the construction of a Jaina *basadi* on the Kanakagiri hill by one Manaleyara in the presence of the king and records the gift of all incomes of the village 'Tippeyur' to Kanasenabhatara. The inscription in fourteen lines sculptured with elephant and other royal insignia on top is found on a well dressed granite slab set up closer to the tank bund in the village.

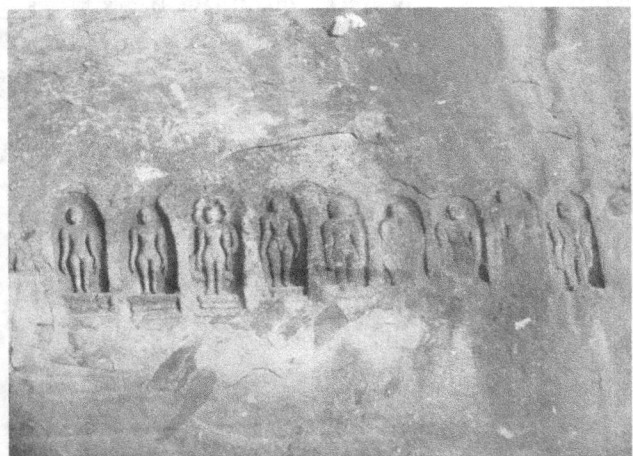 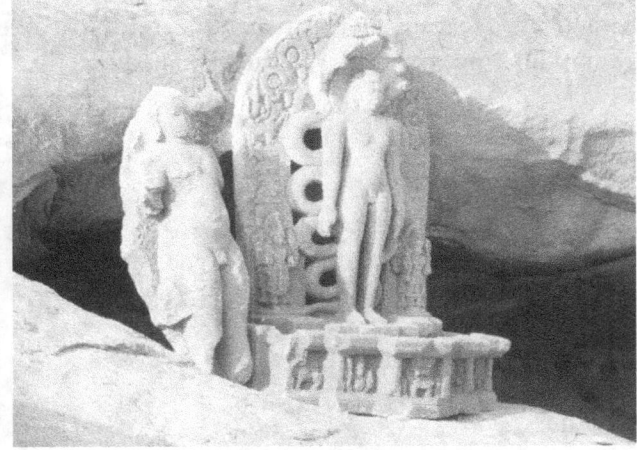

Rock-shelter at Arethippur and Sculpture near the Tank

During the Hoysala period the Jaina establishment at this place enjoyed greater patronage and recognition. Impressive Jina images, both rock cut and structural, are found on the flattish granite hillock called Kanakagiri. The natual depression on the rocky slope was taken advantage to cut a deep 'U' shaped trough. Its southern opening was bounded with cut-stone masonry blocks to retain the rain water. Thus the *belagola* was formed to serve the ritual needs of the Jainas frequenting the spot. In all fourteen Jaina Tirthankaras standing but a few seated are found carved in low relief at the middle height of the scrap facing west. The figure of Suarsvanatha (five-hooded) standing over a lotus pedestal is shown fourth in the right. Vestiges of a brick *basadi* too are visible opposite the water body. Several loose sculptures, broken pillars and inscribed stones are found among the ruins. A 10 feet tall Gommateswara image is installed on the opposite hill.

Besides, these important Jaina monuments described above there are innumerable Jaina vestiges in southern Karnataka datable to the first millennium CE. Important among them are Sivalaya Basadi at Muguru, Sule Devalaya at Manne and Gopinatha Gutta rock shelter at Nandi.

The middle period (Hoysala period)

The end of 10th century CE witnessed a tremendous political change in southern Karnataka. The Ganga royal family which dominated the politics of this region for over five centuries suddenly eclipsed due to the political supremacy of the Cholas on one side and the emergence of the Hoysalas on the other. However, the Hoysalas who emerged as a strong political power offered the same prestigious position and status to Jainism as was extended to by the Gangas. Even the emergence of vaishnavism under the Saint Ramanujacharya as a powerful religion did not affect the power, pomp and popularity of Jainism in the Hoysala country. The golden age of Jainism in Karnataka which commenced during the middle of 10th century CE continued upto the end of 13th century. During this period the best of the religious and cultural achievements may be said to have attained by the Jainas in Karnataka.

The Hoysalas practiced an art tradition which is magnificent and unique by itself. Described as a hybridised form of *Nagara* and *Dravida* styles of architecture, the Hoysala temples contain many other elements, which, to a great extent, are the innovations of highly skilled creative artists. Two modes of architectural styles were preferred for building temples by these artists. The first is the classical mode which is characteristic of their style and the second is the Dravidian style. The classical mode or the Hoysala style also defined as *Vesara* style-a tasteful blend of North and South Indian varieties -consists of a star-shaped plan for the *garbhagriha*. The other parts of the temple plan are *sukanasi*, *navaranga*, *mukhamandapa* all built generally over a platform or *jagati*, slightly bigger in size than the temple proper, providing an open promenade around, for circumambulation.

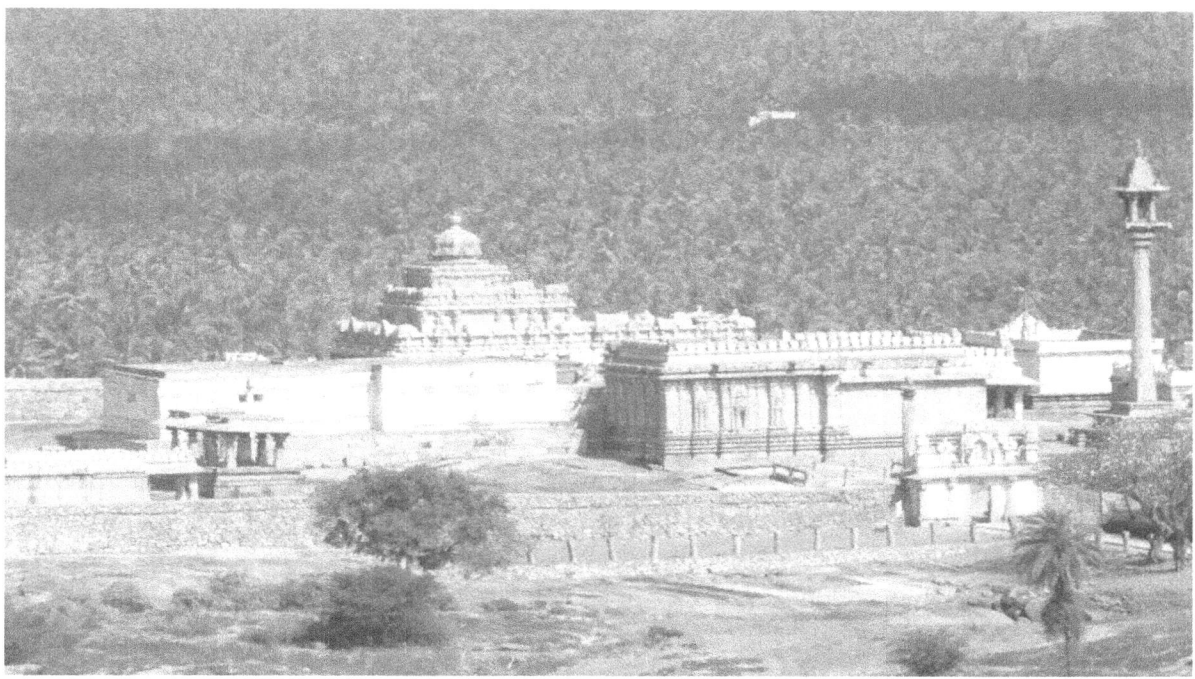

Cluster of Basadis and Manastambha at Chandragiri, Shravanabelagola

Now coming to some of the general characteristic features of the Jaina *basadis* of the Hoysala period we can say that the principal components of the plan of these structures, whether built in pure Dravidian style, or Hoysala style, generally contains a *garbhagriha*, a *sukanasi*, (open or closed) a *navaranga* and a *mukhamandapa*. All these temples are *nirandhara* in character excepting one solitary example (Kattale Basadi on Chandragiri). The plan of the *basadis* of the Hoysala period (excepting those built on the Chandragiri in Dravidian style) may by classified broadly into the following three categories: *basadis* whose walls are laid in straight lines without offsets, *basadis* whose walls have graduated projections and *basadis* whose *vimanas* have stellate plans.

The exterior walls of these structures of this period are usually simple in contrast to the rich sculptural and decorative treatment of the Brahmanical temples. They usually possess the simple decoration of pilasters, sham niches, with turrets above, a sloped *kapota*, parapet and *vimana* or tower. The *vimana* or tower occurs in rare cases. However, they are built in Dravidian or Hoysala styles depending upon the structure on which it is supported.

As the worship of *Yakshas* and *Yakshis* was the trend of the day amongst the Digambara Jainas, each and every *basadi* was adorned with the loose sculptures of respective *Yaksha* and *Yakshi* of the Jina housed in the *garbhagriha*. They are placed either in the *sukanasi* or in the *navaranga*. Every *basadi* was also provided with a *manastambha*, a counterpart of the *dhvajastamba* of the Brahmanical temples. *Manastambha* is a lofty pillar firmly fixed to the ground through a masonry moulded platform. The monolithic shaft supports a capital, a divine figure or a Jina, housed normally inside a small masonry pavilion with a turret above.

Some of the important places in southern Karnataka where good Jaina *basadis* can be seen are Shravanabelgola, Jinanathapura, Halebid, Humcha, Chikkahanasoge, Nitturu, Arasikere and other places. Many of them are either in disrepair or have been renovated during later times thus losing their original shape.

Shravanabelagola: The largest concentration of Jaina *basadis* at one place in Karnataka is to be seen here, where nearly one hundred monuments of various sizes and shapes are existing at present situated on the two hills and in the township as well. Among them some are of Ganga, some are of Hoysala and some of Vijayanagara periods. However, architectural activity at this place on the maximum scale may be said to have taken place during Ganga and Hoysala periods. Of the *basadis* in Shravanabelgola town, the Bhandari Basadi, Akkana Basadi and Nagara Jinalaya deserve special mention. Bhandari Basadi or 'Chaturvimsati Tirthankara Basadi' is a large structure built facing north contains on plan an oblong *garbhagriha*; a similar *sukanasi*, *navaranga*, *mukhamandapa* and a porch all enclosed by a *prakara* wall. This *basadi* is so named because it was got constructed by Hulla, the Bhandari (royal treasurer) of Hoysala Narasimha I in 1159 CE. The king who visited this *basadi* named it as 'Bhavya Chudamani Basadi' and granted the village Savaneru (Sravaneri) for its upkeep. The *garbhagriha* contains the images of all the 24 Tirthankaras, each 3 ft. in height, all placed on a common oblong pedestal. There are three doorways provided for the *garbhagriha* in front to have a clear look of all the images. The central doorway contains the usual delicate and crisp carvings of the Hoysala workmanship. The interspaces of the doorways are provided with *jalandhras*. The central part of the *navaranga* floor contains a huge monolithic slab of 10 feet square. Similar slabs are also found in front of the structure and are a good example to the tremendous transportation capacity of the Hoysala builders.

The only temple in Shravanabelagola to be built in the classical non-ornate Hoysala idiom is the Akkana Basadi, so named as it was constructed by a staunch Jaina lady Achiyakka wife of Chandra Mouli, a Saiva Brahman, a *sandhivigrahi*, and a minister of Ballala II, in the year 1182 CE as evidenced by two inscriptions there. The temple is built out of dark blue schist on a stellate plan. The plan consists of a *jagati*, a *garbhagriha*, a *sukanasi*, a *navaranga* and a *mukhamandapa*.

The *garbhagriha* houses the standing image of Parsvanatha of about 5 ft. height. The *sukanasi* has the seated images of Dharanendra Yaksha and Padmavathi Yakshi. The *navaranga* has four beautifully carved bell moulded pillars and also *bhuvanesvaris* with delicate carvings. The outer walls are non-ornate, hence appear very simple. Plinth having neatly cut mouldings, thin pilasters and occasional *stambha panjaras* of the walls, the *kapota*, the *prastara*, elegantly shaped pyramidal *vimana* with a *sukanasi* projection in front, are all built in conformity with the Hoysala style. The carvings are still unfinished.

The other Jaina temple of the Hoysala period here is the Nagara Jinalaya built in 1199 CE by Pattanaswamy Nagadeva. 'Sri Nilaya' is the other name of this *basadi*. As the merchants of the town (*nagaras*) gave many grants to this *basadi* it came to be known as 'Nagara Jinalaya.' The plan consists of a *garbhagriha*, *sukanasi* and *navaranga*. The *garbhagriha* houses the standing image of Adinatha. The *navaranga* has the image of standing Brahmadeva. He holds a fruit in the left hand and a whip in the right. The pedestal has the carving of a horse.

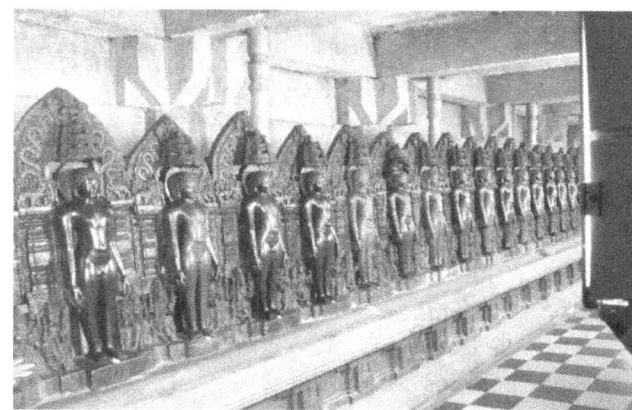 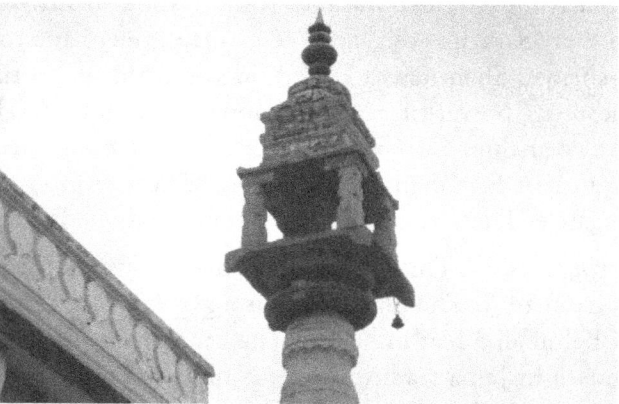

Bhandara Basadi Shravanabelagola and Manastambha

Small hill or Chikkabetta in Shravanabelgola during the 11th and 12th centuries was a beehive of Jaina religious activities. Gangaraja, Santaladevi, and other rich and liberal people built six *basadis* on this hill. However all these monuments, as noticed earlier, are built out of granite and are in Dravidian style. They are 1. Parsvanatha Basadi, 2. Kattale Basadi, 3. Sasana Basadi, 4. Savatigandhavarana Basadi, 5. Terina Basadi, 6. Santiswara Basadi.

Parsvanatha Basadi: This being one of the two tallest structures of Shravanabelagola, houses the standing image of Parsvanatha. It has a seven hooded serpent above. This image carved out of a single block of schist is next only to the colossus of Gommata in height at Shravanabelagola. Not only this sculpture of Parsvanatha is colossal but it is also beautiful with delicate and tasteful decorations of the hooded serpent, sculptured pedestal where mythologically important reliefs are carved.

The temple occupies an area of 69 × 20 feet and on plan consisting of a *garbhagriha*, *sukanasi*, *navaranga* and a porch. Except for the neatly moulded plinth and sloped *kapota*, aesthetically there is nothing noteworthy in the structure. The exact date of construction of this temple is not known. However, it is datable to the beginning of 12th century CE on the basis of an inscription on a pillar in the temple.

In front of this *basadi* is a neatly executed *manastambha* erected by Puttayya in the 17th century. This supports a pillared pavilion with a turret above. The total height of this *stambha* is 65.5 ft.

Kattale Basadi: The biggest of the *basadis* on the small hill. It measures 120 × 40 feet. A *garbhagriha*, *pradakshinapatha* (a strange phenomenon of this temple) an open *sukanasi*, a *navaranga* of 16 pillars, a large *rangamandapa* (a hypostyle hall built adjoining the front of Chandragupta Basadi of Ganga times) are the components of the plan of this structure, The *garbhagriha* houses the seated image of Adinatha flanked by male *chauri* bearers. A label inscription on the pedestal of this image records that Pochavve, mother of Gangaraja caused this *basadi* to be built here. A large stone screen containing many interesting incidents of Jaina mythology, is found placed separating the *rangamandapa* of this *basadi* and the adjoining Chandragupta Basadi.

Sasana Basadi: A structure of *misra* (mixed) type i.e., a neatly plastered brick and mortar structure on a well moulded stone plinth. Its plan has a *garbhagriha*, open *sukanasi*, a *navaranga*, and a *mukhamandapa*. The *garbhagriha* houses the image of Adinatha, 5 ft. in height. *Sukanasi* houses the images of Yaksha Gomukha and Yakshi Chakreswari. The wall decoration on the exterior consists of closely spaced pilasters, *kapota*, *hara* housing Jaina figures. Gangaraja, the able general of king Vishnuvardhana built this *basadi* 'Indrakulagriha' and the king granted a village for its upkeep. The *basadi* has derived its present name because of the presence of a large stone inscription of 1118 CE in front which states that this structure was built by the mother and wife of Gangaraja in 1118 CE. The record was engraved by Vardhamanachari alias Gangachari.

Savatigandharvana Basadi: King Vishnuvardhana's chief queen Shantaladevi, who had the distinctive epithet 'Savatigandhavarini' (a rutting elephant to the co-wives) caused a *basadi* to be built here and enshrined Shantinatha seated on a lion throne in the year 1123 CE. Though built by the chief queen of the most powerful Hoysala monarch, architecturally and artistically this *basadi* has an average quality workmanship. *Garbhagriha, sukanasi, navaranga* are the constituents of the plan. In the *sukanasi* are the figures of Sarvahana and Ambika. The *navaranga* pillars are ordinary and hardly possess the Hoysala elegance. There is also a simple pyramidal *vimana* to the temple, repaired subsequently.

Terina Basadi: This has got its name because of the so called 'car-like' masonry stone platform or *balipitha* in front of it. The plan contains a *garbhagriha*, a *sukanasi* and a *navaranga*. The *garbhagriha* has the image of Bahubali 5 feet in height. The car in front of the *basadi* is called *mandara*. Two classes of *mandaras* are known in Jaina tradition viz., Nandisvara and Meru. This car belongs to the Meru class. It contains the reliefs of 52 Jinas all round. This was got carved by Machikabbe and Santikabbe mothers of Hoysalasetty and Nemisetty respectively in the year 1117 CE. The two sons named were the royal merchants of king Vishnuvardhana.

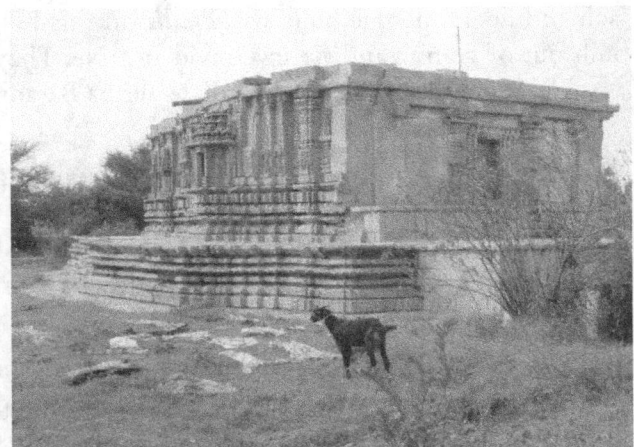
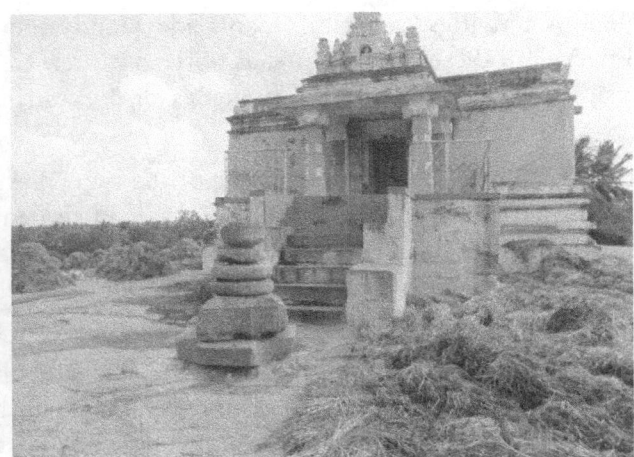

Shantinatha Basadi and Aregal Basadi at Jinanathapura

Santiswara Basadi: Built probably in 1117 CE by Hiri (elder) Echimayya son of Bammanna the elder brother of Gangaraja. Hiri Echimayya was also responsible for constructing the Aregal Basadi at Jinanathapura. *Garbhagriha* open *sukanasi*, a *navaranga* of 10 pillars, a *mukhamandapa* are on the plan of this brick *basadi*. Architecturally this *basadi* is insignificant. It has the standing image of Shantinatha (5 ft 2 inches high) which is interesting. The pedestal of the image has the relief of Indra and Sachi, his consort, on their way to consecrate the Tirthankara. Two attendant images of a later period are also found on the two sides. The *sukanasi* has the usual images of Sarvahana Yaksha and Ambika Yakshi. The Dravidian tower of brick and mortar has lost its original features.

Jinanathapura: This village is situated adjacent to Shravanabelagola, north of Chikkabetta. Gangaraja, general of Vishnuvardhana is said to have founded this village in the beginning of 12th century. There are two *basadis* in this village. The first one is the Parsvanatha Basadi or Aregal Basadi caused to be constructed by Echa, elder brother of Gangaraja, in 1135 CE. This is a very ordinary temple of the Hoysala style having a *garbhagriha*, *sukanasi* and a *navaranga*. The original image in the *garbhagriha* is missing. Instead a Parsvanatha image was installed there in 1889 CE by one Bahubalayya. The temple also contains the loose sculptures of 24 Tirthankaras, Dharanendra, Padmavati, Panchaparamesthis, Navadevatas and Nandi brought from elsewhere.

Shantinatha Basadi: This *basadi* situated to the west of Jinanathapura is the main attraction of this place. This was caused to be built by Vasudaikabandhava Rechana, a minister of Ballala II in about 1200 CE. This *basadi* is, perhaps, the most ornate *basadi* built in the classical Hoysala ornate style. Excepting the *vimana* all other components of this temple are preserved. The *jagati*, *garbhagriha* of stellate plan, *sukanasi*, *navaranga* are the components of this temple. The wall surface, though basically, rectangular contains many indentations. Regular decorations of pilasters, niches with turreted canopies, wall sculptures of average 3 ft. height, meandering creeper scrolls running vertically in the interspaces of closely spaced pilasters are excellently imagined and executed. The subject matter of these figure sculptures, sparing the Tirthankaras, are dancers-male and female, in different poses, gods and goddesses, *Yakshas* and *Yakshis*, attendants, *chauri* bearers. All these sculptures and decorative designs are so beautifully and delicately carved that there are few parallels in the entire gamut of Hoysala sculptures.

In the design and decoration of the interiors also a similar degree of excellence is maintained. The lathe turned pillars of the *navaranga*, the domed ceilings, the wall niches and their turrets are all of superb quality workmanship. The *garbhagriha* houses the standing image of Shantinatha. The sculptural decorations on the outside walls of the Basadi have been studied in depth by Robert Del Bonta and he has identified 73 sculptural images in all.

Halebid: Next group of Jaina monuments, built under the Hoysalas can be seen at Dorasamudra or Halebid, their capital seat. Here are three *basadis* built in a row towards the south of the Hoysalesvara temple.

These *basadis*, almost identical in plan and surface treatment, are of Parsvanatha (1133 CE), Shantinatha (1196 CE) and Adinatha (about the same period). The Parsvanatha Basadi was constructed by Boppa son of Gangaraja, in 1133 CE. In the same year son Narasimha was born to Vishnuvardhana. Hence, the king named this *basadi* as Vijaya Parsva. The plan consists of a *garbhagriha*, *sukanasi* and *navaranga*. The *garbhagriha* houses a tall image of Parsvanatha (14 feet high) with a hooded serpent above his head. The wall surface is treated in a very simple way. The walls are plain with thin pilasters at regular intervals and are devoid of any other decorations. The pillars in the *navaranga* are excellently chiseled and polished. The two other *basadis* are almost identical to this *basadi* with minor variations. A *manastambha* stands outside closer to the Adinatha Basadi.

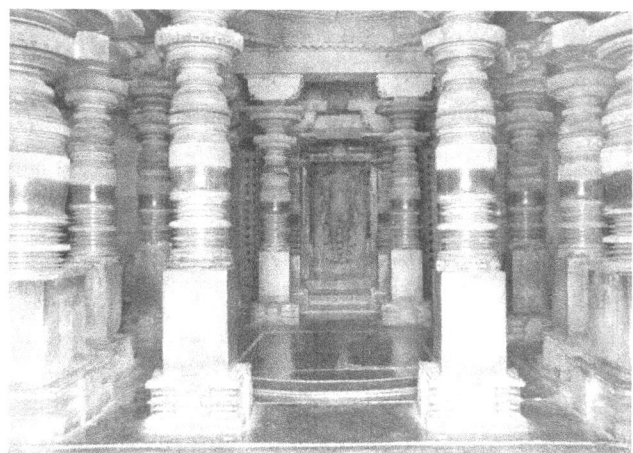
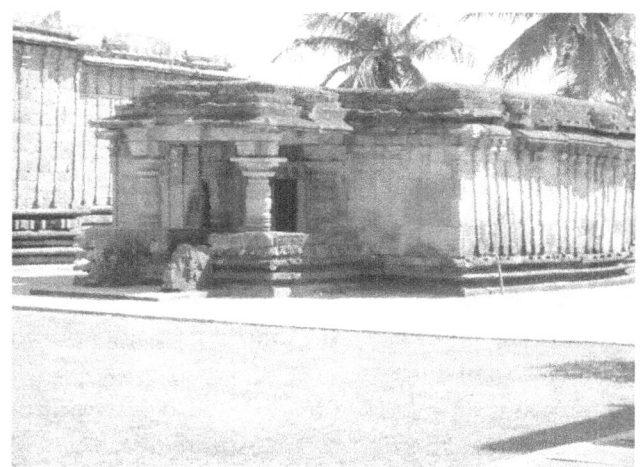

Shantinatha Basadi and Adinatha Basadi at Bastihalli, Halebid

Humcha: Humcha is a small town in the Hosanagara taluk of Shivamogga district. The other names of this place are, Pombuchcha, Patti-Pombuchcha, Hombuja etc. From the beginning of 8th century to 16th century, this place was an active Jaina pilgrim centre. This was also the capital seat of the Santaras of Santalige-1000 province. There are many *basadis* found here in different stages of preservation. The earliest among them is datable to 850 CE called Paliyakkana Basadi, which no longer exists. The remains of Parsvanatha and *hale-basadis* are still to be seen. Panchakuta Basadi the largest among the *basadis* here was built in 1077 CE by Chattaladevi. This *basadi* is referred to in inscriptions as 'Urdhvitilaka.' In front of this structure is a tall ornate *manastambha*. Five *garbhagrihas*, have been built on a common plinth arranged in a row to have a common *navaranga* and *mukhamandapa*. The original sculptures of Neminatha, Shantinatha and Parsvanatha only are remaining in the *garbhagrihas*. The *basadi* has undergone a lot of repairs.

Chikka Hanasoge: This place was an important Jaina settlement since the time of the Gangas. After the Gangas, the Chengalvas patronised Jainism here. Adinatha Basadi of this place, said to have been installed by Sri Rama was reconstructed by Vira Rajendra Nanni Chengalva Rajendra Chola, a feudatory of the Cholas in 11th century CE. This *basadi* is a *trikutachala* repaired and reconstructed in recent years. The structure is of granite. However, the ornate door frames and the sculptures there in are made out of chloritic schist. The three *garbhagrihas* house Adinatha, Shantinatha and Neminatha. All the *garbhagrihas* have *sukanasis* which open to a *navaranga*. The superstructures on these *garbhagrihas* are completely lost.

Nitturu: A town in Tumkur district has an ornate Shantiswara Basadi of the Hoysala period (12th Century CE). *Garbhagriha, sukanasi, navaranga* and *mukhamandapa* are the components of this temple. The treatment of the exterior is quite ornate having a moulded *adhisthana*, pilastered wall, niches with turrets, and other floral patterns. The designs of the pillars of the *navaranga* are varied and attractive. The *bhuvanesvaris* are deep and contain notable decorations. The *garbhagriha* houses the image of Shantinatha.

Arasikere: Sahasrakuta Jinalaya of this town is a beautiful Jaina *basadi* of soap stone built by Dandanayaka Rechimayya, a general of Hoysala king Ballala II in the year 1220 CE. The sculptor who supervised the work was Namoja. The plan of the *basadi* consists of a large *garbhagriha* with 4 pillars, a *sukanasi* with three doorways opening to the three bays of the *navaranga*, a *navaranga*, and a *mukhamandapa*. The *navaranga* is the most attractive part of the entire scheme. The four central pillars and the nine *bhuvanesvaris* are of typical Hoysala workmanship. Particularly noteworthy is the central *bhuvanesvari* which is in the form of a huge inverted lotus flower. The other *bhuvanesvaris* have, besides the usual decorations, unidentified narrative friezes. The *garbhagriha* in the centre has a 'Sahastrakuta Jina Bimba' containing 1008 tiny representations of Jinas carved on a monolithic conventional architectural model. This *bimba* is inscribed and records that it was installed by Recharasa (in 1220 CE), eminent councillor of Kalachuri dynasty, taking refuge under Ballala II. The *basadi* has undergone large repairs. Most parts of the external wall surface are rebuilt. The tower of the *basadi* is missing.

Manastambhas: To the class of Jaina monuments of southern Karnataka may be added the colossal *manastambhas* (huge masonry columns) that are erected in front of the Jaina *basadis*. They are the counterparts of the Hindu *dhvajastambhas* in front of temples like *Garuda Khambha*. The *manastambhas* generally consist of three parts viz., a moulded platform, to suit the size of the pillar, monolithic shaft, and the capital or *Makuta*, the crowning member. The platform is masonry in nature, moulded with attractive forms and also sometimes decorated with relievos. The shaft is made of a single stone and designed suitably. The height of the shaft varies from place to place. The shaft carries the capital, abacus and the crowning member. Here the skill and imagination of the artist really makes the difference. Starting from ordinary capital and abacus type to most complicated and ornate crowning members are found. From an ordinary seated sculpture to turreted *mandapas* with delicate carvings have been found placed on these *manastambhas*. Four Jinas facing four directions called Chaumukha Jinas are generally placed in these pavilions. *Yakshas* may sometimes replace the Jinas, but *Yakshis* are never placed here.

The best specimens of *manastambhas* considered as freaks of architectural skill and taste of the Jaina artists can be seen at Shravanabelagola, Kambadahalli, Halebid, Humcha, Hiriyangadi, Karkala, Mudabidri, Mulki and other places in southern Karnataka.

The dynasties that ruled over parts of northern Karnataka too patronized Jaina faith. Their liberal grants for building Jaina monuments resulted in the construction of numerous *basadis*. However, these constructions were influenced by the architectural trends adopted by the respective dynasties. The monuments built by these dynasties in the northern districts have been considered in a chronological manner taking the particular architectural influences also into consideration.

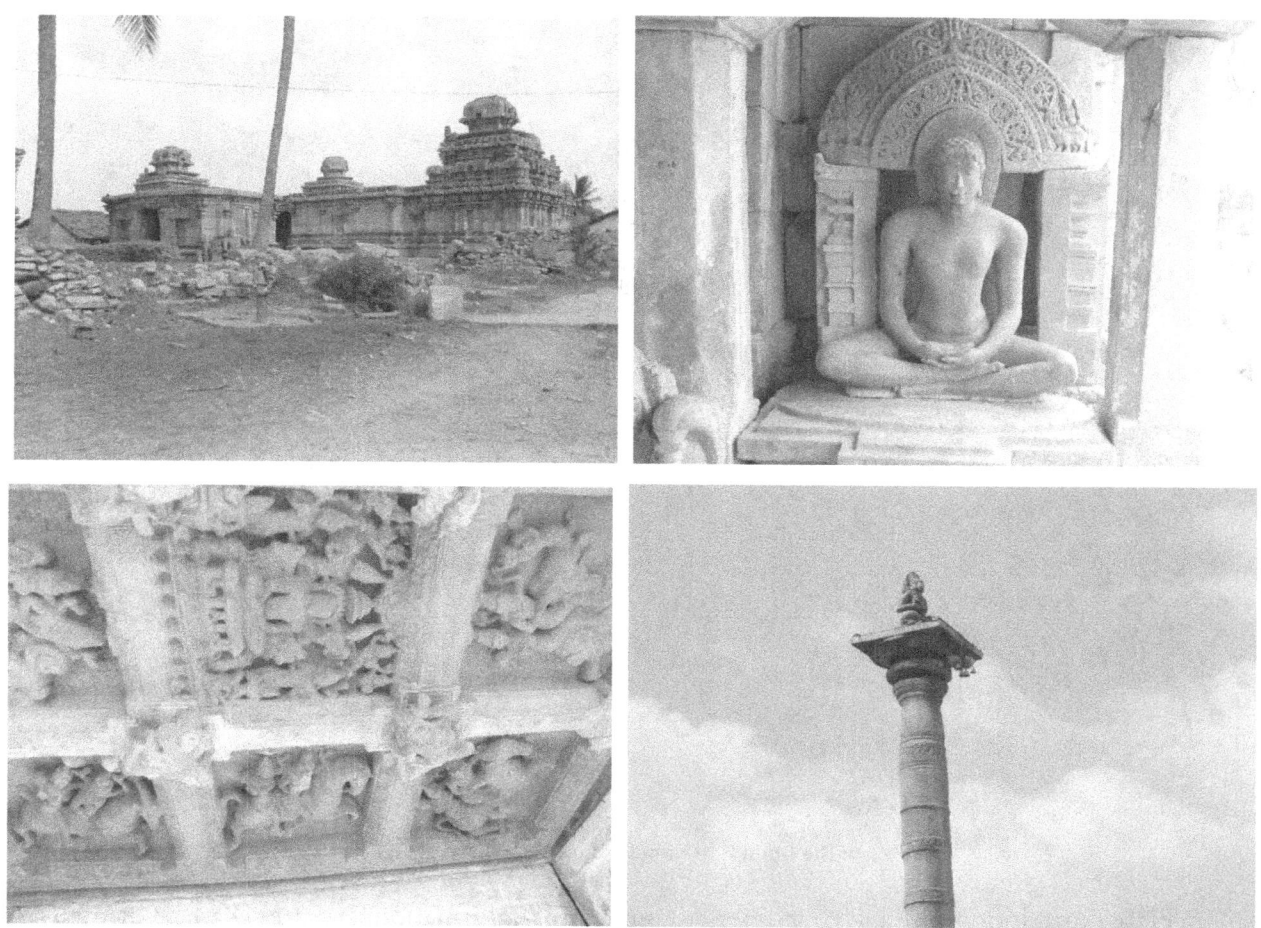

Panchakuta Basadi at Kambadahalli

Kadamba Period: -The existence of Jaina temples during the period of the Banavasi Kadambas is amply evidenced by their epigraphs. The earliest references to a grant by a Kadamba king to a Jaina saint is found in the Halasi copper plate of Kakusthavarma. A reference to a Jaina temple (*chaityalaya*) is also found in the Devagiri copper plate of Mrigesavarma. The inscription states that Mrigesavarma gave a grant for the *sammarjana*, *upalepana*, *archana* and *bhagnasamskara* of the *chaityalaya* located at Brihatparalur. Further he also donated for the enclosure of the *chaityalaya* one *nivartana* of land. In the Devagiri inscription of Vijaya Siva Mrigesavarman a reference is made to *arhatsala* where an image of Jinendra was kept. Mrigesavarman's Halasi inscription of 8th regnal year states that the king built a Jinalaya in memory of his father in Palasika and granted lands to saints of Yapaniya, Nirgrantha and Kurchaka *sangha*. Ravivarma's eleventh regnal year inscription found at Halasi refers to a grant for the *abhisheka* of Jinendra. Another inscription of the same king refers to the worship of Jinendra for which four *nivartanas* of land was granted.

The famous Gudnapur inscription of Ravivarma is more explicit on this point. According to this inscription King Ravivarma built a temple, Kamajinalaya for Manmatha, very near the palace (*rajavesma*) and arranged for its worship by granting lands. At the same time he also gave grants to Kamajinalaya at Hakinipalli and Padmavati temple at Kalliligrama. Dr. B.R. Gopal who has edited this inscription has suggested that this Kamajinalaya is a temple for Bahubali, as Bahubali is described as Manmatha. If this is so, the tradition of erecting Gommata sculptures goes back to the period of Kadambas and to sixth century CE itself. However, Dr. A. Sundara has discovered a sculpture of Rati and Manmatha at the same place.

Whether this was the sculpture worshipped in the Kamajinalya cannot be ascertained. What is more important is the tradition of building Jaina temples for Manmatha and even Padmavati.

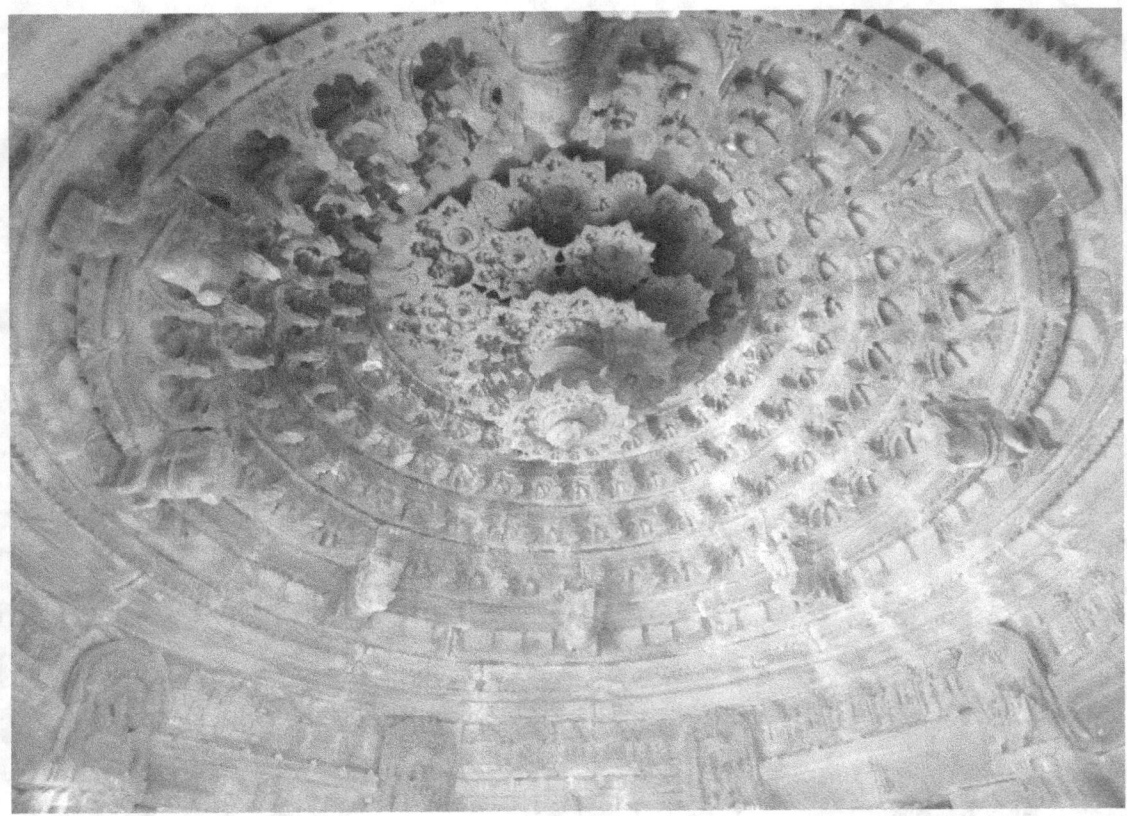

Ceiling of the Open Hall Kamala Basadi Belagavi (Belgaum)

The Halasi inscription of Ravivarma refers to interesting information. It states that the income from the gifted village should be used for eight-day festival in Kartikamasa in the Jinalaya at Palasikanagara. It states at the end wherever Jinendra worship takes place properly, that place will prosper without any fear from enemies and the prowess of the king will improve. The Devagiri plates of prince Devavarma refers to gifts for the worship in the *chaityalaya* and for its repairs.

All the inscriptions referred to above mention gifts for worship and repair to Jaina temples. However, many of them refer to a Jaina temple at Halasi. The Jaina temple now standing at Halasi cannot go back to a period earlier than eleventh century CE. Then the question is what happened to the *basadis* referred to in the inscriptions. Perhaps they might have been built in wood and obviously perished. A. Sundara's field work at Halasi throws very important light on this point. Very close to the Kalleswara temple at Halasi, he discovered an ancient site going back to megalithic and early historic periods. A large number of brick walls of the ancient period have been noticed by him in and around and obviously he thinks that this represents the Jaina temple built during the Kadamba period.

Badami Chalukyan Period: After the rule of the Kadambas of Banavasi most parts of north Karnataka came under the rule of the early or Badami Chalukyan kings. Their contribution to architecture and sculpture is not only well known but unprecedented. Most kings of this powerful dynasty patronised Jainism also though they were followers of Vedic Hinduism. This is attested by many inscriptions including the Aihole inscription of Pulakesi II, composed by the famous poet Ravikirti. The Jaina architectural beginnings made earlier by the Kadambas of Banavasi, crystalised into better structures in stone during the early Chalukyan period. As they used stone as the medium of their architecture, they have come down to us in good numbers.

The Chalukyas of Badami are known for their rock cut temples as well as structural temples. At Badami there are four rock cut temples belonging to Saiva, Vaishnava and Jaina faiths. Incidentally this is an eloquent testimony to the religious tolerance of the kings and the people during the period. The fourth cave is the Jaina cave dedicated to Adinatha Tirthankara. He is seated on the lion pedestal, reclining slightly on the cushion. There is a triple umbrella (*mukkode*) over his head in relief. There are two *chamaradharis* attending on the Tirthankara. On the left wall is a standing sculpture of Suparsvanatha with a seven hooded snake over him. To his right is a *Yakshi* holding a *Chatra*; to the left is a *Yaksha* sitting. On the opposite wall is the sculpture of Bahubali intertwined with creepers. In the inner *mandapa* on both sides are found two sculptures of Mahavira. In addition there are sculptures of twenty eight Jinas. The whole cave is 31 ft. wide and the depth is 16 ft. The entire composition is very elegant.

Another Jaina cave is in Aihole. It has an open *mandapa* and a *sabhamandapa*. In the *garbhgriha* is the sculpture of Mahavira in Padmasana. On the sides are *yaksha* and *yakshi* standing. In the open *mandapa* are high relief sculptures of Parsvanatha and Bahubali. However, this cave is not as refined and elegant as that of Badami.

Structural temples belonging to the Jaina faith too were built by the Chalukayas of Badami. The noteworthy among them are -Meguti Jinalaya at Aihole; the *jinalaya* built by Kumkuma Mahadevi at Lakshmeshwar; during the period of Kirtivarman II. Kaliyamma built a temple at Annigeri; the Jinalaya at Hallur; the Jinalaya built by Dharmagamunda at Adur in Hangal taluk. The Meguti Jinendralaya was built in 634 CE by Ravikirti. The temple has a *garbhagriha*, *antarala* and a *mukhamandapa* perhaps a later addition. There is a narrow *pradakshinapatha* around the *garbhagriha*. In the *garbhagriha* attached to the wall is the sculpture of Mahavira. In the *antarala* was a fine sculpture of Yakshi Ambika sitting in *ardha lalitasana*. Over the *garbhagriha* is another *garbhagriha* which also has a sculpture of Tirthankara. The *adhisthana* has miniature decorations.

The Sankha Jinalaya at Lakshmeshwar is dedicated to Neminatha. Sendraka Durgasakti, a feudatory of Pulakesi II is said to have given gifts to this temple. It is possible that it may be earlier or at least contemporary to the Meguti temple. Many other inscriptions show that this was an important Jaina temple during the period. An inscription of Vinayaditya dated 686 CE refers to a grant to Jaina *acharya* of Devagana and *mulasangha*. Another epigraph of the time of Vijayaditya dated 729 CE mentions a grant to Niravadya Pandita who was to house pupil of Sri Pujyapada. Still another inscription of the time of Vikramaditya II dated 734 CE mentions gifts to Sveta Jinalaya.

The Jain temple at Hallur has *garbhagriha*, *antarala*, and rectangular *sabhamandapa*. The *garbhagriha* has an upper storey and is similar to Meguti temple. The *sabhamandapa* is bigger than *garbhagriha* and *antarala* and has a separate *mukhamandapa* which is in ruins. Thus it shows a more developed architectural feature. The outer walls of the *sabhamandapa* have low relief sculptures of Jaina Tirthankaras. Thus the Chalukyas of Badamis contributed in ample measure to the development of Jaina temple architecture and laid firm foundations for further development during the Rashtrakuta period.

Rashtrakuta Period: Altekar characterises the Rashtrakuta period as the golden age of Jainsim in Karnataka. This is amply demonstrated by a large number of Jaina epigraphs and also generous grants to Jaina temples. Amoghavarsha I used to consider himself purified by the very remembrance of his guru Jinasenacharya. He is also described as a follower of Syadvada. He had appointed the famous Jaina saint Gunabhadra as the teacher for his son Krishna. Krishna gave liberal donations to the Jaina temple at Mulgund. Indra IV was a devoted Jaina and he died committing *sallekhana*. Many of the Rashtrakuta feudatories like Rattas of Saundatti were staunch supporters of Jainism. From all these evidences Altekar estimates that at least one third of the total population of the Deccan during the period were Jainas.

The Jaina monuments of the Rashrakuta period are found at Pattadakal, Malkhed, Lakshmeshwar, Koppala, Bankur, in the present day Karnataka and at Ellora in Maharashtra which was included in the Rashtrakuta empire, The Jaina temple at Pattadakal consists of a *garbhagriha*, *pradakshinapatha*, *antarala*, *sabhamandapa* and *mukhamandapa*. The *garbhgriha* door *jamb* has a fine *makara torana*. Opposite walls of *antarala* have *Devakoshthas* to house *Yaksha* and *Yakshis*. The *sabhamandapa* is square and has four pillars in the centre, The *mukhamanadapa* has been provided with *kakshasanas*, The *garbhagriha* has a *dvitala Nagara sikhara* and it has another *garbhagriha* on the first floor like the Meguti temple, The outer walls in the western and northern sides have Jina sculptures which confirm that this is a Jaina temple, It is believed that this temple was built either during the time of Amoghavarsha I (814–874 E or Krishna I (770 CE). From the stylistic features ninth century CE seems to be reasonable for this temple.

The Jaina *basadi* at Konnur in Dharwad district was built during the period of Amoghavarsha I, by Bankesa in 860 CE. It has a *garbhagriha*, *antarala*, *sabhamandapa* and a ruined *mukhmandapa*. The unique feature of this temple is the star shaped *gabhagriha*, which later became a unique feature of the Hoysala temples in southern Karnataka. There are three niches. in the *garbhagriha* which is also rare. The *antarala* has two pillars while the *sabhamandapa* has twelve pillars. The latter also has two stone *jalandhras*, The *mukhamandapa* is reached through flight of steps.

The Jaina temple at Naregal near Ron was built during the period of Krishna III, by Padmabbarasi, the queen of Ganga Permadi Bhutayya in 950 CE (Now it is referred to as Narayana temple). It is the biggest Rashtrakuta temple in Karnataka, It has a *sikhara* of *Dravida vimana* type over the *garbhagriha*. The main *garbhagriha* of this temple was meant for a Jina, and is square, The other two *garbhagriha*s are rectangular, and have rectangular pedestals from wall to wall with twenty-four holes indicating that both of them were meant for establishing twenty-four Tirthankara sculptures, This is also a unique feature of this *basadi*. This became common in the eleventh century CE.

The Settavva temple at Aihole is another storeyed *basadi*. It is more elaborate in execution. It is also a *trikuta*. Besides it has three *ardhamandapas* and a common *navaranga*.

The Neminatha Basadi at Malkhed, the capital of the Rashtrakutas belongs to ninth century CE. Unfortunately the original structure has been repaired often and hence it is difficult to know its original features (Plate 5-1). The *garbhagriha* has a fine seated Neminatha sculpture. Other sculptures found here are those of Parsvanatha, Dharanendra and Padmavati. Some more Jina sculptures are in the *sabhamandapa* but they seem to belong to later periods.

The *basadi* at Bankur seems to belong to the end of the Rashrakuta period. There are many fine sculptures in this temple. Notable among them are Adinatha, Chandraprabha, Shantinatha, Parsvanatha, Mahavira, Padmavati, high relief sculptures of twenty-four Tirthankaras.

In addition to the above Jaina temples of the Rashtrakuta period many more are also found which are not properly documented. Outside the present Karnataka State, the Rashtrakuta *basadis* are found at Ellora where there are three Jaina cave temples referred to as Chota Kailas, Indrasabha and Jagannathasabha.

The Rashrakuta epigraphs supply evidence for the construction of many more Jaina temples which have not been properly located. Some important epigraphs may be noted below. In 875 CE Krishna II built a Jinendra *bhavana* at Savadatti. In 902 CE Pergada Bittayya built a *basadi* at Bandalike which was later augmented by Hoysalas. In 925 CE Nagayya built a temple at Asundi when Chandraprabha Bhattaraka of Dhora Jinalaya was the administrator. In 932 CE Chandavve built a *basadi* at Nandavara. In 964 CE., a Ratta chief built Jayadhire Jinalaya at Koppal. In 958 CE Jakki Sundari built a Jinalaya at Kakambal.

The above epigraphical references and the extant Jaina monuments prove that the Rashtrakuta period was a golden age from the point of view to Jaina architecture also. However, it has to be admitted that exploration of Rashtrakuta architecture in Karnataka has to be done more systematically. In this connection the good beginning made by S. Rajasekhara in identifying the possible Rashtrakuta monuments in Karnataka on the basis of stylistic evidences and epigraphs is laudable. Further research is bound to yield more Rashtrakuta monuments including Jaina temples in Karnataka.

Kalyana Chalukya Period: With the decline of the Rashtrakutas, most parts of north Karnataka came under the rule of the Chalukyas of Kalyana. Though they are known to be Saivites, they built Jaina temples. Many kings of this dynasty also granted gifts to Jaina establishments and individual saints. The development of *kalamukhas* on the one side and the virashaivism of Basavanna on the other were making great progress in north Karnataka and naturally this did not give enough scope for Jainism to blossom as it did in the earlier Rashtrakuta period. Nevertheless, it flourished through the royal patronage and contributed its share in the development of architecture. Taila, the founder of Chalukya dynasty of Kalyana is well known as the patron of the great Jaina poet Ranna. King Satyasraya had a *Rajaguru* Vimalachandrapanditadeva under whose feet the king is said to have learnt the tenets of Jaina *dharma*. Attimabbe, known as danachintamani is a well known personality of this period. She is said to have made one thousand copies of Ponna's Santipurana and distributed as *sastradana*. She built a Jaina temple at Lakkundi to which the king provided a golden *kalasa*. Somesvara's minister Santinatha persuaded Lakhma to build the Mallikamoda Santinatha Basadi at Baligrama. All these show the existence of Jainism during the period as well as royal patronage.

The Chalukyas of Kalyana were great temple builders all over Karnataka and they brought out new development in various components of temple. This was also adopted in the Jaina temples built by them. This is amply brought out by K.V. Soundararajan when he states "the Jaina temple building efforts went through more or less the same stages of growth and development as the Brahmanical, Jainism nevertheless maintained its entity by taking recourse to certain iconographic specializations which called for a distinctive layout. In surface treatment again, the Jaina temples eschewed all ostentatiously carved richness on the exterior wall or fabric of the temple but were not averse to an extravagant display of ornamentation and figure work in the interior." These distinctive features are found in the Jaina temples built by the Kalyana Chalukyas at Lakkundi and other places. They generally consist of a *garbhagriha*, *antarala*, *navaranga* and *mukhamandapa*. Usually they do not have sculptures on the outer walls. In the *navaranga* pillars are found with small sculptures. The sculptures generally consist of Bahubali, Parsvanatha, Mahavira, other Tirthankaras, *yaksha*, *yakshis*, *Chaumukhastambhas*, *sahasrakut Jinabimba*, *dvarapalas* and *manastambhas*.

The most important Jaina temples of this period are Brahma Jinalaya at Lakkundi, Charantimatha at Aihole and Sankha Jinalya at Lakshmeshwar. The Brahma Jinalaya built by Attimabbe represents a second phase of Kalyana Chalukyan art for it not only represents a progress in architectural work but also uses finer grained schist instead of the usual granite. The latter has influenced its masonry, size and sculpture. The temple is highly imposing with dimensions of 93 ft. and 35 ft. It has a *sikhara* 42 ft. in height, which rises somewhat steeply in three storeys looking like a *chaturasra sikhara*, with a *sukanasi*. The *mukhamandapa* is spacious having entrances in east, south and north. The sculptures of four-faced Brahma and Padmavati are noteworthy.

The Charantimatha group at Aihole was built before 1119 CE on which date king Vikarmaditya VI through his subordinate Kesavayya Setti made arrangements for certain repairs, additions and endowments. The main temple of this group is dedicated to Mahavira. The temple has a *garbhagriha*, *antarala*, *sabhamandapa* and *mukhamandapa*. It has a *sikhara* of the southern *vimana* type. There is also storeyed temple over the *garbhagriha*, a typical character of a *basadi*. The exterior wall is plain without any sculptures. The highly ornate doorways, drooping eaves and cornices of the corridor are highly elaborate and ornate. On the architraves of the front doors of the corridor are carved twenty four Tirthankaras, which add to the beauty of this temple.

Of the two Jaina temples at Lakshmeshwar the more famous is Sankha Jinalaya which consists of a *garbhagriha*, a large *ardhamandapa*, larger *mahamandapa* and a *rangamandapa*. The *rangamandapa* has three entrances to south, north and west. It has a *chaturmukha* structure in diminutive model, each of which carries three figures. It has a *rekhanagara sikhara*. The unique feature of this temple is the *Sahasrakuta Jinabimba* in minute form. There is a *manastambha* in front of the temple. Even though the temple is in ruins and has been renovated later, it presents a rare grandeur and stands as a testimony to the interest of the Kalyana Chalukyas in Jaina architecture. The other Jaina temple in this place is a *trikuta* dedicated to Adinatha.

The other Jaina temples of the Kalyana Chalukya period include Parsvanatha Basadi at Udri, Bandalike, Parsvanatha Basadi at Koppal, a ruined *basadi* at Halasi, Neminatha Basadi at Terdal, a ruined *basadi* within the fort at Belagavi, Parsvanatha Basadi at Ammangi in Belagavi district, a ruined *basadi* at Malkhed and another *basadi* at Sedam. Most of these are in ruins and are simpler in dimensions and designs as compared to the classical *basadis* found at Lakkundi and other two places. However, these constructions show the widespread popularity of Jaina architecture in the north Karnataka region during the Kalyana Chalukya period.

As the Hoysalas did not have a permanent footing in north Karnataka due to the opposition of the Sevunas of Devagiri, there are no Hoysala monuments in this region. They are confined to southern Karnataka.

The Sevuna Period: The Sevunas of Devagiri ruled over most parts of north Karnataka and parts of Maharashtra after the decline of the Chalukyas of Kalyana. Tradition connects the Sevunas with Jainism. As evidenced by Nasikakalpa, Dridhaprahara one of the early kings of this dynasty grew under the care of Chandraprabhasvamin and in recognition of this he named his capital Chandradityapura, after this Jaina saint. Sevunadeva III was a devout Jaina. His Anjaneri inscription opens with an invocation to Pancha Parameshthis namely *arhats, siddhas, acharyas, upadhyayas* and *sadhus*. Singhana II made a large number of grants to Jinalaya at Purikanagara for the worship of Parsvanatha and to the temple of Ananata Tirthankara. King Ramachandta made the grant of a village Hunisehalli for a Jinalaya. His Sarvadhikari is said to have built a *basadi* at the instance of his guru Jinabhattaraka. Apart from these epigraphical references, it is not possible to identify any of the Jaina temples built during the period.

Jaina Influence in Coastal Karnataka

There were two important factors for the flourishing of Jaina religion in the coastal provinces. One, the assimilation of Hindu elements by the Jainas in coastal Karnataka and two, a similar assimilation of the folk forms of worship which were practiced in the locality. The Jainas of coastal Karnataka worshipped goddess Sarawati and this is very much evidenced in the literary works composed between the fifteenth and sixteenth century. Saraswati was considered to be an auspicious goddess by the Jainas of the region.

The merchant class of Jaina *settis* who moved into Karnataka and eventually became domiciled there, were the ones who were the kings' and government's appointed officials in Tululand predominantly covering the coastal region of Karnataka. These *settis* accepted the local Hindu gods like Mahalingeswara, Janardana, Gopalakrishna, Vinayaka, Durgaparameshwari, Rajarajeshwari and others as their clan gods (*kula devata*). They gave grants to the temples of these gods just as they did to Jaina *basadis*. Although this was contrary to Jaina practices, they accepted and practiced *bhuta* worship.

Inscriptions give evidence to the fact that Jainas in coastal region invoked Hindu deities much as they invoked the Tirthankaras. The Govardhanagiri inscription shows that attempts were made by the Jainas to assign the attributes of Siva and Visnu to Nemi Bhattaraka. The Jainas also practiced some Tantric rituals. By these cult practices, the Jainas wielded a considerable influence over the people. Invocation of *yakshini* was prevalent in occult practices among the Jainas. Among the important places where Jaina monuments were built include Angadi, Barkur, Moodbidri, Karkala and Venur. Remains of the tombs of several Jaina ascetics can be seen in Moodbidri of which some are believed to date back to the 8th century CE (Plate 5-2). Both Alupas and Hoysalas patronized Jaina religion in the coastal areas of Karnataka but the major contribution in the flourishing of Jaina monuments was made by the Chautas of Puttige, Bangas of Bangavadi, Samantas of Mulki, Bhairarasa of Karkala and Ajilas of Venur.

5.4 KARNATAKA HISTORY OF ARCHITECTURE-THE HINDU MONUMENTS

The intriguing question is that since when have the Hindu temples been in existence in Karnataka and it gets partially answered if we go to Talagunda and Malavalli and see the pillar inscriptions at both the places. The pillar inscription at Malavalli dates back to the Satavahana period or at least is assignable to the Chutus. Thus the antiquity of the inscription goes back nearly 1900 years. The inscription talks about the god Malapali (Siva) which implies that Siva temples were in existence at that time. The nearby Pranaveswara temple at Talagunda again seems to be of similar antiquity. As per the inscription found here, it is mentioned that the Sivalinga in this temple was worshiped by earlier rulers including Satkarni. This puts back the antiquity of the temple at least to the Satavahana period. However the present structure is not of the Satavahana period but of the early Kadambas (even this structure has been pulled down as the temple is undergoing restoration work by ASI). Explorations around the present structure had revealed brick structure of the Satavahana period. The temple is a small square building consisting of a *garbhagriha* and a *sukanasi*. There is a huge Sivalinga inside the sanctum. The *garbhagriha* doorway jambs are carved out of Kadamba inscription stones, the workmanship of the doorway is of a later period.

Excavation on mounds enclosed by huge brick fortification over a square km in Banavasi exposed an apsidal temple belonging to the Satavahana period. The building consisted of parallel walls and a square platform of baked bricks, paved with terracotta tiles. The existence of a *chaitya* is also mentioned by Hiuen Tsang who visited the site in 7th century CE. Banavasi excavations also unearthed a displaced 20 ft high pillar. On the face of the pillar are engraved inscriptions of the time of the Kadamba king Ravi Varma. Besides describing the Kadama genealogy, the inscriptions articulate construction of temples nearby Banavasi. The two temples finding mention here are the Kama Devalaya at Hakinapalli and Padmavathi Temple at Kallili.

Banavasi excavations threw light on a highly deteriorated fort perhaps the earliest fort built in Karnataka. The fort's exteriors measure 850 metres north-south and 600 metres east-west. During the excavations three distinct phases of construction emerged. These are:

- Period 1 – The earliest phase of brick structure belonging to the Satavahanas and Chutus.
- Period 2 – The next phase was enlargement of the fort with laterite blocks, bricks and mud which belongs to the early Kadamba period.
- Period 3 – The last phase was extension at northern side with full laterite stones datable to the late Kadamba period.

The stratigraphical as well as other typological observations help in bracketing these activities between 2nd century BCE and 5th century CE. Excavations at various other places such as Sannati, Aihole, Gudnapur, Higunda, Vadgaon-Madhavapura, Chandravalli and Togarasi further lend credence to the fact that temples between 2nd and 4th century CE in Karnataka were made in wood or brick architecture. Most early temples of the Gangas of Talakad and Kadambas of Banavasi too were brick structures. Kadambas, however, started using stone as the medium of temple construction in the 4th century and temples at Malavalli (Lokanatha Mahadeva), Talagunda (Pranaveswara), Banavasi (Madhukeswara), Halasi (Hattikeswara, Kalleswara, Rameswara and Varaha Narasimha) suggest that a flourishing style of Brahamanical architecture both in brick and stone was evolving at that time.

Of the early phase of Ganga architecture, inscriptional evidence in respect of Brahamanical and Jaina temples is available but actual remains of temples are not visible on ground. Possibly in a few cases they are the underlying remains of the later enlarged and expanded temple structures. The early brick temples of the Gangas were located at Manne (Someswara and Kapileswara temples), Kodihalli and Honnudike (in Tumkuru district). For some of these temples it is not even possible to ascertain their original ground plans as mere brick wall or basement alone are visible. For instance, while Kapileswara temple at Manne stands largely intact, Someswara temple is recognizable only from the brick plinth under a restructured temple. Brick temples of the 4th and 5th century confirm to be an inheritance of the later Satavahana period and early Kadamba times. Begur temple in Bengaluru was from the time of the Ganga king Durvinita (570–620 CE).

During early period of the Gangas many temples were raised over the mortal remains of the dead king or other members of the royal family. Such sepulchral temples generally consisted of a single chamber without much embellishment with possibly a Linga enshrined inside. The Dadigeswara temple at Kodihalli

(Mandya district) belongs to this class. As the name suggests this temple seems to have been raised in memory of one of the founders of the Ganga dynasty, Dadiga, brother of Madahava I. Inscriptions also reveal that temples called Viniteswara after the king Avinita, Nitimargeswara after the king Nitimarga I and Sivamareswara after Sivamara II were raised and grants were made by the successor kings for their upkeep. All the three named temples are located at Mogenahalli in Ramanagara district. All such temples were just chamber temples with a Linga consecrated in the middle or in an antechamber.

Similar chamber like temples from the Ganga period abound in Kolar district at Madivala (Malur), Dodda Shivara, Uttanur (Uthanur in Google map) and Medithambihalli. The temple at Madivala is dedicated to *Saptamatrikas*. The *Saptamatri* images are fixed over a raised platform at the rear of the shrine. The temple has been modified and buttresses have been provided to keep the chamber walls intact. Similarly the Chowdeswari temple at Medithambihalli has been remodeled though a smaller dolmen like shrine still stands at its original place. These temples had a flat roof devoid of any *sikhara* or *vimana* above the shrine. Very often such temples are also surrounded by hero-stones of various types with vividly sculptured war scenes with the main hero reaching heaven (*Swarga*) after death and shown worshipping a Linga or a goddess.

In spite of their great personal preference to brahamanical cults and vedic rituals, the Gangas couldn't involve themselves in the evolution of any art style of their own but nurtured the extant traditions and upheld the art-idioms of the contemporary period with a large influence of the Pallava and Nolamba traditions. The real marvels of Ganga architecture emerged either in the construction of Jaina shrines or in later periods around the 10th century.

Conventionally, old temples are classified in stylistic groups named after dynasties of kings. In fact, whatever kind of regional styles or traditions guided the structuring of temples, kings only ordered their construction. Even if the temples were commissioned by wealthy people or nobility, the naming of temples got linked with the dynasty under whose rule these were built. Accordingly, it will be in order for us to study the evolution of temple architecture in Karnataka in relation with the region where a temple was built and during the reign of which dynasty was it commissioned. Since Karnataka's borders touch other states which too had extensive temple building activity in their own areas, influences from neighbouring states too added to the art-idiom of the dynasties ruling in Karnataka. Many of these dynasties ruled over areas comprising parts of several of these modern states at the same time. For instance, even though the capital of the Rashtrakutas was at Malkhed in modern Karnataka their most important iconic temple building activity was undertaken at Ellora in modern Maharashtra.

Architecture of the Kadambas of Banavasi

The Kadambas of Banavasi were the ancient royal dynasty of Karnataka from 345 to 525 CE, and made a significant early contribution to the architectural heritage of Karnataka. Dr. G. M. Moraes opines that apart from using some unique features, the Kadambas incorporated a diversity of styles in their architecture (Kadamba architecture), derived from their predecessors and overlords, drawing upon the architectural tradition of the Satavahanas for instance. The Kadambas were the originators of the Karnataka architecture. The most prominent basic feature of their architecture is the *Sikhara* (dome), called Kadamba Sikhara. The *Sikhara* is pyramid shaped and rises in steps without any decoration, with a *stupika* or *kalasa* at the top. Occasionally the pyramids had perforated screen windows. This style of *sikhara* was used several centuries later too, having an influence on the Doddagaddavalli Hoysala Temple and the Mahakuta temples in Hampi. The Kadamba temple *vimana* was usually square in plan, the tower is pyramidal shape and constitutes a series of horizontal step stages decorated with uniform series of quadrangular vertical projections and covering vestibules attached to *vimana*, The stages are more numerous and less elevated, devoid of pavilion ornamentation.

The 5th century monuments at Halasi in Belagavi district are the oldest surviving Kadamba structures. The most prominent feature is the *Kadamba Sikhara* with a *kalasa* on top. Hattikeswara, Kalleswara and

Someswara temples at Halasi form a group of temples. The old Jaina *basadi* containing a sanctum and a sukanasi at Halasi is one of the most ancient stone temples in Karnataka. Kadamba architecture constituted an important link between the architecture of the Satavahanas, Pallavas and Badami Chalukyas. Several features of the Kadamba architecture are visible in the Hoysala Architecture as well. Iswara temple at Malali from the Hoysala period and Keertinarayana temple at Heragu have the typical Kadamba *sikhara*. (Plate 5-3)

The Madhukeshwara (Lord Siva) Temple in Banavasi was built by Kadambas, and has an intricately carved stone cot (Plate 5-4). Originally built by the Kadambas, over a period of time has undergone many additions and renovations, from the Kalyani Chalukyas to the rulers of Sonda. "Kadambotsava," an annual cultural festival is held here in the month of December.

Architecture of the Gangas of Talakad

The Western Ganga style of architecture was influenced by the Pallava, Nolamba and Badami Chalukya architectural features, in addition to indigenous Jaina features. The Ganga pillars with a conventional lion at the base and a circular shaft of the pillar on its head, the stepped *vimana* of the shrine with horizontal mouldings and square pillars were features inherited from the Pallavas. These features are also found in structures built by their subordinates, the Banas.

Other important contributions are the Jaina *basadis* whose towers have gradually receding storeys (*talas*) ornamented with small models of temples. These tiny shrines have in them engravings of tirthankaras (Jain saints). Semicircular windows connect the shrines and decorative Kirtimukha (demon faces) are used at the top. The Chavundaraya Basadi built in the 10th or 11th century, Chandragupta Basadi built in the 6th century and the monolithic statue of Gomateswara of 983 CE are the most important monuments at Shravanabelagola and speak eloquently of the contributio made by the Gangas to Jaina architecture in particular and brahamanical temples in general (Plate 5-5). Some features were added to the Chandragupta Basadi by famous Hoysala sculptor Dasoja in the 12th century. The decorative doorjambs and perforated screen windows which depict scenes from the life of King Chandragupta Maurya are known to be his creation. The Panchakuta Basadi at Kambadahalli (five towered Jaina temple) of 900 CE with a Brahmadeva pillar is an excellent example of Dravidian art. The wall niches here are surmounted by *torana* (lintel) with carvings of floral motifs, flying divine creatures (*gandharvas*) and imaginary monsters (*makara*) ridden by *Yakshas* (attendants of saints) while the niches are occupied by images of tirthankaras themselves

The Gangas built many Hindu temples with impressive Dravidian *gopuras* containing stucco figures from the Hindu pantheon, decorated pierced screen windows which are featured in the *mandapa* (hall) along with *saptamatrika* carvings (seven heavenly mothers). Some well known examples are the Arkesvara Temple at Alur, Kapileswara temple at Manne, Rameswara temple at Narasamangala, Nagareswara temple at Begur and the Vaidyanatheswara temple at Vaidyanathapura (Plate 5-6). At Talakad they built the Maraleswara temple, the Arkeswara temple and the Pataleswara temple. Unlike the Jaina temples where floral frieze decoration is common, Hindu temples were distinguished by friezes (slab of stone with decorative sculptures) illustrating episodes from the epics and *puranas*. Another unique legacy of the Gangas is the number of *virgals* (hero stones) they have left behind; memorials containing sculptural details in relief of war scenes, Hindu deities, *saptamatrikas*, Jaina tirthankars and ritual death (such as the Doddahundi hero stone). The outer compound of the Siddappa temple at Dodda Shivara in Kolar district is a veritable museum of hero stones from the Ganga period.

Architectural contribution of the Chalukyas of Badami

The structure and format of a temple became realistic and aesthetic only by the 6th–7th century CE. Stylistic orientation and classification of temples as *Dravida*, *Nagara* and *Vesara* which we talk about so liberally now was achieved during this period only. 3rd to 6th centuries CE was a period of experimentation with style and structure of temples and at the same time of the evolution of canonical literature on art and architecture. Chalukyas of Badami partook in this experimentation and evolved highly indigenous architectural styles which were to form the foundation of nearly all temple building activities in future.

Badami Chalukyas came to power in the second half of the 6th century. The earlier Kadamba architecture did influence the Badami Chalukyas to some extent but they were not content with just one style of temple building. They came up with new styles of temple building even borrowing features from the northern temples of the Gupta period. This experimentation eventually led to the evolution of the Chalukya style of architecture. It won't be wrong to say that Aihole, the first temple building site of the Badami Chalukyas in fact was the cradle of Indian architecture. Aihole, Badami, Pattadakal and Mahakuta became the centres of the Badami Chalukyan School of Architecture, where they experimented both with the rock-cut and structural temples. (Plate 5-7)

Salient features of their experimentation are:

- They produced both rock-cut and structural temples;
- They experimented with all three architectural styles of the Hindu temple building viz. *Dravida*, *Nagara* and *Vesara*. *Vesara* style in fact is indigenous to Karnataka having been introduced by the Badami Chalukyas;
- Unlike the apsidal ended rock-cut temples of the north and central India, they went for the square and rectangular formats;
- Shrine in the body of the building was housed with nothing on the exterior to mark its position from outside in the initial stages. Later the tower (*vimana*) was added over the shrine (*garbhagriha*) to give the shrine that distinguishing look from the rest of the buildings;
- They experimented with all sizes of temples from small, medium, large, single celled to with *garbhagriha* and additional structures;
- The experimentation was centred at Aihole, Badami and later at Pattadakal;

The first phase of Badami Chalukya temple construction was notable for the excavation of caves at Badami and Aihole and a continuation of the well established architectural tradition of western India. The second phase was remarkable for a rapid development of structural activities of the temples at Aihole, Bdami, Mahakuta and Pattadakal. The importance of the early period lies in the fact that the temples built on different plans served as models for the later generations. The basic requirements of temples were fully developed in view of the ritualistic demands of the times.

The Badami Chalukyas built temples either on the banks of rivers or near tanks and wells. Majority of the temples in Badami are built around a huge tank called the Agastya Lake. Temples in Aihole and Pattadakal are built on the banks of the river Malaprabha and temples in Mahakuta are built around the Visnu Pushkarni.

The early temples of Badami Chalukyas had flat roofs with gradually inclining sides. This kind of roof is high and flat with slabs of the inclining roof inserted underneath to let off rain water. In temples with *pradakshinapatha* this kind of roof is found around the entire hall. Such arrangement can be seen in the Chikkigudi and Durga temples at Aihole. The inclining roof became the characteristic feature of the Badami Chalukyan temples.

The *adisthana* of Badami Chalukyan temples has a *kapota* and a *gala* moulding. The *kapota* mouldings occur as the top most moulding and are generally decorated with *kudu* motifs. The temples of Ladkhan, Huchchimalli, Chikkagudi at Aihole contain plain *gala* whereas the Meguti, Huchchappayya and Durga temples contain excellently carved reliefs of *yakshas* and scenes from the epics and *puranas* as also animals like lions and elephants besides floral reliefs.

The early phase temple walls are simple without much decoration whereas the second phase temple walls are more decorative being decorated with *koshthas* or niches, tops having simple and small *jalandharas* but with progress in time the *jalandharas* became large and articulate. The geese (*hamsa*) motif in a row underneath the nave is another characteristic of Badami Chalukyan temples. Such geese motifs can be seen at the Ladkhan temple in Aihole and Jambulinga temple in Pattadakal.

The pillars of the Badami Chalukyan temples in general are square and the shaft is decorated with *pattas* and medallions. The pillars do not possess vase, capital and abacus. The *pattas* and medallions are often designed with pearl chains, *kirtimukhas*, floral designs, musicians, dancers, animal figures, *mithunas* and *gandharvas*. In spite of the predominantly square shape of the pillars, the pillars with octagonal and sixteen sided shafts too occur, as in Meguti temple.

The *garbhagriha* is generally built at a higher level than the pillared hall or *sabhamandapa*. The same feature has been adopted in the caves and structural temples. The door jambs are fluted and divided into vertical *sakhas*. The *sakhas* are filled with pilasters, rosettes, figures of sculptures and floral motifs. The lower part of the door jambs usually bears a panel with river goddesses, *mithunas* and motifs.

The ceiling of nave in the temples is always broad and flat while that of the aisles is always inclining. The flat ceiling of the nave in the temples is always made up of massive stone blocks. The ceiling is invariably square and bears well executed reliefs. The major temples like the Galaganatha, Ladkhan, Huchchimalli, Huchchappyyagudi, Huchchappayya Matha and Durga at Aihole; the temples of Virupaksha and Papanatha at Pattadakal contain large sized reliefs on ceilings. The deities carved on the ceilings are Kartikeya, Trimurtis, Nataraja, Narayana on Ananta, *Nagas* and *Gandharvas*. The ceiling relief of Siva and Parvati riding Nandi in the Huchchappayya Matha is more articulate.

The Badami Chalukyan temples are adorned with all three kinds of *sikharas* over the *garbhagriha* viz. *Dravida*, *Nagara* and *Vesara*. The Sangameswara temple at Pattadakal, the Malagatti Sivalaya at Badami, the Mahakuteswara temple at Mahakuta are some of the temples with pure form of *Dravida sikhara*. The temples of Durga, Surya, Huchchimalli and Huchchappayya at Aihole, Jambulinga, Galaganatha, Kasivisvanatha and Papanatha at Pattadakal are adorned with *Nagara sikhara*.

Architecture of the Rashtrakutas

Numerous inscriptions issued by various kings of the Rashtrakuta dynasty help in recognising a large number of temples built during their reign. The study of epigraphs suggests a great outburst of both Hindu and Jaina temples by the Rashtrakutas in northern Karnataka. The Rashtrakuta architects continued the Badami Chalukyan tradition of temple style and began the introduction of new ideas, motifs and new set of plans which included the erection of *dvikuta* and *trikuta* temples often necessitated by religious considerations. The Traipurusha concept resulted in the consecration of the *trimurtis* either in separate *garbhagrihas* or in the same *garbhagriha*. The Navalinga temple at Kuknur built over a period of time ultimately resulted in the conglomeration on nine shrines in one temple complex.

The Rashtrakuta architects continued to use the red sand stone for building temples. In closing stages of their reign, the architects also used schist stone building temples at Sogala and Hooli. The Rashtrakuta architects continued to construct temples having *garbhagriha*, *ardhamandapa*, *sabhamandapa* and added a separate *mandapa* for the Nandi image opposite the main shrine. The Markandeswara temple at Sirwal is a good example of the separate Nandi pavilion. Among the *dvikuta* temples constructed during the Rashtrakuta reign are the Narayana temple at Savadi and Jodkalasa temple at Sudi. The Someswara and Narayan temples at Naregal originally a Jaina *basadi* built in 950 CE, is divided into two temples under different names. The temple consists of a *garbhagriha*, an *antarala* or *ardhamandapa* and a *sabhamandapa* or *navaranga*. This *navaranga* opens into a large *mukhamandapa* and the sides of the *mukhamandapa* are adjoined by *garbhagrihas* making it a *trikuta* plan.

The Rashtrakuta temples are generally built on a low or medium *adisthana* which indicates the continuation of a few mouldings of the Badami Chalukyan style of *adisthana*. The Rashtrakuta temples have two dominant types of wall decoration, the first one is simple and plain and the second one is wall decorated with a series of narrow tetragonal pilasters. Often pilasters exhibit a square bell in top position. In addition to the pilasters, *panjaras* crowned by *sikharas* are also noticed from the Jaina Basadi at Pattadakal and Kalleswara temple at Bagali. *Hamsa* (swans or geese) motifs just above the wall and below the *kapota* or eave became a common feature under Rashtrakutas. (Plate 5-8)

The Rashtrakuta temples have two types of pillars. The first type of pillars are square, heavy and simple without carvings and the second type of pillars are slender with graceful proportions richly engraved with figure sculpture and chain beads. A third type of pillars that appear in later Rashtrakuta temples are square at the bottom with an octagonal bell shaped shaft followed by a cushion lid and square abacus. Pillars in the Kalleswara temple at Bagali are the most beautiful with stellate shafts. Another interesting development that took place during the Rashtrakuta times was the shifting of the *makaratorana* from the *garbhgriha dvara* into the *ardhamandapa* as an independent unit.

Nolamba architecture

Although Nolamba-Pallavas (hereinafter referred to as Nolambas) had their capital in Hemavathi in modern Andhra Pradesh, they ruled over the areas bordering Andhra Pradesh either independently or as feudatories during their nearly 300 years' rule. At least three of their temple complexes contribute significantly to the monuments of Karnataka. These are the Kalleswara temple at Aralaguppe, Bhoganandiswara temple at Nandi and Ramalinga Group of temples at Avani. Nolambas' influence extended to the districts bordering Andhra Pradesh and hence their temples are mostly located in Tumukuru, Chitradurga, Ballari, Kolar and Rural Bengaluru districts only.

Nolamba temples are generally simple shrines architecturally, yet embellished with sculptural elements which provide grace to the monuments. Consisting of a *garbhagriha*, an *antarala* and a *mukhamandapa*, some temples have a later period Nandi *mandapa* and an *agramandapa* in addition. No Nolamba period temples have *antarala* doorways. Although the *garbhagriha* doorways tend to be relatively simple usually with three decorative bands (*sakhas*) and small door guardians (*dvarapalas*) at the base, the *mukhamandapa* entrances are sculpturally intricate. Commonly, five bands (*panchasakhas*) doorways are adorned with miniature relief musicians, dancers, *mithunas, ganas* and other mythological creatures entwined within meandering lotus vines (*kalpavalli*) or other decorative motifs. These are protected by *dvarapalas* at the base on both sides and auspicious signs (usually dancing Siva) above.

In some temples, ceiling panels with figural sculptures pleasantly distract from the temple's austerity. Kalleswara temple at Aralaguppe has a central panel in the *mukhamandapa* depicting Siva encircled by the *Ashtadikpalas*. The panel is divided into nine bays with dancing Siva (Natesa) at the centre and the other eight bays being occupied by the *Ashtadikpalas*. Because of their sculptural refinement and because of their iconic presentation, pillars are critical to the Nolamba temples. These pillars have square shafts with small upper cylindrical section leading to the cushion capital. The centre of the shaft has square panels on all four sides with relief sculptures. The *chaturasa* sections have *kirtimukhas* which spew bejeweled strands in the centre and sides of the panels. Above the *kirtimukha* is a *kalpavalli* which usually has figural sculptures at the top and sides. Above the *chaturasa* area on the four corners ubiquitous small lions are represented.

Among the Nolamba temples in Karnataka Bhoganandiswara, Kalleswara (Aralaguppe), Mahendreswara (Bargur) and the Ramalinga Group of temples at Avani occupy the central place. While the Mahendreswara temple is a surprisingly humble monument built of brick, yet it is the one of the only temples to have irrecusable Nolamba royal sponsorship of construction. In the Lakshmaneswara temple at Avani, a portrait of Tribhuvanakartabhatara, the religious overseer of Avani identified by an inscription can be seen on the north wall of the *vimana*. A figure on the south wall probably portrays the Nolamba king Vira Nolamba (also known as Anniga). Tribhuvanakarta ruled the '*Avaniya Sthana*' during the reign of two Nolamba kings, Anniga and Iriva, and during his forty years of control is reputed to have built two tanks and fifty temples.

Two temples of the Nolambas are described here in order to get a general impression of the art and architecture of the Nolambas and these are, Bhoganandiswara temple at Nandi and Kalleswara temple at Aralaguppe.

Bhoganandiswara temple: The original temple in the complex of the Bhoganandiswara temple ensemble, identified as one of the oldest grand temples of Karnataka, dates back to the early 9th century. The earliest inscriptions referring to the construction of the temple for Siva, according to the Archaeological Survey of India, are from Nolamba dynasty ruler Nolambadiraja and the Rashtrakuta emperor Govinda III dated 806 CE and copper plates of the Bana rulers Jayateja and Dattiya of about 810 CE. The temple was later under the patronage of successive notable South Indian dynasties: the Ganga dynasty, the Chola dynasty, the Hoysala Empire and the Vijayanagara Empire. The architectural style is *Dravidian*. The temple is located at a distance of 60 km from Bangalore. The temple is protected as a monument of national importance by the Archaeological Survey of India.

The temple complex has two large shrines: the Arunachaleswara shrine to the south and the Bhoganandiswara shrine to the north. It has the sculpture of a king considered to be that of Rajendra Chola added during the time when the temple was under the control of the Cholas. In between there is a small intervening shrine called with Umamaheswara shrine with a *kalyana mandapa* (marriage alter) supported by ornate pillars in black stone with reliefs depicting the Hindu gods Siva and his consort Parvati, Brahma (the creator) and Saraswati, Visnu (the preserver) and his consort Lakshmi, the god of fire Agni and his consort Swaha Devi, and decorative creepers and birds in bas-relief. This is typical to Hoysala architecture.

According to the art historian George Michell, the temple is a typical 9th–10th century Nolamba construction with pilasters on the outer walls of the shrines, perforated decorative stone windows which contain figures of a dancing Siva (south wall of the Arunachaleswara shrine) and Durga standing on a buffalo head (north wall of Bhoganandiswara shrine). Pyramidal and tiered towers (*sikhara*) rise from the two major shrines. Each major shrine has a large *linga* in the sanctum (the universal symbol of the god Siva) with a sculpture of Nandi (the bull) in a pavilion facing the shrine. During the 16th century Vijayanagara period, a pavilion with elegant pillars was added in between the two major shrines. The pillars crafted out of grey-green granite have relief sculptures of attendant maidens. The minor Uma Maheswara shrine was added in between the two major shrines (behind the pavilion) during the post Vijayanagara rule. The minor shrine has a procession of deities and sages in wall relief. The wall that links the two major shrines was cleverly constructed so as to be indistinguishable from the two original shrines. A spacious pillared hall was also added in front of the two major shrines.

The Arunachaleswara and the Bhoganandiswara forms of Siva represent, according to Hindu legend, two stages in the life of the god Siva: childhood and youth. The Umamaheswara shrine has reliefs depicting the third stage, Siva's marriage to the goddess Parvati. Hence this shrine is popular with newlyweds who come to seek blessing. The Yoganandiswara temple (of the Western Ganga dynasty) on top of Nandi hills represents the final "renunciation" stage in the life of Siva and hence this temple is devoid of any festivities. The large shrines each have a sanctum (*garbhagriha*), a vestibule (*sukanasi*) and a closed hall (*navaranga* or *mandapa*). The vestibule and hall are provided with perforated stone screens called *jali*. Each shrine has a *Nandi mandapa* in front (hall with the sculptured image of Nandi the bull) facing the sanctum. The outer bounding wall (*prakara*) of the complex has two minor shrines for *Devi*, the female form of divinity (divine core of all Hindu goddesses). To the north of the shrines is a second compound with a *navaranga mandapa* (pavilion) with *Yalli* pillars. Beyond this compound is a large stepped temple tank (*kalyani* or *pushkarni*), locally called "Sringeri Teertha" (the mythical source of the Pinakini river) where lamps are lit on certain festive days.

Bhoganandiswara temple is the most architecturally impressive and best preserved Nolamba period monument. Sculptures on the *vimana* superstructure and *hara* (cloistered parapet) level throughout the temple are exquisitely carved and feature an encyclopedic iconographic scheme. Facing east the temple consists of a *garbhagriha*, an *antarala* and *mukhamandapa*. The Bhoganandiswara *adisthana* has a *jagati*, a *tripatta-kumuda*, a *kantha* with mostly *makaras* and some *bhuta* reliefs. Protruding from the north of *vimana* adisthana, the *pranala* is shaped into a squatting, pudgy *gana* from whose large mouth the sanctum *abhisheka* water drains.

A unique portrayal of the *Kiratarjuniyam* episode is delineated on the south *antarala panjara*. Seated in the centre are Siva and Parvati disguised as *kiratas* (hunters). Kneeling below them is a small male in *anjali*. Identified by the bow to the side, the lower male is Arjuna receiving grace by Siva whose foot touches Arjuna's head. Two semi-circles of figures surround Siva and Parvati. The inner circle has *ganas* and *vidyadharas*, the outer circle narrates portions of *Kiratarjuniyam*. In the lower left Arjuna in *ekapadasana* (standing on one foot) performs *tapas* (penance) and a *linga* is depicted over his head. A boar pierced by two arrows is rendered in the upper right of the outer circle. Below the boar two small figures, Siva (*kirata*) and Arjuna fight. Exhausted by his futile attempt to defeat the *kirata*, Arjuna realizes the hunter is Siva and requests the boon of receiving from Siva the *pasupatastra* (weapon). *Kiratarjuniyam* is a Sanskrit *kavya* (poetic epic) written by Bharavi in the 6th century CE (or may be earlier). It describes a combat between Siva and Arjuna in Indrakeeladi hill (near Vijayawada). The contents of the *kavya* feature *vira rasa*, the mood of valour. (Plate 5-9)

The otherwise granite temple has exquisite black schist sculptures placed at the *griva-sikhara* level. The *kalasa* at the temple apex also is black stone. Facing the four directions, four couchant Nandis are in the corners of the *griva* platform. The other four sculptures are standing deities, Siva in the south, Brahma in the west, the north image is Visnu flanked by *Garuda* and *Gadadevi*, and in the most important front (east) is Siva leaning on Nandi as *Vrsabhantikamurti*.

The adjacent Arunachaleswara temple is similar to the Bhoganandiswara temple but with some notable variations and later alterations. Like the Bhoganandiswara temple, the Arunachaleswara temple has a *garbhagriha*, *anatarala* and *mukhamandapa* and is approximately the same size. The *adisthana* and wall elements on the Arunachaleswara are more elaborate. The *adisthana* mouldings are a *jagati*, a *kapota* with *nasikas*, a *kantha* with lions, elephants and *makara* reliefs, a *gala* and *padma-pattika*. The *pranala* is *makara* shaped with a man or *bhuta* standing in the open mouth.

The *mukhamandapa bhadrakosthas* are actually *jalavitayanas* with Natesa in the south window and in the north window a *kalpavalli* with dancers and musicians in its three swirls. The south Natesa is in *lalita* pose on top of Apasmara displaying in his eight hands: gajahasta (main R), *damaru* (UR), *trisula* (mid R), *pustaka* (LR), *abhaya* (main L), *naga* (UL), *ghanta* (mid L), *kapala* (LL) (Plate 5-10). A drummer and cymbals player sit to the left sides. Flanking the niche are elephants, *yallis* and above *makaras* ridden by *ganas* and a central *kirtimukha*.

Bhoganandiswara superstructure is an earlier construction than the Arunachaleswara tower is evident upon close inspection. The Arunachaleswara images tend to be stiffer, less fluid, more stylized and some of the ornamental motifs are variants of earlier forms. An Umamaheswara shrine constructed between the Bhoganandiswara and Arunachaleswara temples during the Vijayanagara period or slightly after the Arunachaleswara superstructure exhibits the same traits. (Plate 5-11)

The *mukhamandapa* and *garbhagriha* of Arunachaleswara temple have lantern roofs with central lotus medallion. Possibly a feeble attempt was made to replicate the Bhoganandiswara temple ceiling: two *dikpalas*, Indra (E) and Isana (NE) are roughly carved in low relief. The inappropriateness of Arunachaleswara lantern roof shape for *dikpala* images might have been the cause of abandoning the work.

Kalleswara temple: The dating of the Kalleswara temple at Aralaguppe is confirmed by two inscriptions. One inscription in the temple dated 895 C.E. (*saka* 817) describes the commissioning of the temple by a Nolamba king under his overlord, the Western Ganga King Rachamalla II (870–907 CE). The inscription also records the grant made by King Rachamalla II himself to the construction of this temple (called *Kalladegula* in the inscription). The other inscription, a hero stone in the temple tank (*pushkarni*), confirms that this region was under the overall control of the Western Ganga Dynasty during this period. The Western Gangas and Nolambas had close links with regards to "cultural art" and they would have, in their commission, common guilds of architects (*sthapatis*) and sculptors (*silpis*).

The plan of the sanctum (*garbhagriha*) is a square pyramidal one, with a plain exterior with simple pilasters, a vestibule (*antarala*) separating the sanctum from a closed hall (*mukhamandapa*) with an exceptionally well sculptured section called the *mahamandapa* or *navaranga*. The superstructure over the shrine (*sikhara*) and vestibule (*sukanasi*) have been renovated at a later period but the base on which the temple stands (*adhisthana*) is original in construction. The doorjamb (*sakha*) and the lintel above the main door have exceptional art. The doorjamb exhibits seated door keepers (*dvarapalas*) at the base, bold scrolls of decorative creepers that run along the sides of the main door and contain *Yaksha* (benevolent spirits from Hindu mythology) and *Yakshis* (or *Yakshinis*, their female counterparts). Above the door, forming the lintel (*lalata*) is a sculpture of Gajalakshmi (a version of the goddess Lakshmi) with elephants showering her from either side.

The walls are flat without projections and recesses except for the recess at the *antarala* dividing the *vimana* from the *mukhamandapa* and articulated by *brahmakanta* pilasters. *Jalavitayanas* are built into the *mandapa* and *vimana* walls. The walls and superstructure are built of bricks, the *adisthana* and *upana* platforms are granite. The brick *Phamsana* superstructure has a *sukanasi* in front.

Although the exterior is unimposing, the granite *mukhamandapa* entrance is finely sculpted with bands and reliefs. The inner and outer bands have *kalpavallis* with females, males or *ganas* within the meandering lots swirls. In the central *sakha* on each side is an opaque *stambhasakha* with a female carved three-quarters up to the height of the *stambha*. Within the *mukhamandapa* are four lathe-turned (*proto-srikara*) pillars. Two more lathe-turned pillars demarcate the *antarala* entrance. These pillars have sixteen sided and octagonal bands under the bell shaft.

The central black coffered portion of the *mukhamandapa* ceiling is divided by beams into nine panels (Plate 5-12). On the beams which circumscribe the central panel there are lotus pendants and attached to each pendant is a garland bearing *vidyadhara*. Carved in the round except for the portion of the back attached to the pendant the graceful flying *vidyadharas* are oriented towards the central panel carrying Natesa. His upper two hands hold alternate shaped tridents (*trisulas*). Sculpted in high relief, the three dimensionality of the body is strikingly conveyed. The lord of dance, Natesa is accompanied by three *Bhuta* musicians. A flutist sits to Natesa's right. An elegant open-hooded cobra facing Apasmara is below the flutist. To the left a *Bhuta* sits playing a three-sided drum (*trimukhavadya*) and above a *Bhuta* plays cymbals. The *ashtadikpalas* are portrayed in their assigned directional realms, each *dikpala* mounted on his *vahana* along with his consort. (Plate 5-13)

Chola architecture in Karnataka

Cholas ruling from Tanjavur from the days of Rajaraja I (985–1016 CE) started encroaching upon the areas commanded by the Gangas. This resulted in the annihilation of the Gangas power and their area of control fell into the hands of the Cholas between 1004 to 1014 CE. Cholas ruled over this region for over a century. Cholas took control of Talakad, the capital of the Gangas and made it their provincial headquarters and called it Rajarajapura. Cholas' first inscriptional record in Karnataka dates back to 991 CE. This inscription found in Kempanapura near Chamarajanagar describes an *agrahara* founded by Rajaraja Chola at Mundigod near Kollegal and also the Lakshminarayana temple there. He also founded *agaraharas* at Honganur and Kudlur near Channapatna and constructed Narayanaswamy temple at Malurpatna near Channapatna in 1007 CE. The famous Aprameyaswamy temple was founded at Dodda Malur by the Chola general Aprameya around the same time. (Plate 5-15)

Rajaraja's son Rajendra I (1016–1044 CE) consolidated the position of the Cholas in the erstwhile Ganga region and built Kailaseswara temple at Dodda Malur on the western bank of the river Kanva.

He also built the Muktinathswara or Mukeswara temple at Binnamangala near Nelmanagala. The Cholas, in their over 100 years reign, built temples at Malur, Begur, Bannur, Mudigonda, Kolar, Marehalli, Vagata and many other places. The famous Kolaramma temple though initially built by the Gangas was renovated and expanded by the Cholas. Cholas excavated various water tanks during their reign, the more notable among them being the Bellandur tank in Bengaluru and the Malurpatna *kere*. Though Cholas did not leave any remarkable impact on Karnataka's art and architecture, their temple building activity was quite widely visible. They did not build temples on grand scales as they did in the areas now called Tamil Nadu but they followed the typical Chola idiom even in the temples built in Karnataka. In order to understand their architectural style in Karnataka two of their temples have been described here – Kolaramma temple at Kolar and Narayanaswamy temple at Malurpatna.

Kolaramma temple: Through the epigraphy records, history of Kolar can be traced back to a pre-Christian era when it was called 'Kuvala-pura,' later it became the capital of the Ganga dynasty. The Gangas ruled large parts of southern Karnataka till about 10th century. Since then, the town has developed chaotically but around some impressive monuments. The most outstanding among these monuments are the Kolaramma and the Somesvara temples. Both being protected monuments, they have fortunately remained free from vandalism largely, and have been preserved in a fairly good state.

Much older of the two monuments, the Kolaramma temple is believed to have been built by Rajendra Chola around 1040 CE even though its original foundation may have been laid by the Gangas. Numerous Tamil inscriptions testify to the Chola occupation of Kolar around this time. The temple is an ordinary structure built in the Dravidian style, with a richly-carved doorway. It is believed that the *mahadvara* and *mukhamandapa* lay buried under the ground with only a few portions visible. A former government official got it removed as part of relief work in the past and the inscribed stones around the temple were brought to light. The Mysore Archeological Report gives details of these unearthed inscribed slabs. Most of them are in fragments and contain Chola inscriptions in Tamil. (Plate 5-14)

According to the Mysore State Gazetteer, the deity in the sanctum was Mahishasuramardini, known popularly as Kolaramma. This had replaced the original image of Kolaramma as it was mutilated due to medieval vandalism. However, later the Kolaramma's image was replaced by *Saptamatrika* figures.

Being a malevolent deity, any one experiencing Kolaramma's direct gaze is believed to be prone to calamities. So her image has been shifted to a side to protect the devotees from her direct gaze. The devotees can still have her *darshan* through a mirror placed in the opposite corner. The Mysore Archaeological Report mentions another stone image, about six feet tall, as Kapalabhairavi, which, people call Mukanancharamma, owing to its nose having been broken during vandalism in the past. According to some, this is the real image of Kolaramma, which, owing to its mutilation was removed from its place. A scorpion of immense proportion is carved on the wall of the *garbhagriha* above the *Saptamatrikas*. This leads to another intriguing question as to whether the original deity was Mahishamardhini or Bhairavi, as iconographic texts prescribe scorpion as an attribute of the latter and not the former who is associated with lion.

The ground plan of the temple complex has a rather strange look. The main shrine of Kolaramma is to the north of the campus and faces east. The later added larger shrine faces north and the two share a four-pillared *mandapa*. Both shrines comprise a *garbhagriha* and an *ardhamandapa*. The treatment of the external wall surface parts is identical.

The Kolaramma shrine houses images of the *Saptamatrikas* together with Ganapati and Virabhadra, the pride of the place being given to Chamunda, whose image is larger than the rest. To meet the need to accommodate as many as nine deities the *garbhagriha* is oblong, it is supported by a low *upana* and a high *adisthana* consisting of several mouldings including a *jagati* and a *tripatta kumuda*. These mouldings and the *garbhagriha* walls are covered with inscriptions. There is an animated *bhutagana* frieze below and a lion carved above the cornice. The superstructure consists of a high *griva* and *sala sikhara*.

The other shrine houses stucco images of the *Saptamatrikas* much bigger than those in the main shrine. Its *ardhamandapa*, which is supported by a row of four pillars, contains a life size image of a female deity and there is no superstructure over the *garbhagriha*. The two shrines and the *mandapa* common to them are surrounded by a *prakara*. The entrance to the temple complex is on the east wall but not in line with the axis of the main temple. At the entrance to the main shrine, there are two sculptures, Bhairava on the left and Bhairavi on the right.

One of the most outstanding examples of plastic art in the Kolaramma temple is the slab depicting a battle scene, now placed on the front platform of the entrance. It is a *viragal* (hero stone), probably belonging to the Ganga period measuring 4.5 feet in height. The slab is covered with relief work of horses, elephants, soldiers, celestial nymphs and celestial cars. The upper portion of the slab is vacant. It could have probably been the space reserved for inscription, which for some unknown reason was not engraved. The atmosphere in the stone carving is surcharged, with clashing of swords of the soldiers, galloping of the horses, the agony of the dying heroes, the anguish, and turmoil portrayed realistically and with great effectiveness. In the centre of the slab, there is a huge standing figure of a man with a curious dagger and a shield. Behind him are three attendants, one holding an umbrella and two holding the royal insignia. These fit in symmetrically well in the space. Opposite these figures is a king riding an elephant with a number of horsemen behind. The other hero stone slabs in the temple mostly contain only one standing armed human figure.

Narayanaswamy temple: Narayanaswamy temple is located at Malurpatna reachable by a narrow rural road taking off from the Bangaluru-Mysore highway about 3 km south-west of Channapatna. Eight inscriptions have been recorded on the walls of this temple over a period of time from 1107 to 1030 CE and these relate to various gifts made to the temple or for the upkeep of the temple. The temple is referred to as Jayangondasola-Vinnagar-Devar in these inscriptions. Jayagondasolan was one of the surnames of the Chola king Rajaraja I. As such the temple should have been built by Rajaraja I to get his surname associated with the name of the temple. (Plate 5-16)

Structurally of less importance than other Chola temples in Karnataka, Jayangondasola-Vinnagar-Alvar temple is a tiny piece of beauty with its walls covered over with meticulously engraved inscriptions in impeccable calligraphy. The temple faces west and it being without the *griva* and *sikhara* it must have been an *ekakuta* and *ekatala* temple. The *garbhagriha* measuring some 4.5 metres by 4 metres along the axis of the temple speaks of a relatively smaller temple. The *ardhamandapa* is just about 2.5 metres along the axis and 3.2 metres across. From the basement to the foot of the *griva*, the height is 2.2 metres. The wall enclosure (*prakara*) should have been about 20 by 15 metres going by the foundation stones of the walls visible at the site. A temple dedicated to Visnu but it is too austere by the standards of Vaishnavite temples generally.

Alupa architecture

The Alupas built some fine temples in their area of rule. The Panchalingeswara temple at Barkur, Brahmalingeswara temple at Brahamavar, Kotilingeswara temple at Koteshwar and the Sadasiva temple at Suratkal are attributed to them. They used sculptural styles from their various overlords over the centuries. Details of some of their architecturally significant structures follow.

Rajarajeshwari Temple, Polali: In modern Mangaluru district, Polali Rajarajeshwari Temple is one of the oldest temples and has the earliest inscription of the Alupa dynasty, written in 8th-century in Kannada language. The principal deity of the temple is Rajarajeshwari. The idol of Rajarajeshwari is completely moulded from clay with special medicinal properties. The temple portrays Hindu architecture with roofs adorned with wooden carvings of gods and copper plates. The temple has been referred to in many ancient inscriptions, including the *Markandeya Purana* and travel accounts of ancient travellers. According to an inscription discovered in the vicinity of the temple, the temple around the clay idol was built in 8th century CE. It is a widely held belief that the temple was built by King Suratha and that the king offered his own crown studded with precious jewels to be placed on the head of the deity. The king, having lost most of his kingdom in a war and being betrayed by his own ministers, is believed to have taken refuge under a sage named Sumedha in forests in a location near the temple. The clay idol of the main deity in the temple is historically believed to be up to 5000 years old. The king is reported to have carved the clay idol of Rajarajeshwari himself and offered penance to the deity in return for his kingdom. Many ancient inscriptions alluding to the temple were reported around the temple but were lost over time primarily due to the neglect of their keepers. The remaining inscriptions which are available today were obtained in Kariyangala village, Ammunje and in the temple itself and are now under custody of the Government of Karnataka. (Plate 5-17)

The region surrounding the temple was ruled by many dynasties including Kadamba, Chalukya, Alupa, Rashtrakuta, Hoysala and Vijayanagara. Most of these dynasties spent a lot of resources on the temple and donated agricultural lands for the benefit of the temple. Kings from the Alupa dynasty which ruled the region around 8th century were particularly noted to have contributed to the development of the temple. In later years, Queen Chennammaji of Keladi is reported to have visited the temple and gifted the temple with a grand chariot.

Records written by historian Abdul Razzak in 1448 CE suggest that the temple was initially built from molten brass. He recorded that the temple had four platforms. An image of the deity, 5 to 6 feet in height, with red rubies for eyes was present on the highest of the platforms. Today, the idol of the main deity is a stucco image of a height of 10 feet. The clay used for making the idol was specially prepared with herbal mixtures for added strength. The temple also has smaller idols for other deities including Subramanya, Bhadhrakali, Mahaganapati and Saraswati. During a religious event named *Lepashta Gandha*, the idols are coated with a special soil mixture with eight medicinal properties once every 12 years. The soil used for coating was prepared hundreds of years ago and is not prepared freshly on each occasion. The roof of *mukhamandapa* has many Gods and Goddesses exquisitely carved in wood. The roofs of other sections of the temple like *garbhagriha* and the *dhvajastambha* are covered in copper plates.

Manjunatheswara Temple, Kadri: In modern Mangaluru district, Kadri has the other important and old temple that belonged to the era of Alupas. The temple has several finest bronze statues installed by the king Kundavarma, which bears inscriptions of him dated 968 CE. In the inscription of Lokeswara statue, king Kundavarma is compared to Arjuna in bravery. The temple of Manjunatheswara on the hills of Kadri is a very beautiful and popular temple in Mangaluru. It was converted to a complete stone structure during the 14th century. The idol of Manjunathaswamy of the temple is called as oldest of the south Indian temples. It is believed that Parasurama who was living in Sahyadri, killed the *kshatriyas* who were cruel and donated the lands to Kasyapa. He prayed to Siva for a place to live. Siva assured Parasurama that if he performed a penance at Kadali kshetra, Siva would reincarnate as Manjunatha for the betterment of the world. As per Siva's orders Parasurama threw his axe into the sea and created a place for his penance (Plate 5-19). Yielding to Parasurama's prayers Siva appeared to him as Manjunatha along with goddess Parvati and stayed at Kadri for the betterment of the world. As per the orders of Manjunatha the *saptakoti mantras* become the seven *thirthas*.

This temple has Hindu and Buddhist history. Buddhism was practised here till the 10th century CE. But after the fall of Buddhism the devotion of Manjusri and Avalokiteswara continued in this region. The Natha cult was embraced towards Buddhism and continued their Tantric Siva tradition as well. As a result many Buddhist temples came in Hindu vortex. According to historian M. Govinda Pai this temple was known as *Kadri Manjunatha* where *Manjunatha* relates to Siva and *Kadri* is derived from *Kadri Vihara* which was Buddhist monastery of Vajrayana cult.

King Kundavarma of Alupa dynasty has left an inscription on the base on Avalokiteswara image stating he was devotee of Siva. This image was not of Buddha, but of Bodhisattva who was being worshiped as integrated form of Siva. Further M. Govinda Pai has concluded this was center of Bodhisattva Manjusri's cult.

And later these Bodhisattvas were identified as Saivite deities. Sivalinga and Bodhisattva were worshipped together for centuries at this place until this was converted completely to Saivite temple. *Kandarika Vihara* provides firm inscriptional evidence for this transformation.

In front of the temple, at a height there are a number of water ponds. There's a garden surrounding the ponds. When one walks down from there in front of the temple is a huge *deepastambha*. During the Hindu month of *kartika*, *deepotsava* is held here. There are statues of Matsyendranatha, Gorakanatha, Shringinath, Lokeswara, Manjusri and Buddha in the temple.

Mahishamardini Temple, Neelavara: In times, Alupas changed their capital from Mangaluru to Udyavara, Udyavara to Mangaluru and then again to Barkur depending on the political situation and demand. To be in centre to their ruling place, they even shifted their capital to Barkur from where they could look after the vast territory which spread up to Ankola in the north Karnataka coastal region. During this period they patronised several temples in the areas surrounding Barkur (which was their capital). Neelavara is one such holy place where Mahishasuramardini temple has several Alupa inscriptions of later period establishing that the Alupas gave grants for the temple. (Plate 5-18)

The stone inscriptions available here establish the antiquity of the temple. The four-handed statue of the goddess Mahishamardini is found with *chakra* in the left hand, slitting open the throat of Mahishasura with the sphere in the hand. The goddess is found stamping Mahishasura with the right leg. Dr. Gururaj Bhat, the illustrious historian of Karnataka maintained that the statue could have belonged to the 10th century CE.

Historicity establishes that the Alupas who ruled long here had made Udyavara to be their capital. The inscription issued by Veerapandyas in 1258 CE, throws much light over the fact that distribution of the revenue generated in this village those days also included the share to be given to the temple. The inscriptions found in the vicinity of Neelavara also establish that the Hoysalas ruled here around 1333 CE. *Grama Sabhas* (village councils) offered land cess to the temples recorded in inscriptions. An inscription of 1344 CE of Kulasekhara, the ruling king then has reference to donations made to Durga Bhagavathi, the ruling deity of the temple.

Panchalingeswara Temple, Vittla: Panchalingeswara Temple is the largest temple of Vittla (Vittal) region. Vittla comprises of 16 villages and is located in Bantwal taluk of Dakshina Kannada district. The temple is unique for its antiquity and rare artistic splendour. It is faced to the west and the sanctum has three-tiered roof. The shape of the temple is that of the back of an elephant (apsidal) rare style in temple architecture of south India. The sanctum of the temple has five lingas – Sadyojotha, Vamadeva, Aghora, Thathpurusha and Isana. These are supposed to be the five features of Siva. The legend has it that the temple is a creation of the Pandavas. (Plate 5-20)

Vittla temple is one of the temples and places of worship run by the Domba Heggade dynasty. Panchalingeswara was the chief deity of the Heggade dynasty. Early mention about Domba Heggade dynasty dates back to 1257 CE in Vogenadu inscription. Dr. P. Gururaj Bhat, a renowned historian, has pointed out that Panchalingeswara Temple must have been constructed in the 7th/8th century CE. No proper record is available to tell how many times it was renovated in the past, yet there is evidence that it was renovated in 1436CE, 1744 CE and 1894 CE.

The people of Vittla and devotees of the temple spread world over have joined for the cause of renovating the temple to give it a modern structural stability while retaining the earlier historic architecture. In 2002 a concrete plan was drawn up to renovate this beautiful temple of antique architectural value. A committee was formed and a detailed blueprint was prepared. A clear direction for renovation was sought in '*Astamangala Prasne.*' Dr. Veerendra Heggade has been guiding the committee as its honorary President. The committee comprises 305 members from all the villages. The three stage roof of the temple requires about 12,000 cubic feet of timber. Most of the timber required for the work is secured from Tirthahalli, Sullia and Kasaragod. Carpenters work continuously to keep the temple in good condition.

Anantheswara Temple, Udupi: Diagonally opposite to the main entrance of the Krishna Mutt, and adjacent to the Chandramouliswara temple, stands one of the oldest Alupa temples namely Anantheswara temple. An old belief is that lighting a lamp at the ancient Anantheswara temple takes away evil and sins. It is one of the biggest temples in Udupi. The main idol is the Linga, whose adornment makes it to look like the Face of Siva. From a small window on the left, the site where saint Madhvacharya disappeared is seen.

Both Vittla Panchalingeswara and Udupi Anantheswara temples have the elephant-back type curvilinear (apsidal) structure similar to the Durga temple in Aihole. The temple appears to be a structure of 7th century CE. The unique noteworthy feature of the architecture of South Kanara temples is their roof. Being in a region of high rainfall, the temple roofs evolved from grass, clay tiles and eventually with the copper-plates.

Temples of Barkur: The temples at Barkur have a distinct architecture. The sloping terracotta-tiled roofs bear resemblance to the temples of Kerala, but they do not have *gopurams*, a common feature of the *Dravidian* style of architecture of the south Indian temples. The 900-year-old Chowlikere Ganapati temple was constructed during the Chola Period. The Bairagi Ganapati temple is entirely hewn out of stone with a slanted stone roof and etched stone pillars. The stone walls of this temple display beautiful sculptures and it is apparent that this mammoth structure has withstood the ravages of time. The Panchalingeswara Temple, dedicated to Siva, is Barkur's largest temple, and is one of the oldest in the town. Its double-storied gateway, with a pillared verandah on either side, is most alluring. The rear side of the temple has an elephant-back-like curvilinear structure. The pillars that surround the circumambulatory path of the temple are decorated with carvings depicting mythological characters. (Plate 5-21)

Another interesting monument in the town is the Katthale Basadi. A 20-feet monolithic stone pillar is erected at the entrance. The temples were elegantly designed with carvings and embellishments, but are now in ruins. The twenty-four dents in the stone are the only evidence of the existence of idols of the twenty-four Jaina thirthankaras. There are three main structures in a big courtyard with a victory pillar at the entrance. Archaeologists say that they were built between the 8th and 12th Century CE. Built by the Alupa rulers, the Jaina *basadi*, unlike most south Indian temples built in the *Dravidian* style, does not have a *gopuram*. The sanctum sanctorum is surrounded by stone walls otherwise known as *prangana*, with sloping stone pillars over it. The original Mahavira idol was destroyed but has been replaced by stone tablets with animal figures that are a later addition.

Katthale Basadi consists of *navranga* with Nagakali, Siva, Visnu and Jain deities with separate temples. It proves the existence of changing kingdoms with various rulers trying to control the city both politically and in terms of religion.

Kalyani Chalukya architecture

Kalyani Chalukya or Later Chalukya architecture is the distinctive style of ornamented architecture that evolved during the rule of the Kalyani Chalukya Empire in the Tungabhadra region of modern Karnataka, during the 11th and 12th centuries. Kalyani Chalukyan political influence was at its peak in the Deccan Plateau during this period. The centre of cultural and temple-building activity lay in the Tungabhadra region, where large medieval workshops built numerous monuments. These monuments, regional variants of pre-existing *dravida* temples, defined the *Karnata dravida* tradition. Temples of all sizes built by the Chalukyan architects during this era remain today as examples of their architectural style.

The capital of Kalyani Chalukyas was shifted to Basavakalyan from Malkhed and it attained the celebrity status of a metrolpolis as a centre of wealth and prosperity besides being a centre of educational and spiritual importance at that time. Most of the many splendid monuments of the Kalyani Chalukyas in Basavakalyan do not exist now but from a few epigraphs it is evident that there were temples dedicated to Bhumeswara, Madhukeswara, Mahakaleswara, Pampeswara, Someswara, Malayavati and Narayana in the city and donations and grants were made to these temples by the kings, *dandanayakas*, provincial officers, merchants and various *mahajanas*. Some stone images and sculptures of the Kalyani Chalukyan times such as Nataraja, Bairava, Varaha, Mahishasuramardini, Surya, Anantasayana, Kesava, Tirthankaras, Siva-Parvati, Ravana etc. and other sculptural remains that survived here have been kept inside the fort now. (Plate 5-22)

Siva temple at Narayanpur, an ancient village 3 km east of Basavakalyan speaks eloquently about the art and architecture of the Kalyani Chalukyas. The village is mentioned in the inscriptions as Tribhuvana Tilaka Shri Rama Narayanapura, Rayanarayanapura and Viranarayanapura. The Siva temple constructed as a *trikutachala* consists of a *garbhagriha* and two-pillared *mandapas*. There are two ornamented pillars at the entrance. The *mandapa* has four highly ornamented pillars with four *dikpalas* on top of each pillar. Beautiful sculptures of *madanikas* have been kept at various places in and outside the temple. The ceiling of the *mandapa* has a beautiful floral design. On either side of the doorway to *garbhagriha*, *madanikas* and *dvarapalas* have been carved with high ornamentation of *yalli* design. The upper portion of the door has a small Ganesha and row of gods and goddesses depicting *swarga* (heaven). Many old statues including those of Siva, Parvati and Narasimha slaying Hiranyakashapu are kept in the temple hall. Many images of Visnu in different forms and Lakshmi found in the temple suggest that the temple may originally have been dedicated to Visnu. A broken *makaratorana* lying outside the temple has a central image of Visnu riding the *Garuda* and flanked by *madanikas* on both sides. (Plate 5-23)

There is another temple to the left beyond the well of similar design. This temple in ruins has a Sivalinga in its dilapidated *garbhagriha*. Scattered and loose sculpture can be noticed near that tank as well.

Most other notable of the many buildings dating from this period are the Mahadeva Temple at Itagi, the Kasivisveswara Temple at Lakkundi, the Mallikarjuna Temple at Kuruvatti and the Kalleswara Temple at Bagali. Other monuments notable for their craftsmanship include the Kaitabheswara Temple in Kubatur and Kedareswara Temple in Balligavi, both in the Shivamogga district, the Siddhesvara Temple at Haveri, the Amriteswara Temple at Annigeri, the Saraswati Temple in Gadag, and the Dodda Basappa Temple at Dambal. (Plates 5-24 and 5-25)

The surviving Kalyani Chalukya monuments are temples built in the Saiva, Vaishnava, and Jaina tradition. The centre of these architectural developments was largely the region encompassing the present day Dharwad district; present-day Haveri and Gadag districts and some temples in Ballari, Shivamogga and Kalaburgi districts. In these districts, over seventy monuments have survived as evidence of the widespread temple building of the Kalyani Chalukyan workshops. The influence of this style extended beyond the Kalyani region in the northeast to the Ballari region in the east and to the Mysore region in the south. In the Bijapur-Belgaum region to the north, the style was mixed with that of the *Hemadpanti* temples. Very few Kalyani Chalukyan temples can be found in the Konkan region.

Though the basic plan of the Kalyani Chalukya style originated from the older *dravida* style, many of its features were unique and peculiar to it. One of these distinguishing features of the Kalyani Chalukyan architectural style was an articulation that can still be found throughout modern Karnataka. The only exceptions to this motif can be found in the area around Basavakalyan, where the temples exhibit a *nagara* (North Indian) articulation which has its own unique character.

In contrast to the buildings of the early Badami Chalukyas, whose monuments were clustered around Pattadakal, Aihole, and Badami, these Kalyani Chalukya temples are widely dispersed, reflecting a system of local government and decentralisation. The Kalyani Chalukya temples were smaller than those of the Badami Chalukyas, a fact discernible in the reduced height of the superstructures which tower over the shrines.

The Kalyani Chalukya art evolved in two phases, the first lasting approximately a quarter of a century and the second from the beginning of 11th century until the end of their rule in 1186 CE. During the first phase, temples were built in the Aihole-Banashankari-Mahakuta region (situated in the Badami Chalukya heartland) and Ron. A few provisional workshops built them in Sirwal and Gokak in the Belagavi district. The structures at Ron bear similarities to the Rashtrakuta temples in Kuknur and Mudhol, evidence that the same workshops continued their activity under the new *Karnata* dynasty. The mature and latter phase reached its peak at Lakkundi (Lokigundi), a principal seat of the imperial court. From the mid-11th century, the artisans from the Lakkundi School of architecture moved south of the Tungabhadra River. Thus the influence of the Lakkundi School can be seen in some of the temples of the Davangere district, and in the temples at Hirehadagalli and Hoovina Hadagalli.

Influences of Kalyani Chalukya architecture can be discerned in the geographically distant schools of architecture of the Hoysala Empire in southern Karnataka, and the Kakatiya dynasty in present-day Andhra Pradesh. Sometimes called the *Gadag style* of architecture, Kalyani Chalukya architecture is considered a precursor to the Hoysala architecture of southern Karnataka. This influence occurred because the early builders employed by the Hoysalas came from pronounced centres of medieval Chalukya art. Further monuments in this style were built not only by the Kalyani Chalukya kings but, also by their feudal vassals. The Kalyani Chalukyan temples' architectural style can be described in brief as under:

Basic layout: A typical Kalyani Chalukya temple may be examined from three aspects viz. the basic floor plan, the architectural articulation, and the figure sculptures.

The basic floor plan is defined by the size of the shrine, the size of the sanctum, the distribution of the building mass, and by the *pradakshinapatha* (path for circumambulation), if there is one.

Architectural articulation refers to the ornamental components that give shape to the outer wall of the shrine. These include projections, recesses, and representations that can produce a variety of patterns and outlines, either stepped, stellate (star-shaped), or square. If stepped (also called "stepped diamond of projecting corners"), these components form five or seven projections on each side of the shrine, where all but the central one are projecting corners (projections with two full faces created by two recesses, left and right, that are at right angles with each other). If square (also called "square with simple projections"), these components form three or five projections on a side, only two of which are projecting corners. Stellate patterns form star points which are normally 8, 16, or 32 pointed and are sub-divided into interrupted and uninterrupted stellate components. In an interrupted stellate plan, the stellate outline is interrupted by orthogonal (right-angle) projections in the cardinal directions, resulting in star points that have been skipped. Two basic kinds of architectural articulation are found in Indian architecture: the southern Indian *dravida* and the northern Indian *nagara*.

Figure sculptures are miniature representations that stand by themselves, including architectural components on pilasters, buildings, sculptures, and complete towers. They are generally categorised as figure sculpture or other decorative features. On occasion, rich figure sculpture can obscure the articulation of a shrine, when representations of gods, goddesses, and mythical figures are in abundance. Figural sculpture and deity sculpture of Kalyani Chalukya period has been dealt with in detail under the section devoted to sculptural history.

Kalyani Chalukyan temples fall into two categories-the first being temples with a common *mandapa* (a colonnaded hall) and two shrines (known as *dvikuta*), and the second being temples with one *mandapa* and a single shrine (*ekakuta*). Both kinds of temples have two or more entrances giving access to the main hall. This format differs from both the designs of the northern Indian temples (*nagara* style), which have a small closed *mandapa* leading to the shrine and the southern Indian temples (*dravida* style) which generally have a large, open, columned *mandapa*.

The Kalyani Chalukyan architects retained features from both northern and southern styles. However, in the overall arrangement of the main temple and of the subsidiary shrines, they inclined towards the northern style and tended to build one main shrine with four minor shrines, making the structure a *panchayatna* or five-shrined complex. Kalyani Chalukyan temples were, almost always, built facing the east.

The Sanctum (cella, *garbhagriha*) is connected by a vestibule (*ardhamandapa* or ante-chamber) to the closed *mandapa* (also called the *navaranga* or *sabhamandapa*), which is connected to the open *mandapa*. Occasionally there can be two or more open *mandapas*. In Saiva temples, directly opposite the sanctum and opposite the closed *mandapa* is the *Nandi mandapa*, which enshrines a large image of Nandi, the bull attendant of Siva. The shrine usually has no *pradakshina*.

The pillars that support the roof of the *mandapa* are monolithic shafts from the base up to the neck of the capital. Therefore, the height of the *mandapa* and the overall size of the temple were limited by the length of the stone shafts that the architects were able to obtain from the quarries. The height of the temple was also constrained by the weight of the superstructure on the walls and, since Kalyani Chalukyan architects did not use mortar, but built by the use of dry masonry and bonding stones without clamps or cementing material.

The absence of mortar allows some ventilation in the innermost parts of the temple through the porous masonry used in the walls and ceilings. The modest amount of light entering the temples comes into the open halls from all directions, while the very subdued illumination in the inner closed *mandapa* comes only through its open doorway. The vestibule receives even less light, making it necessary to have some form of artificial lighting (usually, oil lamps) even during the day. This artificial source of light perhaps adds mystery to the image of the deity worshipped in the sanctum.

From the 11th century, newly incorporated features were either based on the traditional *dravida* plan of the Badami Chalukyas, as found in the Virupaksha and Mallikarjuna Temples at Pattadakal, or were further elaborations of this articulation. The new features produced a closer juxtaposition of architectural components, visible as a more crowded decoration, as can be seen in the Mallikarjuna Temple at Sudi and the Amriteswara Temple at Annigeri.

The architects in the Karnataka region seem to have been inspired by architectural developments in northern India. This is evidenced by the fact that they incorporated decorative miniature towers (multi-aedicular towers depicting superstructures) of the *Sekhari* and *Bhumija* types, supported on pilasters, almost simultaneously with these developments in the temples in northern India. The miniature towers represented shrines, which in turn represented deities. Sculptural depictions of deities were generally discreet although not uncommon. Other northern ideas they incorporated were the pillar bodies that appeared as wall projections. Well-known constructions incorporating these features are found at the Kasivisveswara temple and the Nanneswara temple, both at Lakkundi.

In the 11th century, temple projects began employing soapstone, a form of greenish or bluish black stone, although temples such as the Mallikarjuna Temple at Sudi, the Kalleswara Temple at Kuknur, and the temples at Konnur and Savadi were built with the formerly traditional sandstone in the *dravida* articulation. Soapstone is found in abundance in the regions of Haveri, Savanur, Byadgi, Motebennur and Hangal. The great archaic sandstone building blocks used by the Badami Chalukyas were superseded with smaller blocks of soapstone and with smaller masonry. The first temple to be built from this material was the Amriteswara Temple in Annigeri in 1050 CE. This building was to be the prototype for later, more articulated structures such as the Mahadeva Temple at Itagi.

Soapstone was also used for carving, modelling and chiselling of components that could be described as chubby. However, the finish of the architectural components compared to the earlier sandstone temples is much finer, resulting in opulent shapes and creamy decorations. Stepped wells are another feature that some of the temples included, for example at Sudi and Lakkundi.

As developments progressed, the Kalyani Chalukyan builders modified the pure *dravida* tower by reducing the height of each stepped storey and multiplying their number. From base to top, the succeeding storeys get smaller in circumference and the topmost storey is capped with a crown holding the *kalasa*, a finial in the shape of a decorative water pot. Each storey is so richly decorated that the original *dravida* character becomes almost invisible. In the *nagara* tower the architects modified the central panels and niches on each storey, forming a more-or-less continuous vertical band and simulating the vertical bands up the centre of each face of the typical northern style tower. Old and new architectural components were juxtaposed but introduced separately. Some superstructures are essentially a combination of southern *dravida* and northern *nagara* structures and are termed "*Vesara Sikhara*" (also called *Kadamba Sikhara*).

The characteristically northern stepped-diamond plan of projecting corners was adopted in temples built with an entirely *dravida* articulation. Four 12th century structures constructed according to this plan are extant: the Basaveswara Temple at Basavana Bagevadi, the Rameswara Temple at Devur and the temples at Ingleshwar and Yevur, all in the vicinity of the Kalyani region, where *nagara* temples were common. This plan came into existence in northern India only in the 11th century, a sign that architectural ideas traveled fast.

Stellate plans: A major development of this period was the appearance of stellate (star-shaped) shrines in a few temples built of the traditional sandstone, such as the Trimurti temple at Savadi, the Parameswara temple at Konnur and the Gauramma temple at Hire Singgangutti. In all three cases, the shrine is a 16-pointed uninterrupted star, a ground-plan not found anywhere else in India and which entirely differentiates these temples from the 32-pointed interrupted star plans of *bhumija* shrines in northern India.

The stellate plan found popularity in the soapstone constructions such as the Doddabasappa temple at Dambal as well. Contemporary stellate plans in northern India were all 32-pointed interrupted types. No temples of the 6, 12, or 24 pointed stellate plans are known to exist anywhere in India, with the exception of the unique temple at Dambal, which can be described either as a 24-pointed uninterrupted plan, or a 48-pointed plan with large square points of 90 degrees alternating with small short points of 75 degrees. The upper tiers of the seven-tiered superstructure look like cogged wheels with 48 dents. The Doddabasappa temple and the Someswara Temple at Lakshmeshwar are examples of extreme variants of a basic *dravida* articulation. These temples prove that the architects and craftsman were consciously creating new compositions of architectural components out of traditional methods. (Plate 5-26)

In the early 13th century, 12th century characteristics remained prominent; however, many parts that were formerly plain became decorated. This change is observed in the Mukteswara temple at Chaudayyadanapura (Chavudayyadanapura) and the Santeswara temple at Tilavalli. The Mukteswara temple with its elegant *vimana* was renovated in the middle of the 13th century. In the Tilavalli temple, all the architectural components are elongated, giving it an intended crowded look. Both temples are built with a *dravida* articulation. Apart from exotic *dravida* articulations, some temples of this period have *nagara* articulation, built in the stepped-diamond and the square plan natural to a *nagara* superstructure. Notable among temples with a stepped-diamond style are the Ganesha Temple at Hangal, the Banashankari temple at Amargol (which has one *dravida* shrine and one *nagara* shrine), and a small shrine that is a part of the ensemble at the Mahadeva temple. At Hangal, the architects were able to provide a *sekhari* superstructure to the shrine, while the lower half received a *nagara* articulation and depictions of miniature *sekhari* towers. The style of workmanship with a square plan is found at Muttagi and the Kamala Narayana Temple at Degoan.

Temples built in and around the Kalyani region (in the Bidar district) were quite different from those built in other regions. Without exception, the articulation was *nagara*, and the temple plan as a rule was either stepped-diamond or stellate. The elevations corresponding to these two plans were similar because star shapes were produced by rotating the corner projections of a standard stepped plan in increments of 11.25 degrees, resulting in a 32-pointed interrupted plan in which three star points are skipped in the centre of each side of the shrine. Examples of stepped-diamond plans surviving in Karnataka are the Dattatreya Temple at Chattarki, the Someswara Temple in Kadlewad, and the Mallikarjuna and Siddheswara at Kalgi. The *nagara* shrine at Chattarki is a stepped diamond of projecting corners with five projections per side. Because of the stepped-diamond plan, the wall pillars have two fully exposed sides, with a high base block decorated with a mirrored stalk motif and two large wall images above. The shapes and decorations on the rest of the wall pillar have a striking resemblance to the actual pillars supporting the ceiling.

The other type is the square plan with simple projections and recesses but with a possibility of both *sekhari* and *bhumija* superstructures. The plan does not have any additional elements save those that derive from the ground plan. The recesses are simple and have just one large wall image. The important characteristic of these *nagara* temples in the Kalyani region is that they not only differ from the *dravida* temples in the north Karnataka region but from the *nagara* temples north of the Kalyani region as well. These differences are manifest in the articulation and in the shapes and ornamentation of individual architectural components, giving them a unique place in Kalyani Chalukyan architecture. Temples that fall in this category are the Mahadeva Temple at Jalsingi and the Suryanarayana Temple at Kalgi. The plan and the *nagara* articulation of these temples are the same as found to the north of the Kalyani region, but the details are different, producing a different look.

Architectural elements: The Kalyani Chalukya decorative inventiveness focused on the pillars, door panels, lintels (*torana*), domical roofs in bays, outer wall decorations such as *Kirtimukha* (gargoyle faces common in Kalyani Chalukya decoration), and miniature towers on pilasters. Although the art form of these artisans does not have any distinguishing features from a distance, a closer examination reveals their taste for decoration. An exuberance of carvings, bands of scroll work, figural bas-reliefs and panel sculptures are all closely packed. The doorways are highly ornamented but have an architectural framework consisting of pilasters, a moulded lintel and a cornice top. The sanctum receives diffused light through pierced window screens flanking the doorway; these features were inherited and modified by the Hoysala builders. The outer wall decorations are well rendered. The Chalukyan artisans extended the surface of the wall by means of pilasters and half pilasters. Miniature decorative towers of multiple types are supported by these pilasters. These towers are of the *dravida* tiered type, and in the *nagara* style they were made in the *latina* (mono aedicule) and its variants; the *bhumija* and *sekhari*.

The Jaina temple at Lakkundi marked an important step in the development of Kalyani Chalukya outer wall ornamentation, and in the Mukteswara temple at Chaudayyadanapura the artisans introduced a double curved projecting eave (*chhajja*), used centuries later in Vijayanagara temples. The Kasivisveswara Temple at Lakkundi embodies a more mature development of the Kalyani Chalukyan architecture in which the tower has a fully expressed ascending line of niches. The artisans used northern style spires and expressed it in a modified *dravida* outline. Miniature towers of both *dravida* and *nagara* types are used as ornamentation on the walls. With further development, the divisions between storeys on the superstructure became less marked, until they almost lost their individuality. This development is exemplified in the Dodda Basappa temple at Dambal, where the original *dravida* structure can only be identified after reading out the ornamental encrustation that covers the surface of each storey.

The walls of the *vimana* below the *dravida* superstructure are decorated with simple pilasters in low relief with boldly modeled sculptures between them. There are fully decorated surfaces with frequent recesses and projections with deeper niches and conventional sculptures. The decoration of the walls is subdued compared to that of the later Hoysala architecture. The walls, which are broken up into hundreds of projections and recesses, produce a remarkable effect of light and shade, an artistic vocabulary inherited by the Hoysala builders in the decades that followed.

An important feature of Kalyani Chalukya roof art is the use of domical ceilings and square ceilings. Both types of ceilings originate from the square formed in the ceiling by the four beams that rest on four pillars. The dome above the four central pillars is normally the most attractive. The dome is constructed of ring upon ring of stones, each horizontally bedded ring smaller than the one below (corbelling). The top is closed by a single stone slab. The rings are not cemented but held in place by the immense weight of the roofing material above them pressing down on the haunches of the dome. The triangular spaces created when the dome springs from the centre of the square are filled with arabesques. In the case of square ceilings, the ceiling is divided into compartments with images of lotus rosettes or other images from Hindu mythology.

Pillars are a major part of Kalyani Chalukya architecture and were produced in two main types: pillars with alternate square blocks and a sculptured cylindrical section with a plain square-block base, and bell-shaped lathe-turned pillars. The former type is more vigorous and stronger than the bell-shaped type, which is made of soapstone and has a quality of its own. Inventive workmanship was used on soapstone shafts, roughly carved into the required shapes using a lathe. Instead of laboriously rotating a shaft to obtain the final finish, workers added the final touches to an upright shaft by using sharp tools. Some pillars were left unpolished, as evidenced by the presence of fine grooves made by the pointed end of the tool. In other cases, polishing resulted in pillars with fine reflective properties such as the pillars in the temples at Bankapura, Itagi and Hangal. This pillar art reached its zenith in the temples at Gadag, specifically the Sarasvati Temple in Gadag city.

Notable in Kalyani Chalukya architecture are the decorative door panels that run along the length of the door and over on top to form a lintel. These decorations appear as bands of delicately chiseled fretwork, moulded colonettes and scrolls scribed with tiny figures. The bands are separated by deep narrow channels and grooves and run over the top of the door. The temple plan often included a heavy slanting cornice of double curvature, which projected outward from the roof of the open *mandapa*. This was intended to reduce heat from the sun, blocking the harsh sunlight and preventing rainwater from pouring in between the pillars. The underside of the cornice looks like woodwork because of the rib-work. Occasionally, a straight slabbed cornice is seen.

From the 11th century, architectural articulation included icons between pilasters, miniature towers supported by pilasters in the recesses of walls, and, on occasion, the use of wall pillars to support these towers. These miniature towers were of the southern *dravida* and northern *bhumija* and *sekhari* types and were mostly used to elaborate *dravida* types of articulation. The miniatures on single pilasters were decorated with a protective floral lintel on top, a form of decoration normally provided for depiction of gods. These elaborations are observed in the Amriteswara Temple at Annigeri. These miniatures became common in the 12th century, and the influence of this northern articulation is seen in the Kasivisveswara temple at Lakkundi and in the nearby Nanneswara temple.

The miniature towers bear finer and more elegant details, indicating that architectural ideas traveled fast from the north to the south. Decoration and ornamentation had evolved from a moulded form to a chiseled form, the sharpness sometimes giving it a three-dimensional effect. The foliage decorations changed from bulky to thin, and a change in the miniature towers on dual pilasters is seen. The 11th century miniatures consisted of a cornice (*kapota*), a floor (*vyalamala*), a balustrade (*vedika*) and a roof (*kuta*) with a voluptuous moulding, while in the 12th century, detailed *dravida* miniature towers with many tiny tiers (*tala*) came into vogue. Some 12th-century temples such as the Kalleswara Temple at Hirehadagalli have miniature towers that do not stand on pilasters but instead are supported by balconies, which have niches underneath that normally contain an image of a deity.

Influence of Kalyani Chulkyan architecture on later monuments: The Kalyani Chalukya dynastic rule ended in the late 12th century, but its architectural legacy was inherited by the temple builders in southern Karnataka, a region then under the control of the Hoysala empire. Broadly speaking, Hoysala architecture is derived from a variant of Kalyani Chalukya architecture that emerged from the Lakshmeshwar workshops. The construction of the Chennakesava temple at Belur was the first major project commissioned by Hoysala king Vishnuvardhana in 1117 CE. This temple best exemplifies the Kalyani Chalukyan taste the Hoysala artisans inherited. Avoiding over-decoration, these artists left uncarved spaces where required, although their elaborate doorjambs are exhibitionistic. Here, on the outer walls, the sculptures are not overdone, yet they are articulate and discretely aesthetic. The Hoysala builders used soapstone almost universally as building material, a trend that started in the middle of the 11th century with Kalyani Chalukyan temples. Other common artistic features between the two dynasties are the ornate *Salabhanjika* (pillar bracket figures), the lathe-turned pillars and the *makaratorana* (lintel with mythical beastly figure). The tower over the shrine in a Hoysala temple is a closely moulded form of the Chalukya style tower.

The Mahadeva Temple at Itagi dedicated to Siva is among the larger temples built by the Kalyani Chalukyas and perhaps the most famous. Inscriptions hail it as the 'Emperor among temples.' Here, the main temple, the sanctum of which has a *linga*, is surrounded by thirteen minor shrines, each with its own *linga*. The temple has two other shrines, dedicated to Murtinarayana and Chandraleswari, parents of Mahadeva, the Kalyani Chalukya commander who consecrated the temple in 1112 CE.

The Siddheswara temple in the Haveri district has sculptures of deities of multiple faiths. The temple may have been consecrated first as a Vaishnava temple, later taken over by Jainas and eventually becoming a Saiva temple. The hall in the temple contains sculptures of Umamaheswara (Siva with his consort Uma), Visnu and his consort Lakshmi, Surya (the sun god), *Naga-Nagini* (the snake goddess), and the sons of Siva, Ganapati and Kartikeya. Siva is depicted with four arms, holding his attributes: the *damaru* (drum), the *aksamala* (chain of beads) and the *trisula* (trident) in three arms. His lower left arm rests on Uma, who is seated on Siva's lap, embracing him with her right arm while gazing into his face. The sculpture of Uma is well decorated with garlands, large earrings and curly hair.

Some temples, in a departure from the norm, were dedicated to deities other than Siva or Visnu. These include the Surya (portrayed as Suryanarayana) shrine at the Kasi Vishveswara temple complex and a Jaina temple dedicated to Mahavira, both at Lakkundi; the Taradevi temple (built in a Buddhist architectural style) at Dambal in the Gadag district; the Mahamaya temple dedicated to a tantric goddess at Kuknur, and the Durga temple at Hirekerur.

Hoysala architecture

Hoysala influence was at its peak in the 13th century, when it dominated the southern Deccan Plateau region. Large and small temples built during this era remain as examples of the Hoysala architectural style, including the Chennakesava Temple at Belur, the Hoysaleswara Temple at Halebid, and the Kesava Temple at Somanathapura. Other examples of Hoysala craftsmanship are visible in the temples at Belavadi, Amritpura, Hosaholalu, Mosale, Arasikere, Basaralu, Kikkeri and Nuggihalli.

Study of the Hoysala architectural style has revealed a lesser extent of northern architectural influence while the impact of the *Dravidian* style is more distinct. Temples built under Hoysalas till the mid-12th century reflect significant Kalyani Chalukya influences, while later temples retain some features salient to Kalyani Chalukyan art but have additional inventive decoration and ornamentation, features unique to Hoysala artisans. Some three hundred temples are known to survive in present-day Karnataka state and many more are mentioned in inscriptions, though only about hundred have been documented. The greatest concentration of these is in the Malnad (hill) districts, the native home of the Hoysalas.

The *Karnata Dravida* tradition which covers a period of about seven centuries began in the 7th century under the patronage of the Chalukya dynasty of Badami, developed further under the Rashtrakutas of Manyakheta (Malkhed) during the 9th and 10th centuries and the Kalyani Chalukyas of Basavakalyan in the 11th and 12th centuries. Its final development stage and transformation into an independent style culminated during the rule of the Hoysalas in the 12th and 13th centuries. Medieval inscriptions displayed prominently at temple locations give information about donations made toward the maintenance of the temples, details of consecration and on occasion, even architectural details.

Hoysala temples were not limited to any specific organised tradition of Hinduism and encouraged pilgrims of different Hindu devotional movements. The Hoysalas usually dedicated their temples to Siva or to Visnu but they occasionally built some temples dedicated to the Jaina faith as well. While king Vishnuvardhana and his descendants were Vaishnava by faith, records show that the Hoysalas maintained religious harmony by building probably as many temples dedicated to Siva as they did to Visnu though a preponderance of Vaishnanite temples is visible currently more on account of their rich ornamentation. Most of these temples have secular features with broad themes depicted in their sculptures. This can be seen in the famous Chennakesava temple at Belur dedicated to Visnu and in the Hoysaleswara temple at Halebid dedicated to Siva. The Kesava temple at Somanathapura is different in that its ornamentation is strictly Vaishnava. Generally Vaishnava temples are dedicated to Kesava (or to Chennakesava, meaning "Beautiful Visnu") while a small number are dedicated to Lakshminarayana and Lakshminarasimha (Narayana and Narasimha both being *avatars*, or physical manifestations of Visnu) with Lakshmi, consort of Visnu, seated at his feet. Temples dedicated to Visnu are always named after the deity. The Saiva temples have a Sivalinga, symbol of fertility and the universal symbol of Siva, in the shrine. The names of Siva temples can end with the suffix *-eswara* meaning "Lord of." The name "Hoysaleswara," for instance, means "Lord of Hoysala." The temple can also be named after the devotee who commissioned the construction of the temple, an example being the Buceswara temple at Koravangala, named after the devotee Buci. The most striking sculptural decorations are the horizontal rows of mouldings with detailed relief, and intricately carved images of gods, goddesses and their attendants on the outer temple wall panels. (Plates 5-27 and 5-28)

The Doddagaddavalli Lakshmi Devi (Goddess of Wealth) temple is an exception as it is dedicated to neither Visnu nor Siva. The defeat of the Jaina religion following Western Ganga dynasty (of present-day south Karnataka) by the Cholas in the early 11th century and the rising numbers of followers of Vaishnava Hinduism and Virasaivism in the 12th century was mirrored by a decreased interest in Jainism. However, two notable locations of Jaina worship in the Hoysala territory were Shravanabelagola and Kambadahalli. The Hoysalas built Jaina temples to satisfy the needs of its Jaina population, a few of which have survived in Halebid containing icons of Jaina Tirthankaras. They constructed stepped wells called *Pushkarni* or *Kalyani*, the ornate tank at Hulikere being an example. The tank has twelve minor shrines containing Hindu deities.

The two main deities found in Hoysala temple sculpture are Siva and Visnu in their various forms and *avatars* (incarnations). Siva is usually shown with four arms holding a trident and a small drum among other emblems that symbolize objects worshiped independently of the divine image with which they are associated. Any male icon portrayed in this way is Siva although a female icon may sometimes be portrayed with these attributes as Siva's consort, Parvati. Various depictions of Lord Siva exist: showing him naked (fully or partially), in action such as slaying a demon (Andhaka) or dancing on the head of a slain elephant (Gajasura) and holding its skin up behind his back. He is often accompanied by his consort Parvati or shown with Nandi the bull. He may be represented as Bhairava, another of Siva's many manifestations.

A male figure depicted holding certain objects such as a conch (symbol of eternal, heavenly space) and a wheel (eternal time and destructive power) is Visnu. If a female figure is depicted holding these objects, she is seen as his consort, Lakshmi. In all the depictions Visnu is holding four objects: a conch, a wheel, a lotus and a mace. These can be held in any of the icon's hands, making possible twenty-four different forms of Visnu, each with a unique name. Apart from these, Visnu is depicted in any of his ten *avataras*, which include Visnu sitting on Ananta (the celestial snake and keeper of life energy also known as Sesha), Visnu with Lakshmi seated on his lap (Lakshminarayana), with the head of a lion disemboweling a demon on his lap (Lakshminarasimha), with head of a boar walking over a demon (Varaha), in the Krishna *avatar* (as Venugopala or the cow herder playing the venu-flute), dancing on the head of the snake Kaliya, lifting a hill such as Govardhana), with his feet over head of a small figure (Vamana), along with Indra riding an elephant, with Lakshmi seated on *Garuda*, and the eagle (stealing the *parijata* tree).

The focus of a temple is the centre or sanctum sanctorum (*garbhagriha*) where the image of the deity resides, so temple architecture is designed to move the devotee from outside to the *garbhagriha* through ambulatory passageways for circumambulation and halls or chambers (*mandapas*) that become increasingly sacred as the deity is approached. Hoysala temples have distinct parts that are merged to form a unified organic whole, in contrast to the temples of Tamil country where different parts of a temple stand independently. Although superficially unique, Hoysala temples resemble each other structurally. They are characterised by a complex profusion of sculpture decorating all the temple parts chiseled of soft soapstone (chloritic schist), a good material for intricate carving, executed mostly by local craftsmen, and exhibit architectural features that distinguish them from other temple architectures of south India.

Most Hoysala temples have a plain covered entrance porch supported by lathe turned (circular or bell-shaped) pillars which were sometimes further carved with deep fluting and moulded with decorative motifs. The temples may be built upon a platform raised by about a metre called a *"jagati."* The *jagati*, apart from giving a raised look to the temple, serves as a *pradakshinapatha* or "circumambulation path" for circumambulation around the temple, as the *garbagriha* (inner sanctum) provides no such feature. Such temples will have an additional set of steps leading to an open *mandapa* (open hall) with parapet walls. A good example of this style is the Kesava temple at Somanathapura. The *jagati* which is in unity with the rest of the temple follows a star-shaped design and the walls of the temple follow a zig-zag pattern, a Hoysala innovation.

Devotees can first complete a ritual circumambulation on the *jagati* starting from the main entrance by walking in a clockwise direction (towards the left) before entering the *mandapa*, following the sculptural clockwise-sequenced reliefs on the outer temple walls depicting a sequence of epic scenes from the Hindu epics. Temples that are not built on a *jagati* can have steps flanked by elephant balustrades (parapets) that lead to the *mandapa* from ground level. An example of a temple that does not exhibit the raised platform is the Buceswara temple in Korvangla, Hassan District. In temples with two shrines (*dvikuta*), the *vimanas* (the shrines or cellae) may be placed either next to each other or on opposite sides. The Lakshmidevi temple at Doddagaddavalli is unique to Hoysala architecture as it has four shrines around a common centre and a fifth shrine within the same complex for the deity Bhairava (a form of Siva). In addition, four minor shrines exist at each corner of the courtyard (*prakara*).

The *mandapa* is the hall where groups of people gather during prayers. The entrance to the *mandapa* normally has a highly ornate overhead lintel called a *makaratorana* (*makara* is an imaginary beast and *torana* is an overhead decoration). The open *mandapa* which serves the purpose of an outer hall (outer *mandapa*) is a regular feature in larger Hoysala temples leading to an inner small closed *mandapa* and the shrine(s). The open *mandapas* which are often spacious have seating areas (*asana*) made of stone with the *mandapa's* parapet wall acting as a back rest. The seats may follow the same staggered square shape of the parapet wall. The ceiling here is supported by numerous pillars that create many bays. The shape of the open *mandapa* is best described as staggered-square and is the style used in most Hoysala temples. Even the smallest open *mandapa* has 13 bays. The walls have parapets that have half pillars supporting the outer ends of the roof which allow plenty of light making all the sculptural details visible. The *mandapa* ceiling is generally ornate with sculptures, both mythological and floral. The ceiling consists of deep and domical surfaces and contains sculptural depictions of banana bud motifs or lanterns and other such decorations.

If the temple is small it will consist of only a closed *mandapa* (enclosed with walls extending all the way to the ceiling) and the shrine. The closed *mandapa* well decorated inside and out, is larger than the vestibule connecting the shrine and the *mandapa* and has four lathe-turned pillars to support the ceiling, which may be deeply domed. The four pillars divide the hall into nine bays. The nine bays result in nine decorated ceilings. Pierced stone screens (*Jali* or Latticework) that serve as windows in the *navaranga* (hall) and *Sabhamantapa* (congregation hall) is a characteristic Hoysala stylistic element.

The bigger Hoysala temples possess *koshthas* in the form of miniature shrine on the walls. The *koshthas* are built in the prominently projected portion of thee *garbhagriha* walls. These *koshtha* shrines housed images are related to the main deity of the temple. The railings are divided into compartments by pilasters and the space between the pilasters is carved with reliefs. The upper and lower portions of the railing are ornamented with scrolls and floral motifs. The door frames of Hoysala temples are richly carved with scrolls and other reliefs. The door *sakhas* varies from three to nine in numbers.

The ceilings of the bigger Hoysala temples are richly carved and made up of square, octagonal, circular portion with pendant hanging in the centre. The smaller and earlier temple ceiling in the *navaranga* and *sabhamandapa* is simple without much decorative and generally depicts *padma.* The central ceiling of *sabhamandapa* of Chennakesava temple at Belur is an exquisite piece of art made up of square, octagonal and circular portions with pendant hanging in the centre in relief with tiny figures of different forms of Visnu, incidents from Bhagavata and the Mahabharata, a king or queen in the darbar, musicians, dancers, drummers, *yakshas* and *yakshis*. The lower face of the lotus pendant facing downwards contains a marvelous relief of Ugra Narasimha with ten arms. The Parsvanatha Basadi at Bastihalli has beautifully chiseled ceiling dominated by the figure of Dharnendra in the centre of the ceiling. One of the domical bays in the ceiling at Kesava temple at Somanathapura has a design that is akin to a Borromean motif.

A porch adorns the entrance to a closed *mandapa*, consisting of an awning supported by two half-pillars (engaged columns) and two parapets, all richly decorated. The closed *mandapa* is connected to the shrine(s) by a vestibule, a square area that also connects the shrines. Its outer walls are decorated, but as the size the vestibule is not large, this may not be a conspicuous part of the temple. The vestibule also has a short tower called the *sukanasi* or 'nose' upon which is mounted the Hoysala emblem or Hoysala crest depicting a man engaging a lion. In Belur and Halebid, these sculptures are quite large and are placed at all doorways.

The outer and inner *mandapa* (open and closed) have circular lathe-turned pillars having four brackets at the top. Over each bracket stands sculptured figure(s) called *salabhanjika* or *madanika*. The pillars may also exhibit ornamental carvings on the surface and no two pillars are alike. This is how Hoysala art differs from the work of their early overlords, the Kalyani Chalukyas, who added sculptural details to the circular pillar base and left the top plain. The lathe-turned pillars are 16, 32, or 64 pointed; some are bell-shaped and have properties that reflect light. The Parsvanatha Basadi at Halebid is a good example.

The *vimana*, also called the cella, contains the most sacred shrine wherein resides the image of the presiding deity. The *vimana* is often topped by a tower which is quite different on the outside than on the inside. Inside, the *vimana* is plain and square, whereas outside it is profusely decorated and can be either stellate (star-shaped) or shaped as a staggered square, or feature a combination of these designs, giving it many projections and recesses that seem to multiply as the light falls on it. Each projection and recess has a complete decorative articulation that is rhythmic and repetitive and composed of blocks and mouldings, obscuring the tower profile. Depending on the number of shrines (and hence on the number of towers), the temples are classified as *ekakuta* (one shrine), *dvikuta* (two shrines), *trikuta* (three shrines), *chatushkuta* (four shrines and *panchakuta* (five shrines).

Most Hoysala temples are *ekakuta*, *dvikuta* or *trikuta*, the Vaishnava ones mostly being *trikuta*. There are cases where a temple is *trikuta* but has only one tower over the main shrine (in the middle). So the terminology *trikuta* may not be literally accurate. In temples with multiple disconnected shrines, such as the twin temples at Mosale, all essential parts are duplicated for symmetry and balance.

The highest point of the temple (*kalasa*) has the shape of a water pot and stands on top of the tower. This portion of the *vimana* is often lost due to age and has been replaced with a metallic pinnacle. Below the *kalasa* is a large highly sculptured structure resembling a dome which is made from large stones and looks like a helmet. It may be 2 m. by 2 m. in size and follows the shape of the shrine. Below this structure are domed roofs in a square plan, all of them much smaller and crowned with small *kalasas*. They are mixed with other small roofs of different shapes and are ornately decorated. The tower of the shrine usually has three or four tiers of rows of decorative roofs while the tower on top of the *sukanasi* has one less tier making the tower look like an extension of the main tower and this constitutes the 'nose' of the *vimana*. One decorated roof tier runs on top of the wall of a closed *mandapa* above the heavy eaves of an open *mandapa* and above the porches.

Below the superstructure of the *vimana* are temple "eaves" projecting half a meter from the wall. Below the eaves two different decorative schemes may be found, depending on whether a temple was built in the early or the later period of the empire. In the early temples built prior to the 13th century, there is one eave and below this are decorative miniature towers. A panel of Hindu deities and their attendants are below these towers, followed by a set of five different mouldings forming the base of the wall. In the later temples there is a second eave running about a metre below the upper eaves with decorative miniature towers placed between them. The wall images of gods are below the lower eaves, followed by six different mouldings of equal size. This is broadly termed 'horizontal treatment.' The six mouldings at the base are divided in two sections. Going from the very base of the wall, the first horizontal layer contains a procession of elephants, above which are horsemen and then a band of foliage. The second horizontal section has depictions of the Hindu epics and *puranic* scenes executed with detail. Above this are two friezes of *yalli*s or *makara*s (imaginary beasts) and *hamsa*s (swans). The *vimana* (tower) is divided into three horizontal sections and is even more ornate than the walls.

In Hoysala art Hardy identifies two conspicuous departures from the more austere Kalyani Chalukya art, ornamental elaboration and a profusion of iconography with figure sculptures, both of which are found in abundance even on the superstructure over the shrine. Their medium, the soft chlorite schist (soapstone) enabled a virtuoso carving style. Hoysala artists are noted for their attention to sculptural detail be it in the depiction of themes from the Hindu epics and deities or in their use of motifs such as *yalli*, *kirtimukha*, aedicula on pilaster, *makara* (aquatic monster), birds (*hamsa*), spiral foliage, animals such as lions, elephants and horses, and even general aspects of daily life such as hair styles in vogue. *Salabhanjika*, a common form of Hoysala sculpture, is an old Indian tradition going back to Buddhist sculpture. *Sala* is the sala tree and *bhanjika* is the chaste maiden. In the Hoysala idiom, *madanika* figures are decorative objects put at an angle on the outer walls of the temple near the roof so that worshipers circumambulating the temple can view them. (Plate 5-29)

The *sthamba buttalikas* are pillar images that show traces of Chola art in the Klayani Chalukyan touches. Some of the artists working for the Hoysalas may have been from Chola country, a result of the expansion of the empire into Tamil-speaking regions of southern India. The image of *mohini* on one of the pillars in the *mandapa* (closed hall) of the Chennakesava temple at Belur is an example of Chola art.

General life themes are portrayed on wall panels such as the way horses were reined, the type of stirrup used, the depiction of dancers, musicians, instrumentalists, and rows of animals such as lions and elephants (where no two animals are identical). Perhaps no other temple in the country depicts the Ramayana and Mahabharata epics more effectively than the Hoysaleswara temple at Halebid.

Erotica was a subject the Hoysala artist handled with discretion. There is no exhibitionism in this, and erotic themes were carved into recesses and niches, generally miniature in form, making them inconspicuous. These erotic representations are associated with the *Shakta* practice. (Plate 5-30)

Apart from these sculptures, entire sequences from the Hindu epics (commonly the Ramayana and the Mahabharata) have been sculpted in a clockwise direction starting at the main entrance. The right to left sequence is the same direction taken by the devotees in their ritual circumambulation as they wind inward toward the inner sanctum. Depictions from mythology such as the epic hero Arjuna shooting fish, the elephant-headed god Ganesha, the Sun god Surya, the weather and war god Indra, and Brahma with Saraswati are common. Also frequently seen in these temples is Durga, with several arms holding weapons given to her by other gods, in the act of killing a buffalo (a demon in a buffalo's form) and Harihara (a fusion of Siva and Visnu) holding a conch, wheel and trident. Many of these friezes were signed by the artisans, the first known instance of signed artwork in India.

5.5 KARNATAKA HISTORY OF SCUPLTURE

Stone becoming the medium of art expression and communication at the time of Ashoka led to development of sculpture and plastic art of an indigenous nature. It led to imparting a semblance of a linear expressiveness that endowed the form with plastic coherence in models even though the artist gave unequal treatment to each single part of the subject. The sculpture of this phase consisted mostly of relief carvings on stone slabs and stone railings. Even gateways of *stupas* were decorated by depiction of stories and legends of Buddhism.

Serving as a vehicle of communication according to the needs of the expanding religion, the art of this period was mainly narrative. The intention of the artist was to present various episodes and incidents in one and the same relief composition. The figure of the main actor in the narration was usually highlighted in some form or the other to distinguish him/her from the other characters in the episode. Chronological order of events in an episode or sequence of events was maintained by creating relief compositions in a distinguished order. The forms were conceived not in terms of depth but those of surface and hence the figures were presented above and not behind each other. Objects were large or small not according to nearness or distance as the optical impression would demand but in accordance with the functional importance of each object. Unique examples of such narrative depiction in art can be seen in the carved pillars of the Arkeswara temple at Alur, Begur hero stone inscription, Kolaramma temple hero stone and episodes from the Epics carved in panels on the outside walls of several Hoysala temples. *Kiratarjuniyam* legend has the unique distinction of having been depicted on temple wall carvings right from the Badami chalukya times till the Hoysala period.

The antiquarian evidence collected in archaeological excavations suggests the beginning of art-activities in Karnataka from the Mauryan period. Important archeological sites of this period in Karnataka like Brahmagiri, Chandravalli, Banavasi, Maski, Sannati and Kanganahalli have yielded antiquities of significant importance. Good number of stone sculpture, terracotta, brick structures, *stupas, chaityas* have been found at these locations. However, art activity really gained momentum during the Satavahana phase, particularly for the Buddhist art. The emergence of Jaina and Brahamanical (or Vedic or Hindu) art in Karnataka can be mainly noticed during the 4th to 6th centuries CE when the Kadambas of Banavasi and the Gangas of Talakad ruled the middle and southern parts of Karnataka.

Excavations at Sannati and Kanganahalli have brought out a whole range of artifacts of the early Buddhist period in Karnataka. It has three important historical sites – two habitational and one Buddhist site with remains of two *stupas*. Out of the two *stupas*, first one is existing only in the form of a large circular base. More than hundred sculptures were salvaged and preserved from this site in the Government Museum at Kalaburgi. The second *stupa* is almost intact and undergoing excavation. It has over one hundred fifty inscriptions in Brahmi script paleographically assignable to period from 1st century BCE to 3rd century CE and these are mostly commemorative or donative in nature. Ranamandala near Sannati is Satavahana site as indicated from the epigraphs found there mentioning the names of the Satavahana rulers. (Plate 5-31)

Kanganahalli is a small village near Sannati. The excavations here revealed remains of a massive *stupa*, many brick built structures in the form of *chaitya griha* and votive *stupas* along with several members of the *stupa*–like fragments of sculptured veneering slabs, members of railings, pillars, capitals, Buddha *padas*, sculptures of *yaksha* and four images of Buddha.

The sculptural panels depict scenes from Jataka stories and life of Lord Buddha and portrait of many donors in singular or as couples. The excavations conducted at the site during the years 2000–01 and 2001–02 laid bare ruined remnants of a number of brick built structures like paved and sheltered passages connecting them. It also exposed part of a possible monastic complex to the north west of the main *stupa*. Limestone had been used for the construction of *stupa* and for carving sculptures. Antiquities such as lead coins bear names of Satavahana king like Satakarni, Pulumavi and Yajnasri. The remains of the site can be dated from 1st cent BCE to 3rd century CE. The most important discovery was the sculpture representing Ashoka from the site at Kanganahalli. This identification of the ruler is made on the basis of a small label inscription on the lower part of the same sculpture panel *-raya asoka* in Brahmi script. The artistic representation of this panel needs to be understood in the context of its social, political, cultural as well as religious connotations of that period. Narrative themes quite often seen at Sannati and Kanganahalli are the Jataka stories. Jataka "Suja Somiya" is one such example, represented on different slabs. Interestingly, there are a few Jatakas in relief inscribed with names.

In southern Karnataka, the sculpture of this period (Mauryan and post-Mauryan) distinguishes itself by an extremely low and flattened relief and the carvings seem to be attached to the surface almost like linear sketches (Plate 5-32). Though only a few fragments of relief carvings are available in the south from this period. Preference for slimness and elongation of limbs of the human characters in the reliefs, along with a precision in outline was a distinguished feature of the southern art. The tradition of creating relief carvings in the nature of a narrative however continued right till the 14th century CE as is evident from the narration of war history on the pillars of the Arkewara temple at Alur of the Ganga period and at many Hoysala temples in the friezes on their outer walls.

Though not much by way of antiquity records has come down to us from the period 2nd century CE to 5th Century CE other than a few artifacts from the Chutus and the Kadambas, art and sculpture were undergoing a massive transformation during this period. One *Naga* image contains the famous inscription of Shivaskanda Nagashri of Chutu family engraved on its frame. This *Nagapratima* kept at the Madhukeshwara temple at Banavasi from the 2nd century CE and a few scattered pieces of sculpture in a store room of the same temple are perhaps among the few items of evidence from that period. Scattered sculpture from various locations in coastal Karnataka and Uttara Kanara regions like Gokarna, Idagunchi, Haigunda, Gudnapur and Talagunda dating back to the Kadambas were mostly of the Brahamanical order. Carving of the sculptures in the round is a hallmark of the Kadamba art. The Talagunda inscription of the Kadamba Kakusthavarman while giving genealogy of the Kadamba rules, states that the king got a tank constructed for the service of the Siva temple there. This Linga is said to have been worshipped earlier by the Satakarni from the Satavahana family. This clearly establishes that Brahamanical or Vedic religion was practiced in Karnataka over two thousand years ago.

The human figure, termed as the image became the conscious medium of divine concept as gods began to be seen in anthropomorphic form. New canon of beauty evolved leading to the emergence of new aesthetic ideal. Youthful forms of characters depicted followed the newly establishing aesthetic and ritualistic canons. Elaborate draperies, jewelry, adornments and postures depicting movements or emotions of the character portrayed started becoming part of the overall compositions. The local material forms like trees, creepers, wooden architectural forms and natural spirits and animals started becoming part of the new art style.

The intellectual discipline lies further at the root of various attitudes (*asanas*) and gestures (*mudras*) for proper rendering of the different actions and moods reflected in the figures. A general classification in respect of attitudes is that of standing (*sthanaka*), seated (*asana*) and reclining (*sayana*) positions. At the same time the canonical literature on the Brahamanical iconography too was evolving lending further and newer dimensions to art and sculpture of the time. The aesthetic canon evolved clearly formulated the language and grammar of gestures. These gestures, *mudras* as they are known in the canonical and dramaturgical literature consist of definite conventions in finger plays and hand poses, each with a distinctive and significant meaning. Sculptures with several hands, multiple faces and manifestations too became common. Chaturmukha Brahma or Panch-mukha Linga and Mahishasurmardini with several arms too became part of the Brahamanical iconography. *Vahana* (vehicle of the deity) too occupied a central place in the iconography of this period. Location of these sculptures in different parts of the temple also started determining the getup and looks of the sculptures. Carving sculptures at different places of the temple involved different operational and sculpting methods and the sculpture possessed varying features resultantly. Sculptures appeared on temple pillars, temple walls, under *mandapas*, on the ceilings and on the periphery of the temple with all their different respective features. (Plate 5-33 and 5-34)

Codification of iconography and image cult was gaining currency in Jainism too around the same time. With monks adopting permanent residency in *basadis* instead of the earlier wandering ways, veneration of icons might have emerged as a consequence of these changes. Further, social conventions and Hindu customs and practices might have influenced Jainism to adopt in these areas. Though evidence of image creation and worship exists from the times of Mahavira, the progress in this direction became faster with a proper codification of Jaina iconography. Appeal of Jainism to common and ordinary people increased with the development of the image and temple cult, the prominence given to the *yaksha* and *yakshis* and the adoption of Tantric practices. These developments resulted in the formulation of ritual texts, Jaina *puranas*, *puja* rituals and canonical guidelines for iconography.

Devotees usually tend to seek favours and the benign grace of the deity in a temple. They may not expect such favours from the bodiless and fully-enlightened Jinas or monks. *Yaksha* and *yakshis* thus became the icons for seeking such favours and boons. *Yakshis*, as the female divinities generally gained more influence than their male counterparts viz. *yakshas*. Tribal rituals and imagery of those times where the role of mother goddess was supreme influenced the organized religions significantly. Simultaneously, the martial goddesses like Mahishasurmardini in Hinduism too were become prominent. This led to the development of a standardized set of seven mothers, the *saptamatrikas* from about the 4th century CE. These were joined by *Yoginis* and the goddess of knowledge, *vidya-devis* with Sarawati as the presiding deity. All these female deities were associated with supernatural abilities, with power to cure illnesses, grant children and to protect and fulfill wishes of their followers.

Tantric form of veneration was gaining currency in all three prominent religions of those times. Buddhism, Jainism and Hinduism all had their respective tantric icons and rituals during 6th and 7th century CE. Tantric form of worship included magical incantation, meditating on esoteric diagrams (*yantras* and *mandalas*) and rites to ward off evil spirits. Padmavati, Kushamandini and Jvalamalini were the important *devis* worshipped by the followers of Tantric form of Jainism during those times, which practice still continues with some reforms. Yakshi Jvalamalini is the *shasana-devata* of Chandraprabhanatha. Her genesis is attributed to the *puranic* pantheon and is hailed as a fire goddess. The cult of Padmavati is assignable to Simhanandi, the founder of the Ganga empire in Karnataka. The first *basadi* dedicated to goddess Padmavati was built in 490 CE by the Kadamba king Ravi Varma in the village Kallili in Uttara Kannada. The Western Gangas too were ardent devotees of the goddess Padmavati as the rulers considered that benevolence of the goddess offered them protection in all respects.

Padmavati was also the tutelary deity of the Rashtrakutas and adorned a basadi in Saundatti during the rule of the Rattas. From 14th century onwards, this goddess has been worshipped as a Hindu goddess now called Renuka or Yellamma. A magnificent idol of goddess Padmavati adorns the Brahma Jinalaya in Lakkundi constructed by the Kalyani Chalukyas. The image is placed at the entrance of the *garbhagriha* (sanctum sanctorum) on to left as one enters the temple, Chaturmukha Brahma (four-faced Brahma) being on the right of the entrance.

The development of gods and goddesses in Buddhism was due to the influence of Tantric Buddhism commencing sometime in the 7th century CE. In the Dambal inscription of the Kalyani Chalukyas, praise of goddess Taradevi is striking. The goddess is believed to remove fear from the lion, elephant, fire, serpent, thieves, water, sea and spirits. A broken image of Taradevi was found at the Koliwad temple. Likewise Balligavi inscriptions of 1064 and 1067 CE too are clearly Tantric Buddhist records. They talk about a grant of land for worship of Tara Bhagavati, Lokesha Devata and Buddhadeva which implies that there was a Tara Bhagavati temple in Balligavi.

It is necessary to understand some technical issues about plastic arts before going into its description.

What is Relief Sculpture? Definition and Meaning

In plastic art, relief sculpture is any work which projects from but which belongs to the wall, or other type of background surface, on which it is carved. Reliefs are traditionally classified according to how high the figures project from the background. Also known as *relievo*, relief sculpture is a combination of the two-dimensional pictorial arts and the three-dimensional sculptural arts. Thus a relief, like a picture, is dependent on a background surface and its composition must be extended in a plane in order to be visible. Yet at the same time a relief also has a degree of real three-dimensionality, just like a proper sculpture.

Reliefs tend to be more common than freestanding sculpture for a number of reasons. First, a relief sculpture can portray a far wider range of subjects than a statue because of its economy of resources. For instance, a battle scene, that, if sculpted in the round, would require a huge amount of space and material, can be rendered much more easily in relief. Second, because a relief is attached to its background surface, problems of weight and physical balance do not arise -unlike in statues and other freestanding sculptures where weight and balance can be critical. Third, because reliefs are carved directly onto walls, portals, ceilings, floors and other flat surfaces, they are ideally suited to architectural projects -typically the greatest source of sculptural commissions -for which they can provide both decorative and narrative functions. (Plate 5-35)

Types of Relief Sculpture

There are three basic types of relief sculpture: (1) low relief (*basso-relievo*, or bas-relief), where the sculpture projects only slightly from the background surface; (2) high relief (*alto-relievo*, or alto-relief), where the sculpture projects at least half or more of its natural circumference from the background, and may in parts be wholly disengaged from the ground, thus approximating sculpture in the round. (Sculptors may also employ middle-relief (*mezzo-relievo*), a style which falls roughly between the high and low forms); (3) sunken relief, (incised, or intaglio relief), where the carving is sunk below the level of the surrounding surface and is contained within a sharply incised contour line that frames it with a powerful line of shadow. The surrounding surface remains untouched, with no projections. Sunken relief carving is found almost exclusively in ancient Egyptian art, although it has also been used in some beautiful small-scale ivory reliefs from India.

Hindu Temple Sculpture

Organic and inorganic matter is perceived as a potential residence for a deity or spirit, particularly the sacred images produced for veneration in a temple or domestic shrine. The image is generally required to be beautiful to encourage the deity to enter it, and the material from which it was made must be unblemished. Divine energy is believed to be infused by ritual, and the final task of the ceremony is to open the eyes of the image by means of a specific chanted *mantra* (spoken or sung religious formula) and the completion by the artist of this part of his work.

To be ritually effective and sacred an image must be given the correct preparation and invocation, after which it is perceived not only as an icon or symbol but is also believed to hold a numinous presence. The image is also said to emanate a particle of the divine whole, the divine perceived not in man's image as a separate entity but as a formless, indescribable omnipresent whole. The image allows the worshipper to catch a reflection of the deity whose effulgence transcends what the physical eye can see. This divine effulgence is beheld in man's inner vision. An image is a *murthy* not because it resembles the deity it represents but because it conforms to prescribed measurements and symbolic conventions.

Hindu images have a very distinct appearance. The deities possess human or animal characteristics but represent superhuman beings. They are portrayed sometimes with many upper limbs, sometimes with more than one head. They express mood and movement in their posture and gesture; they hold emblems and can be placed in dynamic relation to other figures or symbolic animals. They inhabit realms beyond our normal existence. This mythical world and the gods who inhabit it express the Hindu belief that 'the Universe is boundlessly various, that everything occurs simultaneously and that all possibilities are not mutually exclusive.' Hindu aniconic and iconic symbols seek to represent forces and energies -aspects of a single supreme undifferentiated Iswara which is unmanifest and in real terms unrepresentable.

Because temples and the accompanying rituals to enshrined deities had an intricate role within regional polity. Royalty required overlord deities for legitimacy and sustenance and regional temple styles so evolved are often labelled as dynastic art. Ostentatious temples speak of dynastic puissance. While it might be true that royalty, or their surrogates, had some impact on the appearance of monuments within their realm, dynastic artistic styles did not necessarily emerge as being peculiar or unique to a certain dynasty. Style discrepancies within a given political realm are frequent. Contributing to regional diversity are temples built by smaller dynastic families which, even if politically subordinate to a regional sovereign, constructed monuments according to their own requirements. Adopting styles from other neighbouring dynasties too was common besides extending or reforming the style of another to suit own aesthetic needs.

Two generalizations regarding Karnataka monuments can be stated simply: One, Karnataka is a region where architectural and sculptural elements labeled "northern" and "southern" were utilized freely. This is true during the period of Chalukyas of Badami where temples with northern superstructures sit beside temples with southern characteristics and remains true throughout the region's history. This mixing and sharing of elements and motifs demonstrates how easily artisans appropriate ideas to suit their immediate needs in order to formulate new regional mannerisms or it also suggests migration of artists and sculptors from one land to another. Secondly, Karnataka sculptors favor ornamental surfaces. Architectural elements (such as doorways, pillars, ceiling panels) usually are embellished as are images' clothing and jewels. This trend starts with the sculptures of the Chalukyas of Badami which are distinguished from other southern traditions because they are more decorative relative to the contemporaneous austere Pallava tradition, for instance and climaxes with the Hoysala sculptures which are famed for their surface exuberance.

Growth and evolution of sculpture and plastic arts in Karnataka over the centuries is described as under:

6th century CE

Although some early sculptures from Karnataka are known, such as the 3rd century Buddhist images from Sannati which are stylistically akin to the famous Amaravati (Andhra Pradesh) sculptures, the first substantial artistic monuments are associated with the Chalukyas of Badami dynasty active from the mid-6th to mid-8th centuries. During their height the Badami Chalukyas controlled most of the Deccan, their most formidable rivals, the Pallavas were to the south. The Badami Chalukyas first excavated cave temples at Aihole and Badami and then constructed structural monuments throughout their realm. Of the four cave temples at Aihole and another four at Badami, the only one with irrefutable dating is the Cave 3 at Badami thanks to a pilaster epigraph dated to the Saka era 500 (578 CE). The Cave 3 has served as the stylistic index upon which to establish a relative chronology for the other caves; however, disagreement among scholars remains. There is a noticeable style variance between Aihole and Badami cave sculptures. While some scholars think the Aihole sculptures are later, after the Pallava invasion of Badami during 642 CE because the sculptures have a more "southern" appearance than Badami images, others have argued convincingly that the earliest Badami Chalukyan cave excavation is the Aihole Ravana Phadi from the mid-6th century (550–60 CE), mostly because of architectural considerations.

The Ravana Phadi facade has two chubby, and now abraded, wealth images--Padma and Sankha Nidhis -within framed niches and two standing door guardians with, surprisingly, Scythian clothing. The interior sculptures display motifs and mannerisms that become common in Badami Chalukya images but here they are in their early forms. Much of the ceiling and walls have sculptural panels with the most striking composition in a shrine to the left of the main hall depicting Siva Natesa (Dancing Siva) along with Parvati, Ganesha, Karttikeya, Bhrngi and *Saptamatrikas* (Seven Mothers). The over life-sized Natesa swirls with motion, emphasized by his encircling eight arms, while the *Matrikas* stand in elegant but frozen repose. Carefully incised striated clothing and jewels ornament the figures. These figures display the ethnicity (fleshy, rounded faces) and body form of following Badami Chalukya figures, although here the figures are slightly more slender.

Of the four cave temples at Badami, Cave 1 is dedicated to Siva, Cave 2 and 3 to Visnu, and Cave 4 is Jaina. Cave 3, the grandest shrine, has imperial sponsorship: Mangalesa dedicated in Saka 500 (578 CE) to Visnu on behalf of his brother King Kirtivarman (566–598 CE). The epigraph is inscribed next to a large sculptural panel on the veranda showing Varaha (Visnu in his boar incarnation) rescuing the earth goddess (*Bhu*) and, no doubt, the king identified with Varaha. Varaha, the earth protector, was the Badami Chalukyan dynastic emblem. Another veranda panel, and one that also might have imperial symbolism, shows a majestic Visnu seated in "royal ease" pose upon Sesa (the cosmic serpent) whose outstretched hood circumscribes Visnu's head. As creator and sustainer, Visnu sits supreme. A third veranda panel has a huge Visnu Trivikrama with one leg stretched high above other figures symbolizing Visnu's trickery and conquest over king Bali. Although each of these panels might reflect imperial pretense, they accurately demonstrate the Badami Chalukyan sculptors' skills and tendency towards surface design. Along with the gracious and tender loving couple (*mithuna*) pillar bracket figures, the deity ceiling panels, and other subsidiary figures and carvings that decorate the shrine, these reliefs best characterize the earliest phase of Karnataka sculptural style.

7th-mid 8th centuries CE

The Badami Chalukyas became avid supporters of structural temples, the largest number of early Indian temples date from this period. Major sites include Badami, Mahakuta, Pattadakal, Aihole, and Alampur (in Andhra Pradesh). Additionally, temples or ruins are located at Sandur, Satyavolu, Nagaral, and Banavasi. At first most sculptural reliefs were subsidiary and decorative, but soon large sculptures, such as deity images in niches or loving couples on pillars, became well intergraded with the architecture. Door guardians (*dvarapalas*), for instance, start as small, symbolic images but by the end of the Badami Chalukyan period they are intimidating life-sized protectors.

A few shrines might date earlier, but the first to have a datable inscription, to 634/5 CE, is the Meguti Jaina temple at Aihole. Except for reliefs of animals and *ganas* (dwarfs) the walls lack large imagery. Other shrines from the 7th century at Aihole, such as the Gaudargudi and Huccapayya-math, have doorway floral and scroll reliefs and other animal and *gana* reliefs that are exquisitely lyrical, yet lack monumentality. This early pattern of nicely executed subsidiary panels is seen at the Upper Sivalaya and Lower Sivalaya temples at Badami. In addition to scroll, *gana*, animal motifs, both shrines have small narrative reliefs: the Upper Sivalaya has Ramacharita and Krishnacharita scenes and the Lower Sivalaya has Krishnacharita scenes, now at the Badami Museum.

Variously dated from the mid-7th to the early 8th century, the Melagitti Sivalaya at Badami, designed by the architect Aryaminci Upadhyaya, is a finely proportioned temple that has large niche sculptures. From this period onwards wall imagery becomes increasingly popular. Besides the *gana*, animal, floral wall reliefs and ornamental doorways encountered elsewhere, this temple has increased number of relief panels, many of which show deities. Originally the temple probably was dedicated to Surya who is prominently displayed in the central panel over the shrine doorway and is seen elsewhere along with Surya associated guardians on the temple walls. In the exterior wall niche, to the south, is a majestic Visnu and the north wall niche has a Siva. Presented frontally, and though well executed, the figures are broad with rather tubular limbs.

Two temples at Aihole, the Lad Khan and the Durga temple, considered enigmatic in form (each for separate reasons) are now usually assigned dating from late 7th-early 8th century. Both temples have graceful, loving couples (*mithuna*) in high relief on exterior pillars. These figures, though a bit stocky and tubular still, are compositionally sophisticated as seen in the manner in which bodies twist and embrace. The faces convey contentment, a sign of the sculptors' growing skills. Doorways, pillar reliefs, and ceiling panels, too, are more elaborately carved at these temples. At the Durga temple, originally dedicated to the Sun god, not only are there an increased number of exterior pillar loving couples (*mithuna*), there are additional deity niche figures in the ambulatory. The Siva and the Durga niche sculptures are among the finest works from the Badami Chalukyan period. In graceful *tribhanga* pose, multi-armed Shiva leans on his bull Nandi with the self-absorbed dignity befitting of the deity. Durga, too, stands in *tribhanga*, but the arrangement of the many arms and her position over her pathetically defeated foe, the buffalo demon (Mahishasura) suggests an active god (whereas Siva appears passive).

The grandest in scale and final phase of Chalukyan temples are from Pattadakal. The three largest shrines have dynastic affiliation. Vijayaditaya (696–733 CE) had the Vijayeswara, now known as the Sangameswara, built but left unfinished at his death. During the reign of his son and successor, Vikramaditya II (733–745 CE), the Virupaksha was founded (745 CE) by the king's senior queen Lokamahadevi; and the sister to Lokamahadevi queen Trailokyamahadevi founded (in 755 CE) the Trailokeswara (now called Mallikarjuna). Mixed together are sculptural manners of previous monuments, blending elements from Telengana with more localized idiosyncrasies. The large door guardians, loving couples, deity niche figures, pillar reliefs, etc., epitomize the Badami Chalukyan sculptural style at its climactic finish.

The Virupaksha, originally called Lokeswara, was built to celebrate Vikramaditya II's victory over the Pallavas (Plate 5-36). Many of the niche figures are of Siva forms to whom the temple is dedicated. Contained within deep niches, these figures are sturdy, yet slender, often dramatically posed: for example on the forehall, south wall, Natesa dynamically conveys motion. Especially theatrical are the large guardians carved in high relief on porch pilasters. Whereas most guardians appear at rest, because their backs are engaged to the pilasters, one guardian in particular, on the south porch, has only his right side engaged which successfully conveys the illusion that he is stepping away. Other porch reliefs include loving couples, similar to the ones mentioned from Aihole, except here they take on an even greater urbane demeanor. Numerous figural sculptures cover the superstructure and elsewhere. As was the case since Badami Chalukyan cave temples, the interior is embellished with ceiling, doorway and pillar reliefs. Of the two subshrines, one is dedicated to Ganesha and the other to Durga--the latter one powerfully shows the victorious goddess. These temple sculptures are testament to the glory of the Bdami Chalukyan dynasty and the early Karnataka sculptors.

Scattered sculpture of Badami Chalukya period can be seen in the museums at Aihole and Badami as well. Particularly interesting is the Lajja Gouri image kept in the Badami museum. Sculpture at Mahakuta temple complex has certain degree on uniqueness that needs special mention. The walls of the Mahakuteswara temple have central projections defined by double sets of pilasters accommodating diverse icons of Siva, conveniently marked with modern painted Kannada and English labels. Curiously, they are all two-armed, a feature hardly found elsewhere in Badami Chalukyan representations of Siva. Immediately to the south of the Mahakuteswara temple is the Sangameswara temple. A small porch gives access to the sanctum, the outer walls of which are embellished with the naked figure of Lakulisa (south), gracefully posed Ardhanariswara (west), Harihara (north) and all in pilaster niches. Other scattered sculpture in the temple complex includes images of Varaha, Visnu and Virabhadra. There is also a *Pushakarni Tirtha* in the complex which houses a *chaturmukha sivalinga* (four human faces on Linga's sides).

Mid 8th-late 10th centuries CE

In the mid-8th century the Rashtrakutas seized control over the Deccan and for the next two centuries they remained India's paramount rulers. Karnataka and Maharashtra formulated the Rashtrakuta's nucleus; it is in the latter area, at Ellora, where the greatest imperial Rashtrakuta monuments were built. No doubt the most effort and finance during the late 8th-mid 9th century was concentrated at Ellora and it is there that the finest sculptures remain. Temple sites in Karnataka include Aihole, Pattadakal, Kuknur, Hallur, Sirwal and Bagali. However, the Kalleswara temple at Bagali has erotic sculpture on its outer walls which makes it different from the other temples. Most of the other monuments are sculpturally unimpressive. Malkhed, once a Rashtrakuta capital, now has little more than ruins with uninspired pillars reliefs to show of its past glory. A Jaina *basadi* of Rashtrakuta times houses some remaining sculpture of *Yaksha* and *Yakshi* with some Jinas in sitting postures.

Generally temples in Karnataka built during Rashtrakuta times tend towards conservatism: while some elements popularized during the previous century continued, most sculptural embellishments were reduced. Interior pillar relief narratives lessened, and deity ceiling panels often were replaced by a large full blossomed lotus motif. Exterior niche figures were eliminated or minimized. For example, at Sirwal over 20 shrines were constructed during the Rashtrakuta period (early 10th century). While these temples might be of architectural interest, sculpturally they lack distinction--exterior wall articulation is obtained through engaged pilaster variations, rather than additive sculpture.

Local architectural mannerisms developed during the Badami Chalukya period dominate at Aihole during the late 9th-early 10th century. This is seen at the Kontigudi group, shrines 2 and 3, and Hallibasappa temple. The exterior walls of these shrines, however, do not have niche figures nor any significant sculptural embellishments. Also the interior pillar and doorway reliefs lack the crisp elegance seen in earlier temples. Figures are stiff and crudely proportioned, no longer showing the relaxed naturalism attained during the height of the Badami Chalukya idiom. Yet, a contemporaneous set of pillars from Kadur, now maintained at the Department of Archaeology, Government of Karnataka, Mysore, have vigorous reliefs depicting Saiva narratives bordered by exuberant animal and floral motifs. During this period there is a trend towards subregional idioms.

Especially within Karnataka Rashtrakuta realm many questions have yet to be answered regarding who actually sponsored the temples and how best to discuss "idiom." Only at Ellora can we discuss an imperial Rashtrakuta style. Elsewhere much of the Rashtrakuta vast empire was overseen by feudatories, people with their own subregional identification and self-interest. In Karnataka numerous other examples of this complex mixture of subregional sculptural styles are available.

For example, pillars in the Navalinga group at Kuknur are carved in a manner that shares characteristics with pillars popularized in Nolambavadi. Variant pillar shapes, including the proto-"lathe turned" type, seen at the Rashtrakuta period Jaina temple at Pattadakal, develop simultaneously in Nolambavadi and Gangavadi. The Kalleswara temple at Bagali, most often noted for the small erotic sculptures on the exterior wall below the superstructure, has architectural and sculptural elements also shared with temples in Nolambavadi. In Karnataka there is not a distinct "Rashtrakuta" sculptural style, rather there is a mixture of elements that vary locally. Although this is a 10th century proclivity, there are some monuments distinctively identifiable as "Ganga" or "Nolamba"-two dynastic families that, although less militaristically powerful than the Rashtrakutas, played important roles in the history of Karnataka.

The Gangas of Talakad were the longest sustaining dynastic family in Karnataka, having a presence in southern Karnataka from the mid-4th century to early 11th century. Situated as they were between the dominating dynasties in northern Karnataka (Chalukyas of Badami, Rashtrakutas, and Chalukyas of Kalyana) and competing dynasties in the deeper south, Tamil Nadu (i.e., Pallavas, Pandyas and Cholas), the Gangas had to contend with a politically precarious position. Many elements displayed in their temples, most of which date from the 10th century, are shared with contemporaneous monuments elsewhere. This is a propensity observed above with Rashtrakuta period temples, and does not infer artistic inferiority following political subordination. Although the Rashtrakutas were the dominating political power of their time, their artistic presence in Karnataka was muted. The Gangas, however, sponsored a monument, at Shravanabelagola, unique in art history. Other important Ganga sites include Manne, Kambadahalli, Begur, Varuna, Alur, Gangavara and Narasamangala. The Ganga capital Talakad and temples are now mostly buried under silt from the Cauveri river though some of these have been excavated and are accessible. (Plates 5-37 and 5-38)

As the preeminent supporters of Jainism (Digambara sect) in the south, the Gangas were responsible for developing the sacred Shravanabelagola site. On the smaller hill, the Chandragiri (ancient Katavapra, where legend has it Chandragupta Maurya resided as a Jaina ascetic), there are a number of shrines dating from the 9th to 13th centuries. The Chandragupta *basadi* is sculpturally noteworthy for the 12th century carvings, especially the stone screens with some 90 episodes from the life of Chandragupta Maurya and Bhadrabahu, executed by the artist Dasoja (who has other signed sculptures at the Hoysala temples from Belur and Halebid). Nearby is one of the finest of the Ganga period temples, the Chamundaraya *basadi*. Sponsored by Chamundaraya, general and minister to Ganga king Racamalla IV (974–999 CE), the temple dates 982 CE with the superstructure completed (995 CE) through the aid of Chamunda's son Jinadevana.

The exterior walls, though void of sculptures, have above them on all sides handsomely rendered images of seated Jinas, *yakshas* and *yakshis*. More of these figures grace the upper stories of the superstructure. These images have an understated, naturalistic and relaxed mien.

At the summit of the larger hill, the Vindhyagiri, stands the world's tallest monolithic free-standing sculpture (height 18 metres) called, in Kannada, Gommateswara. Sponsored by Chamundaraya, dedicated in 983 CE, this image is of Bahubali, the son to the first Jain Tirthankara Risabhanatha (also called Adinatha). Nude except for the vines which grew around his legs and arms during his years of meditation, Bahubali stands majestically upright. As deserving for a Jaina saint, he is ideally proportioned with wide shoulders and hips, thin waist, and alert face with the slightest smile signifying his blissful enlightenment. Still in pristine condition after a thousand years, Bahubali over the centuries has served as model for other Jaina colossi in Karnataka, none of which equal in artistic charm. In comparison, the largest other Gommateswara monolith is 12.6 m high at Karkala, dedicated in 1432 CE. Other images include one at Venur (dedicated 1604 CE, 10.6 m), Gommatagiri (14th century, 5.5 m), and the recent, one at Dharmasthala (1973 CE, 11.9 m).

Kambadahalli is another Jaina centre with Ganga period temples. The five shrine Panchakuta *basadi*, dating from 975, and the twin shrine Shantinatha *basadi* from late 10th century have quite a few Jaina images sculpted in the same handsome style as the Shravanabelagola images. Sculptures here, especially *Yakshi*, *Yaksha* and guardian figures, are more richly bejeweled than in coeval northern Karnataka (Rashtrakuta) temples. Some Gangavadi temples have large lotus motif ceilings, a trait shared with Rashtrakuta period temples, but here (also at Begur and Narasmangala) there are *Ashtadikpala* ceiling reliefs. This is a characteristic shared with temples in Nolambavadi where ceiling panels and sculptures in general, often are elaborately carved.

The Saiva temples at Begur (twin temple complex) and at Narasmangala (the Ramalingeswara temple) have architectural characteristics which demonstrate a sharing of elements with monuments in lower Dravidadesa (Tamil Nadu). At Shravanabelagola and Kambadahalli exterior wall space is broken only by engaged pilasters (similar to temples in northern Karnataka), but at Begur and Narasmangala walls are broken into deep recessions and projections, edged with pilasters. To further illustrate how regional "styles" are mixing and sharing in the 10th century: a partial set of Matrikas from Begur, now at the Karnataka Government Museum, Bengaluru, are low relief granite figures with little attention to ornamentation-similar to Dravidadesa sculptures-whereas other sculptures within the twin shrines (e.g., especially two Mahisasuramardini and a Surya) are carved from dark schist and appear stylistically related to images from Nolambavadi. Also related in style to temples in Nolambavadi, especially the ones at Nandi and Avani, are the *Ashtadikpala* ceiling panels and pillar reliefs. A peculiar feature at the Ramalingeswara temple, Narasmangala, is the stucco images on the superstructure which might date from the time of the temple. Among the stucco images, the central *sala-koshtha* has a seated Yogadakshinamurthi. At the northern side is a Bhikshatana Siva and on its left a graceful Siva (Chandrasekhara)-Parvati is shown. Another noteworthy aspect of the Narasamangala temple complex is its *ashta-parivara* disposition. Basements of six shrines have been noted around the main temple. Almost all the loose images that were consecrated in these shrines are now pooled together in a covered shed at the south-west. Mahishasurmardini, however stands majestically at the north-west basement of a shrine. Images of Chandikesa, Saptamatrikas, Ganesha, Bhairava, Virabhadra and a goat faced Daksha are all housed in the shed at the south-west.

A few km away from Narasamangala is Alur. In the open compound surrounding the Arkeswara temple there are housed several Ganga period sculptures under the open sky. The sculpture here include the four-armed Durga, Yogadakshinamurthi, Saptamatrikas (independent images like at Narasamangala), Ganesha and the family deity of the Gangas, *Kiltabel Eretti Bhatari* or Kali with drawn sword. Various *Viragals* and *Mastikallus* too are there in the temple compound.

The Nolamba (Nolamba-Pallava) dynasty was at times politically (and matrimonially) related with the Gangas, while at other times in direct competition. From the 8th to the early 11th century, southeast

Karnataka and limited contiguous sections of Andhra Pradesh and Tamil Nadu formulated Nolambavadi, the territory controlled by the Nolambas. Monuments from Hemavati, the Nolamba capital, located in the portion of Andhra Pradesh (Anantapur district) which protrudes into and separates Tumakuru district of Karnataka rightfully belongs within a discussion of Karnataka sculptures. Here a distinguished sculptural (Nolamba) idiom was centred with stylistically related monuments at Pathasivarama, Baragur, and Aralaguppe (latter two in Tumakuru district as is the less important site Nonavinakere). Elsewhere in Nolambavadi, although architectural and sculptural traits are shared, there are idiomatic shifts. Temples from Nandi and Avani (Kolar district) blend elements from Hemavati with characteristics from Gangavadi monuments. Generally, ornamentation becomes increasingly popular in Nolambavadi: doorways, pillar reliefs, perforated window carvings, and ceiling panels, all which are sculptural elements developed during the Badami Chalukya period but reduced since, are areas of attention. This trend intensifies in the 11th century during the Kalyani Chalukyan period. The Nolambavadi monuments, especially from Hemavati, are a crucial link in understanding 11th century sculpture. The Nolambas, along with artisans presumably, moved to Ballari district becoming absorbed into the Chalukyan realm.

Possibly the most elegant late 9th or early 10th century temple in Karnataka is the Bhoganandiswara at Nandi. The exterior walls are without niche images but the windows have perforated carvings of lively dancers, musicians, *ganas*, or deities. On all sides above the walls and throughout the superstructure are deities (mostly Saiva forms, to whom the temple is dedicated) and subsidiary figures sculpted exquisitely. The naturalistic, relaxed figures are surrounded by ornamental exuberance, seen in animal, vegetative, celestial beings motifs. The otherwise granite temple has eight (four couchant Nandis interspersed with two Sivas, a Brahma and a Visnu) black schist sculptures at the tower's top (*griva-sikhara* level) which are especially majestic.

In the same compound the contemporaneous Arunachaleswara temple is a close duplicate of the Bhoganandiswara. The superstructure of the former duplicates the format (same motifs and iconography) of the latter; however, the Arunachaleswara tower was rebuilt during the Vijayanagara period (16th century). Only the walls of the Arunachaleswara date from the 10th century, which includes some fine perforated window carvings. Although scholars have recognized the similarity of the twin shrines, and noted that the Arunachaleswara has later period stucco figures at the top of the tower, it has not previously been noted that the complete Arunachaleswara tower is by much later sculptors who are trying to archaize their work in order to conform to the earlier Bhoganandiswara model. A Vijayanagara period shrine, recognizably in a 16th century style, also was built in-between the Nolamba period Bhoganandiswara and Arunachaleswara temples.

Another Nolamba centre was Avani (ancient Avantikaksetra, a site rich with Ramayana lore) where many epigraphs and shrines proclaim their presence. The Laksmaneswara temple dates to the reign of King Vira Nolamba (also called Anniga, 923–40 CE), except for the tower which is a Vijayanagara period replacement. During the 10th century exterior walls lacked significant deity reliefs-at Nandi and Shravanabelagola, for instance, sculptures appeared above the walls-yet there are carved on the Laksmaneswara walls deities (mostly goddesses) or attendants, plus a portrait of Vira Nolamba and the religious leader Tribhuvanakara. Having the wall reliefs, and the peculiar iconographic scheme, makes this temple a curiosity. The mostly renovated Bharateswara temple has an inscription claiming Nolamba Queen Divambika (980 CE) had it built. Both temples have interior ceiling panels with a central Siva and Parvati circumscribed by *Ashtadikpalas* akin to the panels at the Bhoganandiswara at Nandi.

The prevailing goddess imagery on the Laksmaneswara is a visual reminder that goddess worship became increasingly popular during the 10th century onwards. Another coeval goddess image from Avani (locally called Mutyalamma, "the pearl-like mother"), once enshrined in a separate shrine but now at the Karnataka Government Museum, Bengaluru, is a striking image demanding attention-as the defeated foe below the seated goddess has learned. Further attesting to the importance of goddess worship in this area, and another vigorous image both in presence and style, is the enshrined Kolaramma goddess (at the

Kolaramma temple) in nearby Kolar. Within an 11th century shrine, Kolaramma might date from the late 10th century.

During the Nolamba period ornamentation is not superfluous nor is it detrimental to the form, rather there is an elemental balance. This is seen in the ubiquitous pillar reliefs, the intricate doorways and especially in the ceiling panels, climaxing with panels at Aralaguppe, Kallesvara temple. There, carved in high relief, Siva dances with extreme vigor surrounded by four celestial garland-bearers (carved in the round and attached at their backs to the ceiling) and by *Ashtadikpalas*. Also at Aralaguppe a large (Height: 1.5 m) Umasahita stele exemplifies the late 10th century trend towards heighten embellishment.

Southwest Karnataka, ancient Tulunadu (South Kanara district and adjacent northern Kerala), was the traditional land of the Alupa dynasty. Alupas temple sites include Udayavara, Polali, Ullala, and Kadri. Although worship of the *Saptamatrikas* and Durga was popular in this area, it is three exceptional Buddhist bronzes at Kadri that are most noteworthy. In 968 CE, the Alupa King Kundavarma (950–980 CE) inscribed and installed a bronze image of Lokeswara. Generally considered to represent the Mahayana Halahala Lokeswara-seated, he is three-faced and six-armed (some have argued he is a form of Siva-this image is probably the largest bronze in Karnataka (Height: 1.37 m). Truly a bronze masterpiece and not an isolated example: at the same site there is another coeval image of Avalokiteswara, this one with one head and four arms. These two images are superbly cast imbuing grace. A third image, and possibly slightly later in date, is a seated Buddha which displays stylistic affinities with Buddhas from Nagapattinam (Tamil Nadu).

Although the Buddha image does display resemblance with bronzes from Chola territory, other bronzes in Karnataka hastily have been incorrectly labelled "Chola" style. For instance, the Kali (Directorate of Archaeology and Museums, Karnataka) bronze from Malangi, near Talakad, though often called "Chola," is more likely of "Ganga" idiom. A number of Jaina bronzes are in the Ganga idiom, some are at the Shravanabelagola *math*, others in various collections are fine examples. A Somaskanda (Karnataka Government Museum, Bengaluru) from Nandi, might be Nolamba idiom. This latter one is close in style to Kalyani Chalukya, 11th century, bronzes. Once Karnataka bronzes receive systematic study answers to proper idiom appellation will clarify. At such time bronzes from Karnataka labelled "Chola" might receive new review.

11th-13th centuries CE

After 973 CE, when the Rashtrakutas were irremediably defeated, until 1189 (except for a 25 year hiatus when the Kalachuris controlled) Deccan paramountcy belonged to the Chalukyas of Kalyani. Mostly in northern Karnataka temple construction by Kalyani Chalukyas proliferated during this period. Major sites include Lakkundi, Haveri, Hangal, Ittagi, Gadag, and Dambal; however, many other lesser known sites also exist. Famed for their architectural innovations, temples during the Kalyani Chalukyan period became divergent in form with heightened dependency on sculptural embellishments. Greater attention to minute details was made possible by using a malleable fine-grained greenish or blue-black chloritic schist. Besides figural images, a popular wall motif is a pilaster crowned by a miniature pavilion (early forms are at the 11th century Jaina temple at Lakkundi and the Siddheswara at Haveri). Artisans' knowledge of disparate architectural traditions is indicated by the pavilion form which duplicates temple superstructure shapes from other regions of India. Pillar reliefs are less common during this period because the actual form of the pillar is intricately shaped-the "lathe-turned" type is popular and remains so into the 14th century. Occasionally pillar bracket figures are used. When carved, ceiling panels have elaborate *Ashtadikpalas* and doorways, too, are ornate.

Example of the mature Kalyani Chalukya temple is the Mahadeva at Ittagi. Sponsored by Mahadeva, a general to King Vikramaditya VI (1077–1127 CE), the monument was dedicated in 1112 (Saka 1034). It is the architectural elements, such as the elaborately carved miniature pavilion motif that decorates the walls (above the deep niches or engaged pilasters) and repeats up the tower (the top most part is rebuilt), or the open eastern pavilion with its numerous complex lathe-turned pillars, that distinguishes this (and coeval Chalukyan) temple. Lively small scale figural reliefs are rendered on the walls and pillar bases. The interior lantern ceiling has attendants watching the spirited dancing Siva. The 12th century Kasivisveswara temple at Lakkundi has increased figural wall reliefs and doorway carvings which are especially elaborate. Composing the doorway are base female and guardian figures, above them bands of jewels and vegetative motifs interwoven with dancing and embracing couples, musicians, *ganas*, *yallis*, etc., all of which are carefully sculpted in high relief. The walls and superstructure have small scale figural carvings (complimenting the pilaster-pavilion, or deep niche pavilion wall motif), many of which are Saiva themes, and delineated throughout the temple are energetic *ganas* and *yallis*.

Figural sculpture on friezes and panels changed during the period. The heroes from the Hindu epics Ramayana and Mahabharata, depicted often in early temples, become fewer, limited to only a few narrow friezes; there is a corresponding increase in the depiction of Hindu gods and goddesses in later temples. Depiction of deities above miniature towers in the recesses, with a decorative lintel above, is common in 12th-century temples, but not in later ones. Figures of holy men and dancing girls were normally sculpted for deep niches and recesses. The use of bracket figures depicting dancing girls became common on pillars under beams and cornices. Among animal sculptures, the elephant appears more often than the horse: its broad volumes offered fields for ornamentation. Erotic sculptures are rarely seen in Kalyani Chalukyan temples; the Tripurantakesvara temple at Balligavi and Kalleswara temple at Bagali being the exception. Here, erotic sculpture is limited to a narrow band of friezes that run around the exterior of the temple or on panels in the *sikhara*.

In what was a departure from convention, the Kalyani Chalukyan figure sculptures of gods and goddesses bore stiff forms and were repeated over and over in the many temples. This was in contrast to the naturalistic and informal poses employed in the earlier temples in the region. Barring occasional exaggerations in pose, each principal deity had its own pose depending on the incarnation or form depicted. Consistent with figure sculpture in other parts of India, these figures were fluent rather than defined in their musculature, and the drapery was reduced to a few visible lines on the body of the image.

Kalyani Chalukyan deity sculptures were well-rendered; exemplified best by that of Hindu goddess Saraswati at the Saraswati temple in Gadag city. Much of the drapery on the bust of the image is ornamentation comprising jewellery made of pearls around her throat. An elaborate pile of curls forms her hair, some of which trails to her shoulders. Above these curly tresses and behind the head is a tiered coronet of jewels, the curved edge of which rises to form a halo. From the waist down, the image is dressed in what seems to be the most delicate of material; except for the pattern of embroidery traced over it, it is difficult to tell where the drapery begins and where it ends.

The Kalyani Chalukyan kings were Saivites and they (worshippers of the Hindu god Siva) dedicated most of their temples to that god. They were however tolerant of the Vaishnava or Jaina faiths and dedicated some temples to Visnu and the Jaina Tirthankaras respectively. There are some cases where temples originally dedicated to one deity were converted to suit another faith. In such cases, the original presiding deity can sometimes still be identified by salient clues. While these temples shared the same basic plan and architectural sensibilities, they differed in some details, such as the visibility and pride of place they afforded the different deities.

As with all Indian temples, the deity in the sanctum was the most conspicuous indicator of the temple's dedication. The sanctum (*garbhagriha* or cella) of a Saiva temple would contain a Siva *linga*, the universal symbol of the deity. An image of Gaja Lakshmi (consort of the Hindu god Visnu) or an image of Visnu riding on *Garuda*, or even just the *Garuda*, signifies a Vaishnava temple. Gaja Lakshmi, however, on account of her importance to the Kannada-speaking regions, is found on the lintel of the entrance to the *mandapa* (pillared hall) in all temples irrespective of faith or sect. The carving on the projecting lintel on the doorway to the sanctum has the image of a *linga* or sometimes of Ganapati (Ganesha), the son of Siva in the case of Saiva temples or of a seated or upright Jaina saint (Tirthankara) in the case of Jaina temples.

The great arched niche at the base of the superstructure (*sikhara* or tower) also contains an image indicative of the dedicators' sect or faith. Above the lintel, in a deep and richly wrought architrave can be found images of the Hindu *trimurti* (the Hindu triad of deities) Brahma, Siva and Visnu beneath arched rolls of arabesque. Siva or Visnu occupies the centre depending on the sect the temple was dedicated to. Occasionally, Ganapati and his brother Kartikeya (Kumara, Subramanya) or the *shaktis*, the female counterparts, can be found at either end of this carving. Carvings of the river goddesses Ganga and Yamuna are found at either end of the foot of the doorway to the shrine in early temples.

Though the temple is increasingly becoming elaborate in shape and embellishments, the sculptures are not overwhelmed by ponderous extras. Some sculptures during this period are outstanding for their elegant understatement. Most figural sculptures have delicate ornaments with volume that overlay and supplement the slightly elongated bodies. Sculptors successfully created a vigorous style which was transported to southern Karnataka: inscriptions indicate some sculptors moved from Kalyani Chalukyan to Hoysala territory bringing with them mannerisms that strongly contribute to the "ornate style."

The proclivity towards profuse ornamentation culminates when the Hoysalas, erstwhile feudatory to the Kalyani Chalukyas, seized power over southern Karnataka (1006 to 1346 CE). Originating from the Malanad hills (in the Western Ghats), Hoysalas moved east, into the heartland of former Gangavadi, and established their imperial capital at Halebid (ancient Dorasamudra, in Hassan district). A period of extensive temple construction, the "ornate style" is best known and synonym for "Hoysala style"; however, majority of temples were not so complex and closely resemble Kalyani Chalukyan temples (for example the Lakshmidevi temple at Dodda Gaddavalli, dedicated in 1113 CE with its *Phamsana sikharas*, or the Malleswara temple at Kikkeri). The famous ornate temple sites include Belur, Halebid, Mosale, Javagal and Somnathapura. Complex in shape, they have stellate shrine plan, the exterior surface of these monuments are veiled with sculptural embellishments. Interiors, too, are ornate with extensively carved doorways, ceilings, and pillar bracket figures. Pillars are lathe-turned or other elaborate forms. Figural sculptures tend to have portly bodies which are overlayed with profuse ornamentation, often with delicate filigree motifs. Along with the decor efflorescence is a practice of artists often inscribing their names to their work. Artist signed works during other periods but at Hoysala monuments this is especially common; not a statement of individuality, although individual masters can be identified, sculptors harmonized (competing workshops had to work together on monuments) within a style norm. In addition to the famous sites mentioned above, many other Hoysala period sites exist: to name a few, Nuggehalli, Basaralu, Koravangala, Arsikere, Aralaguppe, and Amritapura. These locations were Sri Vaisnava or Saiva centres-this was a time of active *bhakti* (devotional) movements-and Jainism enjoyed continued support especially at Shravanabelagola.

The Kesava (Chennakesava, or Vijayanarayana) temple at Belur, dedicated in 1117 CE, was erected to commemorate Visnuvardhana's (1108–1147 CE) victory at Talakad over the Cholas who had occupied portions of southern Karnataka. The first of the famed ornate Hoysala shrines, this monument's walls are covered with richly embellished iconic panels. The original appearance of the temple is altered by the perforated stone screens between the exterior pillars of the *mandapa* added during the reign of Ballala II (1173–1220 CE). Encountering this temple (and the ones at Halebid and Somnathapura) is visually overwhelming. Placed below the *mandapa* roof there are 38 (and 4 more in the interior) figural bracket images (Kannada: *madanakai*) depicting females in alluring poses. With delicately carved ornaments over the plump seductive bodies, a lace foliate motif overhead, these figures, 22 in number all of which are signed by the artists justly deserve the acclaim they have received. (Plates 5-39 and 5-40)

During Visnuvardhana's reign two temples at Halebid were constructed, the Jaina Parsvanatha Basadi (1133 CE) and the Hoysaleswara (1121–1160 CE). Also at Halebid, the Hoysala capital, the Jaina Shantinatha Basadi (1196 CE) and Kedareswara (1219 CE) were built during the reign of Ballala II, the king who secured regional paramountcy by defeating the tottering Kalyani Chalukyas in the north and to the south intruded deep into Chola territory and politics. The famed twin shrined Hoysaleswara was first sponsored in 1121 CE by Visnuvardhana's officer Ketamalla, but not completed until about 1160, during the reign of Narasimha I (1142–73 CE), by the architect Kedaroja. Shrouding this temple's surface is sculptural scenes and motifs. The temple basement has small relief bands with thousands of figures extending around the monument, and above on the main wall surface there are over 400 high relief figural sculptures. Interior, too profusely ornate, has detailed coffered ceilings, carved and lathed-turned pillars, bracket figures, and doorways richly decorated with intimidating almost like-sized guardians. Though sculpturally prodigious with accoutrements, figures retain a vitality which subsequently in later Hoysala sculptures erodes. At the ornate and best architecturally preserved Hoysala temple, the Kesava at Somnathapura which was founded in 1268 CE by Somanatha, general to king Narasimha II (1254–92 CE), some of the figural sculptures appear more frozen and stubby compared to their predecessors. The inventiveness and grandeur of embellishments which characterises the Hoysala ornate style, in its final 13th century phase becomes repetitive and restrictive.

All the sculpture decorating the temples at Belur and Halebid is governed by uniform decorative, anatomical and stylistic principles. The themes that appealed to the Hoysala Artist seem to be human and animal forms, floral and geometric patterns in different architectural contexts. On the ceilings and perforated screens one finds abstract patterns while the doorways, basements and railings are embellished with smaller figures, scrolls and motifs. The outer walls are filled with large reliefs of divinities and their entourages. Perhaps more than passion or romance it is female beauty that is celebrated. Young women engaged in music, dance, sport and self-adulation adorn the surfaces. These young women or '*Sursundaris*' as they were known, epitomize the concept of female beauty. For example, a series of a lady admiring or adorning herself, plucking fruits, feeding a parrot, dancing or surrounded by nature are depicted all around the temples. As is evident by their sheer numbers, sculptors seemed to favour dancers in various postures, celebrating the vibrant lines their bodies made.

It is evident that ornaments were important features of the sculptures. The entire body, male and female, is bedecked with intricately carved ornaments studded with jewels, stones and strings of pearls. There is a specific ornament for each part of the body, from head to toe and every inch of the body is covered. The most conspicuous and unusual ornament is the 'Vaijayanti,' a long string resembling a waist band which emerges from the back of the hip, curves widely on the knees and disappears below the left vertical portion of the 'Hara' or the necklace. Most often there are 3 varieties of necklaces worn by the figures. The individuality of the Hoysala School stands out in the detailed, intricate and elaborate finish of the ornaments. This is seen even in the other accessories worn by the figures, such as pendants, crowns, weapons, etc.

Most of the figures on the outer walls are those of cult deities and their attendants. The groups consisting of Brahma, Visnu and Mahesh (the divine trilogy of the Creator, Protector and Destroyer), the *Dashavatara* or the 10 incarnations of Visnu or the popular couple of Siva with his consort Parvati are the favourite subjects. There are also the figures of *Yakshas* (divine courtiers), either in miniature relief around the deities or in large size guarding the doorways. All deities are flanked by two or more miniature attendants and stand on curved but plain pedestals. The sculptors used dance and music, play and sport to lend rhythmic movement to the sculptures and so all the figures are lifelike. Even the creeper canopies surrounding the deities have their own characteristic features and stand apart one from the other.

The mouldings of the basements of the temples are decorated with motifs of animals. Elephants seem to find a special place in art of the Hoysalas extensively and elaborately. The artists have carved perfect movements of this majestic animal in the wall friezes. There are over 1200 elephants depicted on the outer walls of the temples at Halebid in various descriptions, with or without Mahouts, in war or at play, they all have the same sort of conspicuous decorations adorning them.

Horses too seem favoured. They appear as embellished representations of those that were a part of the cavalry units of the Hoysala army. Vivid and realistic, they express the sheer spirit of the animals of those times carrying in their saddles weapon wielding warriors. The powerful and expressive depiction by sculptors of the different ways in which riders and horses attack or succumb to their enemies and the ways in which they ride and charge into battle suggest that as much as imagination, experience seems to have played its role in guiding the hand that created them. This is further evidence by their attention to proportion, detail and symmetry. Besides being proportionate in size, the horses are dressed and decorated with restraint, fitted with a saddle, bridle, reins, stirrups and bells.

The lion, being the symbol of the dynasty, holds a place of special importance. Apart from the crest, over 1400 lions appear on the friezes at Halebid. Unlike the manner in which horses and elephants are treated, the lion takes on exaggerated expression. Perhaps because of its symbolic nature, this splendid creature goes beyond realistic representation, moving instead into symbolic realms.

Another animal that makes its appearance is born from the world of imagination. It is known as the *Makara* or sea elephant. Local legend says that it is a combination of 7 Animals, each symbolic of some virtue. For example it has a crocodile's mouth for 'grip' and a monkey's eyes for 'sharpness.' It is invariably presented with its upraised head or snout, wide open jaws revealing long sharp teeth and the tongue and tail resembling bursting flames.

Apart from this fantastic creature, bulls too find a place of importance especially as the vehicle of Siva. The two Nandis at the Hoysaleswara Temple at Halebid are apt tributes to the power and beauty of this animal. Carved out of monolithic stone blocks of eight or nine feet, and exquisitely carved to highlight the finest of detail including the folds of the skin and adorned with elaborate ornamentation, these Bulls are awesome in their appearance. Other animals such as monkeys, camels, mice, buffalos, rams and birds like peacocks, swans and small birds too are present in most reliefs. The artists have used an infinite variety of stylized foliage and scroll creepers. Vegetative motifs and floral patterns surrounding deities in which one can see monkeys playing and birds flying seem to compete with nature itself. The finish given to every minute detail captivates one's eye. You can see here the nail of the deity piercing through the skin of the elephant, appearing on the other side. One also notices the fingers of a drummer through the ropes on the drum, the skin of stone relenting to the magical touch of master sculptors.

The most remarkable feature of these temples is the reliefs which present continuous narratives, entire episodes captured in single compositions. Although the epics have always played a major role in Indian Art through the centuries, nowhere else would one find entire stories depicted in sculptures as one does on the outer walls of the temple at Halebid. Not only are complete stories from the Bhagvad Gita, the Mahabharata and Ramayana depicted in a series but sometimes a single relief is enough to recount the entire story. For example the story of Krishna lifting mountain Govardhana or Narasimha annihilating Hiranyakashyapu or Ravana shaking Mount Kailasa or Abhimanyu entering the Chakravyuh of the Kauravas are all depicted in a single relief panel each. These reliefs served a triple purpose. Not only did they enhance the beauty of the structure but they also revealed various manifestations of the God to his devotees and entertained and educated them by means of stories. Many of these reliefs are also found at the twin temples at Mosale in smaller carvings. Particularly interesting is the comparison between the sculpture of Ravana shaking the Mount Kailasa at Hoysaleswara and Chennakesava temple at Belur. While the one at Hoysaleswara is about 4.5 feet in height, the one at Belur has been carved in a panel measuring barely one foot in either dimension but the degree of similarity between the two is amazingly striking.

The artists who worked on these temples were masters of their craft, is obvious. But their commitment and artistry would have come to naught if there was no royal patronage. The kings accorded them respect and patronage. The kings from various dynasties accorded agreeable conditions of work and good fortune to the artists of the time. Only men of great skill and patience whose work was valued by society at that time could have produced such master pieces. Just as warriors were needed to defend boundaries, artists were required by the royal families to promote their religious, political and social interests. They were considered an important part of society. Many of the honoured architects and sculptors of those times find their names engraved in various inscriptions. List of some of the very well known among them is placed below.

Erotic sculpture in Karnataka: An increasingly prevalent motif in temple iconography from the first century CE was the erotic or loving couple known as the *mithuna* image. *Mithuna* couples were most commonly found on thresholds and weak architectural junctures. Evidence from ancient texts, supports the suggestion that they fulfilled a magico-protective function and were remnants of ancient non-Vedic fertility rituals. The *Silpasastras*, *Puranas* and other authoritative texts implicitly recognized the auspicious (*mangala*) and protective-defensive (*raksartham-varanartha*) aspects of erotic depictions. Texts such as the Agni Purana and the Brihatsamhita also suggest that doors of the inner sanctum, or *garbhagriha*, should be protected by such imagery. The early depictions of *mithuna* couples were small, discreet and held to be purely magico-religious in function. (Plate 5-41)

The form of these images pointed to the continuity of primitive and popular cultural elements or an 'other Hinduism' in the ancient Indian society. The dramatic and overt appearance of large and aristocratic couples as *mithuna* is found in sites such as Aihole, Badami and Pattadakal, and have been explained by the growing power and involvement of the aristocracy in patronage. Gradually from 900 CE, there was a profusion of a more consistent, blatant and sophisticated treatment of sexual depictions of the *mithuna* couple. By 950 CE *mithuna* was already represented in sculptural decorations of the temples in Mahakuta, Aihole, Badami (Cave 1) and Pattadakal. Mithuna figures also appeared on the walls of Jaina *basadis* besides the Hindu temples belonging to the Saiva, Vaishnava and Shakta sects. Different regions of India display varied treatment in the placing and emphasis of the *mithuna* or *maithuna* figures. For example, the Sun temple in Modhera shows erotic figures on the plinth, shafts of pillars and lintels in a crude manner, while in Bhubaneswar, Konark and Khajuraho they are more bold and prominent. However, temples in Aihole, Badami, Pattadakal and Mahakuta from the times of Chalukyas of Badami (6th to 9th century CE) were the earliest to depict bold erotic representations on their walls or by the side of their entrances.

Several scholars of Indian art have attempted to interpret the significance of the growing proliferation of these *mithuna* images. Scholars have noted the persistence of primitive pre-Aryan cults and practices with the ancient associations of the magico-protective function of sexuality and the influence of ideas of *tantrism* on pleasure loving aristocrats to be one of the principal causes of such depictions. They also note the concept of the stimulation of generative powers expressed in the king/concubine relationship and the use of punning or tantric *sandhyabhasa* (intentional language) to express deeper, more abstract philosophical ideas. One example of the continuity of these primitive beliefs is the association of haircutting and sexual intercourse depicted on temples such as Bhubaneswar, Konarak and Ratnagiri in Odisha and Balligavi and Bagali in Karnataka. The offering of hair was a widespread practice associated with the Vedic royal consecration ceremony and was linked to the offering of heads and purification enjoined by medieval *puranic* literature and this practice still continues in many parts of India. Kramrisch had claimed that the *mithuna* image echoed the *Upanishadic* texts which used the metaphor of the loving embrace of man and woman to symbolize union or *moksha*.

The proliferation of the *mithuna* image which reached its height in the tenth to eleventh century CE seems to be a result of the following factors. First, the continuity of primitive magico-protective beliefs and customs; second, the growing influence of *tantrism* on the aristocratic pleasure-loving court, images inspired by but not necessarily addressed to *tantrikas* (the followers of Tantra); third, the relationship between frieze narratives and sophisticated dramatic art which involved the use of punning and double meaning; fourth, the use of obscenities, courtesans and *mithuna* couples for their regenerative potential (which included ancient ideas of magico-protective ritual); fifth, the concealment of a *yantra* which expressed the deep universal meaning of union, and sixth, for the purpose of ornamentation (*alankara*). Even the *Silpa* canons suggest that the purpose of the erotic image was to give delight.

Erotic sculpture continued to be part of the sculptural representations on the walls and friezes on the basement even in the Kalyani Chalukya and Hoysala temples.

5.6 SOME OF THE GREAT ARCHITECTS AND SCULPTORS OF KARNATAKA

In ancient days the sculptural art and architectural science were handed down from father to son. There are a number of inscriptions in Karnataka in support of this fact. Thus the art was practiced by the members of the same family or caste. These *silpis* or sculptors believe that they are the descendants of Vishwakarma, the divine Architect in heaven. The names of artists had suffixes 'acharya' (achari) or 'oja' (upadhyaya). In Chalukyan context they also had the suffix 'manchi.' The Vishwakarmas are able to work in different media like stone, wood, gold, iron and copper and they are called sculptor, carpenter, goldsmith, blacksmith, and coppersmith respectively.

Names of many of the Vishwakarmas or *silpis* appear in several of the inscriptions pertaining to construction and decoration of various temples commencing from the 4th century CE. The Vishwakarmas themselves too etched their own names and description at certain strategic point in the temple or its walls or at the basement (*adhisthana*). For instance, the name of the sculptor, Nelavalke is autographed on the right wing of *Garuda* on eaves of Cave 3 in Badami.

Southern Karnataka region held by the Western Gangas was deeply influenced by Tamil language and culture. The composers, engravers and artists too may have either come from Tamil speaking regions or must have been influenced by the Tamil culture.

Description of some of the well known architects and sculptors in Karnataka from 2nd century CE onwards is given below. Most of the description that follows is taken from the extracts of inscription and hence the language used is as from the inscription records.

Damoraka: Damoraka (Damodaraka) was the Acharya *sthapati* or architect and the *guru* of the sculptor ***Nataka (Nartaka)*** who made the image of the *Naga* or cobra on the slab on which the inscription was inscribed in 2nd century CE. The *Nagapratima* with the inscription is lying at the Madhukeswara temple in Banavasi.

Narasobba: An architect of the 7th century CE about whom it is written thus in an inscription at Aihole – "there has not been, and there shall not be, in Jambu-dvipa (India) any wise man, proficient in (the art of) building houses, temples equal to Narasobba.

Revadi Ovajja: Revadi Ovajja of the Sarvasiddhi Acharya, versed in the secret of Kanarese stone masons, probably the builder of Papanatha temple at Pattadakal in 8th century CE.

Subha-deva (754 CE) of Sandilya-gotra, sculptor or architect (*rupkara*) son's son of the sculptor ***Siva-vardhamana***, son of the sculptor *Siva*, or rather (*bhuyah*) the Acharya ***Jnana-Siva***, who is the disciple of the disciple's disciple at the feet of him, the venerable and worshipped ***Payo-bhakshin***, who had the appellation of ***Siva-sasana*** (and) who has come here (Pattadakal) from Mrigathanika-hara-vishaya on the north bank of the river Ganga-there has been set up in (?) gateway (*dvara*) of his own particular (?, style) shrine, this great stone pillar, which bears the mark of the seal of the trident and is octagonal at the upper part and square immediately below. (Pattadakal pillar inscription of Kirtivarman II).

Sri Gundan: An architect who built the temple of the god Virupaksha at Pattadakal (originally, Lokeswara), as mentioned in the inscription for Loka-mahadevi, the Queen and consort of the Badami Chalukya king Vikramaditya, the second. (8th century CE)

Visvakarmmacharya: An artist and painter (776 CE), "By the abode of all arts, skilled in painting pictures (*sarvakaladhara-bhuta-chitra-kalabhijnena*) was this Sasana written. (Narasamangala, Western Gangas)

Bidigoja: An inscription discovered on a rock at Shravanabelagola mentions a sculptor named ***Bidigoja***, with the honorary prefix Srimart, somewhere about 900 CE and two other records at the same place of the date unspecified mention *Chandraditya* and *Nagavarma* as having carved Jinas, animals and other figures of Jainism.

Jakanacharya: The architect of the temple at Halebid and Belur. He came from a small village near Tumkur and became a sculptor of fame. His son *Dankanacharya* too became a sculptor of repute and was involved in the building of several Hoysala temples. (12th century CE).

Malitamma: The earliest records of the Hoysala sculptors seem to be those of the Amriteswara temple at Amritapura built in 1196 CE. The fifteen signatures comprise *Malitamma*, each four times, and *Padumanna, Baluga, Majaya, Subujaga, Padumaya* and *Muhana,* each one. The last named signed in *Nagari* characters, an indication that he came from the north.

Ballanna: A shrine of goddess Nimaja was set up in the temple in 1261 CE. The sculptors who executed the marvelous statues and figures on the outer walls of this especially on the western side have not given their names except here and there, the following are the only ones: *Ballanna, Bochana, Changa, Devoja, Harisha of Odeyagiri, Harisha of Tanagundur, Kalidasi, Kedaroja, Ketana, Mabalaki, Machanna, Manibilaki, Masa* son of *Kanimoji* and *Revoja.*

It is apparent from the above details that architects, engravers and sculptors came to Karnataka from various parts of India. If there were migrants from the north, Tamil influence too is visible on the arts and architecture of Karnataka. No wonder then that Karnataka is the only state where one finds temples of all types viz. *Nagara, Dravida* and *Vesara* type of architecture. Architects and sculptors were suitably rewarded by the rulers for their exquisite works. Even incentives were given for completing a temple building job before the contracted date.

6

IMPORTANT HERITAGE CIRCUITS

6.1 BANAVASI AND AROUND

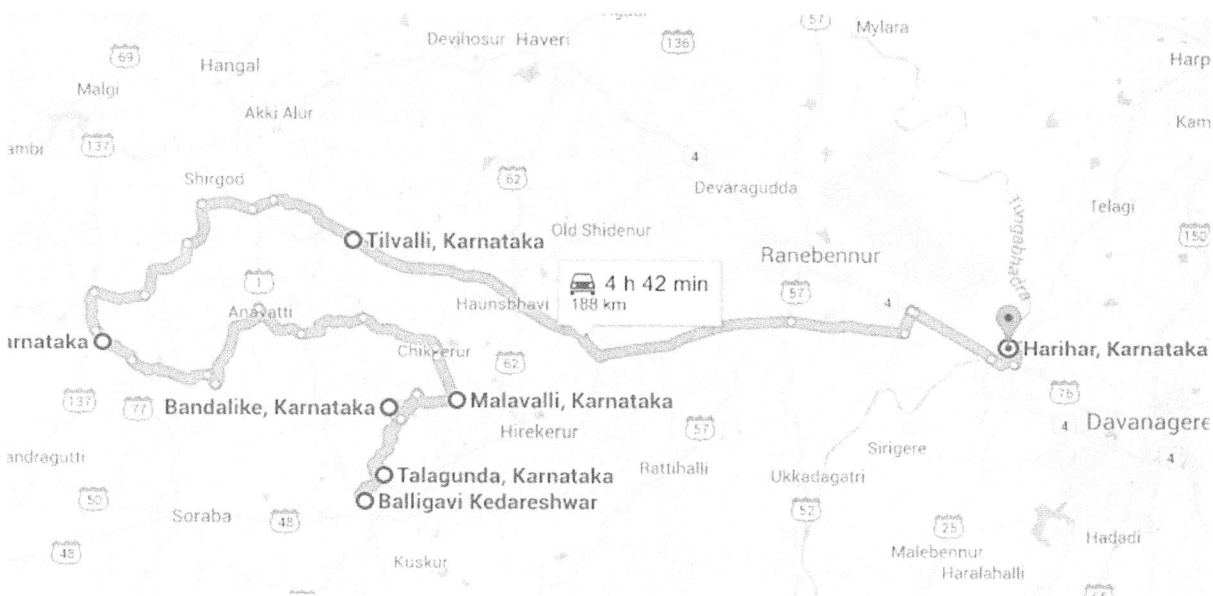

Banavasi holds the pride of a place in the history of Karnataka. It enjoys the reputation of being the capital town of the first indigenous Kannada dynasty, the Kadambas. Though it rose to the position of a capital town during the Kadambas, it was already playing the same role during the rule of the Chutus who were feudatories under the Satavahanas. If the pre-historic period is not taken into consideration; Banavasi might emerge as the oldest town of Karnataka, probably contemporary to Shravanabelagola. However, its antiquity prior to the Mauryas is still not established probably due to inadequate number of excavations carried out at this site.

With the all round distribution of Ashoka's inscriptions in southern India, it can be safely assumed that Banavasi was under Ashoka's dominion and more particularly because the place was an important Buddhist religious centre in those times. After the disintegration of the Mauryan empire, there were different regional powers in north and south India and Banavasi came under the Satavahanas. Nasik cave inscription of the Satavahana king Gautamiputra Satakarni was issued from the victorious camp of Banavasi. Satavahana activities around the Banavasi region are also attested from various coins and a solo Satavahana memorial inscription found here.

The Chutus ruled after the Satavahanas and Banavasi became their capital. Though there are not many inscriptions of this dynasty, Malvalli pillar inscription adequately testifies to their influence in the region around Banavasi. Many of their coins have also been discovered here. They were prominently Buddhists as is evident from their inscriptions. After the Chutus, Banavasi became the celebrated capital of the first indigenous Kannada dynasty, the Kadambas. Though it was their capital city, there is only one Kadamba inscription found here.

While the power of the Kadambas was on decline, another south Indian dynasty, the Badami Chalukyas, was on the rise. Badami Chalukya inscriptions mention defeat of the Kadambas at the hands of the king Kirtivarman I. However it seems that he was not able to conquer Banavasi as this victory is attributed to his son, Pulakesin II. In his Aihole *prashashti*, it is mentioned that Banavasi appeared to be a water-fort (*Jaladurga*) due to its being surrounded by river Varada on three sides.

Since then, Banavasi remained a province under the Badami Chalukyas. It would have been an important province as at one point of time it was being governed by the brother-in-law of the Badami Chalukya king Vijayaditya. The Shiggaon plate mentions that Vijayaditya visited Banavasi to see his brother-in-law, the Alupa king Chitravahana in 708 CE. Chitravahana's father, Gunasagara, was the first Alupa king who was made the governor of the Kadamba-mandala by the Badami Chalukya king Vikramaditya I as evidenced from Kigga inscription.

From various inscriptions it is clear that it was under the Rashtrakutas for sometime, being governed by their feudatories. After them, it was Chalukya Rajaditya and Chellaketana families who governed this region. With the Kalyani Chalukyas taking over most of the Karnataka into their control, Banavasi also came under them.

Kadambas of Hangal administered Banavasi-12000 under the Kalyani Chalukyas. They continued their rule even after the fall of the Kalyani Chalukyas. With the fall of the Kalyani Chalukyas, Karnataka went into the hands of two powerful dynasties, the northern part to the Seunas and the southern to the Hoysalas. Both these dynasties tried their best to prove their supremacy but none succeeded. Due to its strategic location, being situated at the border of the Hoysala and Seuna territories, Banavasi became the point of tussle between these two dynasties. Both had their small stints over Banavasi however it did not remain with them for long. Hoysala Vishnuvardhana conquered Banavasi in 1135 CE for a small time but later driven out by the Kadamba Mallikarjuna. Seuna Singhana II also ruled over Banavasi in about 1215 CE.

Banavasi enjoys a mythological link too. A Banavasi Kaifiyat provides a legend for the origin of the Madhukeswara linga. It is told that Madhu and Kaitabha, two demons, were killed by Visnu on instance of Siva. However, as both the demons were great devotees of Siva, two lingas were consecrated after their names as Madhukeswara and Kaitabheswara. It is believed that an aspect of Siva himself is enshrined in these lingas.

John Wilson points to a reference of "Story of Allama Prabhu about subduing Maya." Once Siva and Parvati were seated in their court and Chandeswara arrived. He saluted Siva only with one hand. Parvati asked Siva that everybody salutes him with two hands but why Chandeswara saluted only with one hand. On this, Siva turned into his ardhanariswara form. Chandeswara then turned to right where half-Siva was and saluted him alone.

Parvati got enraged over this and turned Chandeswara into a skeleton which was later known as Bhringi. Then Parvati said to Siva that she has conferred her half body to Bhringi and Brahma, Visnu and rest are concentrated in her, then who is greater, Bhringi or Siva? Siva asked Parvati to send a part of her essence to the mortal world and he would send Bhringi there and she might then examine its spiritual truth.

Thus Parvati was born as Maya or Mohinidevi as the queen of the Banavasi king named Mamakara raja. She got associated to the musicians of the Madhukeswara temple at Banavasi. Bhringi was born as Allama Prabhu at Karure. Later Allama Prabhu subdued the musicians of Madukeswara temple and Mohinidevi, and obtained the title 'Niranjani.'

With such rich history and culture, it is not surprising that Banavasi was known by its many names in its past. The town has been identified with Banauasei mentioned by Ptolemy. As per a local Kaifiyat, it was known as Kaumadi in the Krita Yuga, Jayanti in the Treta Yuga, Beindivi in the Dvapar Yuga and Banavasi in the Kali Yuga or present age. The various names with this the town has been referred in the past are Vaijayanti, Vanavasi or Vanavasaka and Sanjayanti.

Banavasi in Literature – Banavasi has been mentioned in literature of different periods and of different languages.

Few prominent references are listed below:

- **Mahabharata** – Mahabharata places Vanavasaka in the southern India
- **Ramayana** – Ayodhya Kanda's chapter 9 mentions Vaijayanti which most probably refers to present Banavasi.

Other references in literature are found in Mahavamsa (a Buddhist text), Varaha-Mihira's Brihatsamhita, Pampa's Vikramarjuna Vijaya and Chamarasa'a Prabhulinga Leele.

Banavasi also finds mention in the travelogues of Xuanzang (602–664 CE) and Francis Buchanan (nineteenth century CE). Close to forty inscriptions of the past have been found in Banavasi which reveal a lot about its history.

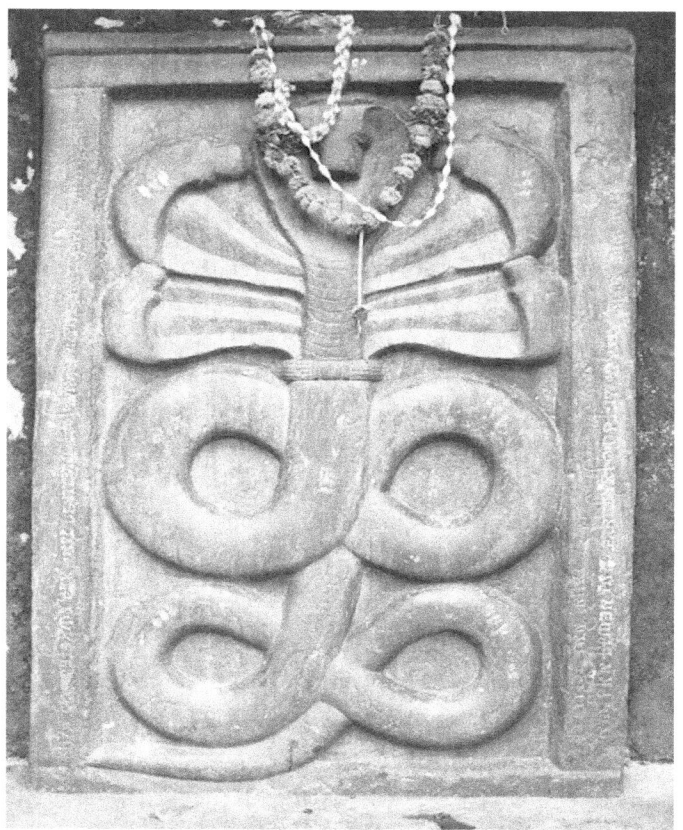

Nagapratima of the Chutus in Madhukeswara temple

There are many temples of different antiquities in Banavasi. Madhukeswara temple is the oldest and the most important one.

Madhukeswara temple is the epicenter of the town as the town has grown around it. The temple was originally considered to be dedicated to Madhava, one of the twenty-four incarnations of Visnu. However at present it is dedicated to Siva who is represented in his linga form. Due to its honey-like color, this linga, and consequently the temple, is named as Madhukeswara. The temple has undergone substantial additions and alterations from the times of the Kadambas to Kalyani Chalukyas and right up to the Sonda (Sode) chiefs. (Plate 6-1)

The present temple compound has a *prakara* wall housing the main temple and various other subsidiary structures. This *prakara* wall along with many of its subsidiary structures can be dated to the Sonda period of sixteenth century CE. The *prakara* wall has two entrances, main entrance from the east, and another entrance from the north. Two magnificent stone elephants are placed outside the eastern entrance. On entering inside the compound, a visitor is greeted with two tall *dipastambhas*.

The temple faces east. The main temple was probably constructed by the Kadambas and comprises of a square *garbhagriha*, a small *sukanasi* and a pillared *navaranga* hall. A *pradakshinapatha* (circumambulatory path) around the *garbhagriha* puts the temple in *sandhara* temple category. At present the *garbhagriha* enshrines a large Sivalinga however it seems that it was placed at some later period.

There are two niches on either side of *sukanasi* in the *navaranga* hall. There is an image of Adimadhava in one of the niches, many believe that this might be the original image of this temple. The sculpture depicts features and style which may be attributed to the Kadamba period. Super structure above the *garbhagriha* is a later renovation, in the Vijayanagara times, which is carried in the Kadamba stepped *sikhara* style.

A later *navaranga* of the Kalyani Chalukya times was constructed in 11th or 12th century CE. It has three entrances, one on east, south and north. In contrast of the square base pillars of the original *navaranga*, this *navaranga* hall has ornate lathe turned pillars. Local tradition mentions that it was here where Allama Prabhu defeated the dancer queen Shantala. On the eastern entrance of this hall, a large stone Nandi is placed. The local guide and priest will tell you the engineering behind the turned face of the Nandi as with one eye he sees the Sivalinga and with another the Parvati temple. The slanted roof of this *mandapa* reminds of the various similar Kalyani Chalukya structures strewn across the Western Ghats region.

During the period of the Sonda chief Sadashiva, Parvati temple was added. The exquisite Trailokya mandapa which is at present kept under the *navaranga* hall was also donated by the Sonda chief, Sadasivarajendra of sixteenth century CE. Virabhadra temple on the right of the main temple was built in 1369 CE by one Nagappa during the Sode Nayaka rule. A stone cot of majestic craftsmanship was also a gift of a Sode chief, Raghu Nayaka. *Rangamandapas* were added to the Parvati and Narasimha temple during the Vijayanagara rule in 1552 CE. Narada and Parvati temples around the *prakara* were added during the Vijayanagara period. Many other small shrines were also added to house *dikpalas*, Ardha-Ganapati, two-armed Narasimha etc. The unique Ardh-Ganapati statue is only finished in half such as cut vertically into two parts. It is said that this sculpture represents Ganesha in his bachelorhood, without his wife. Two-handed Narasimha image is also worth noticing as there are legends about the eyes of this sculpture that they look different in different period of the day. Narasimha here is shown in his peaceful (*saumya*) attitude.

A small museum is set up on the left of the eastern entrance of the temple compound with several sculptures just strewn around the hall.

Very few vestiges of the Banavasi Fort are left now. This might be among the earliest forts built in Karnataka. The fort was built at the sharp curve of river Varada, with exterior measuring 850 m, north-south and 600 m east-west. Total length of periphery is about 2140 m. During an excavation around the fort area, three separate and distinct phases in construction were observed:

- The earliest phase was of brick structure which belongs to the late Satavahanas and the Chutus
- The next phase was the enlargement of the fort with laterite blocks, bricks and mud which belongs to the early Kadambas
- The last phase was extension at northern side with full laterite stones datable to the late Kadambas

Till now only one major excavation has been carried out here on the behalf of the Dr M. Sheshadri of The Department of Post-Graduate Studies and Research in Ancient History and Archaeology of the Mysuru University. The excavation was conducted for three seasons beginning from 1969–70 and ending 1971–72. The most important discoveries of the excavations are:

- Inscribed pottery bearing a Brahmi inscription datable to third century BCE
- Two apsidal brick structures of the Satavahana period which are among the largest such structures in Karnataka
- Due to missing evidences, it cannot be said with certainty if these structures were Buddhist or Hindu
- A stone Skanda sculpture was found in one of the structure which suggests its Hindu affinity; however it might be a later addition. 11 coins including 1 punch-marked, 3 Satavahana and 2 Chutu coins were also discovered.

Balligavi

Balligavi is an open air museum of the Karnataka temple architecture and the cradle to the *kalamukha* and *lingayat* (Virashaivism) sects. Though now reduced to a small hamlet, in its golden era of the bygone times, Balligavi enjoyed the status of the royal city of the province. The village Baligavi is variously known as Ballegave, Belgami or Belligave in various agencies' records. This confusion is not of the modern origin, in the ancient times, this village had been known variously as Belgami, Belligave, Balligave, Balligame, Belligamve, Ballegavi, Baligrama, Balipura and Balinagara. The name Balligavi also figures in the Google maps and hence has been used thus in this write up.

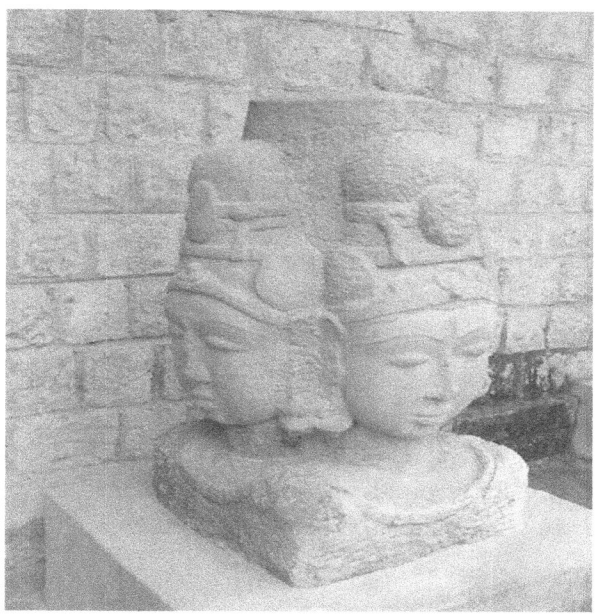

Chaturmukha Brahma dated to Satavahana Period (Balligavi Museum)

Balligavi is situated in Shikarpur taluk of Shivamogga district in Karnataka. Brimmed with natural beauty, idyllic atmosphere and away from the hustle and bustle, Balligavi looks a serene and quiet village. It was also known as Dakshina Kedara, famous for its Kedareswara temple which is compared with Kedarnath in north India. The importance and beauty of this village is evident in its inscriptions. It has been extolled for its inspirational beauty and surroundings. Balligavi is compared with Amaravati, Bhogavati-pura and Alkapura in its inscriptions. An inscription describes this royal city of Balligavi as "with clusters of lotus, with swarms of bees, with mango groves filled with beautiful swans, parrots and cuckoos, surrounded with climbing betel vines, areca palms, begonias, and muchukunda, Balligave was like the twining curls of the lady the Kuntala country."

As per a legend, Balligavi was inhabited by the *asura* (demon) king Bali from whom it got its name Balipura. King Bali, though with demon ancestry, was a pious king known for his charities. As king Bali had won over the heavens from the gods, there was an immediate need to reinstate the balance in the Universe. Lord Visnu took over this task upon himself and appeared on the earth in his Vamana incarnation with an idea to exploit the charitable nature of the king. This story is told in various mythological texts and epics.

This legend is supported in an inscription found here. This inscription dated 1181 CE, tells how the *rajaguru* Vamasakti-deva explained the greatness of the city. He told, "The *rakshasa* Bali having in his time dwelt in this kshetra, made gifts and in the course of *manvantaras* been considered as Indra himself, I literally know not how to praise the greatness of Balipura."

Another legend links this place with the Pandavas of Mahabharata even though Balligavi does not find any mention in the epic directly. An inscription dated 1036 CE, tells that the Pandavas, while performing Rajasuya sacrifice, after taking tributes from Vibhishana of Lanka, visited Balligavi and setup the Panchalingas. From Mahabharata, we come to know that Sahadeva was assigned to conduct the southern conquest during the Rajasuya. Sahadeva did not visit Lanka but sent his messengers. Vibhishana, the king of Lanka, sent back the messengers with bounties paying tributes to the Pandavas.

Balligavi is also famous as the birth place of Allama Prabhu, a twelfth century *lingayat* saint, the one among the Trinity of *lingayatism*. Allama Prabhu, Akka Mahadevi together with Basavanna constitute the Trinity of *lingayatism*. Akka Mahadevi was born in Udutadi, situated near Balligavi. Thus Balligavi held a special regard for the *lingayats* (Virashaivas). Being an ancient centre of the *kalamukhas*, it provided ideal environment fostering the *lingayat* movement.

Harihara, the first poetic biographer of Allama Prabhu, tells that Allama was born in the caste of temple performers in Balligavi. He grew up into a handsome youth, expert in playing *maddale*, a kind of drum. While performing once at the temple he fell in love with the temple dancer Kamalathe. She reciprocated, and they got married. But misfortune stroke the couple, a fatal illness took away Kamalathe. Like all legendary lovers, Allama went insane. This lasted, till he discovered a hidden garden and temple where his future guru Animisha was waiting for him. Initiated into secrets of 'linga,' Allama became enlightened.

Inscriptions play a major role in understanding the political history of a place. More than hundred and thirty-five inscriptions of this place have been published till now. Situated at a strategic location, being the bed rock of the Karnataka culture, Balligavi commanded the impact of rule of almost all the major dynasties of Karnataka. All of these different rulers left their imprint on the cultural heritage and socio-religious conditions of the town.

The earliest inscription at Balligavi is dated 685 CE and refers to the rule of the Badami Chalukya king Vinayaditya (680–696 CE). This inscription mentions about a village fair attended by high officials. This suggests that by this time the town had already gained its fame enough to hold religious fairs attended by large crowds. This definitely takes back the antiquity of the town by a few centuries. Support of its antiquity comes from a Chaturmukha Brahma sculpture, found at Balligavi, which few scholars have dated to Satavahana period.

The political history of Karnataka was in turmoil after the fall of the Badami Chalukyas. Balligavi fails to throw any light on this intervening period, between the fall of the Badami Chalukyas and the advent of the Kalyani Chalukyas. But it appears from literary records that the Rashtrakutas were in command during this period. But probably Balligavi did not get their attention and as a result we fail to find any inscription of theirs.

From the Badami Chalukyas, the political history of Balligavi directly leaps to the early eleventh century where it finds itself under the Kalyani Chalukyas. The earliest Kalyani Chalukya inscription at Balligavi is dated 1019 CE, referring to the reign of the Kalyani Chalukya king Jayasimha II (1015–1042 CE). This is an important inscription, as it connects the Kalyani Chalukyas with the immemorial city of Ayodhya. It is told that fifty-nine of the Chalukya kings ruled at Ayodhya. It further mentions that the first Kalyani Chalukya king Tailapa drew away the Rattas and acquired the Chalukya throne. Mention is also made of the conflict between the Chola king Rajendra-Chola with then Kalyani Chalukya king Jayasimha II.

By the time of king Jayasimha II, the town was already adorned with many temples as inscriptions lend references of Muligamatha, Panchalinga temple etc. Balligavi was also established as a famous *kalamukha* center referred as *Kalamukhi Brahmachari-sthana* in its inscriptions. The priest of this *kalamukha* center was Vadi-Rudragana-Lakulisvara-pandita.

King Jayasimha II, also known as Jagadhekamalla, would have setup Jagadhekamalla-deva at Balligavi as a reference of it comes in a later inscription dated 1047 CE. Somesvara I (1042–1068 CE) succeeded Jayasimha II. During his time, was setup the very famous Ganda-Berunda pillar, and establishment of the Berundeswara temple in front of the god Jagadhekamalla-deva.

By the time of Somesvara I, Balligavi was already established as the place famous for its five *mathas*. Among these five *mathas* were Berundeswara temple, Panchalinga temple and Tripurantaka temple. Somesvara I not only patronized the Hindu religion, but equally supported other religions. We learn about Chamunda-rayarasa, the governor of Banavasi-12000, making grants to Jaina temple at Balligave. He also constructed habitations for the Vaishnava, Saiva, and Jaina *munis*. Another minister Dandanayaka Rupa-bhattayya caused to be made Jayanti Buddha Vihara and setup Tara Bhagwati worship. These are some glaring examples of communal harmony practiced during the Kalyani Chalukya rule.

Kalyani Chalukya rule at Balligavi provided a stable political condition. This is evident from numerous Kalyani Chalukya inscriptions at Balligavi, providing a continuous history of about two-hundred fifty years of their rule. This stable political situation resulted in a prosperous merchant community at Balligavi. A very detailed inscription of the time of Somesvara I, mentions various countries where this merchant community was engaged in business. These various countries in which the merchant community was engaged were Chera, Chola, Pandya, Maleya, Magadha, Kausala, Saurastra, Dhanushtra, Kurumbha, Kamboja, Gaula, Lala, Barvvara, Parasa, Nepala, Ekapada, Lambakarnna, Stri-rajya and Gholamukha.

This wealthy merchant community also supported the religious activities at Balligavi. Various grants, temple construction and other works of merit were performed with support of this merchant community. This also resulted in establishment of a sculptor guild at Balligavi which grew to its zenith during the Hoysala period. Mention of Dasoja and his son Chavana will not be out of place here. Dasoja is one of the most famous artists of Sarasvatigana, an important artist guild of early medieval Karnataka.

A very important inscription at Balligavi provides details on the death of king Somesvara I and accession of king Somesvara II. We are told that on 29th March 1068 CE, Sunday, king Somesvara I having performed the rites of supreme *yoga* in the Tungabhadra at Kuruvatti, the master of the world ascended to heaven. The supreme *yoga* rites in the inscription might be the *sallekhana* practice of Jainas as the inscription is also dedicated to Jaina religion. The same inscription further tells that on 11th April, 1068 CE, Friday, under the *pushya* star, in the sign of cancer, king Somesvara II ascended the throne.

With accession of Somesvara II (1068–1076 CE), we come to know the alliances between the Kalyani Chalukyas and other minor dynasties of Karnataka. The two important alliances evident in Balligavi inscriptions were the Gangas and the Nolambas. The inscriptions inform about Vikrama-Ganga-Permmadi Udeyaditya and Vira-Nolamba-Singi-Deva ruling under the supremacy of Somesvara II. The Gangas and Nolambas were the buffer states between the Cholas and Kalyani Chalukyas.

Enmity between the two brothers from the Kalyani Chalukya clan, Somesvara II and Vikramaditya VI, is a well-known fact. In his later inscriptions, Somesvara was at Bankapura many times, and this suggests that he was trying to control the insurgency from his younger brother. But at last, Vikramaditya VI (1076–1126 CE) was able to overthrow his brother and with his accession started the golden period of the Kalyani Chalukyas.

Vikramaditya VI is the most successful Kalyani Chalukya rulers. He consolidated the Chalukya power in the Deccan plateau, and also kept his feudatories in control. He successfully put away the Chola threat by defeating the combined army of the Cholas and Somesvara II. Vikramaditya VI is attributed to have the largest number of inscriptions being issued during any Indian king's reign. And Balligavi is not an exception here, majority of its inscriptions are from the period of this great king.

Various feudatories of Vikramaditya VI are found in inscriptions at Balligavi. Famous among them are the Nolambas and the Kadambas. During the rule of Vikramaditya VI, which spans for great fifty years, *kalamukha* sect flourished to its zenith. Kedareswara and Pachalinga temples at Balligavi were the major centeres of this movement, though the former was more glorified than the latter. Kedareswara temple received a continued patronage from the king and his ministers. The Acharya of the temple, Somesvara-pandita, attained the status of the *rajaguru*. The temple did not lose its sheen even after the fall of the Kalyani Chalukyas and it gained same respect during the Kalachuri and the Hoysala rule.

The period after Vikramaditya VI was of varied political troubles for the Kalyani Chalukyas. Their powerful feudatories started raising heads, and this resulted in the reduction of the Chalukya territories. Vikramaditya VI was followed by his son, Somesvara III (1126–1138 CE). Many inscriptions of this king are found at Balligavi suggesting that the town continued to be the center of the drama.

Somesvara III was followed by Jagadhekamalla II (1138–1151 CE). There are two inscriptions from this king found at Balligavi but those are not from Balligavi proper but from Govindapura in the near vicinity. Jagadhekamalla II was succeeded by Tailapa III (1151–1164 CE) and inscriptions tell about him making donations to Kedareswara temple at Balligavi. Tailapa III found himself in troubled waters very early in his rule. The Hoysalas and the Kalachuris were getting stronger. The Kalachuris were able to capture Kalyani, the capital of the Kalyana Chalukyas, forcing them to move to another capital, Annigeri in this case. Balligavi was the mute witness of this transition.

An inscription, dated 1158 CE, at Balligavi refers to the third regnal year of the Kalachuri king Bijjala II (1130–1167 CE). This suggests that the Kalyani Chalukyas were ousted in about 1156 CE by the Kalachuris. There is another inscription dated 1159 CE, where Bijjala II acknowledges the supremacy of the Kalyani Chalukyas. But his later inscriptions till 1162 CE do not mention the Kalyani Chalukyas as his overlords. Again in 1164 CE, we see Bijjala II acknowledging the Kalyani Chalukyas as his overlords. This suggests that during the rule of Bijjala II, the fate of Balligavi oscillated between the Kalachuris and the Chalukyas.

Since 1168 CE, from the rule of the Kalachuri king Sovideva (1168–1176 CE), no more references occur to the Kalayani Chalukyas at Balligavi. This confirms the Kalachuri rule over Balligavi. After Sovideva, Sankama (1176–1180 CE) and Ahavamalla (1180–1183 CE) ruled from the Kalachuri line over Balligavi till 1183 CE in Balligavi. The Kalachuris were strong supporter of the *pasupata* sect therefore the *kalamukha* center of Balligavi was further strengthened during their rule with various donations and grants. Vamasakti-deva, the priest of the Kedareswara temple, attained the status of *rajaguru* during the Kalachuri rule.

Balligavi got another chance to witness another transition, and this time it was from the Kalachuris to the Hoysalas. Year 1184 CE brings Balligavi under the Hoysala rule. Under Ballala II (1173–1220 CE), Jainism received the much needed booster which was missing during the Kalyani Chalukya rulers. But with Ballala II soon converting into Vaishnava, the attention moved back to the Hindu temples.

After the brief period of forty years of Hoysala rule, Balligavi was again forced to witness one more historical transition. This time it was from the Hoysalas to the Seunas. Ballala II was pushed back by the Seunas. Year 1215 CE, brings in the Seuna king Singhana II (1200–1247 CE), into Balligavi making grants to Kedareswara temple. The Seuna rule brought back stability to the region. After Singhana II, Kannara (1247–1261 CE), Mahadeva (1261–1271 CE) and Ramachandra (1271–1309 CE) would have ruled Balligavi. We have inscriptions only from the last Seuna ruler at Balligavi.

Balligavi boasts of a very rich cultural and archaeological heritage. A major reason behind this would be the patronage it received at the helm of various dynasties ruling this region. Though the fate of kingdoms changed hands many times, but Balligavi kept its reputation high throughout. At one point of time, there were about forty five different temples adorning this royal city. Of these, thirty were associated with Siva, three with Visnu, seven to Jaina faith, two with Buddhism and one to Aditya.

Balligavi provided support and habitation for all the major communities of the time, Hindu, Buddhist and Jaina. The rulers of the land supported all these with much or less the same fervor. There are inscriptions giving us instances where the same person at one instance provided grants to some Hindu temple, and at the other instance provided habitation for all communities.

From its inscriptions, it is also learnt that there were five *mathas*, seven Brahmapuris and three *agraharas* at Balligavi. The five *mathas*, includes Berundesvara temple, Panchalinga temple, Tripurantaka temple, Mulasthana temple and Kodiya Matha attached to the Kedareswara temple. Among these, the Kedareswara temple emerges as the most prominent temple enjoying support

These catalytic conditions gave birth to a new tradition of sculptural art which blossomed in the hands of the artist guilds at Balligavi. Coming from this guild, the most famous was Dasoja and his son Chavana who migrated to Belur with Shantala, the chief queen of the Hoysala king Vishnuvardhan. Dasoja was the crest jewel of Saravatigana. Some other important artists from this town were Mavoja, Chavundoja, Somoja, Barmoja, Kalloja Chattayya, Mammatoja. An inscription at Balligavi mentions two sculptors, Bavana and Ravana, who were from Gaurisa Dasa community. *Acharyas* of the Kodiya Matha were said to be their religious teachers. It is told that these two, in order to clear an aspersion on their own race of the sculptors, set up an image of the god Kusuveswara and presented that to Gautamadeva, attached to the god Kedareswara.

Balligavi was also adorned with few Buddhist temples and *viharas*. In 1065 CE, minister Rupabhattaya, under king Somesvara I, constructed a Buddhist *vihara* and provided worship for Tara Bhagawati and other gods of Buddhist pantheon. Two years later, 1067 CE, a lady Nagiyakka, caused to be made Tara Bhagawati and made some land grants. Nothing is left of these structures now.

Kedareswara Temple is the main temple of the village and probably the oldest one. This temple is situated behind the embankment of the Tavarakere (lotus tank). This tank is also mentioned in the Talagunda pillar inscription. Though no foundation inscription is found, but this temple can be dated to ninth-tenth century CE if not earlier. This east facing temple is constructed in *trikutachala* (triple-shrine) fashion. Constructed in the east-west orientation, the temple has three cells, one each on west, north and south. South and west cells have linga inside, while the north cell has an image of Visnu. With this arrangement, it may be said that the linga in the south cell represents Brahma. The cell on the west is adorned with a *sukanasi*, which is missing in case of the other two cells. *Sukanasi* is replaced with an *ardhamandapa* for north and south cells. (Plate 6-3)

All these cells are connected with a six-pillared *mahamandapa* which opens up into a huge *sabhamandapa*. This *sabhamandapa* has polished pillars with sixteen-sides treated with leaf decoration. This might be the place where dance ceremonies were witnessed. The central ceiling of the *mandapa* is decorated with Siva accompanied with *ashtadikapalas*. Siva is shown with Nandi, Ganesha and Kartikeya in the central panel, while Indra, Agni, Yama, Nrriti, Vayu, Varuna, Kubera and Isana surround him.

As per an inscription, a *mandapa* of the temple was completed in 1103 CE and the *rajaguru* was happy that it was completed within the contract time. Being pleased, the *rajaguru* provided certain grants to the architects, Bisadoja, Chavoja and Singoja.

All the three cells have towers on top with projections bearing Hoysala crests. These crests would have been added later. The crest on the north tower has fallen down, the other two are intact. These three towers are similar in form to each other with the wall details repeated at each level (*tala*).

In the same complex, on the north-west of the main temple, there is another shrine which is very similar to the Kedareswara temple. This is a *trikutachala* structure and known as temple of Prabhudeva. Prabhudeva would be the original name of Allama Prabhu before attaining the enlightenment. The western and southern cells have lingas inside while the northern one has a Virabhadra image.

Tripuranteswara Temple is situated in the north-west corner of the village and would be contemporary of the Kedareswara temple. From the foundation inscription of the temple, it is evident that it was constructed in 1070 CE under the reign of the Kalyani Chalukya king Somesvara II. This is a double temple, having two parallel shrines facing east. Both these shrines are built upon a high rising platform (*jagati*). The shrine to the north has its *garbhagriha* (sanctum) on the west and adorned with *antarala* (vestibule) and *ardhamandapa*. The shrine to the south also has its sanctum with all other attachments as that of the north shrine (Plates 6–2 and 6–4). The shrine on the south is exquisitely carved and suggests its supremacy on the other one. Its entrance is flanked with *dvarapalas* (guards) on either side. These *dvarapalas* are of carved with superior craftsmanship. On either side of these *dvarapalas*, there are provided pierced windows. These windows carry medallions depicting various dancers. Total of sixteen dancers are on a window, out which only three are female.

In the *ardhamandapa* of this shrine, there is an elaborately carved lintel supported on two free standing pillars. There are two female attendants on extreme sides of these pillars. These female figures very much resemble with the *salabhanjika* figures. Mysore Gazetteer mentions that the lintel piece of this temple is a perfect marvel in delicate imagery and workmanship. Both shrines are connected to the *mahamandapa* (hall) which has massive square based circular pillars supporting the roof. On the central piece of this roof, depiction of *ashtadikapalas* is found. This common *mahamandapa* has two entrances, at the east and the south.

The plinth of the temple is decorated with friezes at the base. These friezes contain various depictions of daily life activities, erotic sculptures and stories. Among the stories are found some famous stories from Panchatantra which include depiction of the 'Monkey and Crocodile' story, the 'Rams and Jackal' story and the 'Swans and Tortoise' story. This temple holds an important place among other few temples where depiction of Panchatantra stories is found.

Bherundeswara Pillar is the most striking object standing in the village of Balligavi. This pillar is located on a cross-road, where it stands in its full majesty. This huge pillar, about 9 m high, has its base enclosed by a small structure. It is raised over a two-tiered platform of about 3 m in height. Now known as *Garudakhamba*, this pillar was originally erected to support a life-like statue of Ganda Berunda.

This pillar was erected by Mahamandaleswara Chamunda-rayarasa in 1047 CE, when he was ruling over Banavasi-12000, Santalige-300 and Hayve-500. Chamnuda-rayarasa was under the service of the Kalyani Chalukya king Somesvara I. The inscription mentions that this pillar was erected in front of god Jagadekamalleswara. God Jagadekamalleswara would have been setup by the Chamunda-rayarasa as he was also known by the title Jagadhekamalla. No remains of this temple survive except this singular pillar standing tall.

The statue of Ganda Berunda is no more on the top of the pillar. It is kept inside the enclosure on which this pillar is standing. It is kept inside a locked gate. Ganda Berunda represents a mythological bird, having half-bird and half-human body. As per Hindu Mythology, Ganda Berunda fought with Sharabha for about eighteen days resulting in the death of the latter. Sharabha was an incarnation of Siva to get rid of Narasimha.

This figure of Ganda Berunda is in standing posture, with slight bent knees, supposedly ready to sweep down to its prey. The heads are of an eagle, with strong beak. Ganda Berunda was the royal insignia of the Wodeyar dynasty of Mysore. Later, it was adopted as an official emblem of the Karnataka Government.

Someswara temple would have been established by the time of the Kalyani Chalukya king Somesvara I (1042–1068 CE), though there is no foundation inscription. On the plan, the temple is consisted of a *garbhagriha* (sanctum), an *antarala* (vestibule) and a pillared hall which also serves as *mukhamandapa*. The doorways of the sanctum and *antarala* are exquisitely carved.

There is a Sivalinga inside the sanctum. Inside the *mukhamandapa*, there are two niches on either side of the doorway on the west wall. These niches are empty at present. The entrance door of this *mandapa* is flanked with pierced windows on either side, provisioning for a sunlit hall inside. The temple is built on a plinth and provided with elephant balustrade steps. The exterior wall is plain, devoid of any decoration.

Panchalinga temple is towards the north of the village, near Jiddi tank. There is an image of Umamaheswara which needs attention. Uma is seated on Siva's lap while he himself is resting on a *simhasana*. He wears a tiara on which he is shown with Visnu and Brahma. Beneath him are shown Ganesha, Kartikeya, Bhringi and Nandi. The sculpture is of great artistic value.

Jalasayana temple is located to the north-west of the village is an island, Sitahonda. On this island is located the Jalasayana temple. Many of the statues from this island had been moved to Shivamogga museum. The main statue of Visnu in reclining posture is still in the shrine. This image was caused to be made by Govindamayya in 1114 CE. He also caused to be made twenty four images depicting twenty-four forms of Visnu.

Bandalike

Bandalike, referred as Bandanike or Bandhavapura in inscriptions, is situated in Shivamogga district of Karnataka. As per the inscriptions, the town was the capital city of Nagarakhanda-70 region, which was included in Banavasi-12000 province. The town started gaining importance since tenth century onwards. The earliest inscription, dated 912 CE, found here refers itself to the rule of the Rashtrakuta king Krishna II. During this period, the town was governed by the Sattara chiefs. It is told that Jakkiyabbe, wife of Nagarjuna Sattara, performed *sallekhana* here at Bandalike. Bandalike was already established as a celebrated Jaina pilgrimage centre by then.

Emergence of the Kalyani Chalukyas saw the departure of the Rashtrakutas from Karnataka. The earliest Kalyani Chalukya inscription found at Bandalike is dated 1015 CE and belongs to the reign of the Chalukya king Jayasimha II. The Sattaras continued to rule over here under the Kalyani Chalukya kings. During the reign of the Kalyani Chalukya king Vikramaditya VI, region Nagarakhanda-70 was under Mahamandaleshwara Bopparasa. He is said to be born in the Kadamba *vamsa*. Many inscriptions of Bopparasa and his wife, Siriya Devi, have been found here. Bopparasa had a long reign and made various grants to temples and *basadis*.

The Kalyani Chalukyas were eclipsed under the emerging Kalachuri power. The Kalachuris, under Bijjala II, took over Basavakalyan, the celebrated capital of the Kalyani Chalukyas. Inscription dated 1163 CE, belonging to Bijjala II marks the start of the Kalachuri rule at Bandalike. Bopparasa continued to serve Nagarakhanda-70 under the Kalachuris. Inscriptions of Bijjala II, Sovideva, Sankama and Ahavamalla, belonging to the Kalachuri line who ruled in succession, are found at Bandalike. This suggests that Bandalike enjoyed quite an importance during the Kalachuri rule. All of their inscriptions are for grants to or building of Siva temples. Probably Jaina character of the town took a hit during their rule.

The Kalyani Chalukyas, under Somesvara IV, ousted the Kalachuris and reinstated themselves at Basavakalyana. An inscription, dated 1185 CE, here suggests revival of the town under the Kalyani Chalukyas. But it was a short lived rule as they were soon ousted by the Hoysala Ballala II. The earliest Hoysala inscription found here is dated 1203 CE and belongs to the reign of Ballala II. Long standing fight for this region between the Hoysalas and the Seunas is also revealed from the inscriptions at Bandalike. Ballala II has his inscriptions dated in 1203 and 1215 CE while Seuna Singhana II has inscriptions dated 1215 and 1224 CE. It is a known fact that Seunas were victorious at last and ruled over this region.

As evident from above, that the inscriptions at Bandalike are good resources to understand the political history of this part of Karnataka region. Starting from the Rashtrakutas, to the Kalyani Chalukyas, to the defeat of the latter in the hands of the Kalachuris, later reinstatement of the Kalyani Chalukyas and then the fatal blows from the Hoysala Ballala, expansion of the Seunas and the final authority of the Vijayanagara empire, inscriptions at Bandalike are the mute witnesses of this changing political drama. There are about 31 inscriptions found here. All these are published in the Epigraphia Carnatica vol. VII.

There are many ruined temples in this village. The main three temples, Shantinatha Basadi, Trimurti and Someswara Temple are under the protection of ASI (Archaeological Survey of India). Virabhadra temple, Sahastralinga temple and Hanuman temple are other main temples in the village.

Shanthinatha Basadi is located on the right side of the tank, locally known as Nagarakere or Nagaratirtha. The *basadi* consists of a *garbhagriha* (sanctum sanctorum), an *antarala* (vestibule), a four pillared *mahamandapa* (hall) and a thirty two-pillared *mukhamandapa*, all in north-south orientation. The *mukhamandapa* has entrances on its three sides. Slanted back-rest type arrangement is present on the parapet wall of the *mukhamandapa*. There is no image now in the *garbhagriha* but once there would have been a Jaina tirthankara image, probably of Shantinatha. The well-carved *antarala* doorway is provided with perforated *jalis* (screens) on its either side. This kind of *jali* work was very prominent during the Chalukyas times, specially the Kalyani Chalukyas. (Plate 6-5)

No foundation inscription is found for this *basadi*. The earliest inscription found in vicinity of the temple belongs to the Rashtrakuta period and dated 912 CE. However this inscription does not mention about this *basadi*. Therefore this date cannot be taken on its face value. The inscription mentions *sallekhana* of a lady at the Bandalike *tirtha*. However, it is confirmed that Bandalike had assumed the status of a Jaina *tirtha* by that time.

A later epigraph, dated 1200 CE, records repair and maintenance of Pancha Basadi of Hiriya-Mahalige, therefore it does not apply to this *basadi*. It is curious why such an inscription is engraved on a pillar of the *mandapa* of this *basadi* where it mentions repairs of another *basadi*. Another inscription dated 1204 CE, mentions grants and endowments by Boppa-setti, the ruler of Nagarakhanda-70 region, to this *basadi*.

Someswara Temple also referred as Anekal Somayya and Boppeswara temple was built by Boppa Setti, the ruler of Nagarakhanda-70, in 1274 CE. The temple consists of a *garbhagriha* (sanctum), an *antarala* (vestibule), a pillared *mandapa* (hall) with an insignificant porch, all arranged in east-west orientation. The porch has not survived. The entrance doorway to the *mandapa* had four *sakhas* (divisions). At the base of it are depicted *dvarapalas* and female figures. On the *lalatabimba* of the lintel is Gajalakshmi. On either side of the above door are highly ornate, sculptured, screens which have perforations alternating with narrative friezes depicting select episodes from epics, Ramayana and Mahabharata. The left side screen depicts episodes from the Ramayana, whereas the right side screen depicts episodes from the Mahabharata.

Inside the sanctum is a Sivalinga with Nandi in *antarala* facing the linga. The *antarala* doorway has two perforated screens on is either side. On the *lalatabimba* of *antarala* doorway is Siva in dancing *mudra*. He is accompanied with Ganesha, Brahma, Visnu and Mahishasuramardini. In the *mandapa* are provided niches, two each on either side but all are empty at present. Just behind this temple, there is a *mandapa* known as Mahanavami Mandapa. An inscription found here, dated 1207 CE, mentions grant from the Hoysala queen, Abhinava-Ketala-Devi, the wife of the Hoysala king, Ballala II.

Trimurti Narayana temple is the largest temple at Bandalike. This east facing temple is *trikutachala* (triple celled) in design. All the three cells are adorned with *antaralas* (*sukanasi*), which connect to a common *mandapa*. The tower of the western cell has fallen while the other two towers are in good state of preservation. West and south cells have Sivalingas while the northern cell has an image of Visnu. (Plate 6-6)

Harihar

Harihar is a town situated in Davangere district of Karnataka. The earliest historical reference comes from a Badami Chalukya grant of Vinayaditya, where mention of Hareshpura is found. B L Rice narrates a tradition about an *asura* (demon), named Guhasura, who had his capital at Harihar, on the bank of Tungabhadra. His kingdom was so big that its eastern gate was at Uchchangi-durga, the southern at Govinahalu, the western at Mudanur and the northern at Airani. By performing severe penance, he got a boon from Brahma that he could not be killed by Visnu or Siva in their individual capacity. This made him almost invincible.

To put an end of all his cruelties, Siva and Visnu took a combined form, Harihara, combining half-Visnu and half-Siva characteristics. The descent of Harihara happened at Kudalur, at the confluence of Tungabhdra and Haridra rivers, where there are some impressions on the rock which local people point out as the footprints of Harihara. On the request from the dying demon, the place was named Guharanya kshetra. Praise of lord Harihara is found in an inscription dated 1224 CE

The earliest historical occupation of this town appears to be that of the Kadambas. After the defeat of the Kadambas at the hands of the Pallavas, the place would have been under their regent till it was taken back by the Kalyani Chalukyas. Pandya, claiming their Yadava ancestry, defeated the Chalukyas in the middle of twelfth century CE. But their rule did not last for long as the Hoysalas wrestled it from the Pandyas.

The town is famous and known from Harihareswara temple which is the main attraction here. There are many other monuments of later period in the town.

- Harihar was an early Harihara worship centre as the earliest historical reference of the place is of the Badami Chalukyan period. There is no foundation inscription found in the temple. Statements from various historians about the renovation and construction are given below.
- Henry Cousens mentions that the temple was built by Polava, a minister of Hoysala king Narasimha II, in 1224 CE.
- Adam Hardy mentions that the temple was rebuilt by Poladeva-dandanayaka, an officer of Hoysala king Narasimha II in 1124 CE.
- R Gopal (referring to Mysore Archaeology Report 1937) mentions that the Hoysala king Narasimha II made a grant to this temple.
- Shrinivas V Padigar mentions that the temple underwent extensive renovation under the patronage of Somanatha-dandanayaka, a general of the Hoysala king Narasimha III, who also built the Kesava temple at Somanathapur.

It is very probable that the original temple was of very small proportions, and the present complex which we see today was built in the Hoysala period. The temple faces east and has a *garbhagriha*, *antarala*, *mandapa* and *mahamandapa*.

Mahamandapa is supported on 58 pillars and has five openings, two each on north and south and one on east. This is not a closed *mandapa* but an open one with its wall rising to half height and the remaining space is left open for air to pass through. On the top of these half walls, a stone is placed in slanted position appearing like a back-rest of a seat. This kind of open *mandapa* style is observed at many temples of Kalyani Chalukya and Hoysala period. (Plate 6-7)

The central block of *mahamandapa* ceiling is split into nine parts using four cross-beams. Eight portions or panels of it are occupied with *ashtadikpalas* (eight directional regents) riding over their respective mounts. The ninth and central part had a Harihara image which was later removed and placed in shrine at the rear of the temple. *Mandapa*, which is connected to the *mahamandapa* on the east, is supported on four central pillars and has an opening at north and south.

The main image of lord Harihara, in *garbhagriha*, is badly mutilated as all the original arms are lost. A stone screen is placed to cover up his lower portion as it is lost. The most striking feature of the icon which helps date its original portions is the presence of a single-beaded necklace and absence of *yajnopavita*. Padigar dates this image to fifth-sixth century CE. The tower of the temple is lost. There are many Hoysala inscriptions found at Harihar. These all inscriptions are detailed in Epigraphia Carnatica vol XI (original series).

Tilvalli

Tilivalli is a small village in Hangul taluk of Haveri district of Karnataka. J Burgess counted 16 inscriptions at the village. Dharwad gazetteer mentions twenty-six inscriptions here.

Santeswara temple is an east facing temple and consists of a *mandapa*, *antarala* and a *garbhagriha*. The temple is 75 feet long and 57 feet wide. The *mandapa* is supported on 44 pillars, and provided with three entrances, one each at east, north and south. (Plate 6-8)

Central ceiling of the *mandapa* has *ashtadikpalas* on its offsets. *Antrala* doorway is provided with perforated panels on either side. Door jambs are plain and devoid of any sculptures. There are niches provided on either side of the doorway and as well of the side walls, north and south. Southern niche has *Saptamatrikas*, western left niche has a modern *veena* player sculpture. Right western niche has Mahishasuramardini while the northern niche has some modern sculptures.

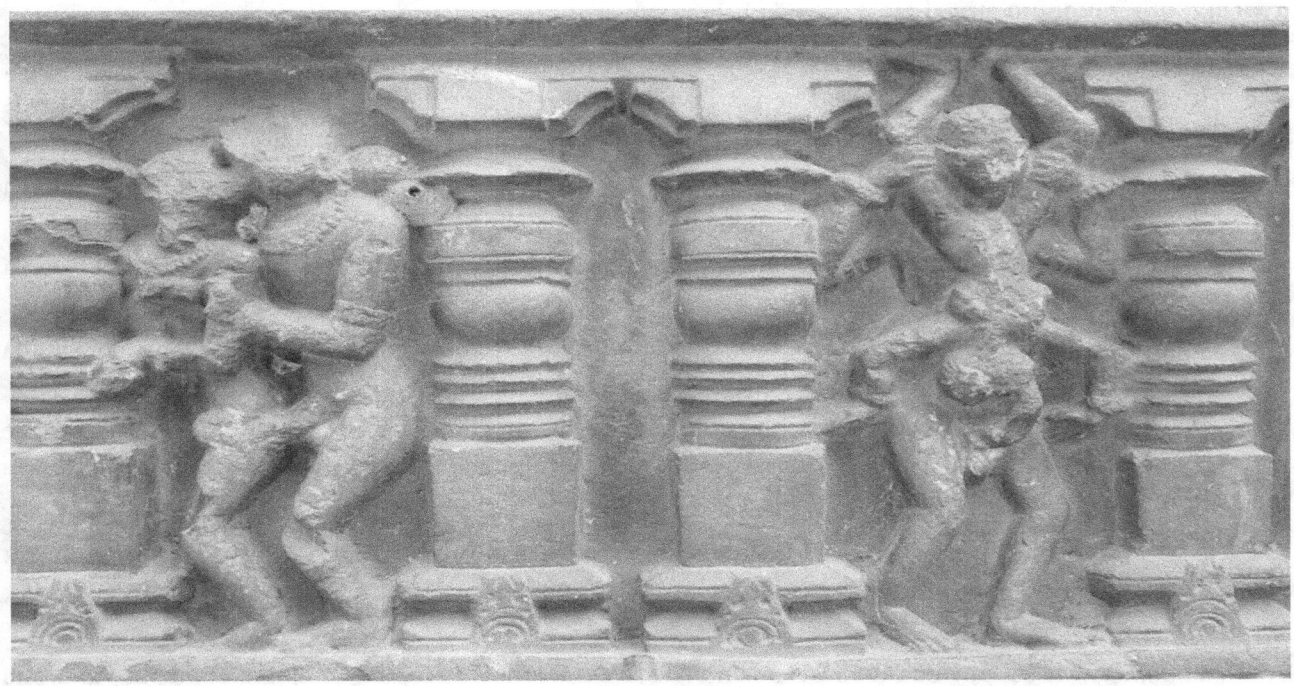

Amorous Couple, Tilvalli

As per an inscription, the temple was constructed by Savanta Kalideva, a subordinate of the Suena king Singhana II, in memory of his father in 1237 CE. The temple was referred as Savanteswara and the priests were from *kalamukha* lineage.

6.2 GADAG AND LAKKUNDI SCHOOL OF ARCHITECTURE

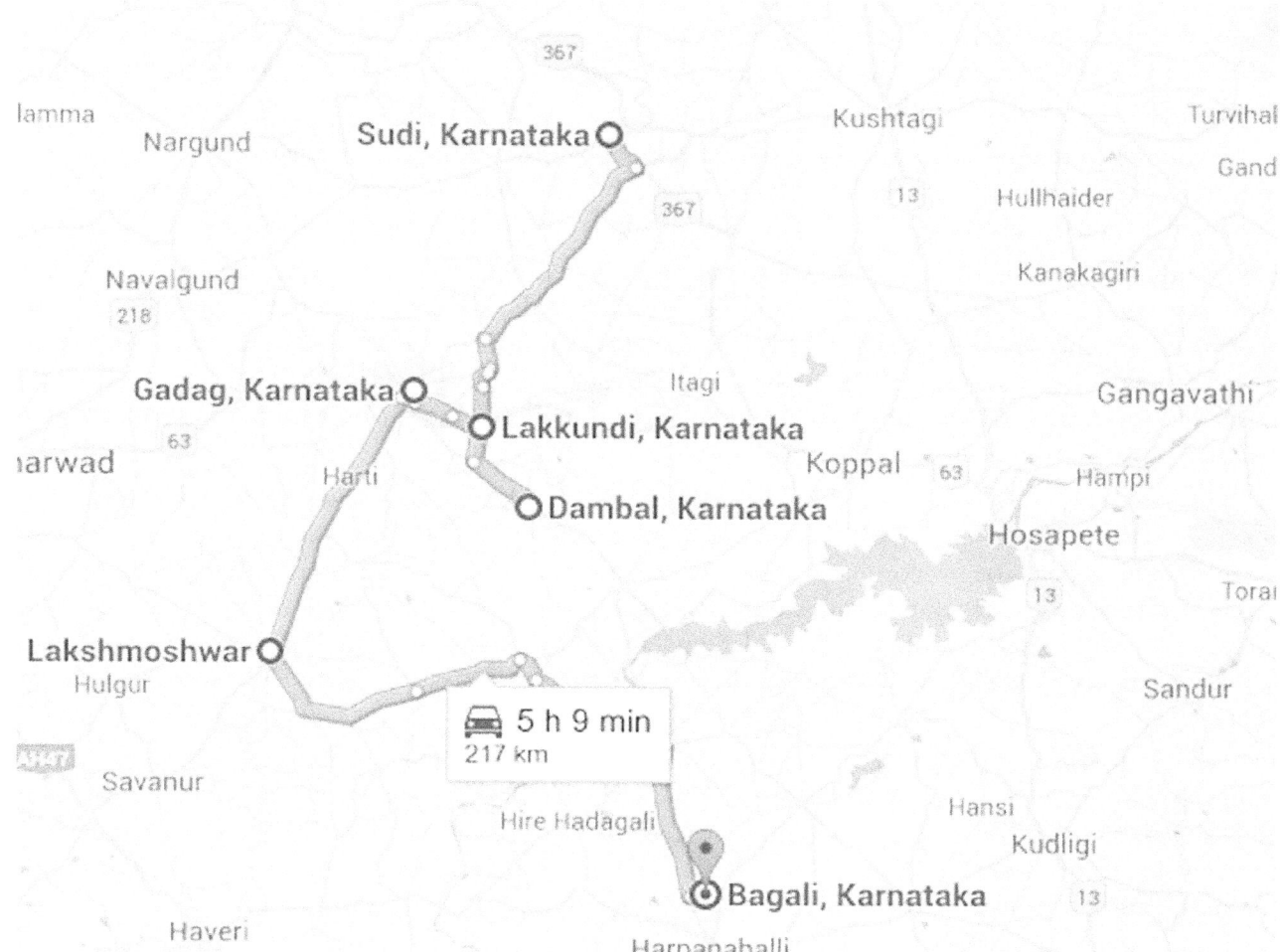

Gadag

Gadag is the main town of the district bearing the same name. Before the formation of a separate district, the town was part of Dharwad district which was the part of Bombay Presidency during the British times. Dharwad Gazetteer mentions that the town was described as a *Maha-agrahara* founded by Janamejaya of the Mahabharata times.

During the reign of the Kalyani Chalukyas in the eleventh century CE, the town was known as Kardugu as mentioned in the earliest inscription dated 1002 CE found here. It was situated in Belvola-300 region. The name changes to Galdugu during the reign of Vikramaditya VI in the start of the twelfth century CE.

During the reign of the Yadavas at the end of twelfth century CE, the name changes to Kratupura and the god in the principal temple here is referred as Swyambhu Madhaveswara. However, from the times of Siddhanti-Chandrabhushana-pandita-deva, who later became the *rajaguru* of the Hoysalas, the god is referred as Swyambhu-Trikuteswara. From the start of the thirteenth century CE, the town was known as Gadugu. The present name, Gadag, is a derivation of this name.

During the Kalyani Chalukyas' times Gadag, being a prominent *kalamukha* centre, was abuzz with architectural activity. Many artists from this town were involved in construction of temples at other sites. Nagoja was such artist who worked in the Chennakesava temple at Belur. Inscriptions suggest that Nagoja hailed from Gadag and was a devotee of the god Trikuteswara.

There are many temples and other religious structures at Gadag, but only a few of considerable antiquity remain now. Scholars aver that Gadag temples are examples of the 'local style' created in northern Karnataka in the twelfth century CE in an interaction between idioms of the Tungabhadra region and Hoysala style. Where the Someswara temple shows the amalgamation of the local style with the Hoysala, the Rameswara temple is strictly in the local style.

Trikuteswara temple complex is located in the southern part of the city at present which was part of a fort in the past. However there are very few vestiges of this fort left at present. There are two main temples and a tank inside the complex. Trikuteswara is the main temple of the complex. (Plate 6-9)

The temple was built as a double temple having two shrines facing each other. The principal shrine faces east and has two *mandapas*, a small closed *mandapa* followed by a large *mandapa*. With this large *mandapa* is attached the second shrine facing the principal shrine. The entrance to the temple was provided from the *mandapas*, the one on the north is later closed by building a shrine against that. The principal shrine has three Sivalingas set upon a single *pitha*. This is probably the reason why the name of the god is Trikuteswara, the lord of three mountains.

The interior of the temple is very simple and devoid of any decoration. However the exterior is in quite contrast. A distinctive feature which is witnessed in many temples of this period, open space between the parapet wall and beam below cornice is absent here. This open space is usually adorned with slanted slabs similar to back-rest seats. But in this temple, this space is closed with perforated stone screens. These perforated screens are decorated with medallions and have openings on each alternate square section. James Fergusson puts the temple as one of the most complete illustrations of the Kalyani Chalukya style of architecture.

The top part of the basement has stone slabs sloping outwards. The part below has been carved with panels depicting *sikharas* separated with pilasters. Under the *sikhara* are shown dancers, musicians, demigods, gods, ascetics and elephants. Continuous whitewash over a long period has resulted in the obliteration of the major features of these figures. The *sikhara* over the principal shrine is of later origin built in brick and mortar. The *sikhara* over the eastern shrine has not survived or it was never there.

Saraswati Temple is situated within the same complex as of the Trikuteswara temple. It is situated on the south of Trikuteswara temple facing north. The entrance is provided from the north. Henry Cousens states that some of the best works of the Kalyani Chalukyan style are seen in this temple. Apart from the outer decoration, particular attention is to be attributed to the pillars supporting the *mandapa* as these are the best specimen of the Kalyani Chalukyan work.

The temple is constructed on a simple plan, consisting of a *garbhagriha*, *antarala* and a *mandapa*. The *mandapa* is supported on fourteen pillars. Four pillars supporting the central ceiling are in one pattern and the remaining are executed in pairs. The central ceiling is worth noticing as it reflects the wooden construction techniques which were followed before stone was used in temple construction. The ceiling has ribs crossing and re-crossing each others. Lotus pendants hang at their intersections.

The central four pillars have base similar to the basements seen on temples of this period. These are square at base, recessing to octagon and then to round near the capital. The facets of the square and octagonal sections are decorated with miniature carvings however these are much defaced and deteriorated. The facets on octagonal sections have images of *ashtadikpalas* (eight directional guardians). (Plate 6-10)

The two pillars standing on either side of the entrance are the most elaborately worked of all, and there are, perhaps, no other pillar throughout the whole extent of Kalyani Chalukyan craft left which are equal to these for the crowded abundance of minute work which covers their surfaces. The ornaments consists of repetitions of miniature shrines, tiny pilasters, panels containing Lilliputian gods, goddesses and attendants, rampant lions, and host of other details. Inside the *garbhagriha* (sanctum) is placed a mutilated image of goddess Saraswati. The image is quite large in size and resting above a pedestal. All her hands are broken away.

Someswara Temple at present is not in use and probably abandoned long back. The temple is simple in plan consisting of a *garbhagriha*, *antarala*, a *mandapa* with two porches attached to that. The temple is carved profusely all around however the repetitions across make it rather monotonous. Scheme of miniature shrines is used across the base of the temple. Wall above the basement has panels depicting various gods. *Sikhara* of the shrine is lost except its remaining three stories. There is a Sivalinga inside the *garbhagriha*.

Rameswara temple is situated near the Someswara temple. The temple is in much deteriorated condition. It is devoid of external decoration.

Veeranarayana temple is the main temple at present in Gadag. The temple was built during the Kalyani Chalukya times however it received continuous patronage till the Vijayanagara rulers. Kannada poet Kumara Vyasa composed his monumental work in this temple sitting before the image of the god. The temple is located within a huge complex. Photography is not allowed inside hence no pictures are attached except the temple entrance. However there is nothing much of interest as well. The old structures are overshadowed by modern constructions.

There is a museum in Gadag which is maintained by Karnataka State Archaeological Department. It is a big museum having various galleries and housing many artifacts. One can purchase books published by department from here.

Dharwad Gazetteer mentions about 34 inscriptions found at Gadag, the earliest inscription from the Rashtrakuta king Indra III dated 918 CE. While some of these are scattered all over Gadag and Betigere, many others cannot be located.

Lakkundi

Lakkundi is a small village in Gadag district of Karnataka. The village is referred as Lokkigundi in its inscriptions. It is said to be a *maha-agrahara* settlement consisting of one thousand *mahajanas*. As per legends, this *agrahara* was established by Rama of the Ramayana period. The earliest inscription found here is of the Kalyani Chalukya period. This and the other major earlier inscriptions are of Jaina order which suggest influence of Jainism in this area during those times.

In the later period of the Kalyani Chalukyas, the Kalachuris ruled over this region as their feudatories. After the Kalyani Chalukyas, the region came under the Suenas (Yadavas of Devagiri). They patronized various Siva temples here. During the Kalyani Chalukya times, Lakkundi had a royal mint as evidenced from its inscription. A part of earnings from the mint was donated to the temples here.

In 1192 CE, the great Hoysala king Ballala II established himself at Lakkundi as his capital. According to a tradition, between 1187 and 1192 Lakkundi was the scene of a battle between Ballala II and Jaitugi, the son of Suena king Bhillama. In this battle, Jaitugi is said to have lost. Since then the region was under the rule of the Hoysala kings. About thirty-five inscriptions have been found at Lakkundi, which describe the history of temple building activity in the town.

As per the Bombay gazetteer, the important temples at Lakkundi were: Chandramauleswara, Ganesha, Gokarneswara, Halagund Basavanna, Iswara, Kashivishveswara, Kumbhargiriswara (or Nadayadeva), Lakshminarayana, Mallikarjuna, Manikeswara, Nagardewara, Nanneswara, Nilkantheswara, Someswara, Virabhadra, Virupaksha and Vishvanatha. A list of eleven of these temples can be found at the Lakkundi Heritage Centre under the control of ASI.

Brahma-Jinalaya an east facing temple is the oldest Jaina temple at Lakkundi. The temple consists of a *garbhagriha*, *antarala*, *navaranga*, an open *mandapa* and *mukhamandapa*. Balustrade entrance flanked the *mukhamandapa*. The open *mandapa* is supported on twenty-eight pillars. As observed in other Kalyani Chalukya period temples, there is no slanted-backrest seating like arrangement in this open *mandapa*. *Navaranga* has four pillars in center to support the ceiling above the central stage.

The *antarala* doorway has Gajalakshmi on its *lalata bimba*. The *garbhagriha* doorway has an image of Mahavira on its *lalata bimba*. The *garbhagriha* is a square sanctuary and it houses a Mahavira image standing above a *simha*-pedestal. On his left is shown Yakshi Padmavati and on his left is a *yaksha*.

Inside the *navaranga*, on either side of the *antarala* doorway, are placed two exquisite sculptures, one of Padmavati and one of four-faced Brahma. Brahma is shown standing in *sambhaga* posture. He is shown with his four heads and four hands. Because of this image, the temple is probably known as Brahma-Jinalaya.

The *sikhara* of this temple is very noteworthy. It is constructed in three stories topped with a crowning member. The first story is taller than the above two stories. It rises above the *garbhagriha* and provides a cavity for another smaller *garbhagriha*. It is topped with two stories of same design. The crowning member is square in shape and has a pot-finial above it. The whole scheme is executed in *Dravidian* style.

There is another small temple on the north of the main temple. The *mandapa* of the temple has not survived. An image of Mahavira, with broken head, is placed over the platform of the *mandapa*. The *sikhara* of the temple is also lost. As per an inscription, it was constructed by Attiyabbe, the wife of chief Nagadeva, in about 1007 CE. Her son is said to be governing the Masavadi country. The temple was under the priesthood of Archanandi-pandita who belonged to Surasthagana of Mulasangha of Digambar order. (Plate 6-11)

Kashi Vishvanatha (also kknown as Kasi Visveswara) temple has two temples joined by a *mandapa* which at some point of time was covered with a roof above it. The main temple is a Siva temple and faces east. It has a *grabhagriha*, *antarala*, *mandapa* and a porch. Entrance to the *mandapa* is provided on its east and south. (Plate 6-12)

The entrance on the south is an exquisite piece of art and style. It is very elaborately carved and designed. Each doorjamb has eight *sakhas*, with a pilaster in middle. On either side, at the bottom are shown nine guardians and *dvarapalas*. Gajalakshmi adorns the *lalata bimba*. Above the lintel are arranged eleven or twelve male figures either representing *ekadasha* (eleven) Rudras of *dvadasha* (twelve) Adityas, out of which only three have survived. Being a Siva temple, Rudras would be more appropriate here.

The eastern doorway of the *mandapa* rivals in execution with the southern doorway. It has total six *sakhas* and two intermittent pilasters. Gajalakshmi adorns its *lalata bimba*. Many perforated sections are carved on these *sakhas*. It would have been a highly skilled and patient job to execute on these perforated sections. Inside the *mandapa* are found *Saptamatrikas* and Ganesha on either side of the *antarala* doorway. The *garbhagriha* doorway lintel has Siva in middle with Brahma and Vishnu on either side. Siva is shown with Parvati. Below these figures are placed fighting scenes of horses and elephants having rider on few. Inside the *garbhagriha* is a Sivalinga. The god is referred as Kavataleswara and Kavatala-Chamundeswara in inscriptions.

The external walls of the temple are decorated with various sculptures. Among these Ravana lifting mount Kailasa, Siva slaying Gajasura, Bhima fighting with Bhagadatta, Ravana fighting with Indra etc. are notable. These sculptures are much mutilated and spoiled. Noteworthy are the majority of elephant fight themed sculptures on these external walls and presence of elephants on the lintel of the *garbhagriha*.

The other temple, facing opposite to Kashi Vishvanatha temple, is dedicated to Surya. Both these temples are connected by a high raised platform which would have borne ceiling at some point of time. This Surya temple faces west. *Mandapa* doorway lintel depicts Surya with Usha and Pratyusha. Surya is shown in his high boots.

Around the *vimana*, on central niches of all sides, horses of Surya are still intact though the niches are empty now. Inside the *garbhagriha* is a pedestal over which seven horses of Surya with charioteer Aruna are left but image of Surya is missing.

Nanneswara temple built on a high-rising *jagati* stands opposite to Kashi Vishvanatha temple complex on the other side of the road. It consists of an open *mandapa*, closed *mandapa*, *antarala* and *garbhagriha*. The open *mandapa* is supported on sixteen pillars. Entrance to the closed *mandapa* is provided on the east and south. (Plate 6-13)

Southern entrance doorway is devoid of any decoration except plain jambs. *Dvarapalas* are stand at the bottom on a separate pilaster attached to the doorway. Gaja Lakshmi is present on *lalata bimba*. The closed *manda*pa doorway is decorated with three *sakhas* with pilasters on either side. *Dvarapalas* stand here also at the bottom. Gaja Lakshmi is present on *lalata bimba.*

Neelakantha temple, a ruined temple has lost its *sikhara* and *mandapa* walls. There are stones placed over the walls that give the temple an interesting appearance.

Manikeswara temple is a big temple complex as it also houses a *pushkarni* (tank), locally known as Muskinabhavi. This is a *trikuta* (triple-celled) temple. *Sikharas* of all the cells are lost. The main cell houses a Sivalinga. The common *mandapa* is fronted with a porch supported on four front pillars. Perforated panels are present on either side of the *antarala* door-jambs of all the cells. External walls are devoid of any sculptures. Miniature shrines are present on the south and north *vimanas*. (Plate 6-14)

Naganatha temple is a Jaina temple which is now converted into a Hindu shrine. It consists of a front proch, a closed *mandapa*, *antarala* and *garbhagriha*. The porch is supported on two front pillars. The *mandapa* doorway lintel has Gaja Lakshmi. *Mandapa* is supported on four central pillars. The *garbhagriha* has Parshvanatha on its *lalata bimba*. Inside the *garbhagriha*, the snake canopy and pedestal of the original image remains and a Sivalinga is placed over this pedestal.

The Lakkundi Heritage Centre is a museum of sculpture and inscriptions collected from various sites in and around Lakkundi. A great amount of information on the art and architecture of the region can be gathered from here. The Centre is being managed by the Archaeological Survey of India (ASI). Eleven temples and monuments are under the supervision of ASI whereas a large number of them inside the town are protected monuments of the Archaeology Department of the State Government. Excavations at some sites are still being carried out.

Dambal

Dambal is located in Gadag district. The village would have acquired quite a respectable reputation as is evident from the inscriptions found in its near vicinity. It is one among very few places where we find a society patronizing all three major faiths, Hindu, Buddhists and Jaina, prevalent during the early and medieval period. The village has been referred as Dharmavolal and Dharmapura in inscriptions.

The earliest inscription found, dated 1059 CE, was from the reign of the Kalyani Chalukya king Someshvara I and mentions a grant to a Jaina shrine. Someshvara I patronized Shridharacharya who wrote a Jaina purana, Chandraprabhacharite. Shridharacharya might be, probably, responsible for the Jaina influence on the king. But, it is a fact that Jainism witnessed exponential growth during the Kalyani Chalukya rule. In comparison with Jainism, Buddhism did not grow at much pace however at time to time it found patronage from various dynasties. Few Buddhist inscriptions are also found here. As per an inscription, during the reign of the Western Chalukya king Vikramaditya VI two Buddhist monasteries were constructed by the merchant communities of Lakkundi and Dambal at Dambal. The Buddhist monasteries are not traceable now and the Jaina temple is almost lost except few ruins.

The two temples, of Dodda-Basappa and Someswara, are located opposite to each other. There is a ruined fort where ruins of old Jaina temple can be seen. There are no ruins of the Buddhist monasteries mentioned in the inscriptions.

Dodda Basappa temple is east facing temple and is famous for its stellar but almost circular *vimana*. The *vimana* not only has the stellar base buts its *sikhara* (tower) is in continuation with the original base stellar design. The star-points of this stellar plan are located too close together that it gives an impression of a circular structure. The temple consists of a *garbhagriha*, *antarala* and a *mandapa*. The *mandapa* has two openings, one on south and one on the east. (Plates 6–15 and 6–16)

Stellar base temples were mostly promoted by the Hoysala builders however the stellate plan was not their invention. There are temples, though very few, which exhibit the stellar base constructed prior to the Hoysala period. Dodda Basappa temple is among those very few examples. Henry Cousens explains the stellar plan of this temple as, "This is obtained by revolving a square about its center, its angles stopping at points equidistant from one another, the angles and re-entrants angles thus formed, being the perimeter of the plan. The shrine is planned on twenty-four salient angles, and the hall on thirty-two, but the continuity of these is broken where the shrine joins the hall and where the porches come."

Adam Hardy explains that this temple shows the evolution of hybrid of two styles of temple architecture into one structure. It has a *Latina sikhara* over a *Dravidian vimana*. Its stellate *vimana* base is formed by rotating a square around its centre resulting into a star having thirty-two points. The Latina *sikhara* has seven *talas* (storeys) of repeated style. The *vimana* is structured such that one right angle is divided into four angles of 22.5 degrees. 48 such angles are further sub divided and decorated with minute carvings.

There is a *torana* (architrave) before the *garbhagriha* entrance. Usually these *toranas* are placed outside the temple. Images above the lintel are missing but Henry Cousens suggests that these would be of the Hindu Trinity, Brahma, Visnu and Siva, as seen at other similar structures. The doorjambs have intricate carvings including figures of gods and goddesses, *naga naginis* and celestial beings. The *naga naginis* are entwined in complicated prime knots.

In the Kalyani Chalukya temples, usage of miniature shrines as the decorative device over the temple *vimana* was in vogue. In this temple also we see many miniature shrines on the temple walls and *adhishthana*. These shrines provide us very important information about the prevalent temple architecture styles of that time. In this temple we find these miniature temples in *Dravidian* and *Nagara* styles. There is no foundation inscription, the earliest inscription found is dated in 1148 CE and referred the lord as Malabeswara. This inscription is from the reign of the Kalyani Chalukya king Someshvara IV. It might be said that the temple would have been constructed during the 11th-12th century CE.

Someswara or Dabgadi temple is a Hindu temple. However its architecture and style suggests that it was a Jaina shrine originally. The temple has a *mandapa*, *antarala* and *garbhagriha*. The *mandapa* has entrance on its three sides. The *antarala* doorway has pierced stone *jail* at the doorjambs, the feature mostly seen in the Kalyani Chalukyan temples. An inscription found in the temple refers the god here as Madhaveswara.

Lakshmeshwar

Lakshmeswar is a town municipality in Gadag district in Karnataka. It was known as Purigere, Puligere, Hurigere, Huligere and Purikanagara in the past. There are more than fifty inscriptions found in and around Lakshmeswar making it possible to trace back the history of the town.

The earliest reference of the city comes in an inscription of the time of the Badami Chalukya king Pulakesin II (610–641 CE). After the Badami Chalukyas, it came under the Rashtrakutas ruling from Manyakheta or Malkhed. One inscription of the Rashtrakuta king Dhruva (780–793 CE) is found here. After the Rashtrakutas, Western Gangas ruled over this region. Three inscriptions of their dynasty are found here, all belonging to king Marasimha II (963–975 CE).

After the Western Gangas, Lakshmeswar came under the Kalyani Chalukya dominion. An inscription at Annigeri informs that the Cholas invaded the Kalyani Chalukya dominion during the reign of king Somesvara I and ravaged southern provinces and destroyed the city of Pulikaranagara, i.e. Lakshmeswar. The inscription asserts that the Chalukyas defeated the Cholas and stopped further incursions.

During the reign of the Western Chalukya king Vikramaditya VI (1076–1126 CE), Purigere was governed by Mahamandaleswara Lakshmarasa. Purigere division was included in a bigger and important division as it is told that Yuvaraja (Jayasimha III), younger brother of the Kalyani Chalukya king Vikramaditya VI (1076–1126 CE), was governing the divisions along with Banavasi-12000, Purigere-300, Belvola-300, Santalige-1000 and Kandur-1000.

The Kalachuris governed the region as the feudatories under the Kalyani Chalukyas. A Brahmapuri was established during the reign of the Kalachuri king Bijjala in 1166 CE. After them it was the Seunas and after them the Hoysalas. Many inscriptions of the Seunas are found here but no Hoysala inscription is found.

Lakshmeswar is also famous for Pampa or Adi Pampa, the first Kannada writer. He was born in 902 CE. His father abandoned Brahmanism to adopt Jainism. Pampa became the court-poet and a minister under a prince named Arikesari whose court was situated at Lakshmeswar. Arikesari claimed to be a descendant from the early Badami Chalukyas but was then a feudatory under the Rashtrakutas.

It is here in Lakshmeswar that Pampa composed his two poems which made him eternal in the history of the Kannada literature. These two compositions were Adi Purana and Vikramarjuna Vijaya or Pampa Bharata.

From its earliest inscriptions till the last few, Lakshmeswar was all described as a Jaina centre. One of the earliest Kannada dynasty, the Badami Chalukyas, patronized several Jaina temples at this site. The earliest one seems to be the Sankha Basadi which has an inscription assignable to the reign of Pulakesin II (609–642 CE). The priesthood at that time was in the hands of the priest hailing from Devagana of Mulasangha.

Sankha Basadi received continuous patronage under the Badami Chalukyas till the time of Vikramaditya II (733–746 CE). It is also said that the sister of the Badami Chalukya king Vijayaditya constructed a Jaina temple, Anesejjeya Basadi. The priests of this temple seem to hail from Surastragana as is evident from an inscription of the Kalyani Chalukya time. The inscription mentions *nirvana* of two priests by observing *sallekhana*.

The Jaina temples of Lakshmeswar regained the impetus under the Western Gangas. During the times of the Western Gangas, Ganga-Kandarp-Jinalaya was patronized along with Sankha Basadi. Ganga-Kandarp-Jinalaya might have been constructed by Marasimha II. The priesthood was put into the charge of priests hailing from Balakaragana of Mulasangha.

Sankha Basadi is the earliest Jaina *basadi* in Lakshmeswar. Though it is not certain when it was founded however it was in existence in the seventh century CE as is evident from inscriptions found here. The temple received continuous patronage from the Badami Chalukya kings from Pulakesi II to Vikramaditya II. The god is referred as Sankha-Jinendra in an inscription of the Badami Chalukya king Pulakesin II (610–642 CE). The temple seems to belong to Mulasangha monastic order of Jainism which is synonymous with Digambar Jaina order in today's parlance.

Dhruvadevacharya was the main priest of the temple during the time of the Badami Chalukya king Vinayaditya (680–696 CE). He is said to belong to Mulasangha and Devagna. Devagana is one among the four different *ganas* organized and defined by Acharya Arhadbali.

The present structure is the result of recent conservation and renovation. Now it is known as Neminatha Basadi, conch (*sankha*) being Neminatha's symbol therefore it was known as Sankha Basadi in earlier days. It is entered through a big hall, in front of which a high *dipastambha* is erected. This hall seems to have been constructed during the Kalyani Chalukya times. All around the hall is a low parapet wall, which instead of being open is closed on top with pierced window panels.

The space between the parapet wall and window panels is carved with different images of amorous couples, musicians and dancers. Entrance to this hall is provided on three sides. The *sikhara* of the temple is a modern structure.

This large hall is connected to another hall which is smaller in size. This smaller hall would be contemporaneous with the original temple. At present this is reconstructed with original material wherever possible. This hall is connected to the sanctum with an ante-chamber. Inside the sanctum is an image of Neminatha, the 22nd Jaina Thirthankara. It is said that Adi Kavi Pampa composed his Adi Purana seated in this *basadi*.

Anantanatha Basadi is a *trikuta* (triple celled) structure which can be assigned to the Kalyani Chalukya period. The *sikhara* is constructed in the Chalukya *Phamsana* style. A standing image of Anantnatha, the fourteenth Jaina Tirthankara, is kept in the sanctum. The other cells have Parshvanatha and a Jina. All the three cells are connected to a central hall via ante-chambers. This is a live temple and various modern images are installed around.

There are many different *basadis* found in inscriptions which are not traceable at present. The *basadis* finding mention in the inscriptions but are not traceable include Anesejjeya Basadi, Ganga Kandarpa Jinalaya and Permadi Basadi.

Someswara temple finds reference in an inscription dated 1102 CE where god is referred as Muddeswara and Swayambhu Someswara. The Acharya at that time was Mahendrasoma-pandita. Later the god is also referred as Swaymbhu Somanatha or Dakshina Somanatha. (Plate 6-17)

This east facing temple has a large *rangamandapa* which has three entrances, west, south and north. With an ante-chamber, it is connected to another smaller *mandapa* which also has entrance on south and north. These entrances are adorned with porches on outside. The ante-chamber also has entrances on either side.

The external walls have suffered much deterioration. There would have been an arrangement of *ashtadikpalas* on the exterior, only few of these remain, that too in much damaged condition. The image inside the sanctum is unique as instead of Siva represented in his linga form; he is shown here riding over Nandi which is standing over a pedestal.

There seems to be a *ghatika* attached to this temple as grants were made to take care of it. *Ghatika* is an educational institution where Vedic studies were pursued. 13th century witnessed renovation of the temple under Acharya Nageswara who hailed from Saurashtra. It appears that the construction of the temple was motivated from the Somanatha temple in Gujarat. The idea was to introduce Somanatha in Lakshmeswar hence it was referred as Dakshina Somanatha. A dancing girl quarter was attached to the temple. An inscription of the time of Vikramaditya VI, repairs were made to this quarter.

There are many other temples and deities mentioned in inscriptions which are not traceable at present which include Rameswara temple, Kattameswaradeva temple, Swayambhu Lakshmaneswara temple, Virabhadra temple and Kedaradeva temple.

Bagali

It would be hard to explain and understand that how a village, which remained a centre of attraction almost for about six centuries, lost its glory and went into oblivion. Bagali narrates its story in about forty-five odd inscriptions spanning across six centuries and four great dynasties, though at present it has been reduced to a small village. The earliest inscription found here is of the early ninth century CE pertaining to the times of the Rashtrakutas. Later inscriptions are of the Chalukyas of Kalyana, Hoysalas and Vijayanagara rulers. Bagali is referred as Balaguli in inscriptions. Though most of the inscriptions relate to the Hindu traditions and monuments; there is one inscription that talks about a Jaina teacher and a corresponding grant. This suggests that both the religions co-existed at some time, though Jaina faith was not the major one.

Kalleswara temple is built close to the embankment of a huge old tank. The temple has a *garbhagriha*, *antarala*, a *mahamandapa* and a large sized *sabhamandapa*. The temple faces east and has two openings, south and east, one each for the *sabhamandapa* and *mahamandapa*.

Mahamandapa has four central pillars. Few kalyani Chalukyan sculptures are kept in the *mahamandapa* of the temple. These sculptures are of Siva, Umamaheswara, Ganesha, Karttikeya, Surya, Anantasayana, Saraswati and Mahishasuramardini.

The *antarala* doorway is formed with a *makaratorana* supported on two free standing pillars. The *makaratorana* forms five loops resulting in five reliefs. Visnu and Brahma occupy the terminal reliefs while the central relief being Siva as Gajantaka with Natesa over *apsamara*, and Siva in *chaturatandava* on either side. A small image of Nandi is placed in this *mandapa* facing the *garbhagriha*.

The connecting doorway between the *sabhamandapa* and *mahamandapa* has Rati and Kamadeva on both sides of the door jambs. *Sabhamandapa* is supported on fifty-two pillars where each pillar is different in style and execution. The square base of these pillars have miniature images which reflect the superior Hoysala workmanship. (Plate 6-18)

North of the *sabhamandapa* has been extended to form a shrine housing Ugra Narasimha image. The central ceiling of this *mandapa* is ornately carved with the figures of the *ashtadikpalas* (eight directional guardians).

Opposite to the *sabhamandapa*, in east-west axis, detached to the main shrine is another small shrine dedicated to Surya. An inscription found here belonging to the Kalyani Chalukya king Ahavamalla (Tailapa II) and dated 987 CE, mentions consecration of lord Adityadeva which probably is the god enshrined in this shrine. As this temple would have been constructed only after the main shrine; the main Kalleswara temple would have been constructed probably in the early ninth century CE during the Rashtrakuta period. An inscription dated in 1031 CE, is the earliest inscriptional reference to god Kalideva. (Plates 6–19 and 6–20)

This temple is known as the Khajuraho of south India due to few erotic images found on the external walls of its *vimana*. However, the execution and style of these images is not of the same aesthetics and workmanship as those at Khajuraho temples. The images found here depict weird erotic practices, which probably would remain an enigma to everyone.

Sudi

Sudi is a small town in Gadag district of Karnataka. It is referred as Sundi in inscriptions. The earliest reference of Sudi comes in Kalyani Chalukya inscription where it appears that Kuskudi would have been an important region as it was governed by Akkadevi, sister of the Kalyani Chalukya king Vikramaditya V.

In an inscription dated 1069 CE Sudi is mentioned as *rajdhani* Sundi while the governor was the Nolamba king Permanadi Singanadeva, who was a feudatory of the Kalyani Chalukya king Bhuvanaikanalldeva (Somesvara II). It enjoyed the status of the capital town till at least 1084 CE where it is mentioned as *rajdhani* Sundi in an inscription of the Kalyani Chalukya king Vikramaditya VI.

Dharwad gazetteer mentions that the goldsmiths of this town were licensed to mint coins and foremost among them was the royal mint master Uttavoja who struck coins for Vikramaditya VI. An inscription mentions gift of gold by Uttavoja during the reign of the Kalyani Chalukya king Vikramaditya VI.

A Kalchuri inscription found here mentions that Kiskadu (same as Kuskudi of Kalyani Chalukya times) was governed by Sinda chiefs. Later it was governed by local chiefs under the patronage of Seunas. Ultimately it would have passed to Hoysalas but no Hoysala inscription is found here. There are two main temples and three small stand-alone *mandapas* in Sudi. The small *mandapas* either have Nandi or a Sivalinga enshrined. There is also a *kunda* or *kalyani* (tank) in the town near the *mandapas*. A well rounded image of Ganesha is housed in a small shrine in the same compound.

Adam Hardy takes Sudi school of art as a distinguished school with examples like Jodu Kalasa and Mallikarjuna temples in Sudi and Kalleswara temple in Kuknur. He distinguishes the Sudi school from Lakkundi school but there are not many examples of the former in contrast to many found for the latter school. The major difference between these two schools is the treatment of smaller shrines (aedicule) on the *vimana* wall.

Panchalingadeva finds mention in an inscription dated 1113 CE and states that on the north of the town of Sudi, there are several sanctuaries dedicated to the god Panchalingadeva installed by Pandava brethren. Many names of various gods are found in inscriptions. These are Akkeswara, Achaleswara, Nageswara, Kammateshwra and Chakeswara.

Akkeswara is the present day Mallikarjuna temple and Nageswara is probably Jodu Kalasa temple. The other three might be scattered around Sudi. Someshvara-panditadeva is mentioned in an inscription dated 1069 CE with regards to Achaleshvara temple. Someshvara-panditadeva is again mentioned in an inscription dated 1075 CE when a village named Musiyagere was granted to him for the benefit of god Panchalingadeva. Someshvara-panditadeva is again mentioned in another inscription dated 1084 CE and the god mentioned is Achaleswara. All these inscriptional records suggest that all these five temples were in existence at nearly the same time under the priesthood of one person.

The front portion of Mallikarjuna temple is much renovated as it is a live temple. Front *mandapa*, which is open on three sides, is supported on ten pillars, eight pillars supporting the main roof and two supporting a projecting porch. It is a *trikuta* temple where three shrines share a common *mandapa* (hall). This common closed *mandapa* is supported on four pillars. Restoration work in currently on in the temple complex. (Plate 6-21)

A *makaratorana* is setup in front of the main *garbhagriha* (sanctum), which is dedicated to Siva. A small Nandi is placed between the *torana* and the sanctum. The *torana* has Brahma, Siva and Visnu on its lintel. Similar *toranas* are setup in front of other shrines but all not carved. Shrine on north has Umamaheswara while shrine on south has Visnu as Anantasayana. *Ashtadikpala* and all ten incarnations of Visnu can be seen on the *prabhavali* around Visnu.

The *mandapa* and eastern shrine is connected with an *antarala* (vestibule) or *sukanasi*. However there is no Hoysala emblem on top of this. As no Hoysala inscription is found here, it may be surmised that this temple was not patronized under their rule.

An inscription dated 1054 CE mentions that the constitution of the temple was set up by various officers assembled at Vikramapura. The deity is referred as Akkeswara, which would have been drawn from Akkadevi, the governor sister of the Kalyani Chalukya king Vikramaditya V. Therefore it can be said with certainty that this temple was constructed in or around 1054 CE.

Jodu Kalasa temple has two *garbhagrihas* (sanctums) sharing a common *mandapa*. The *mandapa* has entrances on north and south. *Sikharas* on both the sides, east and west, are intact in their full glory with *kalasa* and finial. It is built on a high raised platform (*jagati*). The eastern shrine has a Sivalinga inside. A unique feature of this *garbhagriha* is that there is *makaratorana* on the back wall. A huge Nandi is placed in *mandapa* facing the eastern shrine this suggests that the eastern shrine was the principal among both. The western shrine is empty at present. (Plate 6-22)

The god is referred as Nageswara and the priest was Someshvara-panditadeva An inscription dated 1069 CE mentions that "Nagadeva, the Emperor's (Kalyani Chalukya king Somesvara I) agreeable High Minister, foremost among councilors, radiant with brilliant glory, raised in the excellent town of Sundi for Nageswara a surpassing dwelling pre-eminent in the whole world, so that the (people of the) earth praised it, saying that it is loftier than Himalayas or Kutkila, likewise more spacious than the great Silver Mountain (Kailasa)."

The inscription also mentions that Nagadeva constructed on each side of the temple white plastered buildings such as might be called nest of gods, and a quarter for public women. It further mentions that Nagadeva caused to be dug a pond which may be said to exceed in greatness the Milk Ocean and Manasa lake.

The temple is not being maintained properly, it is protected under the Karnataka State Archaeological and Museums Department. Hopefully efforts will be made soon to restore the temple to its full glory and conserve this heritage.

6.3 THE TUNGABHADRA CIRCUIT

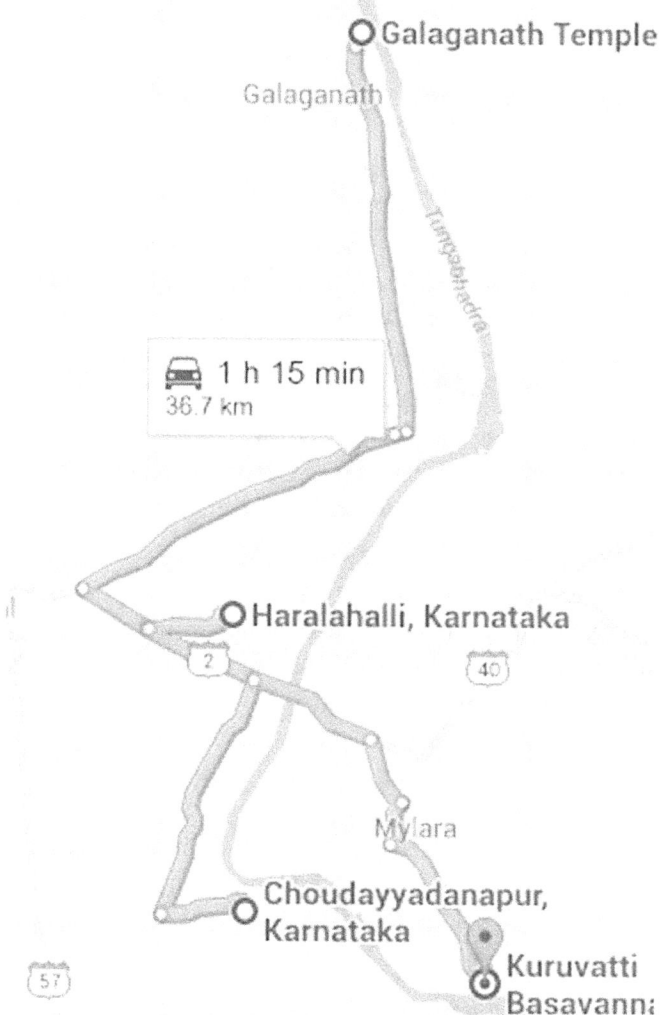

Galaganatha: Galaganatha is a small village in Haveri district located on the west bank of Tungabhadra River near the *sangama* (confluence) of that river with another river, Varada. The town is referred as Hulluni or Pulluni in its inscriptions. The present name Galaganatha seems to have come after the construction of the temple where the god enshrined inside is referred as Galgeswara.

Galaganatha is famous for its Galgeswara temple which enshrines a *sparshalinga*. A legend mentions that if you place an iron rod near the linga and worship lord Siva then the iron will turn into gold. A king when came to know about it, covered the linga with a *galaga*. Somnath temple in Gujarat is famous for its *sparshalinga* where Chandra regained his lost lustre.

This temple is constructed in the serene surroundings of the river Tungabhadra's right bank. The temple faces east and is consisted of a *garbhagriha*, *antarala* and a *mandapa* which has openings on three sides. The *vimana* of the temple is very unique and the largest in region. Its pyramidal shape is due to an architectural adjunct necessitated by the instability of the structure. As the temple lies very near to the bank of Tungabhadra hence this heavy pyramidal buttress around the *vimana* was necessary to save it from collapse. (Plate 6-23)

The *vimana* decoration is simple, having very few images on its *sikhara* (superstructure). The present form of the temple is owed to the skill of two principal architect-artisans Bankoja and Ketoja. The sculpture stored in this temple presents the most unusual picture of plastic art of local flavor exposing to mainstream development and slowly dissolving into it. There are many loose sculptures placed inside the *mandapa* and around the temple.

The image of Surya standing in equipoise over a pedestal which depicts a seven-horse chariot driven by his charioteer Aruna is worth appreciating. Surya is shown holding lotuses in his two hands. Usha and Pratyusha with their bows are shown standing over *makaras* which forms a triple-looped *makaratorana* in the background. Boots, which are mostly present in the Surya images of Northern India, are absent in this image.

An inscribed Mahishasuramardini image was sponsored by a Haihaya chief named Gandaraditya, who claimed descent from the legendary Sahasrarjuna of Mahishmati, the original home of the Haihayas. The eight arms goddess hold sword, trident, *chakra*, arrow, conch, bow and a shield. She is shown standing over a buffalo head, having completed her task of killing the demon, Mahishasura.

The dated image of Visnu is from 1034 CE and was sponsored by Nakimayya. Vishnu standing in equipoise manner holds conch, *chakra* and a *gada* (mace). One of his arm is resting over his hips. Around him are depicted his *dashavatara* (ten incarnations). On the background is seen a five-looped *torana* terminating on rampant lions on either side. *Garuda* and Bhudevi are shown standing on either side of Visnu.

The image of Saraswati is the most outstanding piece of plastic art from here. The four armed goddess is sitting over a half-lotus pedestal. The attributes held in her four hands are almost ruined except books held in her upper left hand. What makes this sculpture unique is the back rest in the form of a frame supported on its flanks by an elephant below, succeeded by a rampant lion above, which is mostly seen in Jaina images.

No foundation inscription is found for this temple. Mention of the *sparshalinga* of this temple was found in an inscription (South Indian Inscriptions vol XVIII, No 246), dated 1263 CE, which mentions that Vira Vikramaditya of the Gutta family worshiped the lord here. However many earlier inscription are discovered here. On the basis of architecture and inscription, this temple can be associated with Kalyani Chalukya king Jayasimha II who ruled in the first quarter of the tenth century CE.

There are five inscriptions found in the vicinity of this temple including one stone built into the bund called *sthapana* of river Varada in front of the Galageswara temple.

Haralhalli

Haralhalli is a small village on the left bank of Tungabhadra river. Bombay gazetteer refers the village as Haralhalli while Dharwad gazetteer refers it as Haralahalli. It now comes under Haveri district and is officially referred to as Haralhalli. Google maps list it as Haralahalli located near Guttal. The town is referred as Gottamgadi in inscriptions, and it would be interesting to find out that how Haralahalli came into vogue from Gottamgadi.

Though now reduced to a small village, it would have been an important town in medieval times. The earliest inscription found here refers to the rule of the Guttas of Guttal. Their ruler Vikramaditya II was ruling under the patronage of the Kalyani Chalukyas. The Guttas were ruling from Guttavolal (modern Guttal) which is not very far from this village. In comparison to Guttal, Haralhalli seems to have more antiquities.

Bombay Gazetteer mentions three temples in town, that of Someswara, Kalleswara and Udchamma. Someswara temple is standing in its full glory, except little damage to its main *sikhara*. Udchamma temple is a live temple of not much antiquity. Kalleswara temple might be another triple-celled structure standing north of Someswara temple. This is referred as Chikkeswara temple in inscriptions. Inscriptions mention two more temples, that of Daseswara and Tulvaleswara, however these are not traceable now.

Someswara temple is triple-celled (*trikuta*) shrine having three towers intact. The main shrine is on west, the subordinate shrines are on south and north. Originally it was a single cell shrine dedicated to *swayambhu* (self-originated) god Someswara. During the rule of the Gutta king Joma II, in twelfth century CE, this single celled structure was converted into a triple-celled shrine on order of the then *kalamukha* priest of the temple, Kalyanashakti.

Joma II added two more shrines, one on north and one on south, and dedicated those to Vikrameswara and Gutteswara. Both of these were dedicated to his predecessors, Vikramaditya and Gutta. Though it is not specified whether northern shrine is for Vikrameswara or the southern however it is not that hard to identify. Vasundhara Filliozat tells that Vikrameswara is name of Visnu and in accordance with the *kalamukha* concept it should be enshrined in the northern cell. In this manner, the southern cell should be enshrining Gutteswara.

Antarala (ante-chamber) doorways are provided with perforated windows. The lintel of the west shrine shows Ganesha, Brahma, Siva, Visnu and Mahishasuramardini inside a *makaratorana*. Lintels of northern and southern *antarala* doorway do not show Ganesha but instead shows standing naked-Siva. This signifies that the western shrine is the main shrine. Tower of the western shrine has four levels while those of northern and southern have three level. This shows the dominance of the western shrine indicating that it is the main shrine. *Mukhamandapa* at the main entrance of the temple has seating areas for temple visitors on both sides of the entrance. (Plates 6–24 and 6–25)

All the cells, on west, north and south, share a common *rangamandapa*. The shrines are connected to it through *sukanasi* (ante-chamber). The *rangamandapa* is square and closed hypostyle structure. It has two niches on all sides, thus eight in total. At present most of these are empty, one housing *saptamatrikas* and one broken man-slaying-lion emblem. Four central pillars of this hall are executed in exquisite beauty. These are remarkable for their regularity in size and shape.

The central ceiling of the *rangamandapa* is divided into nine compartments, each containing a flower with central hanging bud. Ceilings of the cardinal points also have flower decoration with hanging buds. Entrance is provided from east through a porch which is supported on two pillars and two pilasters. Lintel of the doorjamb of the entrance has Gajalakshmi motif. Instead of single door-jamb, a double door-jamb design is used to make the entrance prominently standing out.

There are many icons on the exterior walls of the temple, located above the architrave and on the floors of tower. These icons are the work of more than one artist. The name of few sculptors is engraved on the socle of the sculpture. We find names like Nemoja, Baicoja among the sculptors here. Important icons found here include, Mahishasuramardini, Adi Varaha, Siva as Natesa, Siva as Somanatha, Ganesha, Ugra Narasimha, Yoga Narasimha and Surya. There would have been originally an arrangement of *Ashtadikpalas* around the external walls of the main shrine, however only Indra and Yama have survived. An interesting figure is of a hunter couple, where the man is shown holding a bow and the female is holding a sword.

It appears that the temple is dedicated to dance and music as Siva as Natesa is present on the *sukanasi* stele of the northern and southern shrine. Also are seen various dancers and musicians installed all around the temple, on *vimana* walls and on parapet walls of the porch. The temple was associated to the *kalamukha* sect of Saivism.

Kalleswara or Chikkeswara temple would have been a triple-celled (*trikuta*) structure originally. However at present only two shrines have survived. From the ruins it is clear that there was an additional shrine attached to the common *mandapa* shared by these two shrines. As per inscriptions, it could be Chikkeswara temple which was built during the reign of the Yadava king Singana in thirteenth century CE.

Kuruvathi or Kuruvatti

Kuruvathi (also referred as Kuruvatti) is a village in Ballari district of Karnataka. It is located on the bank of Tungabhadra river. The earliest rulers, known from inscriptions, were the Chalukyas of Kalyana

(Kalyani or Western Chalukya). All of the Chalukya inscriptions are from the reign of Vikramaditya VI. Few inscriptions are from the Gutta kings also ruled as the subordinate of the Chalukyas. The Kuruvatti temple is particularly noteworthy for its exquisite bracket figures, carved screens, polished pillars, and tiers of friezes showing rows of birds, animals, dwarfs, and figures of musicians and dancers.

J F Fleet mentions that an inscription of 1068 CE, found at Balligavi tells that it was at Kuruvatti and in the Tungabhadra river that the Kalyani Chalukya king Ahavamalla-Someshvara I "by supreme act of austerity ascended the heaven." A reference of this is also found in the Vikramankadeva-charita of Bilhana, which mentions that the king in question, being attacked by a malignant fever for which no remedies were found to be of any avail, went to Tungabhadra, and there, after bathing and meditating on Siva, walked into the river until its waters reached his throat, and so ended his own life.

The village would have been an important centre of the *Lakulisa* sect. An inscription refers to Lakulisvara-Pandita who probably was the chief priest at this place. The name suggests that he was a follower of the *lakulisa* sect. This inscription refers the god as Abhinava-Someswara. The name of the lord is probably due to the fact that the temple was constructed in commemoration of king Someshvara's self-sacrifice at this place in river Tungabhadra. The lord is referred as Ahavamalleswara in later inscription, deriving from the title of the Kalyani Chalukya king Someshvara.

When the region came under the Hoysalas, Kuruvatti became an important centre as their *rajaguru*, Lokabharana, made this village his abode. Many inscriptions of the Hoysala period mention Lokabharana as the *rajaguru* of the Hoysala king Ballala II. The chief queen of Ballala II, Padumaladevi, also made a grant at Kuruvatti to god Ahavamalleswara. The village would have acquired quite a reputation during that period that it has been referred as Dakshina-Varanasi in one of the inscription

The earliest information on the monuments of Kuruvatti is from Robert Sewell, who in 1882 CE mentions an old Siva temple and a fort in the village. Next was Alexander Rea, who wrote in 1896 CE in detail about the Mallikarjuna temple in Kuruvatti. In 1910, James Fergusson explained the architecture and other features, deriving most of his information from the works of Rea and others.

Mallikarjuna temple facing east consists of a *garbhagriha*, an *antarala*, a *sabhamandapa* with two *mukhamandapas* on north and south and a detached Nandi *mandapa* in front of the *sabhamandapa*. The two *mukhamandapas* on north and south are the two entrances to the temple, the third entrance is from the east. The Nandi *mandapa* has the original Nandi now under a modern construction. (Plates 6–26 and 6–27)

Garbhagriha is a square room with no decorative element inside. It enshrines a Sivalinga resting over a large *pitha*. The walls of the room have been divided into two halves by inserting a horizontal slab. This slab would have used to keep ritual paraphernalia and movable images. The *antarala* does not have its door but instead it has a *makaratorana* supported on two free standing circular pillars. The niches formed by loops emerging from *makaras* have Siva in middle and Brahma and Visnu on his either sides. A similar *torana* is also found in Dodda Basappa temple at Dambal and Kalleswara temple at Bagali.

Few images are kept inside this *antarala*. Two images of devotees, one showing a couple and one showing two ladies, an image of Bhairava and Siva can be found here. The *sabhamandapa* is supported on four massive central pillars which have square block at the base. This square block is exquisitely carved on all its four faces. There are three entrances to this *sabhamandapa*, one each on south, north and east. All the entrance doorways are profusely carved.

There are three bracket figures left on the eastern entrance. The other bracket figures have been moved to various British museums during their rule. These bracket figures have been considered among the best specimen of the Hoysala period. James Fergusson writes 'All the details are sharp and the carving so good that even at Halebid it would be difficult to prove out any individual piece showing more complete mastery over the material than the brackets representing female figures with encircling wraths on the fronts and inner sides of the capitals at the east entrance.'

There is a royal image put near one of the entrance. Many scholars have suggested that this could be the Kalyani Chalukya king Someshvara with his two queens. As no inscription is found over it hence nothing can be said with certainty however as the temple probably was constructed in memory of this Chalukyan king so it will not be odd to carve out this image also in his memory.

The *vimana* has three projecting niches on its three walls. The niche on the south is empty while that on north has a mutilated image of Narasimha. Miniature models of temple styles are displayed all over the *vimana* wall across its three sides. These shrines are enveloped inside *makaratoranas* which are carved very delicately.

Numerous inscriptions both from the Kalyani Chalukya and Hoysala periods are noticeable inside and around the temple. A few inscriptions are found in Kuruvatti town as well telling about the grants made by kings and history of various events in their lives.

Chaudadanapura or Chaudayyadanapura

Chaudadanapura would have been an important pilgrimage site in the medieval times however at present it is reduced just to a small village. It is located on the southern bank of the Tungabhadra river in Karnataka state. The place has been referred as Gope, Muktikshetra, Sivapura in inscriptions, Chaudadanapura seems to be a later appellation of the same.

A local tradition assigns the present name, Chaudadanapura to 12th century CE. As per the legend Shivadeva Wodeyar, who was living here, donated this place to Chaudayya who was a great devotee of Siva and belonged to the community of boatmen. As the place was donated to him hence it was called as Chaudadanapura.

Viragamottara mentions a place named Muktinilaya located on the banks of Tungabhadra. Muktinilaya is mentioned to be equally revered by Brahma and Visnu. Vasundhara Filliozat suggests that this Muktinilaya might be same as Chaudadanapura, as it has been referred in past as Muktikshetra.

Vasundhara suggests that Chaudadanapura held a considerable importance during the *Lakulisa* movement period. When *lakulisa* sect witnessed a setback during twelfth and thirteenth century CE, Chaudadanapura emerged as a great centre of Virashaivism. However the earliest inscription found in the temple speaks that Muktikshetra was blessed with Brahmans reciting Samaveda, Gayatri etc which are against the *lakulisa* practices.

Story of Chaudadanapura would be incomplete without mention of Shivadeva Wodeyar. It was he who came here and established a great Lingayata centre. An inscription tells that Shivamuddudeva was worshiping Dhavaleswara at Srigiri (Srisailam). From there he came to Muktikshetra, the present Chaudadanapura. He built a temple dedicated to Siva. At some time later, the house of the Guttas, local rulers under the Chalukyas and later Hoysalas, came under the influence of Shivadeva. The Gutta kings paid many visits and made grants to Shivadeva and lord Mukteswara. On receipt of this royal patronage and support, Shivadeva created Shivadevapura, a real seat of Amarganas on the earth. He founded a Virashiava *matha* at Chaudadanapura whose control is still in the hands of his descendants, the Wodeyar family, staying in Dharwar.

The fame of Shivadeva spread to great distances. As per an inscription here, when Kannadevi's husband died, Siddha Revanadeva advised her to go to Mukteswara linga where Shivadeva lives. He asked her to worship lord Muktinatha and get blessings of the saint. Kannadevi came to Muktikhstera and started living there. While living at Muktikshetra built a temple dedicated to Kalideva in memory of her husband.

The village is famous for its Mukteswara temple. There is a *matha* also in the village, except these there is nothing else of interest. Mukteswara temple is the main temple of Chaudadanapura. The temple consists of a *garbhagriha*, *antarala* and a *rangamandapa*, all aligned on the east-west axis. All these elements have an opening on the east except the *rangamandapa* which has two openings, one on east and one on south, both having porches attached. (Plate 6-28)

At a later point of time a modern *mandapa* was added to the temple however the former has no structural connection with the latter. This *mandapa* has an opening on east and west and stood detached from the main temple, however as this is constructed on the same east-west axis of the temple so appears to be a part of the same.

Garbhagriha is square in plan as usual for a Hindu temple. It houses a small linga which is not placed over any *pitha* (base). These types of lingas are assumed to be *swayamvabh*u (self-originating) lingas. As evident from inscriptions of the temple, Siva came here with Uma himself to stay and bless devotees. The *vimana* over the *grabhagriha* is pyramidal shape and has four stories of diminishing size. It is topped with a square dome with its angles protruding up like lotus petals.

Rangamandapa has four pillars in centre which constitute a square of similar size as that of *garbhagriha*. There is a unique Surya image placed in this *mandapa* which was brought from the nearby town of Narsipura. Surya is shown standing below a canopy made of seven hoods of a serpent. A *saptamatrika* panel is also found in a niche in the same *mandapa*.

Iconography of the temple is hard to reconstruct as the temple has been plundered as suggested by Vasundhara Filliozat. She mentions that remains of mortises on the capitals suggests that carved steles were placed on those however none of these exist at present. She numbered such mortises and states that about 160 such carved steles have been removed from the temple. Hence at present the temple gives a look of a deprived one from decoration however it would not been the case when it was constructed.

The tower of the temple has three steles on each side like gable ends. The first stele is empty while others have either Siva in his various forms or a goddess. On south we see Siva as Bhairava accompanied with two ghosts and a dog. On the west we find a seated image of Siva which Vasundhara Filliozat suggests might be of Sadyojatamurti. On north we find Siva as Maheswara.

To the south of the extended *mandapa* of the main temple, there is a small west facing shrine. This shrine is consisted of a cell and a *mandapa*. The shrine was referred as the 'temple of Gomuni' by Walter Elliot, which is also its present nomenclature. As the inscription mentioning construction of a temple by Kannadevi in memory of her husband and dedicating that to lord Kalinath was found inside this temple hence it might be the very same temple constructed by that lady in 1262 CE.

There are few other shrines in the complex however none has any considerable style or architecture. All are small in proportion with their major features already lost. All are made up on a single cell having a Sivalingas inside. A permanent shed has been recently constructed where all the stele inscriptions are put at single place.

There is no proper foundation inscription about this temple. The earliest inscription found here talks about construction of a Siva temple by Attiraja during the reign of the Chalukyan king Vikramaditya VI. This inscription is not dated however the event would have taken place in between 1105 and 1115 CE. As the place mentioned in that inscription is Muktikhstera hence it is not very certain whether the temple mentioned in the inscription was the main temple or a subsidiary shrine.

Another inscription dated in 1225 CE mentions that Shivadeva repaired a dilapidated temple from its base to top till finial. If this was the same temple built by Attiraja, was it possible that within 100 years it had to be repaired in such a large scale. There are nine major inscriptions found at this place. Apart from these, there are few fragmentary records on the steps leading to river Tungabhadra.

6.4 THE CAUVERI CIRCUIT

Talakad

Talakad or Talakadu is a desert-like town on the left bank of the Cauveri River; 45 km from Mysore and 133 km (82 miles) from Bengaluru. It once had over 30 temples, most of which now are lying buried under sand. The extant group of temples, where the eastward flowing Cauveri river changes course as the sand on its banks spreads over a wide area, is a popular pilgrimage site for the Hindus.

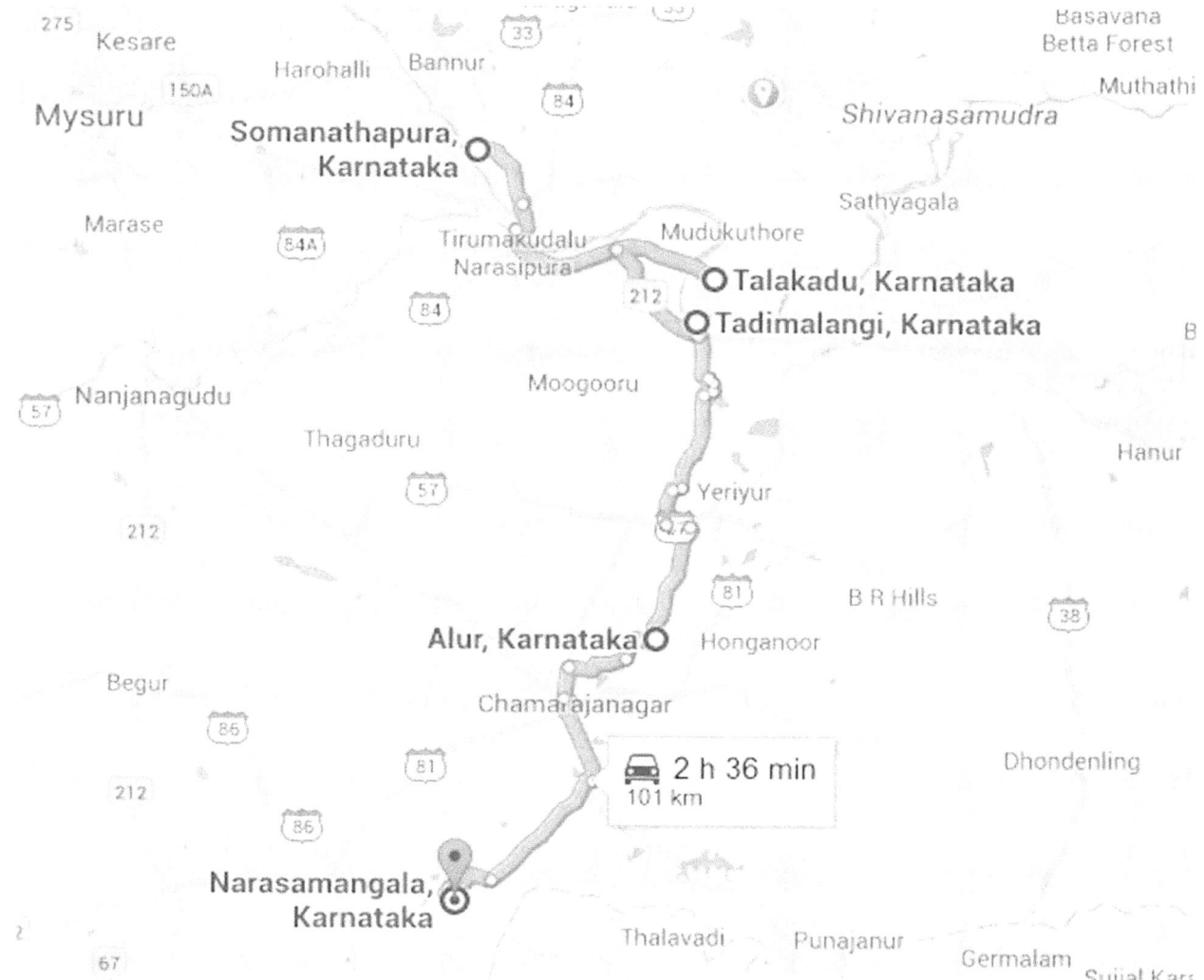

The origin of the town is lost in antiquity; but one tradition is that its name was derived from two *kirata* twin brothers, Tala and Kada. The two hunters Tala and Kada, are believed to have struck a tree with an axe to find blood gushing forth, and upon the bidding of a heavenly voice, dressed the wound of the tree with the tree's leaves and fruits. The tree healed, and the hunters became immortal. Since Siva is believed to have healed himself through this incident, he is referred to as Vaidyeswara. The Panchalingas here are all associated with this legend. Two stone images believed to represent the brothers are supposed to be in front of the temple Virabhadra Swamy. In a later age, Rama is said to have halted here on his expedition to Lanka.

The earliest authentic mention of the city of Talakad or Talakadu is in Sanskrit Dalavana-Purana in connection with the Western Ganga line of kings. Harivarma, who had been assigned to find a place (247–266 CE) and who was according to an old chronicle; installed king at Skandapura (said to be Gajalhatti near Coimbatore where the Moyar flows into the Bhavani), but he resided in the great city of Dalavanapura in the Karnata-desa. Thenceforward Talakad became the capital of these powerful sovereigns who were subsequently known as the Gangas of Talakad.

At the beginning of the 11th century, the Gangas succumbed to the Cholas, who captured Talakad and gave it the name of Rajarajapura. But about a hundred years later it was taken by the Hoysala king

Vishnuvardhana, who drove the Cholas out. After this time it appears that Talakad was composed of seven towns and five *mathas* or monastic establishments. The town of Mayilangi or Malingi, on the opposite side of the river, was also a large place, and had the name of Jananathapura. Down to the middle of the 14th century, it remained a possession of the Hoysalas, and then passed into the hands of a feudatory of the Vijayanagara sovereigns, whose line appears to be known as that of Soma-Raja.

A legend about the "Curse of Talakad" occupies a significant place in the town's history. In 1610 CE it was conquered by the Mysore Raja. Tirumala-Raja, sometimes called Sri Ranga Raya, the representative of the Vijayanagara family at Seringapatam (Srirangapatna), being afflicted with an incurable disease, came to Talakad for the purpose of offering sacrifices at the temple of Vaidyeswara or Vaidyanatheswara. His second wife Alamelamma was left in charge of the government of Srirangapatna ; but on hearing that her husband was on the point of death, she left for Talakad with the object of seeing him before he died, handing over Srirangapatna and its dependencies to Raja Wodeyar of Mysore. It appears that Raja Wodeyar had been desirous of possessing the jewels which were the property of the Rani Alamelamma. Being unable to obtain them, and eager to seize them on any pretext, he raised an army and proceeded against the Rani. Rani Alamelamma thereupon went to the banks of the Cauveri and threw the jewels into the river. She too jumped into the river and drowned herself opposite Malangi, at the same time uttering a three-fold curse, "Let Talakad become sand; let Malangi become a whirlpool; let the Mysore Rajas fail to beget heirs." It is believed that the latter part continues to afflict the royal family.

The old city Talakad is completely buried beneath sand dunes stretching for nearly a mile in length, only the tops of two pagodas being visible. The sand hills used to advance upon the town at the rate of 9 or 10 feet a year, principally during the south-west monsoon and as they pressed it close on three sides, the inhabitants were constantly forced to abandon their houses and retreat further inland. More than thirty temples, it is stated, are beneath the sand, but the Kirtinarayana temlpe is successfully excavated and so are Pataleswara and Maraleswara. The most imposing temple left uncovered by the sand is that of Vaidyanatheswara temple.

In the early part of the last century two temples Anandeswara and Gaurisankara, were unearthed. Four fragmentary records were found on the outer walls of the Pataleswara temple. One of these is an old inscription in Kannada of the Ganga period, the others being in Tamil. The Anandeswara temple is said to have been built by one Chidanandaswami, a contemporary of Haidar.

Among the temples of Talakad, the Pataleswara, Maraleswara, Arkeswara, Vaidyanatheswara and Mallikarjuna temples, the five Lingas believed to represent the five faces of Siva have become famous. In honour of these five Siva temples, a fair is held once every 12 years called Panchalinga Darshana, the last one was held in 2009. The Panchalinga Darshana is held on a new moon day in the month of Kartika. According to a local legend, Ramanujacharya during his sojourn in Karnataka (also called Malnadu) established five Visnu temples of Narayana known as Pancha Narayana Kshetras. Talakad is one of the Pancha Narayana Kshetras where the Kirtinarayana temple was established and the presiding deity in this temple is Kirtinarayana. (Plates 6–29 and 6–30)

Archaeological excavations of the sand dunes at Talakad (or Talakadu) have shown the existence of several ruined temples built during the rule of the Western Ganga dynasty (345–999 CE). However, according to historian I.K. Sarma, only two temples, the Pataleswara and Maraleswara built during the reign of king Rachamalla Satyavakya IV (975–986) are intact. According to the Archaeological Survey of India (ASI), the Vaidyeswara temple; the largest, the most intact and ornate of the group bears Ganga-Chola-Hoysala architectural features. Its consecration is assignable to the 10th century CE with improvements made up to the 14th century. According to the art historian Adam Hardy, the Kirtinarayana temple was built in 1117 CE by the famous Hoysala king Vishnuvardhana to celebrate his victory over the Cholas in the battle of Talakad. It is undergoing restoration work by the ASI. Only its *mahadvara* (grand entrance) is intact. The Vaidyeswara and Kirtinarayana temples are protected as monuments of national importance by the Archaeological Survey of India

Both the Pataleswara and Maraleswara temples have on their original base (*adhishsthana*) a sanctum (*garbhagriha*) and a vestibule (*ardhamandapa*) from the Ganga period. The tower over the shrine may be a Chola period renovation. The pillars and the pilasters in the main hall (*mahamandapa*) are similar to those in the Rameswara Temple, Narasamangala. High quality Ganga workmanship with late Pallava influences is seen in the images of Hindu gods in these temples. These images include the four handed Mahavisnu, Durga standing on the horned head of the demon king (*asura*) Mahisha and Kartikeya in the Maraleswara temple; and the images of Dakshinamurty (a form of Visnu), Trimurti Brahma (three faced Brahma), Simhavahini Durga (Durga riding a lion) and Siva at the Pataleswara temple. Arkeswara temple of the Ganga period is located at a little distance at Vijayapura. Its pillars have circular shafts decorated with dancers and musicians in scrolls. Scattered and wall mounted sculpture of the Ganga period can be noticed in the temple precincts.

The Vaidyeswara temple comprises a sanctum with a *Vesara* tower (a *sikhara* which is a fusion of south and north Indian styles) in stucco, a vestibule that connects the sanctum to a short hall (*ardhamanadapa*) six pillared hall (*mahamandapa* or *navaranga*) and two entrance porches (*mukhamandapa*) facing east-west and southern directions. To the north, within the temple is another large hall (*mahamandapa*) with shrines for deities. The entire complex is built on a platform (*jagati*). The outer walls of the temple are articulated with pilasters, deities from the Saiva faith and aedicula in relief. (Plate 6-31)

The ornate doorjamb and lintel over the entrance doorway to the pillared hall, with the 2 m tall reliefs of door-keepers (*dvarapala*) on either side is typically Hoysala in workmanship. At the rear of the complex is a large bounding wall (*prakara*) that houses independent sculptures from the Ganga, Hoysala and Vijayanagara periods.

According to Adam Hardy, the Kirtinarayana temple has a granite single *vimana* plan (tower over shrine), an *ekakuta* (single shrine) construction, with an open *mandapa* (hall). The temple is similar in plan to the famous Chennakesava Temple at Belur. The temple has a typical stellate (star-shaped) plan with the sanctum, vestibule and open hall (*navaranga* or just *mandapa*) mounted on a platform called *jagati*. These features are, according to historian Suryanath Kamath, standard to Hoysala architecture. The platform serves a dual purpose: improves visual effect as well as provides a path for ritual circumambulation (*Pradakshina*) around the temple for devotees. The sanctum has an image of Narayana (another name for Visnu). The decorative features in the temple are notable. At the entrance to the sanctum, the doorjamb and lintel are ornate, and the lathe turned pillars in the spacious hall support a ceiling that is decorated with floral designs.

Tadimalangi

Tadimalangi and Malangi are located on bank of river Cauveri opposite to Talakad. The two villages adjacent to each other acquire historical significance on several counts. Even the "Curse of Talakad" has its effect on the historical significance of Tadimalangi. A temple has been built in honour of Alamelamma on the bank of the river in Tadimalangi and the entire Wodeyar royal family was present at the time of its consecration in 2006.

A unique gold-gilded cast bronze image of a goddess was reported by the archaeologist MS Nagaraja Rao from Malangi. It measured 34 cm in height (including its base and adornment around the face. It was described as Kali and was believed to be the image of *Bhatari* goddess of the Western Ganga period. The goddess Kiltabal Eretti Bhatari was the royal deity of the Gangas and was highly venerated by the Ganga kings.

Tadimalangi and Malangi passed into the hands of the Cholas after they defeated the Gangas. Janardana temple built near a bund in the fields was a Chola creation. This temple dedicated to Visnu was known as Ravikka-Mannika-Vinnagar in ancient days. There are a few inscriptions of the middle and later Chola periods scattered around the temple. The earliest of them relates to the days of Rajaraja I but the year in which it was written is obliterated. Another inscription belonging to Rajaraja I is from the year 1022 CE and gives the name of the place as Jananathapuram. From another record relating to period of Mahamandaleswara Vira Ganga, it is gathered that one Chibbila Heggade made a grant to provide the illumination in the temple of the god Janardana of Malingi. One inscription on the pillar in the *mukhamandapa* of the temple refers to the gift of the pillar to the temple by Aditya-*gamunda* son of Alagaiyan Vira *gamundan* of Mogur. A large number of patrons and a variety of gifts made to the temple of Iravikulamannika-Vinagar-Alwar at Tadimalangi, an *agrahara*, stand testimony to the fame and popularity this temple had attained. Tadimalangi is one of the earliest centres for the spread of Vaishnavism in Karnataka. Janardana temple now lies in ruins. No worship is performed in the temple now as one of the fingers of the deity got chipped and broken. (Plate 6-32)

Two more temples of the Chola period in the vicinity of Talakad and Tadimalangi are located at Marehalli and Bannur. These temples are Lakshmi Narasimha temple and Hanumanteswara temple respectively.

Narasamangala: Narasamangala is a village about 16 km to the south-west of Chamarajanagar and about 12 km to the south-east of Terakanambi. Since it is an out-of-the-way place, it is accessible only by a narrow road and its importance has not really been publicised. To the south-east of the village is a large mound which is strewn about with wrecks of ancient architecture and sculpture now cleared partially with excavation signboard still in sight. On its eastern slope can be seen the ground relics of ancient brick structures.

The chief monument standing in the place among all the raised platforms is the Rameswara temple. The temple here is a unique creation possessing a brick and stucco *vimana* of great beauty and artistic merit. Another noteworthy aspect of this temple complex is in its *ashtaparivara* disposition. Basements of six other units have been found around the main temple. All the loose images that were once consecrated in these shrines are now pooled together partly conserved in a shed at the south-east. As they stood, the disposition of these *parivara* shrines is as this: Chandikesa and Bhairava at the north, Mahishasuramardini at the north-west, Ganesha and Virabhadra at the south, Surya at the east, Soma at the south-east and the *Saptamatrika* shrine at the south-west. A detached Nandi pavilion stands in front of the principal shrine of Rameswara. (Plate 6-33)

There is an inscription engraved on two slabs to the south of the Rameswara temple. It refers to certain grants made to this temple of Ramaanathadeva in the time of Viraballala III but the temple itself is very much more ancient, being probably at least 400 years older. The structures in comparison with which it can be studied is the Bhoganandiswara temple at Nandi, while its sculptures should be studied along with those of Ellora. This temple was probably built around 800 CE. At that time this area was under the rule of the Gangas and it looks as if we have come across here a genuine Ganga temple dedicated to Siva The structure has a large *garbhagriha*, a narrow *sukanasi*, originally open provided with a smallish doorway, and a *navaranga* of nine *ankanas*. There is no porch. The closed *mandapa* is a later day addition with walls having been built. Outer view is unimportant so far as the *navaranga* is concerned. But the outer wall of the *garbhagriha* and the *vimana* above it are objects of great interest and deserve detailed study. It is remarkable that this brick structure stucco images standing for over a thousand years still look aesthetically enchanting. The basement has the ancient rounded cornice and the topmost basement cornice has rows of lions, sea-horses, *makara*-headed fish, etc.

Above the basement the wall is broken up by pilasters which are either square or octagonal The octagonal pilasters are used more especially for shallow niches over whose canopies stand images of the great gods in various postures.

Under the eaves is a row of *Yakshas* and *Apsaras* and the eaves themselves are ornamented with large and small horse-shoe-shaped windows enclosing *kirtimukhas*. The tower (*sikhara*) itself is composed of two series of turrets, each turret having two storeys. The corner turrets are square in plan with converging rounded domes (*kuta*), while the middle turrets have boat-shaped tops (*sala*). Each face of each turret is ornamented with stucco images of remarkable elegance. Above the second set of turrets is a cornice over which the corners are adorned by bulls. The *sikhara* which is supported on each side by stucco images is shaped like the Bhoganandiswara temple *sikhara*.

The sculptures, some of which are partly damaged, have a character of their own and seem unusual in comparison with the other temples of the State. Sculpture here are quite large in size with broad chests and well developed breasts, thin waists and low bellies, slim limbs, sparse ornamentation, conventional but unobtrusive drapery and dignified faces compel one to find a parallel for them in the sculptures of Ellora.

Some of the more important stucco images on the outer wall and tower are: Two-armed Siva seated, Siva standing with foot on Nandi's head, Andhakasuramardana, Dakshinamurti with a smiling face are on the south side of the tower. On the west side are: Visnu on Garuda, Visnu treading on Bali's head and Ugra Narasimha. On the north side are: Siva and Parvati, Durga seated with *rakshasa* on pedestal and flanked on the west by the Sun and Durga dancing and on the right seated by Brahma and seated Bhairavi.

The *somasutra* or *pranala* emerges from a tiger's mouth and has a *yaksha* sitting on it. The *navaranga* doorway which is of very hard darkish stone (trap) resembles some of the Badami Chalukya doorways. On the right door jamb, the *dvarapala* is standing with his left elbow resting on the handle of his mace, while the *dvarapala* on the left jamb has his body twisted so that his face and the back of his hips are both visible. He has *trisula* in the right upper hand. The jambs and the lintel piece have each three scroll bands in the convolutions of some of which are flowers, *yakshas*, lions, *yallis*, monkeys and swans

The *navaranga*, though only about 18 ft square, has some very interesting features. It has four pillars of hard soapstone with the proto-Chalukyan bell, vase and biscuit-shaped round mouldings with the abacus on a lotus and the brackets bearing deep-cut horizontal *malas* with a central floral band. The pillars flanking the *sukanasi*, however, have octagonal shafts ornamented with floral and beaded hangings and the images of dancers and musicians. Among these images is a king seated at ease and a queen standing admiring a flower. The beams all around the *navaranga* have images of dancing, moving, fighting or wrestling *yakshas* in various poses. (Plate 6-35)

The central ceiling which is flat and divided into nine panels is a beautiful piece of workmanship second only to that of Aralaguppe. In the central panel eight-armed Siva is dancing (*Natesa*) on the body of Andhakasura while an attendant is beating on a vase-shaped *ghara*. Around Siva are the eight *dikpalakas*, each mounted with his consort on his characteristic mount and followed sometimes by attendants. Against the north wall in the *navaranga* is now seated on a high damaged pedestal a large two-handed image of what appears to be Parasurama. Parasurama is seated with one knee resting on seat and the other folded up. His right hand holding a small mace-axe rests on the right knee. His left hand rests on the left thigh. His hair is loose and ends in ringlets. He wears the *inakara-kundala* in his long earlobes and a jewelled diadem and necklace one of which has beaded pendants and hangings. He wears also the *yajnopavita* and a jewelled loin-band on the lower breast.

The *sukanasi* which was open originally is now closed in by a small doorway. The *sukanasi* ceiling has a beautiful large rosette in relief, while on the beams are the usual *yakshas* in various poses which include dancers, wrestlers, playing with cobra, doing *yogasana* etc. The *garbhagriha* which is about 10 feet square and about 7 feet high is low and has a large rosette on the ceiling. Under it on a huge *panipitha* of darkish stone is a large linga about 22 inches in diameter with a flat top and rounded edges. Directly opposite the *navaranga* doorway is a recumbent bull, about 4 feet high, which with its small snout and short curved in horns.

To the south-west of the temple is a small shrine in which are eleven images of a largish size, three facing north, five facing east and three facing south (Plate 6-34). Their sculpture is remarkable because of the slimness of the waist and the fullness of the breasts. There is little doubt that they belong to about the time of the Kolaramma temple and its colossal *saptamatrikas*. The sculptures are in order from the south-east:

Virabhadra is seen playing on the Rudra-*vina*, and holding *trisula* and *damaruga* with Nandi behind. He wears *sarpakundala* and beautiful jewelled diadem

Brahmi or Brahmani (three heads visible) with swan on pedestal and she holds *abhaya*, and stylus

Maheswari with bull on pedestal, *trisula* and *damaruga* in the hands

Kaumari with peacock on pedestal and spear in the hands

Vaishnavi with *garuda* on pedestal and *prayogachakra* and *sankha* held between two fingers in each of the back hands

Varahi with buffalo on the pedestal

Indrani with elephant on the pedestal and *vajrayudha* (double trident) and goad in the back hands

Chamunda with a prostrate man on the pedestal and flames darting from her head. Her eight hands are thus disposed, right *abhaya*, sword, death's head mace, and *damaruga*, left index finger pointing to head, holding *rakshasa's* head, holding *kapala*, and resting on thigh

Gana helping himself to sweets

Daksha-Brahma with a pot belly, dwarfish stout legs and a sheep-shaped head with long hanging ears, no horns.

Bhairava four-handed and seated (holding sword, drum, snake and bowl). The figure has canine teeth, disheveled hair tied with a cobra and the girdle formed by cobra.

In the lantana bushes to the north of the temple was found lying an image of Visnu as Janardana. The image was originally about 6 feet high. The portion beneath the knees is now broken. There are a lot of other loose sculptures scattered in the temple complex. Behind the inscription a portion of the brick basement of the old Janardana temple was found while excavating round about the inscription stone and it is near this spot in the bushes that the image was discovered.

Considering all aspects of temple architecture and sculptural beauty, Rameswara temple at Narasamangala; ranks among the highpoints of Karnataka's art and architecture.

Alur

Alur is a village ten km to the north-east of Chamarajanagar on the right or east bank of a small river Suvarnavati or Honnuhole, a tributary of Cauveri. The site of Hale Alur is in the midst of cultivated fields and tall palms close to the river. There are two temples of the Western Ganga period in Alur.

Deseswara temple is an older structure possibly constructed in two different stages. The *garbhagriha* contains a black image on an octagonal *pitha*, the small *sukanasi*, and the small sized *navaranga* about 12ft x 12ft with its four roundly chiselled trap stone pillars having bell shape and vase moulding appear to belong to the Ganga period. But the outer *navaranga* with its sixteen-fluted granite pillars and its ribbed pillar brackets and hood corners belongs to the renovation effected in early Vijayanagara period. With this is perhaps connected the large stone inscription of the time of Harihara dated 1325 CE, standing on the south side of the temple.

The small bull *mandapa* stands opposite the temple. This *mandapa* is of very recent origin and has no connection with the older construction. The two older pillars on which perhaps the older Nandi *mandapa* rested can still be seen lying outside the temple.

A Tamil inscription was discovered on a large slab in the north side of the *navaranga*. Behind the Deseswara temple on the south-west end of the old compound were found ten sculptures of largish seated figures in granite. These have since been moved to the Arkeswara temple nearby. The sculptures now kept in the Arkeswara temple compound include: the *Saptamatrikas* with Virabhadra to the right and Ganesha to the left and a large seated granite relief of Durga in a vigorous and terrible attitude with eight hands and open mouth, flames darting from her hair. Her hands hold dagger, *vajra*, short sword, long sword, buckler, bell and bowl. The slender waist and limbs and the vigorous attitude of the goddess are characteristic of Ganga workmanship. On her pedestal is a beast whose identity is doubtful. It has the snout of a boar, the legs of an elephant, and the tail of a mongoose or tiger or even crocodile. This is probably the image of *Kiltabel Eretti bhatari*, a form of Kali which was the deity of the royal family of the Gangas.

The temple of Arkeswara was perhaps constructed in the time of the Western Ganga king Butuga II (935–960 CE). It consists of a small *garbhagriha*, a very small *sukanasi* and a *navaranga* of about 12ft x 12ft size with a flat central ceiling divided into nine panels and having Tandaveswara surrounded by the *ashtadikpalakas*. The basement cornices are partly octagonal and partly round There is a small detached bull *mandapa* in front of the temple, containing a bull without trappings except for a head band. In the *navaranga* are kept two images, one of Mahishasuramardini standing on buffalo-head and another of Siva as Kapahka on bull pedestal. (Plate 6-36)

The *navaranga* doorway has on the jambs and the lintel a scroll band with dancing *Apsaras*. On each side of the doorway is a dark stone slab with four vertical panels containing groups of musicians playing on drums, cymbals, flutes, *rudravina* and a violin-like instrument. These depictions unique in their own way as these possibly depict local art forms and nowhere else in temples of the same period have such depictions been seen. (Plate 6-39)

The most unique and original part of the temple lies in the sculptured pillars supporting the *navaranga* grid as well as the detached Nandi *mandapa*. The ornate pillars possess bas-relief scenes pertaining to the epics as well as historical events of the period besides the mythical figures and demigods. The base and shaft of the Nandi *mandapa* pillars are divided into horizontal bands containing fine relief sculptures. Generally they depict epic themes and related court scenes. The south-east pillar has a king seated before a four-handed deity. This might be Arjuna invoking Krishna (Visnu) for the Pandavas' help. The shaft portion depicts fight between Bhima and Duryodhana besides a royal procession.

All *navaranga* pillars are whitish granite and except the south-west pillar; all others are sculptured in bas-relief. The square base is divided into compartments with sculptures on all four sides. Similarly the cubical shaft has also been divided into four panels within neatly bordered lines with flying *vidyadharas* holding the pillar top. These pillars exhibit military exploits wherein a king and his retinue are shown. The story appears to run systematically in an anti-clockwise way from west to north at the base, whereas the shaft part has vertically paneled sculptures.

In the north-east pillar; the top panel depicts a royal couple at ease with the king playing the *vina* and a queen singing. The middle panel minutely portrays military scene. There is a king or a prince mounted on an elephant proceeding through the gateway followed by drummers and carriers. The elephants are shown one with a rider and the other without a rider but guarded by soldiers holding spikes. A person; perhaps the enemy is hurled into the air between the elephants and in subsequent scene an elephant is shown standing in front of the king and holds a person on its trunk. The third panel depicts a *darbar* (court room) scene. The bottom panel shows a king seated over an elephant fighting vigorously with bow and arrows aiming at his opponent. Finally, the king is shown proceeding towards the temple of Mahakali and pays obeisance to the goddess. The deity is eight-handed, seated in *ugra* form with disheveled hair and holding different weapons. In essence the narration depicts a great victory of the king. (Plates 6–37 and 6–38)

While R Narasimhachar considered this as narration of the conquest of Rajendra Chola over the Gangas, other scholars think otherwise. Because of the depiction of the goddess who looks like the royal deity of the Gangas (*Kiltabel Erreti Bhatari*), many conclude that it is about the victory of the Ganga king Butuga II in the Takkolam war against the Cholas. Chola Rajaditya was killed in this battle fought in 950 CE. Similar depiction is also noticed in the Begur Inscription stone now kept in Bengaluru Museum.

There are many more narrations in sculpture form on the pillars of the temple; details of which were carried in the Mysore Archaeological Report for the Year 1937.

Somanathapura

Somanathapura is a town located 35 km from the historic city of Mysore. Somanathapura is famous for the Chennakesava temple (also called *Kesava* or *Keshava* temple) built by Soma, a *dandanayaka* (commander) in 1268 CE under Hoysala king Narasimha III, when the Hoysalas were the major power in South India. The Kesava temple is one of the finest and most complete examples of Hoysala architecture and is in a very well preserved condition. The temple is in the care of the Archaeological Survey of India as a protected heritage site.

Kesava temple is a *trikutachala* temple with three shrines (Plate 6-40). The ceiling of the *mandapa* (hall) is supported by lathe turned pillars, a standard feature in Hoysala monuments. Between pillars, the ceiling is domical and intricately decorated (Plate 6-42). These decorations could include multi-petalled lotuses, banana bud motifs based on stepped ponds and snake like (*ananta*) knots akin to Borromean motifs (symbolising eternity). Of the three shrines, one shrine had the image of the god Kesava, but the image is missing from the sanctum. The other two shrines house images of Janardhana and Venugopala (all three images are forms of the Hindu god Visnu). This is strictly a Vaishnava temple and there are no depictions of any forms of the Hindu god Siva. Other sculptures include depictions of affluence of that age including members of the royal family riding richly decorated chariots, soldiers and commoners riding horses, camel drawn vehicles, dancers, musicians, hunters armed with bows and arrows and accompanied by their dogs, all heading for a hunt. There are sculptures of royal palaces protected by armed guards, intricate carvings of jewellery, such as pendants, necklaces, waistbands and rings and of woman sporting hair styles that were in vogue. The names of many architects and sculptors are etched on stone from which it is evident that the artists were both local and from outside the region. Famous among them are the locals such as Ruvari Mallithamma, Masanithamma, Chameya, Rameya, Chaudeya and Nanjeya while Pallavachari and Cholavachari are prominent artists from Tamil country.

The temple is housed inside an impressive high walled enclosure (*prakara*) and the entrance to the complex is through a porch with tall lathe-turned pillars. The material used for the temple is soapstone (Green schist). The Kesava temple standouts out as one of the finest the Hoysala architects produced. Its symmetrical architecture, fine sculptures on equally prominent shrines, and panel sculptures form a cloister that speaks of good taste. While there are Hoysala temples with better sculpture and others with better architecture, this temple satisfies all requirements. According to the Mysore Archaeological Reports, it was built by the famous architect and sculptor Ruvari Malithamma who was well known for his expertise in ornamentation.

The temple which is built on a *jagati* (platform) is a *trikuta* (triple shrine) and fully satisfies that terminology as all shrines (*vimanas*) have a superstructure (tower) that is intact. Inside the temple, each *vimana* has a vestibule (*sukanasi*) that connects it to the main rectangular *mandapa* (hall). Like the shrines, all three vestibules also have their own tower called the *sukanasi* (or nose), though it is shorter and hence looks like a low extension of the main superstructure over the shrine. The outer walls of all three shrines, their towers and *sukanasi* are equally well decorated, making it overall a very well balanced design. The temple stands on a *jagati* (platform) and the three *vimanas* are located at the back and are connected by a common rectangular closed *mandapa*. The *jagati* closely follows the plan of the temple exterior and there is a gallery with lathe-turned pillars all along the enclosure of the temple complex which adds to the effect. There is one flight of steps that leads to the *jagati* and one that leads from the *jagati* to the *mandapa*. The wide *jagati* invites devotees to follow the ritualistic clockwise circumambulation (*pradakshina*) before entering the hall. The full effect of the rectangular hall is seen only when the temple profile is viewed. The hall has sixteen bays. The mouldings on the outer wall of the *mandapa* have well decorated reliefs and friezes, with pierced windows screens above them. But unusually the hall is not square and is rectangular in plan and so the *vimanas* are only surrounding its rear half.

All the three shrines are 16 pointed stellate (star-shaped) in design and their towers follow the same pattern. Hence the whole structure looks like a rhythmic progression of well decorated projections and recesses (called architectural articulation). The number of points makes the towers look circular in shape. The three *vimanas* are all four storeyed (*talas*). Many wall sections in the upper *talas* of the *vimanas* have been decorated with a seated *yaksha* inside a small *torana*. *Sukanasis* are of intricate full star plan too and often have miniature towers or miniature shrines in the centre of each *tala*. The first *tala* of course contains a *stambha*.

As usual the open hall part has square half pillars resting on a parapet wall that is topped by a slanting railing. The screens between them are elaborately decorated with geometrical patterns. The slanting railing is thin but the parapet wall below is thick.

According to the art critic Gerard Foekema, the temple is of the "New style" because it has two eaves (*chadya*) running around the temple and there are six mouldings at the base of the outer walls. The upper eave is where the tower meets the wall of the shrine. The lower eave is about a metre below the upper eave. Between the two eaves are decorative miniature towers (called aedicule). Below the lower eaves are a panel of Hindu deities in frieze and their attendants. There are nearly two hundred such panels. Below these panels are six horizontal mouldings or friezes of equal size with ornate decorations. The six mouldings of the base are divided into two sections. In the lower section, where the *jagati* meets the temple wall, the orderly placement of friezes starts with sculpted procession of elephants in the lowest moulding, horsemen in the second and a band of foliage in the third. In the upper section, the lowest moulding has depictions from the Hindu epics and *puranic* scenes executed with detail, *yalis* in the second (or *makara*, an imaginary beast) and *hamsas* (swans) at the top. The Ramayana is depicted on the friezes on the south wall, stories of the Hindu god Krishna on the rear and depictions from the epic Mahabharata on the north wall. The overall effect of the decorated towers, wall images and friezes is well balanced.

The sculpture of this temple has certain unusual features not to be seen in other Hoysala temples. For instance a wall image of Visnu has very different details of *chakra* and *sankha*. Even the curls of the garments along the legs and the dress of the two tiny attendants are also uncommon. (Plates 6–41 and 6–43)

6.5 THE MALAPRABHA VALLEY CIRCUIT

Pattadakal

Pttadakal also spelled Paṭṭadakallu is a World Heritage site, a village and an important tourist centre in Karnataka. Pattadakal is located on the left bank of the Malaprabha River in Bagalkot district and is 22 km from Badami and 514 km from Bengaluru. It forms part of the triad of three important heritage sites viz. Aihole, Badami and Pattadakal, all well known for Badami Chalukya monuments. The Pre-Chalukya historical and Archaeological site Bachinagudda is also near Pattadakal. Pattadakal group of monuments were declared World Heritage Site by UNESCO in 1987.

Pattadakal where the Badami Chalukya kings were coronated, was the capital of the Badami Chalukya dynasty between the 6th and 8th centuries. The Badami Chalukyas built many temples here between the 7th and 8th century. There are ten temples at Pattadakal, including a Jaina sanctuary surrounded by numerous small shrines and plinths in fusion of various Indian architectural styles (*Nagara*, *Prasada* and *Dravida vimana*). Four temples were built in *Dravida* style, four in *Nagara* style of Northern India, while the Papanatha temple in a fusion of the two idioms. In all, nine Siva temples and a Jaina *basadi* (called Jain Narayana temple built in the 9th century by the Rashtrakutas), situated along the northern course of the Malaprabha river are situated here.

According to inscriptions, the place was known by the names *Kisuvolal* (Red Town -mostly mountains near Pattadakal gave this name), Raktapura and Pattada Kisuvolal. The literary work Hammira Kavya of 1540 CE quotes the place as Pattashilapura and Hammirapura. It has been mentioned in the 11th and 12th century inscriptions, as well as in the literary work Singirajapurana of 1500 CE and Hammira Kavya as the place where the Badami Chalukya kings were crowned.

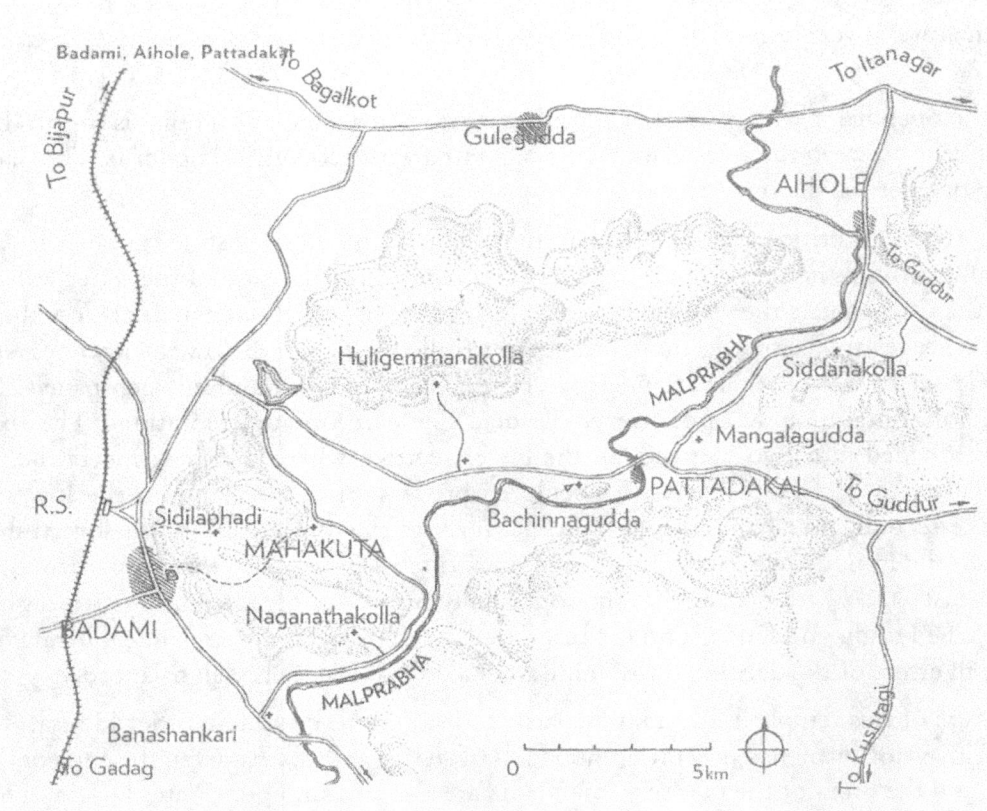

The Badami Chalukya style of architecture originated in Aihole. Architects experimented with different styles, blended the *Nagara* and *Dravida* styles, and evolved their own distinctive style. In the middle of the 7th century, Badami Chalukyan temple building activity shifted from Badami to Pattadakal and reached its pinnacle in Pattadakal. The largest of all the temples in Pattadakal is Virupaksha temple.

There are numerous Kannada language inscriptions at Pattadakal. Important among them; at Virupaksha Temple, there is 8th (733–745 CE) century old Kannada inscription on victory pillar and in the Sangameswara temple, there exists a large inscription tablet (696–733 CE) describing grants made by king Vijayaditya for the construction of the temple.

Virupaksha Temple: This temple, in worship, known as '*Shri Lokeswara-Maha-Sila-prasada*' from the epigraphs, was built by Lokamahadevi, the Queen of Vikaramaditya II (733–745) in about 740 CE to commemorate her husband's victory over the Pallavas of Kanchipuram. It closely resembles the Kailasanatha temple at Kanchipuram on plan and elevation and represents a fully developed and perfected stage of the *Dravidian* architecture.

Facing east, this temple has on plan a square sanctum (*garbhagriha*) with a circumambulatory path (*pradakshinapatha*), an *antarala* with two small shrines for Ganesha and Mahishamardini facing each other in front, a *sabhamandapa* with entrance porches on the east, north and south and a separate *Nandimandapa* in front. The complex is enclosed by high *prakara* walls. Against the inner faces of these walls there were small shrines (originally 32) dedicated to the subsidiary deities (*parivaradevatas*) of which only a few are extant now. The enclosure has been provided with ornate entrance gates (*pratolis*) on both east and west.

The temple is built on a high plinth of five fully evolved mouldings. The outer faces of the walls of the sanctum are divided into a central projection, two intermediate projections and two corner projections with four recesses in between. Likewise, the *mandapa* walls on either side of the northern, eastern and southern porches are divided into two projections and two recesses. All these projections of the sanctum walls carry niches housing images of Saiva and Vaishnava deities like Bhairava, Narasimha, Hari-Hara, Lakulisa while there are perforated windows of various designs in the rest of the recesses. The parapet consists of architectural elements called *kutas* (square), *panjaras* (miniature apsidal shrines) and *salas* (oblong) corresponding to the projections below and the linking courses (*harantaras*) above the recesses. The superstructure over the sanctum is a *Dravida vimana* in three storeys with a *sukasani* projection over the *antarala*. It is square in plan and repeats in its elevation many elements of the parapet and walls beneath. It has a beautifully shaped square roof (*sikhara*) with a round finial *kalasa* above. (Plates 6-44 and 6-45)

The whole of the interior of this temple is embellished with elegant carvings and aesthetically modeled sculptures. Episodes from the Ramayana (e.g. abduction of Sita) *Mahabharata* (e.g. Bhishma lying on a bed of arrows), *Bhagavata* (e.g. Krishna lifting the Govardhana mountain) and *Kiratarjuniyam* (e.g. Arjuna receiving the Pasupatastra from Siva) are depicted on the pillars of the *sabhamandapa* and the pilasters here have the sculptures of amorous couples and Rati and Manmatha. Flora, fauna and geometrical patterns adorn various parts of the temple. Doorjambs (*dvara sakhas*) with their delicate carvings, pillars and pilasters with various types of capitals and carvings on their faces, lintels relieved with animals, birds and architectural motifs, ceilings depicting divine beings and the majestically standing *dvarapalas* all unfold a rich world of plastic art before the connoisseurs and attest to the heights reached by the Badami Chalukyan sculptures.

The *Nandimandapa* situated to the east of the temple, is a square pavilion open on all the four sides. It houses a large image of Nandi on a raised floor. Its flat roof is supported by four pillars and short lengths of walls whose outer surfaces are carved with attendant figures and *Kinnara-mithunas (couples)*. There are a number of inscriptions big and small, engraved in different parts of this temple. Inscriptions in the porch of the eastern gateway record the victory of Vikramaditya II over Kanchipuram and the royal honour and the title of 'Tribhuvanachari' conferred on Anivaritachari Gunda, the architect of the temple and to extol the virtues of Sarvasiddhi Achari, the architect of the southern portion of the temple.

Sangameswara Temple: Founded by king Vijayaditya around 720 CE as Vijayeswara temple, this structure remained incomplete despite several building phases (the columned hall is clearly a later addition). On plan, this temple has a sanctum (*garbhagriha*) housing a *linga*, a small vestibule (*antarala*), a sub-shrine each on either side of the vestibule and a hall (*mandapa*) having massive pillars. A circumambulatory path (*pradakshinapatha*) surrounds three sides of the *garbhagriha*, which is lit by three windows in each of the north, west and south sides. The hall seems to have had entrance porches (*mukhamandapa*) on north, south and east. Only the western and part of the southern walls of the hall are intact. To the east of the hall is a small plinth housing a Nandi image. (Plate 6-48)

The temple is built on a high plinth with five mouldings. The walls are symmetrically relieved into four projections with niches (*devakoshthas*) housing sculptures of Visnu and Siva in various stages of carving. The three intervening recesses have perforated windows. An exquisitely carved frieze of dwarfs (*ganas*) runs below the eave (*kapota*). The round bodied *ganas* appear struggling, as if it were to carry the superstructure. The parapet consists of a string (*hara*) of architectural elements called *karnakutas* (square) and *salas* (oblong) corresponding to the relieved bays below. These elements and the curved linking courses (*harantaras*) are adorned with *kudus* with miniature shrines (*panjaras*) carved in their interior. The superstructure over the sanctum is a perfect example of two tired *dravida vimana* repeating certain elements of the parapet and wall below and crowned with a four sided *kuta sikhara* with a finial (*kalasa*).

Monolithic stone pillar bearing inscription: Engraved on an octagonal pillar set up in front of the Mallikarjuna temple at Pattadakal, this inscription is in the *Siddhamatrika* and Kannada–Telugu characters of the 8th century CE. It opens with invocations to Siva and Haragauri. It refers to the setting up of a *trisula* pillar (*trisula-mudrankita saila-stamba*) by Jnanasivacharya who had come from *Mrigathanikahara-Vishaya* on the northern bank of the Ganga River and was staying in the Vijayeswara temple (modern Sangameswara). This pillar was set up to the south of Vijayeswara Lokeswara temple built by Lokamata (i.e. Lokamahadevi), who was the queen of Vikramaditya Satyasraya the conqueror of Kanchipura, and to the west of Trilokeswara temple (Mallikarjuna) built by Trilokyamahadevi who was also the beloved queen of Vikramaditya and the mother of king Kirtivarma II. A grant of 30 *navaratnas* of land near village Arapunise was made by Jnanasivacharya for the Vijayeswara temple's worship after having bought that land from Aryabhatta who had received it from Vijayaditya. Apparently, it belongs to the reign of Chalukya Kirttivarma-II (744–756 CE).

Mallikarjuna Temple: This temple, called *Trailokeswara Maha Saila Prasada* in an inscription was built around 740 CE by one of the Queens, Trailokyamahadevi of Vikramaditya II (733–45 CE) to commemorate her husband's victory over the Pallavas of Kanchipuram. In general appearance and style it resembles the Virupaksha temple built for the same purpose, at the same time, and most probably by the same guild of architects. These two temples stand side by side and closely resemble each other in their plan elevation, decoration and even the arrangements of sculptural art. Presenting the fully developed southern *vimana* style, this temple consists on plan a sanctum (*garbhagriha*) with circumambulatory path (*pradakshinapatha*) an antechamber (*antarala*) with a sub-shrine each on either side in front, a *sabhamandapa* with entrance porches on the east, north and south and a separate *Nandimandapa* in front. The sub-shrines, originally dedicated to Ganesha and Mahisasuramardhini, are now empty. Only a portion of the enclosure walls (*prakara*) is intact on the southern side and two upright pillars and a few huge stone blocks mark the once existence of the western gateway (*pratoli*). The temple is built on a high plinth comprising five fully evolved mouldings and its wall surfaces are divided in to projection and recesses accommodating sculptures and windows as in the case of the Virupaksha temple. These sculptures are mainly Saivite and unfinished in some cases. Even though the parapet and the superstructure of this temple are similar to those of the Virupaksha temple, there are one or two noticeable differences. Thus, the topmost storey of the superstructure of the Mallikarjuna temple is completely bereft of *hara* elements like *kuta*, *sala* etc., which is considered a transitory stage in the development of southern temple style. Likewise, this temple has a hemi-spherical roof (*sikhara*) as against the square roof of the Virupaksha temple. Further, Nataraja is depicted in the shallow arch of the *sukanasi* of this temple. The epic and puranic episodes carved on the pillars of the *sabhamandapa* include goddesses fighting Mahishasura, churning of the ocean (*samudra-manthana*), Narasimha fighting Hiranyakasipu, "exploits of Krishna," slaying of Maricha etc. The amorous couples relieved on the engaged columns here are slightly bigger in size and better preserved than those in the Virupaksha temple. Even in its ruined state, the well conceived and skillfully executed *Nandimandapa* presents an elegant piece of architecture. Its basement (*adhistana*) has beautifully carved figures of elephants and other animals. Its prominently projecting balconies show nicely shaped sixteen-sided pillars with scroll belts. Graceful female figures are carved in the ornate niches on the walls. (Plate 6-46)

Jambulingeswara Temple: Built probably in the middle of the 7th century CE this temple represents a stage of experimentation in introducing a *sukanasi* projecting from the *sikhara* (over the *mandapa*) in front. Facing the east, this structure consists on plan a square sanctum (*garbhagriha*) housing a linga on the *pitha* with *pranala* on the north and a *mandapa*. To the east of the temple are seen the ruins of a raised platform and basement of a *Nandimandapa* on it. The couchant image of Nandi on this basement is worn out. The temple is built on a high plinth having five mouldings with its topmost moulding (*kapota*) decorated with *kudus*, miniature *ganas* and birds. The walls are decorated with pilasters at the corners and on either side of the side of the windows and niches. Walls of the sanctum have centrally projected ornate *devakoshtha* (niches) having sculptures of Siva (south), Surya (west) and Visnu (north). The ends of the roof slabs of the *mandapa* and the ceiling slabs of the *garbhagriha* resting upon the eave are carved with *vyalas* and *makaras* and a frieze of swans runs below the cornice all round. The superstructure over the sanctum is of the *rekhanagara* (northern) style with a curvilinear profile rising in three diminishing stages, but its *amalaka* and *kalasa* are missing. A small *sukanasi* projecting from the *sikhara* (over the *mandapa*) is seen in the form of a trefoil *chaitya*-arch depicting Natesa with Parvati and Nandi flanked by *nagas* in *anjali* (adorative) posture. (Plate 6-49)

The doorway of the *mandapa* is adorned with three *shakhas* (decorative door-bands). The *stambhasakhas* on either side have *purnakumbhas* below their capitals and there is a frieze of swans over the door. The sanctum doorway has four *sakhas* with dwarfs and attendants carved beneath. The *stambhasakhas* (pilasters) support a flat eave and a pediment above consisting of *kutas and salas*.

Kasivisweswara Temple: Datable to the middle of the 8th century CE this temple was probably the last to be built in the Badami Chalukyan style at Pattadakal. It contains on plan a *garbhagriha* housing a *linga* on a square *pitha* with *pranala* on north, an *antarala* and a *mandapa*. To the east of *mandapa* is a plinth of a small entrance porch (*mukhamandapa*) and further east there is a moulded basement of a *Nandimandapa* retaining two square pillars and a couchant image of *nandi* in the centre. The two carved brackets projecting from the eastern wall of the *mandapa* on either side above the entrance doorways also indicate the once existence of an entrance porch.

The temple is built on a high plinth with the five usual mouldings decorated with the figures of horses, lions, elephants, peacocks, creeper designs and *kudu* motifs. A noteworthy feature of the temple is that its outer walls are symmetrically relieved in to five projections (*pancharatha*) and recesses carried to the superstructure. But for the eastern side, wall surfaces are relieved with pairs of pilasters supporting pediments of *chaitya* arches. On the northern wall of the *mandapa* there are sculptures of Ardhanariswara and Kalabhairava housed in niches. On either side of the *mandapa* entrance the wall surface is relieved with miniature pavilions fashioned in the *Dravida* (Southern) style. The cornice (*kapota*) has *chaitya* arches (*kudus*) for decorative motif and the upper portions of the walls are embellished with dwarfs (*ganas*) carrying garlands, *kirtimukhas* and flying couples.

The superstructure displays the fully evolved *rekhanagara* (Northern) Sikhara rising in five stages with its *amalaka* and *kalasa* missing. A mesh-like design covers its surface completely. The well-developed *sukanasi* projection has a fine sculpture of dancing Umamaheswara within the *Chaitya*-arch. The *mandapa* has an ornate doorway of five *sakhas* with the river goddesses carved below. The *lalatabimba* on the lintel depicts the figure of Garuda holding tails of snakes. Naga in *anjali-mudra* (adoration pose) are seen near the river goddesses. Carvings on the pillars and pilasters of the *mandapa* depict episodes from the *Bhagavata* and *Sivapuranas*. These sculptures including themes like Ravana lifting Kailasa, Kalyansundarmurti, exploits of Krishna etc., testify to the narrative skill of the Chalukyan artists. The elegantly carved central ceiling panel of the *mandapa* depicts Siva, Parvati holding Kartikeya and Nandi, surrounded by the *ashtadikpalas*. Lions and *vyalas* carved on the beams appear to support the ceiling as it were. The *antarala* doorway is similar to that of the *mandapa* and has *Saiva Dvarapalas* on either side.

Papanatha Temple: Dedicated to Mukteswara according to inscriptions, this modest temple seems to have been completed around 740 CE. There seems to have been a change of intention during the course of construction of this temple as can be known from its too narrow circumambulatory path whose floor slabs conceal the external moulding of the *garbhagriha* walls and the buttress like projections of the north and south *garbhagriha* walls into the *ardhamandapa*, both of which are unusual features.

Facing the east, this temple has on plan a sanctum (*garbhagriha*) surrounded by a circumambulatory path (*pradakshinapatha*) with *devakoshtha* pavilions in its three walls, an *ardhamandpa*, a *sabhamandapa* and an entrance porch (*mukhamandapa*) provided with *kakshasana*. Curiously, there is no *Nandimandapa* but an ornate image of Nandi is housed in the eastern half of the *sabhamandapa*.

The temple is built on a plinth of five mouldings, embellished with animal motifs, floral designs and *kudus*. The wall surfaces are relieved with niches (*devakoshthas*) housing Saiva and Vaishnava deities and depicting episodes from the Ramayana. These niches are topped by various designs of *chaitya* arch motifs and interspersed with perforated windows. The three *devakoshtha* pavilions house images of Siva in different forms. A characteristic feature of the temple is its well-developed *rekhanagara* (northern) *sikhara* with an elaborately carved *chaitya* arch enshrining Nataraja on the frontage of the *sukanasi*. The *amalaka* and *kalasa* are, however, missing.

Introduction of narrative panels depicting the episodes from the *Kiratarjuniyam* and the *Ramayana* on the outer wall surfaces is another noteworthy feature of the temple. Significantly, names of the main characters of the episodes as also those of the sculptures like Baladeva, Devaraya, Changama, Revadi, Ovajja, etc., are found engraved in right places.

Pillars of the entrance porch bear *Kinnara* couples and engaged columns have the figures of *dvarapalas*. Lions and *sardulas* are carved at the corners above the entablature and the ceiling panel depicts dancing Siva with Parvati and musicians and flying figures. Pillars and pilasters of the other *mandapas* are relieved with medium-sized graceful sculptures of damsels and couples (*mithunas*) in playful moods. The central bay ceiling of the *sabhamandapa* is adorned with panels depicting Anantasayana surrounded by the *dikpalas*, *nagaraja* and Gajalakshmi from east to west. Here figures of roaring lions are carved projecting from above the entablature. Central ceiling of the *ardhamandapa* has relief sculpture of dancing Siva in the company of Parvati and musicians. The western ceiling here has figure of *Nagaraja*. Both the *mandapas* and the sanctum have ornate doorframes.

Chandrashekhara Temple: This temple, facing east, stands about 15 ft. to the left of the Sangameswara temple and is situated between Sangameswara and Galaganatha temples. The temple measures 33ft in length and 17ft in breadth and stands on an *adhishthana*. On plan, it has a small and receding *garbhagriha* and a closed hall. The *garbhagriha* houses a *linga* on a pedestal. The exterior walls of the temple are decorated with pilasters at regular intervals. There is a niche (*devakoshtha*) on either side of the *garbhagriha*. The doorframe of the shrine is decorated with *sakhas* and there is no dedicatory block on the lintel. There is a *dvarapala* standing on either side of the *garbhagriha*. There is no *sikhara* over the shrine. The doorframe of the hall is also carved with *sakhas*. On architectural grounds, this temple may be assigned to 750 CE.

Kadasiddheswara Temple: This modest temple probably built in the middle of the seventh century CE shows an experimental stage in the development of temple architecture, particularly in the axial expansion of the plan and superstructure. Facing the east, this temple has on plan a square sanctum (*garbhagriha*) housing a *linga* on the *pitha*, an astylar (lacking columns and pilasters), rectangular *mandapa* and probably a *mukhamandapa* as suggested by the plinth and the brackets above the *dvarapalas* flanking the *mandapa* doorway decorated with five bands (*sakha*), which are now worn out. The temple is built on a raised plinth with the usual five mouldings. The wall surfaces are plain but for a frieze of *ganas* carrying garlands at the top. The superstructure is the *rekhanagara* (northern) type having a curvilinear profile with a rudimentary *sukanasi* projection on the east. The *sukanasi* depicts dancing Siva and Parvati in a shallow trefoil (ornamental design with leaves) *chaitya* arch. The niches on the outer walls of the sanctum (*garbhagriha*) house the images of Ardhanariswara (north), Harihara (west) and Siva (south). The doorway of the sanctum has pilasters set among decorated bands (*sakhas*) with Siva and Parvati seated at the centre of the lintel and Brahma and Visnu on either side. River goddesses and attendants are carved at either side below the bands.

Galaganatha Temple: Facing east, this temple, built around 750 CE, is a typical example of a finely evolved *rekhanagara prasada*. It has on plan a sanctum (*garbhagriha*) housing a *linga* and a vestibule (*antarala*), both surrounded by a closed circumambulatory path (*pradakshinapatha*), a hall (*sabhamandapa*) and an entrance porch (*mukhamandapa*). Of these *mandapas*, only the plinth is extant now. The temple is built on a plinth with three highly ornate mouldings depicting dwarfs in playful mood and *chaitya* arch motifs. The outer walls of the circumambulatory path (mostly ruined) had *devakoshta* pavilions at cardinal points, of which only the southern one is intact. It has two round shafted pillars with vases and foliage (*ghatapallava*) at their bases and capitals. The sculpture housed in this pavilion is that of Siva slaying Andhakasura. The eight-armed god wears a wreath of human skulls (*mundamala*) like a sacred thread (*yajnopavita*) and is depicted as piercing the demon with the trident (*trisula*). Windows on either side of this image are divided into square and triangular perforations by bars. Some interesting figures are carved in the box-like projections of the basement moulding to the east. One of these boxes depicts the story of the mischievous monkey from the *Panchatantra* and the figure of a two-faced bird in another box seems to narrate yet another story from the same work. The well preserved northern superstructure (*rekhanagara sikhara*), topped by *amalaka* and *kalasa*, is the most striking feature of the temple. It has a well developed *sukasani*, which is damaged. The outer walls of the sanctum are relieved with niches (*devakoshthas*) created by ornate pilasters at the central portions. These niches are flanked by finely executed trefoil *chaitya* window motifs on the lateral projections. The ornate doorframe of the outer chamber with five *sakhas* depicts the river goddesses at the base and dancing *Siva* on the lintel. (Plate 6-47)

Jaina Temple: Separated from the group of Brahmanical temples, both in terms of time and space, this Jaina temple (locally called as the Jaina Narayana) was built in the 9th century CE probably in the reign of the Rashtrakuta king Krishna II. This three storeyed temple with the two lower storeys being functional, is the last in the temple series at Pattadakal. Certain features exhibited in this temple became in the courses of time essential elements of the temples of the Kalyani Chalukyas. This temple has on plan a square sanctum (*garbhagriha*) with a circumambulatory path (*pradakshinapatha*) whose walls are collapsed, an antechamber (*antarala*), a hall (*mandapa*) and a porch (*mukhamandapa*). It stands on a plinth of triple moulding having projections and recesses. The *garbhagriha* walls show slight central projections (*bhadras*) and a range of thin tetragonal pilasters. The north and south walls of the *mandapa* are divided into seven bays. The recesses between these bays contain narrow niches adorned with projected arched openings (*nasika*) containing the seated Jinas and other figures at places. These walls are crowned by a string of architectural elements called *kuta* (square), *sala* (oblong) and *panjara* (miniature shrine models). Water chutes (*pranalas*) to drain the roof are provided in the recesses (*salilantaras*) just below the roof level.

Walls of the upper shrine reflect the arrangements of the walls of the ground floor on a diminished scale. Its *antarala* front is covered by the basal part of the *sukanasi* projection, while the parapet on the other three sides carries *karnakutas* and *salas*. The third storey of lesser width is relieved on its sides except on the front side. The bays contain kudu-like arches and half-arches as in northern style temples. The subdued *griva* recess over this storey supports a beautifully carved square *sikhara*.

The open porch has peripheral rows of pillars connected by balcony seating (*kakshasana*). All these pillars except the two abutting on the hall as well as the four central ones, though of sand stones, are partially lathe-turned. The exterior of the *kakshasana* is adorned with bas relief figures of *purnaghata*, *nidhis*, *vyalas*, dancers etc., which are partially finished. On the wall of the hall, inside the porch to the either side of the doorway, are large elephant figures with riders. The doorframe of the hall is decorated with six bands (*sakhas*) with *Sankanidhi*, *Padmanidhi* and *purnaghatas* below. There are massive pillars in the hall and *antarala*. The doorframe of the sanctum has five bands, of which a handsome pillaret on either side supports an elegant crocodile (*makara*) with a very florid tail. The *kudu* motifs on the *kapota* tier of the plinth and on the *kapota* of the wall have lost their original shape and have become flat triangular reliefs. The pillar capitals too have lost their original shape and robustness and are transformed in to mere conventional shapes. Likewise, the square *sikhara* with its offsets takes the shape of a twelve ribbed member. All modifications are characteristic of later Kalyani Chalukyan temples that came in to being in the subsequent centuries.

Excavation by the Archaeological Survey of India in the premises of the temple has brought to light the remains of a large temple complex built in bricks and also a beautiful sculpture of Tirthankara standing in *samabhanga* indicating the existence of a temple, probably belonging to the pre or beginning of the Badami Chalukyan rule.

Aihole

Aihole is a village having historic temple complexes and is located 510 km from Bengaluru. A few of the temples here were converted into living apartments for human beings and cattle once the city lost its historical importance around 1400 CE. That is the reason for sometimes the strange names of the temples. For instance, the Lad Khan temple is named after a mendicant who lived here. It seems that after 1400 CE this place went into oblivion and the monuments were occupied by the village folk until recovery by the Archaeological Survey of India nearly a century ago. Many of the temples had become defunct, neglected, not conserved properly as the villagers did not either know their antiquity or were oblivious of the fact that these comprised the rich heritage of the place. The monuments are now under the control and supervision of the ASI. However, the conservation and maintenance effort in respect of some still needs to be strengthened.

Aihole was earlier known as *Ayyavole* and *Aryapura* in its inscriptions. It was established in 450 CE as first capital of Badami Chalukya kings. A place known by as Morera Angadigalu near the Meguti hillocks has a large number of cysts of prehistoric period. The place was an *agrahara*. Aihole has been described as the cradle of temple architecture. Some brick structures of pre-Chalukyan times have also been excavated in this village.

The temples of Aihole are among the most distinctive examples in Indian tradition which range from dolmen chambers on the cliffs of Meguti hill, to the temples of Badami Chalukyas to those of Kalyani Chalukyas charting a history of over a millennium. About 40 megalithic monuments dating back to 3rd and 2nd century BCE have been identified and conserved in situ on the hill. There are five caves of which one relates to Buddhist faith, two to Jaina and two to the Hindu faith. There are about 125 structural temples beginning with the Badami Chalukyas times and coming down to fringes of Hoysala period in the 12th century CE.

The structural temples cover the entire radius of the Aihole village from the Jaina Mena Basadi in the east to Ambiger-gudi in the west and from Ramalinga-Galaganatha group of temples in the south to Tara Basappa temple in the north. There are many partly existing temples and upto plinth level structures scattered all around in the village and in the fields bordering Malaprabha River. A stone fort runs around the village and a few temples are located within the fort compound as well. The walls of the fort can be seen on the Meguti hill also.

The cluster of temples may be grouped and a tentative figure of the number of surviving temples is as under:

S.No.	Name of the Temple Group or Complex	Number
1	Durga and Lad Khan	11
2	Gauri-gudi	5
3	Mallikarjuna	5
4	Kare and Bile	5
5	Jyotirlinga Complex	16
6	Meguti hill site (Buddhist *chaitya*)	4+1
7	Charantimatha (Jaina group)	3
8	Maddina or Basavanna	8
9	Hucchappayya Matha	2
10	Konta gudi	4
11	Veniyar gudi	9
12	Arali Basavanna	2

Contd.

S.No.	Name of the Temple Group or Complex	Number
13	Hucchappayya gudi	1
14	Galaganatha	16
15	Ramalinga devasthana	5
16	Rachi gudi	1
17	Ambiger gudi	3
18	Hucchimalli gudi	3
19	Chikki matha	4
20	Tarabasappa	1
21	Ravanaphadi cave and structural temples	2+2
22	Boyar gudi	2
23	Gardi gudi	1
24	Gaudariswara gudi	1
25	Desayar gudi	1
26	Mena basadi (Jaina) cave temple	1
27	Jaina cave (small)	1

The temples here set models which became the guiding examples for future temple building activity in Karnataka and other southern Indian states. Experimentation with different architectural styles was undertaken by the artisans. The artisans worked on the rocks to create the earliest rock-cut shrines. The experimentation of the artisans ultimately culminated into the full-fledged Badami Chalukya style of architecture.

During their early days the Badami Chalukyas inherited architectural styles largely from the neighbours to the north and south of their kingdom. Usage of curved towers decorated with blind arches came from northern India. Pilastered walls with panel inserts are a southern Indian style. The usage of Deccan style is in their balcony seating, angled eaves and sloping roofs, and elaborately carved columns and ceilings. In short, they artistically brought together the prevailing styles in their neighbourhood to create the Badami Chalukya style.

Typical features unique to Badami Chalukyas architecture include mortarless assembly, an emphasis on length rather than width or height, flat roofs, richly carved ceilings. Sculpturally, the emphasis was on relatively few major figures, which tend to be isolated from each other rather than arranged in crowded groups. The aesthetic sensibility of sculpture from this period also seems to retain a certain classical quality whose impulse does not carry over into later periods of Indian art. Some of the prominent temples in Aihole are described below.

Durga temple: or fortress temple is the best known of the Aihole temples and is very photogenic. It is apsidal in plan, along the lines of a Buddhist *chaitya* with a high moulded *adisthana* and a tower which is curvilinear *sikhara*. A pillared corridor runs around the temple, enveloping the shrine, the *mukhamantapa* and the *sabhamantapa*. All through the temple, there are beautiful carvings. The temple appears to be of the late 7th or early 8th century CE. (Plate 6-50)

The architecture of the temple is predominantly *Dravida* with *Nagara* style features also used in certain areas. The Durga Temple is considered a unique and magnificent temple of the Badami Chalukyan period. It is dedicated to either Visnu or Siva as the representations of Visnu are as numerous as also those of Siva. The most original feature of the temple is a peristyle delimiting an ambulatory around the temple itself and whose walls are covered with sculptures of different gods or goddesses. Two staircases provide access to the porch at the entrance of the temple itself. The sober and square pillars are decorated with characters around the porch and the entrance to the peristyle. The parapet is carved with niches and small animals.

The porch gives access to rooms with pillars (*mukhamandapa* and *sabhamandapa*) to get into the heart of the shrine (*garbagriha*).

The plan of the temple is oblong and apsidal. It means that the corridor with pillars between the porch and the heart of the shrine encompasses the heart of shrine and allows the visitor to perform the *parikrama* (circumambulation ritual). This apse gives outward through openings between the pillars.

The shape of the temple, in Indian traditional architecture, is known as *Gajaprasta* which means the resemblance to the back of an elephant. The temple's unusual apsidal form is thought to imitate the earlier Buddhist *chaitya* halls, but later studies established that apsidal design in Indian architecture is pan-Indian tradition, which was in practice even before Buddhist architecture. The heart of the shrine (*garbagriha*) is surmounted by a tower which laid the design for the future higher towers *sikharas* and *vimanas*.

Lad Khan Temple: dedicated to Siva, is one of the oldest Hindu temples. It was built in the 5th century by the kings of the Badami Chalukya dynasty. It is located to the south of the Durga temple. The temple is named after a person named Lad khan, who turned this temple into his residence for a short period.

The temple consists of a shrine (*garbagriha*) with *mandapa* in front of it. The *mukhamandapa* is situated in front of the sanctum and consists of a set of 12 carved pillars. The *sabhamandapa* leads to the *mahamandapa* and the pillars are arranged to form two concentric squares. The walls have floral patterns on them and the windows have lattice work done in the northern style. Facing the sanctum, a second smaller sanctum is situated above the center of the hall whose outer walls have many carved images.

Originally dedicated to Visnu, now the main shrine houses a Sivalinga with a Nandi. The temple was built in a Panchayatana style, indicating a very early experiment in temple construction. The special feature of this temple is that it starts with a rectangular structure and ends with a square structure. Based on a wooden construction design, the square and rectangular plan has a steep roof, which is an adaptation of wooden styles in stone. (Plate 6-52)

The *mahamandapa* is open to exterior by large windows between the pillars. The roof above the *mahamandapa* shows a turret as a first version of the future towers-*sikharas* and *vimanas*.

Ravanaphadi: cave is one of the oldest rock cut temples in Aihole; located southeast of Hucchimalli temple. This temple dates back to the 6th century, with a rectangular shrine and has two *mandapas*. There is a Sivalinga in the inner room or sanctum sanctorum. This is a Saivite cave temple with a sanctum larger than that of the Badami Cave temples. The sanctum has a vestibule with a triple entrance and has carved pillars. The walls and sides of the temple are covered with large figures including dancing Siva. Ravalphadi rock-cut shrine is the most famous of the three rock-cut shrines at Aihole. This rock-cut shrine has a fine figure of Nataraja dancing, surrounded by *saptamatrikas*, all engraved in high relief and in an elegant styles.

Jyotirlinga Group: at a short distance to the southwest of Ravanaphadi, is the group of temples called Jyotirlinga group. Two small temples here are flat roofed and in front of them are *Nandimandapas*. The remaining temples have a sanctum, *sukanasi* and a front hall in each of the temples. Two of the temples have *nagara* style towers. Two of the temples have inscriptions of the Kalyana Chalukya period. The rest of the temples now dilapidated are of about the 8th to 10th centuries CE. (Plate 6-51)

Meguti Jain temple: stands on a hillock. It is the only dated monument built in 634 CE as evidenced by an inscription of that period. The temple sits on a raised platform, and a flight of steps leads one to the *mukhamandapa*. The pillared *mukhamandapa* is a large one. A flight of stairs leads to another shrine on the roof, directly above the main shrine. From the roof, one can have a panoramic view of the plain with a hundred temples or so. The temple which was possibly never completed gives important evidence of early development in *dravidian* style of architecture. The dated inscription found on the outer wall of the temple records the construction of the temple by Ravikirti, a scholar in the court of emperor Pulakesin II. The first floor includes a pillared hall, and at the wall behind it are three cells. The central room is the shrine cell. The second floor similarly has a verandah and a square cell behind. This is an ordinary structure and is assigned to the 5th century. To the south-east of Meguti is a small Jaina cave, which has a porch, a wall behind and a sanctum in the back which houses a five-foot tall-Bahubali figure and other Tirthankaras are also engraved in other parts against walls.

Enroute to Meguti temple on same hill top there is 6th century two-storied Buddhist Cave temple which has partly rock-cut structure.

Galaganatha group of temples: is one of nearly thirty temples on the bank of the Malaprabha River. The main shrine of the Galaganatha temple enshrining Siva as Galaganatha has a curvilinear *sikhara*, and has images of Ganga and Yamuna at the entrance to this shrine. Galaganatha group of temples comprises about 38 small shrines in which the shrine of Galaganatha is intact, and most of the others are in ruins. The temple has been assigned to the 8th century CE. There is another 10th century *trikutachala* temple also found in this group.

Suryanarayana temple: has a 0.6 m high statue of Surya along with his consorts Usha and Sandhya being drawn by horses. The temple dates from the 7th or 8th century CE and has a four pillared inner sanctum and a *nagara* style tower over it. Suryanarayana Gudi is to the northeast of Ladkhan temple.

Chakra Gudi is a little further to the south from Lad Khan group with a hall and sanctum. Its tower is in *rekhanagara* style. This temple was probably built in the 9th century CE.

Badigera gudi is to the west of Chakragudi which was originally a Surya temple, which has a porch, hall and a cell shrine and over it a *rekhanagara* tower. The temple belongs to the 9th century CE

Triyambakeswara Group: is close to the Charantimatha, towards northeast two of the temples are *trikutachalas*, assigned to the 12th century CE. Nearby is Maddinagudi. There is an idol of Nataraja in the *mandapa* and this is an 11th century CE temple. To the north of Triyambakeswara lie some Jaina *basadis* called Jainanarayana or Yoginarayana. These are Kalyani Chalukya style *trikutachala* structures (11th century). The Parshvanatha idol in the central shrine remains. There are three other shrines here. (Plate 6-55)

Ambigera Gudi Group is situated to the west of the Durga temple outside the fort. There are three temples of this group. The biggest among them has a *rekhanagara* tower. It is supposed to be 10th century structure. The easternmost shrine is a square building open on the west but walled on three sides. It lacks a *sikhara* and seems to have been a subsidiary building to the temple in the middle which is surrounded on three sides by an open verandah roofed by sloping slabs. The sanctuary towards the rear of its interior accommodates a damaged image of Suryanarayana wearing a crown and fluted headdress. (Plate 6-53)

Huchimalli Group of temples, to the north of the village behind the travelers' bungalow is a beautiful temple. The sanctum here has a *pradakshinapatha* and its external walls contain lattices. The sanctum has a northern style *rekhanagara* tower. It is in this temple the *sukanasi* or the vestibule was introduced for the first time. Another small temple to the north of Huchimalligudi is assigned to the 11th century. Its plain exterior with small perforated windows contrasts with the comparatively well preserved tower. The temple is entered through a small porch which has a carved ceiling with a unique image of Kartikeya flying through the air on a peacock. A later inserted screen wall within the temple creates a small square vestibule in front of the linga sanctuary. (Plate 6-54)

Gaudara gudi is very close to the Ladkhan temple, built on the lines of Ladkhan temple. It is standing on high moulded base. An outer wall contains 16 pillars. Between them, stone slabs are fixed to serve as walls. An 8th-century inscription here refers to this as Bhagavati temple.

Jaina temple and Gouri temple: These two temples are located within the walls of the fort like wall surrounding the Aihole village. As one enters, the Jaina temple is the first to be seen and to the north of the Jaina temples is the Gouri temple. It is in Kalyani Chalukya style assignable to the 12th century. Gouri temple is the largest and most elaborate Kalyani Chalukya temple in Aihole. Though partly obscured by the houses that crowd up to its outer walls, the temple incorporates a spacious *mandapa* with porch projections on three sides. The ceiling above has a design of rotated squares crowned with a dome like roof. Set into the *mandapa* walls between the balconies are deep niches topped by *Nagara* styled towers in shallow relief. A finely carved icon of Durga bearing different weapons in her eight hands is placed in the vestibule. A few metres south of the Gouri temple is the Jaina complex. It consists of two open temples linked by an open porch with balcony seating. Installed in the western sanctum is an imposing polished basalt image of Parsvanatha.

Huchappayya Matha is towards west of the village. This temple includes a hall, and a sanctum. Here is an inscription of 1067 CE. The four pillared of its frontal east are graced with human loving couples (*mithunas*) including one showing horse headed woman in the company of a man in fierce expression. The *mandapa* interior has three fine celing panels from entrance and they depict Visnu on Sesha in the company of flying *gandharvas*, siva and Parvati on Nandi and Brahma on his mount *hamsa*. A Nandi placed in the middle of the *mandapa* faces towards the linga installed in the sanctuary.

Kontigudi group of temples situated in about the middle of the bazaar comprises four temples. The first among them has the *Trimurti* idols on the ceiling of the *mandapa*. These temples are assignable to the 7th century with various adjuncts being added during later centuries. Only one among them is dilapidated, and is of about the 10th century.

Charanthimatha Group of temples are located very close to the Kontigudi group to the north east. It is a group of Jaina temples. In course of time they came under the control of one Charantimatha and hence the present name. The principal temple among these is *trikutachala*, and a hall connects the three shrines with a portico in front. It is about 11th or 12th century CE structure, built in the Kalyani Chalukya style. There is a twin *basadi* with one porch serving both and each houses 12 Tirthankars. An inscription here records the date of construction as 1120 CE.

Huchappayya (gudi) temple has a curvilinear tower (*sikhara*) over the sanctum (unlike the Lad Khan temple). The interior of the temple has beautiful carvings. The Huchappayya temple is located to the south of Aihole fort, on the way to the Malaprabha river. This Siva temple has a *mukhamandapa*, a hall and the sanctum, adornd with a *Rekhanagara sikhara*. There are several big square pillars in the porch and hall. Pillars of the porch have finely carved figures of couples, and on the ceiling a fine Nataraja image. Exterior walls of the sanctum have three niches with Narasimha. This temple was constructed in about 8th century CE.

Ramalinga group of temples lies to the south of Veniyar shrines. Chief shrine among this group is Ramalinga. In this *trikutachala* shrine two cells have Sivalinga and the third has image of Parvati. The date of construction is around the 11th century CE. Facing westward, the shrine has two *Kadambanagara* towers.

The Museum and Art Gallery at Aihole in the Durga temple compound is a sculpture gallery maintained by the Archaeological Survey of India. The garden in front of the museum is dotted with hero stones and *sati* stones (*mastikallu*) dating from the 12th century and later. The chief exhibit within the museum is a deeply carved panel portraying Ambika seated beneath a flowering tree brought from the Meguti Jaina temple. A gigantic representation of evil-looking Bhairava and a complete set of *saptamatrikas* too can be seen.

Mahakuta

The **Mahakuta group of temples** is located in Mahakuta, a village on way from Badami to Pattadakal on the road going to Banashankari. It is an important place of worship for Hindus and the location of a well-known Saiva monastery. The temples are dated to the 6th or 7th century CE and were constructed by the early kings of the Chalukya dynasty of Badami. The dating of the temples is based on the style of architecture which is similar to that of the temples in nearby Aihole and the information in two notable inscriptions in the complex: the Mahakuta Pillar inscription dated between 595–602 CE (written in Sanskrit language and Kannada script); and an inscription of Vinapoti, a concubine of king Vijayaditya, dated between 696–733 CE and written in the Kannada language and script.

A natural mountain spring flows within the temple complex and feeds fresh water into a large tank called the *Visnu Pushkarni* and an ablution tank called *Papavinasha Tirtha*. Among the several shrines in the complex, the Mahakuteswara temple, built in the *dravida* style, and the Mallikarjuna temple are the largest. There is a small shrine in the centre of the *Visnu Pushkarni* tank and in it is a Siva *linga* (universal symbol of god Siva) called *Panchamukha linga*, one face for each direction and one on top. (Plate 6-58)

The most important temple here is the Mahakuteswara temple on the north side of the *Pushkarni*. Dating from the latter part of the 7th century this well proportioned monument consists of a porch contained within a later extension, a *mandapa* and a sanctuary with a *sikhara*. Though now whitewashed the outer walls preserve finely carved courtly episodes and battle scenes in the upper panels of the basement. A small pavilion housing a finely finished Nandi stands in front of the temple. The interior of the temple has been remodeled and much of its original detail is no longer in sight. (Plate 6-56)

The Sangameswara temple is built in the contrasting *Nagara* style with a characteristic curvilinear *sikhara*. The temple dates back to the same time as Mahakuteswara temple. A small porch gives access to the *garbhagriha*. The outer walls of the *garbhagriha* are embellished with the naked figure of Lakulisa with curling locks of hair, gracefully poised Ardhanariswara and Harihara (Plate 6-57). A few metres to the rear stands the Virupaksheswara temple in similar *Nagara* style. Icons of Varaha, Visnu and Narasimha can be found in this temple. The southern periphery of the Mahakuta complex is partly occupied by the Mallikarjuna temple which may be considered slightly later copy of the Mahakuteswara temple. Lot of loose sculpture including Virabhadra can be found in the complex mostly around the *Pushkarni*.

The Mahakuta complex has provided historians two important 7th century inscriptions. The Mahakuta Pillar inscription, dated variously between 595–602 CE records a grant made by Durlabhadevi, a queen of Pulakesin I (the father of king Mangalesa). The queen supplemented an earlier grant with an endowment of ten villages, including Pattadakal and Aihole to god Mahakuteswara Natha. In addition, the inscription provides important information about the Badami Chalukyan lineage, their military expeditions, their conquests and early monuments. The pillar goes by the name *Dharma-jayastambha* (Pillar of victory of religion) and is exhibited at the Bijapur Archaeological Museum. The other inscription, ascribed to Vinapoti, king Vijayaditya's concubine, is inscribed in the porch of the Mahakuteswara temple. It describes a grant of rubies and a silver umbrella to the deity *Mahakuteswara* in addition to a piece of land. Wall relief sculptures at the Mahakuta group of temples include *Ardhanariswara* (form of the Hindu god Siva) carved beautifully.

Badami

Badami formerly known as Vatapi, is a town in the Bagalkot district of Karnataka. It was the regal capital of the Badami Chalukyas from 540 to 757 CE. It is famous for rock cut and other structural temples. It is located in a ravine at the foot of a rugged, red sandstone outcrop that surrounds Agastya Lake. Badami is surrounded by many pre-historic places including Khyad area of Badami, Hiregudda, Sidlaphadi and Kutkankeri (Junjunpadi, Shigipadi and Anipadi), where one can see the rock shelters megalithic burial sites and rock paintings.

The name Vatapi has origin in the Vatapi legend of Ramayana relating to Sage Agastya. There were two demon siblings Vatapi and Ilvala. They used to kill all mendicants by tricking them in a peculiar way. The elder Ilvala would turn Vatapi into a ram and would offer its meat to the guest. As soon as the person ate the meat, Ilvala would call out the name of Vatapi. As he had a boon that whomsoever Ilvala calls would return from even the nether land, Vatapi would emerge ripping through the body of the person, thus killing him. Their trick worked until Sage Agastya countered them by digesting Vatapi before Ilvala could call for him, thus ending the life of Vatapi at the hands of Ilvala. Two of the hills in Badami represent the demons Vatapi and Ilvala.

Pulakesin I's son Kirtivarma I strengthened Vatapi and he had three sons Pulakesin II, Vishnuvardhana and Buddhavarasa, when he died they were minors. Kirtivarma-I's brother Mangalesa ruled Vatapi and he tried to establish himself as the king but was killed by Pulakesin II who ruled between 610 to 642 CE. Vatapi was the capital of the Badami Chalukyas, who ruled much of Karnataka, Maharastra, few parts of Tamil Nadu and Andhra Pradesh between the 6th and 8th centuries. The rock-cut Badami cave temples were sculpted mostly between the 6th and 8th centuries. The four cave temples represent the secular nature of the rulers with tolerance and a religious following that inclines towards Hinduism, Buddhism and Jainism. Cave 1 is devoted to Siva, and Caves 2 and 3 are dedicated to Visnu, whereas cave 4 displays reliefs of Jaina Tirthankaras. Deep caverns with carved images of the various incarnations of Hindu gods are strewn across the area, under boulders and in the red sandstone. From an architectural and archaeological perspective, they provide critical evidence of the early styles and stages of the southern Indian architecture.

Badami has eighteen inscriptions among them some inscriptions are important. The first Sanskrit inscription in old Kannada script, on a hillock dates back to 543 CE, from the period of Pulakesin I (Vallabheswara), the second is the 578 CE cave inscription of Mangalesa in Kannada language and script and the third is the Kappe Arabhatta records, the earliest available Kannada poetry in *tripadi* (three line) metre.

Landmarks in Badami include cave temples, gateways, forts, inscriptions and sculptures. An architectural and sculptural description of the four Cave temples follows.

Badami Cave temples are considered an example of Indian rock-cut architecture initiated by the Badami Chalukyas during the 6th century. Badami is situated on the west bank of an artificial lake (Agastya Lake) filled with greenish water dammed by an earthen wall faced with stone steps. Badami is surrounded in the north and south by forts built in later times from the ramparts that crown their summits.

The planning of the four caves is simple. The entrance is a verandah (*mukhamandapa*) with stone columns and brackets, a distinctive feature of these caves, leading to a columned hall (also *mahamandapa*) and then to the small square shrine (*garbhaghrha*) cut deep into the cave. The Cave temples are linked by stepped path with intermediate terraces that offer spectacular views across the town and lake. Cave-temples are labelled 1–4 in their ascending series even though this numbering does not necessarily reflect the sequence of excavation or any chronological order. Important part of historical heritage at Badami cave temples are inscriptions in old Kannada script. There is also the fifth natural cave temple in Badami, a Buddhist temple in natural cave which can be entered kneeling on all fours.

Cave 1: The Cave 1 portrays Lord Siva in his very beautiful incarnation of Nataraja. Lord Siva in this incarnation has 18 arms. Some of the arms have weapons while some of the arms depict beautiful dance postures. The weapons include drums, trident, axe etc. Some arms also have serpents coiled around them. Siva has his son Ganesha and the bull Nandi by his side. They also are in beautiful postures. The two sons of Siva, Ganesha and Kartikeya are seen riding a peacock in one of the carved sculptures on the walls of the cave. Adjoining to the Nataraja, a wall also depicts the adorable goddess Mahishasuramardini. She has been shown in an angry incarnation killing a buffalo with a trident. (Plate 6-59)

The entrance of the cave is like a verandah. The verandah having four columns is very beautifully sculpted with mind blowing images of Siva in different dancing positions and different incarnations. The cave also has carved sculptures of the goddesses Lakhsmi and Parvati to the left of Lord Siva. To the left, there is also a carved sculpture of Harihara having an axe and a serpent in hand. To the right, Ardhanariswara is sculpted on the end of the walls. All the carved sculptures have beautiful ornaments worn by them and are surrounded by animals and birds. The ornaments have designs with lotus carved on them. There is also an image of the *Vidyadhara* couple on the ceiling flying in the air. Beautiful swords are also carved on the walls. The ceiling also depicts Nagaraja, the king of the snakes (Plate 6-60). The Nagaraja is surrounded by a lot of other serpents coiled around him. There are sections in the cave which are orthogonal in shape. The bands in those sections are decorated with jewellery and garlands. There is a cleavage in the rear side of the cave. It led to the formation of a square sanctuary having beautiful images carved on it. (Plate 6-61)

The cave has beautiful bays and pilasters. The system of using columns gives the cave a foliant look. The cave being on a hill cliff gives an excellent view of the town. All the figures of the gods and goddesses are very excellently carved. The cave also has many human figures doing different actions which are neatly carved.

Cave 2: was created in late 6th century CE, is almost same as cave 1 in terms of its layout and dimensions but it is consecrated to Visnu who is shown here as Trivikrama with one foot on Earth and another directed to the north. Visnu in this temple is also represented as Varaha (boar) and Krishna *avatars*. Cave is reached by climbing 64 steps from the first cave. Entrance is adorned with reliefs of guardians.

The entrance of the cave has two armed guardians holding flowers rather than weapons. The end wall of the outer verandah is occupied by sculpted panels, to the right, Trivikrama and to the left, Varaha rescuing Bhudevi. The adjacent side walls have smooth surfaces with traces of paintwork. The columns shows gods and battle scenes, the churning of cosmic ocean, Gajalakshmi and figures around Brahma and figures around Visnu asleep on Sesha, illustration of the birth of Krishna, Krishna's youth, Krishna with *gopis* and cows. The ceiling shows a wheel with sixteen fish spokes in a square frame along with *swastikas* and flying couples. The end bays have a flying couple and Visnu on *Garuda*. The doorway is framed by pilasters carrying an entablature with three blocks embellished with *gavaksha* ornament. (Plates 6-62 and 6-63)

Cave 3: The theme on which the cave 3 is based is Saivite and Vaishnavite combined. The third cave is dedicated to Visnu, and is the best and the biggest, and it has splendid giant figures of Trivikrama, Shankaranarayana, Anantasayana, Paravasudeva, Bhuvaraha, Harihara and Narasimha (Plates 6-64 and 6-65). All these statues are engraved in a vigorous style. An inscription found here records the creation of the shrine by the Badami Chalukya king Mangalesa in 578 CE. Mangalesa was on the throne from 597 to 609 CE. It is common that Indian cave temples were patronised by influential members of royal families. These inscriptions are in Kannada language. The age of cave temple is known with certainty because of the inscriptions on the rock in this cave. Rock-cut temple has north-south orientation providing maximum amount of sunlight in winter. The hall and the verandah dig up to 14.5 m deep into the mountain and the shrine extends the cave some 4 m more inside. The Hall goes up to 4 m high.

Cave 3 is 60 steps away from the cave 2. The temple with its gigantic facade of 21 m wide is adorned of with hefty columns in a row. Below the columns there is a frieze consisting of 30 smaller reliefs of *ganas*.

Splendid embellishments are encompassed in the entire cave, including paintings on ceiling. Four-armed Brahma is the focal point of the murals. There happens to be a lotus medallion on the floor underneath the mural of Brahma, place to beseech. Large number of Visnu's reliefs including standing Visnu, Visnu with a serpent, Visnu as Narasimha Varaha, Harihara and Trivikrama *avatars* epitomize the immensity of vastly admired Indian art. Reliefs stand 4 m tall. (Plate 6-66)

The culture and clothing embedded in the sixth century is clearly visible in the art sculpted in Cave 3. There are some paintings on the ceiling and the style indicates maturity but has lost its original dazzling colour. The bracket figures on the piers here are some of the finest which include couples in amorous poses. (Plate 6-67)

Cave 4: The fourth cave relates with the Jaina faith which is constructed last among all the caves. It is the only Jaina monument of Badami Chalukya period in Badami town and it is a work of the late 6th–7th century. The cave is not as large as the other caves. It is beautiful and rich with decoration. It is located higher than other caves. It has five bayed entrance with square columns which make it more beautiful and attractive at base. The first aisle (a passage between buildings) is treated as verandah. The end walls have

Parshvanatha (right) represented using painting, his head is covered by a metal piece of multi cobra hoods and Bahubali is left to him with his lower legs surrounded by snakes. His two sisters Brahmi and Sundari are here with him. (Plates 6-68 and 6-69)

On the back part of wall, Mahavira is painted on it. This painting shows Mahavira as a savior. He is sitting on lion throne. The sanctum is adorned by the image of Mahavira. The pedestal contains an old Kannada inscription of the 12th century CE which registers the death of one Jakkave. Scores of Jaina Thirthankara images have been engraved in the inner pillars and walls. In addition to it, there are some idols of Bahubali, *Yakshas* and *Yakshis*. Other carvings here are of Padmavati and other Thirthankaras. Some scholars assign the cave to the 8th century.

Cave 5: It is a natural cave of small dimensions located between Cave 2 and Cave 3. One can see a mutilated carved figure of Padmapani holding a lotus. A seated devotee to one side of the Bodhisattva is better preserved. Due to lack of any embellishments and any planned architectural elements, this cave does not get noticed easily by the visitors.

Other Temples at Badami: On the north hill, there are three temples, of which Malegitti-Shivalaya is perhaps the oldest temple and also the finest in Badami, and has a *Dravidian* tower. Out of the two inscriptions found here, one states that Aryaminchi Upadhyaya, as the sculptor who got this temple constructed and the other dated 1543 CE speaks of the erection of a bastion during the Vijayanagara rule. The lower Shivalaya has a *Dravidian* tower, and only the sanctum remains now.

Jambhulinga temple, situated in the town, is presumably the oldest known *trikutachala* temple in Karnataka. An inscription dated 699 CE ascribes construction of this temple to Vinayavathi mother of Emperor Vijayaditya.

The **Bhutanatha group** of temples is a cluster of sandstone shrines dedicated to the deity Bhutanatha. There are two major temples here. Temple No.1, on the east side of the Agastya lake, called the Bhutanatha temple has a superstructure that resembles early South Indian style with its open *mandapa* (hall) extending into the lake, while the smaller temple No.2 on the north-east side of the lake, sometimes called Mallikarjuna group of temples, has a stepped superstructure, commonly found in the Kalyani Chalukya constructions. The inner shrine and *mandapa* (hall) of temple No.1 were constructed in the late 7th century during the reign of the Badami Chalukyas while the outer *mandapa*, facing the lake, was completed during the rule of the Kalyani Chalukyas in the 11th century. Hence the Bhutanatha temples contain architectural forms from different periods. Studies show that these Kalyani Chalukya architects could have belonged to the same early phase workshop that later built the nearby Yellamma temple and the Mallikarjuna group of temples.

In the inner hall of the Bhutanatha temple, a heavy architrave above the columns divides the hall into a central nave and two aisles. The pillars are massive and the central bay in the ceiling of the nave is decorated with lotus rosette. Perforated windows bring dim light into the inner *mandapa*. On either side of the foot of the shrine doorway is an image, that of goddess Ganga on her vehicle, the *makara*, on the right, and on the left that of goddesses Yamuna riding the tortoise. There is no dedicatory block upon the lintel to indicate to which deity the initial dedication was. The Siva *linga* in the shrine appears to be a later addition after the original deity in the sanctum was removed.

The temple is unfinished and at the base of the superstructure (*Sikhara*) are vestiges of Jaina architecture. The image niches on the wall of the shrine and the hall are now empty though some decorative elements like *makaras* (mythical beast) with long tails still remain. To the north of the hall is a small shrine which was originally consecrated for Visnu. Following later Jaina modifications, the temple was eventually taken over by the followers of Lingayatism who built an outer hall and installed a Nandi (vehicle of Siva), and a Siva *linga* inside the sanctum.

The Mallikarjuna group exhibits topological features popularised by the Kalyani Chalukya architects, including plain walls, angled eaves over the open *mandapa* (hall) and pyramid shaped superstructures made of closely spaced horizontal tiers. Badami also has Agasthya Tirtha, temples of Goddess Yellamma, Datttreya and Virupaksha. Bhuthanatha group of temples are most important in Badami after the cave temples.

6.6 THE HOYSALA CIRCUIT

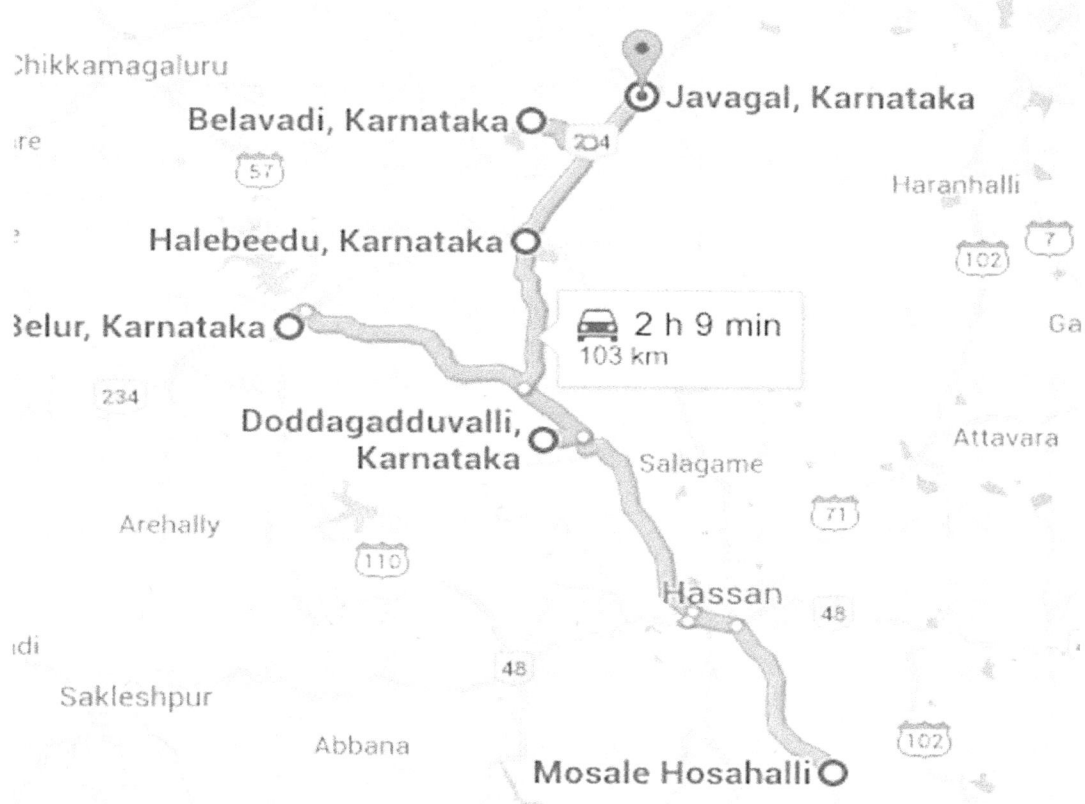

Halebid is located in Hassan district of Karnataka. Also known as Halebidu used to be called Dorasamudra or Dwarasamudra during the Hoysala times and was the regal capital of the Hoysala Empire in the 12th century. It is home to some of the best examples of Hoysala architecture. Most notable are the ornate Hoysaleswara and Kedareswara temples. The city got the name Halebidu (in Kannada meaning the 'Old Encampment/Abode') because it was ransacked two times during the invasion of Malik Kafur.

The temple complex comprises two Hindu temples, the Hoysaleswara and Kedareswara temples and three Jaina *basadis*. In front of these temples there is a large lake called the Dwarasamudra or Hiriya Kere presently. The area of the ancient Dorasamudra (or Dvarasamudra) city comprises two villages today, Halebid and Bastihalli. The Jaina *basadis* are located in the village Bastihalli on way to the Kedraeswara temple. Besides the named temples and the Jaina *basadis*, the other temples in Halebid are: Nagareswara (in ruins), Gudaleswara, Virabhadra and Ranganatha temples located at different spots in the city. There is also an archaeological museum in the Hoysaleswara temple complex.

Consistent with its surrounding topography, the site of the Hoysala capital is framed by hills and reservoirs (some naturally occurring and some man-made). One such hill known as Benne Gudda (Butter Hill) stands to the southern part of the site, midway between the eastern and western sides of the fortification wall that once surrounded the city. Just below Benne Gudda near the Jaina *basadis* one can even notice the remnants of the Hoysala palace. The fort wall is fragmentary today but its massive boulders once encompassed an irregularly shaped area with a diameter of about 2.25 km, generally in all directions.

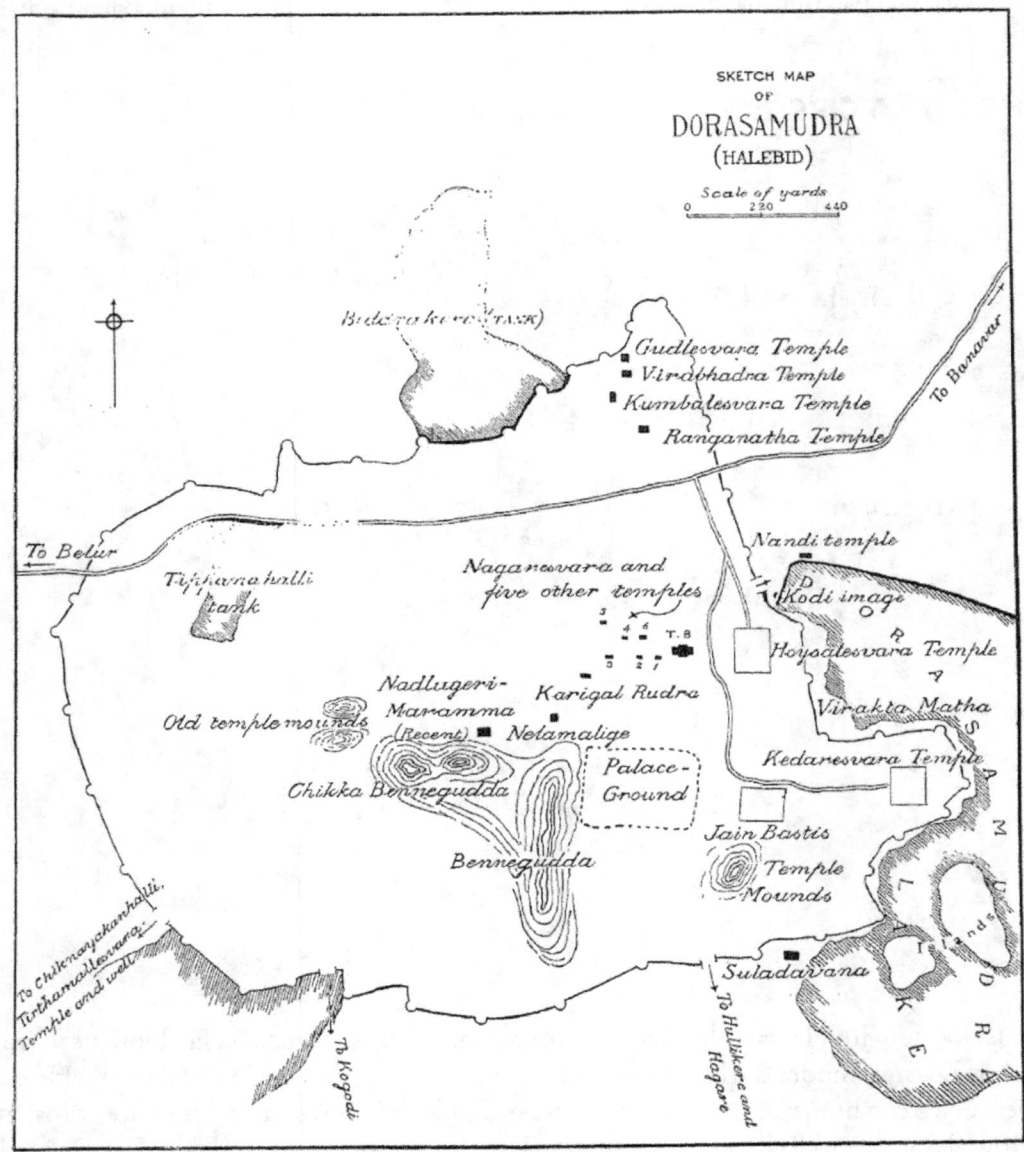

Among the four principal reservoirs that provided water to the city, the largest one is the Dorasamudra tank and it extends for about a km along the southern portion of the fort wall's eastern side. A sketch map of Dorasamudra city published in the Mysore Archaeological Report for the year 1937 is placed in the figure here.

The Hoysaleswara temple, dating back to the 1121 C.E., is astounding for its wealth of sculptural details. The walls of the temple are covered with an endless variety of depictions from Hindu mythology, animals, birds and *shilabalikas* or dancing figures. No two sculptures of the temple are the same. This temple, guarded by a Nandi bull, was never completed, despite 86 years of labour. The Jaina *basadis* nearby are equally rich in sculptural detail. The three Jaina *basadis* are dedicated to the Tirathankaras, Parsvanatha, Shaninatha and Adinatha.

Hoysaleswara temple is a temple dedicated to Hindu god Siva. It was built in Halebid during the rule of the Hoysala king Vishnuvardhana in the 12th century. The construction was started around 1120 CE.

During the early 14th century, Halebid was ransacked and faced invasions from invaders from northern India and the temple fell into a state of ruin and neglect.

According to art critic and historian S. Settar, from contemporary inscriptions it is known that the temple derives its name from the Hoysala ruler at that time, king Vishnuvardhana Hoysaleswara, though interestingly, the construction of the temple was initiated and financed by wealthy Saiva (a Hindu sect) citizens of the city, prominent among who were Ketamala and Kesarasetti. The temple building activity was taken up in competition to the construction of the Chennakesava Temple at Belur, a Vaishnava (a Hindu sect) temple. Surrounded by numerous tanks, ponds and *mandapas*, the temple is built in the vicinity of the large Dorasamudhra lake. The tank preceded the temple by nearly 75 years. It is one of the largest temples dedicated to the god Siva in South India. (Plate 6-70)

The temple is a simple *dvikuta vimana* (plan with two shrines and two superstructures), one for Hoysaleswara (the king) and the other for Shantaleswara (named after Shantala Devi, queen of king Vishnuvardhana) and is built with chloritic chist (more commonly known as soapstone or potstone). The temple complex as a whole is elevated on a *jagati* (platform). According to art historian Foekema, the two shrines which are adjoining, face east and each have a *mandapa* (hall) in front. The two *mandapas* are connected giving a large and imposing view of the hall. Individually, each shrine is smaller than the one at the Chennakesava Temple at Belur and contains a simple *linga*, the universal symbol of the god Siva. The plan of the inside of the temple is simple but the exterior looks different because of the introduction of many projections and recesses in the walls. The towers of the shrines that are missing must have followed the star shape of the shrine, just as in many existing well-preserved towers in other Hoysala temples. The superstructure over the vestibule which connects the shrine to the *mandapa*, called *sukanasi* (a low tower that looks like an extension of the main tower), and the row of decorated miniature roofs above the eaves of the hall are all missing. The temple was built at a height that provided the architects sufficient horizontal and vertical space to depict large and small sculptures. The outer walls of these temples contain an intricate array of stone sculptures. The temple of Halebid, has been described by art critics James Fergusson and Percy Brown as an "outstanding example of Hindu architecture" and as the "supreme climax of Indian architecture."

The temple has four porches for entry and the one normally used by visitors as main entry is actually a lateral entrance (north). There is one entry on the south side and two on the east side, facing two large detached open pavilions whose ceiling is supported by lathe turned pillars. All entry porches have miniature shrines as flanking. In addition there is a sanctuary for the Sun god Surya, whose image stands 7 ft (2.1 m) tall. The pavilions enshrine large images of Nandi. The pavilions share the same *jagati* as the main temple. As in the Chennakesava temple, this temple originally had an open *mandapa* to which outer walls with pierced window screens made with the same material were erected, making the *mandapa* a closed one. The window screens are devoid of any art work. The interior of the temple is quite plain except for the lathe turned pillars that run in rows between the north and south entrances. According to Settar, the four pillars in front of each shrine are the most ornate and the only ones that have the *madanika* (chaste maidens) sculptures in their pillar brackets. There are no other *madanikas* in the temple.

The Hoysaleswara temple is most well known for its sculptures that run all along the outer wall, starting with a dancing image of the god Ganesha on the left side of the south entrance and ending with another image of Ganesha on the right hand side of the north entrance. In all there are two hundred and forty such images. According to the art critic Gerard Foekema, perhaps no other Hoysala temple is as articulate in sculpture as this is and these sculptures are "second to none in all of India." The most intricate of all sculptures are found in the lintels over two of the doorways, one on the south side doorway and the other on one of the eastern doorways. (Plates 6-71, 6-72, 6-73, 6-74 and 6-75)

In this temple the Hoysala architects have broken from the tradition of using five moldings with friezes at the base of the temple, below the large wall sculptures and the window screens. The outer walls have two eaves that run around the temple. The top eave is at the roof of the temple where the superstructure meets the wall, and the second eave is about a metre below. In between there are decorated miniature towers (aedicule). Below the lower eave are the wall sculptures and below them, the eight mouldings. Each of the eight friezes carries an array of decoration. Going from the bottom where the temple wall meets the platform, the lowest frieze depicts charging elephants which symbolize strength and stability, above which, in order, are friezes with lions which symbolize courage, floral scrolls as decoration, horses symbolizing speed, another band of floral scrolls, depictions from the Hindu epics, mythical beasts called *makara* and finally a frieze with *hansas* (swans). According to Foekema, no two animals are alike in a total frieze span of over 200 m. In the epic frieze, the epics are not continuous as they are mixed with other depictions. After the construction of this temple, Hoysala architects used this new kind of horizontal treatment only fifty years later, making it a standard style, though they reduced it to six moulding friezes. A detailed description of the temple's sculpture is furnished in the section of the history of sculpture in Karnataka. However, the major sculptural attractions of the temple include dancing Siva on the lintel at the entrance flanked by two *dvarapalas*, Arjuna disturbed by a celestial dancer, elephants engaged in a fight, Visnu and Lakshmi riding the *Garuda*, Siva killing Andhakasura, Ravana shaking Mount Kailasa, monkeys building the bridge for Rama's army and Bhishma on a bed of arrows.

Garuda pillar: Another interesting object in the temple complex is the rare *Garuda Sthamba* (Garuda pillar). According to Settar, this is different from *virgals* (Hero stone). *Garudas* were elite bodyguards of the kings and queens. They moved and lived with the royal family and their only purpose was to protect their master. Upon the death of their master, they committed suicide. The rare pillar on the south side depicts heroes brandishing knives and cutting their own heads. The inscription honors Kuruva Lakshma, a bodyguard of Veera Ballala II. A devoted officer, he took his life and that of his wife and other bodyguards after the death of his master. This event is narrated in an old Kannada inscription on the pillar. A 8 ft (2.4 m) tall sculpture of Ganesha including the platform rests at the South entrance.

Kedareswara Temple: is a Hoysala era construction. It is located a short distance away from the famous Hoysaleswara Temple. The temple was constructed by Hoysala king Veera Ballala II (1173–1220 CE) and his queen Ketaladevi, and the main deity is *Iswara* (another name for the Hindu god Siva). The temple is protected as a monument of national importance by the Archaeological Survey of India.

According to art historian Adam Hardy, the temple was constructed before 1219 CE and is constructed with soapstone. The usage of soapstone was first popularized by the Western Chalukyas before it became standard with the Hoysala architects of the 12th and 13th centuries. The temple stands on the platform called *jagati* which is typically five to six feet in height and which can be reached by a flight of steps. Hoysala temples normally don't provide a path for circumambulation (*pradakshinapatha*) around the inner sanctum (*garbhagriha*). However, the platform provides this convenience in addition to giving the onlooker a good view of the wall relief and sculptures. The outlay of the main shrine (*vimana*) is star shaped (stellate) with two smaller shrines that have perforated windows (called *Jali*) on the sides. According to the art historian Gerard Foekema, star shaped or "staggered square" (or cross in square) temple plans are quiet common among Hoysala constructions creating multiple projections and recesses in the outer walls. In these projections, the Hoysala architects created repetitive decorative sculptures and reliefs called "architectural articulation." (Plate 6-76)

Since the temple has three shrines, it qualifies as a *trikuta*, a three shrined structure. Often in *trikutas*, only the central shrine has a tower while the lateral shrines are virtually hidden behind the thick outer walls and appear to be a part of the hall itself. Despite being a Saiva temple it is well known for its friezes and panel relief that bear depictions from both the Saiva and Vaishnava legends. The three sanctums are connected to a "staggered square" (indented) central hall (*mahamandapa*) by individual vestibules called *sukanasi*. A porch connects the central hall to the platform. The base of the temple wall (*adhisthana*) around the common hall and the two lateral shrines consist of mouldings, each of which is treated with friezes in relief that depict animals and episodes from the Hindu lore (*purana*). The image of the deity of worship is missing in all three sanctums and the superstructures over all three shrines are lost. Some noteworthy pieces of sculpture worthy of mention are the dancing Bhairava (a form of Siva), Govardhana (the god Krishna lifting a mountain), the god Vishnu as *Varadaraja*, and a huntress. (Plate 6-77)

Ranganatha temple: at Halebid mainly houses the principal deity, Ranganatha. The main reason for importance of this temple is the 6 feet long image of Ranganatha reclining on a hooded serpent. Besides the main deity, there are other images of Brahma seated on the lotus emerging from Ranganatha's navel. There is also an image of Sridevi serving at Ranganatha's feet. One of the many things noticeable in this temple is that the *garbhagriha* is east facing. Sudarshana image is also enshrined in the main sanctum.

Ranganatha temple has a *mukhamandapa* that incorporates the figural blocks from the Nagareswara temple site among other reused material and loose sculpture stored in the temple compound. Ranganatha temple's unadorned *vimana* which remains intact from its *adisthana* to the four tiers of the stepped pyramidal *phamsana* superstructure seems to belong to the temple that originally occupied the location. On its interior the original square *garbhagriha* was not made for the long image of Ranganatha. Although the sculpture dates back to the Hoysala period, it seems to have been brought here from another temple as the sanctum's inner wall bears the marks of a shaft that was removed to accommodate the new image. (Plates 6-78 and 79)

The last published inscription from Dorasamudra is found in the underside of the lintel above the doorway leading into the Ranganatha temple's *garbhagriha*. Dating to 1238 CE, it records granting of a temple associated with one Lakheya *sahani* by his grandson Baicaya *sahani* to the priests or temple functionaries and describes the boundaries of the god (*Vathara*). Because lintel inscriptions are typically engraved on the outward facing sides of their beams and not on the underside, this lintel evidently has been shifted from its original position. It is possible that the lintel originally belongs to this temple and was simply turned when the temple was altered to accommodate the image of Ranganatha.

The temple underwent restoration and renovation work again recently. The new consecration ceremonies were held at the temple on 11th June 2015.

Belur

Belur town is renowned for its Chennakesava temple, one of the finest examples of Hoysala workmanship. Belur was the early capital of the Hoysala Empire. With Halebid which is only 16 km away, this is one of the major tourist destinations in Karnataka. According to inscriptions discovered here, it was also referred to as Velapuri.

The main attraction in Belur is the Chennakesava temple complex which has in its precincts the Chennakesava temple as the centre piece, surrounded by the Kappe Chennigraya temple built by Shantaladevi, queen of king Vishnuvardhana.

There are two more shrines here that are still in use by devotees and there is a *Pushkarni* or stepped well to the right side of the main entrance. The *Dravida* style *rayagopuram* at the entrance was a later addition by the Vijayanagara kings, who considered this deity as one of their *kuladevata* or family god.

The temple is one of the finest examples of Hoysala architecture. It was built by the king Vishnuvardhana in commemoration of his victory over the Cholas at Talakad in 1117 CE. Legend has it that it took 103 years to complete and Vishnuvardhana's grandson Veera Ballala II completed the task. The facade of the temple is filled with intricate sculptures and friezes with no portion left blank. The intricate workmanship includes elephants, lions, horses, episodes from the Indian mythological epics, and sensuous dancers (*Shilabalikas*). Inside the temple are a number of ornate pillars. *Darpana Sundari* (Lady with the mirror) carved on walls of Belur Temple is one of major attractions in the complex.

The Chennakesava Temple: Chennakesava temple was originally called **Vijayanarayana Temple** and was built on the banks of the Yagachi River in Belur.

The temple was commissioned by king Vishnuvardhana in 1117 CE. Scholars are divided about the reasons for the construction of the temple. The military successes of Vishnuvardhana are considered a probable reason. Some scholars believe Vishnuvardhana commissioned the temple to surpass his overlord, king Vikramaditya VI of the Kalyani Chalukya dynasty, after his initial military victories against the Chalukyas. According to another theory, Vishnuvardhana was celebrating his famous victory against the Chola dynasty of Tamil country in the battle of Talakad (1116 CE), which resulted in the annexation of Gangavadi (modern southern Karnataka) by the Hoysalas. Another theory points to Vishnuvardhana's conversion from Jainism to Vaishnavism after coming under the influence of saint Ramanujacharya, considering this is a predominantly Vaishnava temple in sculptural iconography. The Hoysalas employed many noted architects and artisans who developed a new architectural tradition, which art critic Adam Hardy called the *Karnata Dravida* tradition. In all 118 inscriptions have been recovered from the temple complex, covering the period 1117 CE to the 18th century, giving historians details of the artists employed, grants made to the temple and renovations committed during later times.

The temple stands on a raised platform 0.91 m. (3ft.) in height, measuring 54.26 by 47.55m. (178 ft x 156 ft). The shrine consists of a *garbhagriha*, a *sukanasi* (vestibule) and a *navaranga* (central hall) which has entrances from the east, south and north. The east entrance is for the priests and devotees, the south for the "Friday entrance" (*Shukra-vara-bagilu*) and the north is, "the Heavenly entrance" (*Svargada-bagilu*). Manmatha and Rati are sculptured on the eastern doorway, Hanuman and *Garuda* on the southern and female *chauri*-bearers on the northern. The pediments have projected panels with *Garuda* flanked by *makaras* and the sculpture of Narasimha killing Hiranyakashipu (demon) on the east, Varaha killing Hiranyaksha on the south, and Kesava on the north. (Plates 6-80 and 6-83)

The main entrance to the complex is crowned by a *Rajagopura* (superstructure over entrance). Within the complex, the Chennakesava temple is at the centre, facing east, and is flanked by the Kappe Channigraya temple on its right, and a small Sowmyanayaki (form of the goddess Lakshmi) temple set slightly back. On its left, also set slightly back is the Ranganayaki (Andal) temple. Two main *stambhas* (pillars) exist here. The pillar facing the main temple, the *Garuda* (eagle) *stambha* was erected in the Vijayanagar period while the pillar on the right, the *dipastambha* (pillar with lamp) dates from the Hoysala period. This is the first great Hoysala temple, though according to the art critic and historian Settar, the artistic idiom and signature is still Kalyani Chalukyan. Hence, the over-decoration which is seen in later Hoysala temples (including the Hoysaleswara temple at Halebid and the Kesava temple at Somanathapura) is not visible here. According to Settar, during later years, the Hoysala art took an inclination towards craftsmanship, with a weakness for minutiae. The Chennakesava temple has three entrances and their doorways have decorated sculptures called *dvarapalaka* (doorkeepers) on either side. While the Kappe Channigraya temple is smaller than the Chennakesava temple, it is architecturally significant, though it lacks any sculptural features. The Kappe Chennigraya temple became a *dvikuta* (two shrined temple) with the later addition of a shrine to its original plan. The original shrine has a star-shaped plan while the additional shrine is a simple square. The image inside is also that of Kesava (a form of the god Krishna) and was commissioned by Shantala Devi, the noted queen of king Vishnuvardhana. (Plate 6-81)

The building material used in the Chennakesava temple is chloritic schist, more commonly known as (soapstone) or potstone, and is essentially a simple Hoysala plan built with extraordinary detail. What differentiates this temple from other Hoysala temples of the same plan is the unusually large size of the basic parts of the temple. The temple is a *ekakuta vimana* design (single shrine) of 10.5 m by 10.5 m size. A large vestibule connects the shrine to the *mandapa* (hall) which is one of the main attractions of the temple. The *mandapa* has 60 bays (compartments). The superstructure (tower or *Sikhara*) on top of the *vimana* has been lost over time. The temple is built on a *jagati* (platform for circumambulation). There is one flight of steps leading to the *jagati* and another flight of steps to the *mandapa*. The *jagati* provides the devotee the opportunity to do a *pradakshina* (circumambulation) around the temple before entering it. The *jagati* carefully follows the staggered square design of the *mandapa* and the star shape of the shrine. The *mandapa* here was originally an open one. According to art critic Gerard Foekema, the *mandapa* is perhaps the most magnificent one in all of medieval India. The open *mandapa* was converted into a closed one after about fifty years, during the Hoysala rule. This was done by erecting walls with pierced window screens.

The temple wall from the eastern doorway up to the north and the south entrances has a railed parapet (*Jagati*) having beautiful friezes of elephants, a cornice with beadwork surmounted by lion heads (*Simhalalatas*) at intervals, and scroll work with figures in every convolution. Another cornice is decorated with beadwork, and small figures mostly of females. The projecting ornamental niches have beautiful seated figures of *yakshas* and *yakshis*. The eaves are decorated with beadwork and thick creepers running along the edge of the upper slope having miniature turrets, lions and many other small images. The rail also contains figures; some are *mithuna* figures (amorous couples) in panels and with ornamental bands. But the elephant frieze is strangely enough left blank throughout the temple. The rail to the right of the east entrance beautifully illustrates episodes from the Mahabharata. (Plates 6-81, 6-82 and 6-86)

The exquisite sculptures on the outer walls of the *mandapa* are mesmerizing. Details of a few of the sculptured panels are described here. In the first panel, Bhima is seen worshipping Ganapati and Duryodhana falls unwillingly at the feet of Krishna who presses his foot against the earth in order to tumble his throne. Further on the creeper frieze; different scenes from the Ramayana have been carefully sculptured along with tiny seated musicians: Above the rail there are twenty pierced stone windows (perforated screens) surmounted by the eaves, ten on the right and ten on the left of the east doorway, covering the whole temple. Ten of them are decorated with *Puranic* scenes and the rest with geometrical designs. Among them five on the right and five on the left of the east doorway are especially noteworthy. On the top panel is Kesava in the centre flanked by *chauri*-bearers, Hanuman and *Garuda*. Just below this, king Vishnuvardhana, the founder of this temple, holds a *darbar* (royal court). He has a sword in his right hand and a flower in the left. Mahadevi Shantaladevi, the chief queen is seen seated on his left, with her female attendant standing by her side. To his right and a little in front, two religious teachers (*gurus*) are seated with two disciples behind them. One of them is apparently preaching something to the king. (Plate 6-84)

There are also several royal officers and attendants at his beck and call. The king and queen have many pieces of jewellery on their persons, especially unusually large earrings. Then comes a tine scroll and below it a lion with a rider and another standing vigorously facing the visitors, signifying the vigorous rule of Vishnuvardhana.

The next stone screen depicts the story of king Bali making a gift to Vamana (Visnu) and on the top of it Lakshmi and Narayana are flanked by Hanuman and *Garuda*. In the middle panel, Trivikrama (Visnu) is in the centre with his uplifted foot which is being carefully washed by Brahma; Bali is seen standing on the right with folded hands. *Garuda* stands with folded hands and another drags away Sukracharya, the preceptor and minister of Bali. On the lower panel Bali's *Darbar* (royal court) is open to receive gifts.

At the top of the next panel, Lakshmi and Narayana are depicted along with their attendants. In the middle panel, Lord Krishna breaks the pride of the serpent Kaliya (Kaliyadamana) and the lower one depicts a band of musicians. The next screen represents Visnu flanked by *Garuda* and Hanuman. Below this panel, Siva sits on his bull vehicle Nandi, attended by *Garuda* and Kartikeya who in his turn is accompanied by a band of soldiers with flags, swords, spears and shields. Next to this ten *dikpalakas*, including Kubera, are seen, and the rear panel represents a battle scene.

The next screen illustrates the story of Prahlada. On the upper panel, Lakshmi Narayana with *Garuda* and perhaps Hanuman can be seen. On the middle panel, Narasimha kills Hiranykashipu accompanied by *Garuda* and Hanuman. Just below it Prahlada with folded hands is meditating on the deity in different poses; he has *tenkalanamam* on his forehead, which is the significant mark of the Vaishnava faith. The

Vaishnava faith and movement became more active in the South and the perforated screens were added by Ballala II (1173–1220 CE), the grandson of Vishnuvardhana.

The *vimana* (shrine) is at the back of the *mandapa*. Each side of the *vimana* measures 10.5 m and has five vertical sections. Each vertical section comprises a large double storeyed niche in the centre and two heavy pillar-like sections on either side. The two pillar-like sections adjoining the niche are rotated about their vertical axis to produce a star-shaped plan for the shrine. The pillar-like section and the niche bear many ornate sculptures, belonging to an earlier style. There are some sixty large sculptures of deities from both Vaishnava and Saiva faiths. From the shape of the *vimana* it has been inferred that the tower above it would have been of the *Bhumija* style when it existed and not the regular star shaped tower that followed the shape of the *vimana*. The *Bhumija* towers, which are intact on the miniature shrines at the entrance of the hall are actually a type of *nagara* (North Indian) tower, being curvilinear in shape. This shape of tower is quite uncommon in pure *dravidian* architecture. The shrine has a life size (about 6 ft) image of Kesava with four hands. Each hand holds an attribute; the discus (*chakra*), the mace (*gada*), the lotus-flower (*padma*) and the conch (*sankha*), in clockwise direction. The entrance to the shrine is flanked by life size sculptures of door guardians (*dvarapalakas*).

Special attention must be drawn to some interesting sculptures on the outer walls of the *garbhagriha*, for instance, Balarama with a discus (*chakra*) in his left hand and a plough in the right; Chandra holding *kumudas* (water-lilies) in both hands; a sixteen-armed Narasimha slaying Hiranyakashipu; Kayadhu (Prahlad's mother) and *Garuda* are artistic and story-telling. Then there is a *Madanika* (*kirati*) as a huntress to the left of the north doorway with two small female attendants, one with a bamboo *lathi* (rod) carrying a dead deer and a crane apparently shot in the chase. Another small figure is trying to remove a thorn with the help of a needle from the leg of one of the female attendants. This is almost a lyrical ballad in stone. Another *Madanika* in an amorous mood holds a betel leaf apparently for her lover, while her playful attendant squirts scented water with a syringe. Other *Madanika* to the left of the south entrance is dancing under a creeper canopy. The sculptor has a poetic vision; on the top near her head are a lizard, a fly, and a ripe fruit (may be a jack-fruit); the lizard is preparing to pounce on the fly.

The pillars inside the hall are an attraction and the most popular one is the Narasimha pillar which at one time could have revolved on its ball bearings. While all the forty eight pillars are unique and the many ceiling sections are well decorated, nothing surpasses the finish of the four central pillars and the ceiling they support. These pillars may have been hand chiseled while the others were lathe turned. All of these four pillars bear *madanikas* (*Salabhanjika*–celestial damsels). There are 42 of them in the temple complex, one each on the four central pillars inside the hall and the remaining 38 are outside, between the eaves on the outer walls of the hall (Plate 6-85). They are also called *shilabalika* and represent the ideal female form. They are depicted in various forms, such as dancers, musicians and drummers, and are rarely erotic in nature. Some *madanikas* that usually are popular with tourists are the *Darpana Sundari*, "The lady with the parrot," "huntress" and *Bhasma mohini*. Other interesting sculptures inside the *mandapa* are *Stambha buttalika* (pillar with an image in frieze) which is more in the Chola style indicating that the Hoysalas may have employed Chola craftsman along with locals. These images have less decor than regular Hoysala sculptures, the *mohini* pillar being an example.

At the base of the outer walls are friezes of charging elephants (six hundred and fifty of them) which symbolize stability and strength, above which are lions which symbolize courage, and further up are horses which symbolize speed. Above the horses are panels with floral designs signifying beauty above which are sculptures with depictions from the Hindu epics, the Ramayana and the Mahabharata. Hoysala artisans preferred to be discreet about eroticism, mingling miniature erotic sculptures in not so conspicuous places such as recesses and niches. Sculptures depict daily life in a broad sense.

The doorways to the *mandapa* have on both sides an image of "Sala" slaying a lion. Normally this image is placed on the *sukanasi* (tower over the vestibule) adjoining the main tower. Legend has it that Sala killed the lion (or tiger) which was about to pounce on a meditating saint who sought Sala's help. Some historians speculate that the legend may have gained importance after king Vishnuvardhana's victory over the Chola dynasty in the battle of Talakad, the tiger being the royal emblem of the Cholas.

Other important sculptures here are the Narasimha (a form of Visnu) image in the south western corner, *Gajasurasamhara* (Hindu god Siva slaying demon in form of elephant) on the western side, the winged *Garuda*, a consort of the god Visnu standing facing the temple, dancing Kali (a form of Durga), a seated Ganesha, a boy with an umbrella and a king, Ravana carrying and shaking Mount Kailasa, Durga as Mahishasuramardini slaying demon Mahishasura, standing Brahma, Varaha, Siva dancing on Andhakasura, Bhairava, Arjuna shooting a fish seeing its reflection, and the Sun god Surya. The sculptural style of the wall images bear similarities with wall sculptures in contemporary temples of northern Karnataka and adjacent Maharashtra.

The Hoysala artists, unlike other medieval artists, preferred to sign their work in the form of inscriptions. In doing so, they sometimes revealed details about themselves, their families, guilds and place of origin. Stone inscriptions and copper plate inscriptions provide more information about them. Among the sculptors of the Kesava temple at Belur mention may be made of Dasoja, his son Chavana, Chikkahampa, Malliyana, Padari Malloja, Kencha Malliyanna, Masada and Nagoja. Some of the labels give details about their native places, parentage and qualifications. Ruvari Mallitamma was a prolific artist to whom more than 40 sculptures are attributed. Dasoja and his son Chavana who were from Balligavi in modern Shivamogga district made important contributions. Chavana is credited with the work on five *madanikas* and Dasoja accomplished four of them. Malliyana and Nagoja created birds and animals in their sculptures. Artists such as Chikkahampa and Malloja are credited with some of the sculptures in the *mandapa*.

Belavadi

The **Veera Narayana temple** is located in Belavadi, a village in the Chikamagaluru district of Karnataka state, India. The temple was built during the rule of the Hoysala Empire. Known to legend as Ekachakranagara, Belavadi is said to be the place mentioned in Mahabharatha where Pandava prince Bheema killed the demon Bakasura and protected the village and its people. Belavadi is 29 km southeast of Chikmagaluru town on the Chikmagaluru-Javagal highway. It is a short distance from the famous temple towns of Belur and Halebid, and a visit to this town is a rewarding experience.

This ornate *trikuta* (three shrined) temple was built in 1200 CE by Hoysala king Veera Ballala II. The material used is soapstone. Each of the three shrines has a complete superstructure (tower on top of shrine) and is one of the largest temples built by the Hoysala kings. While the famous temples at Belur and Halebid are known for their intricate sculptures, this temple is known for its unique architecture. (Plate 6-87)

The plan of the temple is unique in that two of the shrines face each other and are located on either side of a wide and spacious open *mandapa* (hall) containing thirty seven bays (Plates 6-88 and 6-89). The temple complex has two closed *mandapa*s, one with thirteen bays and another with nine bays, at the end of which is a central shrine. This third shrine is an older construction and exhibits a standard architectural idiom containing all the basic elements of a Hoysala temple. The inner walls of the older shrine are plain, but its roof is well decorated. In all, the temple complex has fifty nine bays (hence it has many pillars), most of the pillars are lathe-turned and bell shaped, while a few have decorative carvings on them. According to Foekema, the outer wall of the temple is of the "old style," with one eave running around the temple where the superstructure meets the wall of the shrine. Below this are miniature decorative towers on pilasters (aedicule). This is followed by a second eave. A panel of Hindu deities and their attendants (frieze) are below this eave followed by a set of five mouldings that form the base of the wall.

The two newer shrines have different plans. One shrine is square in shape while the other is star shaped (stellate). The tower of the shrine has an apex called the *kalasa* (decorative water-pot like structure) below which are three tiers of decorated miniature roofs. The superstructure over each of three shrines is connected to a low protrusion tower called *sukanasi* (tower over the vestibule). The *sukanasi* consist of two tiers of decorated miniature roofs. In all other aspects the two shrines are identical. All shrines have sculptured decoration on the towers, and the sculptures on the walls are bold and are visible from a distance. However, they are not sharp and impressive from close quarters unlike in other Hoysala temples. The important sculptures with fine finish are that of the Hindu god Krishna dancing on the head of *Kalia* the serpent, and the *Garuda* (eagle).

This is a Vaishnava temple and all three shrines have images of the Hindu god Visnu, though in different forms (*avatara*). The central shrine (older shrine) has an 8 ft (2.4 m) tall image of Narayana with four hands and is considered one of the best examples of Hoysala art. It is well elaborated with ornamentation and stands on a *padmasana* (lotus seat). The southern shrine has an 8 ft (2.4 m) tall image of Venugopala (the god Krishna playing a flute) including a *garuda* pedestal and the northern shrine has a 7 ft (2.1 m) tall image of *Yoganarasimha*, sitting in a yoga posture. Decorative sculptures such as *kirtimukhas* (gargoyles) are used to make the shrine (*vimana*) towers ornate.

Doddagadavalli

The **Lakshimi Devi temple** is located in Doddagaddavalli, a village in Hassan District of Karnataka. It is located 16 km from Hassan city and lies on the Hassan-Belur highway. The Lakshimi Devi temple, was built by the Hoysala king Vishnuvardhana in 1114 C.E.

The Lakshimi Devi Temple is one of the earliest known temples built in the Hoysala style. The building material is chloritic schist, more commonly known as soapstone. The temple does not stand on a *jagati* (platform), a feature which became popular in later Hoysala temples. The temple was commissioned by a merchant called Kullahana Rahuta and his wife Sahaja Devi. The temple is a unique *chatuskuta* construction (four shrines and towers) built inside a 7-foot-tall (2.1 m) stone wall enclosure with the entrance through a porch whose roof is supported by circular lathe-turned pillars. Three of the *vimanas* (shrines) have a common square *mandapa* (hall) with nine bays or compartments. The fourth *vimana* is connected to the *mandapa* via an oblong extension consisting of two bays (Plate 6-92). The extension has two lateral entrances into the temple. All the *vimanas* have their original tower (superstructure) intact. The towers are in Kadamba *nagara* style. Each *vimana* has a vestibule connecting it to the central *mandapa*. On top of the vestibule is its own tower called *sukanasi* (or nose because it looks like low extension of the main tower over the shrine). The *sukanasi* is a tier lower than the main tower over the shrine. All the four *sukanasis* are intact and so are the *kalasas* (decorative water pot like structure) on top of the main towers. The Hoysala emblem or crest (the sculpture of a legendary warrior Sala fighting a lion) is mounted atop one of the *sukanasi*. Of the four towers, three are undecorated and they look stepped pyramidal with a pile of dented horizontal mouldings with the *kalasa* on top. The fourth tower is very well decorated (which is typical of Hoysala designs) and this is the tower of the main shrine that houses the Lakshimi Devi image. (Plate 6-91)

The *mandapa* is open and square. The reason for the square plan is the presence of shrines on all four sides of the *mandapa* with no side open for staggering. There is a separate fifth shrine of Bhairava, another manifestation of the god Siva. The shrine is complete with its own *vimana* and tower with a *kalasa* on top, a *sukanasi* with a Hoysala emblem on it. Another unusual feature of the temple is the existence of four more minor shrines at each corner of the temple complex with two sides of each shrine attached to the courtyard wall. Each of these minor shrines has its own tower, *kalasa* and Hoysala emblem. In all, the temple complex has nine towers which is unusual for a Hoysala temple.

According to art critic Gerard Foekema, overall the temple has the older style where there is only one eave running round the temple where the main towers meet the wall of the shrine. At the base of the wall of the shrines are five mouldings, a standard in the old style of Hoysala architecture; between the mouldings and the eaves, the usual panels of Hoysala sculptures depicting Hindu gods, goddesses and their attendants is however missing. Instead, the entire space is taken up by decorative miniature towers on pilasters (called Aedicula). The ceiling of the main hall is supported by eighteen lathe-turned pillars. Inside the main hall, there are two sculptures of large demonic living corpses called *betala*. The main shrine facing east has a 3-foot-tall (0.91 m) image of the goddess Lakshmi with an attendant on either side. The image holds a conch in the upper right hand, a *chakra* (discus) in the upper left, a rosary in the lower right and a mace in the lower left. In the shrines facing north, south and west respectively are the images of Kali (a form of Durga), the god Visnu, and *Boothanatha* Linga (the universal symbol of the god Siva). A sculpture of *Tandaveswara* (dancing Shiva) exists in the circular panel at the centre of the ceiling of the *mandapa*. Other important sculptures are those of *Gajalakshmi* (form of Lakshmi with elephants on either side), Tandaveswara and Yoganarasimha (form of Visnu) found on the doorway of the temple. (Plate 6-90)

Mosale

The Nageswara-Chennakesava temple complex is an elegant example of Hoysala architecture of the early 12th century. It is located in the village of Mosale, about 10 km from Hassan city. The temple was built in 1200 CE during the reign of Hoysala king Veera Ballala II. According to art historian Gerard Foekema, the two temples that are built in the same complex, in an idyllic rural setting, form a perfect twin. This temple complex is protected as a monument of national importance by the Archaeological Survey of India.

By plan, the temples are simple single-shrined structures with all the standard features of Hoysala architecture; a porch entrance into a square closed *mandapa* or *navaranga* (hall with no windows and a thick wall) leading to the sanctum, and a superstructure (*sikhara*) over the main shrine fitting the description of an *ekakuta* (single shrine with top). The sanctum (*garbhagriha*) is connected to the hall by a vestibule called *sukanasi*. The closed hall, whose inner and outer walls are decorated, has four central lathe turned pillars that support a bay ceiling. The temples are constructed next to each other. The Nageswara temple (lord of snakes), dedicated to the Hindu god Siva (represented by his universal symbol, the *linga*) is in the south. The Chennakesava temple (beautiful Visnu), dedicated to a standing cult image of the Hindu god Visnu, is to the north. Since all features are replicated in the temples, Gerard Foekema considers the ensemble a *dvikuta* (two shrines with two towers) though the two shrines stand separated. (Plate 6-94)

The superstructure (tower or *sikhara*) over each shrine is three tiered (*tritala arpita*) and *vesara* in style. It is intact, finely sculptured and has a decorative low extension which is actually the tower over the vestibule (that connects the cella and the hall). The extension tower looks like the nose of the main superstructure and is also called *sukanasi*. The *sukanasi* structure holds the beautiful Hoysala crest that depicts a royal warrior stabbing a lion. At the top of the superstructure of the shrine is a "helmet" like sculptured dome (*amalaka*) whose ground surface area can be 2x2 meters. It is the largest piece of sculpture in the temple. The *amalaka* supports a decorative water pot like structure called the *kalasa* which is the apex of the tower. All these features are intact in both temples.

The decorative features found on the temple outer wall (horizontal treatment) belong are on smaller scales than the Hoysaleswara temple in Halebid but retain similar beauty and symmetry. In this type of decorations, below the superstructure, an eave that projects about half a metre runs all around the temple. Below the eave are decorative miniature towers (aedicula) on pilasters. The large wall images of deities and their attendants are placed below these decorative towers. Some of these images appear damaged, but there are others that require special mention for their elegance and art. The panel images at the Nageswara temple have their names on their pedestals. Some of these are images of Sridevi, Lakshmidevi, Gauri, Maheswari (another name for Parvati), Brahma, Sadasiva (form of Siva) and Bhumidevi (representation of mother earth). The Channakesava temple has sculptures of Garuda (the eagle), Kesava (a form of Visnu), Janardana, Venugopala, Madhava (a form of Krishna) and Bhudevi. Below these images, the base of the wall comprises five different horizontal mouldings, one of which is a row of blocks. (Plate 6-93)

Javagal

The **Lakshminarasimha temple** at Javagal (also called Javagallu) is an example of mid-13th century Hoysala architecture. Javagal is located about 50 km from Hassan city and about 20 km from Halebid. The main deity is Narasimha (a form of the Hindu god Visnu) and the temple was built in 1250 CE by the Hoysala king Vira Someshwara. This temple is a protected monument under the Karnataka state division of the Archaeological Survey of India.

The temple plan is simple and commonly found in other Hoysala temples. It is a *trikuta* (three shrined), though only the middle shrine has a superstructure (tower or *sikhara*) and a *sukanasi* (nose or tower over the vestibule). The three equal size shrines are all square in plan and are connected by a common closed hall (*mandapa*). The closed hall is preceded by an open porch. The lateral shrines are connected directly to the hall while the middle shrine has a vestibule that connects the sanctum (cella) to the hall. Since the lateral shrines have no tower over them and are directly connected to the hall without a vestibule and its corresponding tower like projection, they do not appear like shrines at all from the outside. Rather, they appear absorbed into the walls of hall. The central shrine on the contrary is highly visible from the outside because of its tower, and the *sukanasi* that projects prominently from the tower. The lower part of the shrines (below the roof) have five projections per side, these projections being visible on three sides in the case of the central shrine but only on one side in the case of the lateral shrines. (Plate 6-95)

The temple stands on a platform (*jagati*), a feature common to many Hoysala temples. The platform, in addition to its visual appeal, is meant to provide devotees a path for circumambulation (*pradakshinapatha*) around the temple. It closely follows the outline of the temple, giving it a good elevated look. The tower over the central shrine and the vestibule are intact and highly decorative. Other standard features in a Hoysala temple are the large domed roof over the tower, which is also the largest sculptural piece in a Hoysala temple (called the *amalaka*) and whose shape usually follows the that of the shrine (square or star shape); the *kalasa* on top of it (the decorative water-pot at the apex of the dome); and the Hoysala crest (emblem of the Hoysala warrior stabbing a lion) over the *sukanasi*. Here the emblem and the *kalasa* are missing. The *kalasa* has been replaced during later times with a metallic pinnacle.

The decorative plan of the outer walls of the shrines and the *mandapa* (hall) is of the new kind, with two eaves that run around the temple. According to art historian Gerard Foekema, the wall panel images (one hundred and forty in all), and the reliefs and friezes that abound in this temple have a relaxed quality of workmanship about them, and in no Hoysala temple do these appear more folkish in character. In the new kind of decorative articulation, the first heavy eave runs below the superstructure and all around the temple with a projection of about half a metre. The second eave runs around the temple about a metre below the first. In between the two eaves are the miniature decorative towers (Aedicula) on pilasters. Below the second eave are the wall panel of images of Hindu deities and their attendants in relief. Below this, at the base are the six equal width rectangular mouldings (friezes). Starting from the top, the friezes depict; *hansa* (birds) in the first frieze, *makara* (aquatic monsters) in the second, epics and other stories in the third (usually from the Hindu epic Ramayana, the Mahabharata, and stories of Krishna), leafy scrolls in the fourth, horses in the fifth and elephants in the sixth (bottom frieze).

6.7 IN AND AROUND BENGALURU

Gavipuram

Of the temples in Bengaluru, the Gavi Gangadhareswara temple at Gavipuram and the Chokkanatha Perumal temple at Domlur are among the oldest dating back to the Chola times. Gavi Gangadhareswara temple is a very interesting monument. It is located in a depression behind a hill and is surrounded by a number of other temples, *choultries* and other monuments of religious nature. The temple is in a natural cave and the Linga in the central cave is wrought from a live rock and also the Nandi in front of it. The *pranala* of the Linga is to the right, a special feature. There is to the right of this cella in which the Linga is housed, another cella in which image of Parvati is installed. To its further right there is another small cella where the image of Durga is installed. On the Lings *pitha*, a small metallic Skanda image is placed and that led some scholars to speculate that the temple may have been dedicated to Somaskanda. There is a narrow *pradakshinapatha* built in the rock around the two cellas and one more a little wider outside. In the outer cave like arrangement are installed various images such a *saptamatrikas* and *dikpalas*. The wide cave serves as the *rangamandapa* of the temple and the two pillars in front of the Durga cella and a half metre tall Bhairava image installed outside the temple indicate the Chola origin of the monument. There is also a monolithic parasol atop the hill called Hariharanarayana Gudda to the east of the temple where there is also a park. This Harihara temple houses Linga, Bala Subramanya and Visnu. There are many interesting small monuments on the hill and one of them is a small cave with frontal structure and has two Chola pillars. This is called Gavimatha. (Plate 6-96)

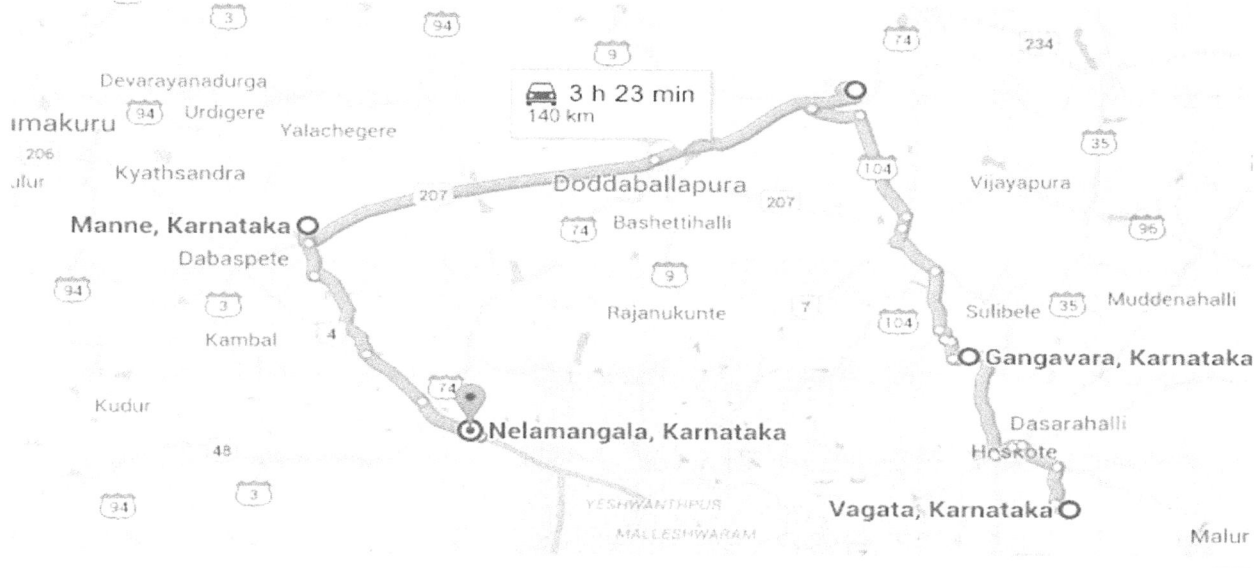

Sun's rays enter the *garbhagriha* from the window on the frontal wall to the cave and two doors, one in the *mandapa* and the other on the *prakara*. Thousands of devotees come in middle January every year on *Makar Sankranti* Day to this cave temple. This is a special day when the sunrays fall on the Sivalinga for one hour as it passes between the horns of the Nandi. Such was the knowledge of architecture and astronomy that the ancient sculptors could craft the horns of the stone bull outside the temple so that the sun's rays would pass through its horns and light up the deity Sivalinga inside the cave. The whole area, uneven in terrain is in quiet surroundings with many papal trees and *Naga* stones. There are many *mathas, choultries* and shrines here and the Kempambudhi tank is in its vicinity with a tower of Kempegouda's times on its bank.

Domlur

An interesting Chola monument in the city is the Chokkanatha temple at domlur called as Desi Manikka Pattanam in earlier records and also Dombalur in Kannada records and Tombalur in Tamil records. The place could have been an important settlement even under the Gangas in view of the fact that a Bhairava image assigned to the 8th century was unearthed behind the Anjaneya temple nearby. The place is described in Ilaipakka (Yelahanka) Nadu in Hoysala records. Though no Chola record is found in the Chokkanatha temple, the pilasters on the parts of the *garbhagriha* and *navaranga* walls of the temple and its name 'Chokka Perumal' make one conclude about its Chola origin. But stylistically it can be grouped with Hoysala times also. The temple which is in an elevated place has part of its *garbhagriha*, *navaranga* and frontal *mandapa* fully renovated. The original structure appears to be the *garbhagriha* and two *ardhamandapas* in front of it and one of them has an underground cella fully covered perhaps meant for storing *vahanas* and valuables of the temple. The *navaranga* pillars have beautiful sculptures like *kolata* scenes, sword dueling, duel between Vali and Sugreeva etc. In the *garbhagriha* are images of Visnu, Sridevi and Bhudevi and outside at the right corner to the front is the Ganesha shrine. There is an inscription slab with Kannada writings on both sides near it. There is also a Tamil inscription on the *adisthana*. There are more than half a dozen records in and around the temple. Hoysala Ramanatha donated 10 *pons* for the temple from the Tombalur (revenue) accounts in 1290 CE. Ballala III's grant of 1301 CE is also seen. A Chola art stone sculpture of Visnu is kept at the entrance of the temple. (Plate 6-97)

South Indian Vaishnavism (the cult devoted to the worship of Visnu and his ten incarnations) was given a new dimension by some of the Tamil saints or *Alwars* with their hymns and the stronghold was the Tamil country, which flourished at first under the *Alwars* up to the 8th century and then by the *Acharyas*. Great religious saints like Ramanuja, Chaitanya also gave a boost in spreading Vaishnavism. The Cholas are credited in bringing Vaishnavism to Karnataka in the late 10th century and early 11th century in a big way which initially was confined to select towns. It was the great Hoysala king Vishnuvardhan who brought it to the heartland of Gangavadi around 1116 CE.

Kadugodi

Kadugodi was a prominent *agrahara* during the Chola times then known as Kadamangalam. In a later record dated 1342 CE by the Hoysala Ballala III, the place is mentioned as Kadugodi Sthala in Toravala Vitti of the southern part of Sannainad. The place name is interpreted as *kadu+gudi* meaning temple in the forest. However, in the light of the Hoysala record this view loses ground and *kodi* stands for a weir.

The place is noted for an ancient temple outside the village locally called Kashi Vishwanatha temple built in Chola style. Several chola inscriptions found on the foundation cornice of this temple repeatedly mention the deity as Rajadiraja Bangishwaram or Vangishwaram Udaiyar. This is a short but spacious structure with squarish *garbhagriha* having short Chola pilasters in its walls (the temple has recently been renovated and some of the original features are no longer regonisable). There is a small Linga described to have been brought from Varanasi and hence the present name Kashi Vishwanatha. The original Linga called Bangishwaram Udaiyar is now missing. The *sikhara* over the *garbhagriha* had totally fallen off but has been reconstructed during recent renovation. The *navaranga* has cylindrical pillars with circular cushions over the round shafts. Inside the *navaranga* is placed one Saptamatrika panel with small but beautiful images of Shanmukha, Surya Narayana and Visalakshmi. There is a small open *mukhamamdapa* in front of the *garbhagriha*.

This temple is on the left bank of the Hoskote canal and is facing east. There are impressive relief sculptures of Nataraja, Umamaheswara on the east wall of the temple. There are two panels depicting Ramayana scenes, loosely placed. There is a series of Tamil inscriptions over the cornice of the foundation and also on the north exterior of the *garbhagriha*. The record dated 1150 CE speaks of a grant made by the Bangiya family of Kadamangalam to god Rajadiraja Bangishwaram Udaiyar of Pattanur in Sannainad under Vikkirama Chola Mandala. The second record on the foundation cornice is dated 1151 CE and it mentions some devotees including Sembabattar son of Nagabattar and others to a grant for the same god. The third record at the same place dated 1150 CE announces certain grants made by Koluttunga Chola to one priest. The last record is dated 1289 CE by Ballala III and it announces tax exemptions made to the same temple and the record mentions Irumbiliur (Ibbalur) or Vira Ballala Chaturvedimangalam. Near Dobighat area is one more Tamil record dated 1043 CE by Rajendra Chola announcing construction of the Pattandur tank with three sluices by one Rajaraja Velan Gavunda of Sannainad. (Plates 6-98 and 6-99)

Chikkajala

Chikkajala, "jala" of the inscriptions was a celebrated *agrahara* under the Hoysalas, then called 'Vishnuvardhana Chaturvedi Mangala.' The place name might have come from *jalari* tree also called *jalla* or *jala*. The place is noted for the Hoysala Chennakesava temple. This temple perhaps was constructed during the Hoysala king Vishnuvardhana's time as later records refer to the temple as Kesava of Vishnuvardhana Charurvedi Mangala.

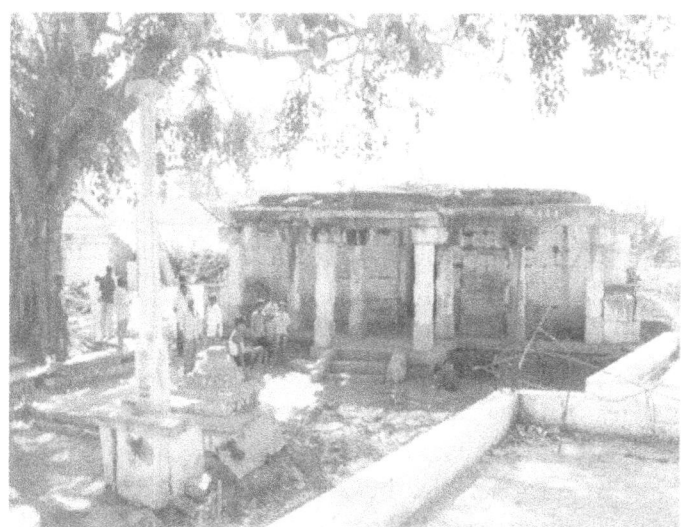

Chikkajala temple as it looked before renovation

The *garbhagriha* with Hoysala pilasters on the wall is now replaced by a renovated structure. The original image of Kesava about one metre tall flanked by his consorts Sridevi and Bhudevi is placed in the *ardhamandapa* and has been damaged. Of the Devi images, one is missing and only the *pitha* on which it was mounted is visible. There are small images of Kesava and his consorts inside the temple compound. The *navaranga* and *mukhamandapa* were perhaps added later during the Vijayanagara times by using some old pillars of the original temple.

There were Tamil inscriptions over the pilasters of the *navaranga* and the *mukhamandapa*. One of them dated about 1275 CE announces the pillar's donation by one Hoysala officer Pemmandai. The second pillar also of the same period states that it was granted by another official Allalar. The third pillar record states that it was donated by two officials Ariyavanigan Maran and Pattanasvami Periyadevan. An inscription on the stone to the south-east of the entrance of the temple dated 1328 CE is of Hoysala Ballala III announcing that one official Hoyadannayaka of Elahakkanad and other subordinate Mayilige Gouda and others granted for the Chennakesava of Jala, the two villages Jala Tarabanahalli and Anoodala. The second record on a stone to the north entrance of the temple dated 1328 CE speaks of several grants for the god by the Sunkada Adhikari Devarasa of Yelhankanad. Facing the temple was a tall *dhvajastambha* was installed by an official Baireya Nayaka son of illustrious commander Sonniyanayaka in around 1409 CE. (Plate 6-100)

The temple was recently renovated and most original features are gone but the older sculptures are all well kept inside the temple compound. The original *dhvajastambha* has now been replaced by a new one. The act of recent renovation is a unique example of religious co-existence as substantial funds were given by an NRI Christian philanthropist Ronald Colaco.

There existed a fort at Chikkajala about a hundred metres from where the temple is located. The fort was a protected monument of the ASI but during a recent widening of the National Highway major parts of the Chikkajala fort went into the land acquired for the Highway. Historians believed that Chikkajala in fact was a pre-historic site as ancient burial grounds were discovered in the vicinity of the fort.

Binnamangala

Binnamangala near Nelamangala is about 60 km away from Bengaluru on the Bengaluru-Pune highway. The Mukthi Natheswara Temple in Binnamangala was apparently built during the period of Kulothunga Chola I (1069–1120 CE) of Tamil Nadu. There is a stone image in front of the temple which mentions in the year 1110 during the 41st year of the Chola king the administrative officer of the region "Udaiyaan Rajaraja Kulothungan alias Kulothunga Chola Athimuurkka Chengiraiyaan, made endowments of surrounding lands and other donations -(devadanam)" to the presiding deity (Siva) of the temple namely (then known as) "Muththeeswarem Udaiya Mahathevar" of the village Vinmamangalam of Kukkanur Nadu of Vikkiramachola Mandala. He arranged these details to be inscribed on a stone and planted therein.

This stone inscription panel can be seen planted within the temple premises. Opposite the temple in the front there are three sculptures, one of which is of interest. This is a sculpture of a devotee wearing a head turban and with clasped hands on a single stone (about 2.5 ft in height) which the nearby villagers hold is the stone image of the Chola king Kulothunga Chola I, whereas from the inscription on the stone panel it is confirmed as that of the Chola admistrative officer of this region under Chola king Kulothunga Chola I of Tamil Nadu, who himself had the name as "Udaiyaan Rajaraja Kulothungan (his royal title) alias Kulothunga Chola Athimuurkka Chengiraiyaan." (Plates 6-101 and 6-102)

The temple is built on a raised *adisthana* (about 3 ft in height). The temple has been renovated recently but most original features have been retained. The temple has squarish *garbhagriha*, a closed hall (*sabhamandapa*) in front of it and an open *mukhamandapa* resting on four pillars. While the pillars of the *mukhamandapa* are simple in design with square, octagonal and square combination in the shaft, the pillars inside the *sabhamandapa* are carved intricately. The exterior walls of the *garbhagriha* and *sabhamandapa* are adorned with Chola pilasters and have various gods and goddesses carved as sculptures in *koshthas*. The deities in the sculptures include Ganesha and Durga standing on Mahisha's head. The loose sculpture scattered around the temple complex include *viragals* and *Naga* images. The tall *dhvajastambha* is erected outside of the complex on raised ground.

Bannerghatta

Bannerghatta has the beautiful temple of Champakadhamswamy located in an elevated place overlooking a small hillock. The temple belongs to the early Hoysala times. Hoysala records there read about making grants to the existing god Damodara, thus the temple in fact may be of even earlier antiquity. The temple is reached through two flights of steps when one reaches the *mahadvara*. The structure is in the *Dravidian* style of architecture. Inside the *garbhagriha* is the image of standing Visnu and his consorts Sridevi and Bhudevi. But locally the deity is called Champakadhamaswamy. It is interesting to note that the name Champakadham is of very late origin occurring in an inscription dated 1819 CE. It is also said that the god is regularly worshipped with offerings of *Champaka* or *Sampige* flowers. There are some *champaka* trees around the temple. Both Hoysala and Vijayanagara inscriptions repeatedly mention the god as Damodara that was the original name of the deity. The *garbhagriha* has a *Vesara sikhara*. There is also a group of five bronze images in the *ardhamandapa*. The decorated *mahadvara* (*gopura*), a lofty structure consists of a number of basement cornices above which rises the wall decorated with pilasters, some combined with *kalasa*. There is a Tamil inscription of the Hoysala general Singeya Dannayaka on the left frame of the doorway dated 1291 CE. It speaks of several grants made to the temple.

In front of the *navaranga* is a compact rectangular *mukhamandapa* having massive Vijayanagara pillars. There is a *sandhara pradakshinapatha* around the *garbhagriha* having a roofed corridor of considerable height as in many Hoysala temples. To the right of the *mukhamandapa* entrance are two small shrines with images of Alwars and Ramanujacharya. A Tamil inscription dated 1278 CE recording a grant for the success of Narasimha's sword and arm was erected by an officer Ketaya Dannayaka who was ruling this region under the Hoysala king Narasimha III. (Plates 6-103 and 6-104)

There is a separate Ammanavaru or Lakshmi temple in the Vijayanagara style to the right of the *mukhamandapa* facing south. To the left of the main gateway is a flight of steps almost circumscribing the Champakadham temple leading to a rocky hill. Over the hill are some stray remains of a fort almost covering the hill. Nearby are remains of an old temple like structure (incomplete) built with huge dressed stones and a tall pillar in the centre. Originally, it is said that this was the site where they wanted to build the temple. At a distance to the south on the hillock named Vahinigiri is the Lakshmi Narasimha temple. Nearby under a tall Ashwatha tree are six *atmabali* stones (self immolation memorial) having fine relief figures. Two km away from here is the famous Suvarnamukhi pond or *kalyani*.

Hulimavu

Hulimavu located on the Bannerghatta Road is noted for a pre-historic rock shelter presently called Ramalinga cave. The place name is found mentioned as Amarapura (*amra* meaning *mavu* or mango) under Sarakeya time in a record dated 1652 CE. Subsequently the place must have got its present name 'Hulimavu' meaning sour mango. The rock shelter is a natural one measuring about 200 feet in breadth and 120 feet in length. It has recently been covered with a brick wall in front with a central doorway. Scholars conclude that this must have been a dwelling for the pre-historic man when the huge ash-mounds near the cave were observed. To the left of the cave is a small in-built sanctum enshrining a Sivalinga installed over a considerably tall *panipitha*. Besides this are processional bronze images of Rama, Lakshmana and Sita. On the right side of the main entrance is the old stone *pitha* having decorative figures around measuring 4 by 7 feet. The *garbhagriha* houses a tall Sivalinga perhaps of the Ganga period. In front of the *garbhagriha* is a *navaranga* having post-Vijayanagara pillars. Outside the temple in an open yard is a broken image of Surya having Ganga features. (plate 6-105)

Manne or Manyapura

Manne is a prosperous village near Dabaspete on Bengaluru-Pune Highway. This is the famous Manyanagara or Ratnapuri Pattana and Srirajya of Sripurusha of the Ganga dynasty who shifted the capital from Kolar to Manne after a setback at the hands of the Rashtrakuta king Krishna I. The earliest record is the copper plates discovered from Manne of the time of Srivikrama (635–650 CE), son of Mushkara. Two more copper plates belonging to the reign of Ganga Marasimha I (796–799 CE) were also found at this place. Both relate to land grants and were issued by the king from the victorious camp of Manyapura after consolidating his position with the help of Rashtrakuta king Govindaa III. The temples known by the names Someswara, Sule Devalaya and Mannaramma indicate the importance of the place during early eighth and ninth centuries. The Kapileswara and Someswara temples reveal the early brick foundations as the Gangas favoured the brick tradition started by the Satavahanas and Kadambas. (Plates 6-106 and 6-107)

The Kapileswara temple located on the tank bund, Chikkakere is in partly dilapidated condition. The temple faces east. The *garbhagriha* fronted by a closed *mandapa* is approachable by a stepped entrance with side banisters or balustrades. Life sized *dvarapalas* flank the entrance. The door frame is of *trisakha* type surmounted by *sala sikhara*. The *adisthana* has preserved its original brick mouldings. The pillars of the *mandapa* have low square over a moulded *padma bandha* base sixteen sided shaft held by *dala padmas*. The pilasters are of simpler type, square shafts with mid-region octagonal and carrying double-armed volute corbels.

The Someswara temple situated in the field has also preserved its original *adisthana* which is simpler one with low *upana* and somewhat higher *jagati*. In this case, the *bhitti* part (outer wall) is also preserved to a height of about 70 cm and the rest of the wall, *prasara* and roof part has been raised of slabs in recent past. A slender granite figure of Chamundi seated, four-handed is an early example of the sculpture in the temple. Based on the archaic structure one can assign the earliest foundation in both the temples to a period earlier than the 7th century CE coinciding with the issue of grant of land by Srivikrama (635–650 CE).

A century later Sripurusha and his successors not only renovated but expanded these temples and gifted lands for their upkeep.

The Akkatangi temple is at the north-east of Manne village closer to the Kapileswara temple and has an eastern stepped entrance. The *prati-bandha* and *adisthana* is buried up to the *tripatta-kumuda* level. The *pada* has plain square pillars. The *sikhara* is missing and on stylistic grounds the temple can be assigned to the ninth century CE.

The *Jinendrabhavanam* of the inscriptions of Sivamara II's time appears to be the Jaina temple in Manne. This temple appears to be have been caused by Prabhutavarsha-Govindarajadeva (802 CE) at the western quarter of Manyapura through his local chief Srivijayaraja. The temple is locally called Sule Devalaya and is in ruined condition.

It consists of large pillared hall, more in length than wide with its sections at the south, north and east partly fallen. The pillars are unusually tall with unworked squarish base parts covered up to a considerable height under ground. Two variants are noticed in the pillars. The peripheral ones are with no capital elements but have octagonal middle and are thinner examples carrying the cross-corbels with beveled arms. The other type has plain ones with thicker shafts roughly worked out squarish shape and left unfinished. These are at the central bay. A special square *ankana* at the south-east bordered within a four-pillared *mandapa* was perhaps segregated for placement of a Jina image. The pillars of this square *ankana* are special class and finely finished. The ceiling slab over the *ankana* possessed within an encircled medallion with flying *gandharvas* couple.

Begur

Begur mentioned severally as Bempur, Veppur, Bevur in inscriptions is perhaps one of the very old towns in Karnataka. It was the headquarters of a Nadu then and popularly called Bempur-12 under the Gangas. According to the hero stone now kept in the Government Museum Bengaluru (known as Begur Inscription), the place was ruled by a Ganga officer Nagattara who in about 890 CE fell in war between Ganga Ereyappa and Nolamba Bira Mahendra while attacking the elephants in the army of the Nolamba prince Ayyapadeva. The place is also considered a pre-historic site as once fields full of ash pits containing bones and pottery were found. It is also said that several circular ovens built of bricks had been erected for the manufacture of glass bangles.

The Nageswara temple complex here consists of five Lingas enshrined separately and known as Nageswara, Nagareswara, Choleswara, Karneswara and Kamateswara. The Nageswara temple is viewed as the most important owing probably to its antiquity. It has a square *garbhagriha* with a *Dravida sikhara* having typical Ganga features with a huge circular *stupika*. This temple is assigned by scholars to Nagattara, the Ganga officer. There is a small but compact *ardhamandapa* connected by a big square *navaranga* having four central cylindrical pillars with cushions at top. Thee *navaranga* ceiling has a well executed *ashtadikpalas* in relief. Around the *garbhagriha* wall below the cornice are some sculptures narrating *Panchatantra* stories. The side wall of the *navaranga* has beautifully executed *jalandharas*. Inside the *navaranga* are the images of Kalabhairava, Ashtabhuja, Mahishamardini, Visnu, Surya, Chandra and Parvati. In the *mukhamandapa* are placed a *saptamatrika* panel and a Nandi facing the circular tall Sivalinga. Over the cornice of the *mukhamandapa* is a Tamil inscription. Another old Ganga record is seen reclining against the wall near the *dhvajastambha* which is assigned to about 900 CE. It is of great interest as it mentions that Nagattara's home servant Buttanasetyy died in battle of 'Bengaluru.' This is the first mention of the place as Bengaluru in records. One inscription dated 1110 CE of the Hoysalas announces that one official Tamattandan of Murusunadu made certain land grants below the tank of Veppur and also caused the surrounding wall to the temple of Nageswara (and the whole temple complex). Another Tamil record dated 1262 CE also of the Hoysala period mentions some grant made to god Tirunagishwaram Mahadevar by one official Sakkanayar and the village granted was Orriya Vanapalli. One record describes the death of Nagattara's daughter Konabbe by *sallekhana*, a Jaina religious ritual of starving oneself to death.

To the left of the Nageswara temple almost adjacent to it is the separate Choleswara temple. The square *garbhagriha* has intact *Dravida sikhara* with a *stupuka* of square base and *kubjas* at different stages. There is a small *ardhamandapa* in front of the *garbhagriha*. The *navaranga* has cylindrical pillars with circular cushions above the shafts mounted with square abacus. These central pillars have beautiful dancing figures in low relief in a band (*mala*). There is a *bhuvanesvari* in the *navaranga* ceiling having an image of Umamaheswara in the centre and *Ashtadikpalas* in the surrounding square panels. Inside the *navaranga* are sculptures of Mahishamardini, Chandikeswara and Surya. The Surya Narayana is four-handed with two holding lotuses and two placed on the waist. To its north-east corner facing south is the small shrine of Ammanavaru or Parvati. (Plates 6-108 and 6-109)

To the right of the Nageswara temple is a separate shrine of Kali-Kamateswara built originally by the Gangas but later renovated by the Vijayanagara rulers. To further south it is a separate shrine of Nagareswara. There is a large Sivalinga inside the square *garbhagriha* having Ganga features. There is an oblong *ardhamandapa*. The *navaranga* has four cylindrical pillars with circular cushions over the shaft and square abacus on top. There are sculptures of Mahishamardini, Ganapati and Bhairava in the *navaranga*. An open Nandi pavilion stands in front of the *navaranga*. Facing the Nandi *mandapa* is a small shrine dedicated to Surya. At a distance from the temple complex to the east is the old Begur tank mentioned in several inscriptions from this place.

Begur must have been a celebrated Jaina centre under the Gangas. Jaina record dated 1422 CE (of the Vijayanagara period) found in the area announces one official Nagiya Kariyappa Dannayaka son of Chokkimayya made a grant for the then existing Chokkimayya Jinalaya.

Agara and Madivala

A Kannada inscription slab of 870 CE of the Ganga ruler Satyavakya and Nagattara (an officer under him at Begur), Siriyamayya son of Irugamayya, chief of Irvvuliyur (modern Ibbalur) fixed sluices of two tanks and built a third tank and secured land for their maintenance. Even today two of the old tanks are seen at Agara. The place has temples dedicated to Venkatarama, Rama and Someswara on the tank bund. The old Someswara temple on the bank of the tank has hero-stone depicting three individual sculptures in high relief. Kannada poet Thimmakavi (Work: Ananda Ramayana) belonged to this place. Madivala was a celebrated *agrahara* under the Cholas and Hoysalas. The place is noted for Someswara temple in the old Tavarakere village. Though the *garbhagriha* faces east, the temple entrance is from the south. The *garbhagriha* has a square shape with typical Chola pilasters projecting from the walls and over which is a *Dravidian sikhara*. Images in the temple include Kalabhairava, Surya, Annapoorna, Dakshinamurthy, Muruga, Srinivasa and Kukkulamma (Plates 6-110 and 6-111). A record dated 1247 CE on the foundation of the temple announces grant of some lands below the big tank of Vengalur (Bengaluru) by an official Pemmattaiyar of Veppur (Begur) for god Sembeswaram (Someswara) at Tamaraikkirai (Tavarakere). The second record dated 1301 CE announces Hoysala king Ballala III granting lands and religious instructions to several *mathas* and *sthanikas*.

Vagata

Vagata, a village located about 6 km from Hoskote which was a very prosperous town under the Cholas. Vagata was known by several names such as Ovattam, Varadaraja-Chaturvedi-Mangalam, Ogata, Bhagirathipura, Yogapuri and so on, under the reign of various kings. The earliest inscription found here has a mention of Raja Rajendra Chola who ruled during the 10th Century. There are many old temples in this village, constructed during the times of the Cholas and Vijayanagara kings. Most important amongst them are the Varadaraja temple, Anjaneya temple, Chandramouleswara temple and the Chowdeshwari temple. The Varadaraja temple is built in *Dravidian* style and dedicated to Visnu. Though the temple is completely renovated, the idol of Visnu, the four pillars of the *mukhamandapa* and the *Garudastambha* have survived all odds and maintained as was originality raised under the Chola architecture. The temple consists of a *garbhagriha*, *antarala*, *sabhamandapa* and *mukhamandapa*. Chola style pilasters can still be seen on the outer walls. There is a Tamil inscription nearby the temple. A few stone slabs with inscriptions and geometric figures etched on them in the shape of *yantras* too can be noticed outside the temple. (Plate 6-112)

The Chowdeshwari temple located on the other side of the lake is one amongst the very few temples dedicated to the *Saptamatrikas* and may have been built during the same time as the Kolaramma temple in Kolar. "*Saptamatrikas*" is a set of seven mothers, representing the motherly aspects of the great goddesses (*devis*) and constitute the female counterparts of the gods Brahma (Brahmani), Maheswara (Maheswari), Kaumara (Kaumari), Visnu (Vaisnavi), Varaha (Varahi), Indra (Indrani) and Yama (Chamundi). Apart from these, there are sculptures of Betala, Veerabhadra, Siva, Chowdeshwari and the Royal priest of Cholas, inside the temple, which are quite interesting. The temple has a simple architecture more reminiscent of the Ganga style architecture consisting of an oblong *garbhagriha* to accommodate the *saptamatrikas*. The *garbhagriha* has a wider *sabhamandapa* in front. An old arch in the shape of a *torana* outside signifies the antiquity of the temple. (plates 6-113 and 6-114)

According to the legend, people feared to visit this temple as it was located in the dense forests. It was then, that a widow named Chikkamma, decided to take up the renovation work of this temple. She approached the king of Mysore and requested him to help the villagers. When the king turned down her request, she returned to her village and found her own way for saving the temple. She sold her Mangalasutra (the sacred thread, made of Gold and other precious stones, tied by the husband to his wife sanctifying marriage) and gathered money. Meanwhile, the king who had refused to help her faced various problems, and on consultation and advice of the royal priest, decided to visit Chowdeshwari temple and perform rituals in order to get rid of all his problems. There is a beautiful *Thoranagamba* (*toranastambha*) just opposite to the temple entrance which lies half buried and pillar that sinks a few inches every year. As per the priest's description, the pillar is sinking ever since Chikkamma renovated the temple and from the time he remembers, it has sunk by almost a foot.

LISTS OF TEMPLES BUILT DURING THE TIMES OF DIFFERENT DYNASTIES

Temples have been built in Karnataka since times immemorial. However, the earliest vestiges of such structures can be traced back to the reign of the Satavahanas only as all earlier structures do not exist any more. Barring pre-historic sites which revealed construction of some sort or the other, signs of any religious structures or shrines haven't really come to sight. Accordingly, the lists of temples furnished here will feature temples about which something is known from historical records or inscriptions left behind by the builders. The lists here commence with the temples of the Ganga and the Kadamba periods and go till the end of the Hoysala period. The lists also include temples built by the Nolambas and Cholas though they were not really dynasties ruling from Karnataka.

List of Temples and Monuments from the times of the Gangas

Name of the Temple	Location	Year of Construction	Principal Deity
Dadigesvara	Kodihalli	5th Centry	Siva
Honnadevi	Honudaki	7th Century	Shakti
Kapilesvara	Manne	7th Century	Siva
Somesvara	Manne	7th Century	Siva
Akka Tangi	Manne	9th Century	Shakti
Kodandarama	Hiremaglur	5th Century	Visnu
Somesvara	Gangavara	8th Century	Siva
Early Sculpture	Devanahalli	8th Century	Visnu
Gangadharesvara	Dodshivara	8th Century	Siva
Vaidyanathesvara	Vaidyanathapura	8th Century	Siva
Vintesvara	Homma	8th Century	Siva
Siddhesvara	Algodu	8th Century	Siva
Somesvara	Kunigal	8th Century	Siva
Sivaramesvara	Kunigal	9th Century	Siva
Sculpture/Somesvara	Hemmige	8th Century	Siva
Virabhadreshwara	Kallattipura	8th Century	Siva
Sriranganathaswamy	Srirangapatna	8th Century	Visnu
Yoganandisvara	Nandi	9th Century	Siva
Kantesvara	Sivarapatna	8th Century	Siva
Chellesvara	Athagur	8th Century	Siva
Ramesvara	Kittur	9th Century	Siva
Varadarajaswamy	Hangala	9th Century	Visnu
Bhagavathi	Meditambihalli	9th Century	Shakti
Mangalesvara	Kudalur	9th Century	Siva
Bhagavathi	Kudalur	10th Century	Shakti
Mahalingesvara	Kunthur	9th Century	Siva
Siva-Bhima (Isvara)	Nagondanahalli	9th Century	Siva

Contd.

Name of the Temple	Location	Year of Construction	Principal Deity
Nagaresvara	Begur	9th Century	Siva
Nagesvara	Begur	9th Century	Siva
Rudresvara	Biskur	9th Century	Siva
Arkesvara	Biskur	9th Century	Siva
Kallesvara	Aralaguppe	9th Century	Siva
Ramesvara	Narasamangala	10th century	Siva
Mahadevesvara	Varuna	10th Century	Siva
Shivaramesvara, Nagaresvara, Nitimargesvara	Mogenahalli	10th Century	Siva
Shambhilingesvara	Alenahalli	9th Century	Siva
Desesvara	Alur	9th Century	Siva
Arkesvara	Alur	10th Century	Siva
Patalesvara	Talkad	10th Century	Siva
Maralesvara	Talkad	10th Century	Siva
Arkesvara	Vijayapura	10th Century	Siva
Nilakanthesvara	Ganiganuru	10th century	Siva
Srikantesvara	Nanjangud	10th Century	Siva
Scattered Scuplture	Kudalur	9th/10th Century	Various/Shakti
Viragals	Nonamangala	7th Century	Hero-stones
Viragals	Kallur	7th Century	Hero-stones
Viragals	Hiregundakal	8th Century	Hero-stones
Viragals	Siva-ganga	Uncertain	Hero-stones
Viragals	Ramenahalli	6th Century	Hero-stones
Viragals (Bhagavathi Temple)	Meditambihalli	9th Century	Hero-stones
Viragals (Bhagavathi Temple)	Uttanur	8th Century	Shakti/Hero-stones
Dolmens	Madivala	8th Century	Sepulchral
Dolmens	Dodshivara	8th Century	Sepulchral
Chamber Temple	Belchawadi	8th Century	Siva
Chamber Temple	Madivala	8th Century	Saptamatrika
Memorial of Dog	Athagur	10th Century	Memorial
Gokals	Hebbeta	10th Century	Memorial
Gokals/Viragals	Hunakunda	9th Century	Memorial
Brick Basadi	Nonamangala	5th Century	Jaina
Sule Devalaya	Manne	9th Century	Jaina
Chandraprabha Basadi	Sravanabelgola	9th Century	Jaina
Chandragupta Basadi	Sravanabelgola	9th Century	Jaina
Chamundaraya Basadi	Sravanabelgola	10th Century	Jaina
Gommatesvara	Sravanabelgola	10th Century	Jaina
Bharatesvara Statue	Sravanabelgola	10th Century	Jaina
Gullakayajji	Sravanabelgola	10th Century	Jaina

Contd.

Name of the Temple	Location	Year of Construction	Principal Deity
Akhanda-Vagilu	Sravanabelgola	10th Century	Jaina
Trikuta Basadi	Kambadahalli	9th Century	Jaina
Panchkuta Basadi	Kambadahalli	9th Century	Jaina
Mana-stambha	Kambadahalli	9th Century	Jaina
Parsvanatha	Talkad	10th Century	Jaina
Sivalaya Basadi	Muguru	10th Century	Jaina
Ruined Jaina site	Kyathanahalli	9th Century	Jaina
Gopinatha gutta	Nandi	8th Century	Cave/rock shelter
Rock Scuplture And Basadi	Arethippur	6th Century	Jaina
Jaina Nishidi	Bastipura	8th Century	Jaina
Arhatpalli Nishidi	Harpanhalli	7th Century	Jaina
Nishidi	Doddahundi	9th Century	Jaina
Nishidi	Asandi/Kadur	9th Century	
Kuge-Brahamdeva Pillar	Sravanabelgola (Chandragiri)	10th Century	Jaina
Tyagada-Brahamdeva Pillar	Sravanabelgola (Doddabetta)	10th Century	Jaina
Ruins of Jaina Temples	Basadi Hoskote (KRS)	9th Century	Gommateswara and Ruins of Jaina Temples

List of Temples and Monuments with the Kadamba Features

Name of the Temple	Location	Year of Construction	Principal Deity
Halmidi Inscription and Hero Stones	Halmidi	5th Century	Inscription and Memorials
Talagunda Inscription	Talagunda	4th Century	Inscription
Praneshwara	Talagunda	4th Century	Siva
Kamala Basadi	Belagami(Belgaum)	11th Century	Jaina
Chikki Basadi	Belagavi(Belgaum)	11th Century	Jaina
Bhava (Mallapalli)	Malavalli	4th Century	Siva
Pillar Inscription	Malavalli	4th Century	Inscription
Bhu Varahaswamy	Halasi	5th Century	Visnu
Malahanikeshwara	Sringeri	9th Century	Siva
Jaina Basadi	Halasi	5th Century	Jaina
Hattikeshwara	Halasi	5th Century	Siva
Kalleshwara	Halasi	5th Century	Siva
Sankar Deva	Kadoroli	5th Century	Siva
Bhutanatha	Torgal	5th Century	Siva
Panchalingeshwara	Munvalli	5th Century	Siva
Ramalingeshwara	Baihongal	5th Century	Siva
Kamalanarayana	Degaon	12th Century	Visnu
Madhukeshwara	Banavasi	5th Century	Siva
Ratnatraya Basadi	Siddapura	5th Century	Jaina

Contd.

Name of the Temple	Location	Year of Construction	Principal Deity
Prasanna Rameshwara	Devarunda	12th Century	Siva
Bettada Bhaireshwara	Bhairapur	12th Century	Siva
Rameshwara	Halasi	5th Century	Siva
Shiva	Yelavatti	5th Century	Siva
Jaina Basadi	Yelavatti	5th Century	Jaina
Veerabhadra	Halmidi	5th Century	Veerabhadra

List of Temples and Monuments of the Badami Chalukyas

Name of the Temple	Location	Year of Construction	Principal Deity
Kalideva	Aminabhavi	6th Century CE	Siva
Rameshwara, Sindeshwara, Hobeshwara	Lakshmeshwar	7th Century CE	Siva
Arjuneshwara, Nandishwara	Banikoppa	7th Century CE	Siva
Mahakuteshwara	Mahakuta	7th Century CE	Siva
Naganatha	Naganathakolla	7th Century CE	Siva
Meguti Jaina Templee	Aihole	7th Century CE	Jaina
Buddhist Chaitya	Aihole	6th Century CE	Buddhist
Mallikarjuna	Aihole	7th Century CE	Siva
Jyotirlinga Complex	Aihole	8th Century CE	Siva
Durga	Aihole	8th Century CE	Surya
Suryanarayana	Aihole	8th Century CE	Surya
Gaudaragudi	Aihole	7th Century CE	Siva
Badiragudi	Aihole	8th Century CE	Siva
Ladkhan	Aihole	7th Century CE	Siva
Chakragudi	Aihole	7th Century CE	Siva
Chikkigudi	Aihole	8th Century CE	Siva
Hucchimalligudi	Aihole	7th Century CE	Siva
Ravanaphadi Cave	Aihole	6th Century CE	Siva
Hucchiapayyamatha	Aihole	8th Century CE	Siva
Jaina Cave	Aihole	7th Century CE	Siva
Kadasiddeshwara	Pattadakal	7th Century CE	Siva
Jambulinga	Pattadakal	7th Century CE	Siva
Galaganatha	Pattadakal	7th Century CE	Siva
Sangameshwara	Pattadakal	8th Century CE	Siva
Mallikarjuna	Pattadakal	8th Century CE	Siva
Virupaksha	Pattadakal	8th Century CE	Siva
Papanatha	Pattadakal	8th Century CE	Siva
Cave Temple 1	Badami	6th Century CE	Siva
Cave Temple 2	Badami	6th Century CE	Siva
Cave Temple 3	Badami	6th Century CE	Visnu
Cave Temple 4	Badami	6th Century CE	Jaina
Jambulinga	Badami	7th Century CE	Siva

Contd.

Name of the Temple	Location	Year of Construction	Principal Deity
Bhutanatha Complex	Badami	8th Century CE	Siva
Lower Shivalaya	Badami	8th Century CE	Siva
Upper Shivalaya	Badami	7th Century CE	Siva
Malegutti Shivalaya	Badami	7th Century CE	Siva
Sangameshwara	Siddanakola	7th Century CE	Siva and Lajja Gouri

List of Temples and Monuments of the Rashtrakutas

Name of the Temple	Location	Year of Construction	Principal Deity
Navalinga	Kuknoor	10th Century CE	Siva
Jaina Narayana	Pattadakal	9th Century CE	Jaina
Kashi Vishwanatha	Pattadakal	9th Century CE	Siva
Jaina Basadi	Malkhed	8th Century CE	Jaina
Malkhed Fort	Malkhed	8th Century CE	Fort and Temples
Siddhalingeshwara	Sirwal	9th Century CE	Siva
Shiva Temples Ensemble	Sirwal	9th Century CE	Siva
Someshwara	Ingleshwar	10th Century CE	Siva
Ambiger Gudi	Aihole	10th Century CE	Siva
Jaina Basadi	Aihole (City)	10th Century CE	Jaina
Veniyargudi	Aihole	10th Century CE	Siva
Jaina Basadi	Hallur	9th Century CE	Jaina
Vishveshwaragudi	Hallur	9th Century CE	Siva
Shantinatha Basadi	Bandalike	10th Century CE	Jaina
Andhakeshwara	Hooli	10th Century CE	Siva
Gavaganeshwara	Kolur	9th Century CE	Siva
Nakhareshwara	Kolur	9th Century CE	Siva
Mulsthaneshwara	Shiggaon	9th Century CE	Siva
Mahadeva	Nidagundi	9th Century CE	Siva
Kogeshwara	Meundi	9th Century CE	Siva
Mallikarjuna	Meundi	9th Century CE	Siva
Ramalingeshwara	Hole Honnatti	10th Century CE	Siva
Brahameshwara	Kalasa	10th Century CE	Siva
Rameshwara	Nagavi	10th Century CE	Siva
Svayambhulinga (Brahamadeva)	Savadi	10th Century CE	Siva
Bhoga Nandishwara	Nandi	9th Century CE	Siva
Sanmukha	Sandur	10th Century CE	Siva
Bhutanatha	Badami	9th Century CE	Siva
Hara (Mahadeva)	Lokapur	9th Century CE	Siva
Huccimali II	Aihole	10th Century CE	Siva
Challeshwara	Atakur	10th Century CE	Siva
Ramalingeshwara	Ramasagara	10th Century CE	Siva
Nandisthana	Ardeshahalli	9/10th Century CE	Siva and Inscription

Contd.

Name of the Temple	Location	Year of Construction	Principal Deity
Panchikeshwara	Salur	9th Century CE	Siva
Mallikarjuna	Ron	9th Century CE	Siva
Someshwara	Sogal	9th Century CE	Siva
Parameshwara	Konnur	9th Century CE	Siva
Trikuteshwara	Gadag	9th Century CE	Siva
Kuntigudi II	Aihole	9th Century CE	Siva
Jadragudi	Aihole	9th Century CE	Siva
Kalmeshwara	Hooli	10th Century CE	Siva
Aralibasappa	Aihole	9th Century CE	River Goddess
Galaganatha	Aihole	9th Century CE	Siva
Ishwara	Gokak Falls	10th Century CE	Siva
Kalbhaireshwara	Mahakuta	10th Century CE	Siva
Adakeshwara	Mahakuta	10th Century CE	Siva
Ishwara 1	Ron	10th Century CE	Siva
Mallikarjuna	Mudhol	10th Century CE	Siva
Ramalingeshwara	Aihole	10th Century CE	Siva
Mallikarjuna	Mudhol	10th Century	Siva

List of Temples of the Nolambas in Karnataka

Name of the Temple	Location	Year of Construction	Principal Deity
Nolamba Narayana	Avani	9th Centry	Visnu
Ramalingesvara Group of Temples	Avani	9th Century	Siva/Shakti
Bhoga Nandisvara	Nandi	9th Century	Siva
Bhimesvara	Anur	10th Century	Siva
Kamesvara	Madigere (Chintamani)	10th Century	Siva
Mahendresvara	Baraguru	9th Century	Siva
Mahadeva	Arakere	11th Century	Siva
Kalideva (Mulstahana)	Vaddanahalli	11th Century	Siva
Nonabesvara	Nonavinalere	10th Century	Siva
Isvara (Mahadeva)	Uttanur	10th Century	Siva
Viragals	Hunakunda	9th Century	Hero-stones

List of Temples of the Alupas

Name of the Temple	Location	Year of Construction	Principal Deity
Rajarajeshwari	Polali	9th Century CE	Shakti
Panchalingeshwara	Vittal	10th Century CE	Siva
Anantheshwara	Udupi	9th Century CE	Siva
Manjunatha	Kadri	10th Century CE	Siva
Mahishamardini	Neelavara	10th Century CE	Shakti
Brahameshwara	Brahmavar	9th Century CE	Siva
Panchalingeshwara	Barkur	9th Century CE	Siva

Contd.

Name of the Temple	Location	Year of Construction	Principal Deity
Kathale Basadi	Barkur	9th Century CE	Jaina
Mahalingeshwara and Baira Ganapathi	Barkur	10th Century CE	Siva
Kotilingeshwara	Koteshwar	10th Century CE	Siva
Mahalingeshwara	Basrur	9th Century CE	Siva
Kuke Subramanya	Sadanur	9th Century CE	Subramanya
Sadashiva	Suratkal	9th Century CE	Siva
Sri Krishna Temple	Udupi	9th Century CE	Visnu
Kilganeshwara	Kigga	7th Century CE	Siva
Shambhukalla	Udayavara	8th Century CE	Siva

List of Temples of the Cholas in Karnataka

Name of the Temple	Location	Year of Construction	Principal Deity
Chokka Perumalswamy	Domlur	11th Century	Visnu
Kolaramma	Kolar	11th Century	Shakti
Muktinathesvara	Binnamangala	11th Century	Siva
Siddesvara	Soladevanahalli	11th Century	Siva
Madesvara	Madigere, Nelamangala	11th Century	Siva
Aprameyaswamy	Doddamalur	11th Century	Visnu
Arkesvara	Chikkamalur	11th Century	Siva
Gopalaswamy	Chikkamalur	11th Century	Visnu
Narayanaswamy	Malurpatna	11th Century	Visnu
Ramadeva	Kudlur	11th century	Visnu
Kasi Visvesvara	Kadugodi	11th Century	Siva
Varadarajaswamy	Vagata	12th Century	Visnu
Somesvara	Agara	11th Century	Siva
Somesvara	Old Madivala	11th Century	Siva
Dharmesvara	Kondrahalli	12th Century	Siva
Sri Madramma	Huskur	11th century	Shakti
Gavi Gangadharesvara	Gavipuram, Bangalore	11th Century	Siva
Mallikarjunaswamy	Hura	12th Century	Siva
Somesvara	Kurudumale	11th Century	Siva
Gopalakrishna	Honganur	11th Century	Visnu
Chamundesvari	Alur	11th Century	Shakti
Vasantha Vallabharaya	Vasanthpura, Bangalore	12th Century	Visnu
Lakshmi Narasimha	Marehalli	11th Century	Visnu
Varadarajaswamy	Uttanur	11th Century	Visnu
Vaidyanathesvara	Talkad	11th Century	Siva
Agastyesvara	Balamuri	11th Century	Siva
Hanumanteswara	Bannur	11th Century	Siva

List of Temples and Monuments of the Kalyani Chalukyas

Name of the Temple	Location	Year of Construction	Principal Deity
Dattatreya	Gokak Falls	11th Century	Dattatreya
Basaveshwara	Gokak Falls	12th Century	Siva
Mahalingeshwara	Gokak Falls	12th Century	Siva
Kadasiddheshwara	Gokak Falls	11th Century	Siva
Tarakeshwara	Hangal	12th Century	Siva
Ganesha	Hangal	12th Century	Ganapathi
Bileshwara	Hangal	12th Century	Siva
Jaina Basadi	Hangal	12th Century	Jaina
Kalleshwara	Hoovina Hadagali	11th Century	Siva
Keshavaswami	Hoovina Hadagali	11th Century	Visnu
Krishna Ensemble	Hoovina Hadagali	11th Century	Visnu
Mahadeva	Itagi	12th Century	Siva
Kalmeshwara	Jalsingvi	11th Century	Siva
Banashankari	Amargol	12th Century	Shakti
Sankarlinga	Saunshi	11th Century	Siva
Dattatreya	Chattarki	12th Century	Dattatreya
Dodda Basappa	Dambal	12th Century	Siva
Siddheshwara	Haveri	11th Century	Siva
Someshwara	Kadlewad	12th Century	Siva
Kotishwara	Kubaturu	12th Century	Siva
Bhimeshwara	Nilgunda	12th Century	Siva
Satyanarayana	Naregal	11th Century	Visnu
Siddheshwara	Ujjini	12th Century	Siva
Parvathi	Umapur	12th Century	Shakti
Mahadeva	Umapur	12th Century	Siva
Siva	Narayanpur	12th Century	Siva
Basavanna	Tambur	12th Century	Siva
Panchalingeshwara	Sedam	12th Century	Siva
Basaveshwara	Kollur	11th Century	Siva
Parvatiparameshwara	Harti	11th Century	Siva
Kalmeshwara	Ingaleshwar	12th Century	Siva
Siva	Salhalli	12th Century	Siva
Ishwara	Ingaleshwar	12th Century	Siva
Veeranarayana	Ingaleshwar	12th Century	Visnu
Basavanna'a birthplace	Ingaleshwar	11th Century	Basavanna
Virupaksha	Lakkundi	11th Century	Siva
Someshwara	Lakkundi	11th Century	Siva
Siddharameshwara	Lakkundi	11th Century	Siva
Brahma Jinalaya	Lakkundi	11th Century	Jaina
Mallikarjuna	Lakkundi	11th Century	Siva
Kumbeshwara	Lakkundi	11th Century	Siva

Contd.

Name of the Temple	Location	Year of Construction	Principal Deity
Naganatha	Lakkundi	11th Century	Siva
Kasivishveshwara	Lakkundi	11th Century	Siva
Nanneshwara	Lakkundi	11th Century	Siva
Nilakantheshwara	Lakkundi	12th Century	Siva
Basaveshwara	Lakkundi	12th Century	Siva
Chandramouleshwara	Lakkundi	12th Century	Siva
Manikeshwara	Lakkundi	12th Century	Siva
Muskinabhavi	Lakkundi	12th Century	Temple Kalyani
Lakshminarayana	Lakkundi	12th Century	Visnu
Virabhadreshwara	Lakkundi	12th Century	Siva
Amraleshwara	Holalu	12th Century	Siva
Lokanatha	Ron	11th Century	Siva
Ishwara 2	Ron	11th Century	Siva
Kallugudi	Ron	11th Century	Siva
Somalingeshwara	Ron	11th Century	Siva
Ramalinga	Ron	11th Century	Siva
Anantasayana	Ron	11th Century	Visnu
Jaina Basadi	Ron	11th Century	Jaina
Trimurti	Savadi	12th Century	Trimurti
Satyanarayana	Savadi	12th Century	Visnu
Kalleshwara	Sogi	12th Century	Siva
Dabbagudi	Sogi	12th Century	Siva
Mallikarjuna	Sudi	11th Century	Siva
Jadkalasagudi	Sudi	11th Century	Siva
Naga-kunda Complex	Sudi	11th Century	Siva
Anantaswami matha	Mulgund	11th Century	Siva
Jaina Basadi	Mulgund	12th Century	Jaina
Siddeshwara	Mulgund	12th Century	Siva
Aravattu Khambodagudi	Nagai	12th Century	Siva
Vira Bhadreshwara	Nesargi	12th Century	Siva
Parameshwara	Konnur	11th Century	Siva
Sambhulinga	Kundgol	12th Century	Siva
Rameshwara	Gundugatti	12th Century	Siva
Dharmaraya	Hagaratagi	12th Century	Dharmaraja
Arjuna	Hagaratagi	12th Century	Arjuna
Bhima	Hagaratagi	12th Century	Bhima
Kalmeshwara	Kamadhenu	12th Century	Siva
Basaveshwara	Basavakalyan	11th Century	Siva
Chalukya Fort	Basavakalyan	11th Century	Fort
Basaveshwara	Anekonda	11th Century	Siva
Basaveshwara	Ablur	12th Century	Siva
Someshwara	Ablur	12th Century	Siva

Contd.

Name of the Temple	Location	Year of Construction	Principal Deity
Amarateshwara	Annigeri	11th Century	Siva
Kalleshwara	Ambali	11th Century	Siva
Someshwara	Bandalike	12th Century	Siva
Trimurti Narayana	Bandalike	12th Century	Visnu
Karpateshwara	Bandalike	12th Century	Siva
Basaveshwara	Basavana Bagewadi	11th Century	Siva
Ramalinga	Chandakarate	12th Century	Siva
Sambhulinga	Itgi	11th Century	Siva
Mallikarjuna	Kalgi	12th Century	Siva
Siddeshwara	Kalgi	12th Century	Siva
Revanna Suryanarayana	Kalgi	12th Century	Visnu
Rameshwara	Kalgi	12th Century	Siva
Ramalinga	Baihongal	12th Century	Siva
Kalmeshwara	Balambid	12th Century	Siva
Baladevarugudi	Balambid	12th Century	Siva
Kalmeshwara	Hosur	12th Century	Siva
Kalmeshwara	Jamkhandi	12th Century	Siva
Rameshwara	Kamadolli	12th Century	Siva
Kalmeshwara	Karmudi	11th century	Siva
Kusumeshwara	Karmudi	11th Century	Siva
Kalikadevi/Umamaheshwara	Hosagunda	12th Century	Shakti
Bhavanisankara	Hubli	12th Century	Siva
Someshwara	Kot Umachige	12th Century	Siva
Rameshwara	Kuppagadde	12th Century	Siva
Baleshwara	Lakshmeshwar	11th Century	Siva
Someshwara	Lakshmeshwar	12th Century	Siva
Lakshmilingeshwara	Lakshmeshwar	12th Century	Siva
Kalika	Lakshmeshwar	12th Century	Shakti
Ananthanatha Basadi	Lakshmeshwar	12th Century	Jaina
Sankha	Lakshmeshwar	12th Century	Jaina
Rameshwara	Nadksale	12th Century	Siva
Mallikarjuna	Nadksale	12th Century	Siva
Chandramoulishwara	Unkal	12th Century	Siva
Santeshwara	Tilvalli	12th Century	Siva
Prabhadeva	Vannur	12th Century	Siva
Jaina Basadi	Yevur	11th Century	Jaina
Basavanna	Yevur	11th Century	Siva
Somanatha-Ishwara	Yevur	11th Century	Siva
Siddheshwara	Sirur	11th Century	Siva
Virupaksha (Gaurigudi)	Aihole	12th Century	Siva-Shakti
Banmkanatha	Ratkal	12th Century	Siva
Kadameshwara	Ratihalli	12th Century	Siva

Contd.

Name of the Temple	Location	Year of Construction	Principal Deity
Jaina Temple (City)	Aihole	11th Century	Jaina
Kalleshwara	Mailar	11th Century	Siva
Sankarlinga	Nimbal	12th Century	Siva
Someshwara	Padaganur	12th Century	Siva
Siddharameshwara	Niralgi	11th Century	Siva
Dandeshwara	Nargund	11th Century	Siva
Virupaksha	Badami	11th Century	Siva
Ramalinga	Malghan	12th Century	Siva
Murulingeshwara	Manoli	12th Century	Siva
Vithala	Muttagi	12th Century	Dattatreya
Ramalinga	Muttagi	12th Century	Siva
Narayana	Belur	11th Century	Visnu
Ishwaragudi	Belur	11th Century	Siva
Sangameshwara	Bewoor	11th Century	Siva
Kalika	Bewoor	11th Century	Shakti
Ramanatheshwara	Chittur	12th Century	Siva
Siva	Degulahalli	12th Century	Siva
Mallikarjuna	Devarnavadgi	12th Century	Siva
Rameshwara	Devur	11th Century	Siva
Ramalingeshwara	Gudur	11th Century	Siva
Kalleshwara	Halavagalu	12th Century	Siva
Bhogeshwara	Yelisirur	11th Century	Siva
Mukteshwara	Chaudayyadanapura	12th Century	Siva
Galageshwara	Galaganatha	11th Century	Siva
Avathu Khambha	Bankapur	12th Century	Siva
Mallikarjuna	Kuruvatti	11th Century	Siva
Prabhulingeshwara	Balligavi	12th Century	Siva
Tripurantakeshwara	Balligavi	12th Century	Siva
Ganda Bherundeshwara	Balligavi	12th Century	Siva
Kalleshwara	Hirehadagali	11th Century	Siva
Trikuteshwara	Gadag	11th Century	Siva
Saraswati	Gadag	11th Century	Shakti
Ugra Narasimha	Narsapur	12th Century	Visnu
Someshwara	Haralhalli	12th Century	Siva
Mallikarjuna	Badami	12th Century	Siva
Rameshwara	Gadag	11th Century	Siva
Someshwara	Gadag	11th Century	Siva
Viranarayana	Gadag	12th Century	Visnu
Kashivishwanatha	Hooli	11th Century	Siva
Tarakeshwara	Hooli	11th Century	Siva
Madaneshwara	Hooli	11th Century	Siva
Panchalingeshwara	Hooli	11th Century	Siva

Contd.

Name of the Temple	Location	Year of Construction	Principal Deity
Suryanarayana	Hooli	11th Century	Surya
Kalleshwara	Kuknoor	11th Century	Siva
Kalabhaireshwara	Mahakuta	11th Century	Siva
Adakeshwara	Mahakuta	11th Century	Siva
Yellamagudi	Badami	12th Century	Shakti
Charantimatha Group	Badami	11th Century	Siva
Ankeshwara	Saundatti	11th Century	Siva
Kalleshwara	Bagali	11th Century	Siva-Surya

List of Temples and Monuments of the Hoysalas

Name of the Temple	Location	Year of Construction	Principal Deity
Lakshmi Narasimha	Adagur	11th Century	Visnu
Mahadeva	Aghalaya	12th Century	Siva
Kesaveshwara	Agraharabelagulli	13th Century	Visnu-Siva
Chennigaraya	Ambale	12th Century	Visnu
Amrateshwara	Amritpura	12th Century	Siva
Narayana	Annekannambadi	12th Century	Visnu
Kesava	Anekere	12th Century	Visnu
Chennakesava	Aralaguppe	13th Century	Visnu
Ishwara	Arsikere	13th Century	Siva
Gangeshwara-Brahmeshwara	Asandi	12th Century	Siva
Virabhadra	Asandi	12th Century	Siva
Mallikarjuna	Basaralu	13th Century	Siva
Madhavaraya	Belluru	12th Century	Visnu
Chennakesava	Belur	12th Century	Visnu
Kappechennigaraya	Belur	12th Century	Visnu
Viranarayana	Belur	12th Century	Visnu
Vasudeva pond	Belur	12th Century	Kalyani
Viranarayana	Belvadi	13th Century	Visnu
Lakshminarasimha	Bhadravati	13th Century	Visnu
Narayana	Brahmasamudra	13th Century	Visnu
Kasivisveshwara	Budanur	13th Century	Siva
Anantapadmanabha	Budanur	13th Century	Visnu
Chennakesava	Channarayapatna	12th Century	Visnu
Chatteshwara	Chatchatanahalli	12th Century	Siva
Chennakesava	Dharampur	12th Century	Visnu
Kesava	Dindagur	12th Century	Visnu
Malleshwara	Dindagur	12th Century	Siva
Lakshmidevi	Dodda Gadduvalli	12th Century	Visnu-Shakti
Trikuteshwara	Gorur	12th century	Siva
Panchalingeshwara	Govindanahalli	13th Century	Siva

Contd.

Name of the Temple	Location	Year of Construction	Principal Deity
Hoysaleshwara	Halebid	12th Century	Siva-Visnu
Kedareshwara	Halebid	13th Century	Siva
Virabhadra	Halebid	12th Century	Siva
Parshvanatha Basadi	Halebid	13th Century	Jaina
Lakshminarasimha	Haranhalli	13th Century	Visnu
Someshwara	Haranhalli	13th century	Siva
Kirtinarayana	Heragu	12th Century	Visnu
Kodandarama	Hiremagalur	6th-12th Century	Visnu
Mallikarjuna	Hirenalluru	12th Century	Siva
Chennakesava	Hirekadaluru	12th Century	Siva
Kesava	Honavara	12th Century	Visnu
Lakshminarayana	Hosaholalu	13th Century	Visnu
Malleshwara	Huliyar	12th Century	Siva
Kesava	Hullekere	12th Century	Visnu
Religious pond	Hulikere	12th Century	Temple Kalyani
Lakshminarasimha	Javagal	13th Century	Visnu
Shantinatha Basadi	Jinanathapur	13th Century	Jaina
Cheluvanarayana	Kalasapur	13th Century	Visnu
Mallikarjuna	Kalasapur	13th Century	Siva
Shambhulingeshwara	Kerasante	12th Century	Siva
Brahmeshwara	Kikkeri	12th Century	Siva
Janardana	Kikkeri	12th Century	Visnu
Bucheshwara	Koravangala	12th Century	Siva
Rameshwara	Kudali	12th Century	Siva
Narasimha	Kudali	12th Century	Visnu
Malleshwara	Machalaghatta	12th Century	Siva
Mahalingeshwara	Mavattanahalli	12th Century	Siva
Siddheshwara	Mirale	12th Century	Siva
Chennakesava	Mirale	12th Century	Visnu
Nageshwara	Mosale	13th Century	Siva
Chennakesava	Mosale	13th Century	Visnu
Yoganarasimha	Mudigere	12th Century	Visnu
Lakshmikanti	Mullur	13th Century	Visnu
Kedareshwara	Nagalpura	12th Century	Siva
Chennakesava	Nagalpura	12th Century	Visnu
Saumyakesava	Nagamangala	13th Century	Visnu
Yoganarasimha	Narasipura	12th Century	Visnu
Shantinatha Basadi	Nittur	12th Century	Jaina
Sadashiva	Nuggihalli	13th Century	Siva
Lakshminarasimha	Nuggihalli	13th Century	Visnu
Rameshwara	Ramanathapur	13th Century	Siva
Lakshmeshwara	Ramanathapur	12th Century	Siva

Contd.

Name of the Temple	Location	Year of Construction	Principal Deity
Agasteshwara	Ramanathapur	13th Century	Siva
Lakshminarasimha	Sagatavalli	12th Century	Visnu
Mahalingeshwara	Santebacchalli	13th Century	Siva
Gadde Rameshwara	Channarayapatna	12th Century	Siva
Eshwara	Malali	12th Century	Siva
Shantishwara	Basavapatna	12th Century	Siva
Yogamadhava	Settikere	12th Century	Visnu
Chennakesava	Shantigrama	12th Century	Visnu
Dharameshwara	Shantigrama	13th Century	Siva
Yoga Bhoganarasimha	Shantigrama	13th Century	Visnu
Akkana Basadi	Shravanabelagola	12th Century	Jaina
Sangameshwara	Sindhagatta	12th Century	Siva
Kesava	Somanathapur	13th Century	Visnu
Lakshminarasimha	Somanathapur	13th Century	Visnu
Panchalingeshwara	Somanathapur	13th Century	Siva
Kirtinarayana	Talkad	12th Century	Visnu
Chennakesava	Tandaga	12th Century	Visnu
Sankareshwara	Turuvukere	13th Century	Siva
Chennakesava	Turuvukere	13th Century	Visnu
Gangadhareshwara	Turuvukere	13th Century	Siva
Chennigaraya	Turuvukere	13th Century	Visnu
Laksminarasimha	Vignasante	13th Century	Visnu
Kedreshwara	Balligavi	12th Century	Siva
Chennakesava	Arakere	12th Century	Visnu
Rameshwara	Arakere	12th Century	Siva
Chennakesava	Salgame	11th Century	Visnu
Narasimha	Maddur	12th Century	Visnu
Himvada Gopalaswamy	Himvada Bette	12th Century	Visnu
Lakshmivaradaraja	Terakanambi	12th Century	Visnu
Veerabhadraswamy	Terakanambi	13th Century	Siva
Hande Gopalaswamy	Terakanambi	13th Century	Visnu
Mulsthaneshwara	Terakanambi	12th Century	Siva
Lakshminarasimha	Raghavpura	13th Century	Visnu
Rameshwara	Raghavpura	13th Century	Siva
Ramalingeshwara	Chunchunakatte	12th Century	Siva
Rama Temple	Chunchunakatte	12th Century	Visnu
Arkeshwara	Hale Yedathe	12th Century	Siva
Pada Teertha	Saligrama	12th Century	Visnu
Yoganarasimha	Saligrama	12th Century	Visnu
Anakartheshwara	Vajamangala	12th Century	Siva
Varadarajaswamy	Varakodu	12th Century	Visnu
Lakshminarasimha	Akkihebbalu	13th Century	Visnu

Contd.

Name of the Temple	Location	Year of Construction	Principal Deity
Konkaneshwara	Akkihebbalu	12th Century	Siva
Venugopalaswamy	Thondanur	12th Century	Visnu
Nambinarayana	Thondanur	12th Century	Visnu
Nrusimhaswamy	Kunigal	12th Century	Visnu
Kodandaramaswamy	Kunigal	12th Century	Visnu
Chennakesava	Kunigal	12th Century	Visnu
Anjaneyaswamy	Kunigal	12th Century	Hanuman
Krigal Rudreshwara	Halebid	12th Century	Siva
Gudaleshwara	Halebid	11th Century	Siva
Ranganatha	Halebid	12th Century	Visnu
Nagareshwara	Halebid	12th Century	Siva
Kumbleshwara	Halebid	11th Century	Siva
Cheluvanarayana	Melkote	12th Century	Visnu
Yoganarasimha	Melkote	12th Century	Visnu
Gommatagiri Jain	Gommatagiri	12th Century	Gommateshwara
Someshwara	Pura	12th Century	Siva
Suryanarayana	Magala	12th Century	Visnu-Surya
Virabhadra	Neralige	13th Century	Siva
Kedareshwara	Balligavi	12th Century	Siva
Harihareshwara	Harihar	13th Century	Siva
Harihareshwara	Hariharpura	13th Century	Siva
Chennakesava	Angadi	10th Century	Visnu
Neminatha Basadi	Angadi	11th Century	Jaina
Mallikarjuna	Sitalayanagiri	13th Century	Siva

GLOSSARY OF TERMS

Abbe	Mother
Abhaya-hasta	The hand gesture of protection
Abhayamudra	Gesture of fearlessness and assurance
Acharya, Achari	Preceptor
Adhara	Support, power of sustaining
Adhisthana	Moulded basement of temple
Adisesha	Mythological serpent on the coils of which Visnu reclines
Adityas	Divinities of the sun taken collectively
Advaita	Non-duality
Agama	Sacred text related to conduct of worship
Agrahara	A grant of land given by royal patrons to brahamanas for their habitat and sustenance
Agramandapa	Fore-hall
Alpa-vimana	Small single-storeyed shrine
Amalaka	Cogged ring-stone on the *vimanas* of Nagara style temples. *Amla* is the fruit of the myrobalan tree
Anahata Chakra	The wheel of the fourth psychic energy centre of awareness or the Heart Chakra
Ankana	Bay or intercolumnation between pillars and pilasters in a hall
Ananda	Bliss
Anandamaya	An abode of bliss
Anantasayana	Visnu sleeping on the endless coils of the snake Ananta.
Antarala	Interior, inner of the middle part
Apsaras	Celestial entertainers or beauties
Ardhamandapa	Half hall articulated with *vimana* in early temples
Ardhanariswara	The androgynous form of Siva representing the union of Siva and Shakti
Arghapitha	Offering platform
Arupa	Formless
Asana	A posture, a seat, a pedestal
Ashta-dikpalas	The guardians of the eight cardinal directions
Ashtakona	Octagonal
Atharvaveda	One of the four Vedas
Avastha	The state of being
Avatara purusha	Incarnation of a deity (generally Visnu)
Avyakta	Unmanifest
Ayaka	Platform or pillar attached to a *Stupa*
Ayudhas	Weapons
Balipitha	Raised platform meant for placing offerings positioned in a temple generally between the *Dhvaja-stambha* and the main entrance
Basadi	Jaina monastery or *vihara*
Bhadra	Auspicious

Bhairava	Name of an *Ugra* form of Siva
Bhitti	Walls
Bhudevi	Consort of Visnu
Bhutamala	Decorative frieze with goblins usually located at the end of the joists of the main beams or columns in the hall
Bhutas	The elements
Bhuvanesvari	The domical ceiling in the assembly hall of the temple
Bindu	Point
Brahamana	A member of the priestly caste of India
Brahmi	An ancient script from which all Indian scripts are derived
Chadya	Eave projection
Chaitya	A sanctuary mostly Buddhist but sometimes Jaina
Chakra	Wheel
Dakshinayana	Southward movement of the sun
Damaru	Small percussion instrument held in Siva's hand
Dandanayaka	Commander-in-chief
Darshana	Revelation
Dasangula	Ten fingers' width or height
Dasavatara	Ten incarnations of Visnu
Devalaya	House of god or temple
Devata	God or goddess
Devi	Goddess
Dhvaja-stambha	Post for a flag or banner
Dikpalas	Guardians of cardinal directions
Dvitala-vimana	Two storeyed temple tower
Ekakuta	A temple with single *garbhagriha*
Gada	Mace
Ganas	Group of gods second in rank in hierarchical terms
Gandharvas	Semi-divine gods of music
Ganita	Arithmetic, mathematics
Garbha	Womb
Garuda-dhvaja	Banner in the form of an eagle
Gavare	Wandering merchant
Gopura or Gopuram	Gateway with or without a tower above in front of the temple
Gorava	Priest, incharge of a temple
Griha	House
Garbhgriha	Sanctum of the shrine
Griva	Neck
Gudhamandapa	Closed hall
Gunas	Qualities, attributes
Hamsa-vallabhi	Decorative frieze of geese
Isana	Lord of north-east direction
Istadevata	Personal god
Jagati	Platfor

GLOSSARY OF TERMS

Jala vitayana or *Jalandharas*	Latticed window, *Jalandharas* have square openings evenly placed vertically and horizontally
Janardana	Epithet for Krishna
Jataka	Tales from Buddha's previous life
Jina	Conqueror
Jiva	Life
Jnana	Knowledge
Jyotisha	Astrology
Kailasa	Abode of Siva, mountain peak in the Himalayas
Kalachakra	Wheel of time
Kalamukha	One of the sects of Saivism
Kalasa	The golden jar
Kaliyuga	The epoch of Kali
Kapalika	One of the sects of Saivism
Kapota	Over hanging cornice
Kavirajmarga	It is the first literary work so far traced in Kannada
Kavya	Poetic composition
Kesava	An epithet for Krishna
Kinnara	Mythical beings with human heads and body of a bird
Kirtimukha	The face of lion projecting religious symbolism, the Face of Glory
Kumuda	An important torus moulding of the basement
Ksetra	Area
Lakulisa	Lord with the club, name of reformer of the *Pasupata* cult, was regarded as an *avatara* of Siva
Lalita	Beautiful
Lasuna	Ridged vase-shaped pillar
Lila	Blissful pastimes
Linga	The phallic symbol of Siva
Lokapalas	The guardians of the world
Mahadeva	One of the names of Siva
Mahajanas	A local body for administering a village
Mahamandaleswara	A feudatory
Mahasthanadhipati	Chief among the feudatories
Makara torana	Arch spewed from the festoon mouths of *makaras*, crocodile type face
Mana-stambha	Pillar of respect, detached pillar in front of Jaina shrines with a deity crowning it
Mandala	Circular design
Manduka mandala	Sacred *mandala* composed of 64 square *padas*
Mantras	Hymns
Matrika	Mother goddess
Maya	Illusion
Meru	Mount Kailasa
Mithuna	A couple
Moksha	Liberation of soul from the worldly affairs
Mudra	Finger and bodily poses or movements

Mukhamandapa	Entrance hall
Mukti	Emancipation
Mulsthana	Main shrine
Mundi	Blunt end
Mulayagana	Dwarf demon symbolic of illusion
Naga	A snake considered to be deity
Nagaras	Merchant guilds
Nagasutra	A string or line in snake motif
Nagapratima	Image of cobra carved in stone
Nakshatra	Star
Namskara mandapa	Prayer hall or place right in front of the shrine where worshippers lie prostrate in front of the deity
Nandi	Siva's vehicle, bull
Nasi	Gable end of a vault, horse-shoe or *chaitya* arch motif
Natha pantha	A religious sect
Natya sala	Hall for musical and dance performances
Navagraha	The nine planets
Navaranga	Square hall with nine bays
Nirandhara	Without ambulatory
Nirupa	Formless
Nirtti	South-west direction
Nritta	Dance movements
Nrittamandapa	Dancing arena in a hall
Ojas	Reciter of *Puranas* at the temple
Padas	Square grids as in *Vastpurushamandala,* also walls or pillars in temple
Padmanabha	Lotus naveled, an epithet for Visnu
Pali	One of the earliest Prakrit dialects adopted by Mauryas and other Buddhists for communication with common people
Prakriti and Purusha	The female and male forces of nature
Pancha	Five
Panchatattva	Five elements
Paramasayika mandala	Sacred *mandala* with 81 square *padas*
Paramatma	The supreme soul
Parameswara	Supreme god-Siva
Pasupati	Epithet of Siva
Pasupata	A sect in Saivism
Pergadde	Headman of village
Phalaka	Abacus, square plank like capital member of a wide pillar
Phamsana	Tiered pyramidal roof type
Pidariyar, Pidari	Local deity
Pitha	9 squares corresponding to the three divisions of a big square, pedestal
Pradakshinapatha	Circumambulatory path around the shrine
Prakara	The boundary wall
Prakrit	A group of languages of ancient India

Pranala	Water chute for letting out lustral water
Prasada	Palacial building
Prastara	Entablature consisting of mouldings above the wall and below the neck
Pratoli	Gatehouse
Puranas	Ancient scriptures, mythology
Puranic	Of the *Puranas*
Rigveda	The first of the four Vedas
Rupa	Form
Sabha	Village assembly
Sabhamandapa	Pillared hall
Saiva	Followers of Siva or *Saivism*
Sakhas	Jambs of a door
Salabhanjika	A word for woman and tree motif
Salas	Schools
Sala sikhara	Barrel vault type roof
Sallekhana	Voluntary starvation till death practiced among Jaina followers
Samantas	Feudatories
Samhita	Treatise
Sankha	Conch shell
Sankara	Epithet for Siva
Sarupa	Body with form
Sastra	A sacred precept or rule or scripture laying down the rules
Satra	Feeding home
Saumya	Calm
Setti	Merchant or tradesman
Shakti	Power, strength, energy and also Siva's consort
Sikhara	Peak of the mountain, structure on top of the shrine, spire of a temple
Silpa-sastra	Ancient treatises on art and architecture like Manasara, Mayamata
Siddhanta	Formula
Soma	Moon
Sthana	Position or place
Sthapati	An architect-builder
Sthapatya veda	Traditional architectural knowledge
Stupika	Finial on the *vimana* of a temple
Sukanasi	Parrot's beak or nose, a projection from the *sikhara-tala*, the entry vestibule
Sutra	Manual of religious rituals
Surya	Sun
Swastika	An ancient symbol, emblematic of the sun. The traditional auspicious cross symbol of Hinduism
Tala	Floor or storey
Talamana	System of measurement used in Hindu architecture and *Silpa*
Tantra	The framework of rituals and order of ceremonies
Tattvas	Elements
Telliga	Oil monger

GLOSSARY OF TERMS

Tirtha	Holy water
Trikuta	Triple-celled shrine or structure
Trikutachala	A temple with three sanctums
Trimurti and Traipurusha	The unified form of Hindu trinity – Brahma, Visnu and Siva
Ugra	Terrific
Upanishad	Ancient writings associated with the secret of the knowledge of the Vedas
Uttarayana	The northward movement of the sun
Vachana literature	It is a unique form of literature in Kannada. It is in poetic prose form meant for common man
Vahana	Vehicle
Vaishnavism	Relating to Visnu
Vaishnavites	Followers of Visnu
Valabhi	Rafter below the cornice beam and joining with *prastatra*
Varaha	One of the incarnations of Visnu
Vastupurushamandala	The *mandala* of Vastu – the site of temple building
Vedangas	Certain class of work regarded as auxiliary to the Vedas
Veda	Sacred knowledge
Vedanta	The end of the Vedas
Vidyadana	Grant for education
Vihara	Monastery
Vimana	Tall tapering roof of the temple shrine
Visnu	The second deity of the trinity entrusted with the preservation of the world
Vitana	Ceiling, the *navagraha* grid with *dikpalas* around a central panel of God-head
Yalli	A hybrid representation of *Kirtimukha* with parrot's body with elephant's head and teeth of crocodile
Yantra	A power diagram
Yoga	Meditation
Yogini gana	A troop of specific demi-goddesses possessed of magical powers
Yuga	Age of the world

REFERENCES

A

Archaeo Astronomy in Indian context: A Programme of the Tata Institute of Fundamental Research – funded by Jamsetji Tata Trust

Asha DM and Chincholi Manjula: Position of Women in Education during Medieval Karanataka, Golden Research Thoughts, Volume 4, Issue 1 July 2014

Archaeological Survey of India: Material for Indian Archaeology-A review 2003–04, Dharwad Circle

A Handbook of Karnataka, Gazetteer Department, Government of Karnataka, 2010

Acharya Prasanna Kumar: Indian Architecture According to Manasara-Silpasastra, Originally published in 1934, Oxford University Press, London

Arjun R: Architecture of Karnataka; The Antiquity and Transformation (From Tekkalakota to Pattadakal), mySOCIETY VIII (1–2) 2013-14, pp 26-44, University of Mysore

Achari Pandit Sri Rama Ramanuja: Hindu Iconology-The Study of the Symbolism and Meaning of Icons, Simha Publications, 2012

Annual Report of the Mysore Archaeological Department for the Year 1930

Annual Report of the Mysore Archaeological Department for the Year 1932

Annual Report of the Mysore Archaeological Department for the Year 1944

Annual Report of the Mysore Archaeological Department for the Year 1935

Annual Report of the Mysore Archaeological Department for the Year 1936

Annual Report of the Mysore Archaeological Department for the Year 1937

Annual Report of the Mysore Archaeological Department for the Year 1941

Annual Report of the Mysore Archaeological Department for the Year 1942

Annual Report of the Mysore Archaeological Department for the Year 1946

Annual Report of the Mysore Archaeological Department for the Years 1947–1956

Acharya PK: Architecture of Manasara-Illustrations of Architectural and Sculptural Objects, 1934

Acharya PK: An Encyclopedia of Hindu Architecture, Oxford University Press, 1946

Aiyangar Krishnaswami S and Sewell Robert: The Historical Inscriptions of Southern India, Didocesan Press, Madras, 1932

Altekar Anand Sadashiv: The Rashtrakutas and Their Times, Oriental Book Agency, 1934

Anantharaman Ambujam: Temples of South India, East West, 2006

Anantharaman TR: The Iron Pillar at Kodachadri in Karnataka

B

Buckee Fiona: Reconstructing a Latina Temple Spire, Temple 45 Sanchi, welsh School of Architecture, Cardiff University, 2010 (Thesis)

Bangalore District Gazetteer, 1990

Bannerjee Shubhendu: Appropriate Vocabulary for a Hindu Temple Design in Auckland, Research Project

Boivin Nicole, Fuller Dorian, Korisettar Ravi and Petraglia Michael: First Farmers in South India-The Role of Internal Processes and External Influences in the Emergence and Transformation of South India Earliest Settled Societies, International Seminar, Lucknow, 18–20 January 2006

Brumm Adam, Boivin Nicole, Korisettar Ravi, Koshy Jinu and Whittaker Paula: Stone Axe Technology in Neolithic South India, New Wvidence from Sanganakallu-Kupgal Region, Asian Perspectives, Vol 46, No. 1, 2007

Bolar Varija R: Temples of Karnataka-An Epigraphical Study, Readworthy, New Delhi, 2010

Bunce Fredrick W: Temples With Multiple Garbhagrihas-An Iconographic Consideration od Selected Indian Monuments, DK Printworld, New Delhi, 2014

Brown Percy: Indian Architecture Buddhist and Hindu, CBS Publishers & Distributors P Ltd, New Delhi, 2014

Balasubrahmanyam SR: Middle Chola Temples, Oriental Press BV, Amsterdam, 1975

C

Cohen Andrew L: The King and the Goddess-The Nolamba Period Lakashamneshwara Temple at Avani, Artibus Asiae Vol 52, No.1/2 (1992) pp 7–24

Correa Charles: The Blessings of the Sky, 1996

Coomaraswamy AK: Indian Architectural Terms

Coomaraswamy Ananda: Introduction to Indian Art, The Theosophical Publishing House, Adyar, 1956

Coomaraswamy AK: A New Approach to the Vedas, Luzac & Co. London, 1933

Coomaraswamy Ananda K: Elements of Buddhist Iconography, Munshiram Manoharlal Publishers Pvt Ltd, New Delhi, 1998

Chandrappa C: Architecture Under the Gangas of Talakadu, Indian Streams Research Journal, Volume 2 Issue 8 September 2012

Chandrappa C: Art and Architecture Under the Hoysalas of Dwarasamudra, Indian Streams Journal, Volume 2 Issue 7 August 2012

Croker Alan: The Temple as a Metaphor for Journey Within, Australia 2008

Chen Andrew L: Indian Subcontinent Sculptures of Karnataka, 7th–18th Centuries, The Dictionary of Art (Groves Dictionary 1996, New York), V 15, pp 525–533

Cohen Andrew L: Why A History of Monuments from Nolambavadi (Nolamba), Artibus Asiae Vol 57 No.1/2 (1997) pp 17–29

Cohen Andrew L: Temple Architecture and Sculptures of the Nolambas, Manohar Publishers, New Delhi 1998

Cohen Andrew L: The Nolamba Style and Vijayanagar Archaizing-The Bhoganandiswara Compound at Nandi (www.academia.edu)

Cousens Henry: Medieval Temples of the Dakhan, Cosmo Publications, New Delhi, 1985

D

Dharwad District Gazetteer, 2002

Datta Sambit: On Recovering the Surface Geometry of Temple Superstructures, School of Architecture and Building, Deakin University, Australia

Datta Tanisha and Adane Vinayak S: Symbolism in Hindu Temple Architecture and Fractal Geometry-"Thought Behind Form," International Journal of Science and Research, Vol 3 Issue 12, December 2014

Dhar Parul Pandya: Indian Art History-Changing Perspectives, DK Printworld (P) Ltd, New Delhi, 2011

Dayalan Dr. D: Digital Documentation of Excavations-Buddhist Site at Kanganahalli, Archaeological Survey of India

Derrett J Duncan: The Hoysalas, A Medieval Indian Royal Family, Oxford University Press, 1957

Dakshina Kanara District Gazetteer, 1973

Davinder Ratnakar and Sarvodaya SS: Art and Architecture Under the Chalukyas of Kalyana, Indian Stream Research Journal, Vol 2 Issue 8, September 2012

Datta Sambit: Infinite Sequences in the Constructive Geometry of Tenth-Century Hindu Temple Superstructures, Nexus Network Journal, Vol 12 No. 3, 2010 pp 471

Draft Karnataka Tourism Policy 2014–19, Department of Tourism, Government of Karnataka

Dhavalkar MK: Masterpieces of Rashtrakuta Art-The Kailas, Taraporevala, Bombay, 1983

E

Elgood Heather: Hinduism and the Religious Art, Cassell London and New York, 1999

Epigraphia Indica Vol X, 1909–10, Parts I, II, VI and VII, Superintendent Government Printing India, Calcutta

Epigraphia Carnatica Vol XIV (Dr. MH Krishna), 1948

Epigraphia Carnatica Vol IX (BL Rice), 1905

Epigraphia Carnatica Vol X (BL Rice) 1905, Basel Mission Press, Mangalore

F

Frett Birch: An Indepth Investigation of Divine Ratios, TMME Vol 3 No. 2 pp 157

Fibier Marianne C Quortrup: When the Hindu Goddess Moves to Denmark-The Establishment of the Saka-tradition, Arahus University

Fergusson James: History of Indian and Eastern Architecture (Vol I & II) John Murray London 1910

Foekema Gerard: Fifteen Golden Examples-Indian Temple Architecture in Karnataka, Simova, 2005

Foekema Gerard: A Complete Guide to Hoysala Temples, Abhinav Publications, New Delhi, 1996

Foekema Gerard: Chalukya Architecture, Volume I,II and III, Munshiram Manoharlal Publishers, New Delhi, 2003

Foekema Gerard: Hoysala Architecture, Volume I & II, Books & Books, New Delhi, 1994

Fritz John M and Michell George: Hampi Vijayanagara, JAICO, 2015

G

Gulbarba District Gazetteer, 1966

Goswami Meghali, Dr. Ila Gupta and Jha Dr.P: Spatamatrikas in Indian Art and Ethos-A Critical Study, Anistoriton Vol 9 Section A051, March 2005

Gokhale Vasudha A: Architectural Heritage and Seismic Design with Reference to Indian Temple Architecture, 13th World Conference on Earthquake Engineering, Vancouver, Canada August 1–6, 2004

Garg Dr. Yogesh and Gupta Amogh Kumar: Content Analysis of Samarangana Sutradhara, ABACUS, A Biannual International Referred Journal on Architecture, Conservation and Urban Studies, Vol 7 No. 2, 2012

Gangamma NT: Art and Architecture Under Rashtrakutas of Malkhed, Review of Research Vol 1 Issue IX, June 2012 pp 1–4

Goswami A: Indian Temple Sculpture, March 1956, Calcutta

Gupta SP and Asthana Shashi Prabha: Elements of Indian Art, DK Printworld, New Delhi, 2009

H

Hardy Adam: Bhoja, Bhojpur and Bhumija

Hegewald Julia AB: Visual and Conceptual Links Between Jaina Cosmological, Mythological and Ritual Instruments, International Journal of Jaina Studies (online) Vol 6 No. 1 (2010) pp 1–20

Harding Phillip Edward: The Propositions of Sacred Space-South Asian Temple Geometry and the Durga Temple of Aihole, Ohio State University, 2004 (Thesis)

Hardy Adam: Dravida Temples in Samarangana Sutradhara

Havell EB: The Ancient and Medieval Architecture of India-A Study of Indo-Aryan Civilisation, John Murray London, 1915

Hardy Adam: Parts and Wholes-The Story of the Gavaksa from the Temples of South Asia

Haedy Adam: A New Hoysala Temple in Karnataka, PRASADA, The Welsh School of Architecture, Cardiff University, 2009

Hegewald Julia AB: The Jaina Heritage-Distinction, Decline and Resilience, Samskriti, New Delhi, 2011

Hiremath RC: Buddhism in Karnataka, DK Printworld (P) Ltd, New Delhi, 1993

I

Indian Archaeology 1963–64 A Review, Archaeological Survey of India, New Delhi

Indian Archaeology 1954–55 A Review, Archaeological Survey of India, New Delhi

Indian Archaeology 1977–78 A Review, Archaeological Survey of India, New Delhi

Indian Archaeology 1979–80 A Review, Archaeological Survey of India, New Delhi

Indian Archaeology 1980–81 A Review, Archaeological Survey of India, New Delhi

Indian Archaeology 1993–94 A Review, Archaeological Survey of India, New Delhi

Indian Archaeology 1994–95 A Review, Archaeological Survey of India, New Delhi

Indian Archaeology 1997–98 A Review, Archaeological Survey of India, New Delhi

J

Jayakrishna Kavita: Dancing Architecture-The Parallel Evolution of Bharatanatyam and South Indian Architecture, Presented at University of Waterloo, Canada, 2011 (Thesis)

Jones Constance A and Ryan James D: Encyclopedia of Hinduism-Facts on Life, New York, 2007

Jones Lang LaSalle Meghraj: Development of Shimoga District as Tourist Destination and Preparation of Tourist Master Plan for Shimoga, KSIIDC Ltd, 2010

Jacob Jose: The Architecture Theory of the Manasara, School of Architecture, McGill University, Montreal, September 2003 (Thesis)

K

Kolar District Gazetteer, 1968

Kern H: The Brhat Sanhita of Varaha Mihira, Calcutta, 1865

Kak Subhash: Art and Cosmology in India, Patanjali Lecture at Center for Indic Studies, University of Massachusetts, Dartmouth, May 5, 2006

Kasdorf Katherine E: Forming Dorasamudra-Temples of the Hoysala Capital in Context, Columbia University, 2013 (Thesis)

Kosuri Lakshmi Shoba: Dravidian Style Hindu Temples-A Graphical Analysis, August 2000, Texas Tech University (Thesis)

Kadambi Hemnath: Sacred Landscapes in Early Medieval South India-The Chalukya State and Society (AD 550–750), The University of Michigan, 2011 (Thesis)

Kramrisch Stella: The Art of India-Traditions of Indian Sculpture, Painting and Architecture, The Phaidon Press, London, 1954

Karnataka Gazetteer, 1982 Vol I

The Karnataka Ancient and Historical Monuments and Archaeological Sites and Remains Act, 1961

Khatri AP: A Century of Prehistoric Research in India, Asian Perspectives, 6, 1962

Karnataka Tourism Vision Group Recommendations, January 2014

Khan Sharmin: History of Indian Architecture-Buddhist, Jain and Hindu Period, CBS Publishers & Distributors P Ltd, New Delhi, 2014

Kamath Dr. Suryanath U: A Concise History of Karnataka, MCC Publications, Bangalore, 2001

Kulkarni Dr. RH: Pre and Early Chalukya Sculpture-Origin and Development, Harman Publishing House, New Delhi, 2009

Krishna Nanditha: The Art and Iconography of Vishnu Narayana, Taraporevala, Bombay, 1980

Kramrisch Stell: The Hindu Temple (Vol I & II), Motilal Banarsidas Publishers, New Delhi, 2015

L

Losty Jeremiah P: Some Illustrated Jain Manuscripts, British Library Journal

Lefevre Vincent: Portraiture in Early India Between Transcience and Eternity, Handbook of Oriental Studies, Volume 25, BRILL Leiden Boston 2011

Lakshminarayanan Arul: Borromean Triangles and Prime Knots in an Ancient Temple, Resonance, May 2007

Lele Vibhakti: Chitpavan Konkanastha Brahmins' History

Lee Risha: Constructing Community-Tamil Merchant Temples in India and China, 850–1281, Columbia University, 2012 (Thesis)

Lochtefeld James G: The Illustrated Encyclopedia of Hinduism, The Rosen Publishing House, New York, 2002

Lorenzetti Tiziana and Scialpi Fabio: Glimpses of Indian History and Art, Reflected on the Past, Perspectives for the Future, Proceedings of the International Conference, Rome April 18–19, 2011

M

Menon Srikumar M: The Curious Case of the Galaganatha Dolmen-Possible Links Between Megalithic Monuments and Early Temples at Aihole, Journal of Multidisciplinary Studies in Archaeology, 2 (2014)

Mercay Jessie J: Fabric of Universe-The Origins, Implications and Applications of Vastu Science, Dakshina Publishing House, Chennai, 2006

Meister Michael W: Phamsana in Western India, Artibus Asiae Publishers Vol 38, No.2/3 (1976) pp 167–188

Moody Robert V: Alice Boner and the Geometry of Temple Cave Art of India, University of Alberta, Edmonton

McCartin Brian J: Mysteries of the Equilateral Triangle, Published Hikari Ltd, 2010

Michell George: The Hindu Temple-An Introduction to its Meaning and forms, The University of Chicago Press, Chicago and London

Muller Max: On Ancient Hindu Astronomy and Chronology, Oxford, 1862

Menon Srikumar M and Vahia Mayank N: Investigating Megalithic Astronomy-The Role of Remote Sensing, Third International Conference on Remote Sensing in Archaeology 17–21 August 2009, Tiruchirrapalli

Meister Michael W: Measurement and Proportion in Hindu Temple Architecture, Interdisciplinary Science Review, Vol 10 No. 3, 1985

Mysore Gazetteer (C Hayavadana Rao) 1930

Mandya District Gazetteer, 2009

Muller Fredrich Max: The Vedas, Susil Gupta (India) Limited, Calcutta, 1956

Mysore Government Museum Annual Report, 1954–55

Muddi Smt. Veena: Vamana-Trivikrama in Badami Chalukya Sculpture, GRA (Global Research Analysis) Vol 2 Issue 9, September 2013

Moraes George M: Kadamba Kula-A History of Ancient and Medieval Karnataka, BX Furtado & Sons, Bombay, 1931

Menon Srikumar M, Vahia Mayank N and Rao Kailash M: Recent Survey of a Megalithic Stone Alignment at Byse

Ministry of Tourism and Culture, Department of Tourism, Market Research Division: Final Report on 20 Year Perspective Plan for Development of Sustainable Tourism in Karnataka, March 2003

Masataka Suzuki: Bhuta and Daiva-Changing Cosmology of Rituals and Narratives in Karnataka, Senri Ethnological Studies, 71, p 51–85 (2008)

Michell George: Southern India-A Guide to Monuments, Sites and Museums, Roli Books, 2013

Michell George: Bdami, Aihole, Pattadakal, JAICO, 2011

Murthy Dr. MS Krishna: Jaina Monuments in Southern Karnataka, Ahimsa Foundation www.jainsamaj.org

Murthy Dr. AV Narasimha: Jaina Monuments in North Karnataka, Ahimsa Foundation www.jainsamaj.org

Menon Shrikumar: A Peek into Sculptors' Legacy, Deccan Herald (Supplement, Spectrum) 24 November, 2015

N

Newsletter Archives, Exotic India art Pvt Ltd: Tantra-The Art of Philosophy, 2000

Narasimha AN: A Grammar of the Oldest Kanarese Inscriptions, University of Mysore, 1941

Nagabhushanam P, Snagurmath P, Patil ML and Sukhija BS: Ancient Gold Mining Activity in Hutti-Maski Greenstone Belt, Karnataka, Radiocarbon Perspective, Current Science, Vol 95 No. 3, august 2008

O

Oijevaar KJ: The South Indian Hindu Temple Building Design System, September 2007, Delft University of Technology, the Netherlands

P

Palmer Martin J: Expressions of Sacred Space-The Temple Architecture in the Ancient Near East, February 2012, University of South Africa (Thesis)

Paddayya K: Archaeology in Karnataka-Achievements and Issues Ahead, ICHR Sponsored Seminar August 26–27, 2010

Panchmukhi RS: Karnatak Inscriptions, 1941

Pattar Dr. Shreekant: The Architects and Sculptors of Early Chalukya Art, Kannada Shasanagala Sasnkrutika Adhyana, 2002 pp 485

Premsing Dr. Chawan: Jewellery and Ornament During Chalukyan Era, Indian Streams Research Journal, Vol I Issue IX October 2011

Pappu Shanti: Introducing Indian Prehistory Teaching South Asia, An internet Journal of Pedagogy, Vol 1, No. 1, Winter 2001

Pattnaik Devdutt: 7 Secrets of the Goddess, Westland Ltd, 2014

R

Ragavan Deena: Heaven on Earth-Temples, Rituals and Cosmic Symbolism in the Ancient World, Oriental Institute Seminar, University of Chicago, 2–3rd March 2012

Raghu MN: Opportunities of Tourism in Kolar District of Karnataka-A Study, IJSR August 2014

Ramaswamy Vijaya: Metallurgy and Traditional Metal Crafts in Tamil Nadu, Indian Journal of History of Science, 29(3), 1994

Rian Iasef Md, Park Jin-Ho, Ahn Hyung UK and Chang Dongkuk: Fractal Geometry as the Synthesis of Hundu Cosmology in Kandariya Mahadev Temple Khajuraho, Building and Environment, 42(2007) pp 4091–4107

Risch Roberto, Boivin Nicole, Petraglia Michael, Gomez-Gras David and Korisettar Ravi: The Prehistoric Axe Factory at Sanganakallu-Kupgal (Bellary District), Southern India, http://intarch.ac.uk/journal/issue26/26/toc.html

Rao N Kameshwara and Thakur Priya: Aspects of Observational Astronomy in India-The Vidyasankara Temple at Sringeri, Journal of Astronomical History and Heritage, 14(2) pp 136–144, 2011

Rajarajan RKK: Aihole Revisted, AION 72/1–4, 2012, pp 211–222

Roy AB and Sethumadhav MS: The 'Mystic' Sand Dune Covered Temples of Talakad, Mysore District, Karnataka-Evidence of Earthquake Related Destruction, Current Science Vol 107, No. 2, July 2014

Rambach Pierre and Vitold De Golish: The Golden Age of Indian Art, Vth-XIIth Century, DB Taraporevala Sons & Co Ltd, Mumbai, 1995

Rao TA Gopinatha: Elements of Hindu Iconography, Vol II-Part I, The Law Printing House, Madras, 1916

Rao TA Gopinatha: Elements of Hindu Iconography, Vol I-Part I, The Law Printing House, Madras, 1914

Roy Mira: The Concept of Yantra in Samarangana Sutradhara of Bhoja, Indian Journal of History of Science, 19(2) pp 118–124, 1984

Rao MVK: Gangas of Talakad, Madras, 1936

Rice B Lewis: Mysore-A Gazetteer Complete for Government of West Minster, Archibald Constable & Company, 1897

Reu Pandit Bisheshwar Nath: History of the Rashtrakutas (Rathodas), The Archaeological Department, Jodhpur, 1933

Rao N Kameswara: Aspects of Prehistoric Astronomy in India, Bull. Astr. Soc. India, 2005, 33 pp 499–511

Rao Shankaranarayana AV: Temples of Karnataka, Vasan Publications, Bangalore, 2012

Ramesh KV: Inscriptions of the Western Gangas, ICHR, 1984

Rao Rekha: Science and Golden Ratios in Mandala Architecture, DK Printworld, New Delhi, 2011

S

Sweetman Will: The Prehistory of Orientalism, Colonialism and the Textual Basis for Batholomans Ziegenbal's Account of Hinduism, The New Zealand Journal of Asian Studies, 6, 2 (December 2004) pp 12–38

Shylaja BS and Kydala Geetha: Inscriptions as Records of Celestial Events, Indian Journal of History of Science, 46–2(2011) pp 335–343

Smythies Adrian Greville: The Architecture and Iconography of the Hindu Temple in Eads, Tennessee, University of Alabama at Buckingham, 2006 (Thesis)

Saini Shilpi: The Representation of Women in Early Sculptures of Khahuraho, 2012, JNU

Sharma Anuradha: Hinduism and the Arts, http://faithandhearts.com, April 2007

Suri Anil: The Evolution of Hindu Gods

Stencil Robert, Gifford Fred and Moron Eleanor: Astronomy and Cosmology at Angkor Wat, Science 1976, 193, pp 281–287

Suvarthan Uthara: A Fragmentary Brahmi Inscription from Banavasi, Museum of Anthropology, Ann Arbor, Michigan

Sastri Dr. S Srikantha: The Gangas of Talkad

Sastri Dr. S Srikantha: The Cholas in Karnataka

Sastri Dr. S Srikantha: Political History of the Kadambas

Sala Nicoletta: Fractal Geometry and Self-similarity in Architecture-An Overview Across the Centuries, The International Society of the Arts, Mathematics and Architecture

Shukla AK, Mishra J and Ajatshatru: Implementation of Fractals art in Ceiling Decoration, International Journal of Emerging Trends and Technology in Computer Science, Vol 2 Issue 3 May-June 2013

Sharma Shaan: Taming of Monsters-Expansion of the Application of Fractal Geometry, College of William & Mary, April 17, 2015 (Thesis)

Sardar Dhrubajyoti and Kulkarni SY: Role of Fractal Geometry in Indian Hindu Temple Architecture, International Journal of Engineering Research & Technology, Vol 4 No. 05, May 2015

Shylaja BS: The Zodiacal Pillars of Sringeri, Current Science, Vol 92 No. 6, March 2007

Shimoga District Gazetteer, 1975

Srinivasan KR: Jaina Art and Architecture Under the Gangas of Talakad

Sircar Dinesh Chandra: The Successors of the Satavahanas in Lower Deccan, University of Calcutta, 1939

Sastri H Krishna: South Indian Images of Gods and Goddesses, Madras Government Press, 1916

Sharma SR: Jainism and Karnataka Culture, Secretary Karnatak Historical Research, Dharwar, Dharwar, 1940

Sundara A: The Traditional Date of Asoka Maurya-Archaeological Evidences in Karnataka, A Consideration Paper Originally Published in Puratattva

Suvarthan Uthara: Complexity of the Periphery-A Study of the Regional Organisation at Banavasi, 1st to 18th Century AD, University of Michigan, 2013 (Thesis)

Shrigoundekar Gajanan K: Manasollasa Vol I, Central Library, Baroda, 1925

Salvini Mattia: The Samaranganasutradhara, Mahidol University

Sadhale Abhijit: Kadamba Temples Architecture and Iconography-Continuity, Assimilation and Development of Varied Influences, Goa abhijitsadhale@gmail.com

Settar S and Korisettar Ravi: Prehistory-Archaeology of South Asia, ICHR, 2001

Sarma IK: Temples of the Gangas of Karnataka, Archaeological Survey of India, New Delhi, 1992

Sastri Nilakanta KA: A History of South India-Prehistoric Teimes to the Fall of Vijayanagar, Oxford University Press, 1975

Saha Anju: Our Heritage Revisited-A Glimpse into Ancient Indian Texts, March 2015

Saraswati SK: A Survey of Indian Sculpture, Munshiram Manoharlal Publishers, New Delhi, 1975

Soundararajan J: Early Chalukyan Temples-Art, Architecture & Iconography, with Special Reference to Aihole, Sharada Publishing House, Delhi, 2009

Suresh Dr. KM: Temples of Karnataka-Ground Plans and Elevations, Bharatiya Kala Prakashan, Delhi, 2003

Swarup Shanti: The Arts and Crafts of India and Pakistan, DB Taraporevala, Bombay, 1957

Sundara A: Roots of Culture of Karnataka Archaeological Approach-Problems and Prospects, Journal of Karnataka Studies, May 2007-April 2008

T

Tumkur District Gazetteer, 1969

Trivedi Prof Kirti: Hindu Temple-Models of Fractal Universe, Paper Presented at the International Seminar on Mayonic Science and Technology, 28–31 January 1993

Timalsina Sthaneshwar: Imagining Reality-Images and Visualization in Classical Hinduism, Southeast Review of Asian Studies, Vol 35 (2013) pp 50–69

Thakur Priya: New Archaeological Readings in Southern India with Special Reference to Buddhist Art, International Journal of Social Sciences and Humanities, Vol I December 2012 pp 47–51

U

UNESCO: India-Group of Monuments at Pattadakal

UNESCO Courier: Twenty Five Centuries of Buddhist Art and Culture, No. 6, June 1995, 9th Year

V

Vahia NM and Halkare Ganesh: Aspects of Gond Astronomy, Journal of Astronomical History and Heritage, 16(1), 2013 pp 29–44

Vardia Shweta: Building Science of Indian Temple Architecture, Universidade do Minho, Portugal, 2008 (Thesis)

Vardia Shweta and Lourenco Paulo B: Building Science of Indian Temple Architecture, International Conference, Chennai 13–16 February 2013

Vahia MN: Origin and Growth of Astronomy-Indian Context, TIFR, Mumbai

Venugopal Jayadevi: Vastu Purusha Mandala-A Human Ecological Framework for Designing Living Environments, Paper Submitted at the International Conference on Advancement in Architecture and Civil Engineering, June 2012

Venkataraman Subasini: The Iconometrical Perspective of the Early Chola Images, International Journal of Computer Applications, Vol 22 no. 7, May 2011

Veliath Cyril: The Mother Goddess in Indian Sculpture, Bulletin of the Faculty of Foreign Studies, Sophia University, No. 37, 2002

Venkateswara SV: Critique of South Indian Art, The Half-yearly Mysore University Journal, Vol I No. 2, July 1927

Vincent Fr M: Varuna-A Cultural Study with Special Reference to the Inscriptions and Sculpture, mySociety VI(12), 2011 pp 110–118

Vimala Sangoli: Jaina Monuments at Halasi and Belgaum Fort in Belgaum Region, International Indexed and Referred Journal, April 2013, Vol IV Issue 51–52

Vaastuyogam, Heritage of India, Pattadakal, January 2013

Vyasanakere P Jayanth, Sudeesh K and Shylaja BS: Astronomical Significance of the Gavi Gangadhaeshwara Temple in Bangalore, Current Science, Vol 95 No. 11, December 2008

Vahia Mayank N, Menon Srikumar M and Abbas Riza: Megaliths in Ancient India and Their Possible association with Astronomy, International Conference on Oriental Astronomy, Japan, September 2010

X,Y,Z

Yaguchi Naomichi: On the Spatial Units of the Hoysala Temples-A Study of Spatial Composition of the Hoysala Temples

Websites:

Websites where several subjects/articles of interest can be seen:

http://karntakaitihasaacademy.org/

http://puratattva.in/

https://www.wikipedia.org/

http://www.kamat.com/

https://www.scribd.com/

http://www.whatisindia.com/inscriptions/

https://www.academia.edu/

http://www.templenet.net/

http://templesofkarnataka.com/

http://www.historydiscussion.net/

http://hoysalatemple.blogspot.in/

http://www.indian-heritage.org/index.html

Websites from where specific information can be obtained:

http://www.megalithindia.in/2014/04/the-enigma-of-nilaskal-and-byse.html

http://www.vagata.org/culture_tradition.php

PICTURES FOR CHAPTERS 5 AND 6

Pictures for Chapter

Plate 5-1:	Jaina Basadi at Malkhed	325
Plate 5-2:	Tombs of Jaina Ascetics at Moodbidri	325
Plate 5-3:	Kadamba Sikhara at Iswara Temple Malai and Malahanikeswara Temple Sringeri	325
Plate 5-4:	Madhukeswara Temple Banavasi	326
Plate 5-5:	Gommateswara at Shravanabelagola	326
Plate 5-6:	Gangadhareswara Temple Gangavara and Vaidyanatheswara Temple Vaidyanathapura	326
Plate 5-7:	Temples of Badami Chalukyas at Aihole, Pattadakal, Mahakuta and Badami	327
Plate 5-8:	Navalinga Temple Kuknur, Panchalingeswara Temple Hooli, Someswara Temple Hooli and Narayana Temple Naregal	328
Plate 5-9:	Kiratarjuniyam Bhoganandiswara Temple Nandi	328
Plate 5-10:	Siva Dancing Carved on Perforated Window Bhoganandiswara Temple	329
Plate 5-11:	Sikharas of Arunachaleswara and Bhoganandiswara Shrines	329
Plate 5-12:	Natesa Surrounded by Ashtadikpalas and Vidyadharas Kalleswara Temple Aralaguppe	330
Plate 5-13:	Umasahita Sculpture and Doorway Kalleswara Temple Aralaguppe	330
Plate 5-14:	Kolaramma Temple Kolar	331
Plate 5-15:	Aprameyaswamy Temple at Doddamalur	331
Plate 5-16:	Narayanaswamy Temple at Malurpatna	331
Plate 5-17:	Rajarajeshwari Temple at Polali	332
Plate 5-18:	Mahishasuramardini Temple at Neelavara	332
Plate 5-19:	Kadri Manjunatha Temple Mangaluru	333
Plate 5-20:	Panchalingeswara Temple Vittla	333
Plate 5-21:	Panchalingeswara Temple, Kattale Basadi and Baragi Ganapati Temple at Barkur	334
Plate 5-22:	Basavakalyan Fort	334
Plate 5-23:	Broken Makaratorana and Interior of Siva Temple Narayanpur	335
Plate 5-24:	Two Views of Mahalingeswara Temple Gokak Falls	335
Plate 5-25:	Basaveswara Temple at Bagewadi and Amruteswara Temple at Annigeri	335
Plate 5-26:	Sikhara of Dodda Basappa Temple Dambal (Wikipedia)	336
Plate 5-27:	Domical Ceiling Chennakesava Temple Belur with Ugra Narasimha in Pendant	336
Plate 5-28:	Twin Temples of Mosale -Nageswara and Chennakesava	337
Plate 5-29:	Friezes on the Adisthana of Chennakesava Temple Mosale	337
Plate 5-30:	Erotic Sculpture on the Outer Wall of Porch Somanathapur	338
Plate 5-31:	Sketch Map of Sannati and Kanganahalli Sites	338

Plate 5-32: Linear Sketch and Yantra Drawings, Malavalli   332
Plate 5-33: Frame of a Person in Navatala as per Talamaana   333
Plate 5-34: Some Mudras for Sculpture   340
Plate 5-35: Sculptures in Low and High Relief from Mallikarjuna Temple Ron and Badami Cave 2   340
Plate 5-36: Sculptures on the Outer Wall of the Mandapa, Virupaksha Temple Pattadakal   341
Plate 5-37: Stucco Images on the Sikhara of Rameswara Temple Narasamangala   341
Plate 5-38: Matrikas from Arkeswara Temple Alur   342
Plate 5-39: Krishna Lifting Mount Govardhana and Arjuna Aiming at the Fish Looking at Reflection in Water   342
Plate 5-40: Mark the Fingers Running Through the Strings on the Drum   343
Plate 5-41: Amorous Couples on Column Brackets Cave 3 Badami   343

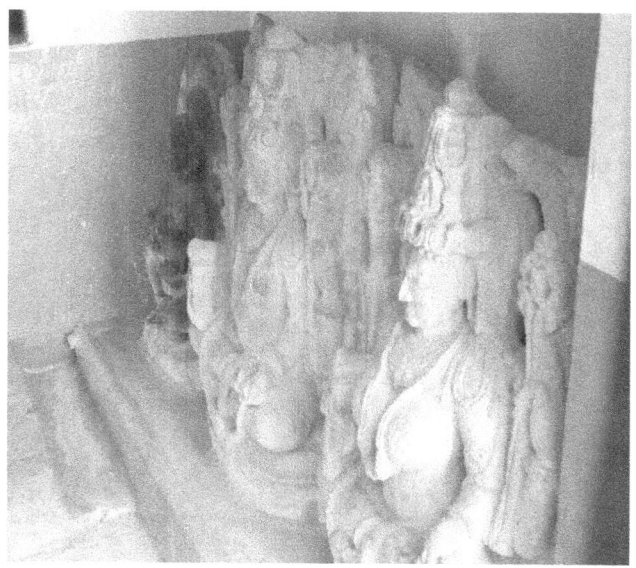 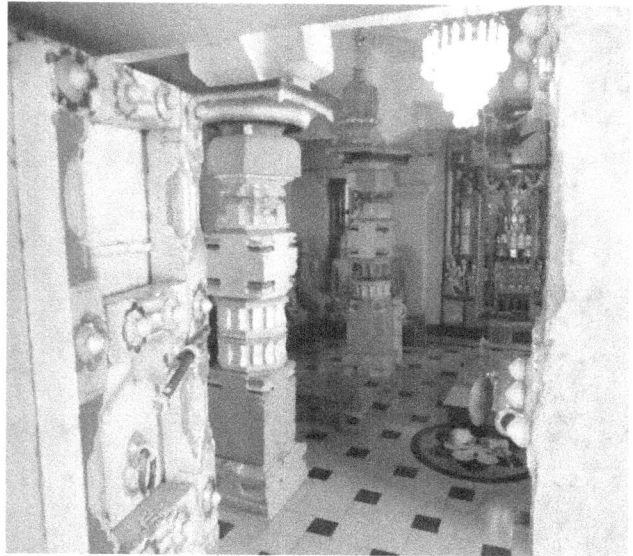

Plate 5-1: Jaina Basadi at Malkhed

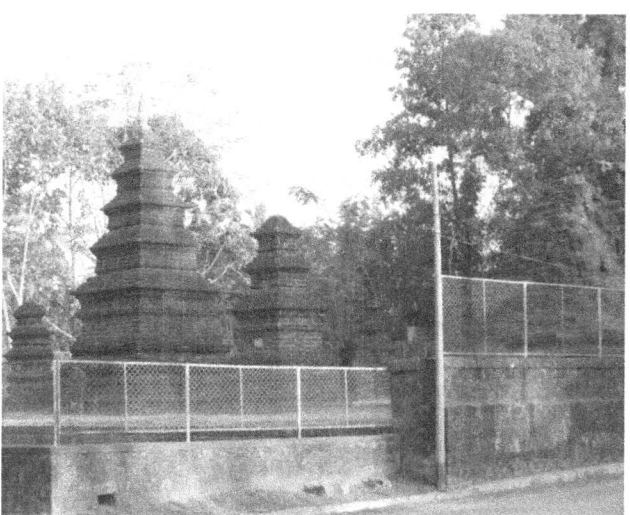 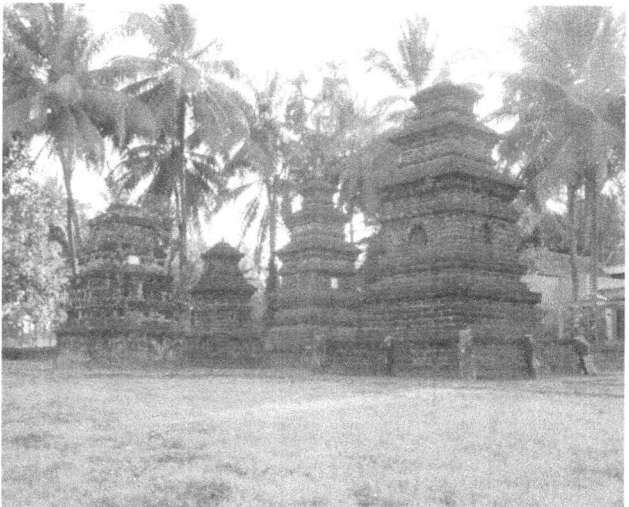

Plate 5-2: Tombs of Jaina Ascetics at Moodbidri

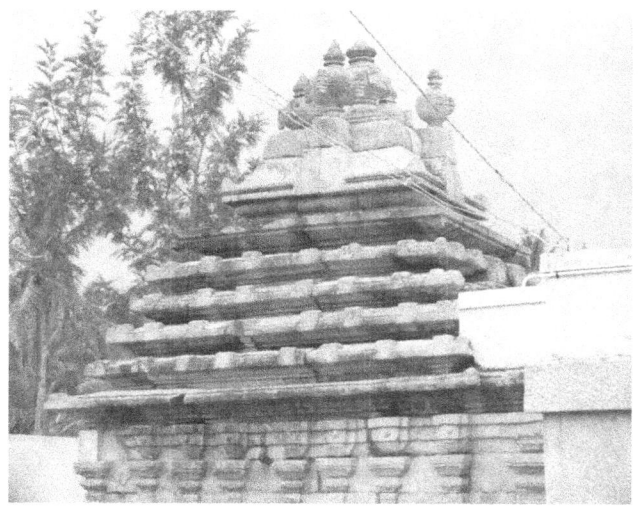 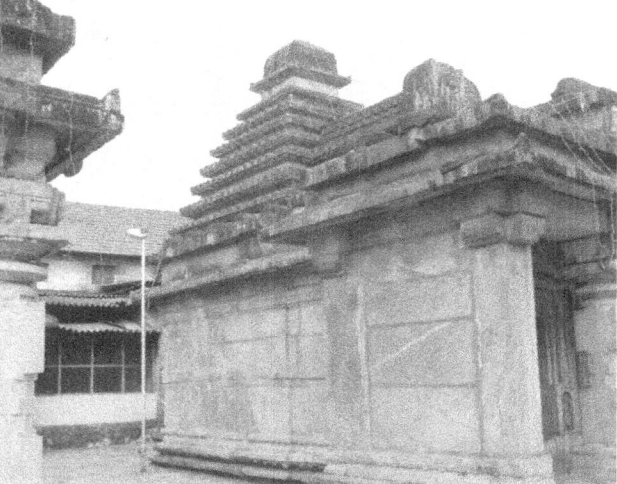

Plate 5-3: Kadamba Sikhara at Iswara Temple Malai and Malahanikeswara Temple Sringeri

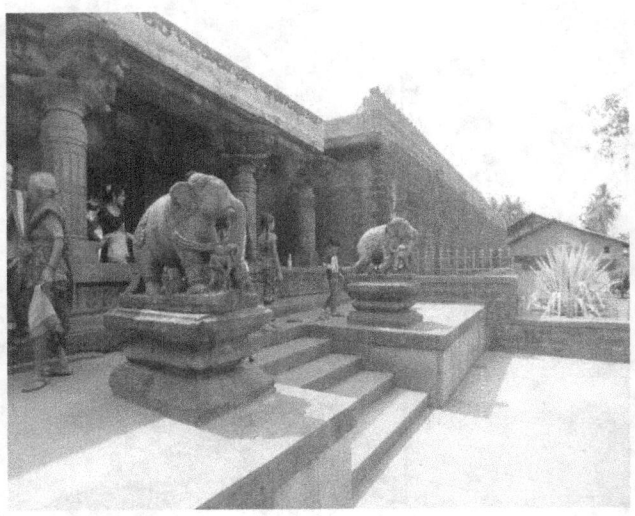 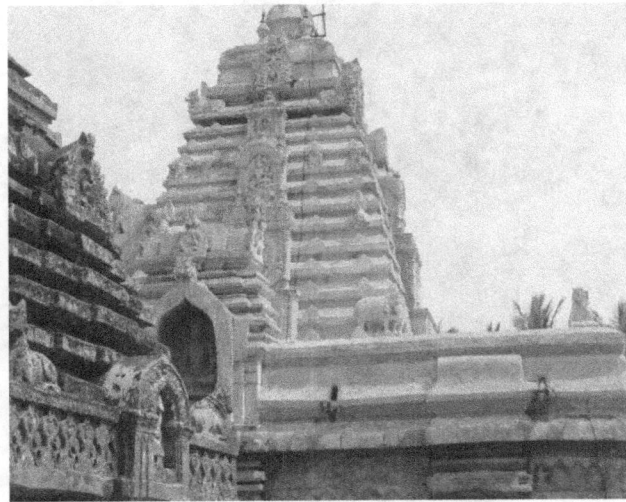

Plate 5-4: Madhukeswara Temple Banavasi

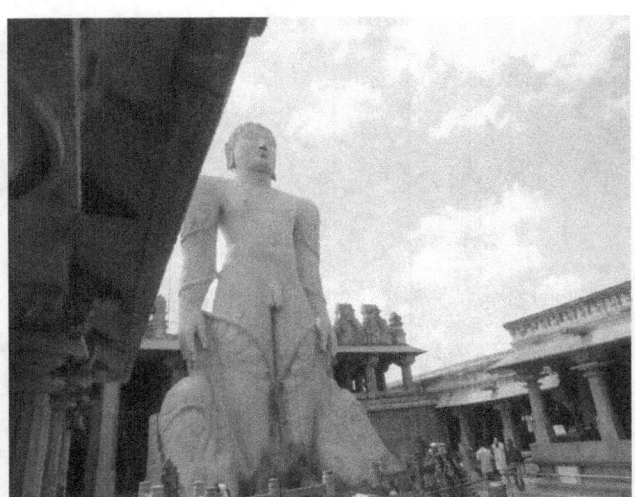 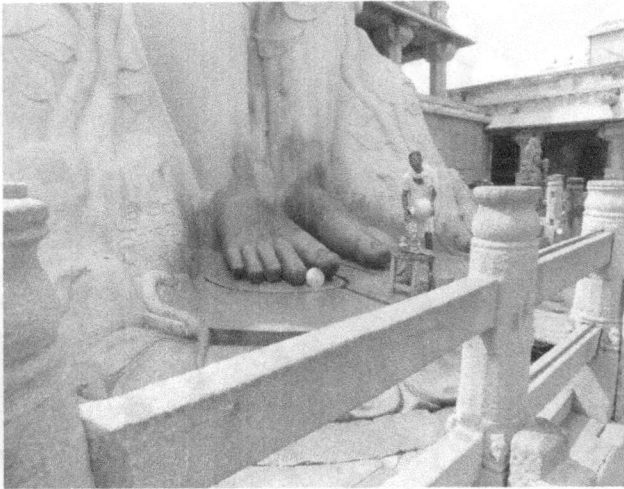

Plate 5-5: Gommateswara at Shravanabelagola

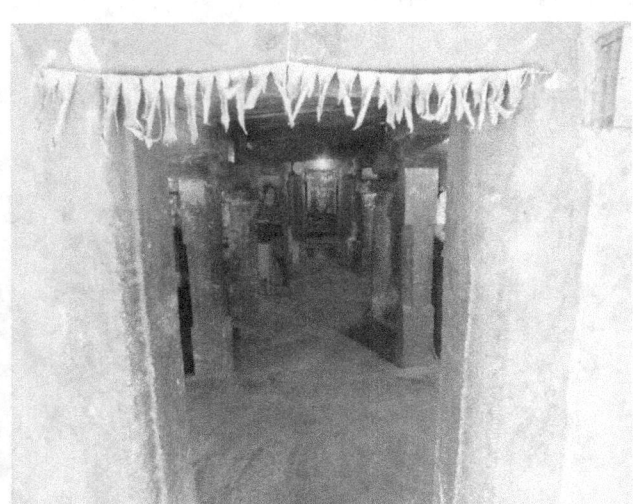 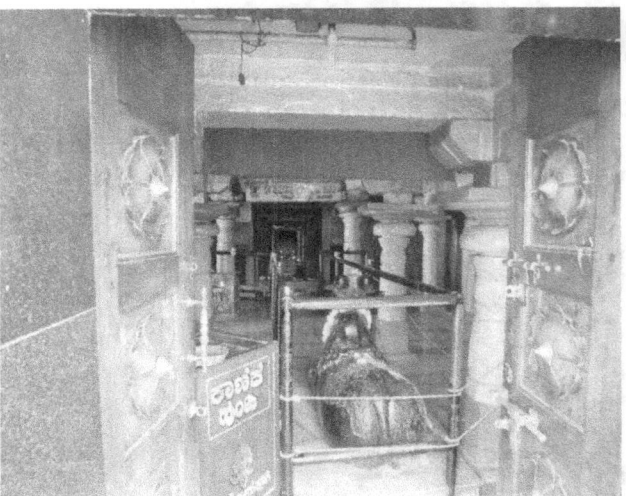

Plate 5-6: Gangadhareswara Temple Gangavara and Vaidyanatheswara Temple Vaidyanathapura

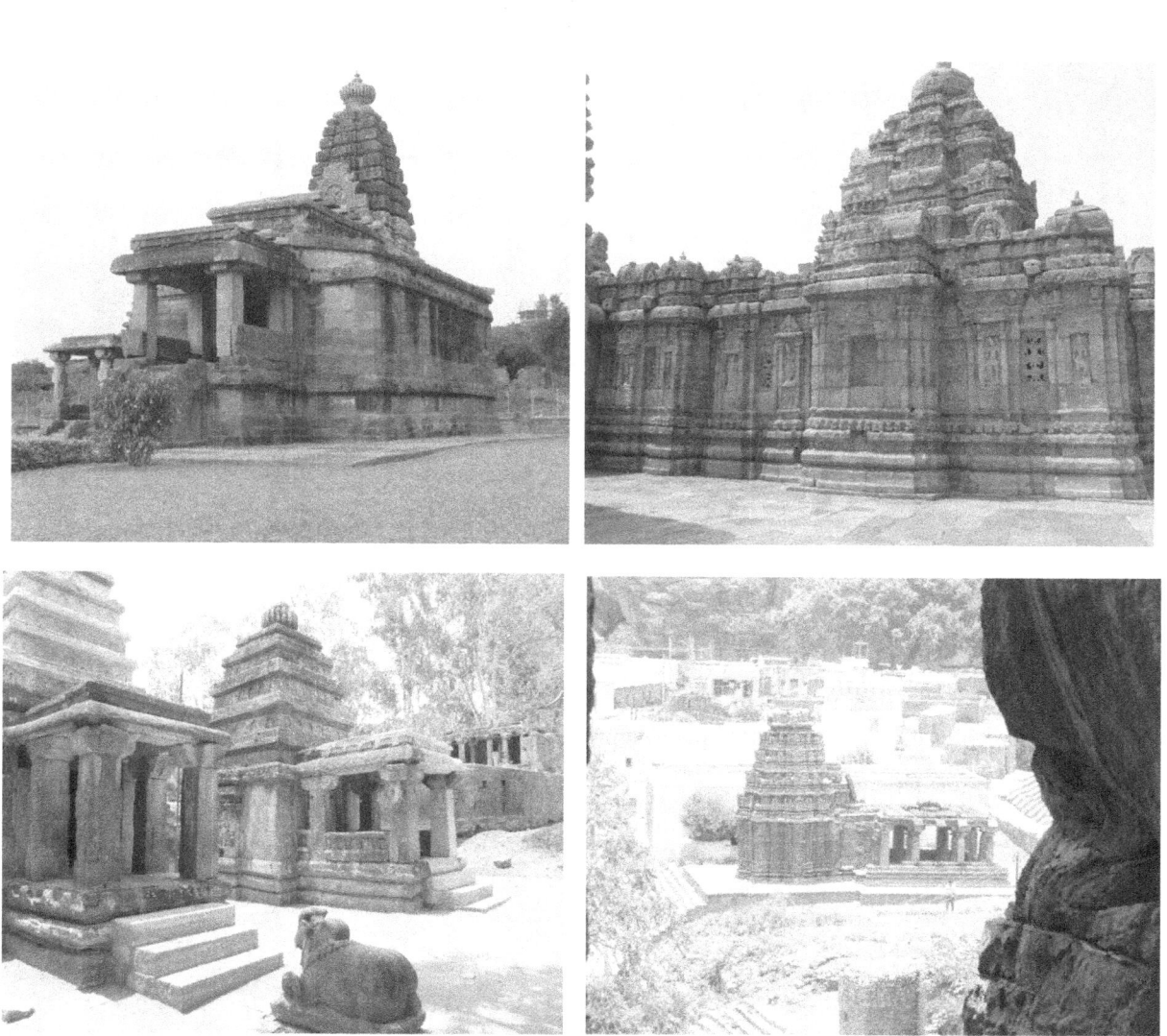

Plate 5-7: Temples of Badami Chalukyas at Aihole, Pattadakal, Mahakuta and Badami

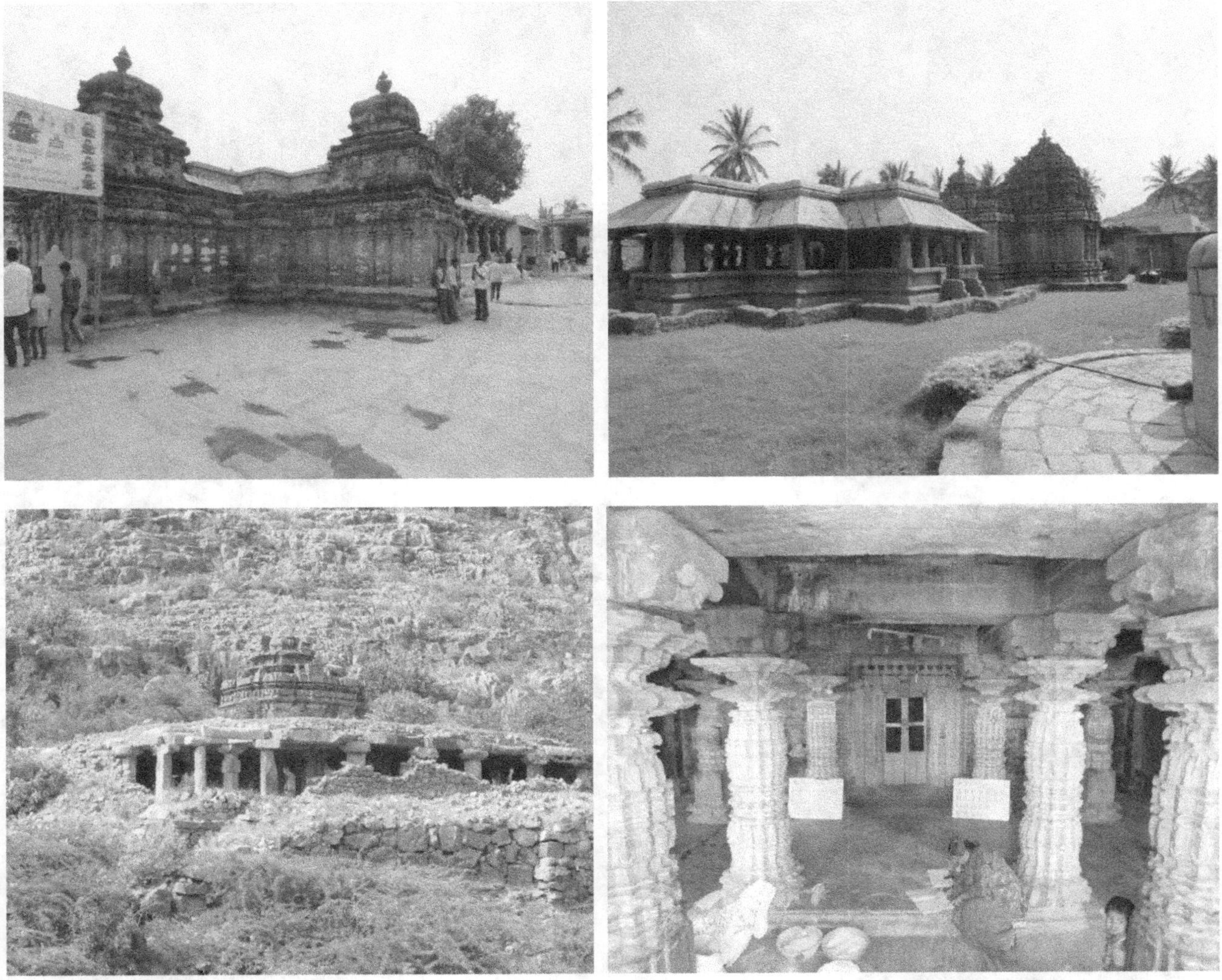

Plate 5-8: Navalinga Temple Kuknur, Panchalingeswara Temple Hooli, Someswara Temple Hooli and Narayana Temple Naregal

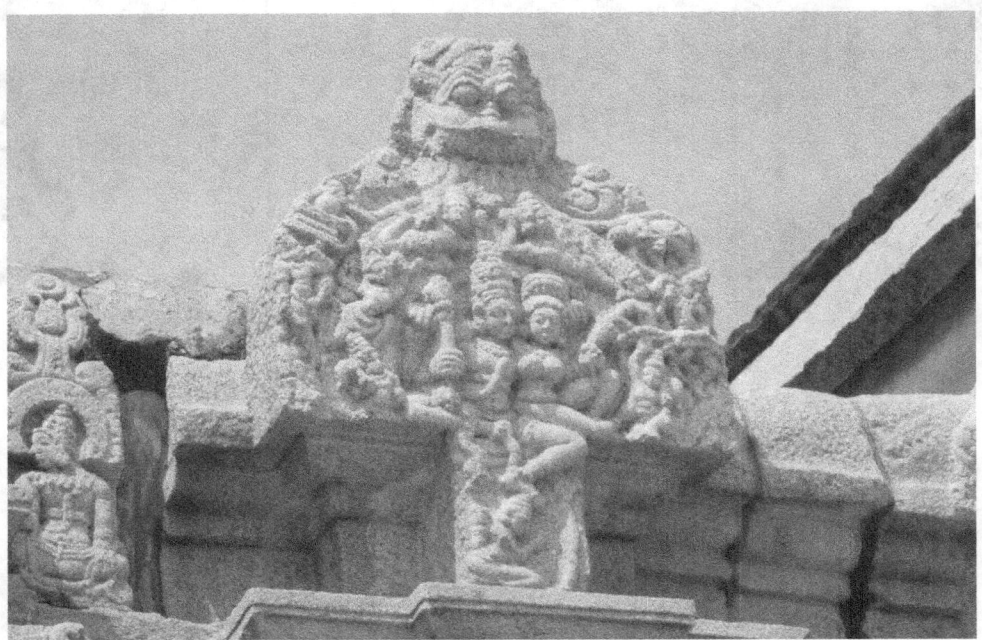

Plate 5-9: Kiratarjuniyam Bhoganandiswara Temple Nandi

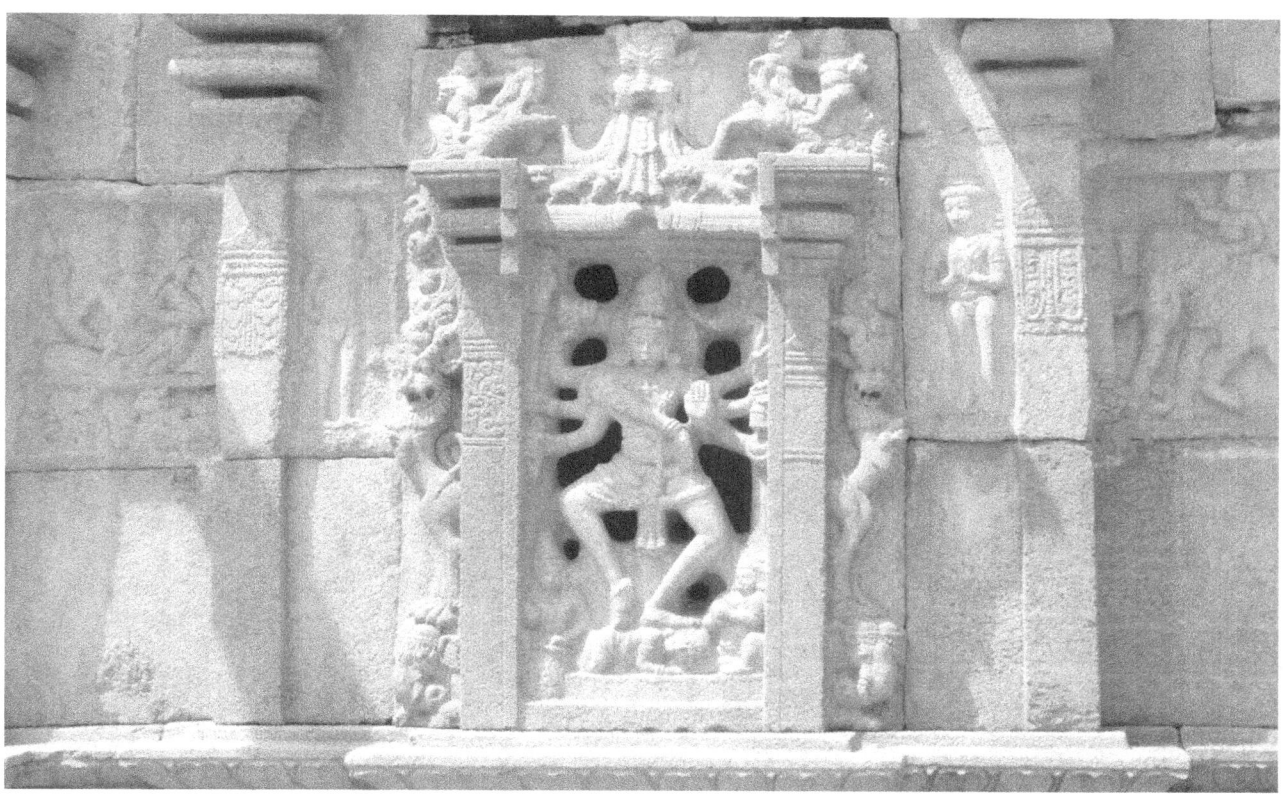

Plate 5-10: Siva Dancing Carved on Perforated Window Bhoganandiswara Temple

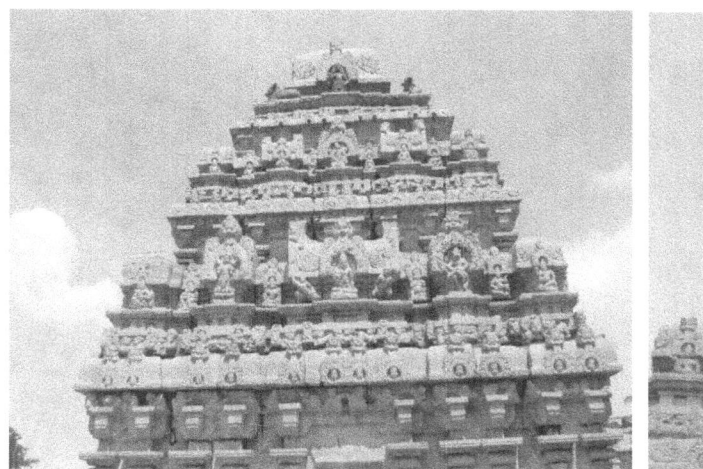 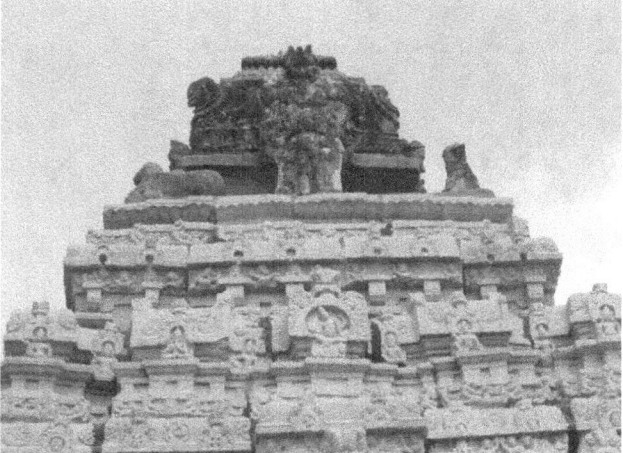

Plate 5-11: Sikharas of Arunachaleswara and Bhoganandiswara Shrines

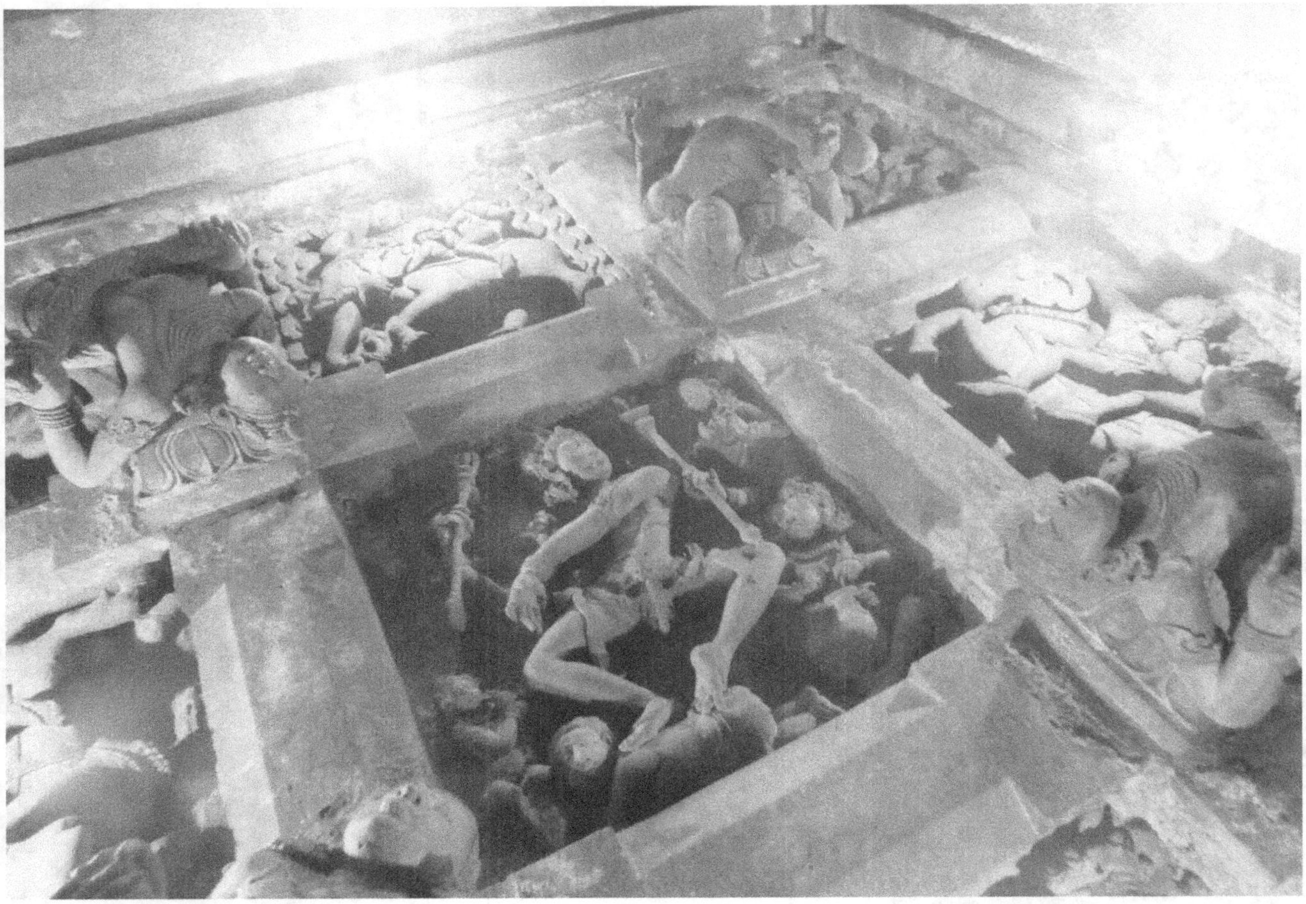

Plate 5-12: Natesa Surrounded by Ashtadikpalas and Vidyadharas Kalleswara Temple Aralaguppe

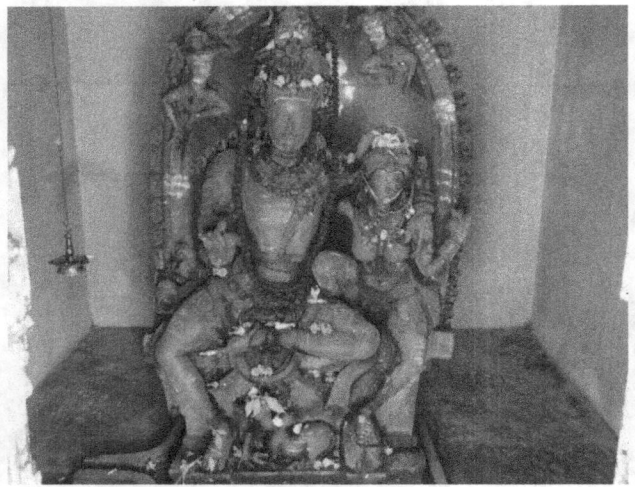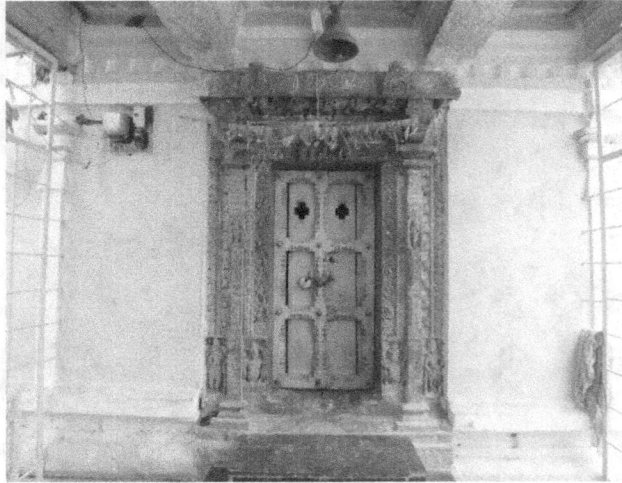

Plate 5-13: Umasahita Sculpture and Doorway Kalleswara Temple Aralaguppe

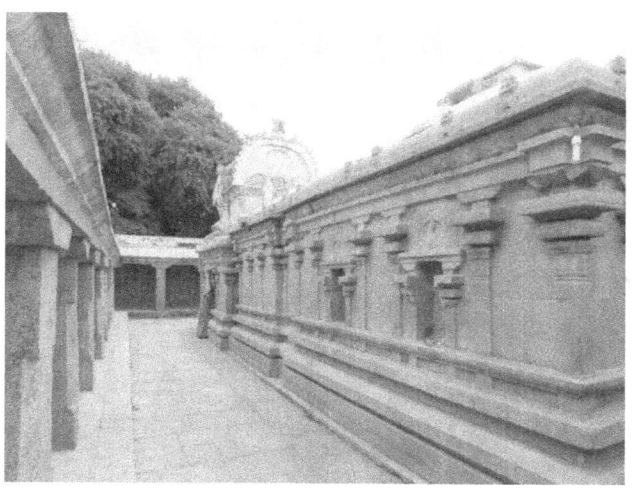 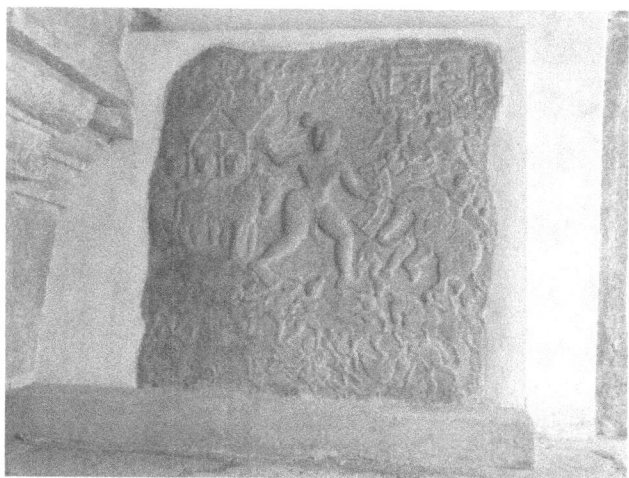

Plate 5-14: Kolaramma Temple Kolar

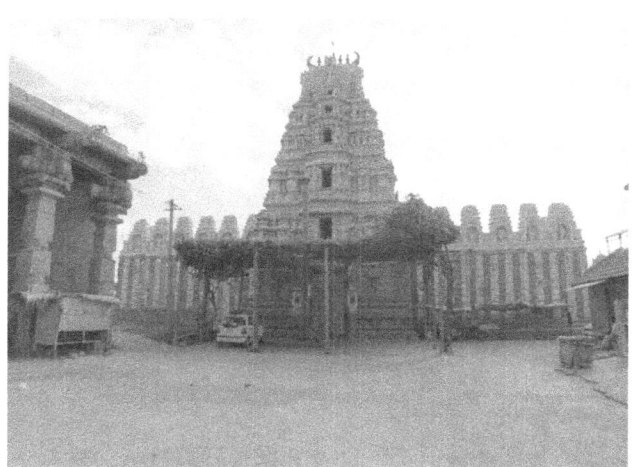 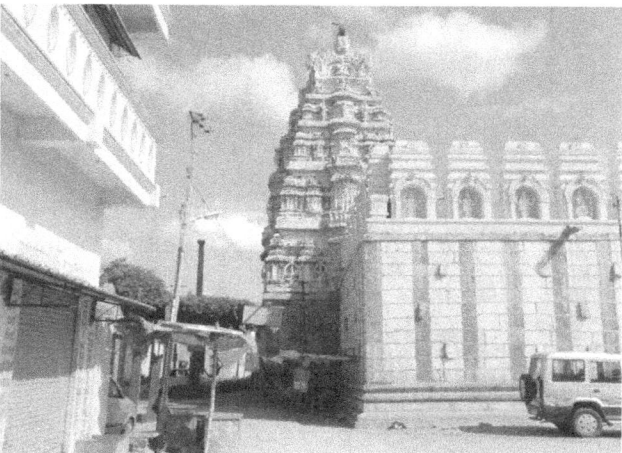

Plate 5-15: Aprameyaswamy Temple at Doddamalur

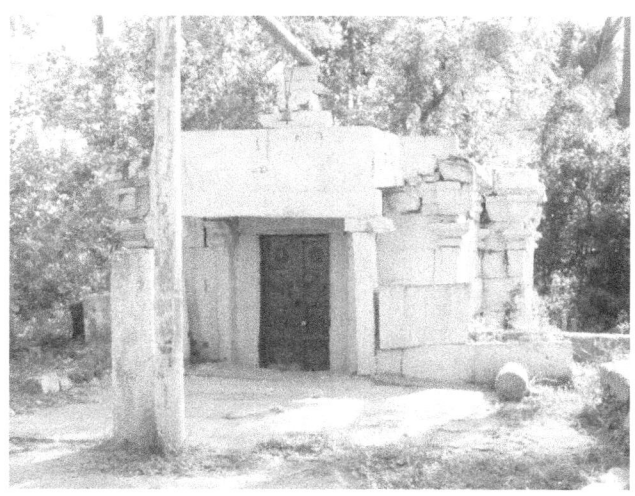 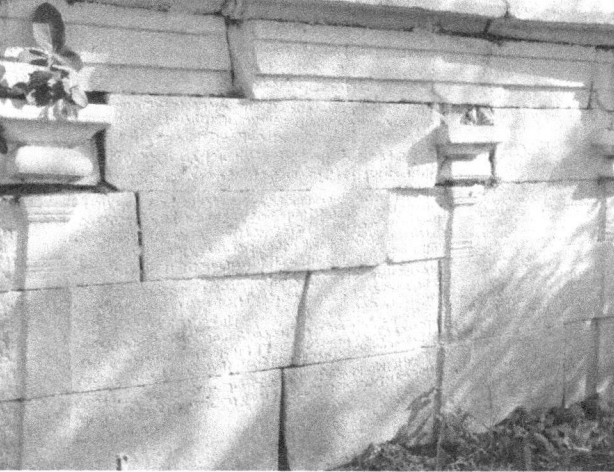

Plate 5-16: Narayanaswamy Temple at Malurpatna

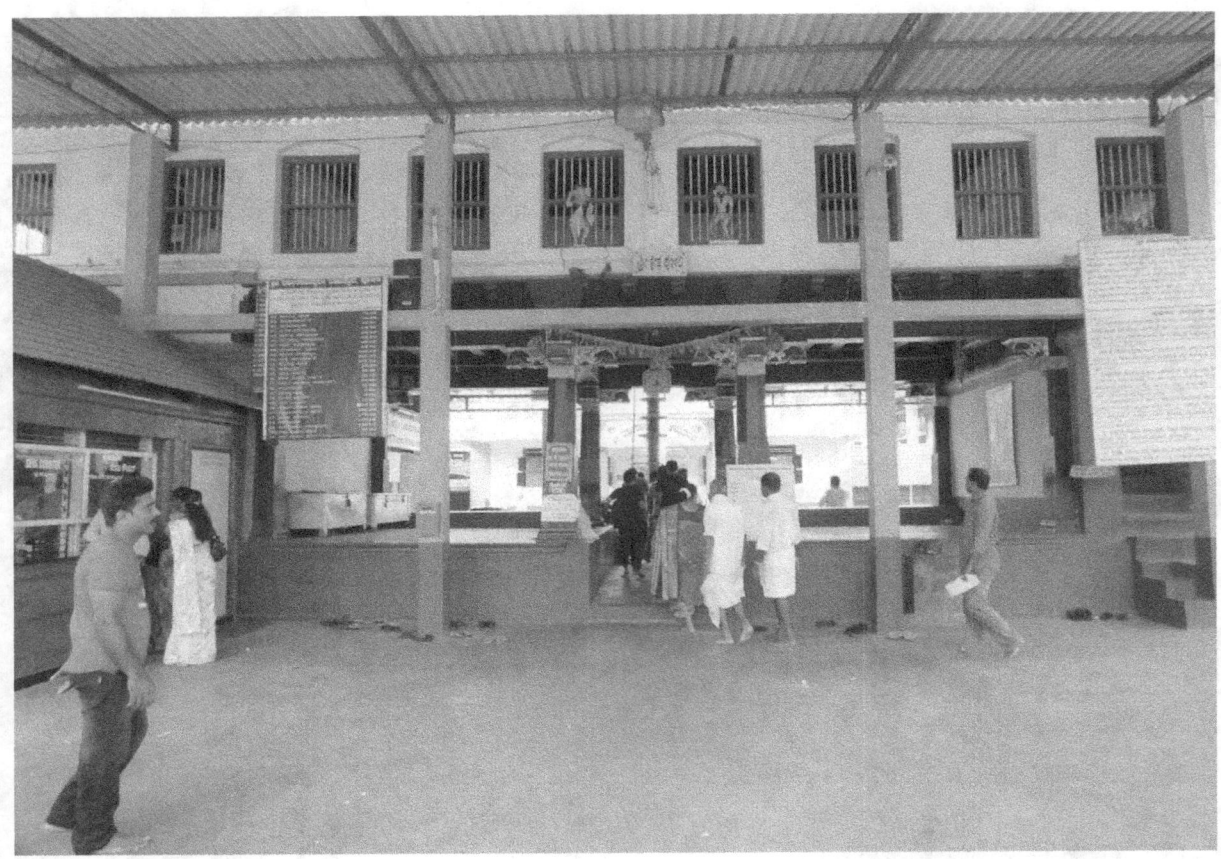

Plate 5-17: Rajarajeshwari Temple at Polali

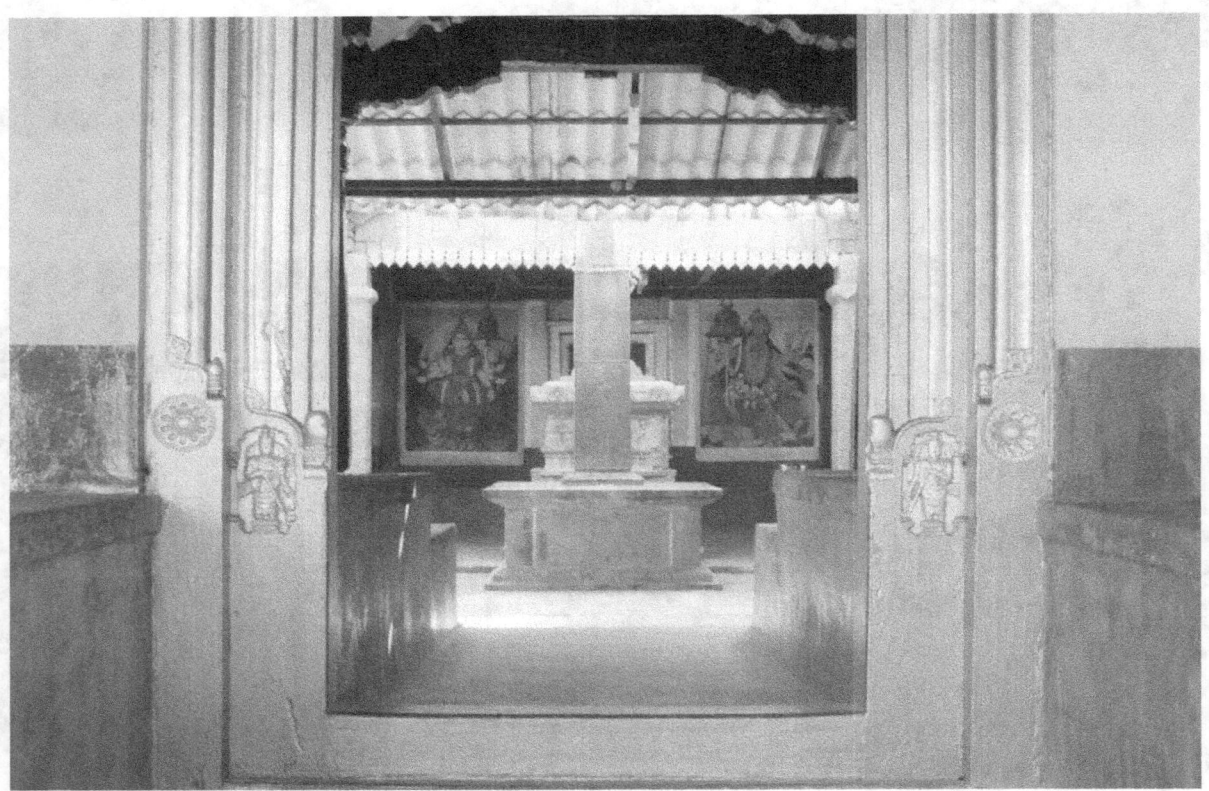

Plate 5-18: Mahishasuramardini Temple at Neelavara

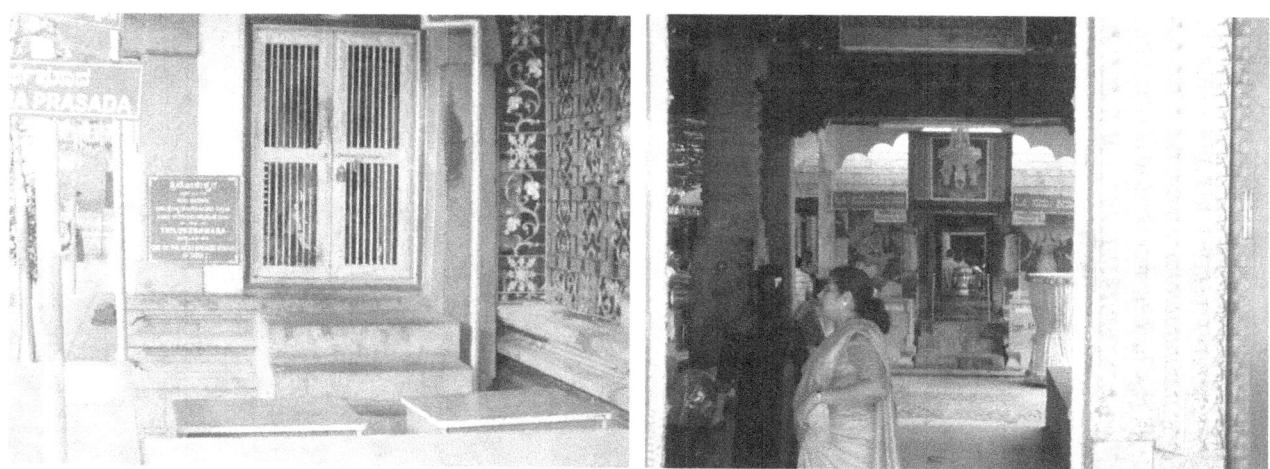

Plate 5-19: Kadri Manjunatha Temple Mangaluru

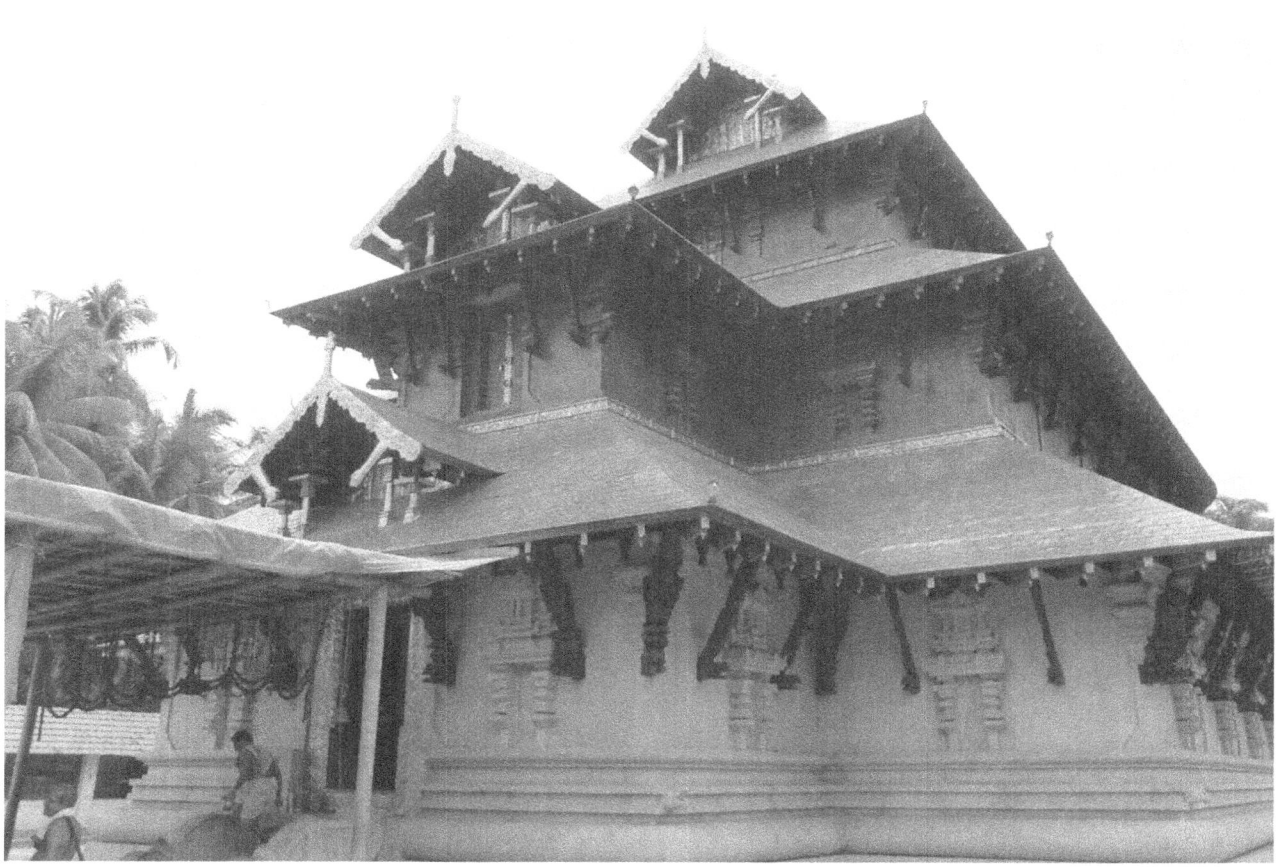

Plate 5-20: Panchalingeswara Temple Vittla

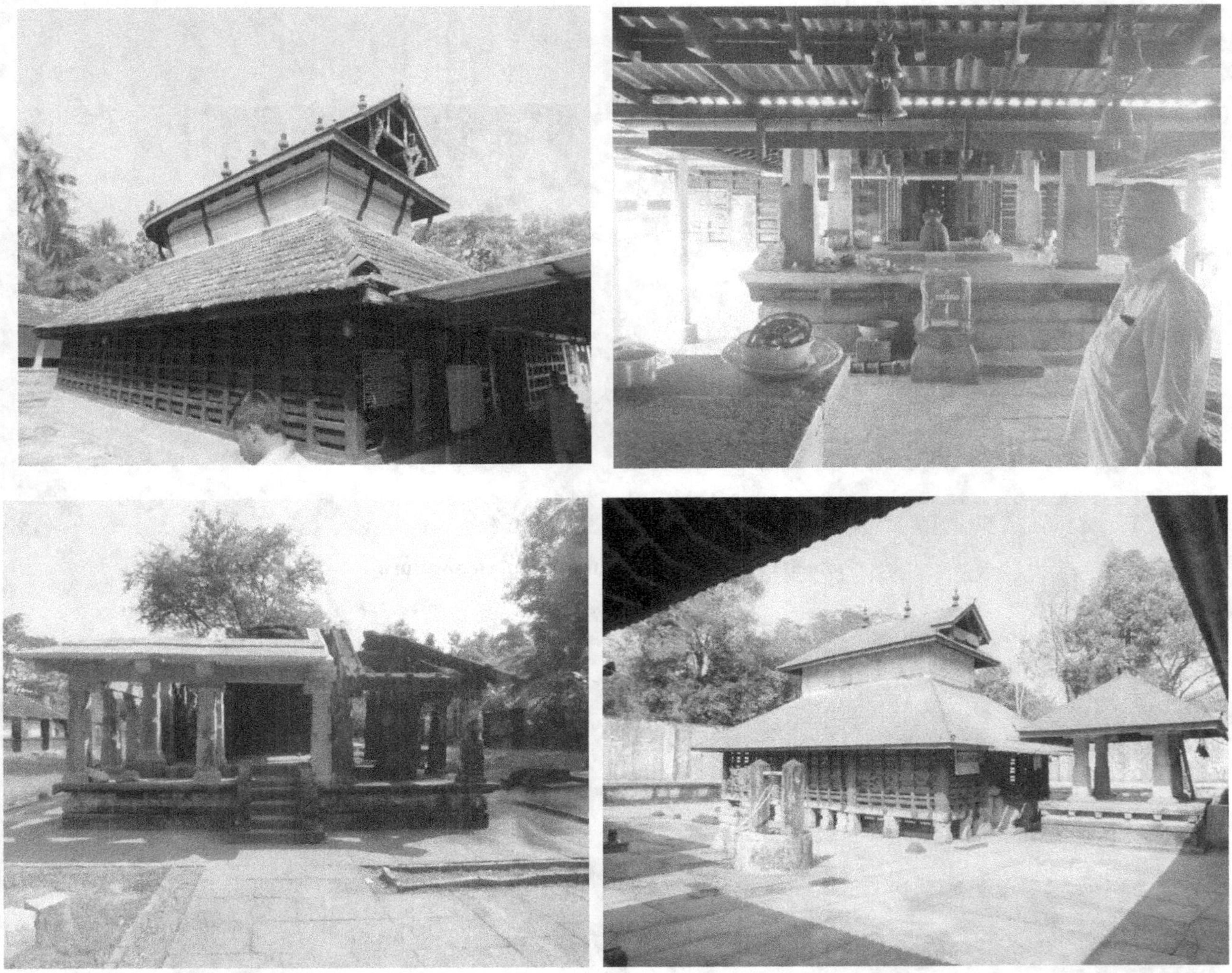

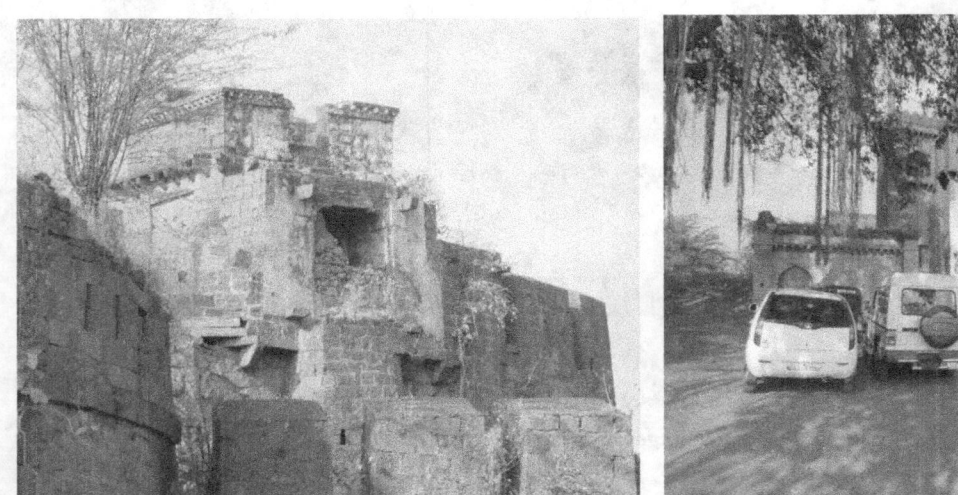

Plate 5-21: Panchalingeswara Temple, Kattale Basadi and Baragi Ganapati Temple at Barkur

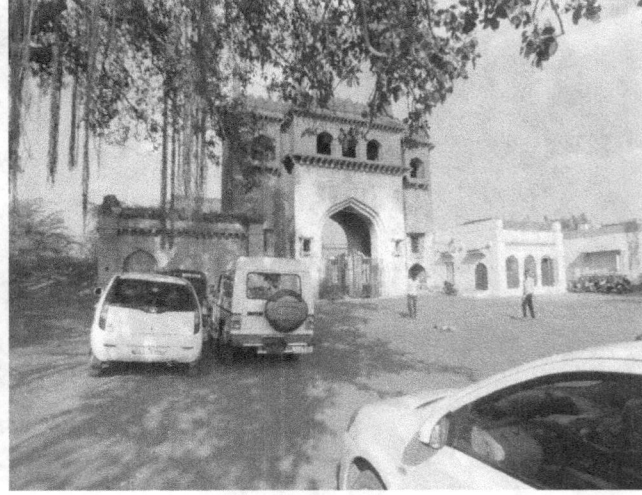

Plate 5-22: Basavakalyan Fort

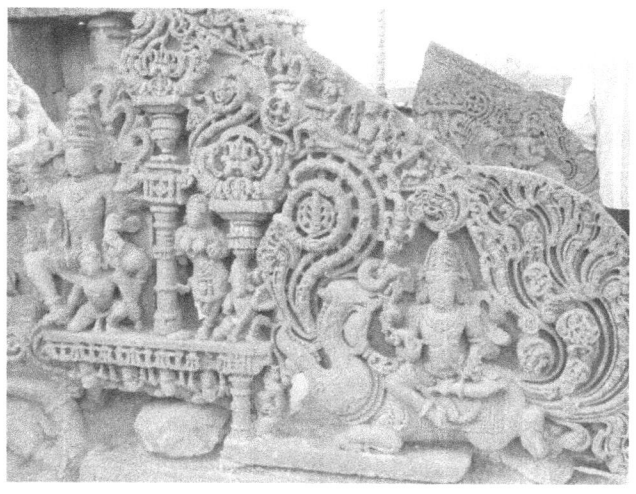
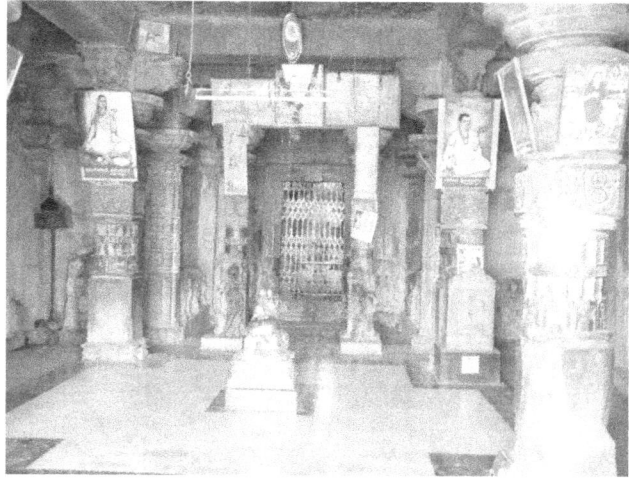

Plate 5-23: Broken Makaratorana and Interior of Siva Temple Narayanpur

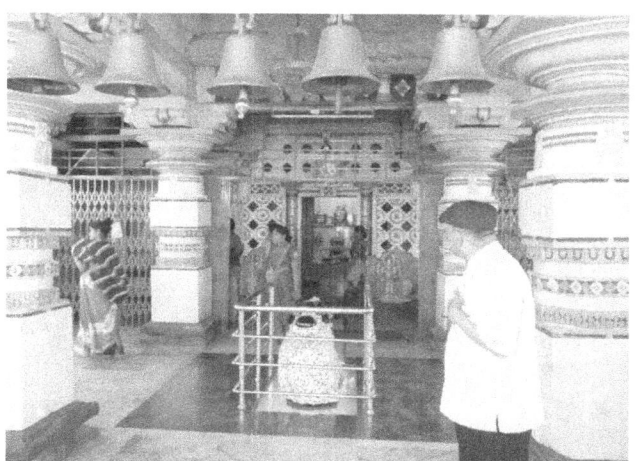
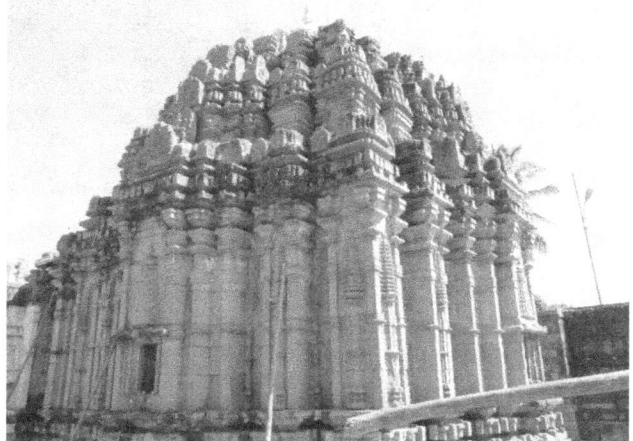

Plate 5-24: Two Views of Mahalingeswara Temple Gokak Falls

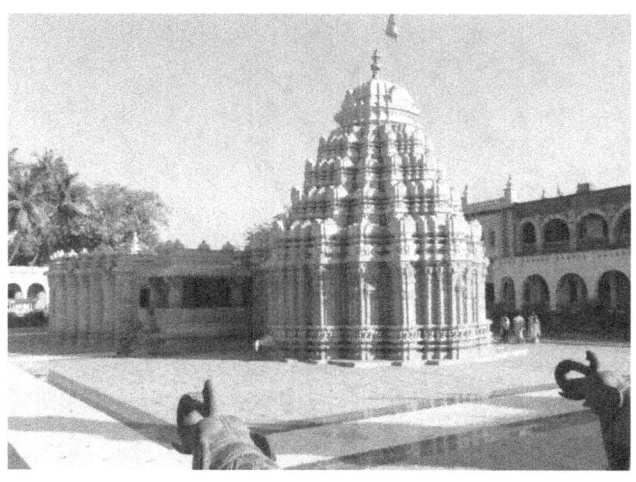
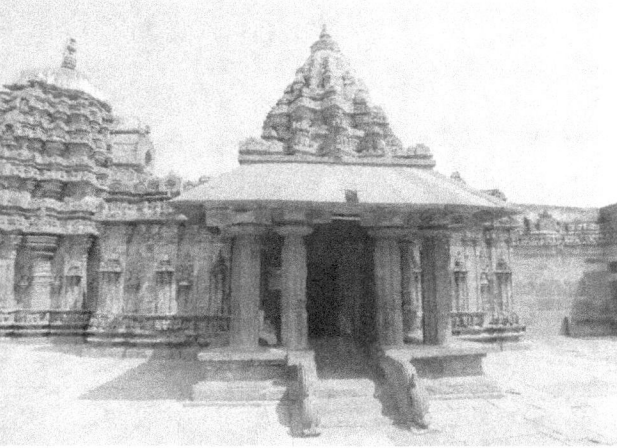

Plate 5-25: Basaveswara Temple at Bagewadi and Amruteswara Temple at Annigeri

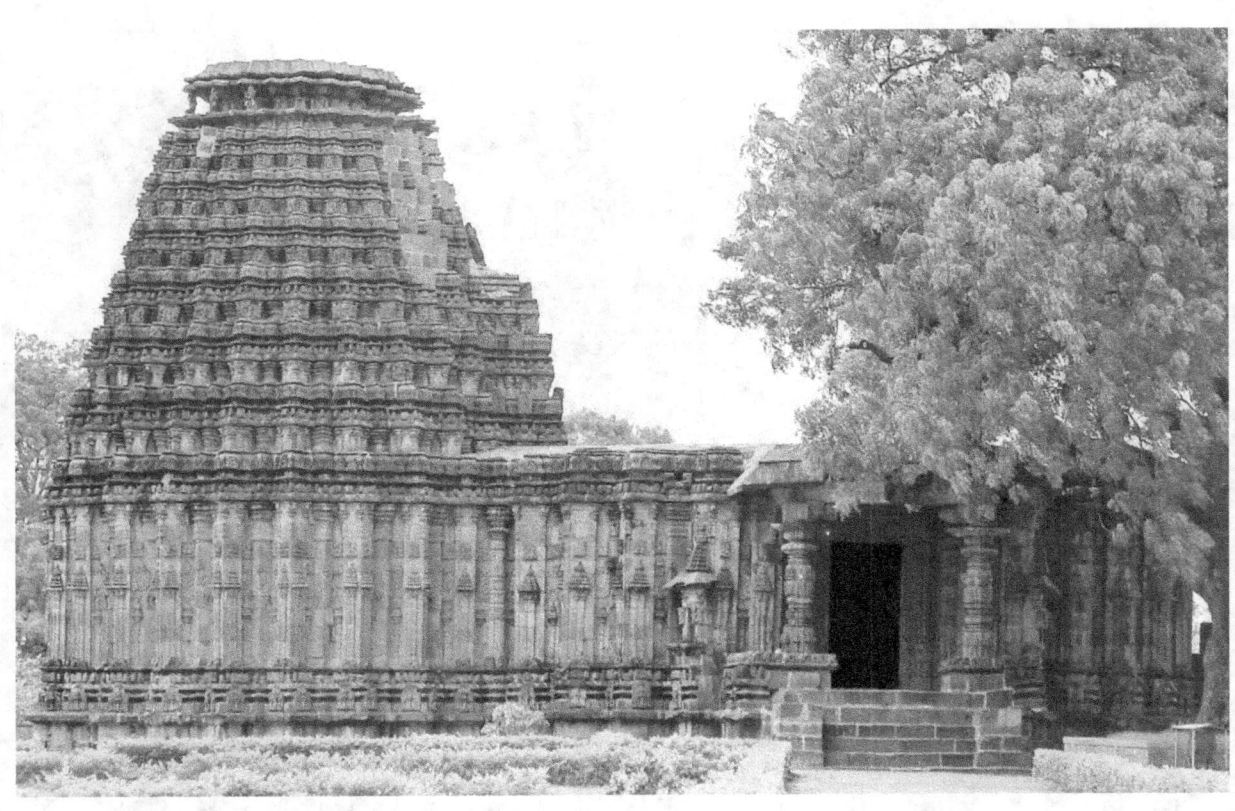

Plate 5-26: Sikhara of Dodda Basappa Temple Dambal (Wikipedia)

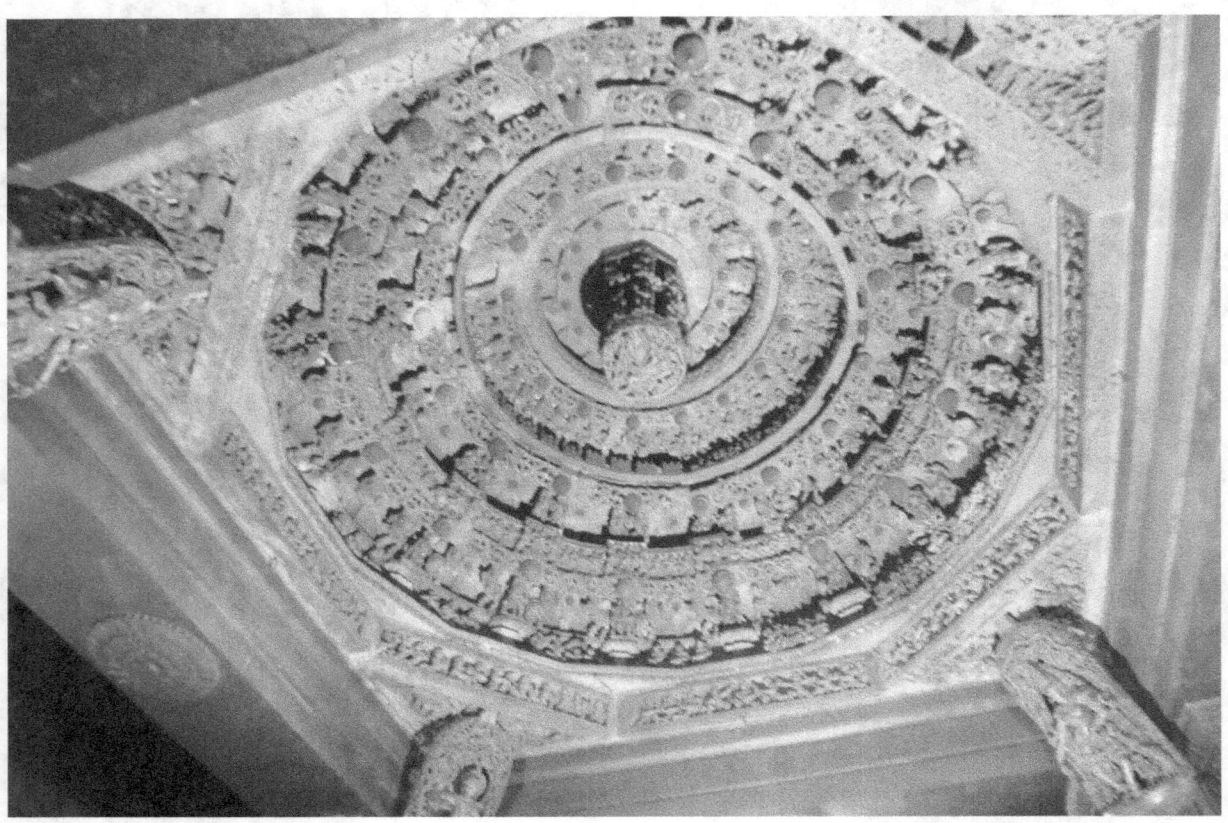

Plate 5-27: Domical Ceiling Chennakesava Temple Belur with Ugra Narasimha in Pendant

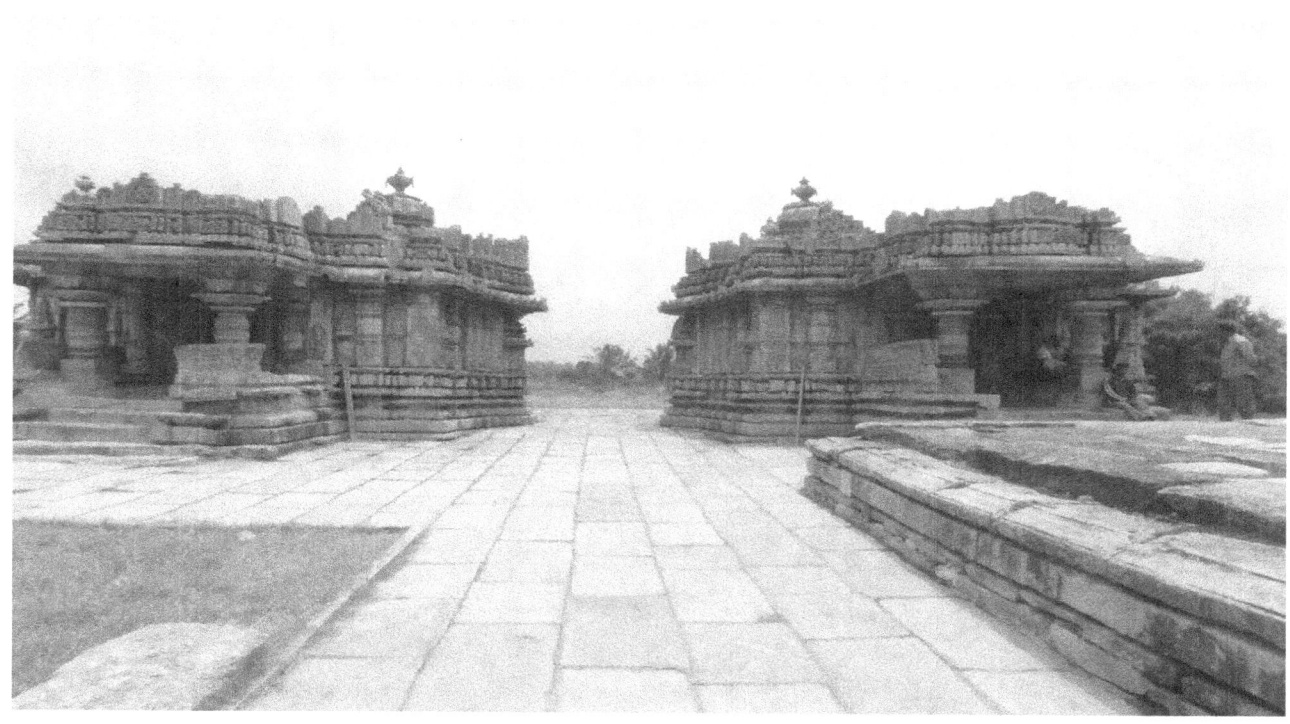

Plate 5-28: Twin Temples of Mosale - Nageswara and Chennakesava

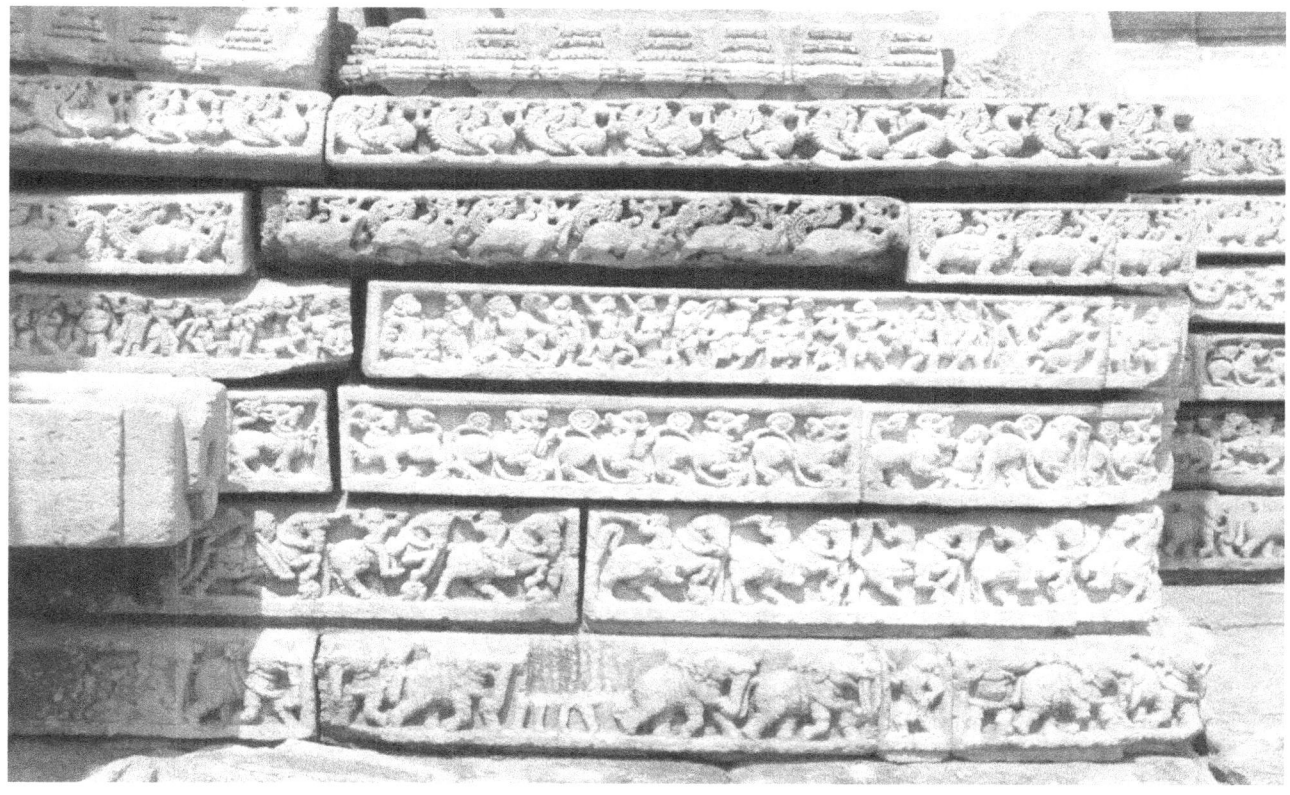

Plate 5-29: Friezes on the Adisthana of Chennakesava Temple Mosale

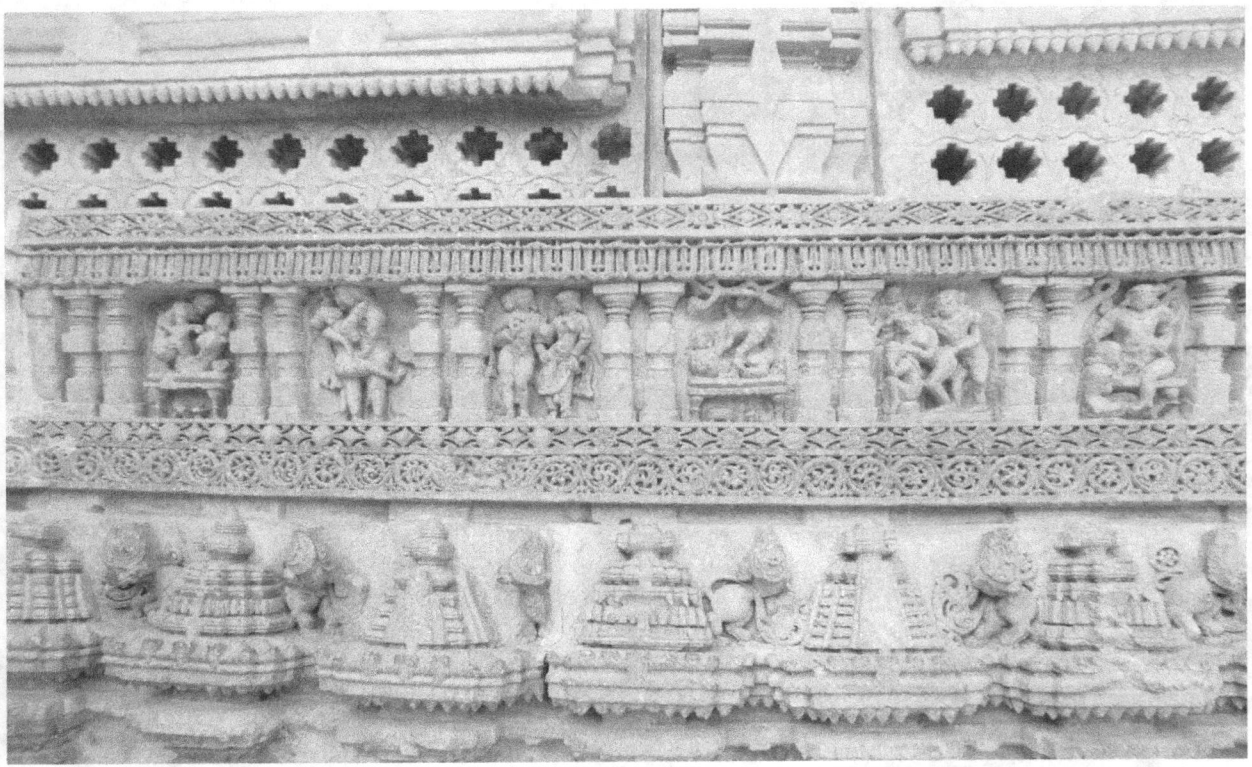

Plate 5-30: Erotic Sculpture on the Outer Wall of Porch Somanathapur

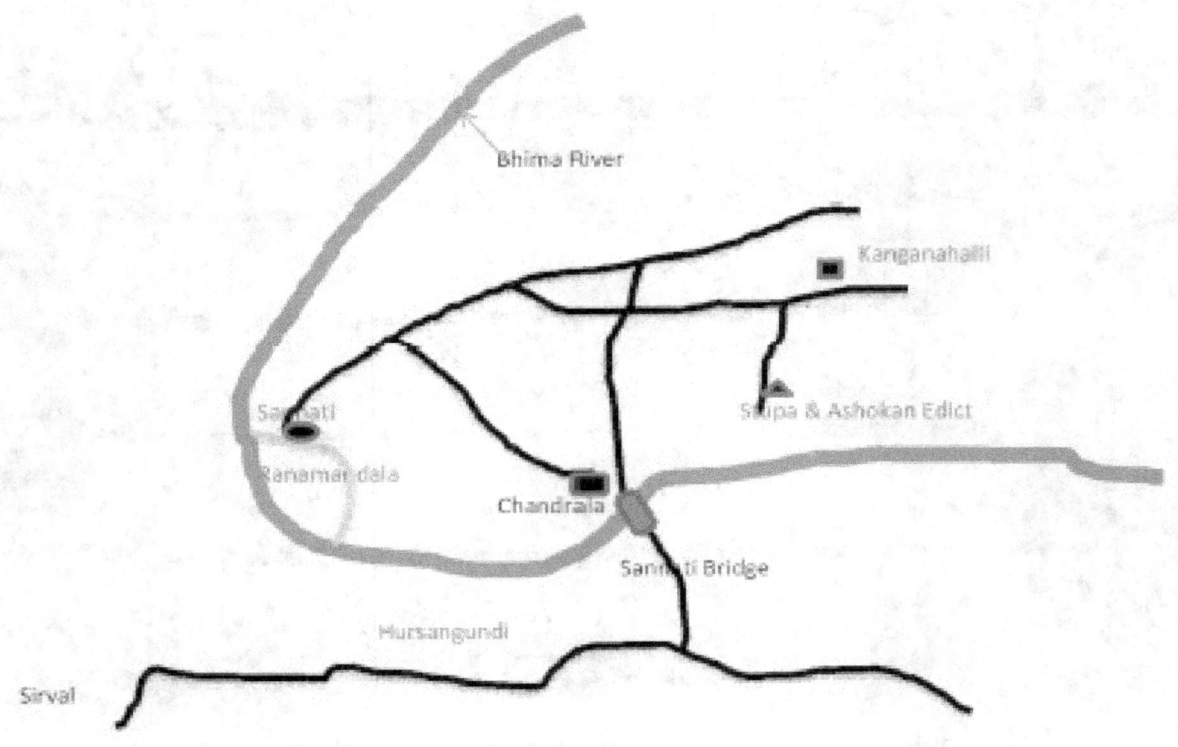

Plate 5-31: Sketch Map of Sannati and Kanganahalli Sites

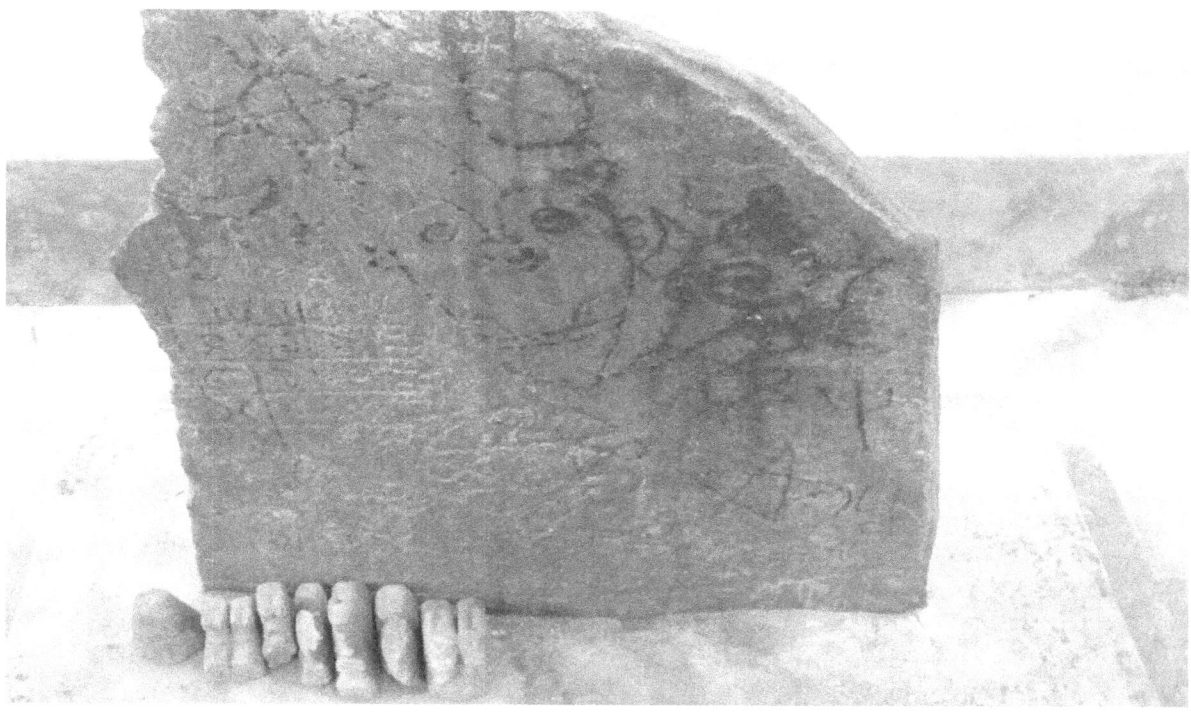

Plate 5-32: Linear Sketch and Yantra Drawings, Malavalli

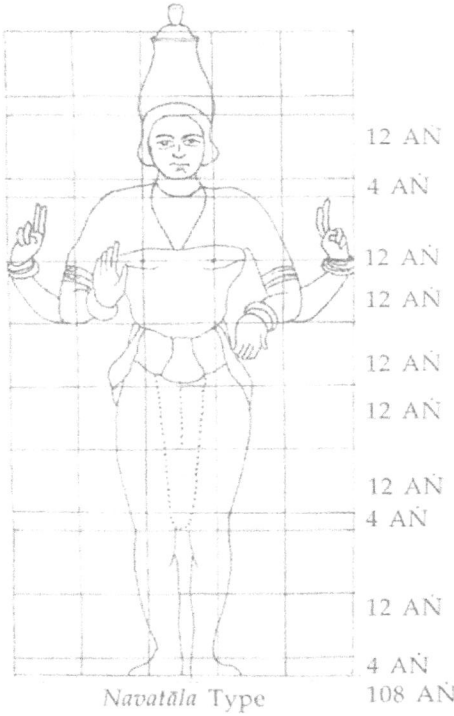

Plate 5-33: Frame of a Person in Navatala as per Talamaana

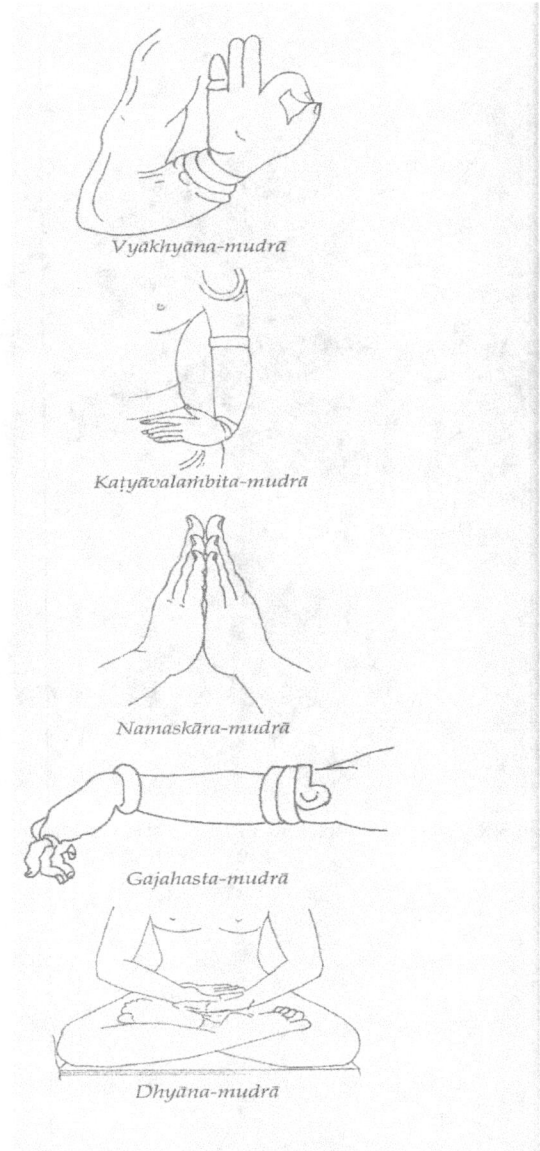

Plate 5-34: Some Mudras for Sculpture

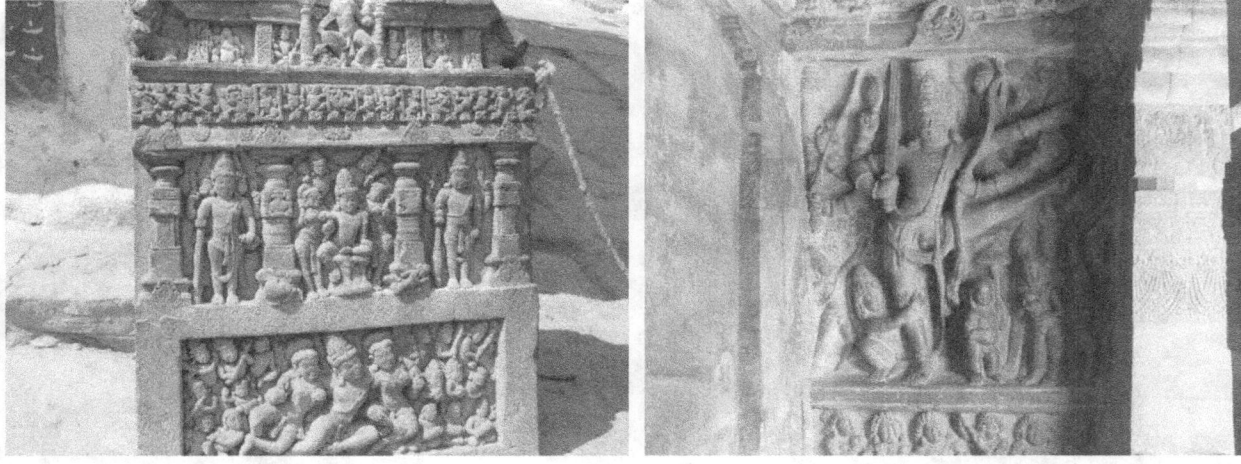

Plate 5-35: Sculptures in Low and High Relief from Mallikarjuna Temple Ron and Badami Cave 2

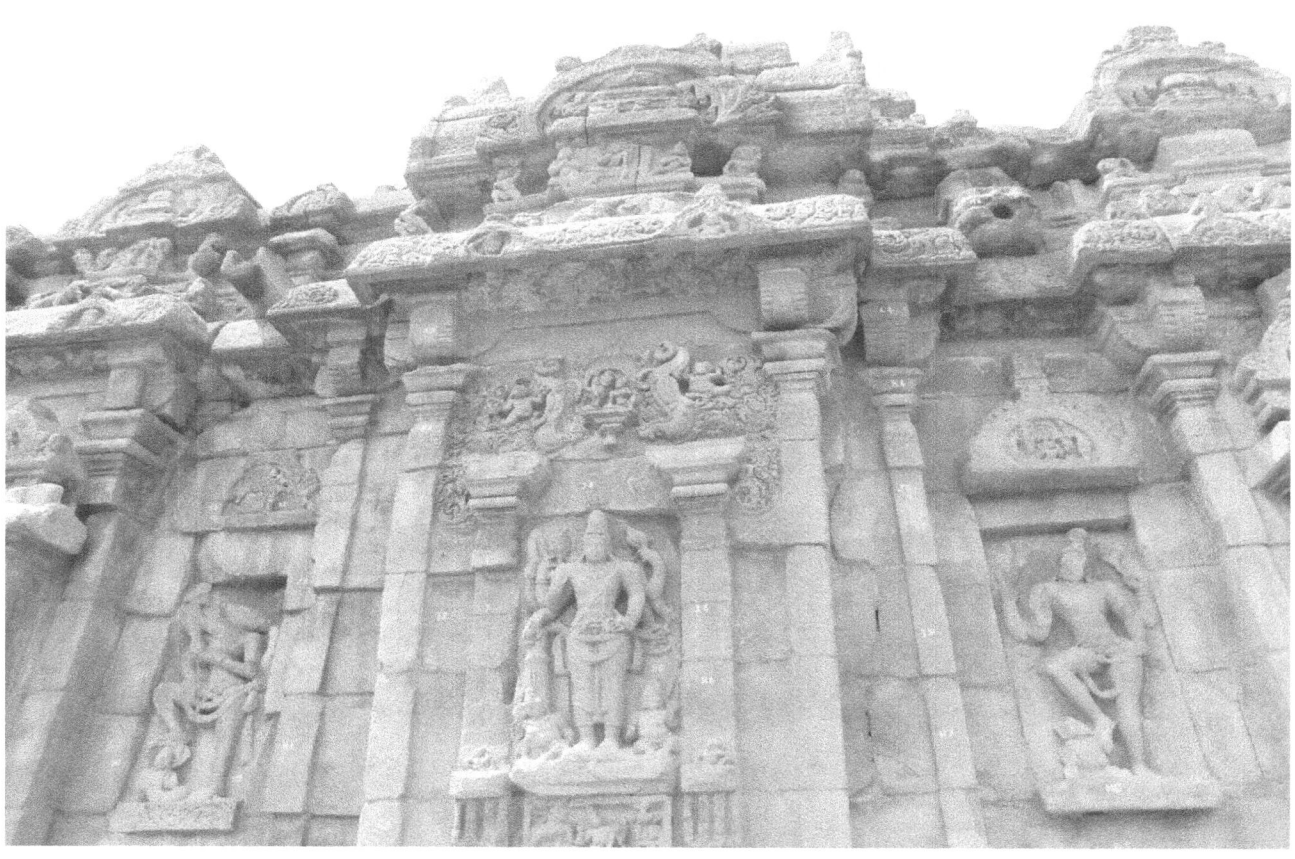

Plate 5-36: Sculptures on the Outer Wall of the Mandapa, Virupaksha Temple Pattadakal

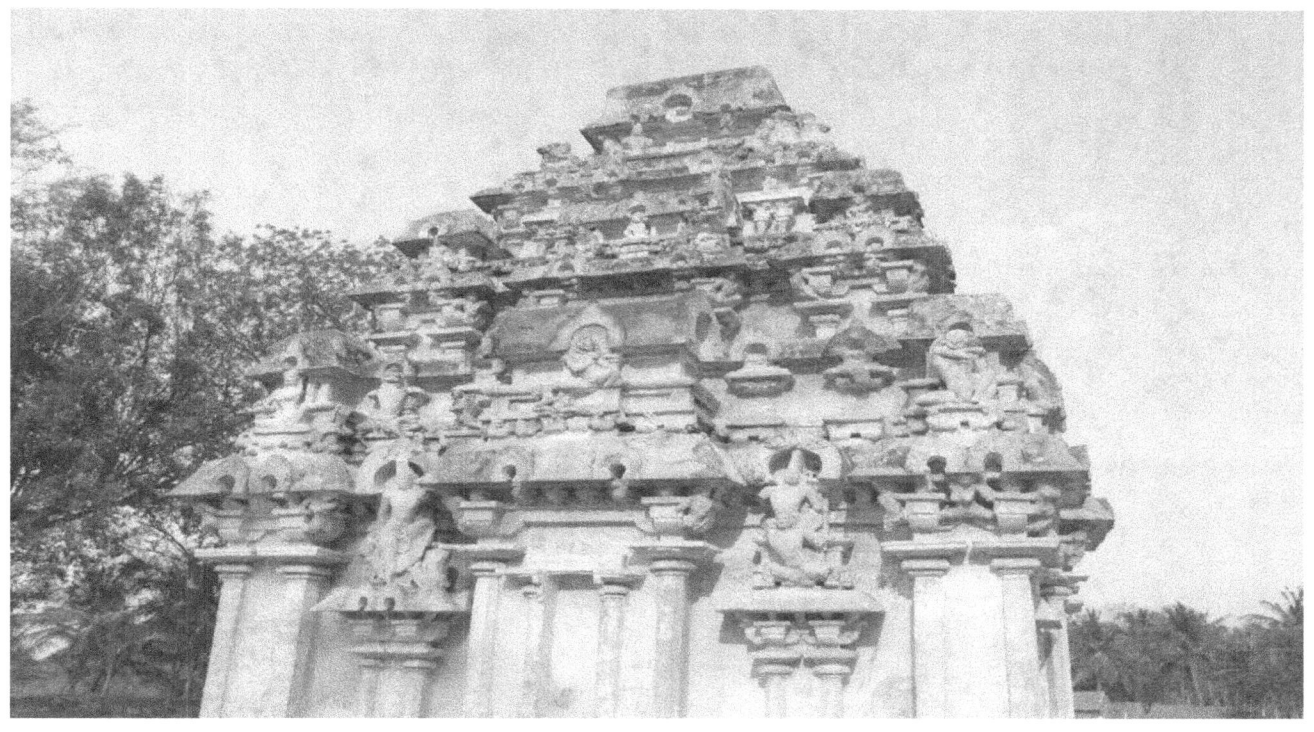

Plate 5-37: Stucco Images on the Sikhara of Rameswara Temple Narasamangala

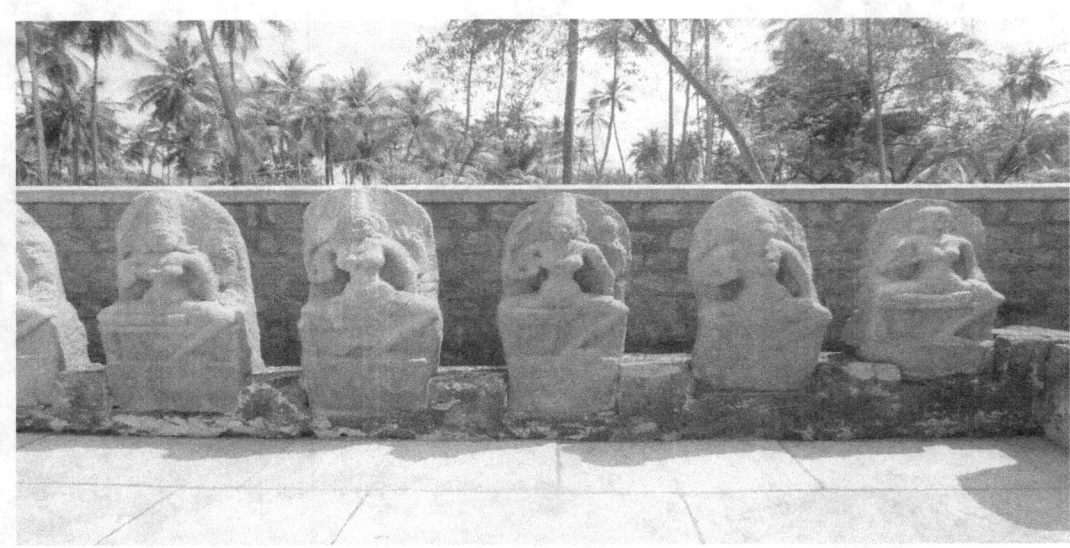

Plate 5-38: Matrikas from Arkeswara Temple Alur

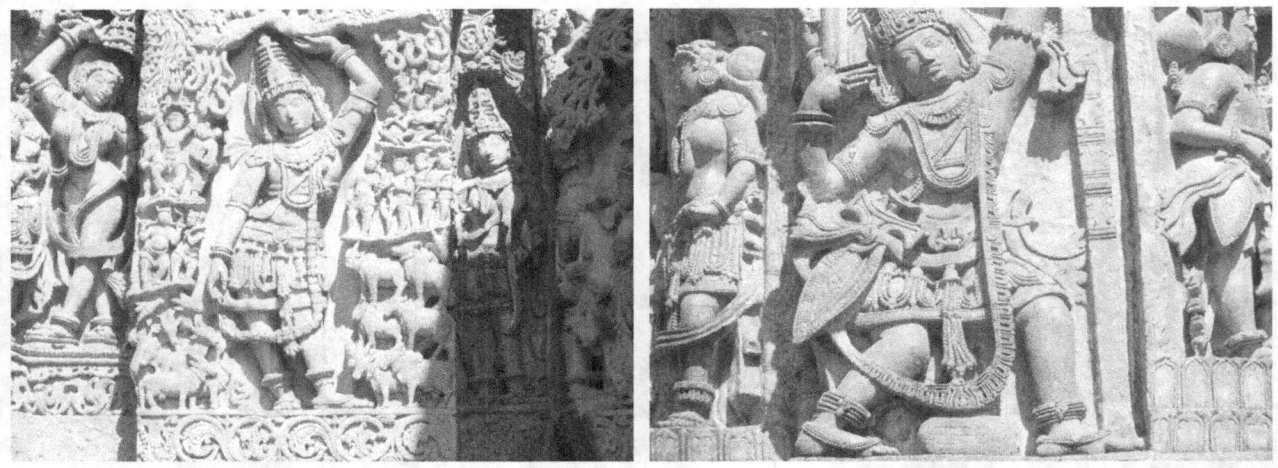

Plate 5-39: Krishna Lifting Mount Govardhana and Arjuna Aiming at the Fish Looking at Reflection in Water

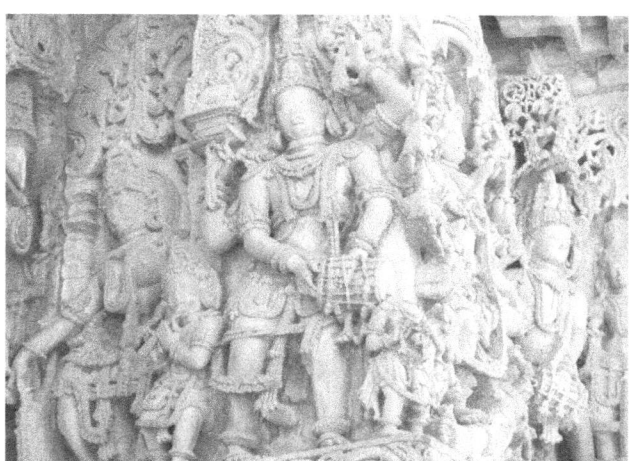 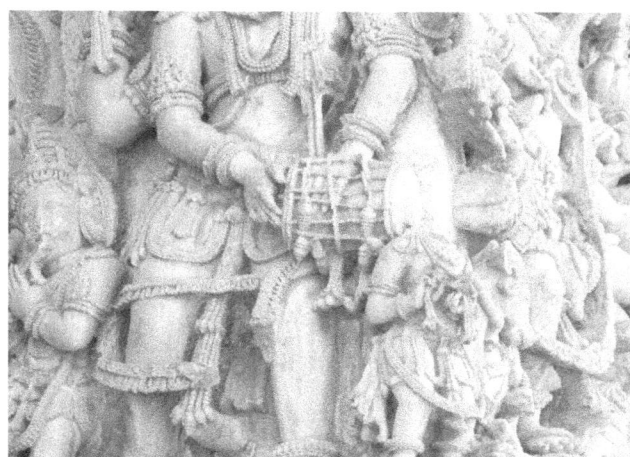

Plate 5-40: Mark the Fingers Running Through the Strings on the Drum

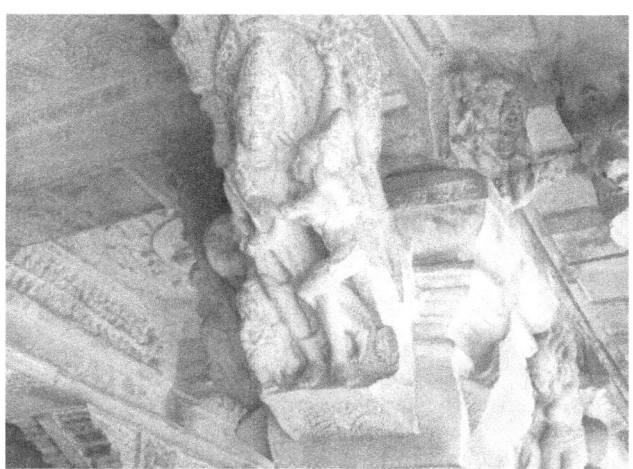 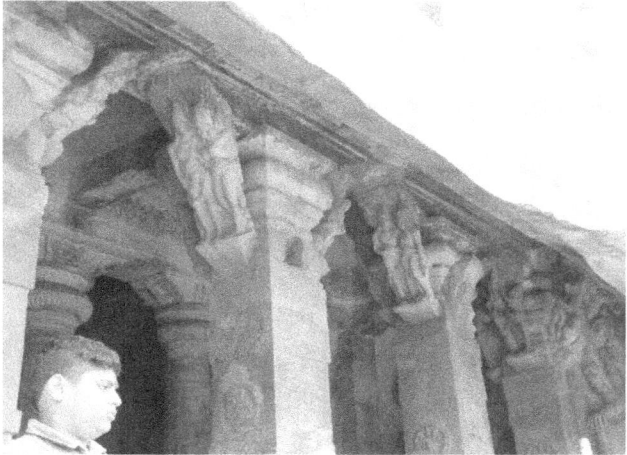

Plate 5-41: Amorous Couples on Column Brackets Cave 3 Badami

PICTURES FOR CHAPTER 6

Plate 6-1:	Madhukeswara Temple Banavasi and Trailokya Mandapa on the Left of Garbhagriha	349
Plate 6-2:	Tripurakanteswara Temple Balligavi	349
Plate 6-3:	Kedareswara Temple Balligavi and Hanumana Image from Balligavi Museum	350
Plate 6-4:	Panchatantra Tales and Erotic Images in Friezes on Adisthana of Tripurakanteswara Temple Balligavi	350
Plate 6-5:	Shantinatha Basadi Bandalike	351
Plate 6-6:	Trimurti Narayana Temple Bandalike	351
Plate 6-7:	Harihareswara Temple and Mahishasuramardini Templee at Harihar	352
Plate 6-8:	Santeswara Temple Tilvalli	352
Plate 6-9:	Trikuteswara Temple Gadag	352
Plate 6-10:	Saraswati Temple Gadag and its Ornate Pillars	353
Plate 6-11:	Brahma Jinalaya Lakkundi	353
Plate 6-12:	Kasi Visveswara Temple Lakkundi	354
Plate 6-13:	Nanneswara Temple Lakkundi	354
Plate 6-14:	Manikeswara Temple and Mallikarjuna Temple at Lakkundi	354
Plate 6-15:	Naga-Nagini Entwined in Dvarasakhas at Dodda Basappa Temple Dambal	355
Plate 6-16:	Dodda Basappa Temple Dambal Makaratorana in front of Antarala and Garbhagriha, Nandi, Entrance Gate and Ornate Pillar Base (Night Pictures)	355
Plate 6-17:	Someswara Temple Lakshmeshwar	356
Plate 6-18:	Kalleswara Temple Bagali	356
Plate 6-19:	Kalleswara Temple Bagali Doorway to Gudhamandapa Guarded by Rati and Kamadeva	356
Plate 6-20:	Closed Mandapa, Antarala and Garbhagriha of Kalleswara Temple Bagali	357
Plate 6-21:	Mallikarjuna Temple Sudi (Under Restoration)	357
Plate 6-22:	Jodu Kalasa Gudi Sudi	358
Plate 6-23:	Vimana of Galgeswara Temple at Galaganatha	358
Plate 6-24:	Garbhagriha and Antarala Doorway with Perforated Screens on Sides and Torana on the Lintel, Someswara Temple Haralhalli	359
Plate 6-25:	Vimanas of the Trikuta Someswara Temple Haralhalli	359
Plate 6-26:	Ornate Doorway and Torana in front of Antarala Mallikarjuna Temple Kuruvatti	360
Plate 6-27:	Mallikarjuna Temple Kuruvatti	360
Plate 6-28:	Mukteswara Temple Chaudayyadanapura	361
Plate 6-29:	Pataleswara Temple and Maraleswara Temple at Talakad	361
Plate 6-30:	Kirtinarayana Temple Talakad	361

Plate 6-31:	Vaidyeswara Temple Talakad	362
Plate 6-32:	Alemalamma Temple and Janardana Temple at Tadimalangi	362
Plate 6-33:	Three Sides of Vimana and Adisthana with Pranala of Rameswara Temple Narasamangala	363
Plate 6-34:	Sculptures at Rameswara Temple Narasamangala	363
Plate 6-35:	Navaranga Ceiling Rameswara Temple Narasamangala	364
Plate 6-36:	Tandaveswara Surrounded by Ashtadikpalas Navaranga Ceiling Arkeswara Temple Alur	364
Plate 6-37:	Battle Scene Carved on Navaranga Pillar Arkeswara Temple Alur	365
Plate 6-38:	Siva as Kaphaka on Bull Pedestal Alur	365
Plate 6-39:	Door Panels of the Arkeswara Temple Entrance, Alur	366
Plate 6-40:	Kesava Temple Somanathapura Main Entrance	366
Plate 6-41:	Images of Varaha and Visnu Seated on Sesha Somanathapura	367
Plate 6-42:	Domical Ceiling and Visnu with Lakshmi Seated on His Lap, Somanathapura	367
Plate 6-43:	Saraswati Holding Veena and Book in Her Hands, Somanathapura	368
Plate 6-44:	Virupaksha Temple at Pattadakal	368
Plate 6-45:	Sculpture on the Walls of Mandapa and Garbhagriha, Virupaksha Temple	369
Plate 6-46:	Mallikarajuna Temple Pattadakal	369
Plate 6-47:	Galaganatha Temple Pattadakal	370
Plate 6-48:	Sangameswara Temple Pattadakal	370
Plate 6-49:	Jambulinga Temple Pattadakal	371
Plate 6-50:	Durga Temple Aihole	371
Plate 6-51:	Jyotirlinga Complex of Temples Aihole	371
Plate 6-52:	Ladkhan Temple Aihole	372
Plate 6-53:	Ambigeragudi Aihole	372
Plate 6-54:	Huchapayya Matha and Hucchimalligudi Aihole	373
Plate 6-55:	Triambakeswara Complex Aihole	373
Plate 6-56:	Ganesha and Nandi Pavilion in Front of Mahakuteswara Temple, Mahakuta	374
Plate 6-57:	Sangameswara Temple Mahakuta	374
Plate 6-58:	Chaumukha Sivslinga under the Mandapa in the Kalyani, Mahakuta	375
Plate 6-59:	Dancing Siva Nataraja Badami Cave 1	375
Plate 6-60:	Nagaraja and Flying Vidyadhara Couple on the Ceiling of Cave 1 Badami	376
Plate 6-61:	Siva and Parvati with Nandi and Bhringi, Cave 1 Badami	376
Plate 6-62:	Fish Spokes Chakra on the Ceiling of Cave 2 Badami	377
Plate 6-63:	Swastikas Joined Together and flying couples in the Corner Panels, Cave 2 Badami	377
Plate 6-64:	Shankaranarayana Cave 3 Badami	378
Plate 6-65:	Narasimha Cave 3 Badami	378
Plate 6-66:	Ceiling Sculpture Cave 3, Visnu Surrounded by Ashtadikpalas in a Circle	379

Plate 6-67:	Amorous Couples on Column Brackets Cave 3 Badami	379
Plate 6-68:	Bahubali with Creepers and Snakes Entwined Around his legs Cave 4 Badami	380
Plate 6-69:	Parsvanatha with Five-hooded Snake Covering His Head, Cave 4 Badami	380
Plate 6-70:	South Entrance of Hoysaleswara Temple Halebid	381
Plate 6-71:	Siva Dancing and Surya on the Outer Walls of Hoysaleswara Temple	381
Plate 6-72:	Makaratorana at the South Entrance of Hoysaleswara Temple Halebid	382
Plate 6-73:	Trivikrama and Goddess Lakshmi Hoysaleswara Temple	382
Plate 6-74:	Hoysaleswara Temple Halebid, Abhimanyu and Chakravyuh	383
Plate 6-75:	Ravana Shaking Mount Kailasa, Hoysaleswara Temple	383
Plate 6-76:	Complete Side View of Kedareswara Temple Halebid	384
Plate 6-77:	Inside Kedareswara Temple, 32 Pointed Stellate Pillar and Navaranga Ceiling	384
Plate 6-78:	Ranganathaswamy Temple Halebid Entrance	384
Plate 6-79:	Image of Ranganathaswamy, Halebid	385
Plate 6-80:	Makaratorana with Narasimha Riding on Garuda's Shoulders, Chennakesava Temple Entrance Belur	385
Plate 6-81:	Garuda and Hanumana Attending on Visnu and Lakshmi, Carving on Perforated Window	386
Plate 6-82:	Eight Armed Visnu Seated Under the Eave, Chennakesava Temple Belur	386
Plate 6-83:	Complete View of the Entrance, Chennakesava Temple Belur	387
Plate 6-84:	King and Queen with Their Retinue on Perforated Window and Darpanasundari on Column Bracket, Belur	387
Plate 6-85:	Madanikas With the Drum and Mirror in Hand, Belur	388
Plate 6-86:	Krishna Playing Flute on Both Sides of Visnu-Lakshmi Sculpture, Andal Temple Belur	388
Plate 6-87:	Veeranarayana Temple Belavadi	389
Plate 6-88:	Open Hall with 37 Bays and Lathe-turned Pillars Belavadi	389
Plate 6-89:	Ceiling of Navaranga with Krishna Playing Flute and Surrounded by Gopikas and Cows, Belavadi	390
Plate 6-90:	Goddess Kali Lakshmidevi Temple Doddagadavalli	390
Plate 6-91:	Lakshmidevi Shrine Doddagadavalli	391
Plate 6-92:	Lakshmidevi Chatushkuta Temple, Doddagadavalli	391
Plate 6-93:	Three Different Sculptures of Garuda from Chennakesava Temple Mosale	392
Plate 6-94:	Sikharas of Nageswara and Chennakesava Temples Mosale	392
Plate 6-95:	Lakshmi Narasimha Temple Javagal	392
Plate 6-96:	Gavi Gangadhareswara Temple Gavipuram	393
Plate 6-97:	Chokkaperumal Temple Domlur	393
Plate 6-98:	Kashi vishwanatha Temple Kadugodi	393
Plate 6-99:	Dakshinamurthy and Kalabhairava Images, Kashi Vishwanatha Temple Kadugodi	394
Plate 6-100:	Chennakesava Temple Chikkajala (Renovated)	394

Plate 6-101:	Muktinatheswara Temple Binnamangala	394
Plate 6-102:	Kulothunga Chola Image and Temple Wall Sculpture, Binnamangala	395
Plate 6-103:	Gateway Pilasters and Inscription Champakadhamaswamy Temple Bannerghatta	395
Plate 6-104:	Ramanujacharya and Alwars, Champakadhamaswamy Temple Bannerghatta	395
Plate 6-105:	Hulimavu Temple	396
Plate 6-106:	Kapileswara and Someswara Temples, Manne	396
Plate 6-107:	Akka Tangi Temple Manne	396
Plate 6-108:	Nagareswara Temple Begur	397
Plate 6-109:	Nageswara Temple Begur	397
Plate 6-110:	Someswara Temple Madivala Bengaluru	398
Plate 6-111:	Someswara Temple Agara Bengaluru	398
Plate 6-112:	Varadaraja Temple Vagata and Inscriptions Outside Temple	399
Plate 6-113:	Chowdeswari Temple Vagata	399
Plate 6-114:	Images of Saptamatrikas in the Garbhagriha Chowdeswari Temple Vagata	400

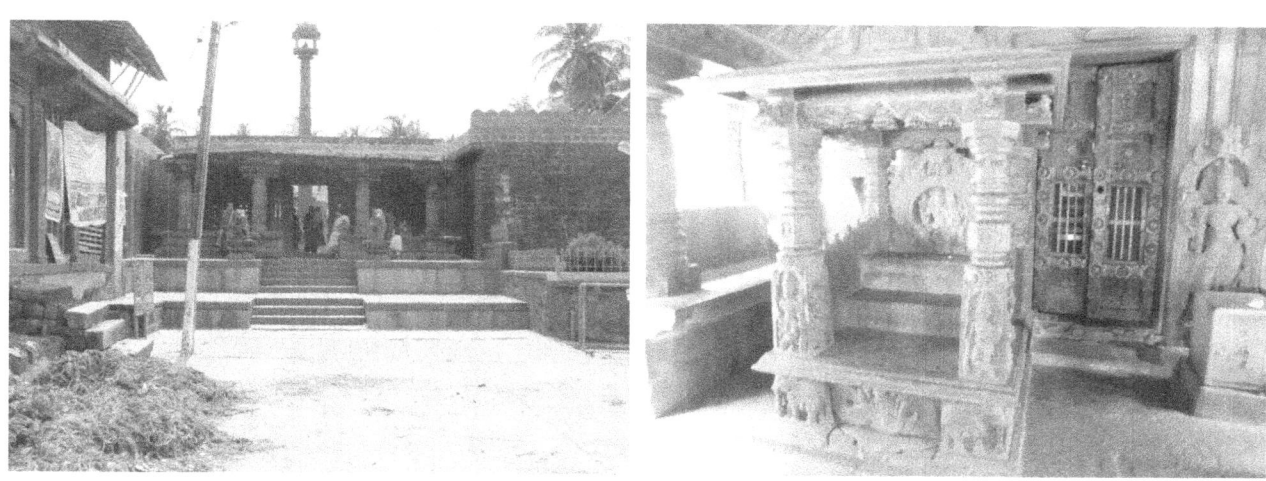

Plate 6-1: Madhukeswara Temple Banavasi and Trailokya Mandapa on the Left of Garbhagriha

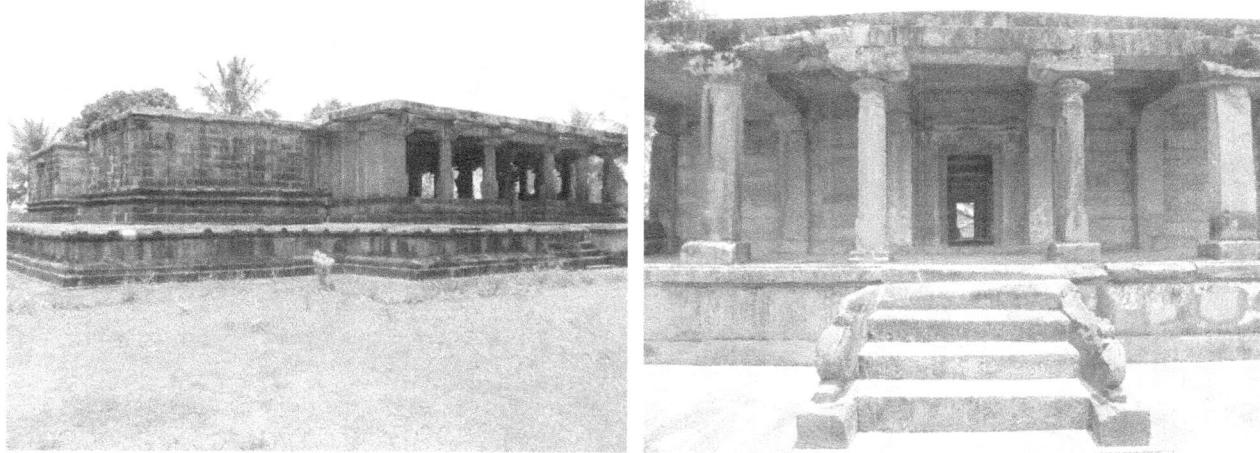

Plate 6-2: Tripurakanteswara Temple Balligavi

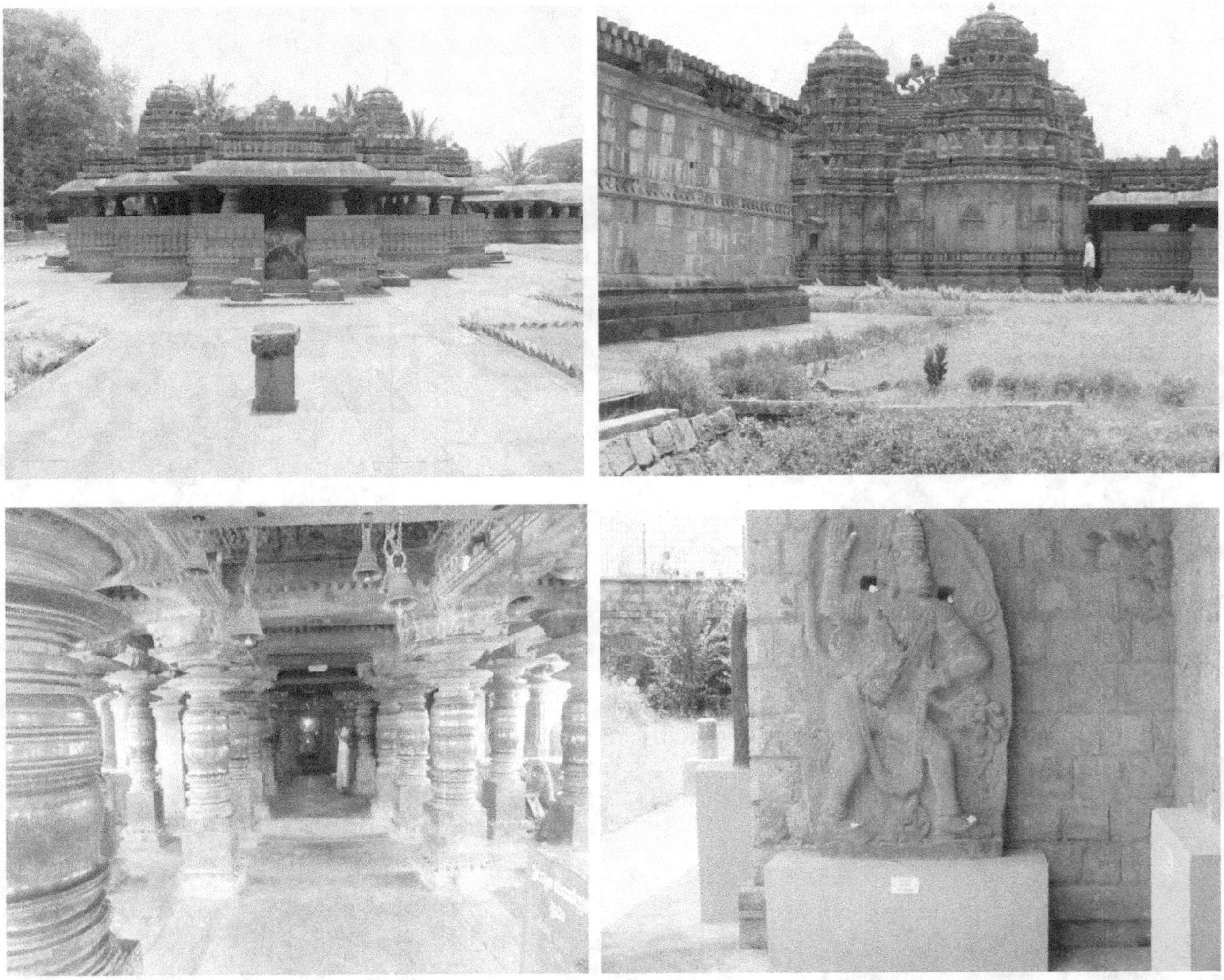

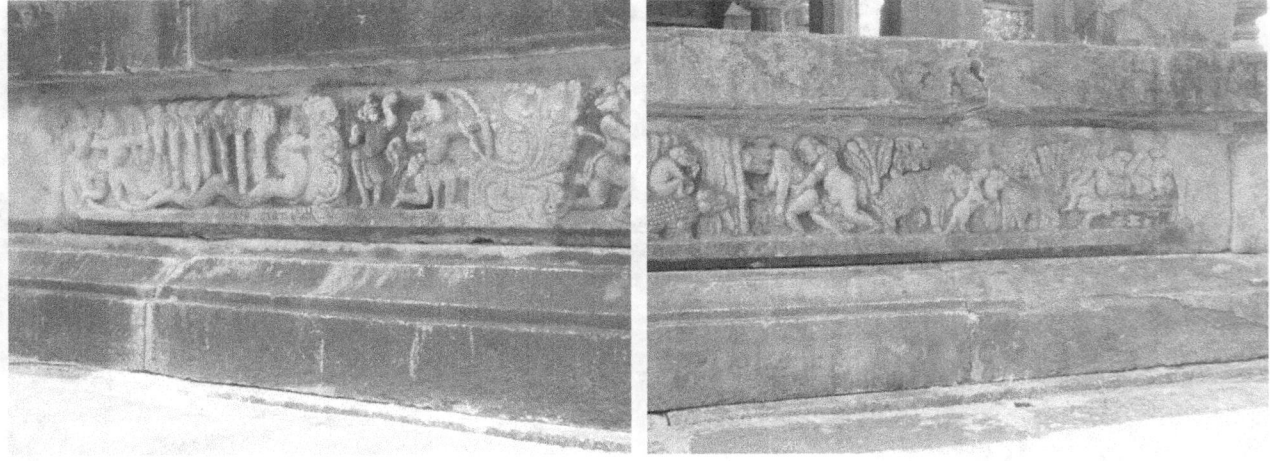

Plate 6-3: Kedareswara Temple Balligavi and Hanumana Image from Balligavi Museum

Plate 6-4: Panchatantra Tales and Erotic Images in Friezes on Adisthana of Tripurakanteswara Temple Balligavi

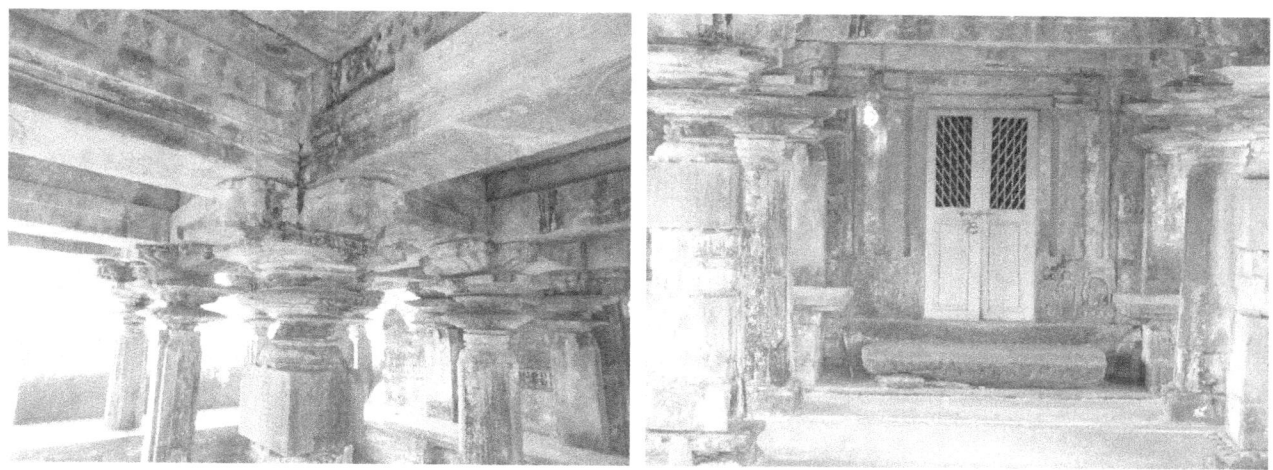

Plate 6-5: Shantinatha Basadi Bandalike

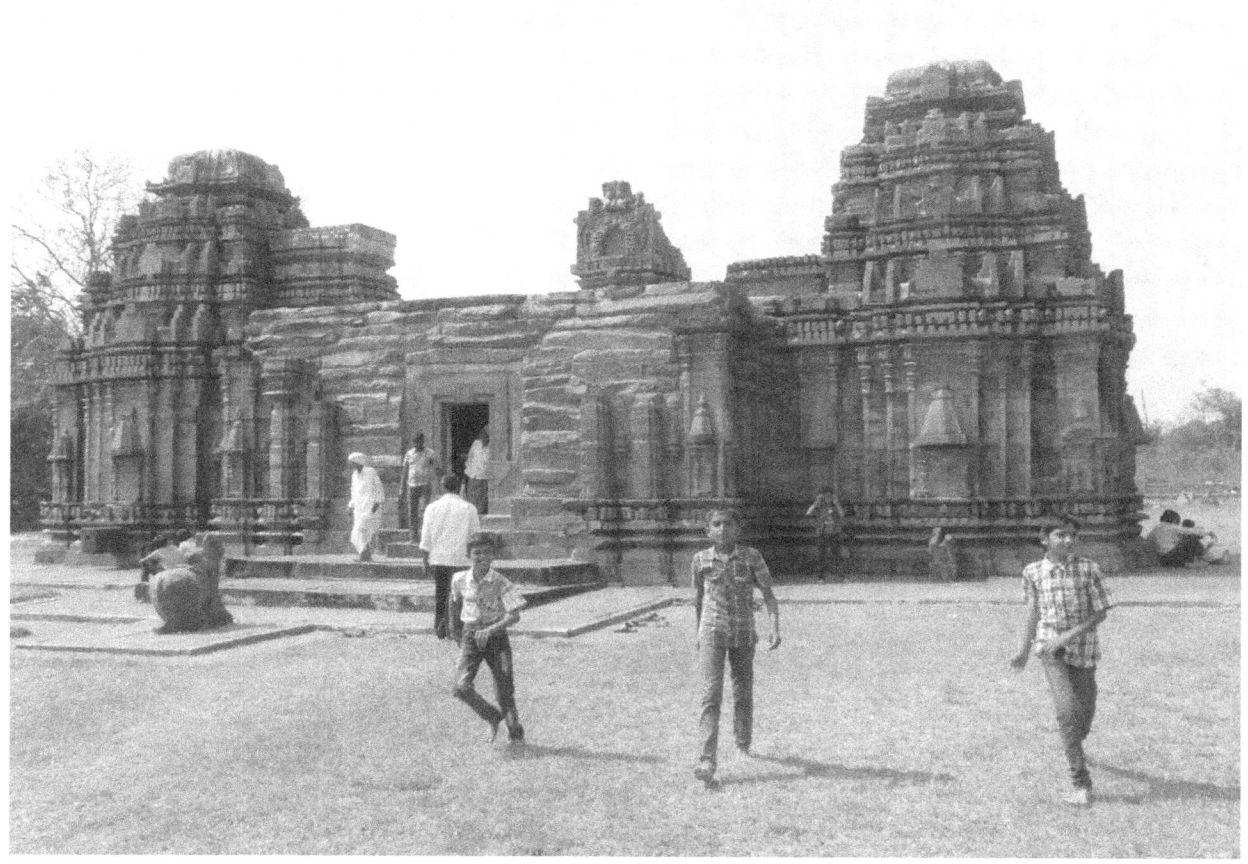

Plate 6-6: Trimurti Narayana Temple Bandalike

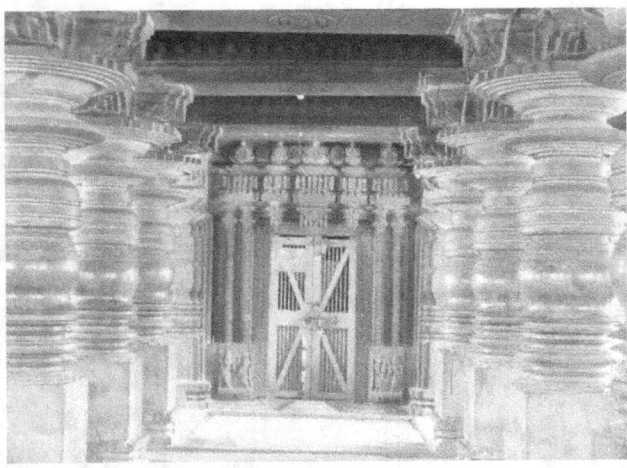 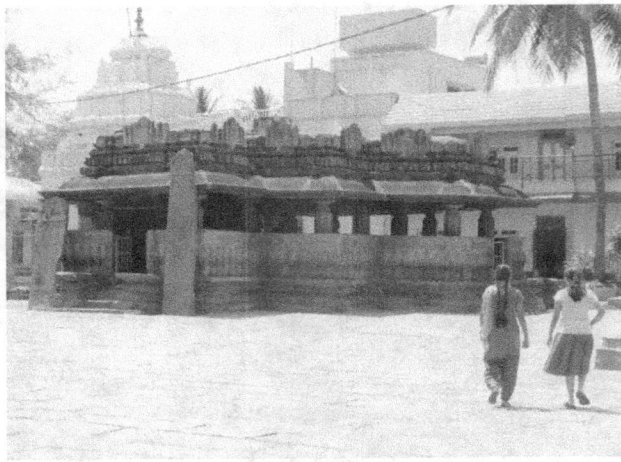

Plate 6-7: Harihareswara Temple and Mahishasuramardini Templee at Harihar

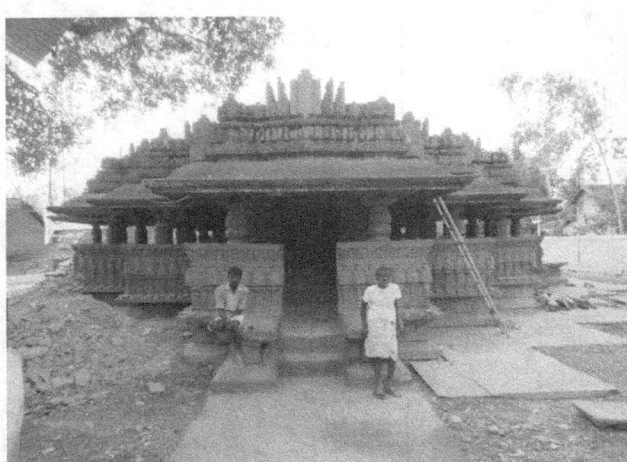 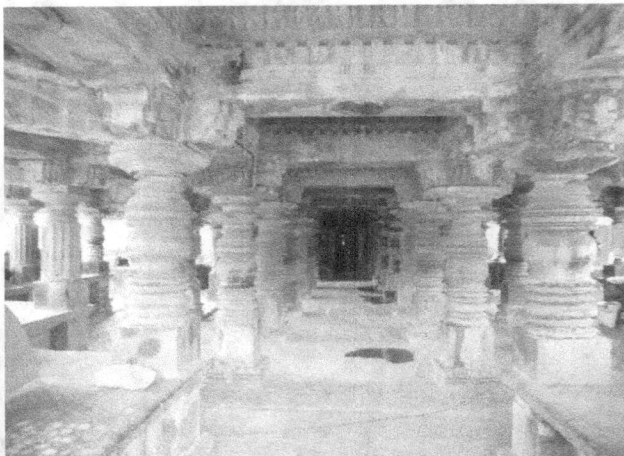

Plate 6-8: Santeswara Temple Tilvalli

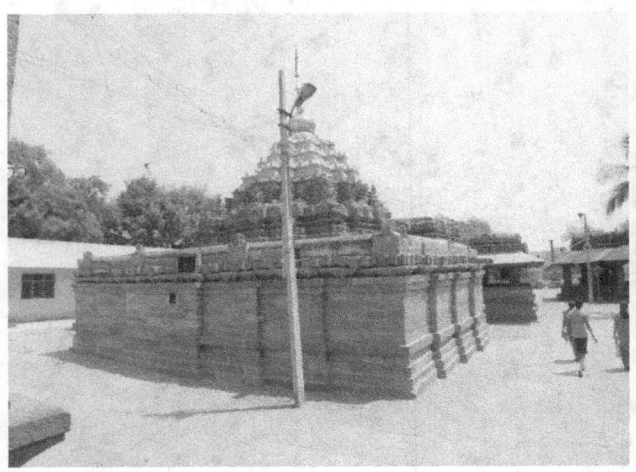 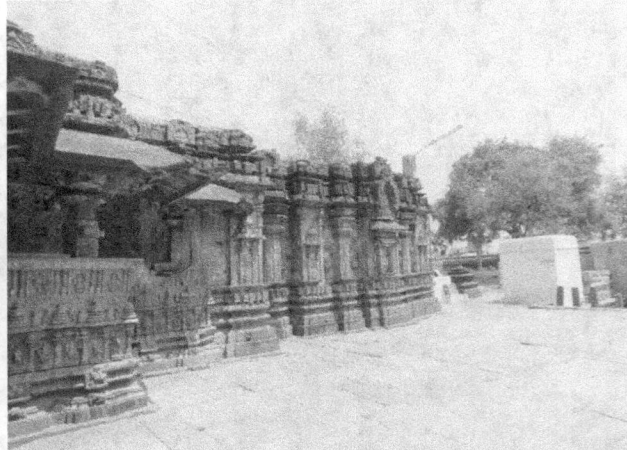

Plate 6-9: Trikuteswara Temple Gadag

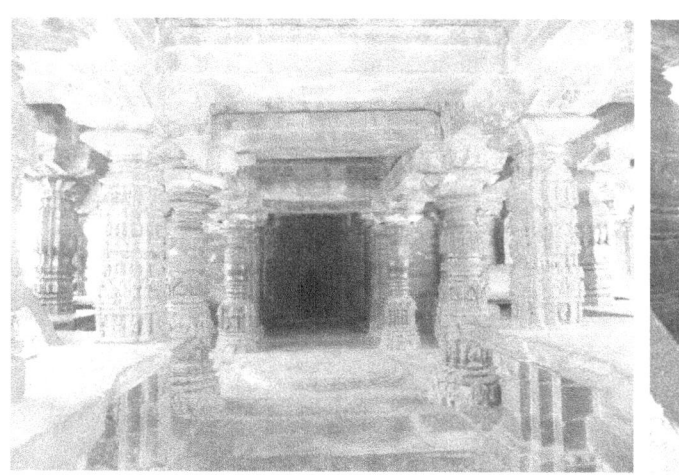
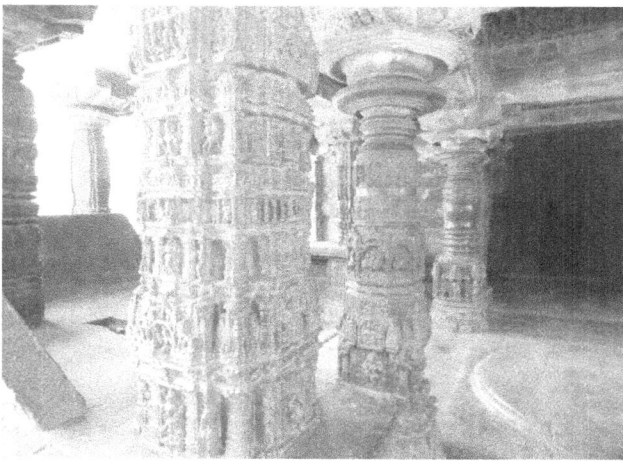

Plate 6-10: Saraswati Temple Gadag and its Ornate Pillars

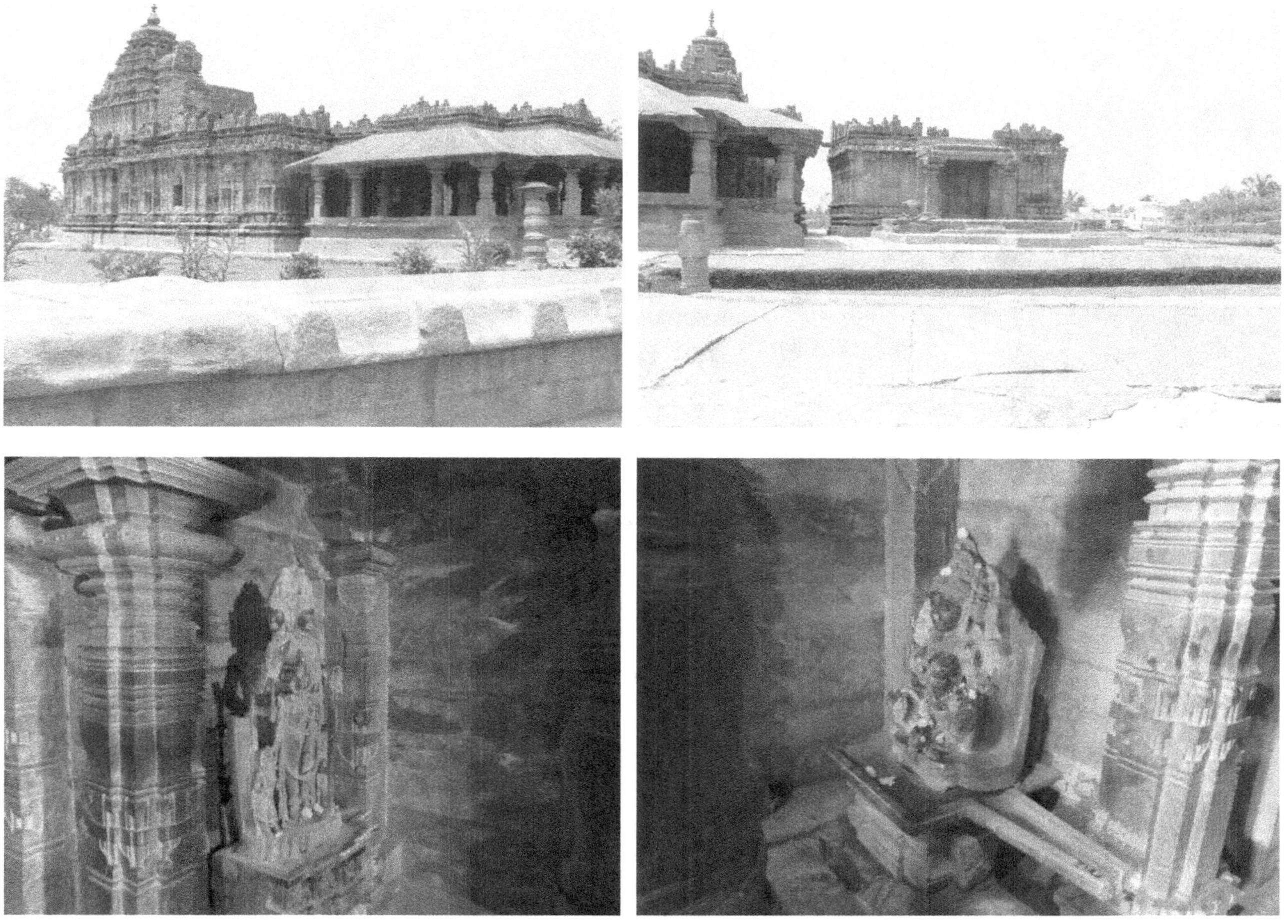

Plate 6-11: Brahma Jinalaya Lakkundi

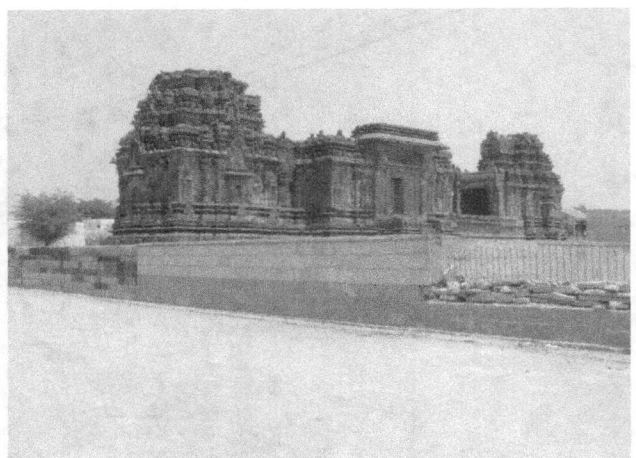 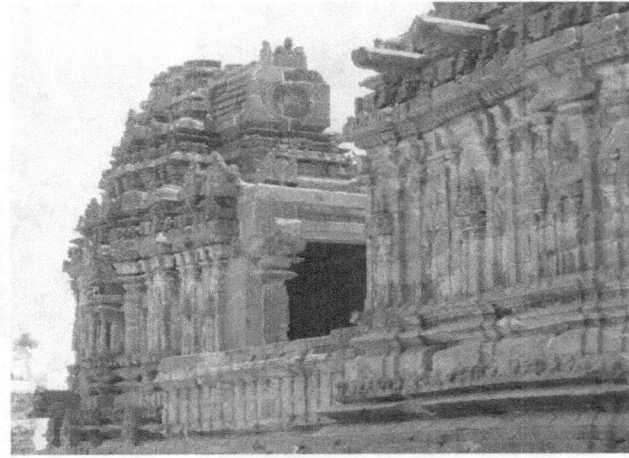

Plate 6-12: Kasi Visveswara Temple Lakkundi

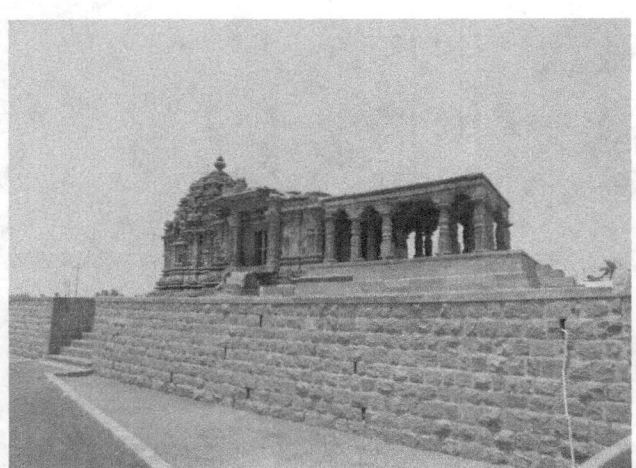 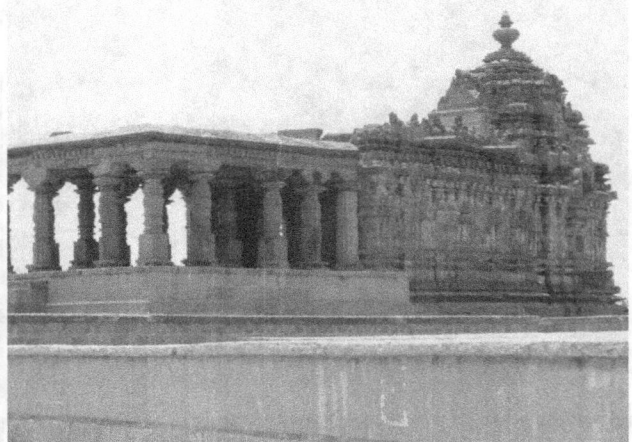

Plate 6-13: Nanneswara Temple Lakkundi

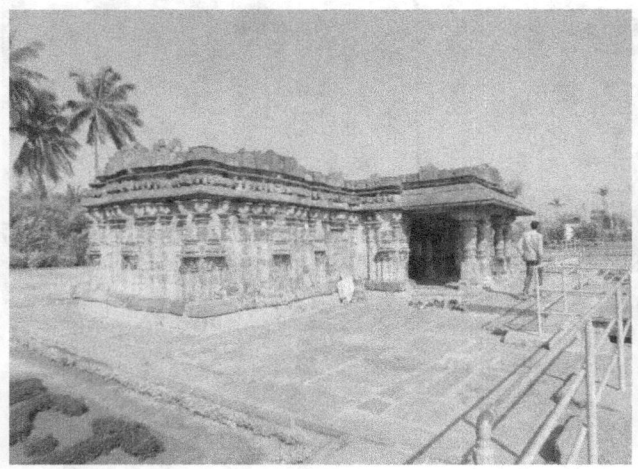 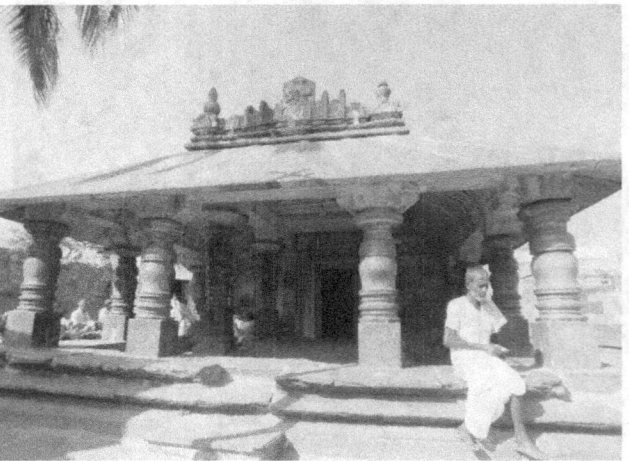

Plate 6-14: Manikeswara Temple and Mallikarjuna Temple at Lakkundi

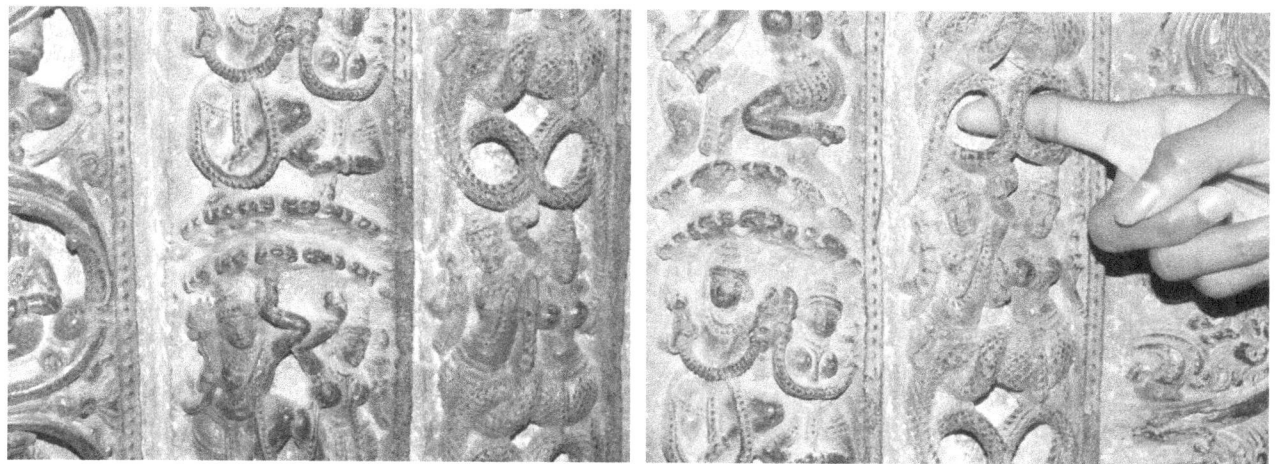

Plate 6-15: Naga-Nagini Entwined in Dvarasakhas at Dodda Basappa Temple Dambal

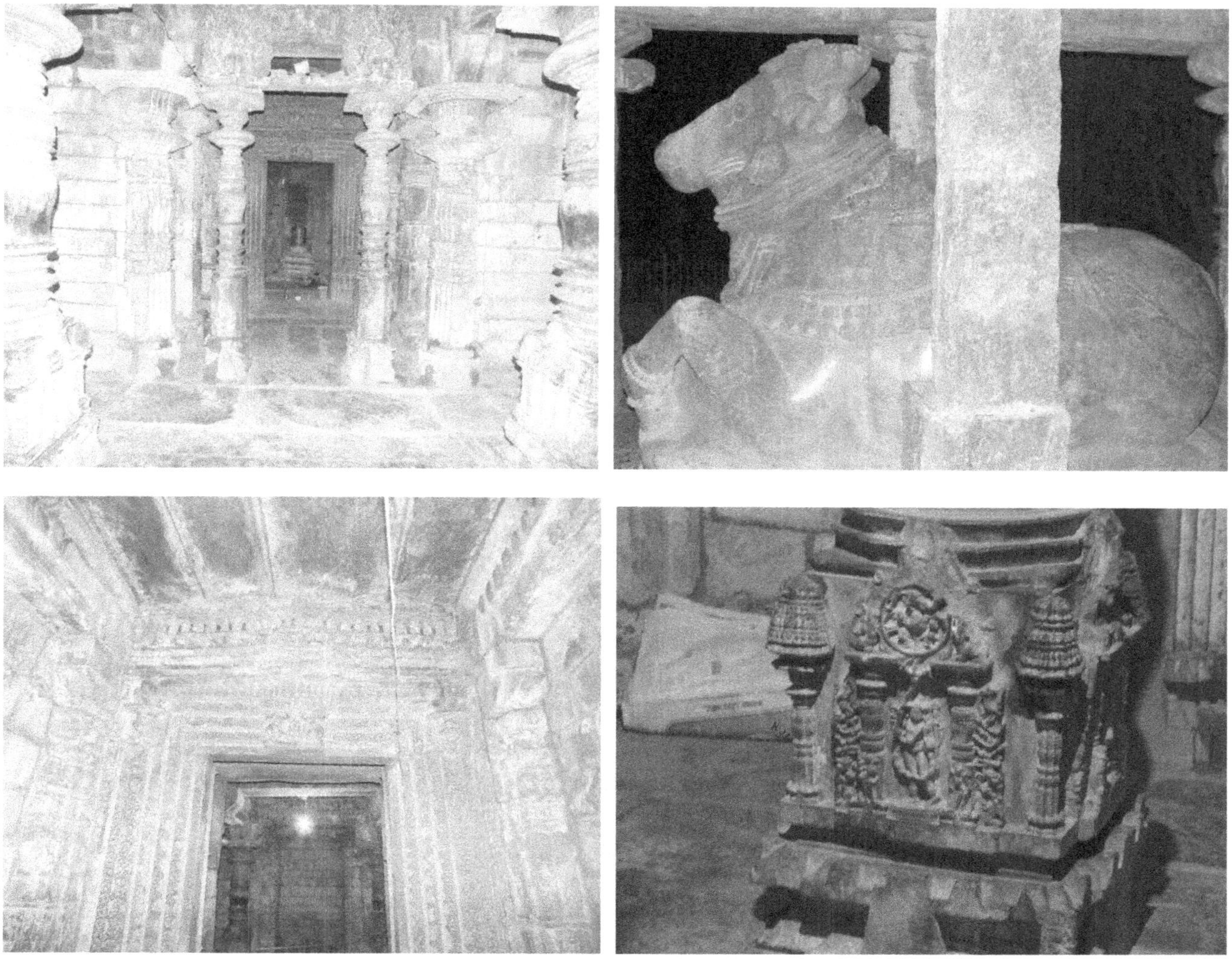

Plate 6-16: Dodda Basappa Temple Dambal Makaratorana in front of Antarala and Garbhagriha, Nandi, Entrance Gate and Ornate Pillar Base (Night Pictures)

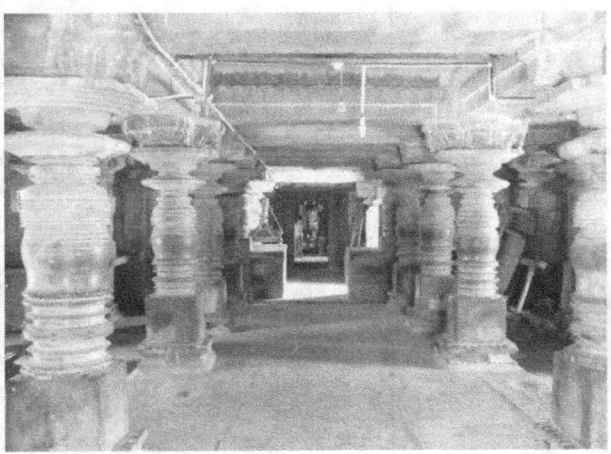 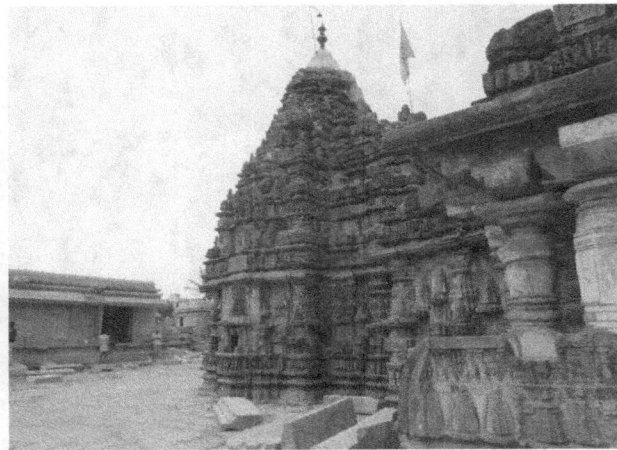

Plate 6-17: Someswara Temple Lakshmeshwar

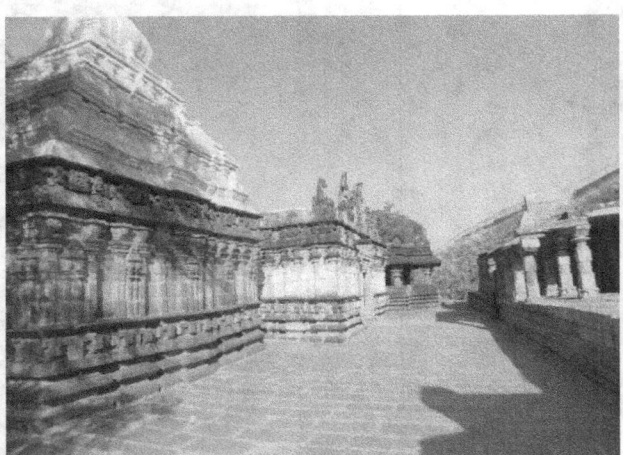 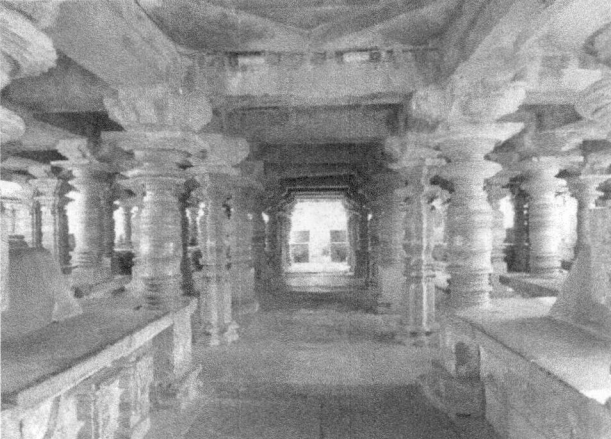

Plate 6-18: Kalleswara Temple Bagali

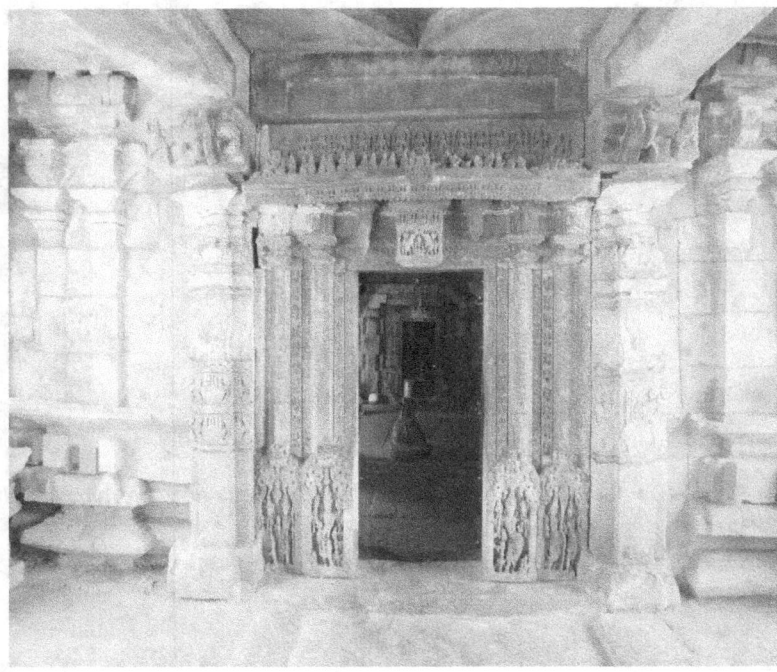

Plate 6-19: Kalleswara Temple Bagali Doorway to Gudhamandapa Guarded by Rati and Kamadeva

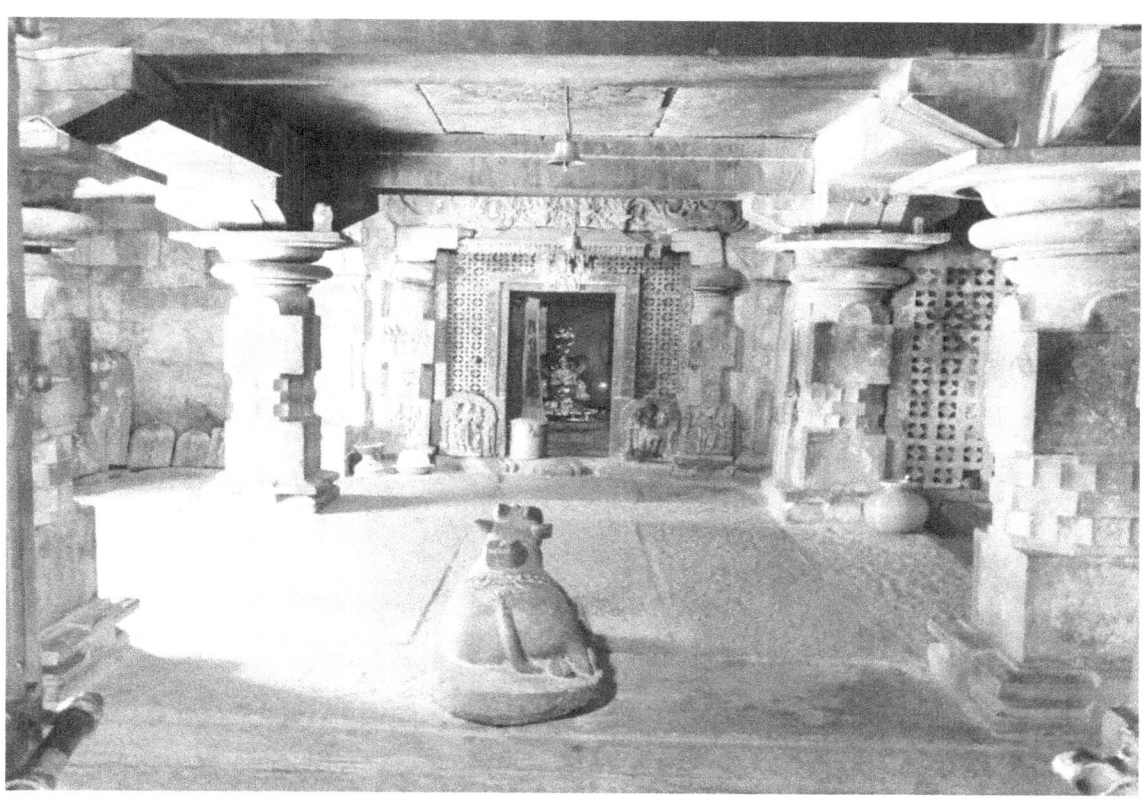

Plate 6-20: Closed Mandapa, Antarala and Garbhagriha of Kalleswara Temple Bagali

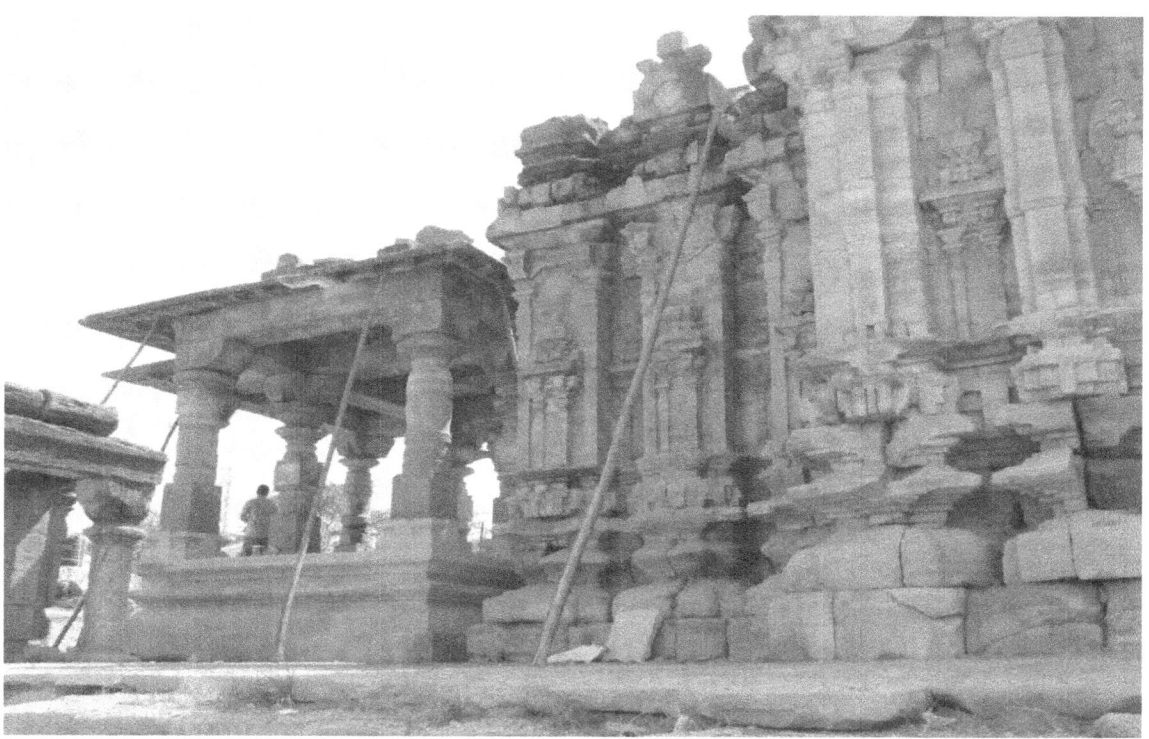

Plate 6-21: Mallikarjuna Temple Sudi (Under Restoration)

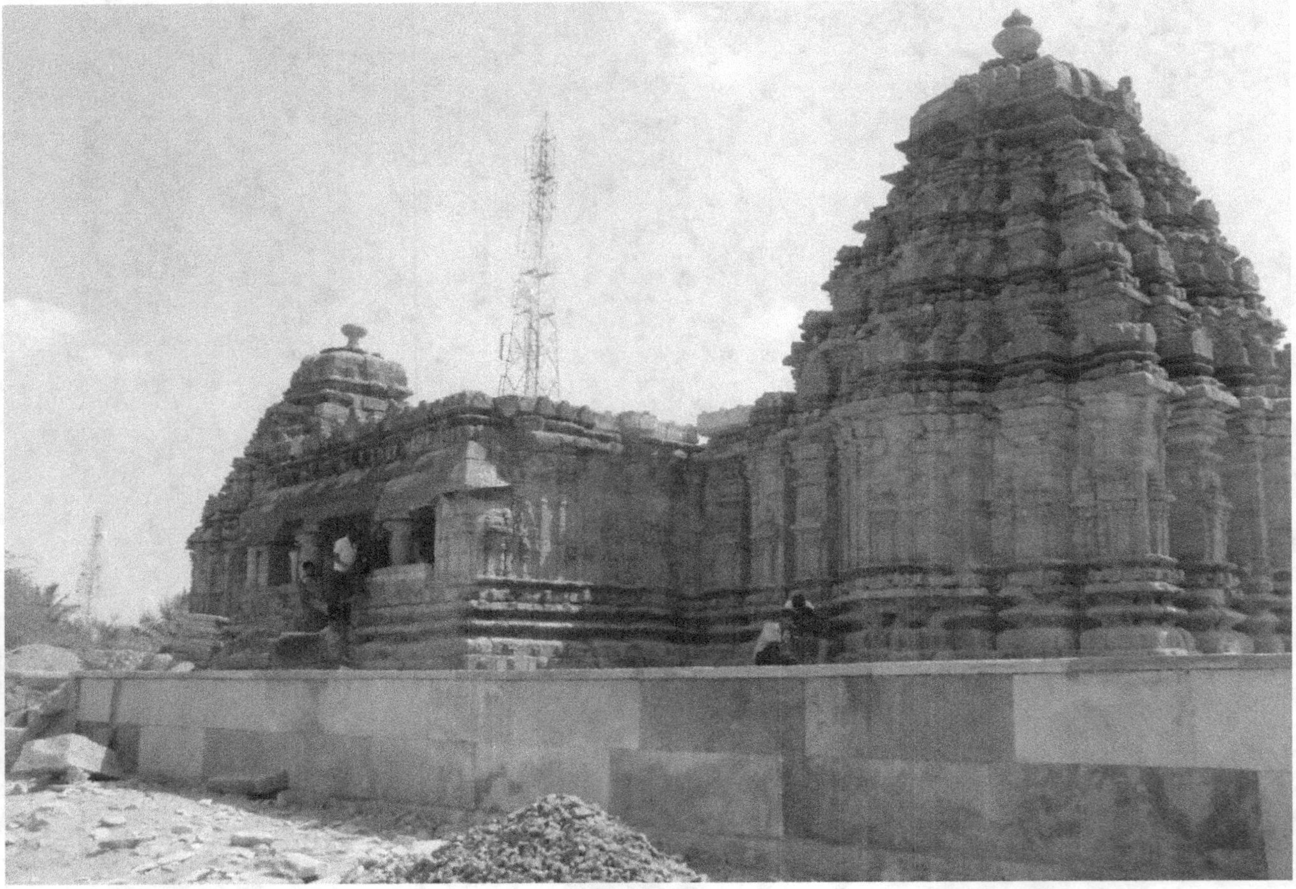

Plate 6-22: Jodu Kalasa Gudi Sudi

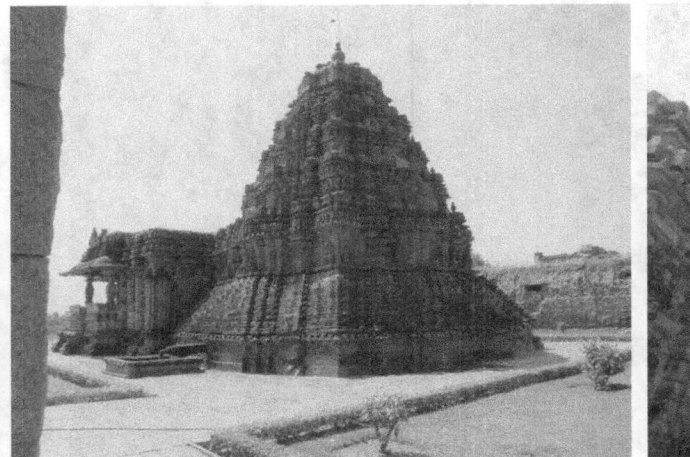
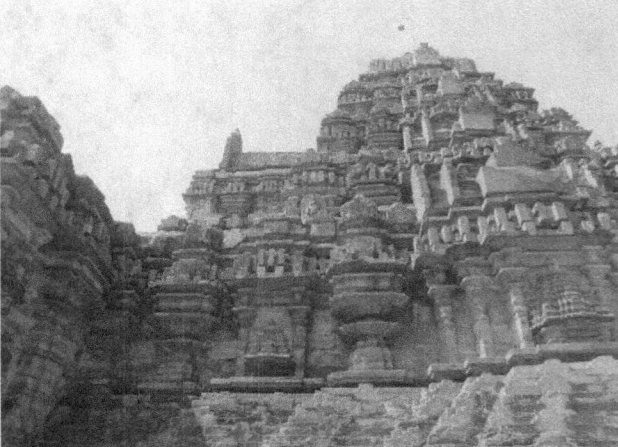

Plate 6-23: Vimana of Galgeswara Temple at Galaganatha

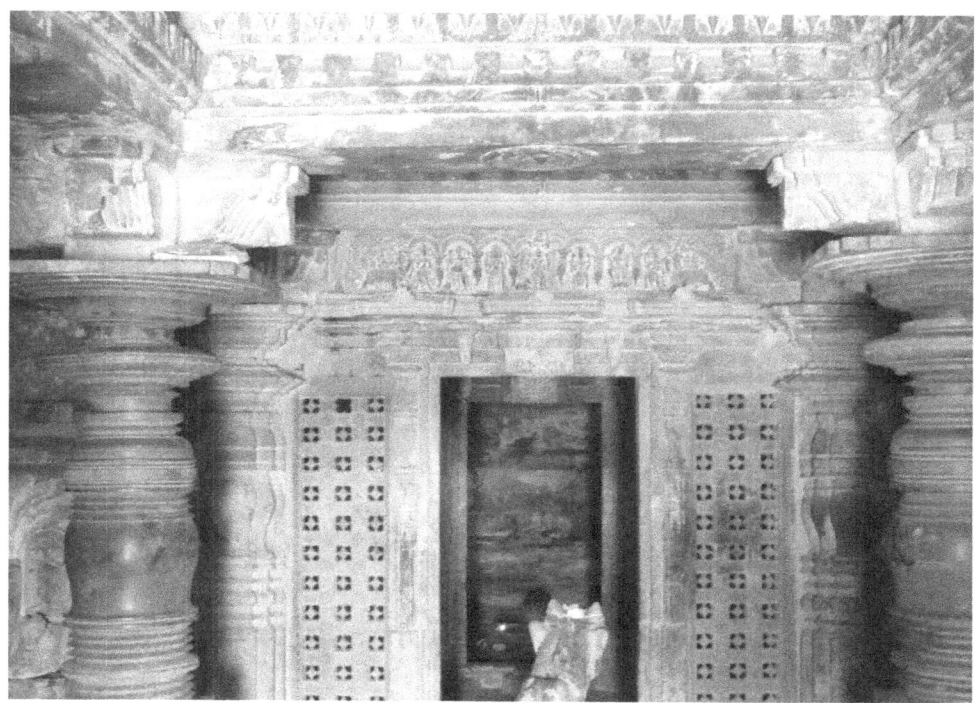

Plate 6-24: Garbhagriha and Antarala Doorway with Perforated Screens on Sides and Torana on the Lintel, Someswara Temple Haralhalli

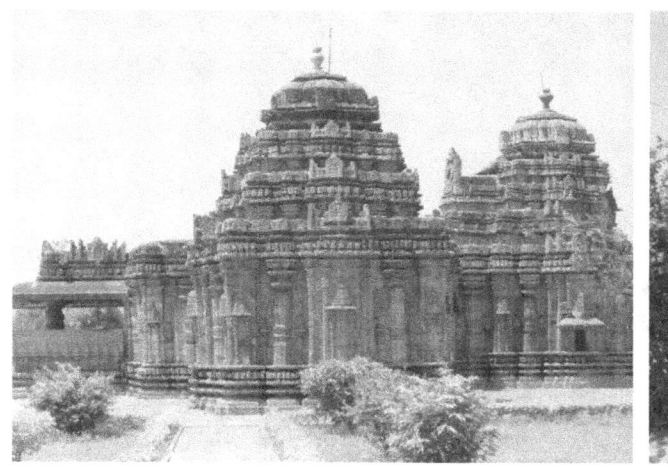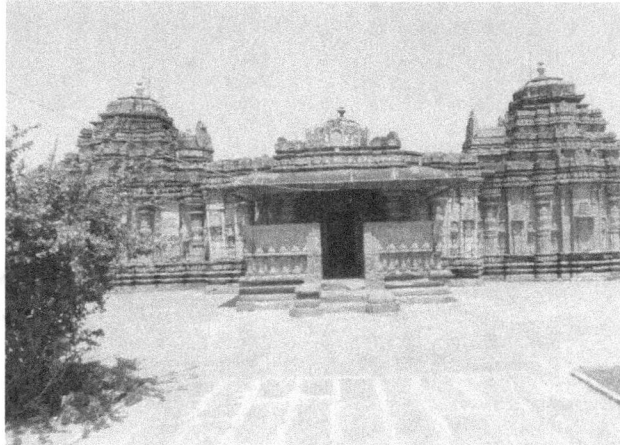

Plate 6-25: Vimanas of the Trikuta Someswara Temple Haralhalli

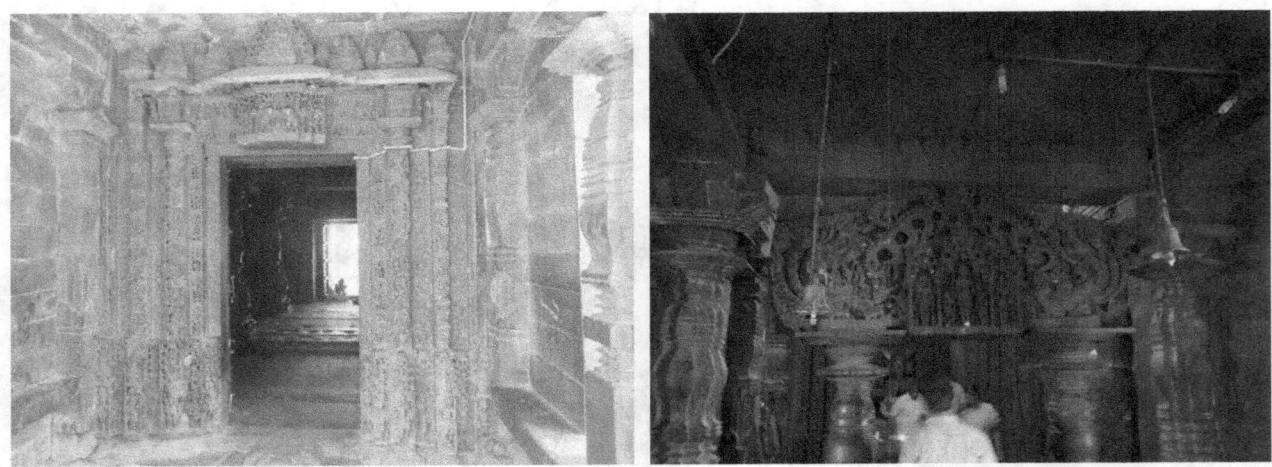

Plate 6-26: Ornate Doorway and Torana in front of Antarala Mallikarjuna Temple Kuruvatti

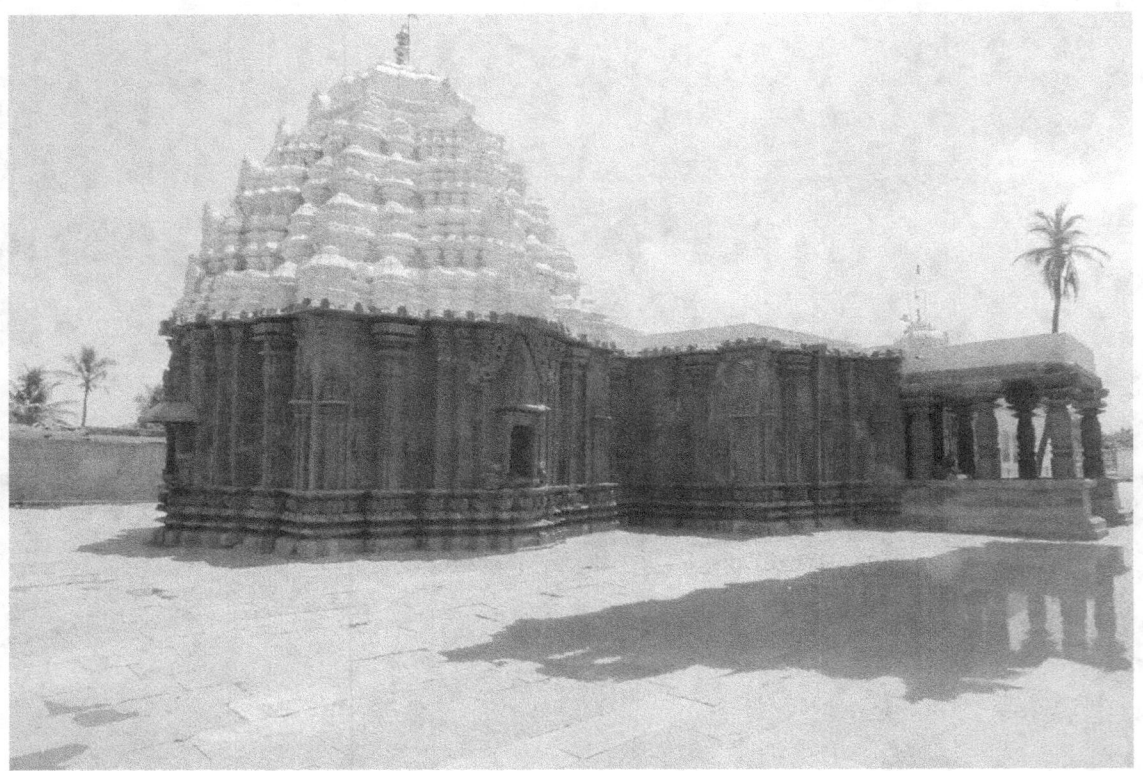

Plate 6-27: Mallikarjuna Temple Kuruvatti

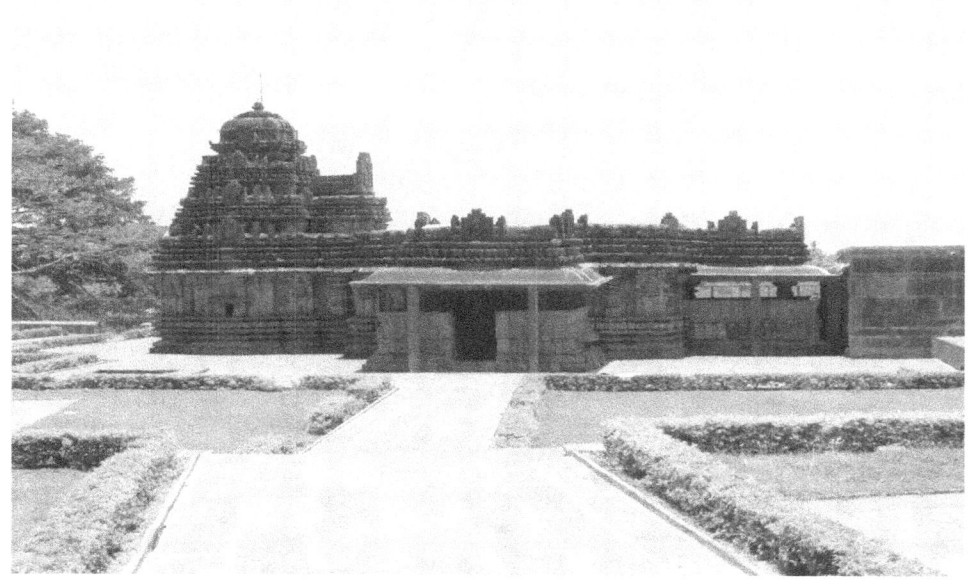

Plate 6-28: Mukteswara Temple Chaudayyadanapura

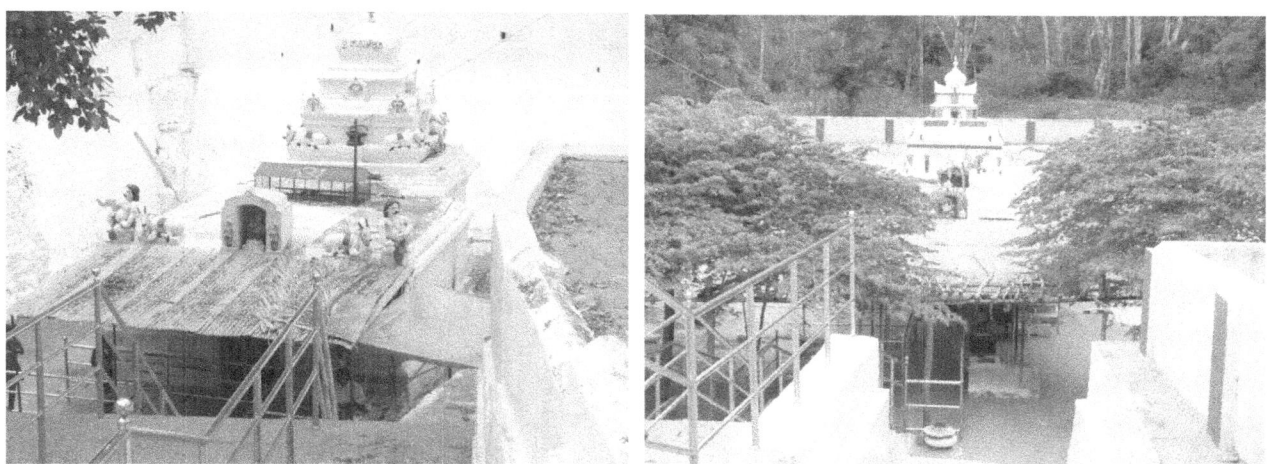

Plate 6-29: Pataleswara Temple and Maraleswara Temple at Talakad

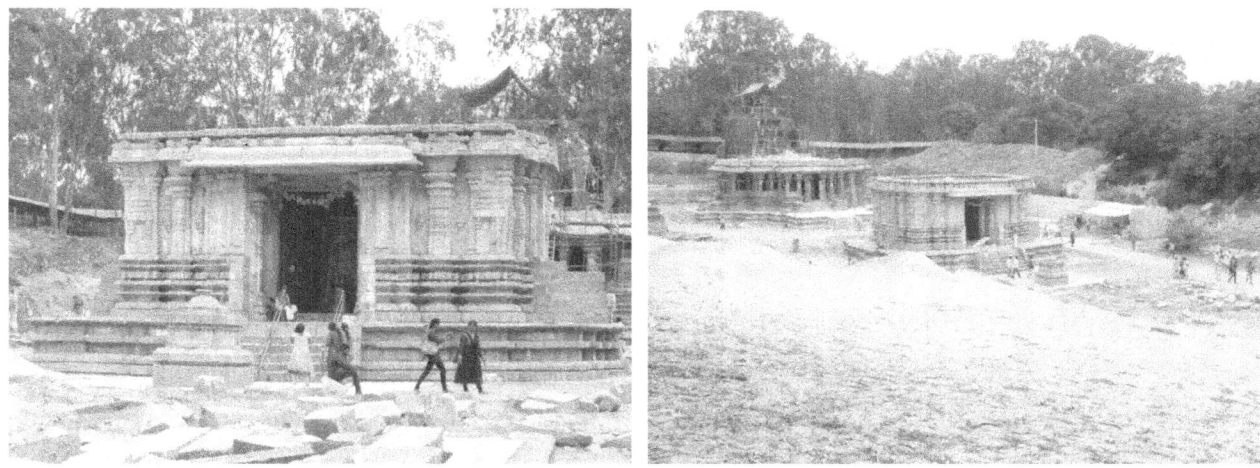

Plate 6-30: Kirtinarayana Temple Talakad

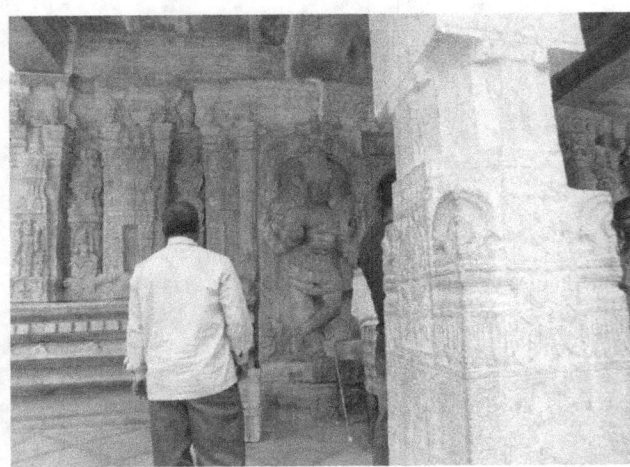 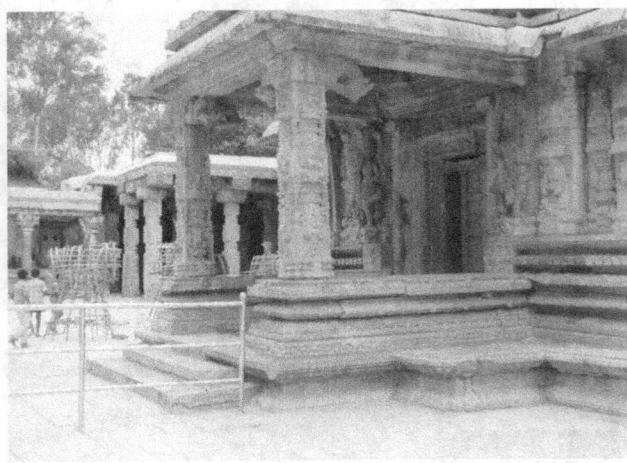

Plate 6-31: Vaidyeswara Temple Talakad

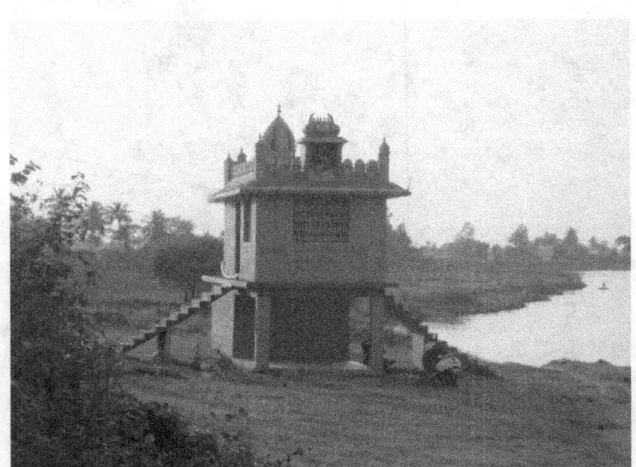 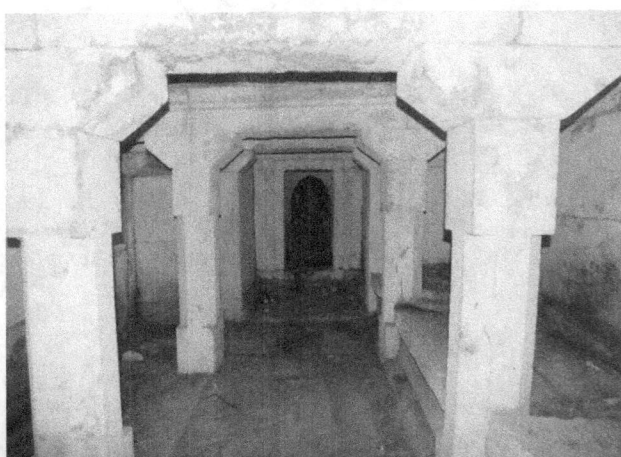

Plate 6-32: Alemalamma Temple and Janardana Temple at Tadimalangi

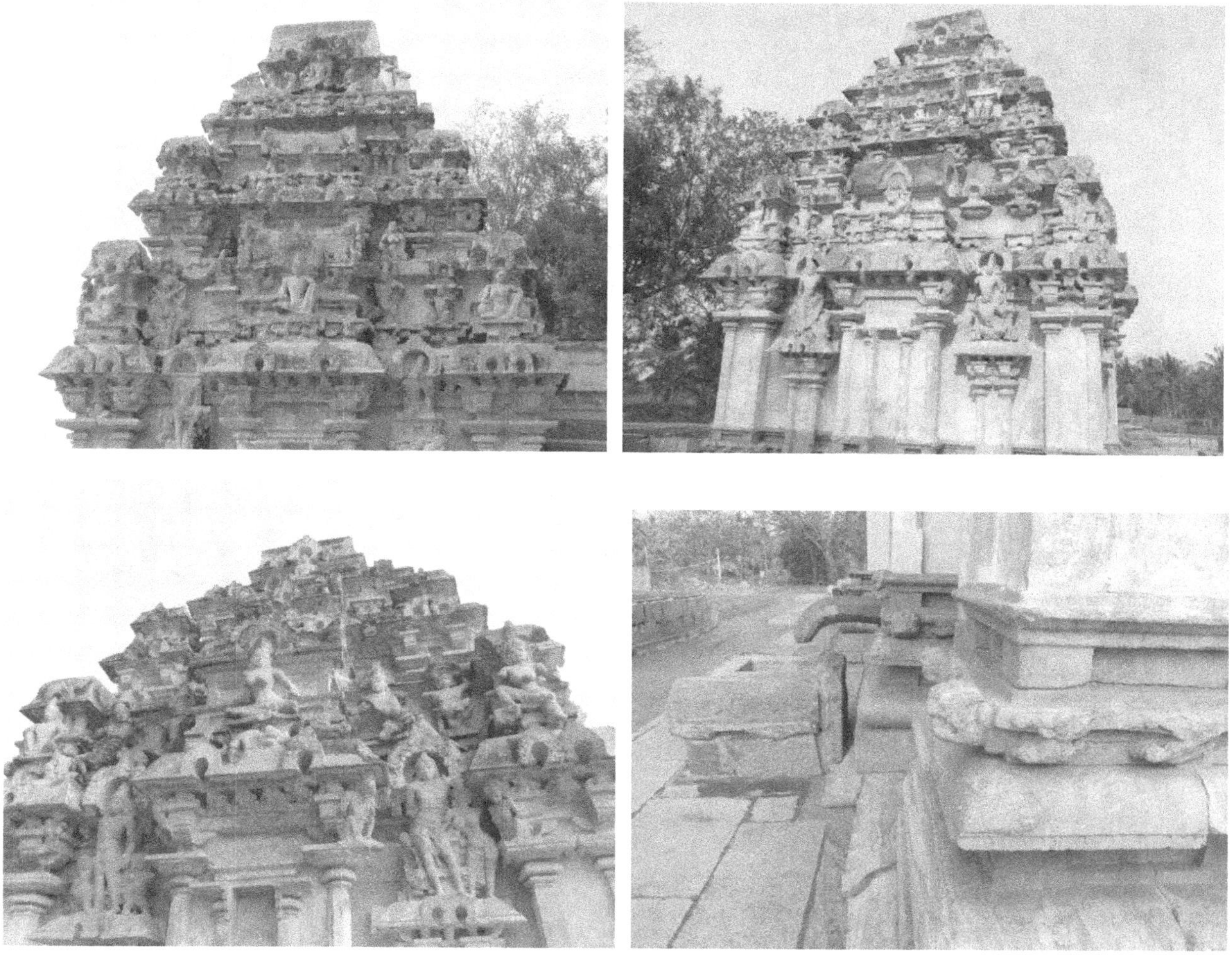

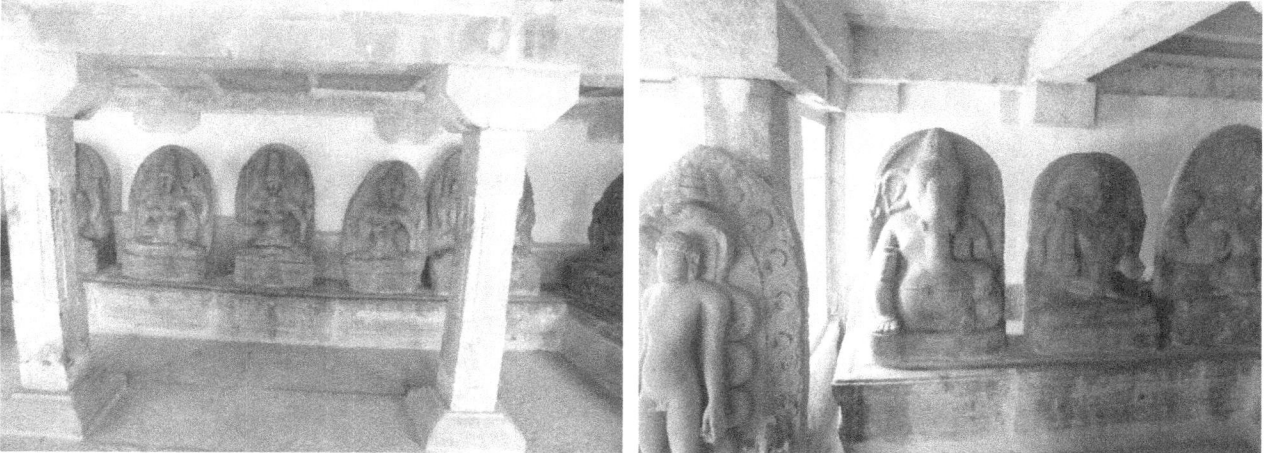

Plate 6-33: Three Sides of Vimana and Adisthana with Pranala of Rameswara Temple Narasamangala

Plate 6-34: Sculptures at Rameswara Temple Narasamangala

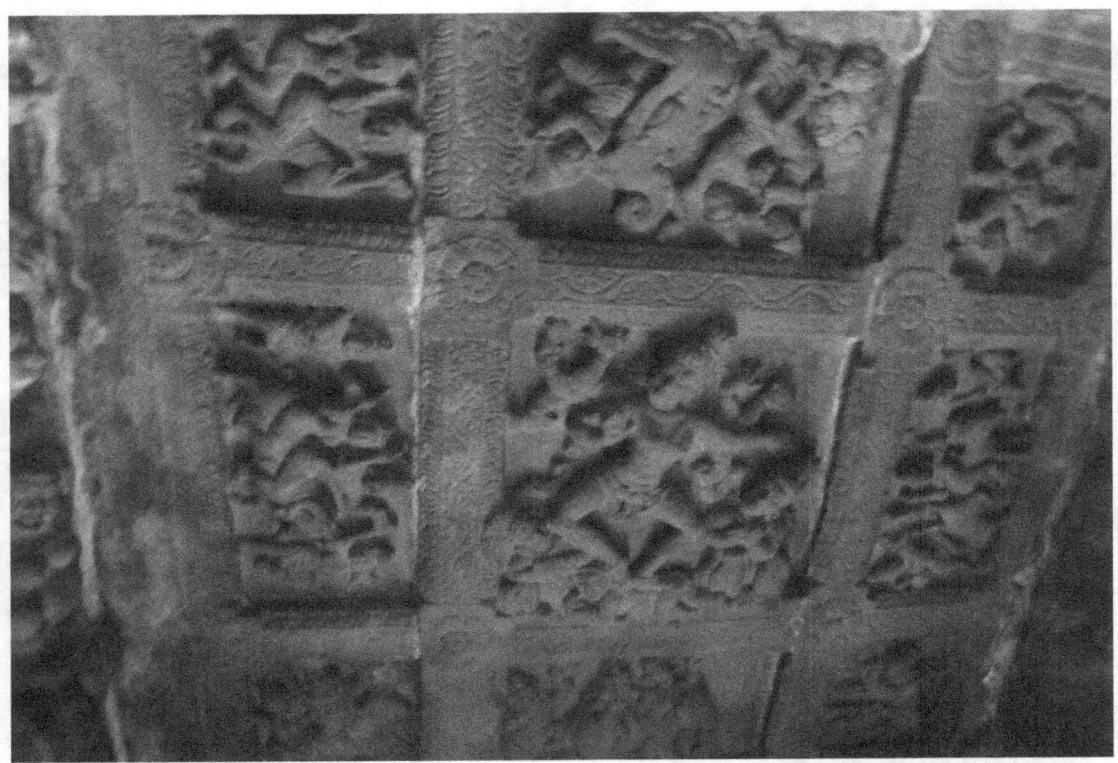

Plate 6-35: Navaranga Ceiling Rameswara Temple Narasamangala

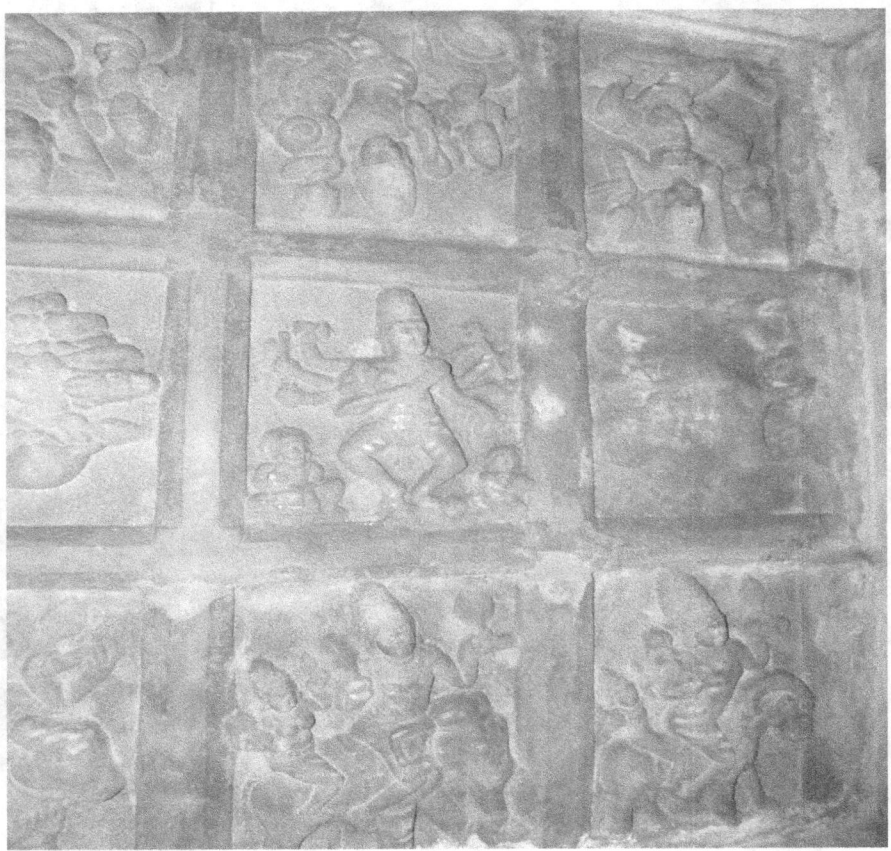

Plate 6-36: Tandaveswara Surrounded by Ashtadikpalas Navaranga Ceiling Arkeswara Temple Alur

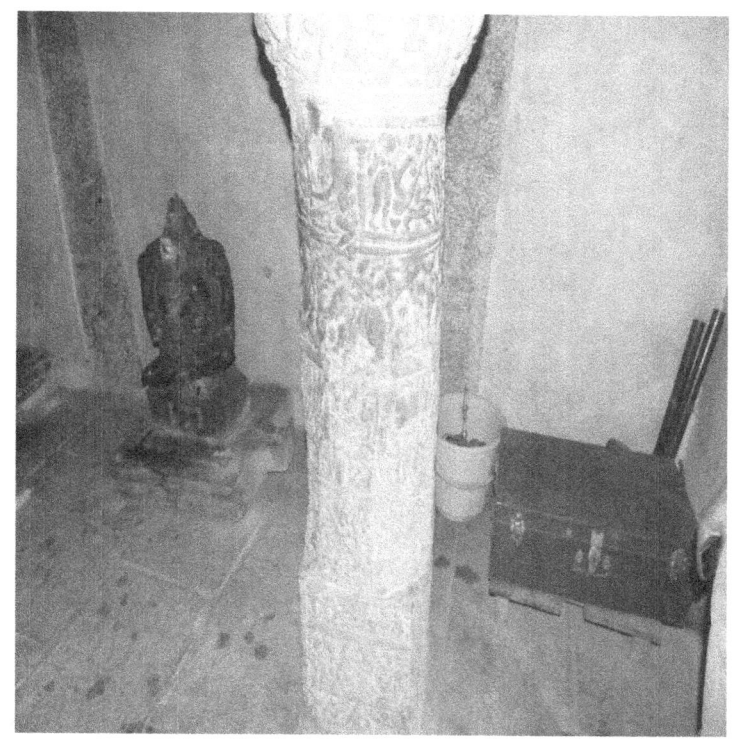

Plate 6-37: Battle Scene Carved on Navaranga Pillar Arkeswara Temple Alur

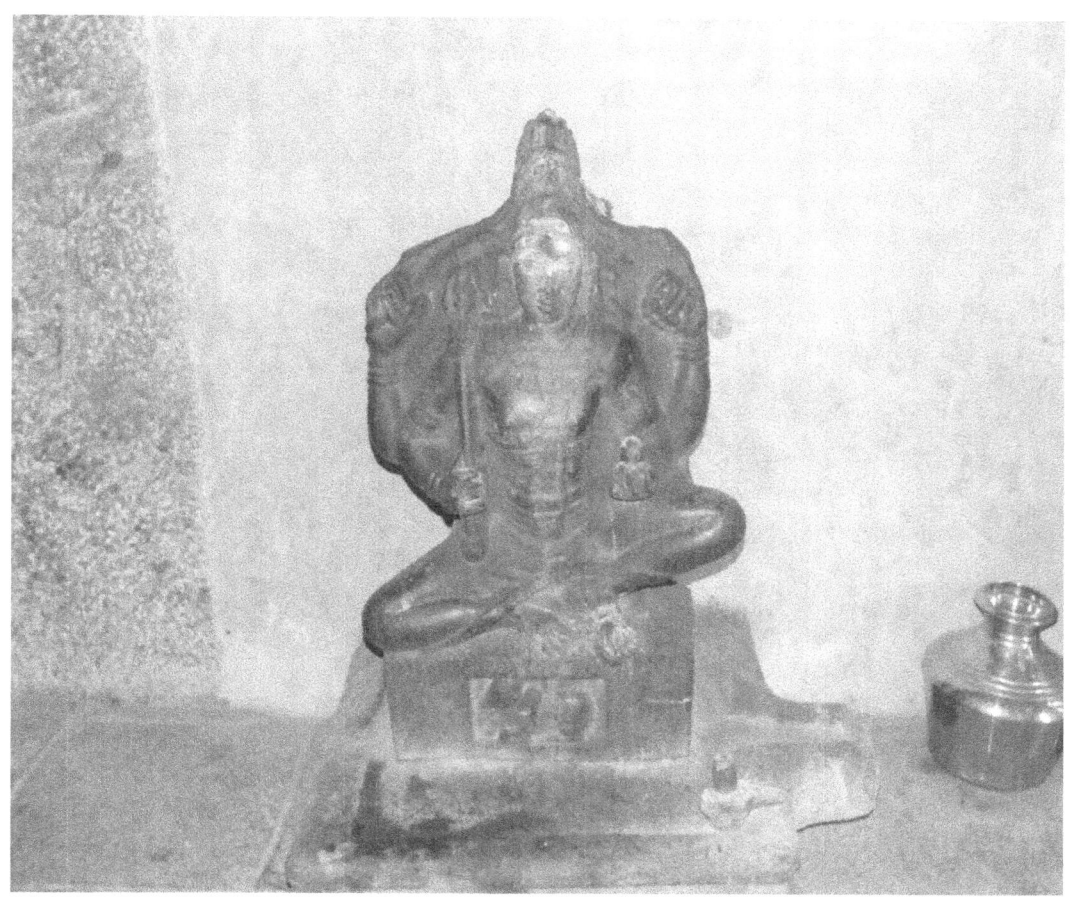

Plate 6-38: Siva as Kaphaka on Bull Pedestal Alur

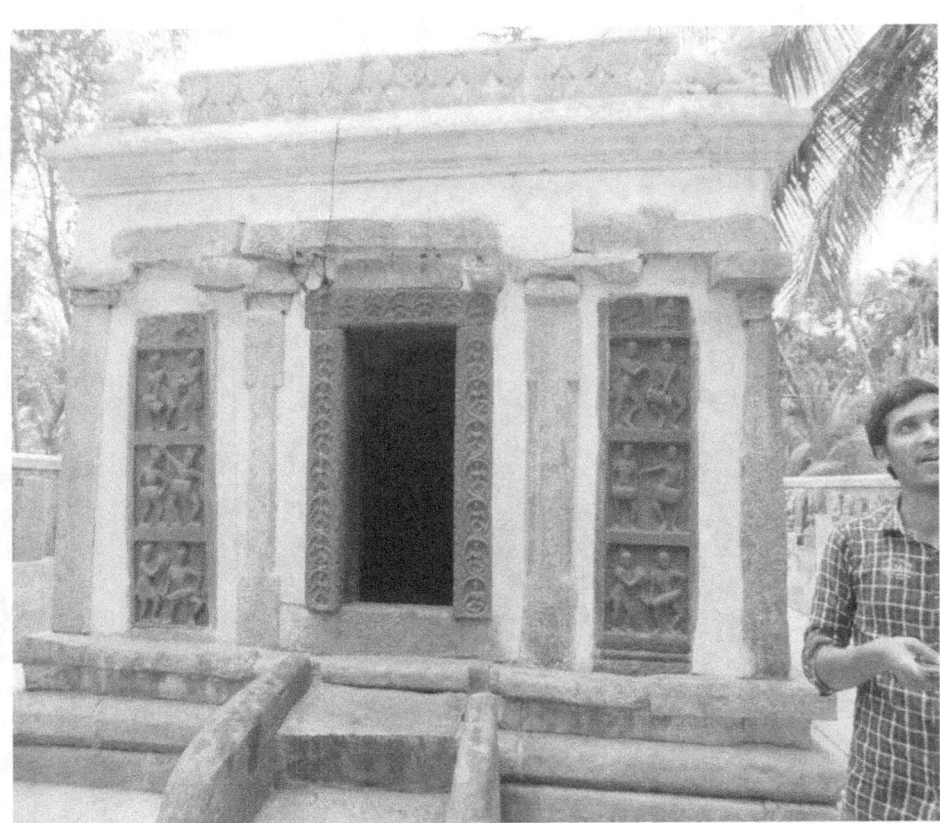

Plate 6-39: Door Panels of the Arkeswara Temple Entrance, Alur

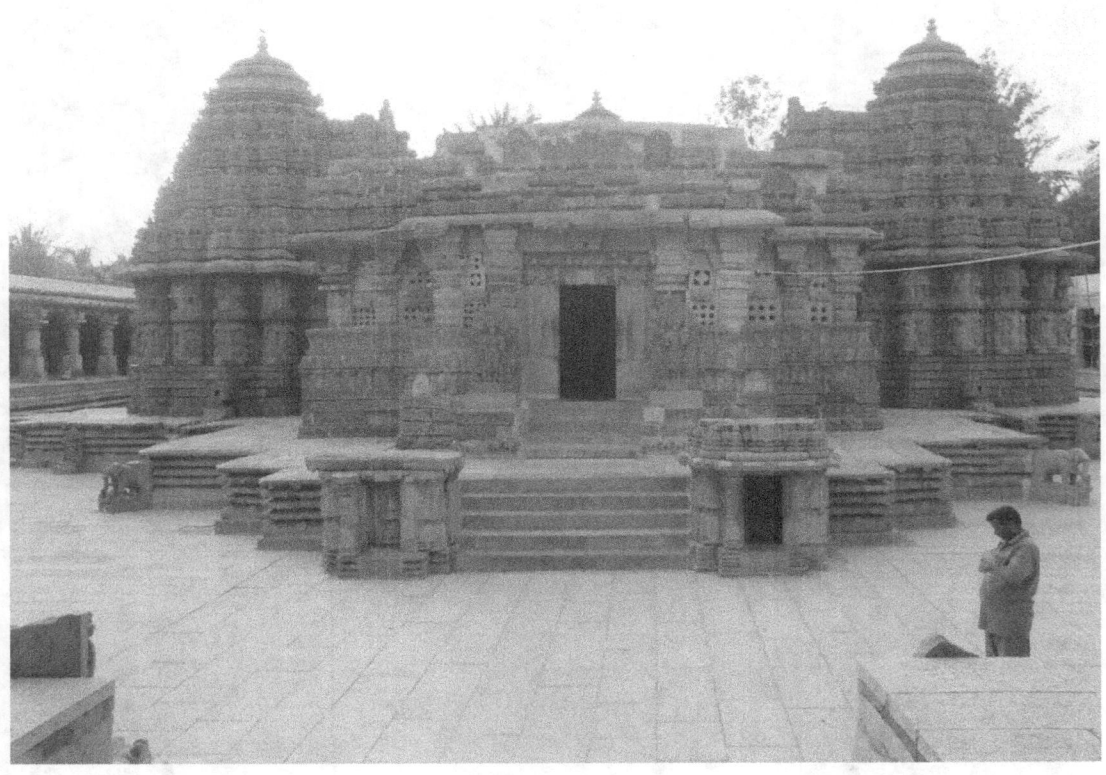

Plate 6-40: Kesava Temple Somanathapura Main Entrance

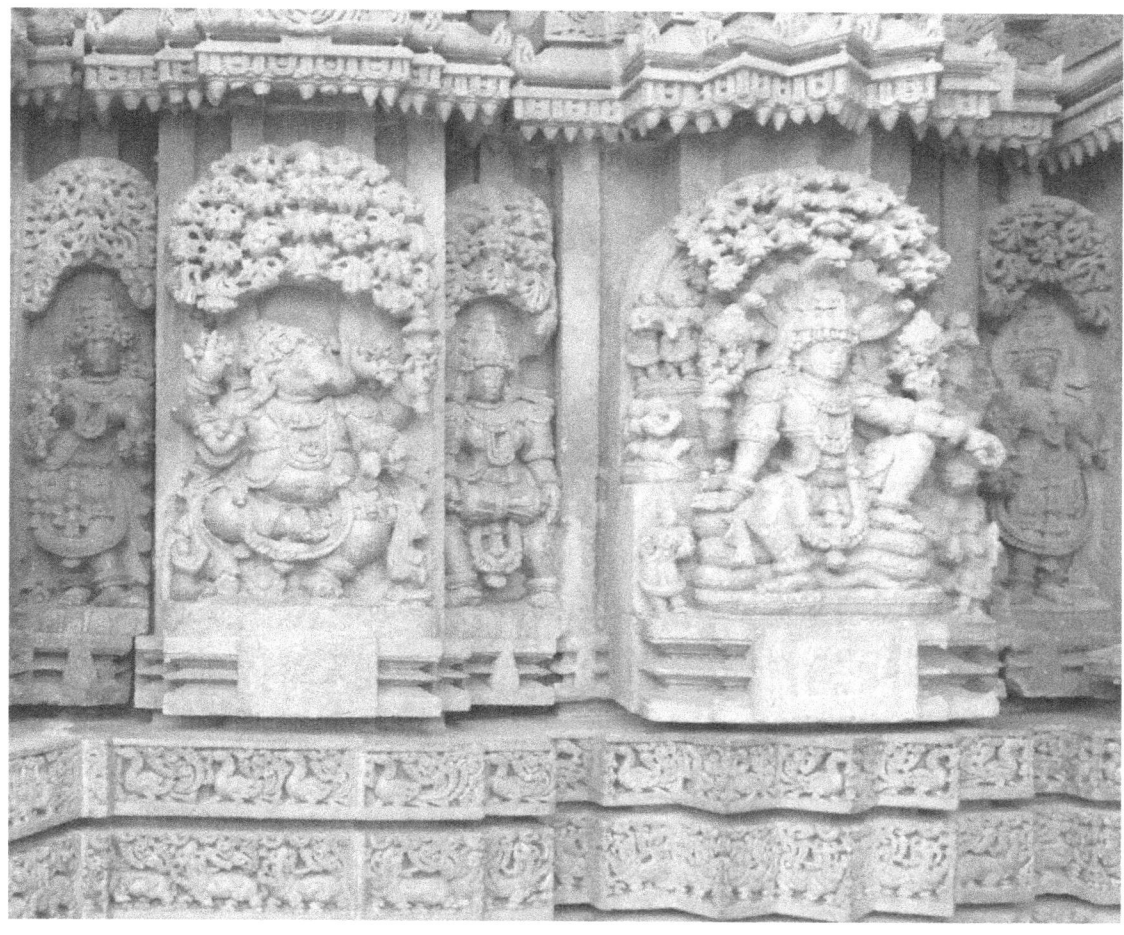

Plate 6-41: Images of Varaha and Visnu Seated on Sesha Somanathapura

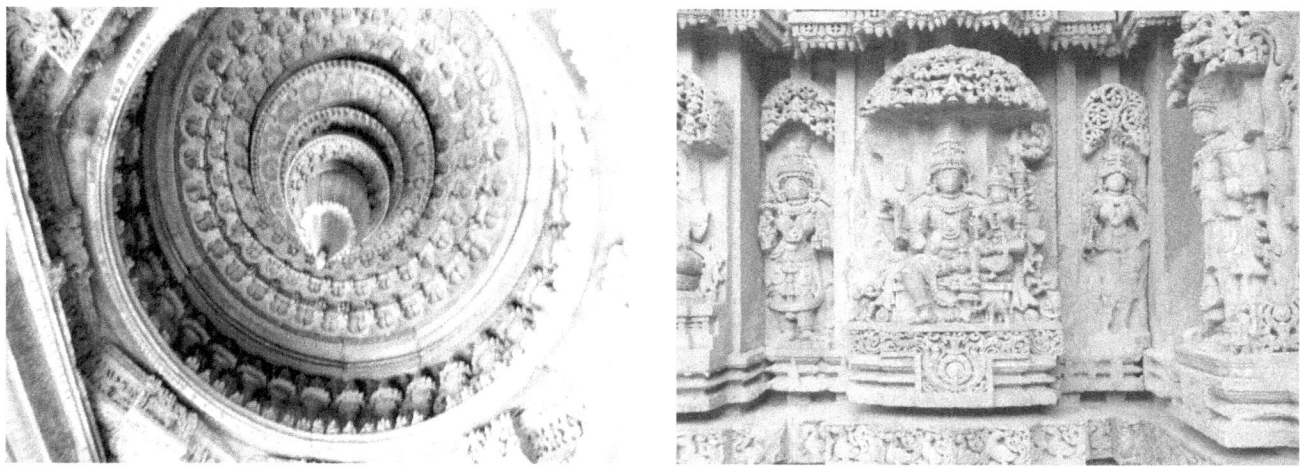

Plate 6-42: Domical Ceiling and Visnu with Lakshmi Seated on His Lap, Somanathapura

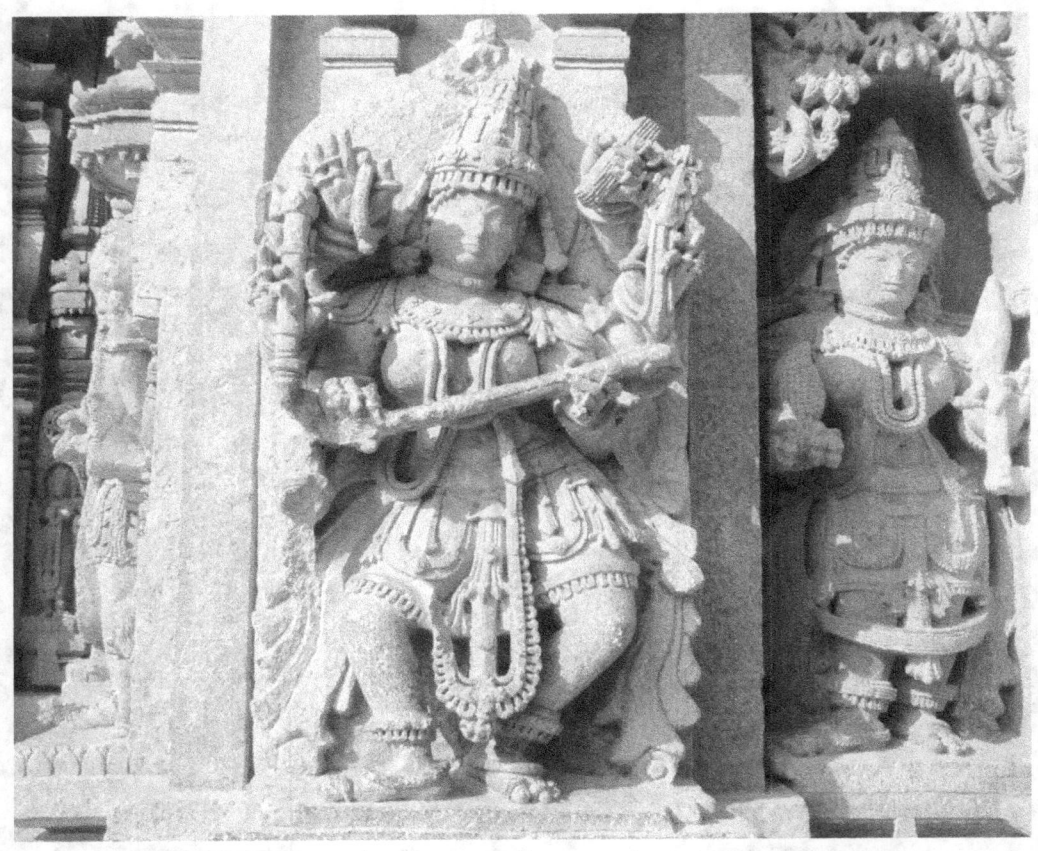

Plate 6-43: Saraswati Holding Veena and Book in Her Hands, Somanathapura

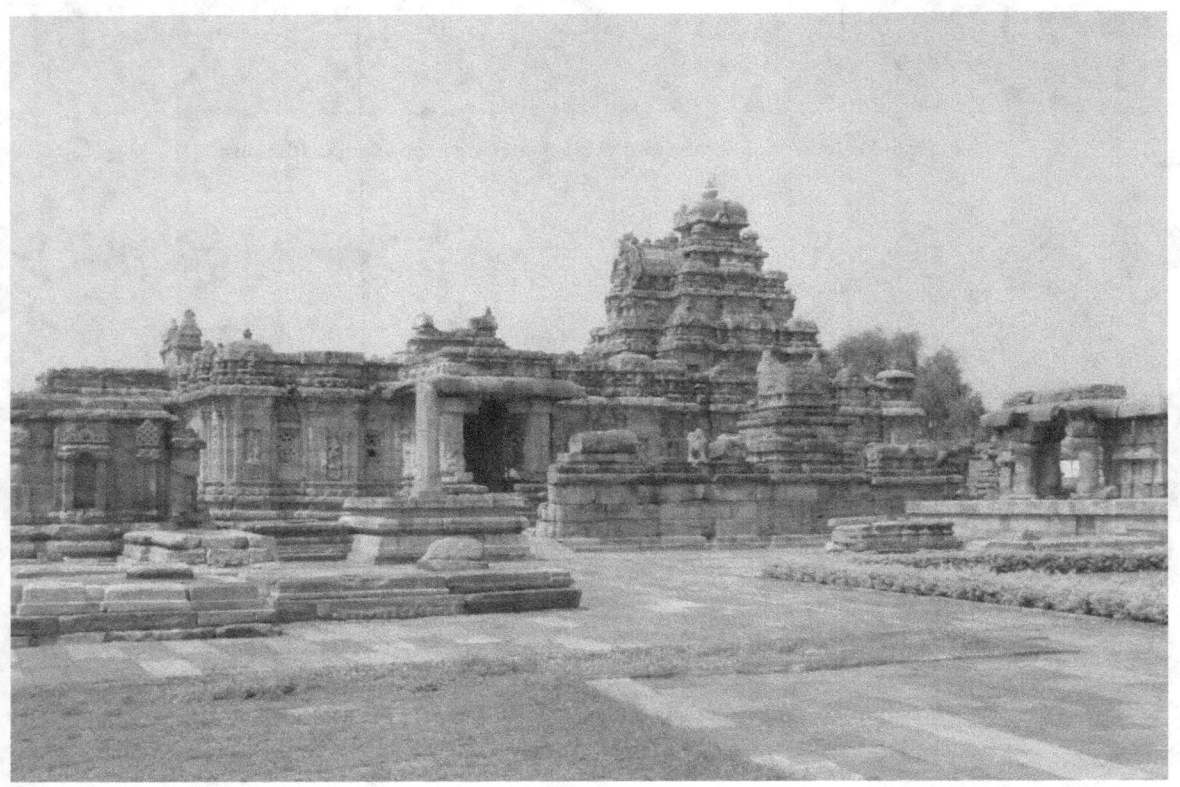

Plate 6-44: Virupaksha Temple at Pattadakal

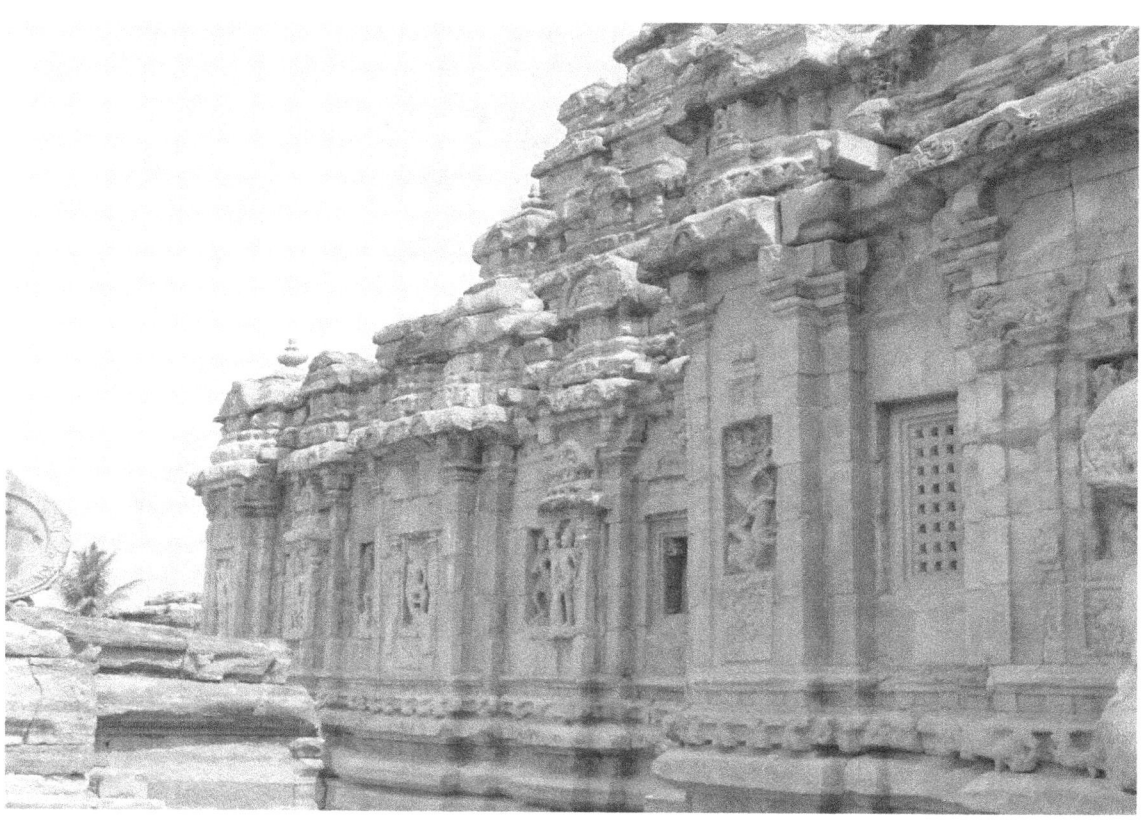

Plate 6-45: Sculpture on the Walls of Mandapa and Garbhagriha, Virupaksha Temple

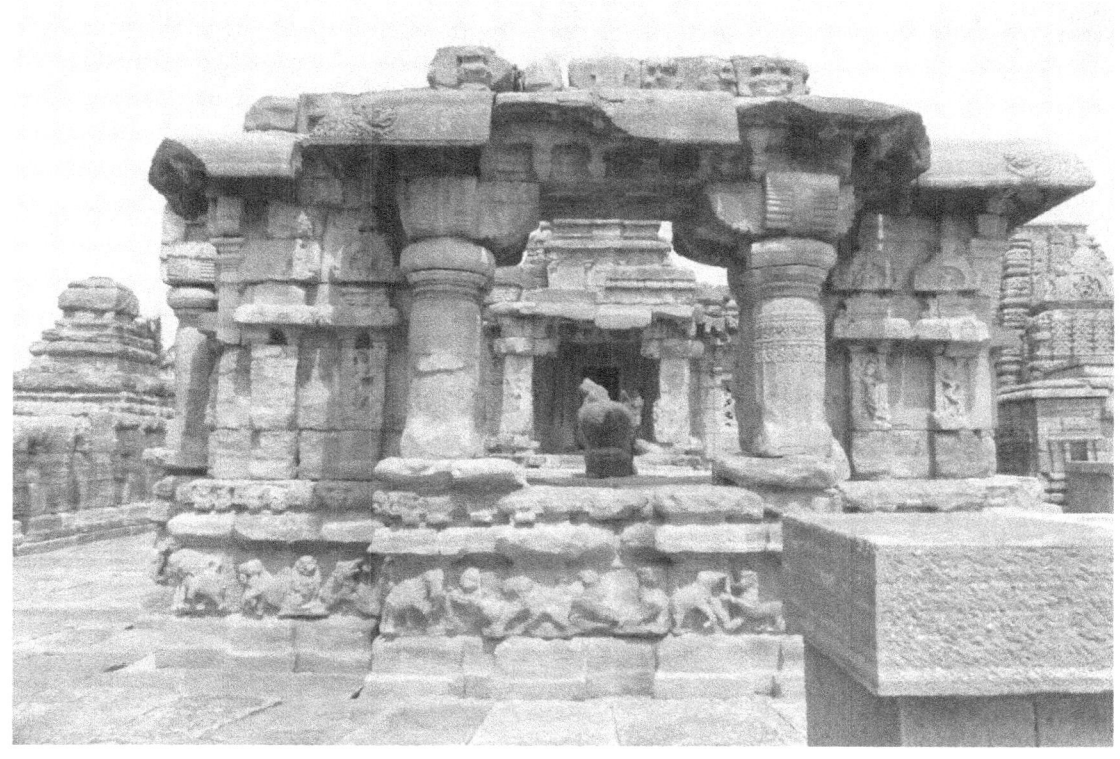

Plate 6-46: Mallikarajuna Temple Pattadakal

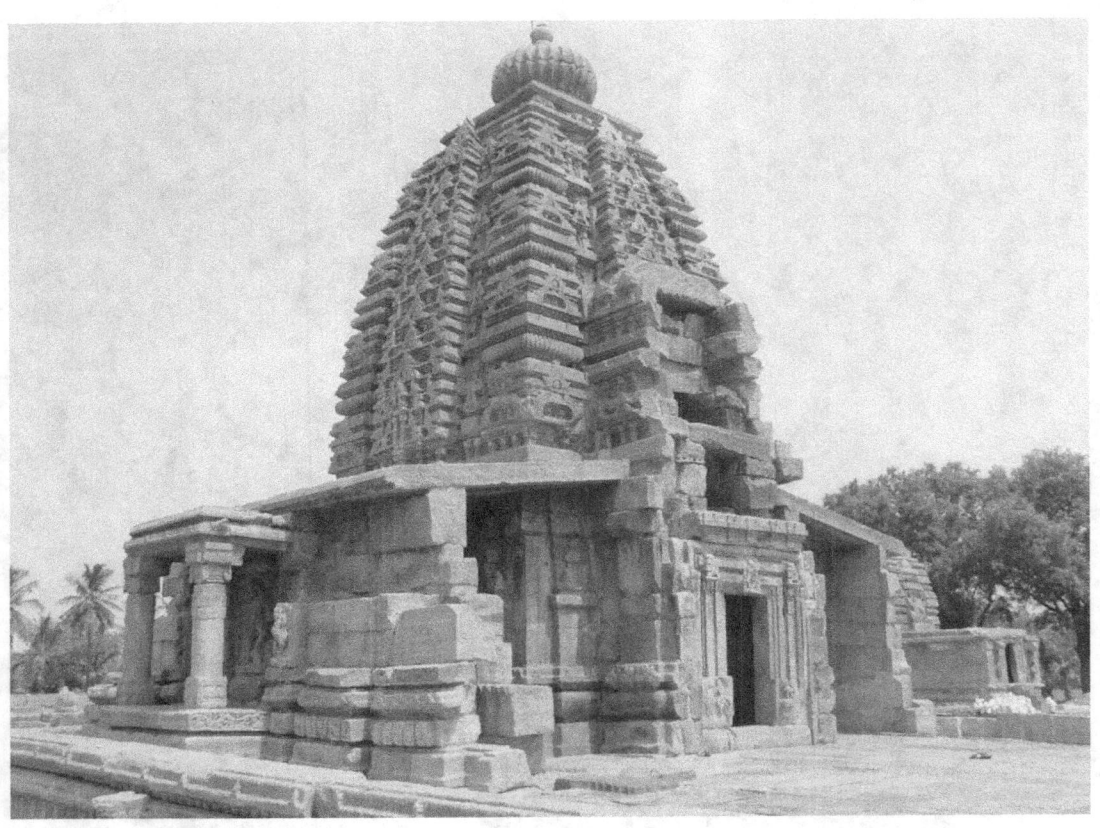

Plate 6-47: Galaganatha Temple Pattadakal

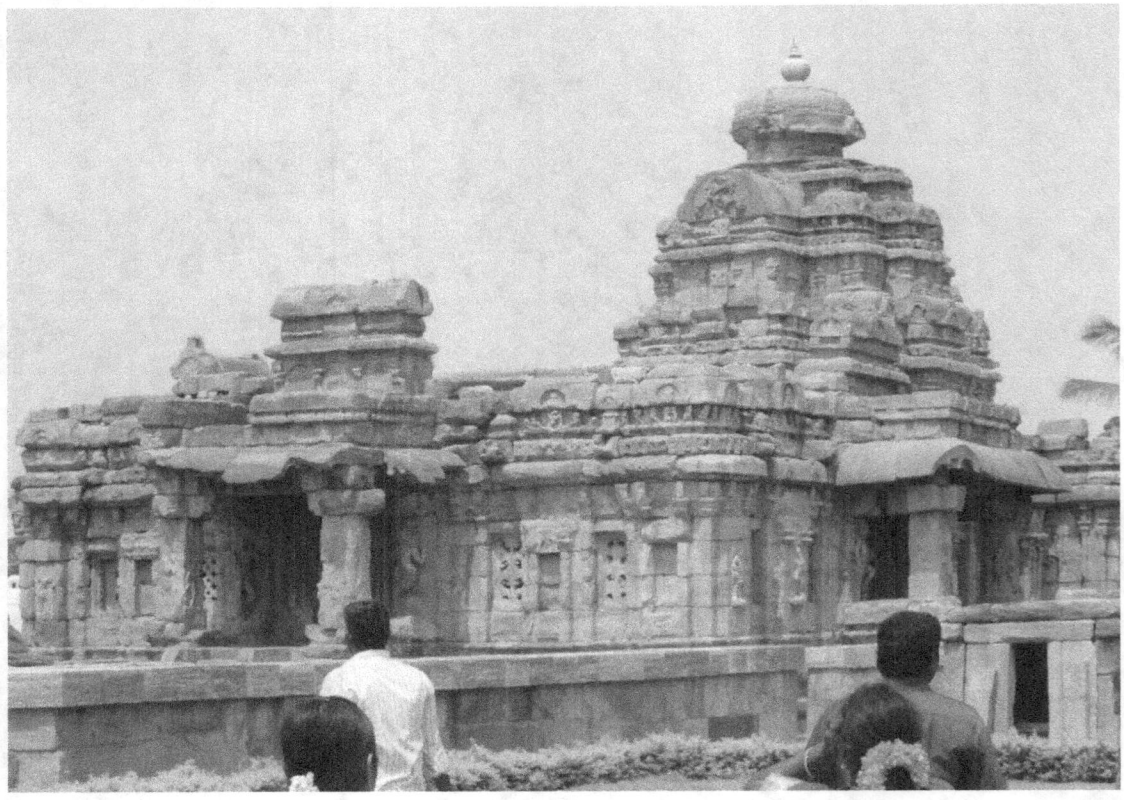

Plate 6-48: Sangameswara Temple Pattadakal

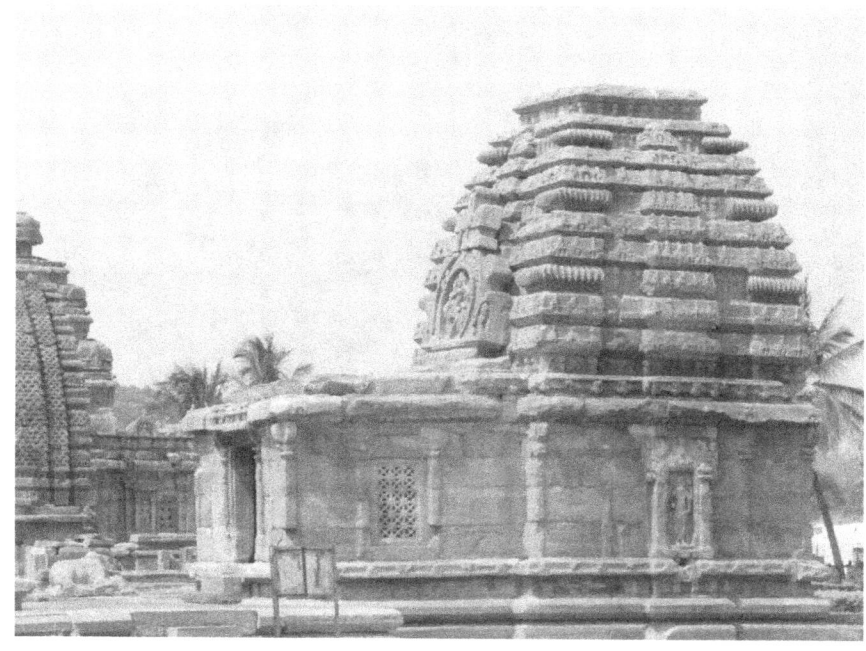

Plate 6-49: Jambulinga Temple Pattadakal

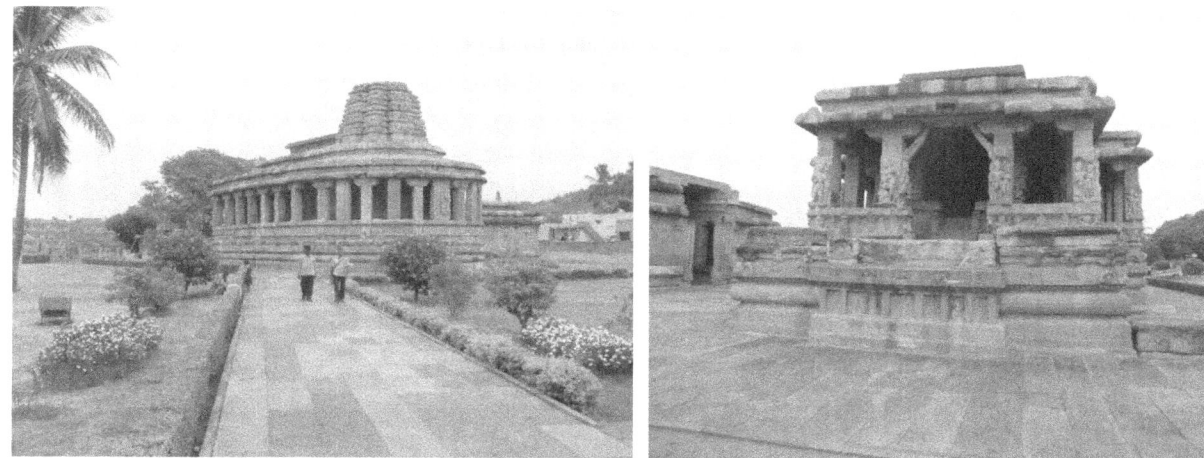

Plate 6-50: Durga Temple Aihole

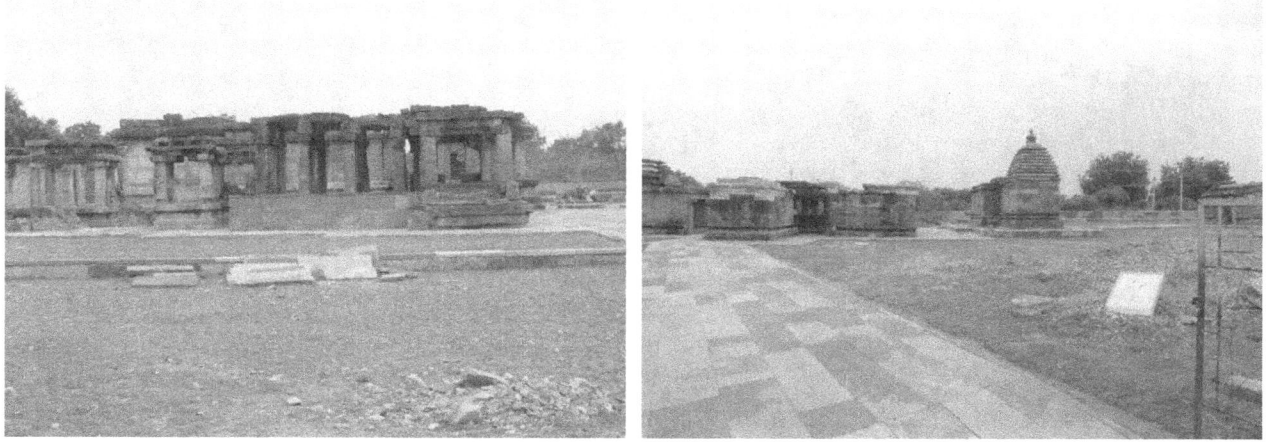

Plate 6-51: Jyotirlinga Complex of Temples Aihole

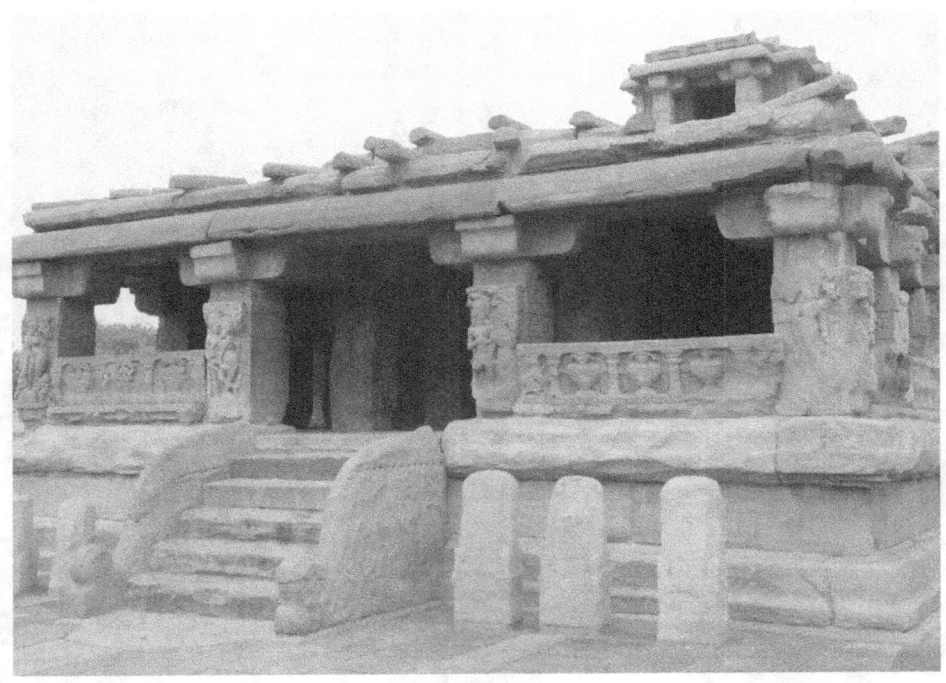

Plate 6-52: Ladkhan Temple Aihole

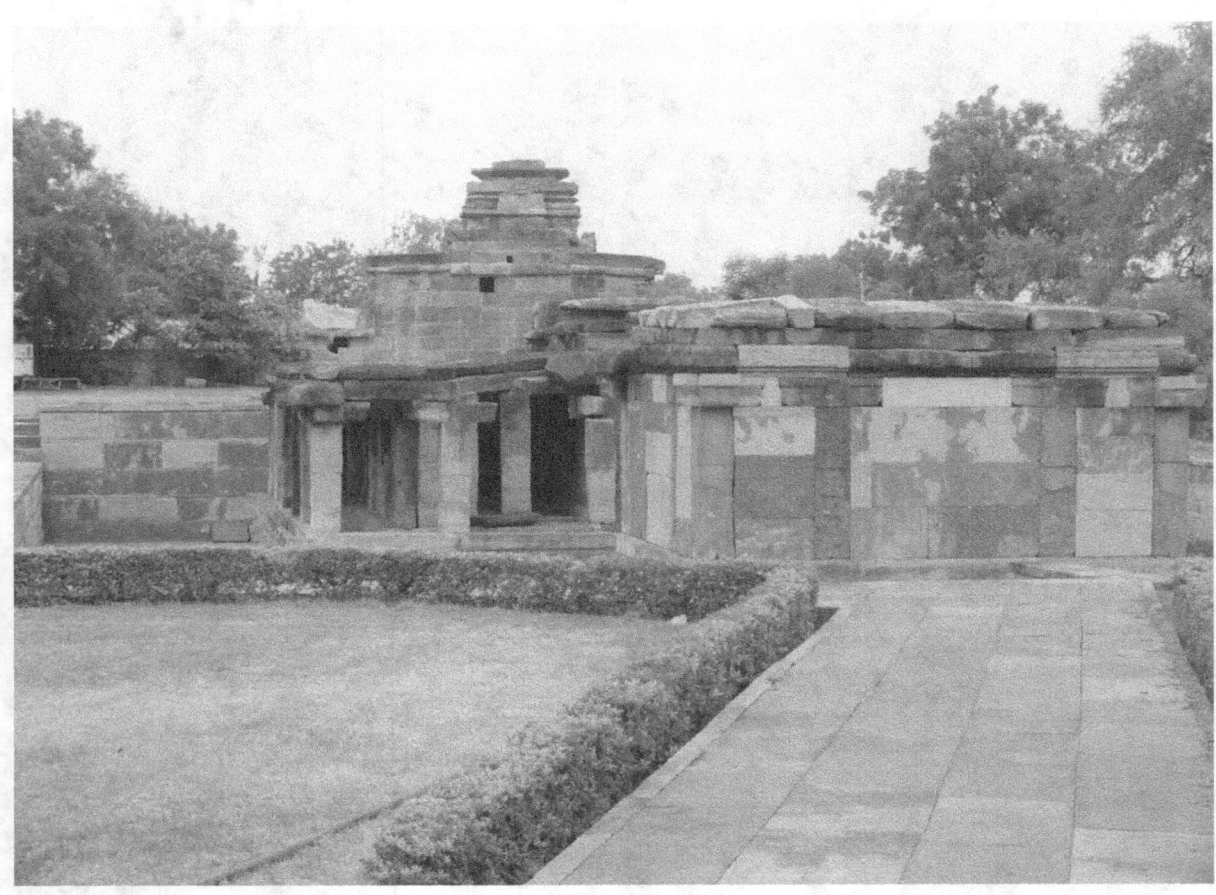

Plate 6-53: Ambigeragudi Aihole

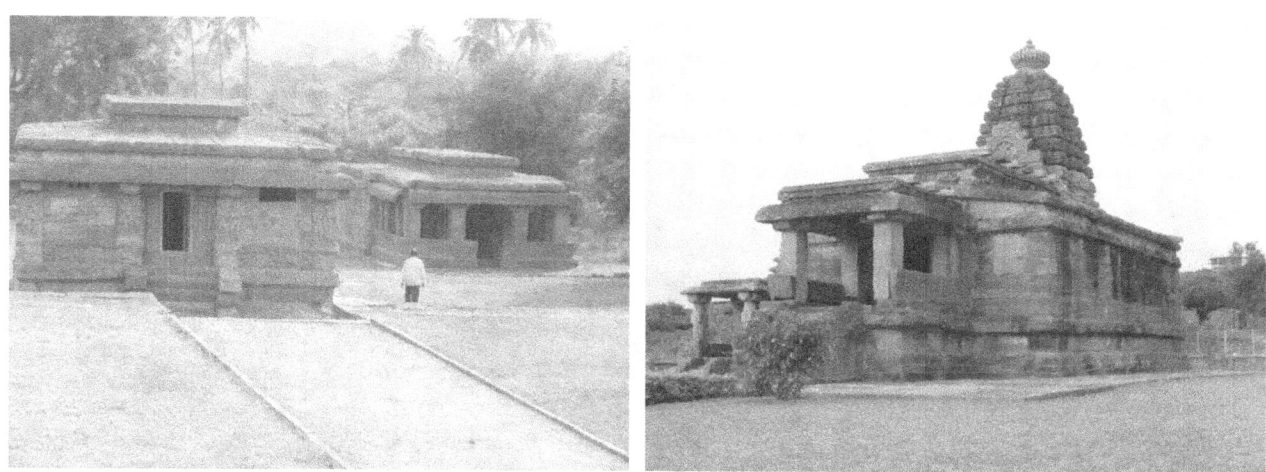

Plate 6-54: Huchapayya Matha and Hucchimalligudi Aihole

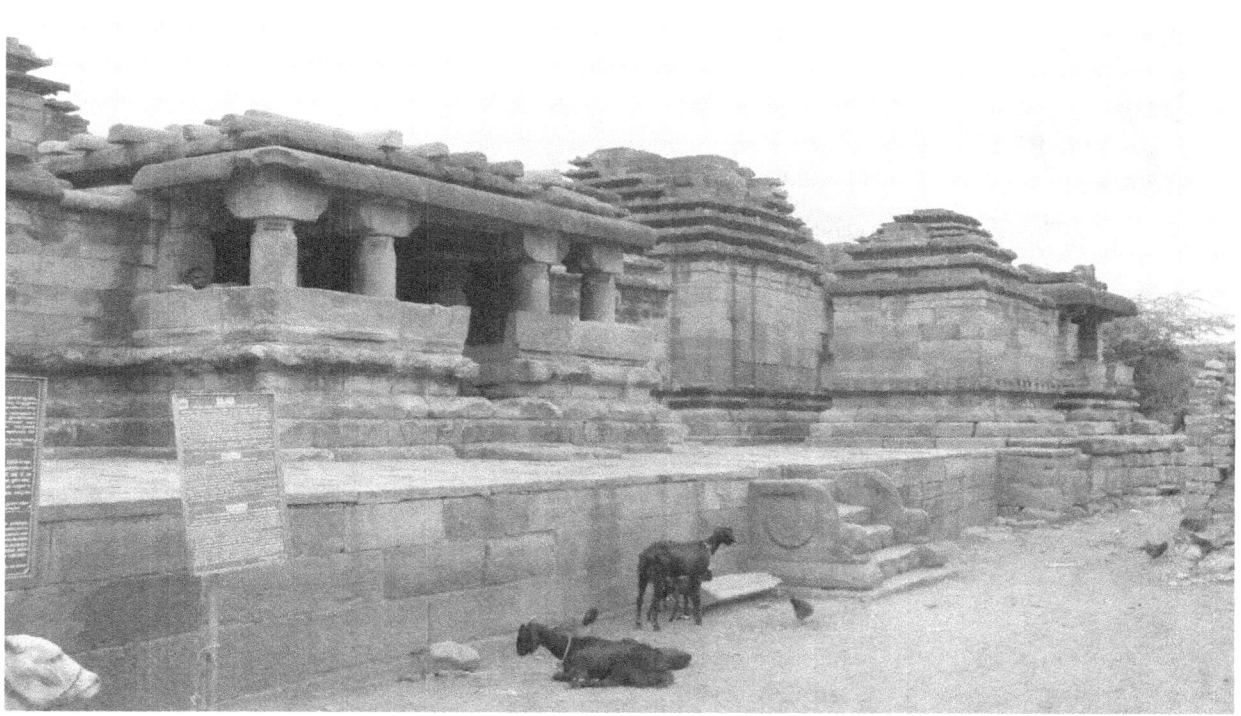

Plate 6-55: Triambakeswara Complex Aihole

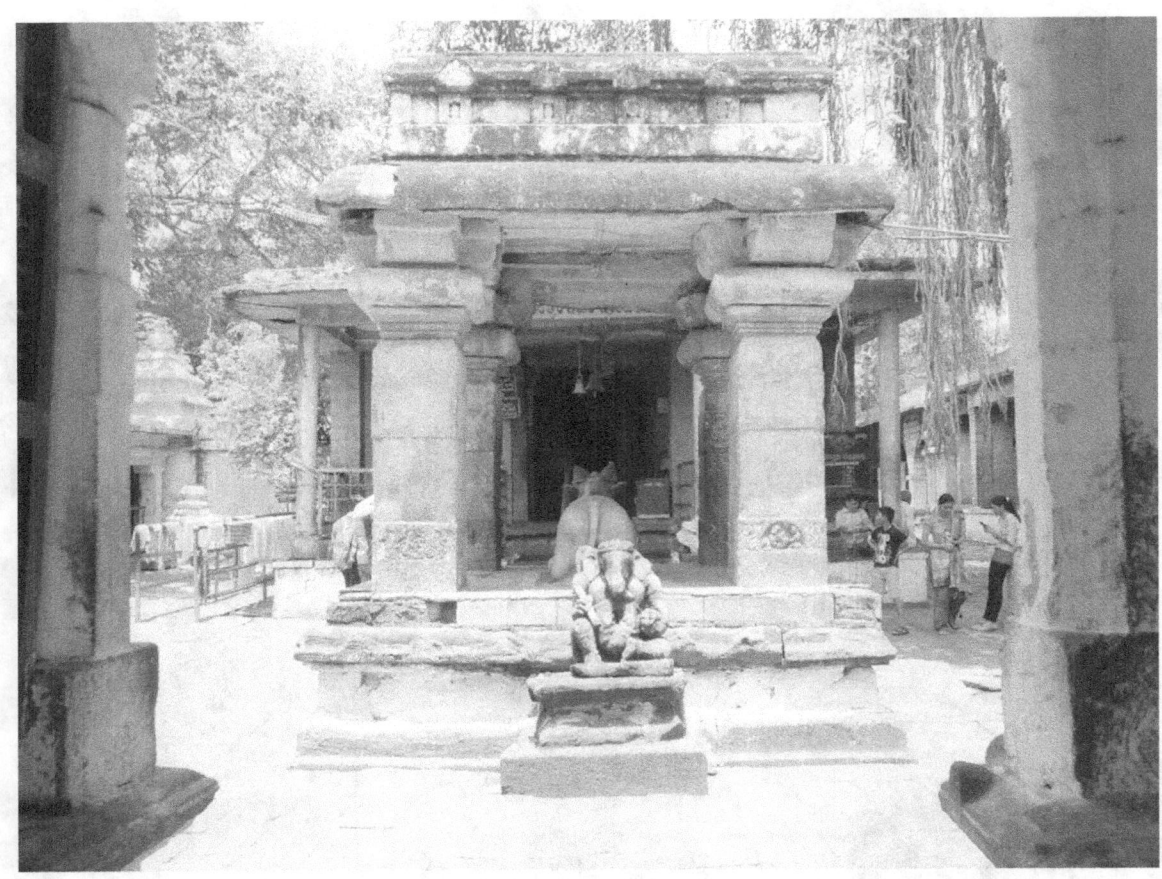

Plate 6-56: Ganesha and Nandi Pavilion in Front of Mahakuteswara Temple, Mahakuta

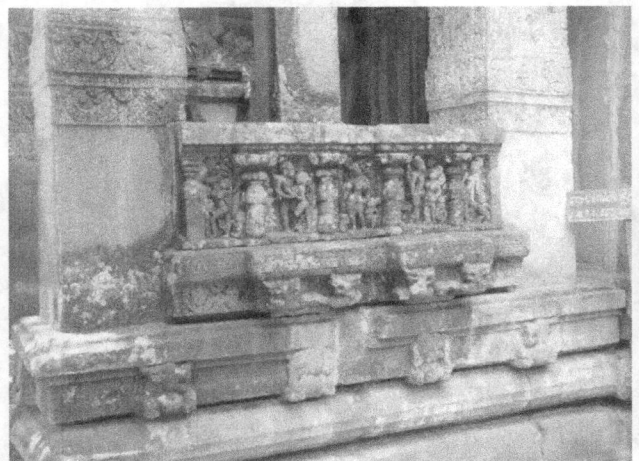 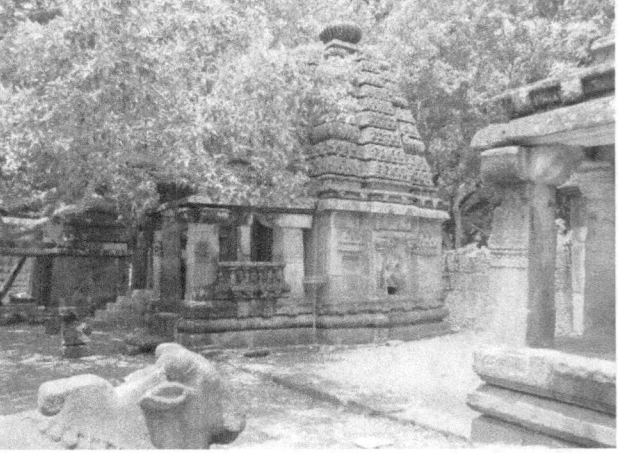

Plate 6-57: Sangameswara Temple Mahakuta

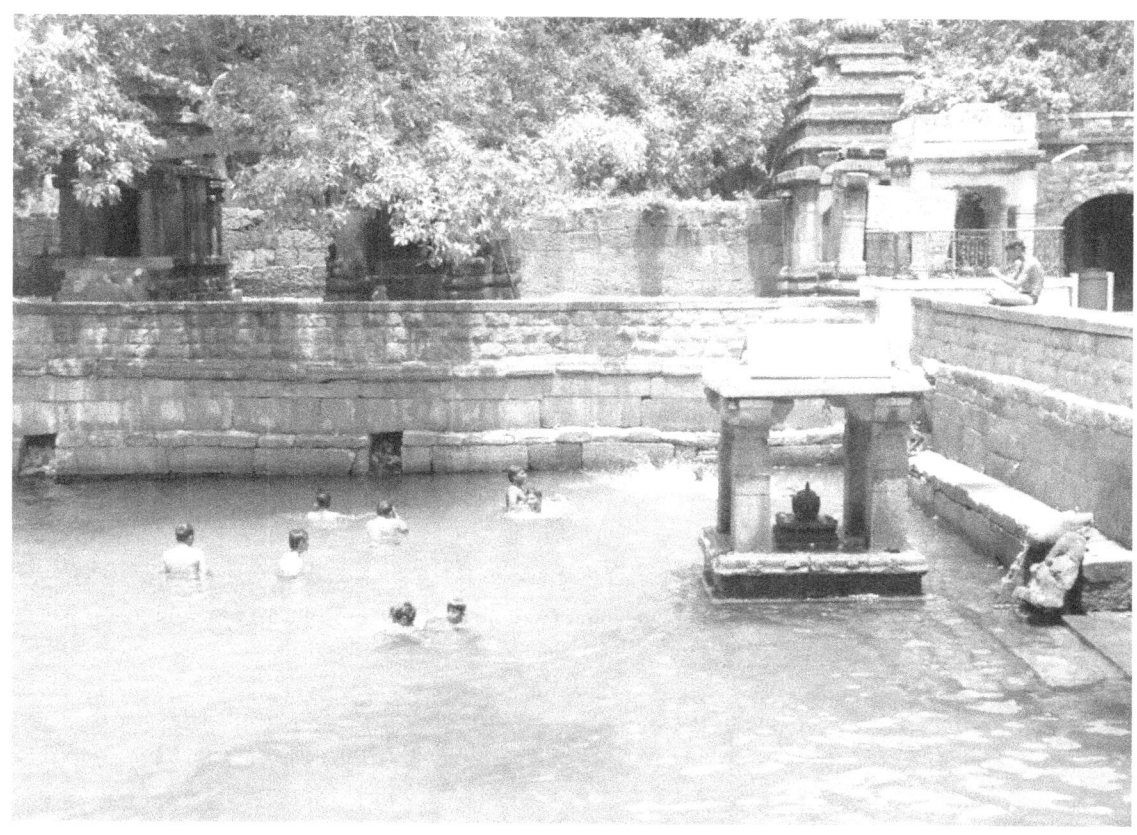

Plate 6-58: Chaumukha Sivslinga under the Mandapa in the Kalyani, Mahakuta

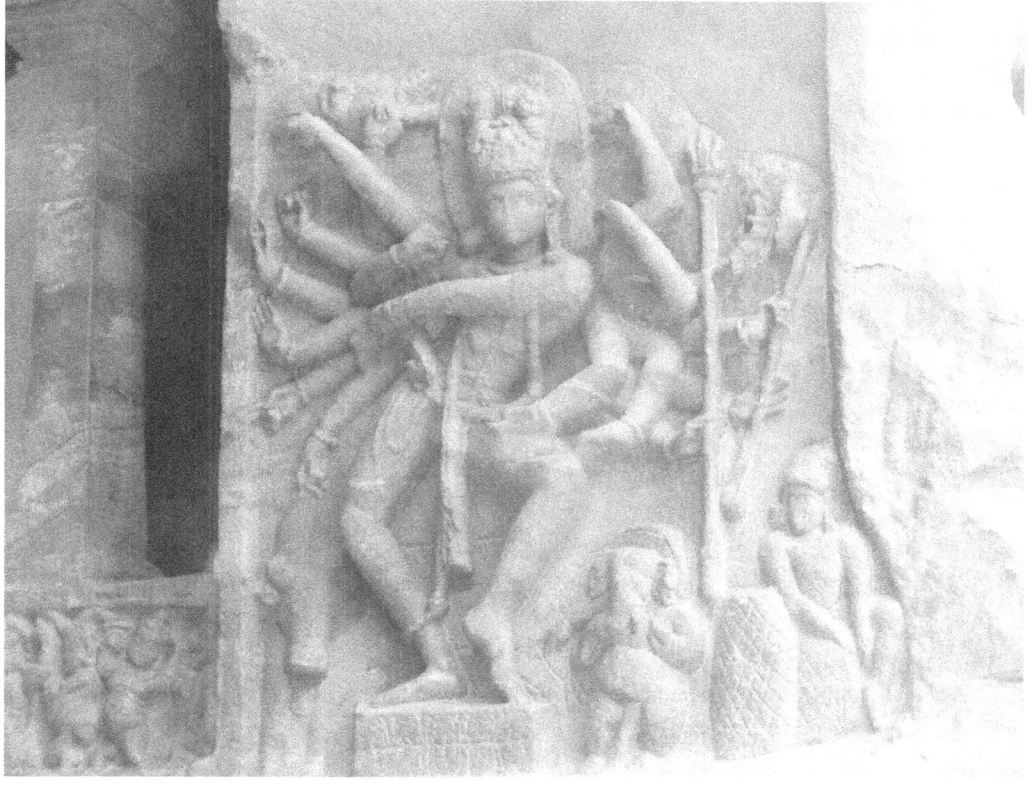

PLATE 6-59: DANCING SIVA NATARAJA BADAMI CAVE 1

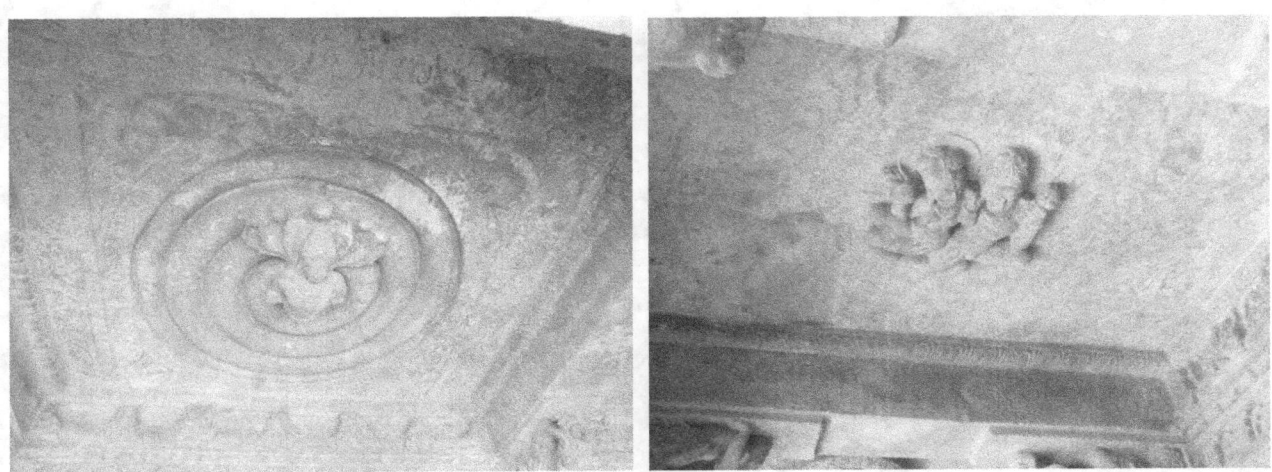

Plate 6-60: Nagaraja and Flying Vidyadhara Couple on the Ceiling of Cave 1 Badami

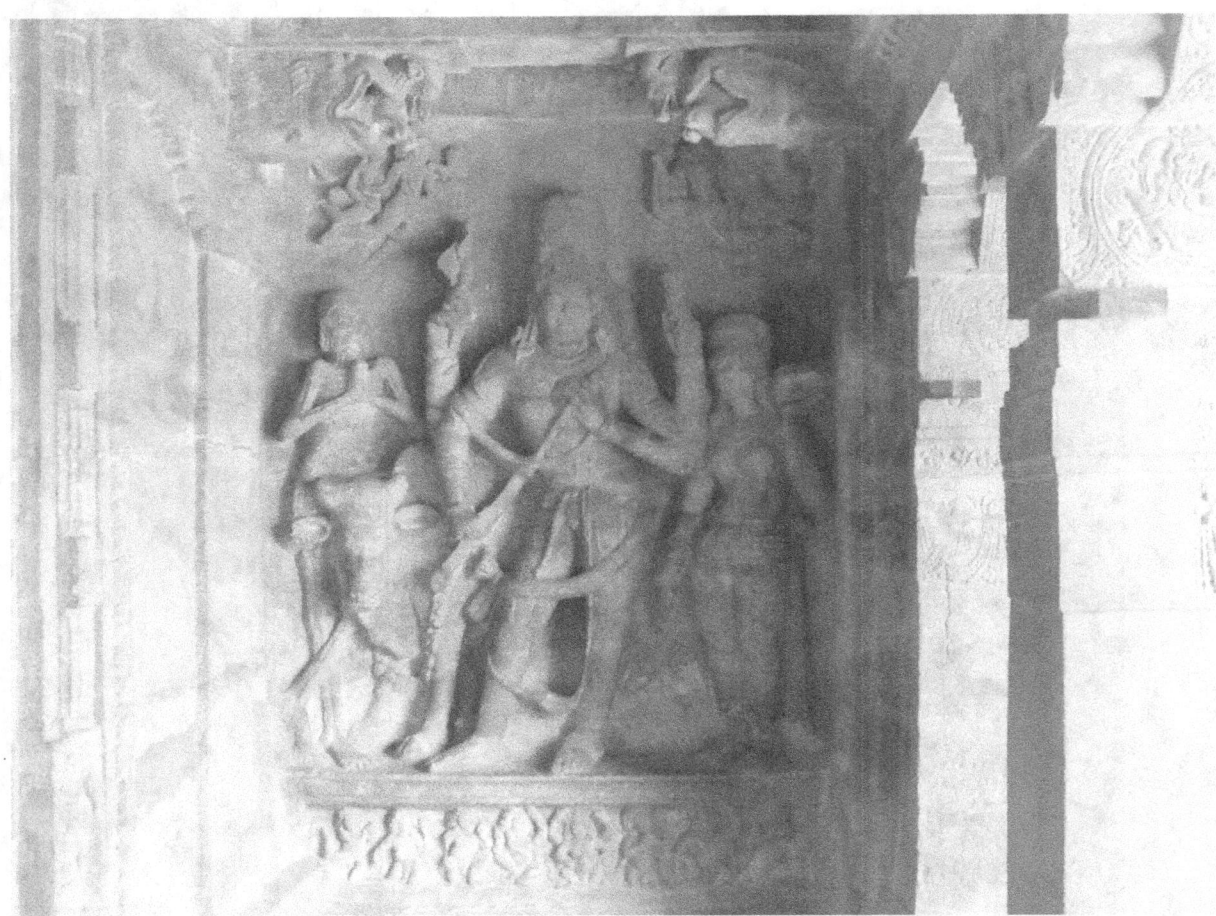

Plate 6-61: Siva and Parvati with Nandi and Bhringi, Cave 1 Badami

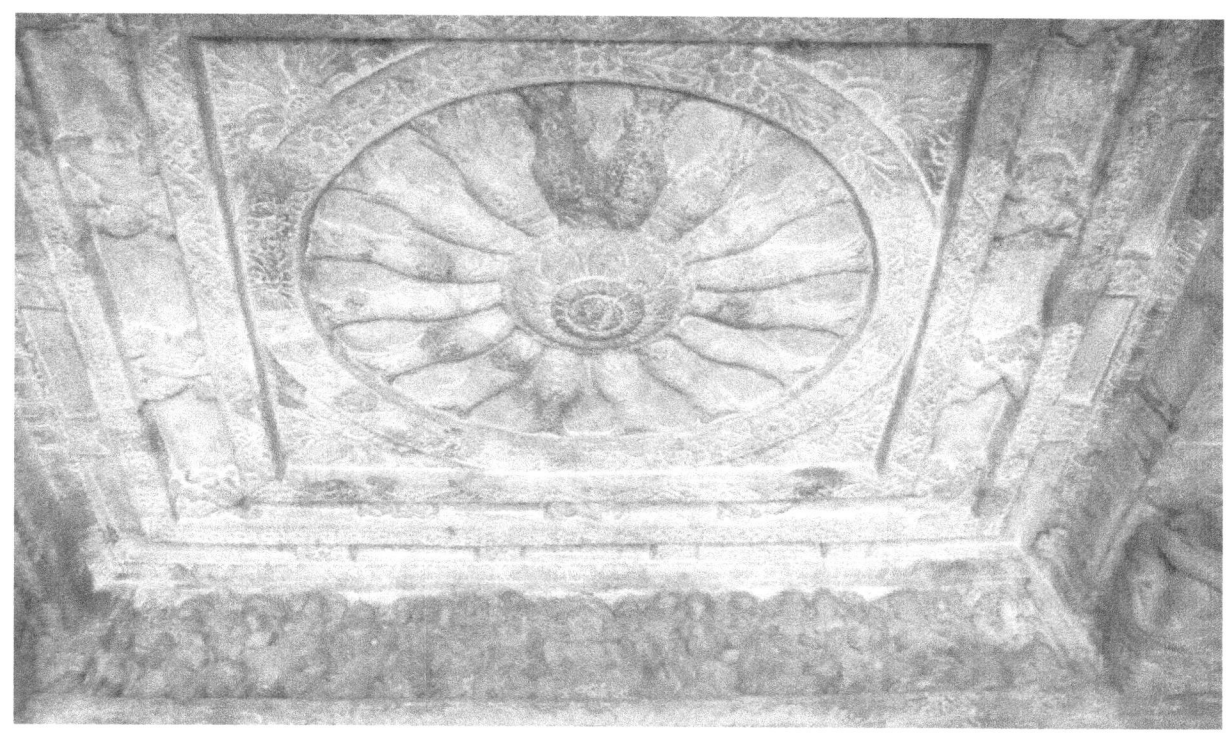

Plate 6-62: Fish Spokes Chakra on the Ceiling of Cave 2 Badami

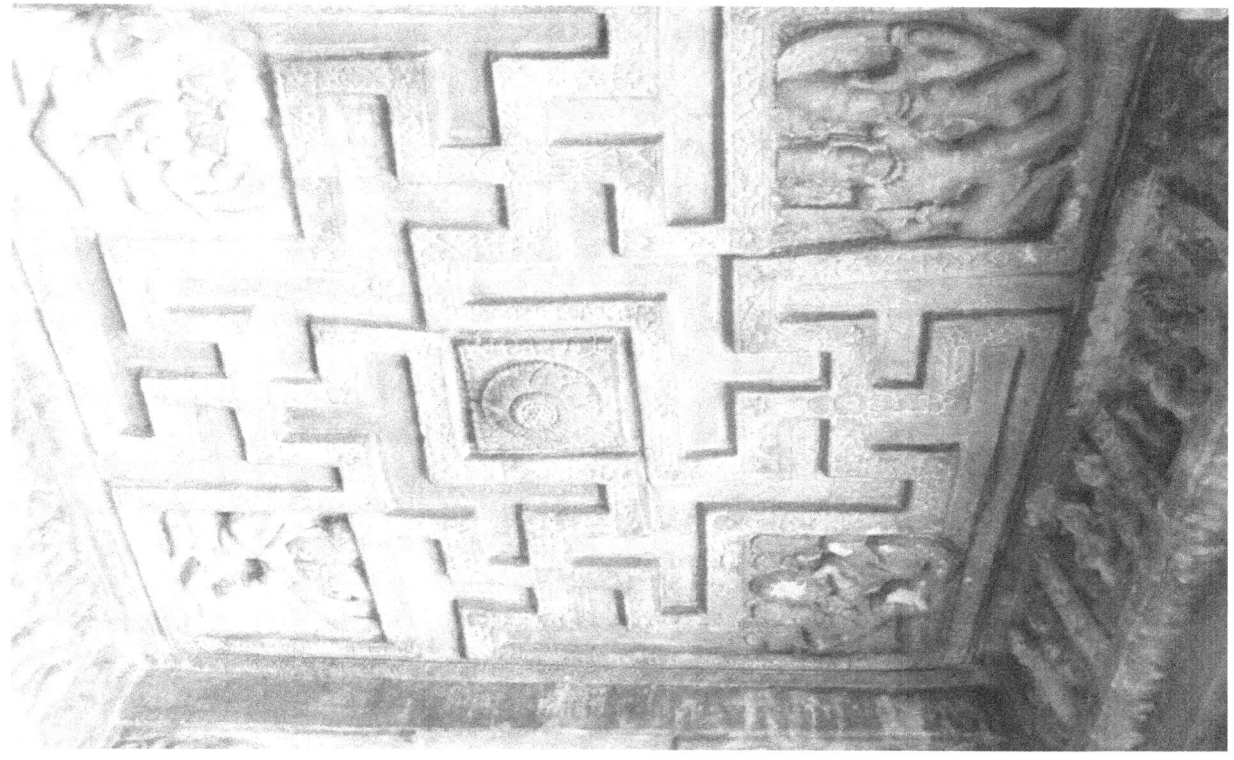

Plate 6-63: Swastikas Joined Together and flying couples in the Corner Panels, Cave 2 Badami

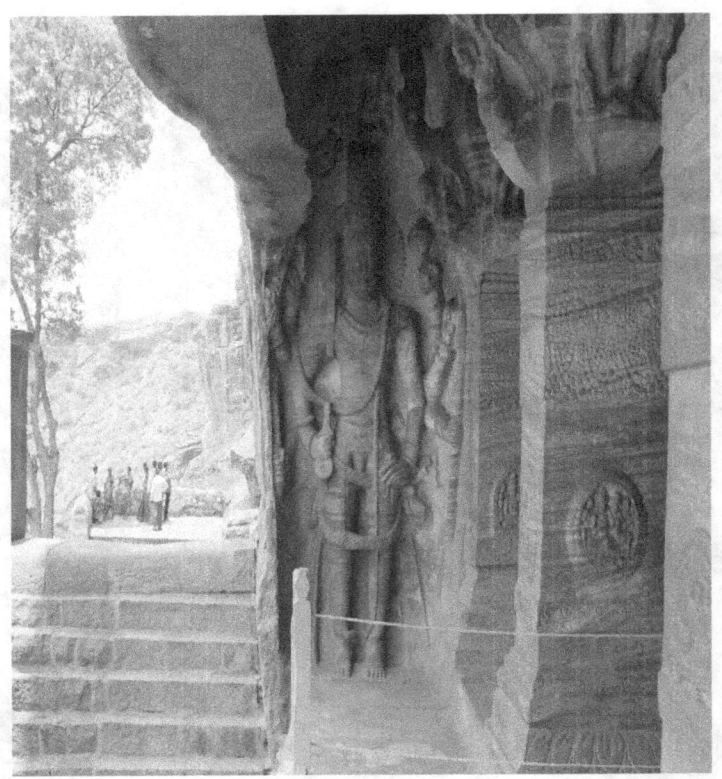

Plate 6-64: Shankaranarayana Cave 3 Badami

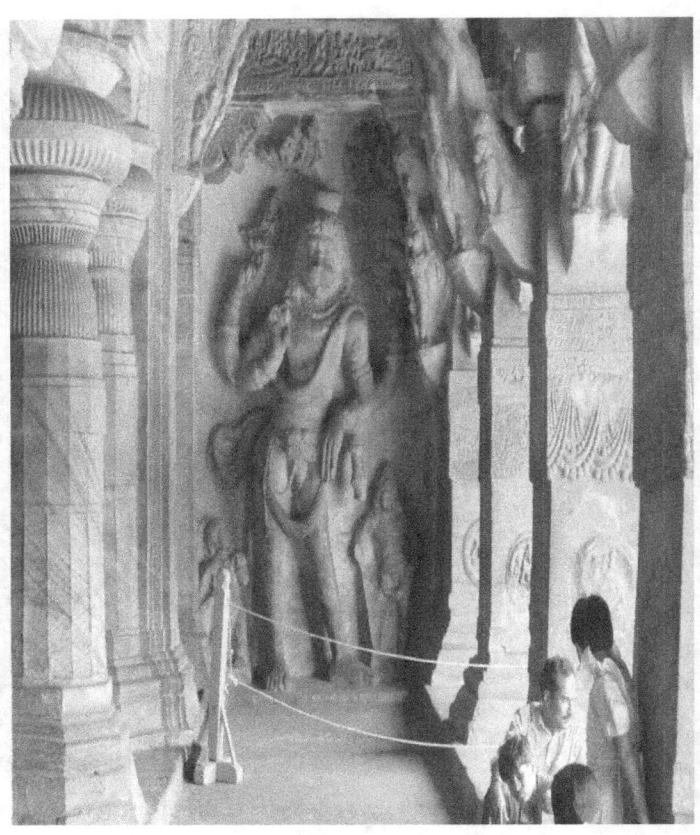

Plate 6-65: Narasimha Cave 3 Badami

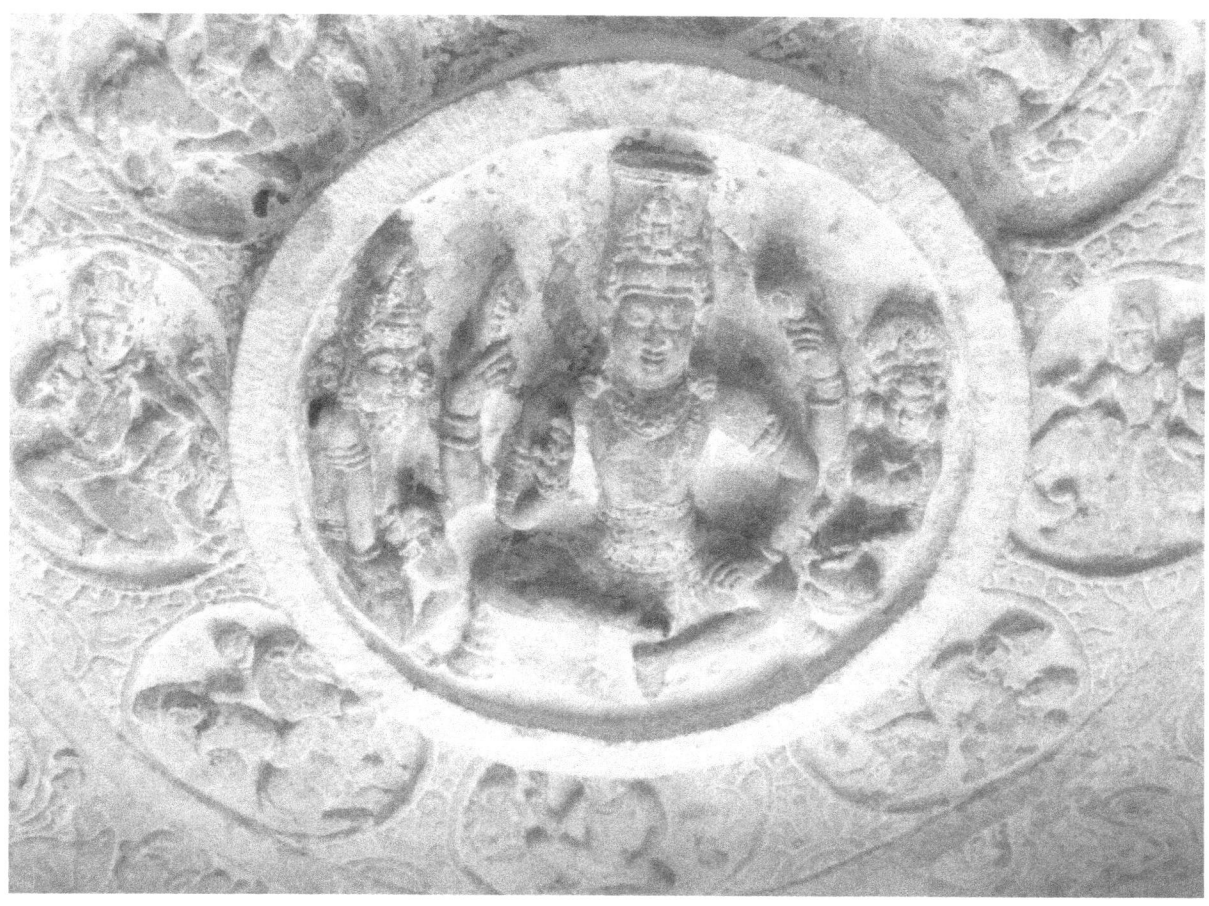

Plate 6-66: Ceiling Sculpture Cave 3, Visnu Surrounded by Ashtadikpalas in a Circle

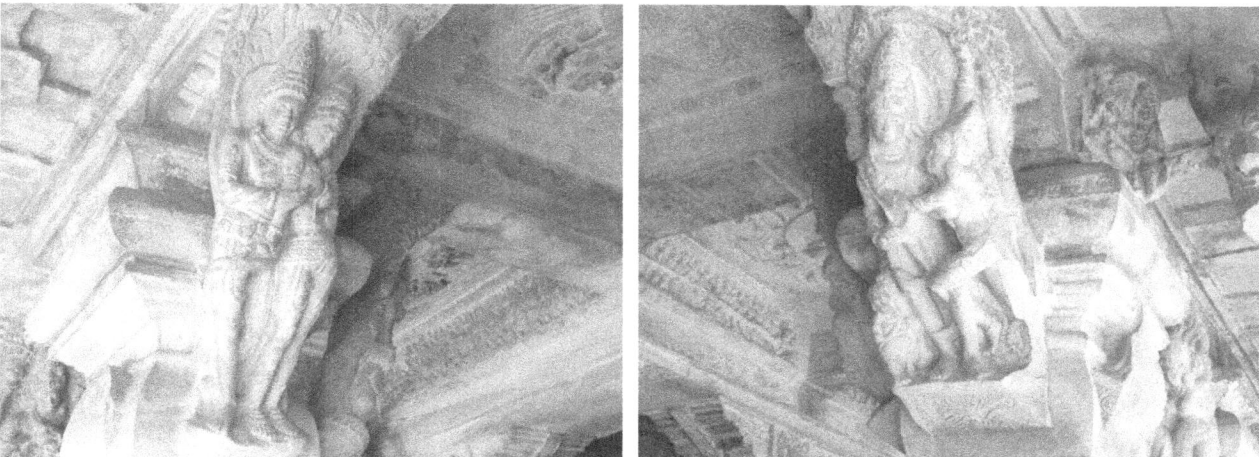

Plate 6-67: Amorous Couples on Column Brackets Cave 3 Badami

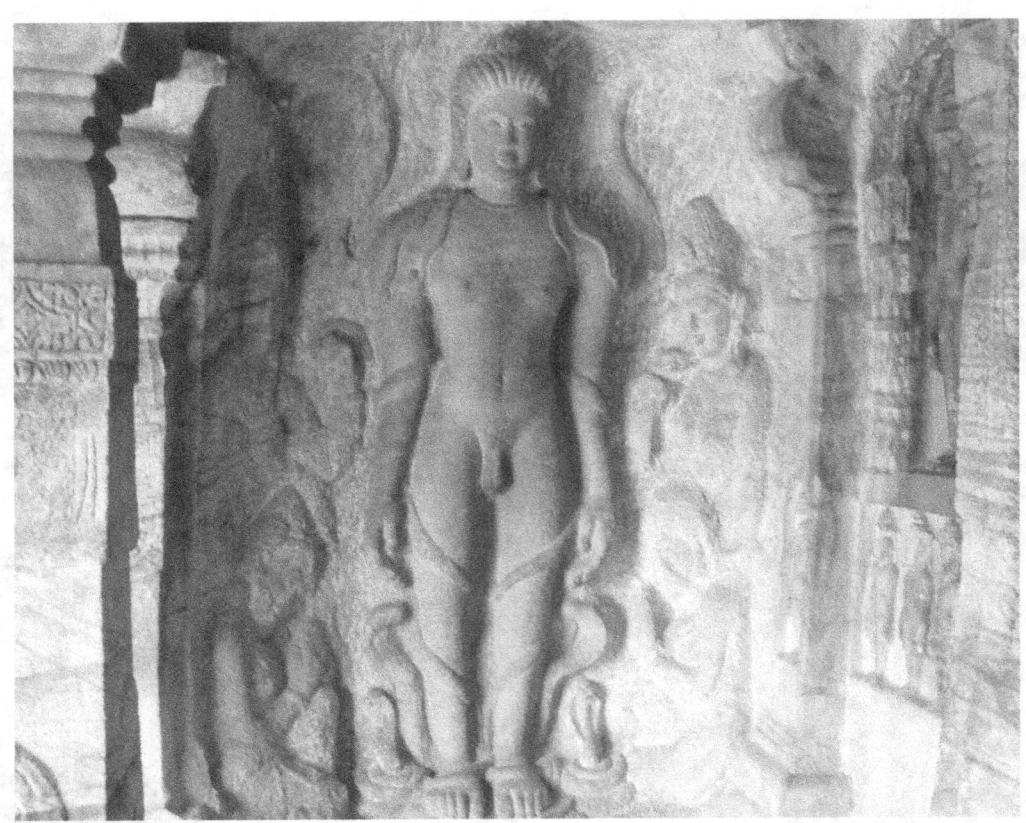

Plate 6-68: Bahubali with Creepers and Snakes Entwined Around his legs Cave 4 Badami

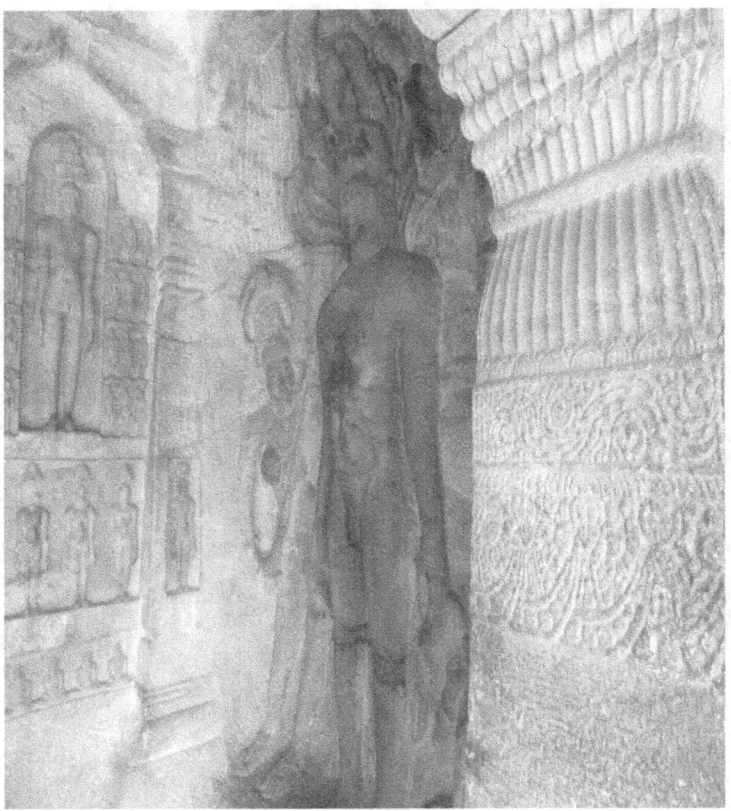

Plate 6-69: Parsvanatha with Five-hooded Snake Covering His Head, Cave 4 Badami

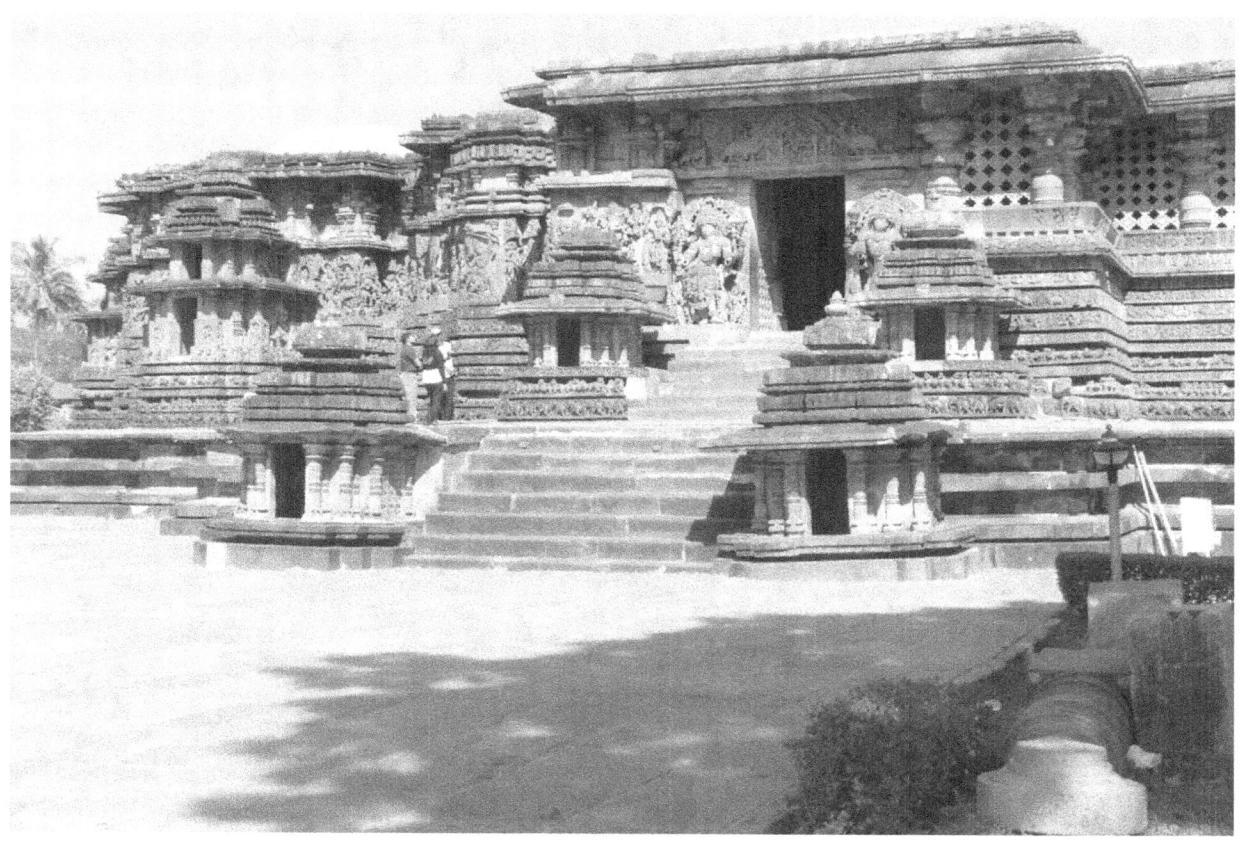

Plate 6-70: South Entrance of Hoysaleswara Temple Halebid

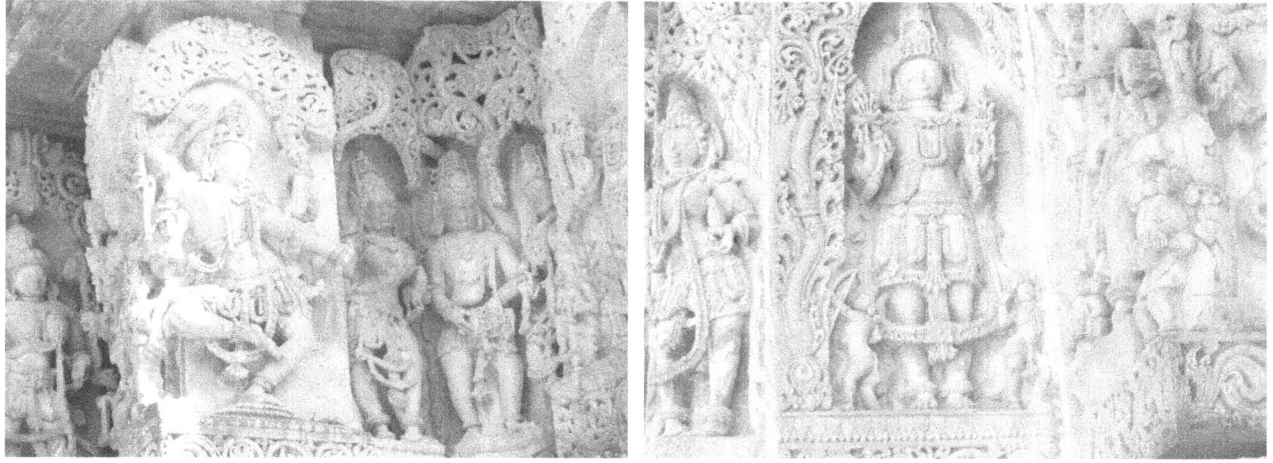

Plate 6-71: Siva Dancing and Surya on the Outer Walls of Hoysaleswara Temple

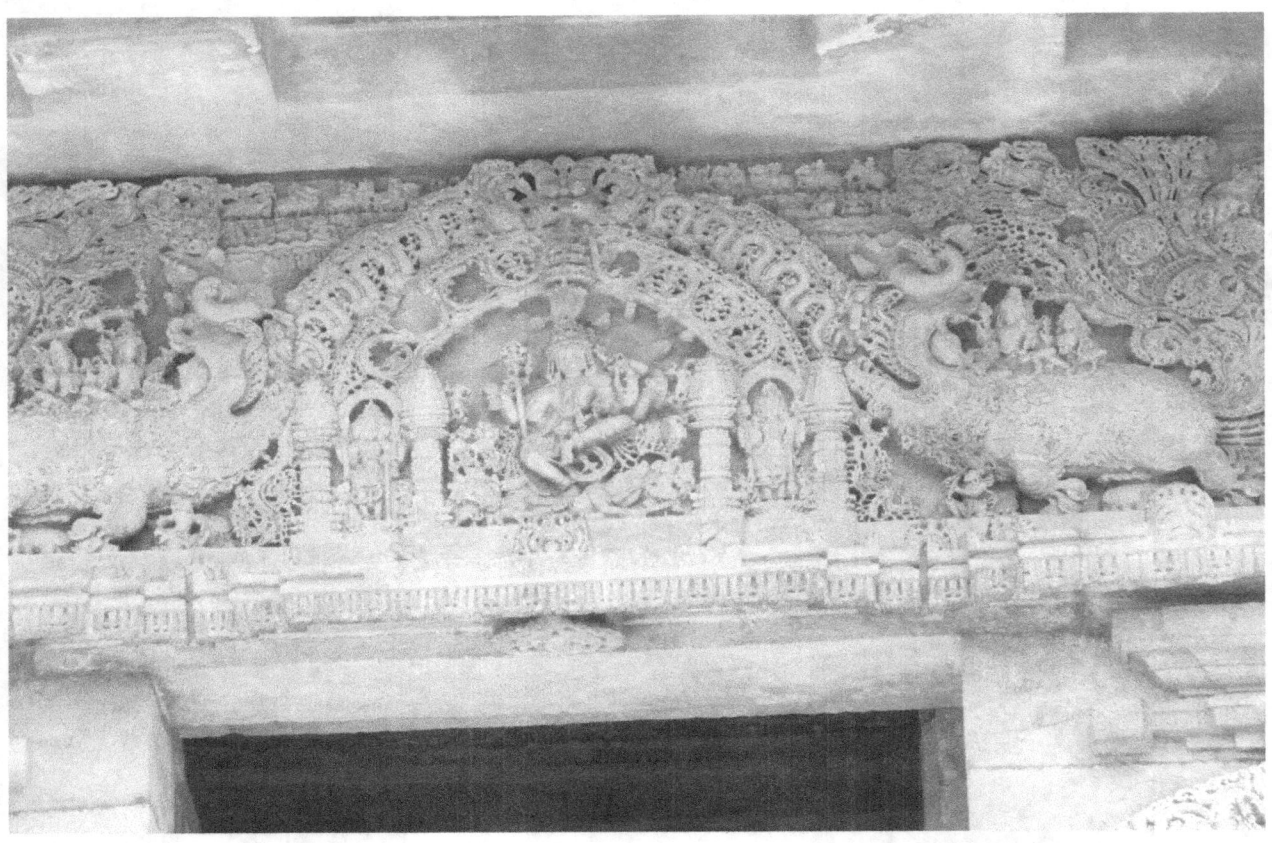

Plate 6-72: Makaratorana at the South Entrance of Hoysaleswara Temple Halebid

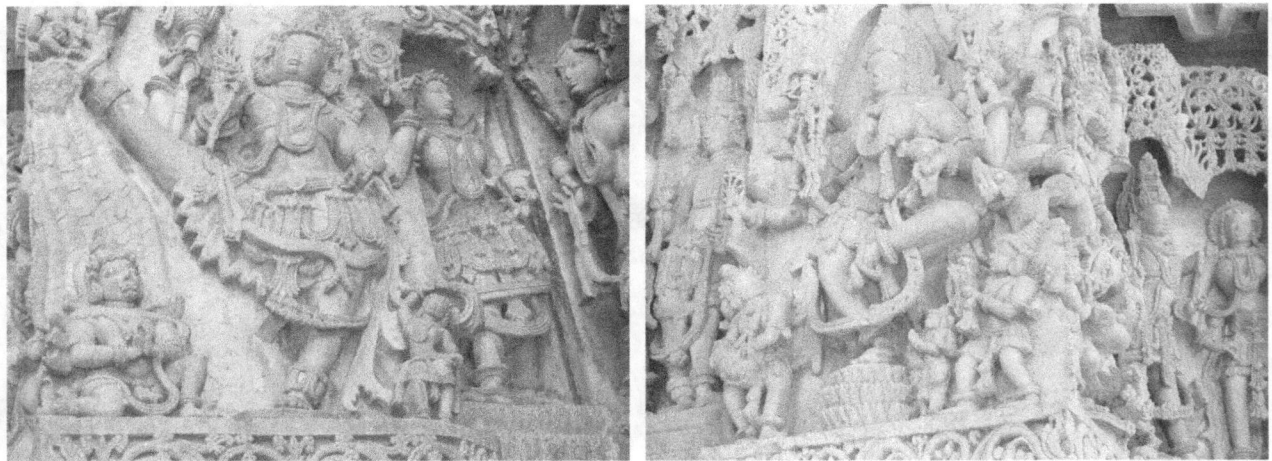

Plate 6-73: Trivikrama and Goddess Lakshmi Hoysaleswara Temple

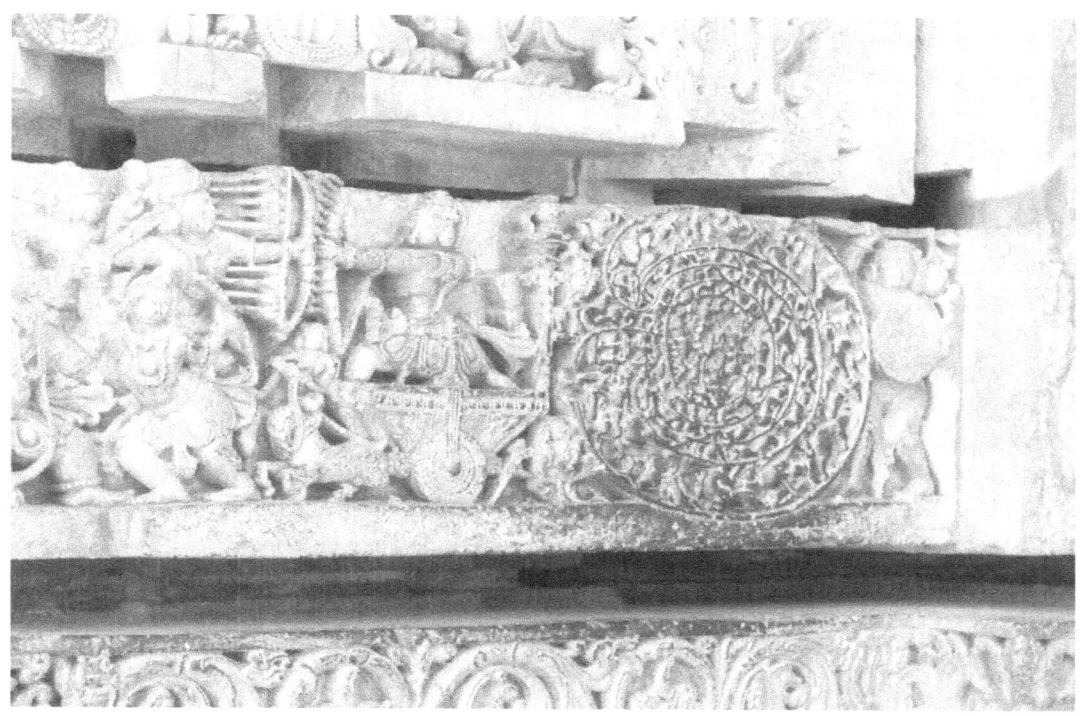

Plate 6-74: Hoysaleswara Temple Halebid, Abhimanyu and Chakravyuh

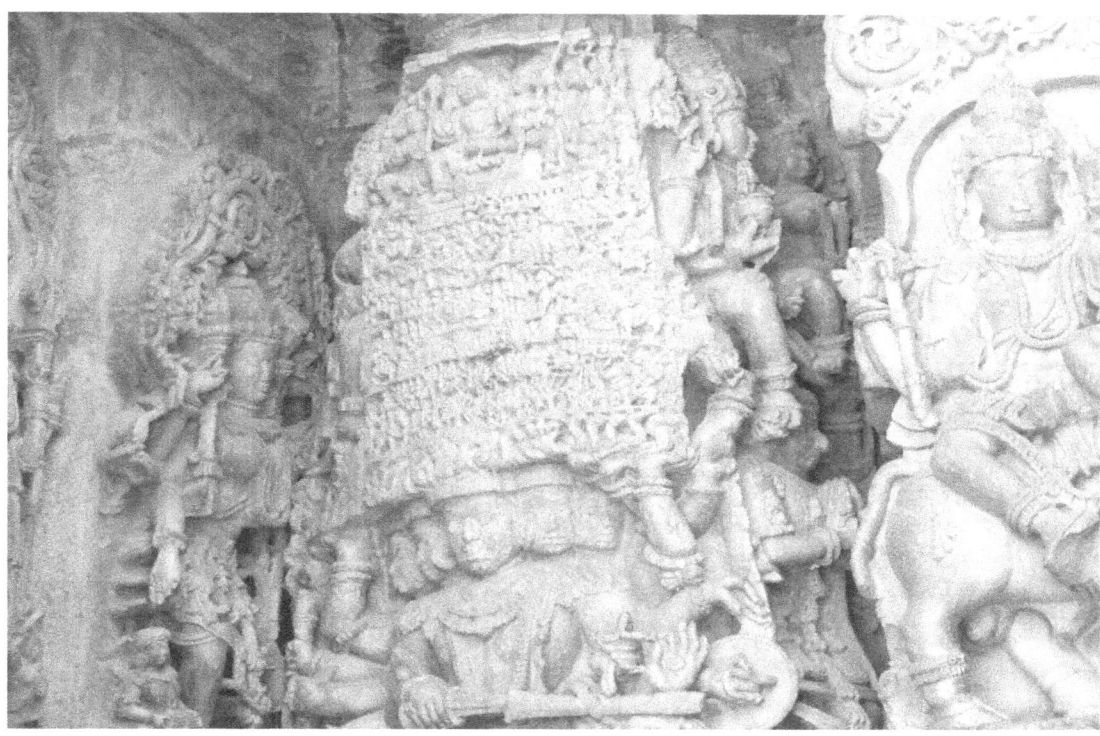

Plate 6-75: Ravana Shaking Mount Kailasa, Hoysaleswara Temple

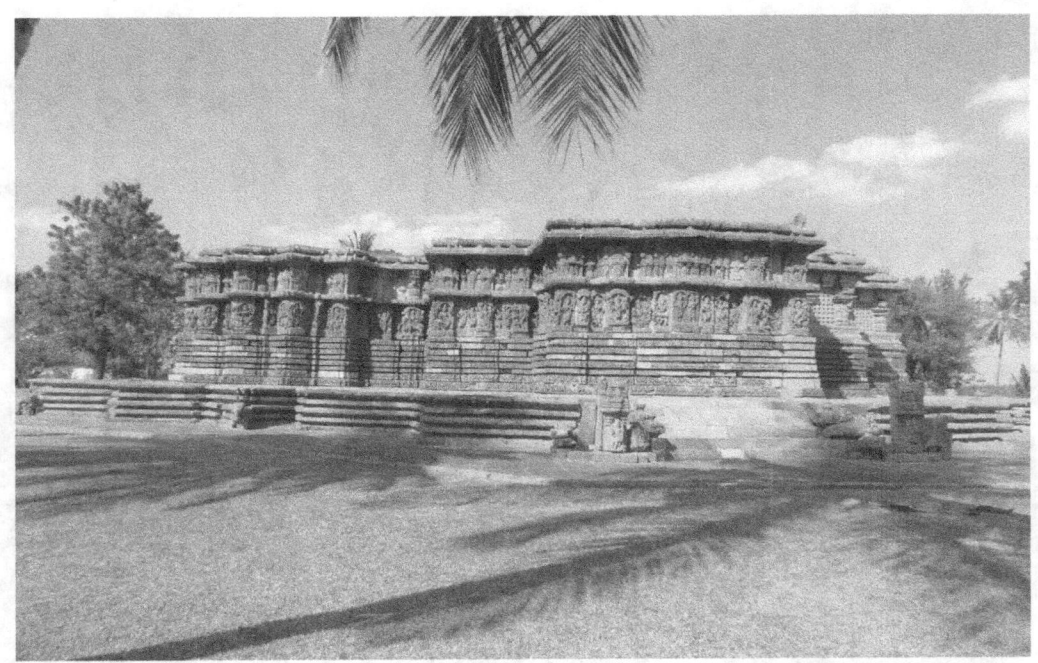

Plate 6-76: Complete Side View of Kedareswara Temple Halebid

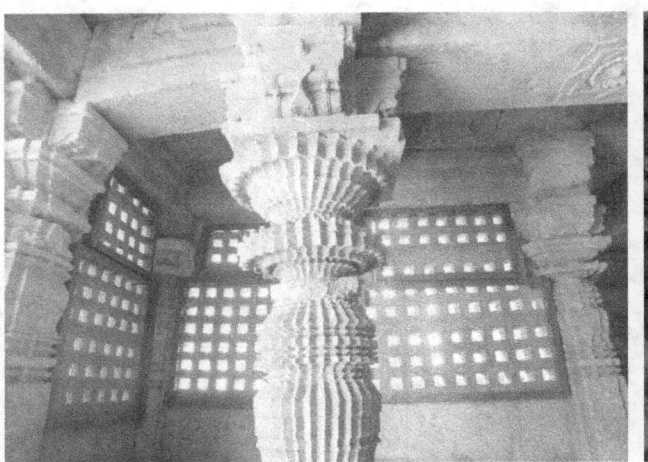 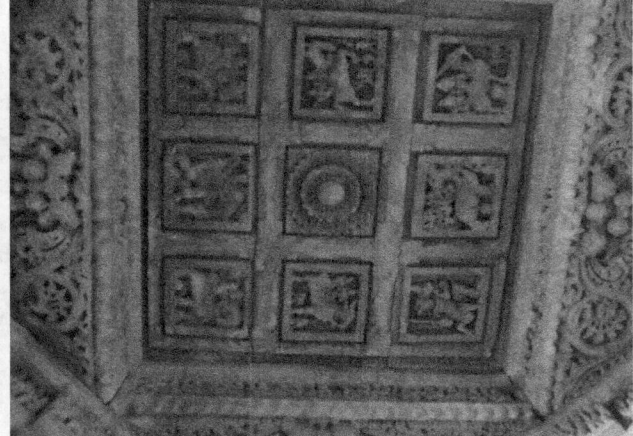

Plate 6-77: Inside Kedareswara Temple, 32 Pointed Stellate Pillar and Navaranga Ceiling

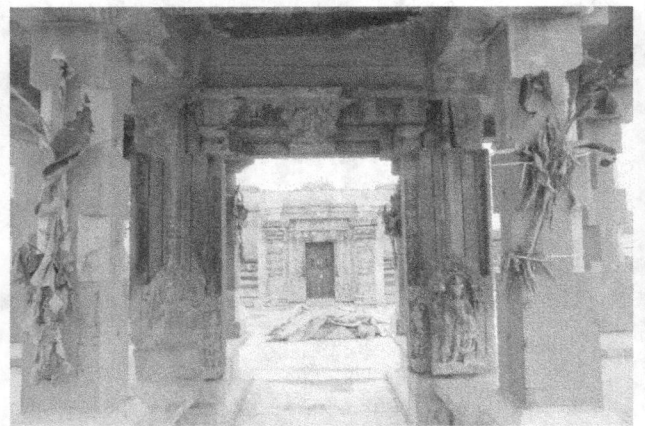 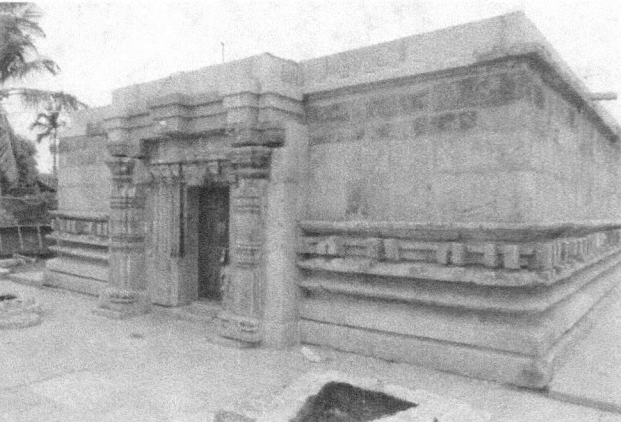

Plate 6-78: Ranganathaswamy Temple Halebid Entrance

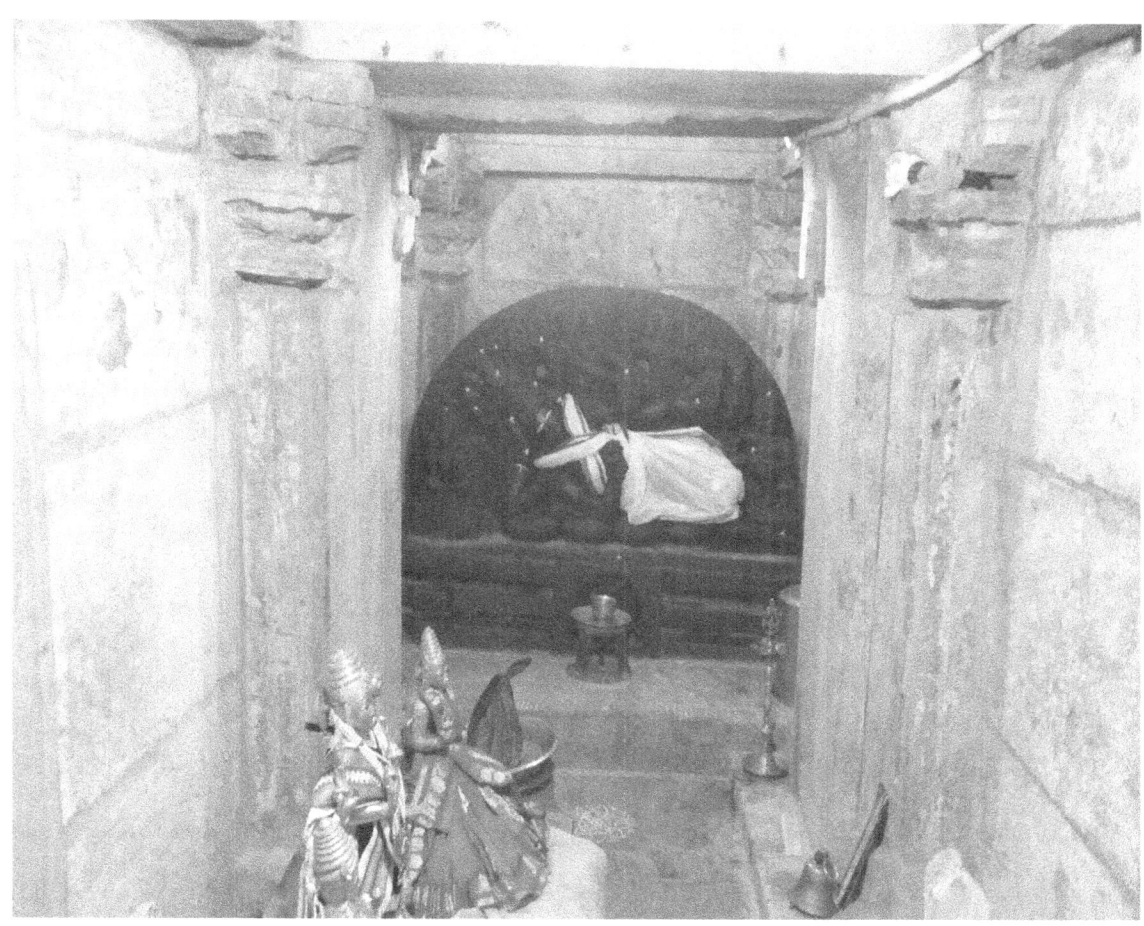

Plate 6-79: Image of Ranganathaswamy, Halebid

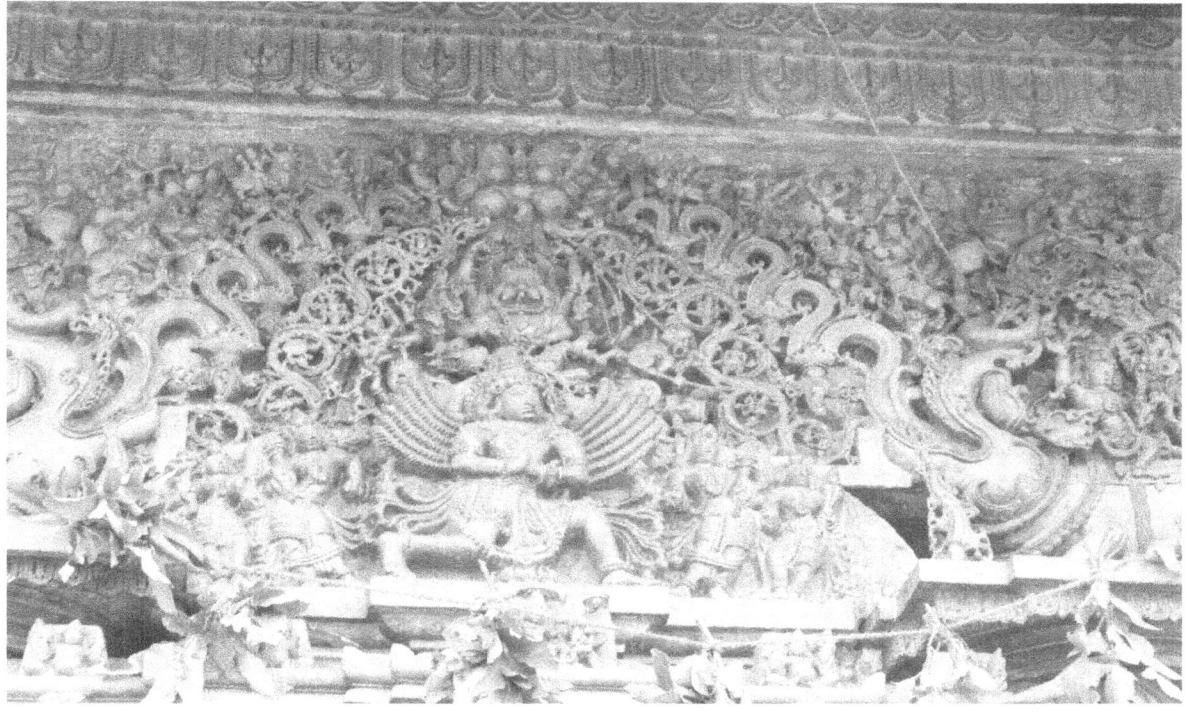

Plate 6-80: Makaratorana with Narasimha Riding on Garuda's Shoulders, Chennakesava Temple Entrance Belur

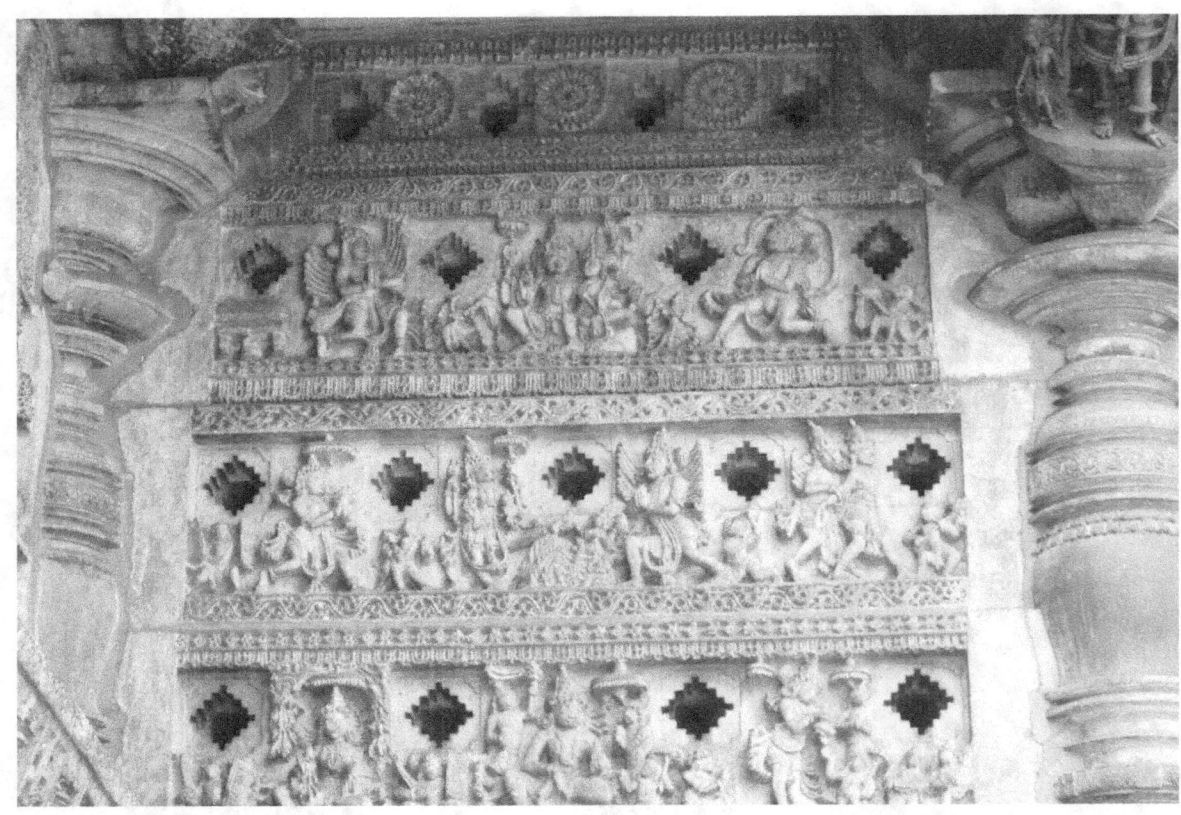

Plate 6-81: Garuda and Hanumana Attending on Visnu and Lakshmi, Carving on Perforated Window

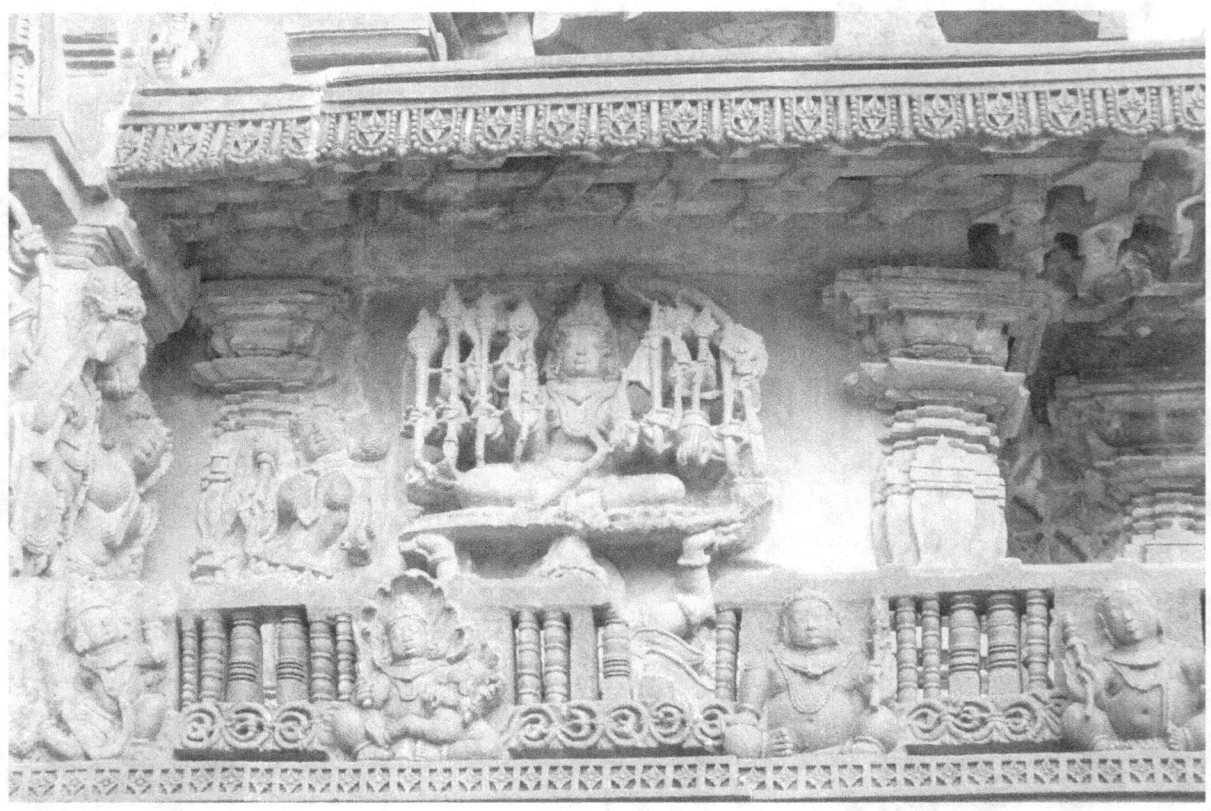

Plate 6-82: Eight Armed Visnu Seated Under the Eave, Chennakesava Temple Belur

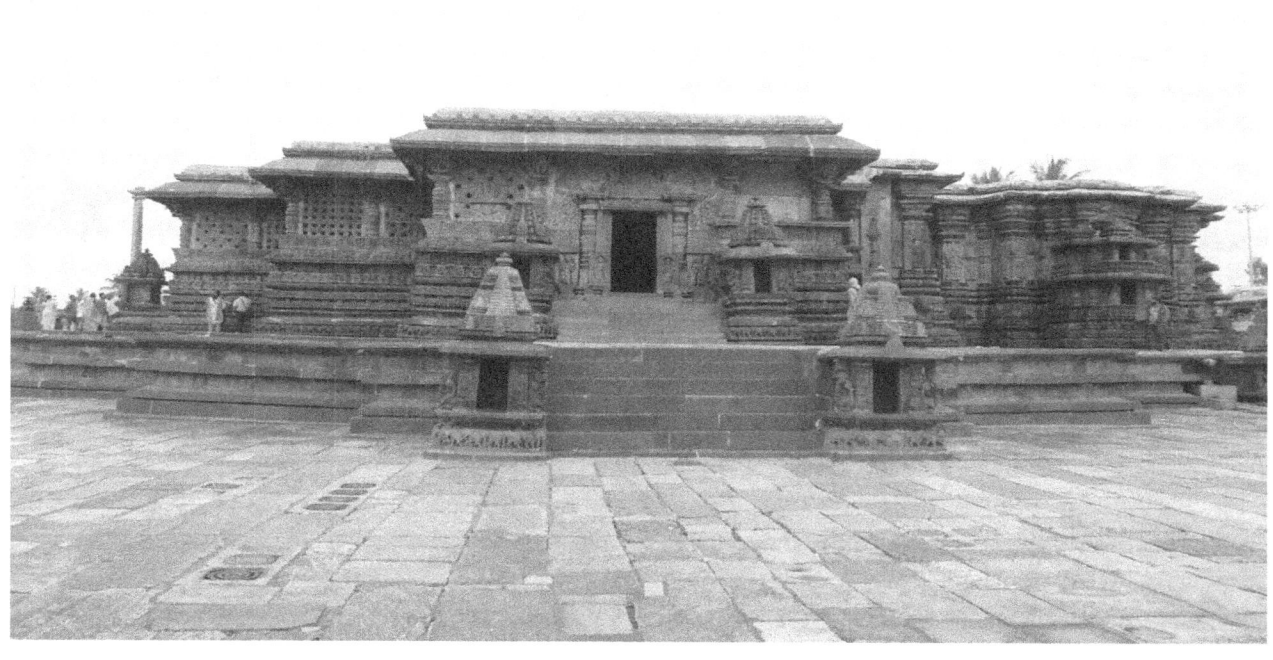

Plate 6-83: Complete View of the Entrance, Chennakesava Temple Belur

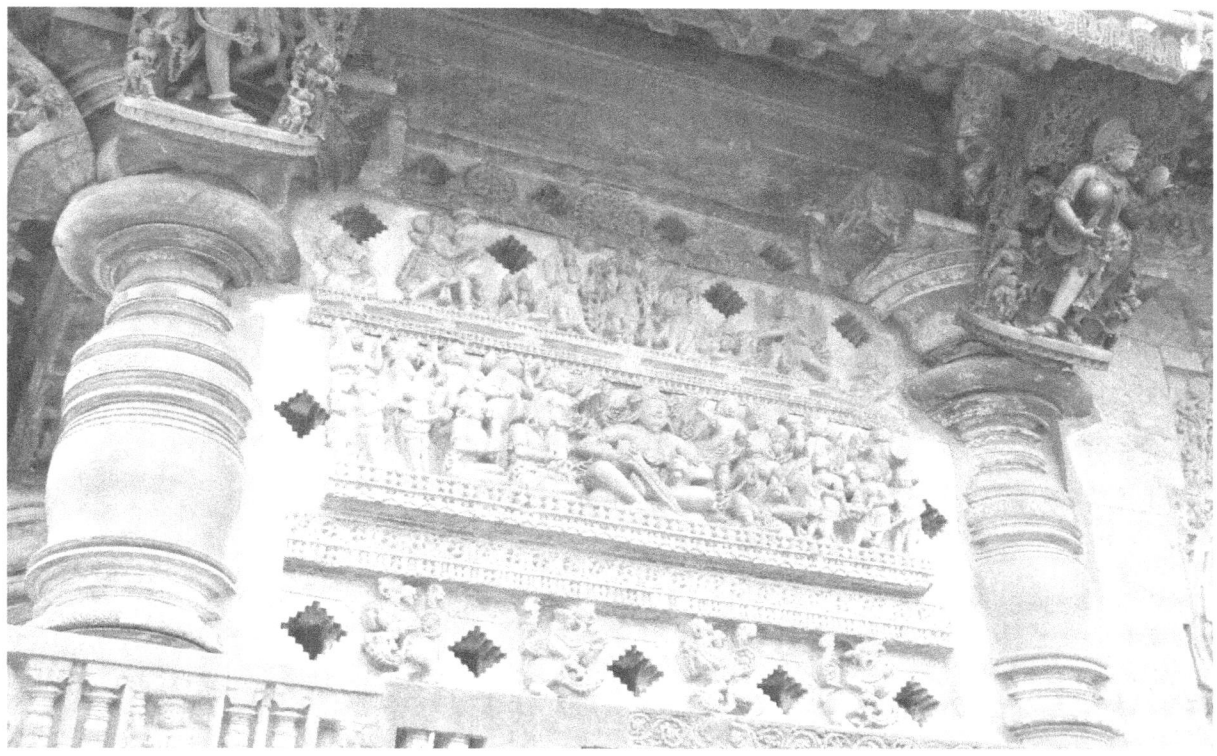

Plate 6-84: King and Queen with Their Retinue on Perforated Window and Darpanasundari on Column Bracket, Belur

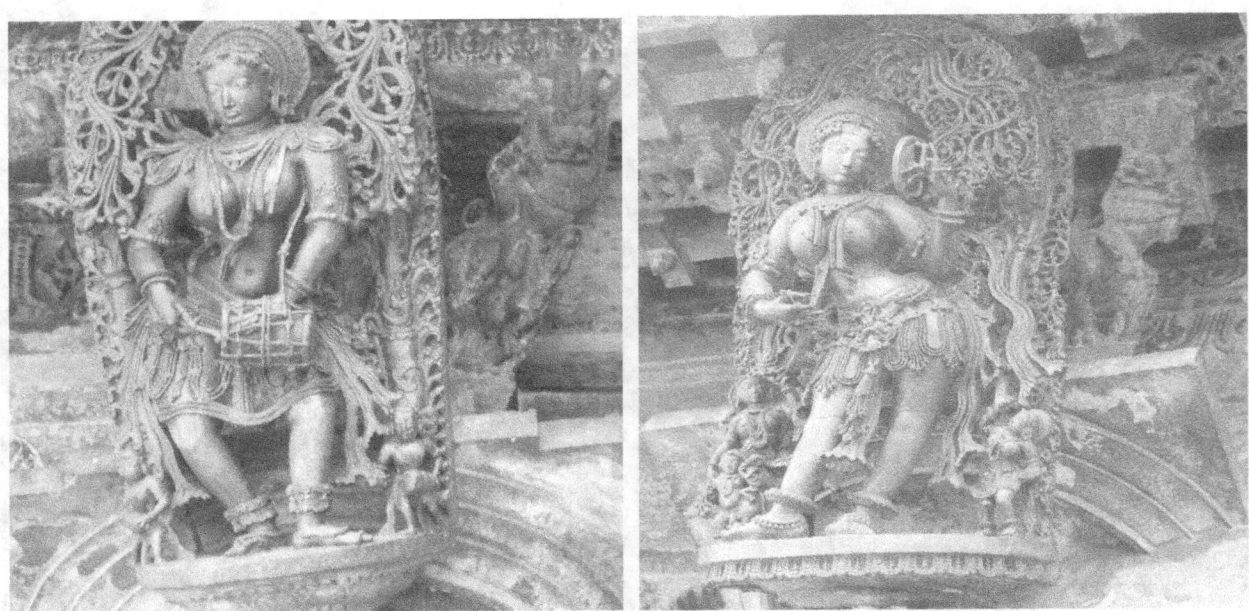

Plate 6-85: Madanikas With the Drum and Mirror in Hand, Belur

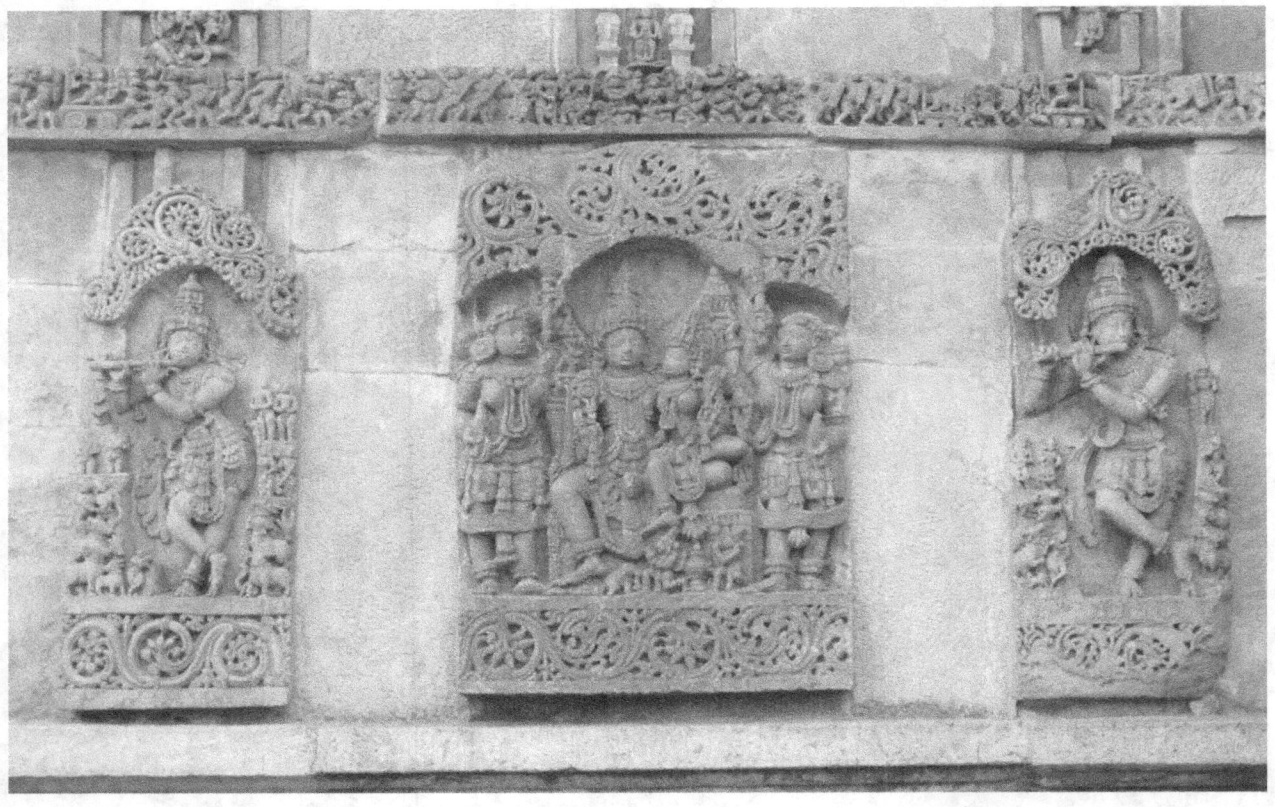

Plate 6-86: Krishna Playing Flute on Both Sides of Visnu-Lakshmi Sculpture, Andal Temple Belur

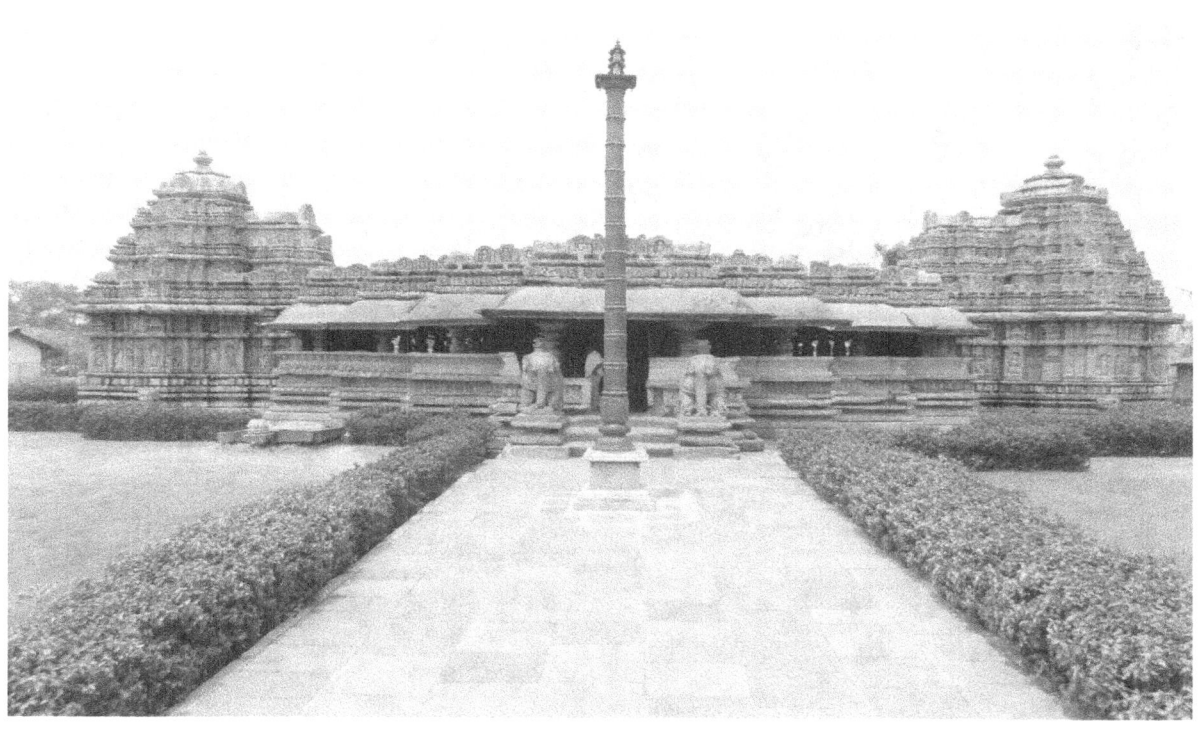

Plate 6-87: Veeranarayana Temple Belavadi

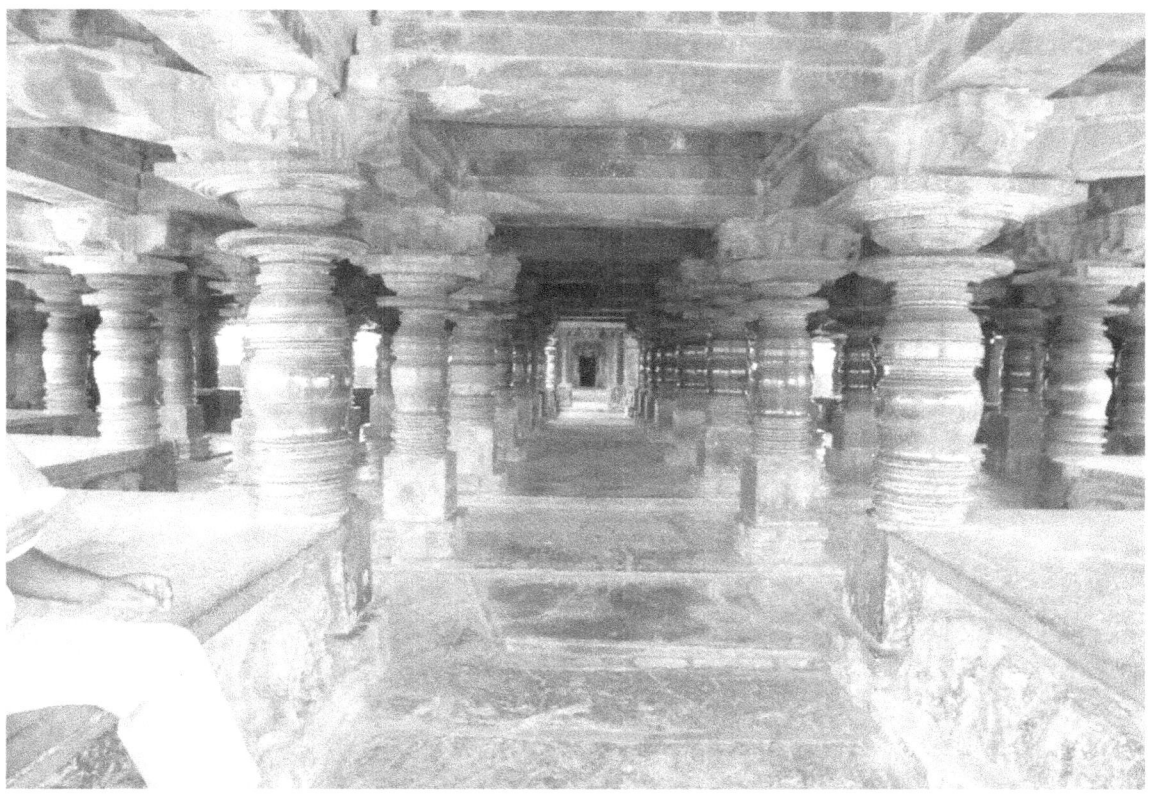

Plate 6-88: Open Hall with 37 Bays and Lathe-turned Pillars Belavadi

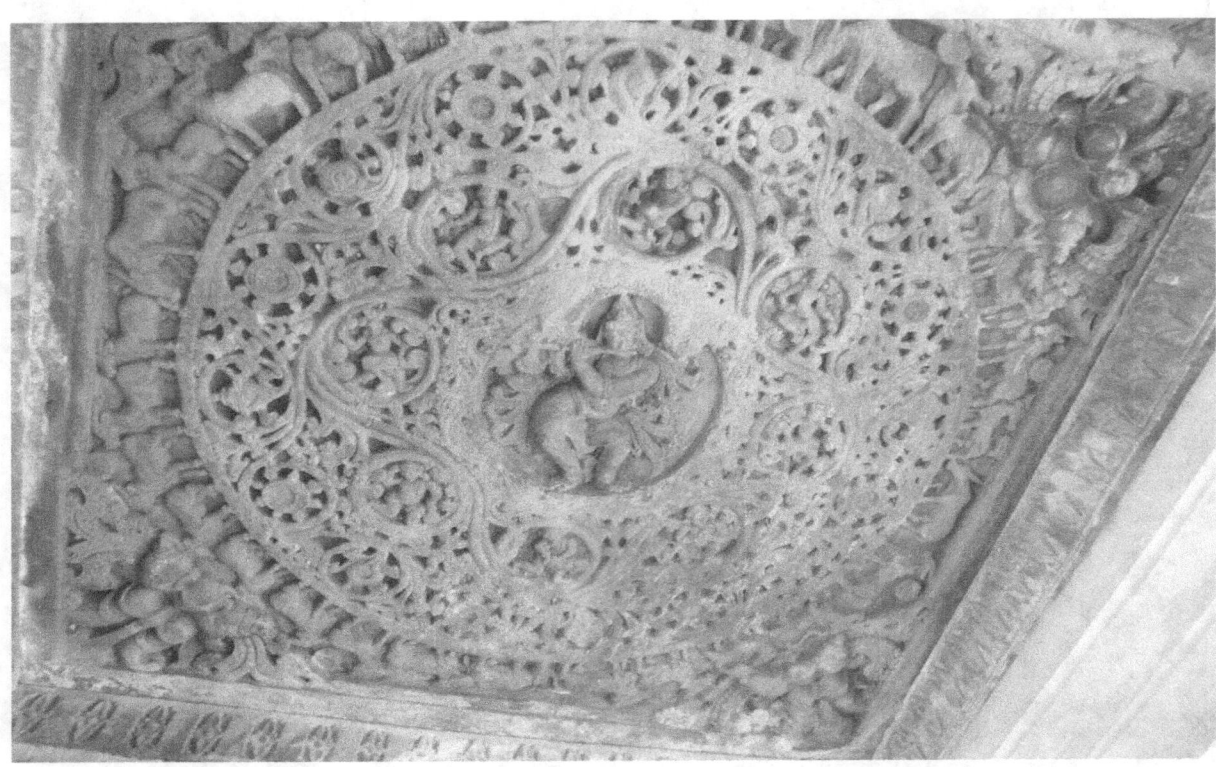
Plate 6-89: Ceiling of Navaranga with Krishna Playing Flute and Surrounded by Gopikas and Cows, Belavadi

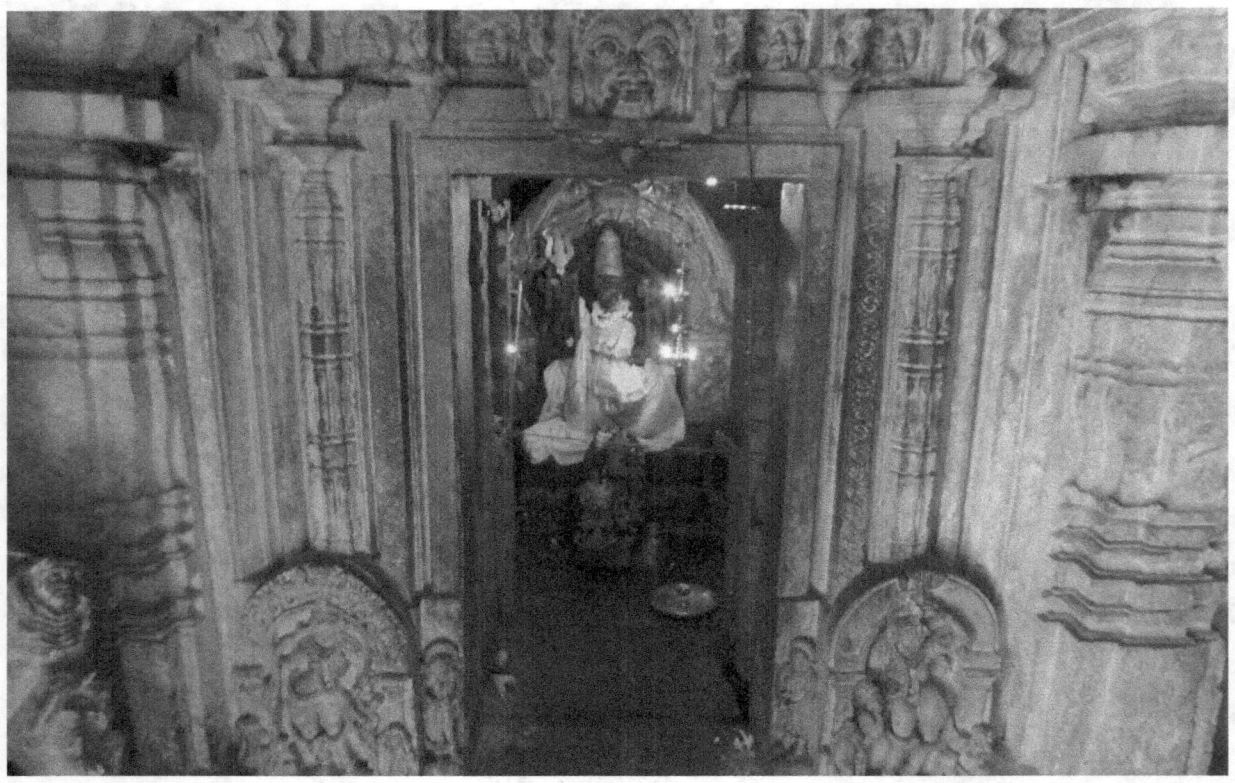
Plate 6-90: Goddess Kali Lakshmidevi Temple Doddagadavalli

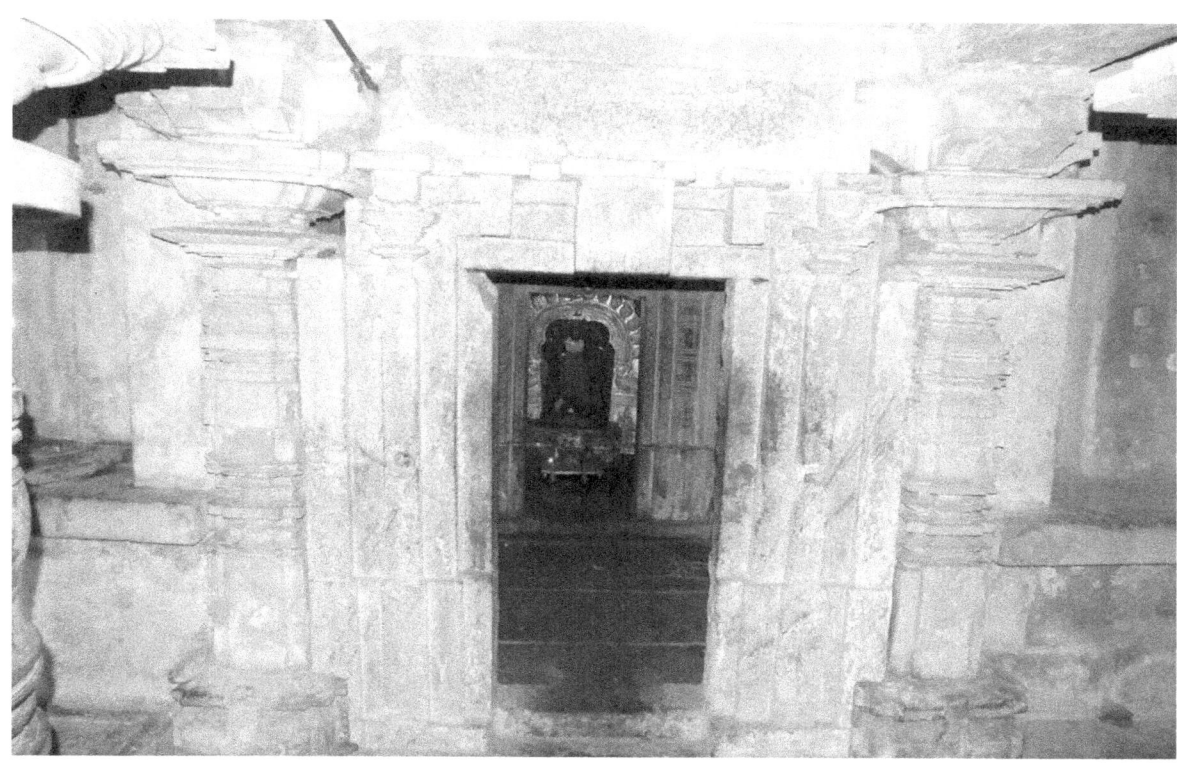

Plate 6-91: Lakshmidevi Shrine Doddagadavalli

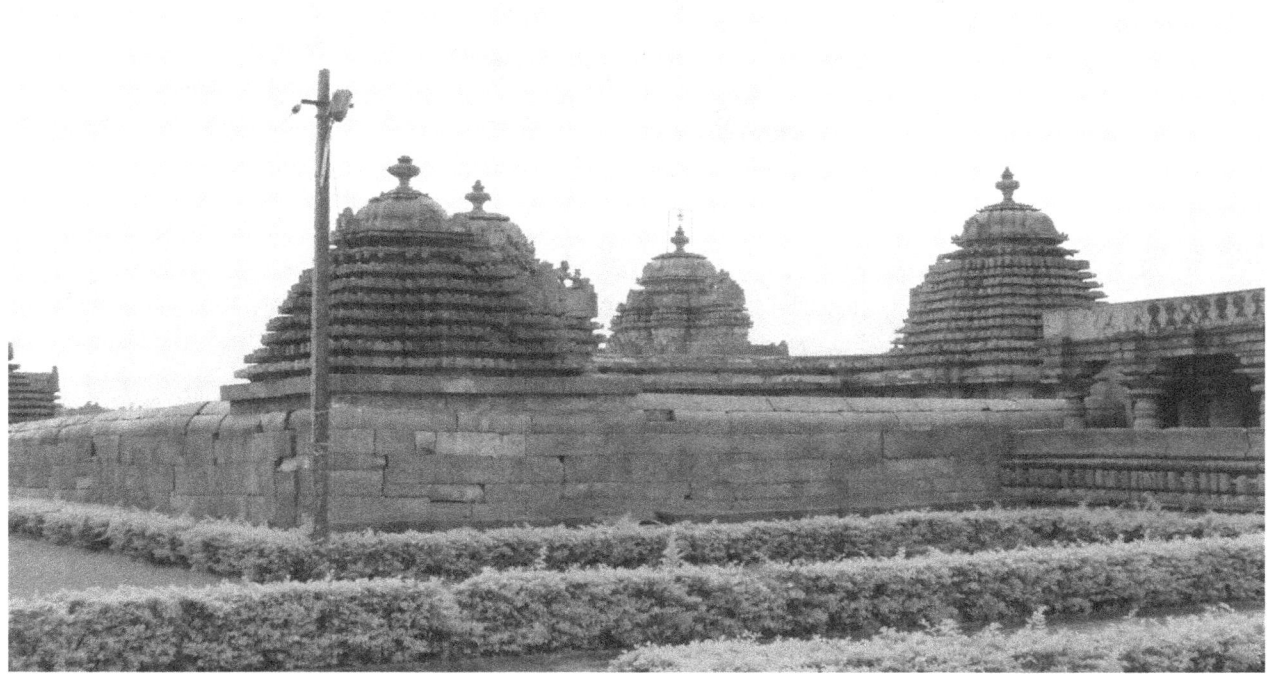

Plate 6-92: Lakshmidevi Chatushkuta Temple, Doddagadavalli

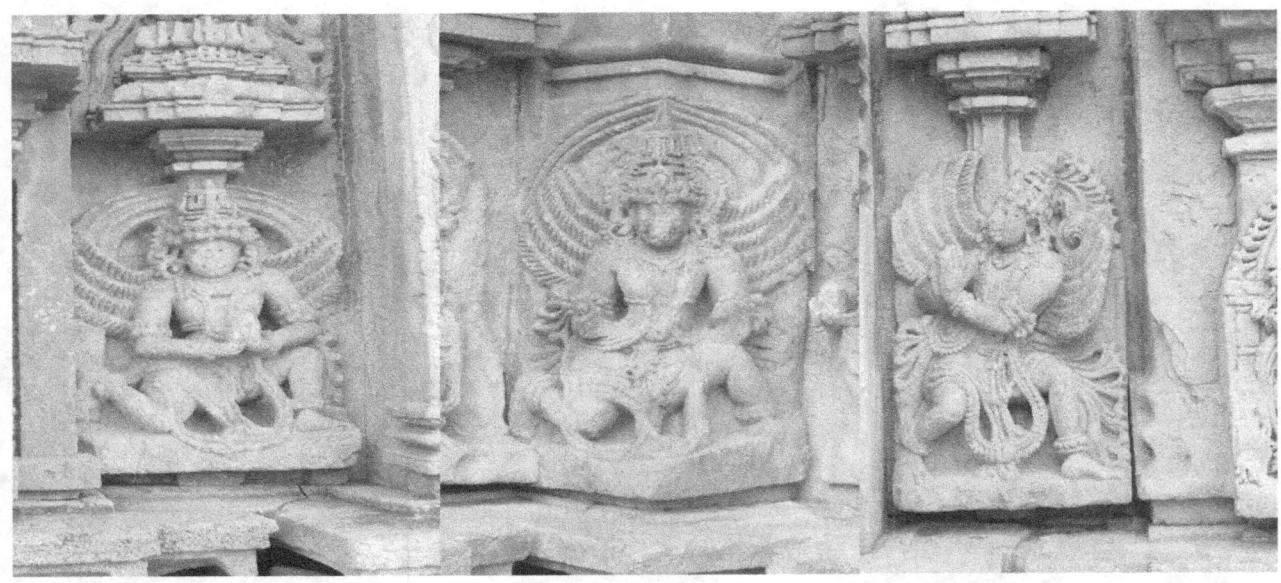

Plate 6-93: Three Different Sculptures of Garuda from Chennakesava Temple Mosale

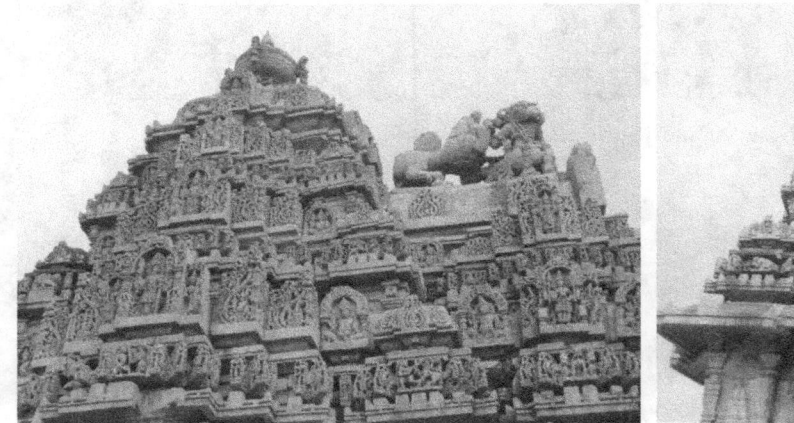
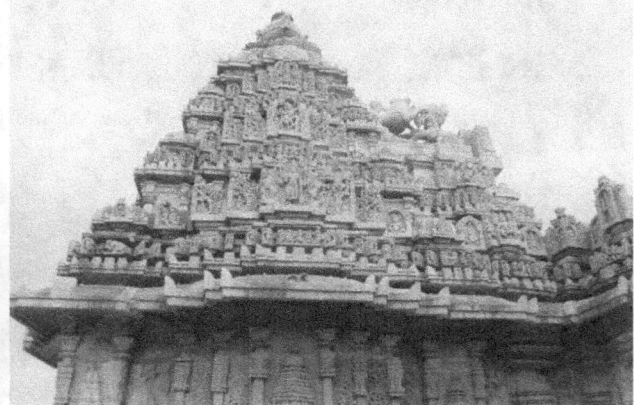

Plate 6-94: Sikharas of Nageswara and Chennakesava Temples Mosale

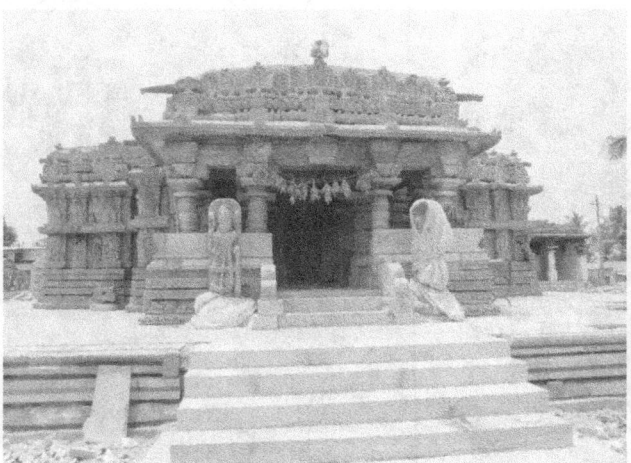
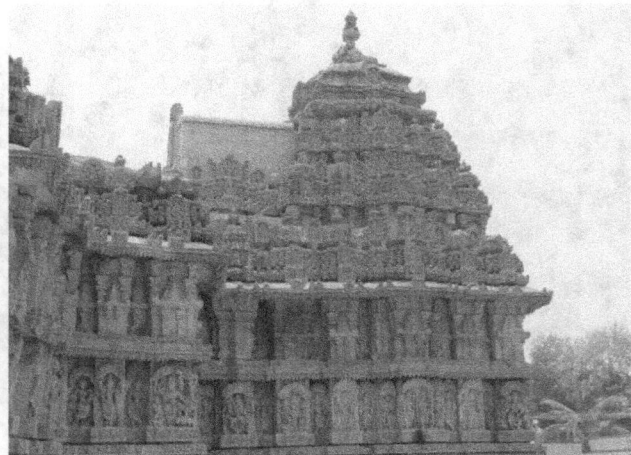

Plate 6-95: Lakshmi Narasimha Temple Javagal

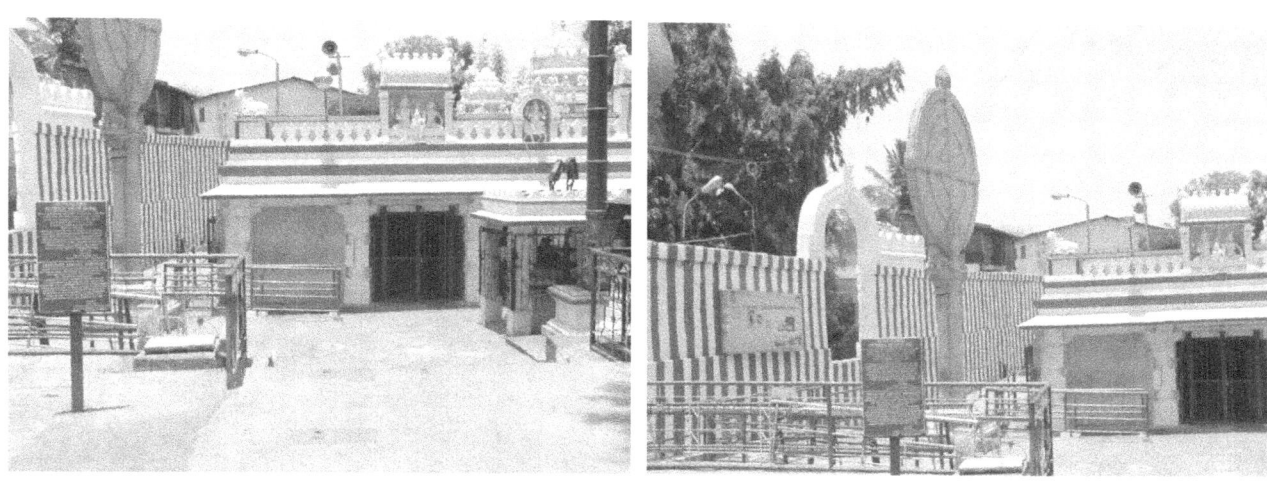

Plate 6-96: Gavi Gangadhareswara Temple Gavipuram

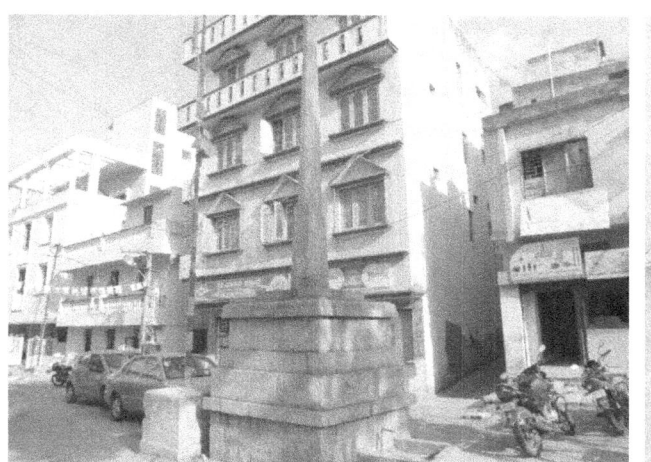 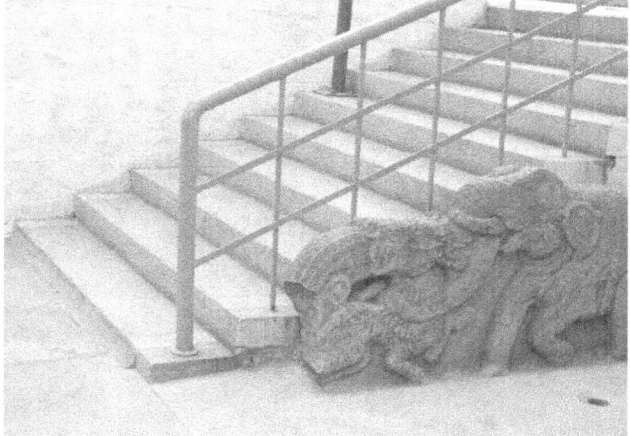

Plate 6-97: Chokkaperumal Temple Domlur

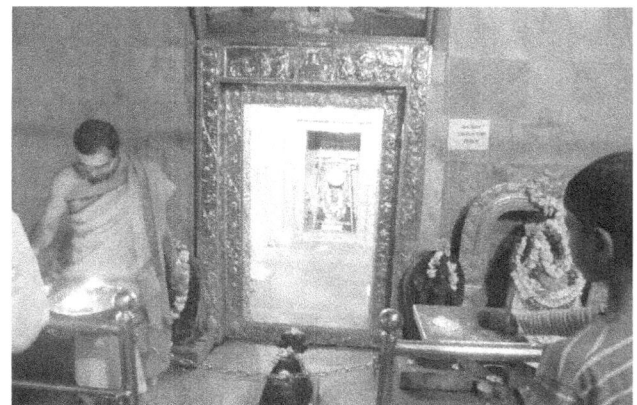 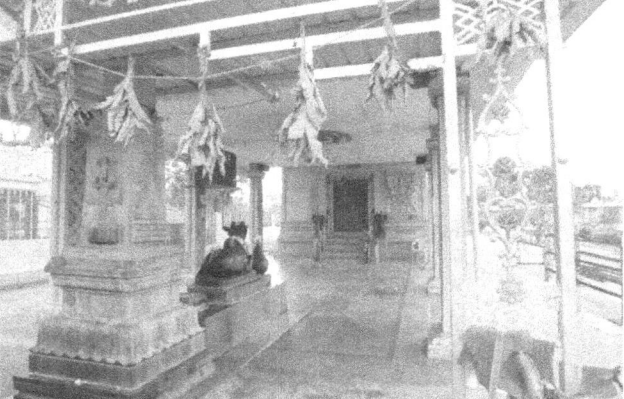

Plate 6-98: Kashi vishwanatha Temple Kadugodi

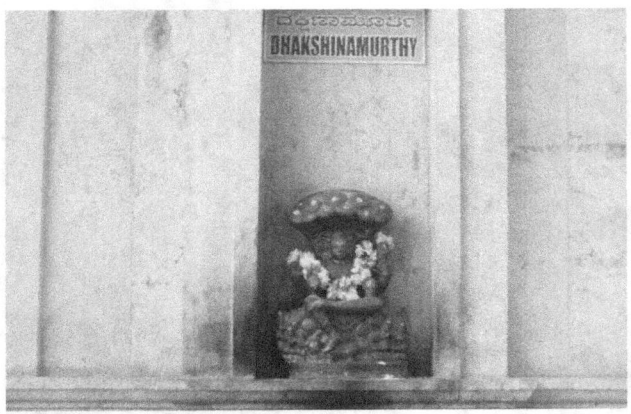 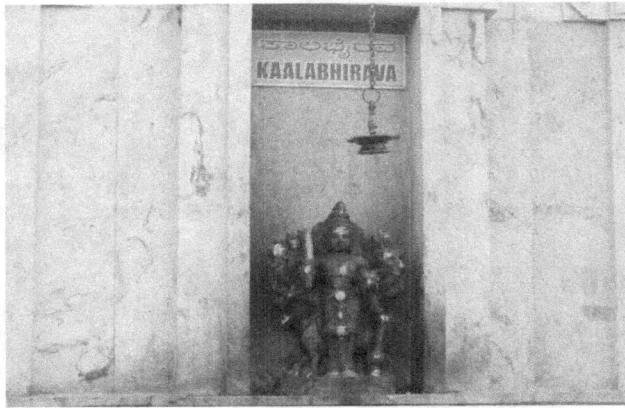

Plate 6-99: Dakshinamurthy and Kalabhairava Images, Kashi Vishwanatha Temple Kadugodi

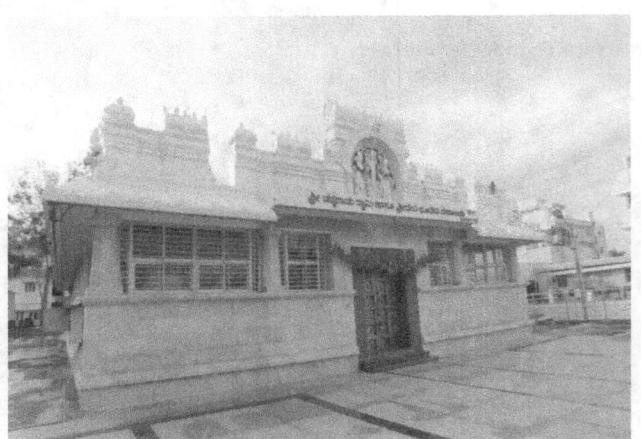 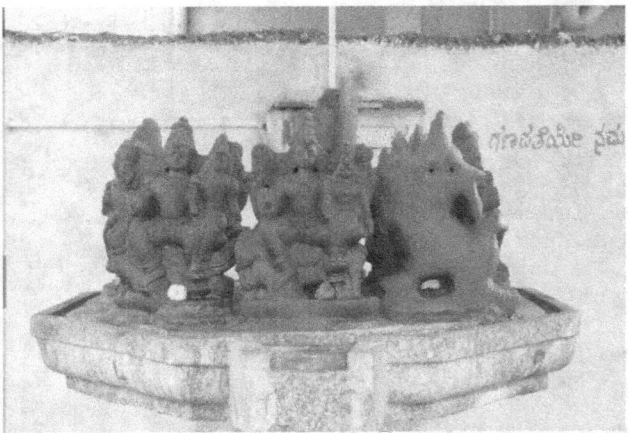

Plate 6-100: Chennakesava Temple Chikkajala (Renovated)

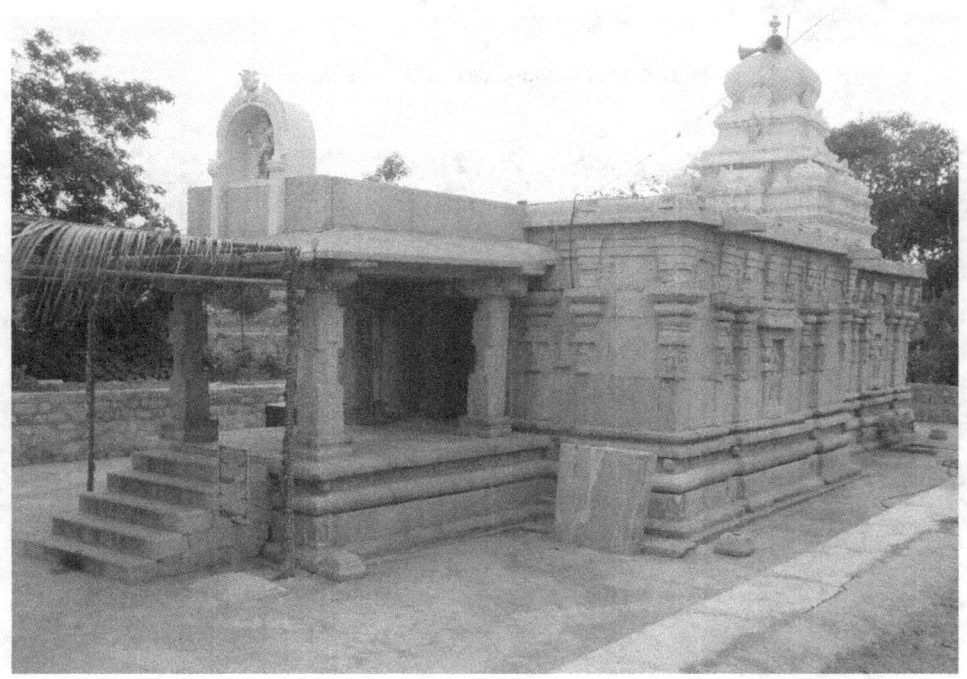

Plate 6-101: Muktinatheswara Temple Binnamangala

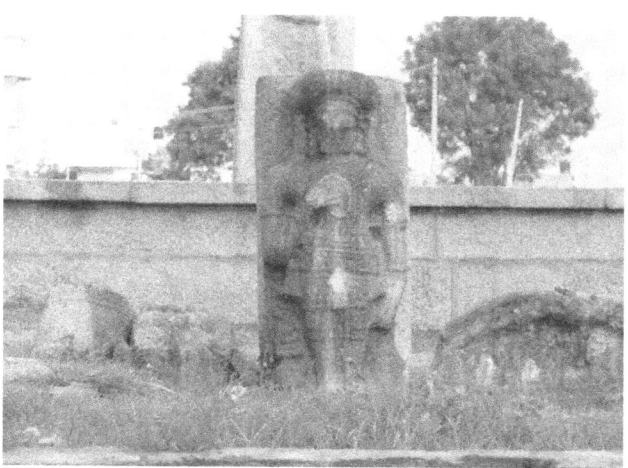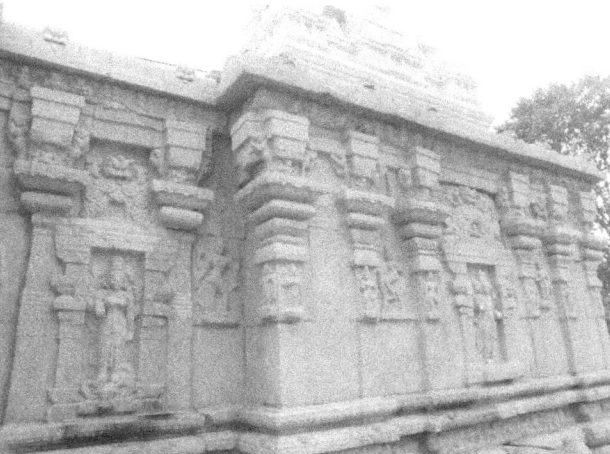

Plate 6-102: Kulothunga Chola Image and Temple Wall Sculpture, Binnamangala

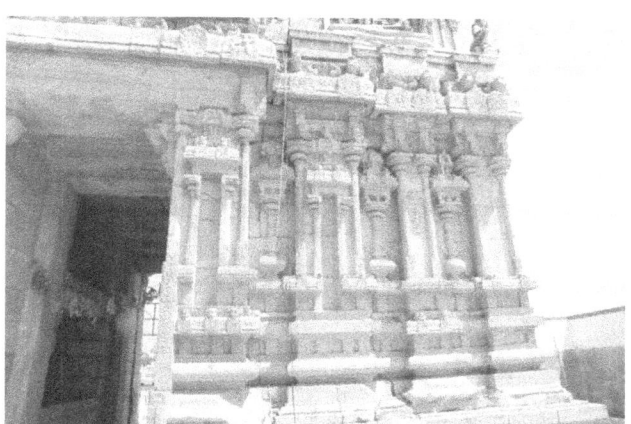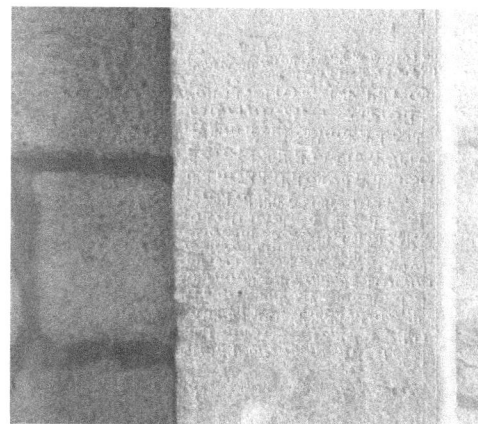

Plate 6-103: Gateway Pilasters and Inscription Champakadhamaswamy Temple Bannerghatta

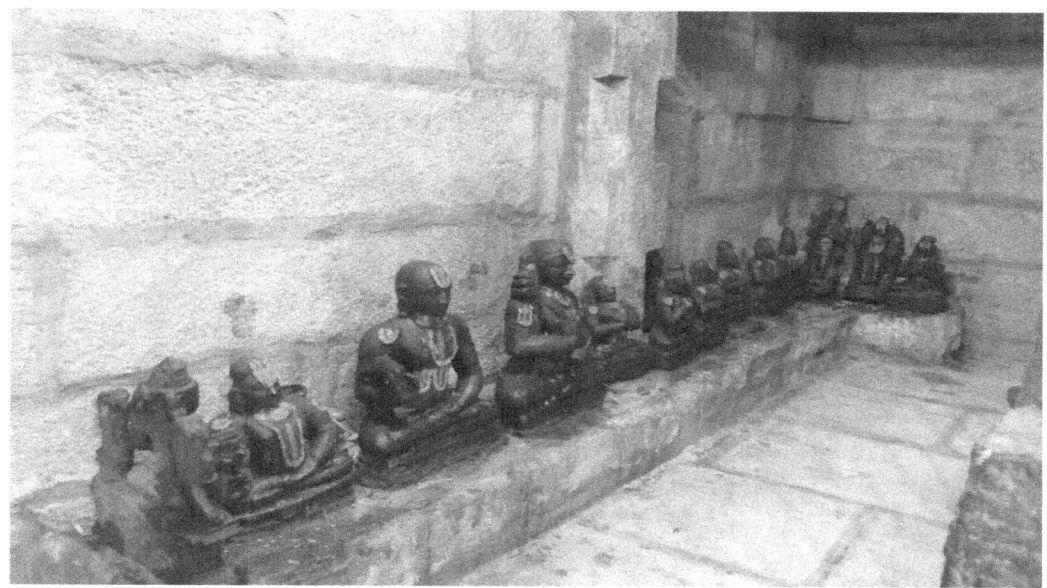

Plate 6-104: Ramanujacharya and Alwars, Champakadhamaswamy Temple Bannerghatta

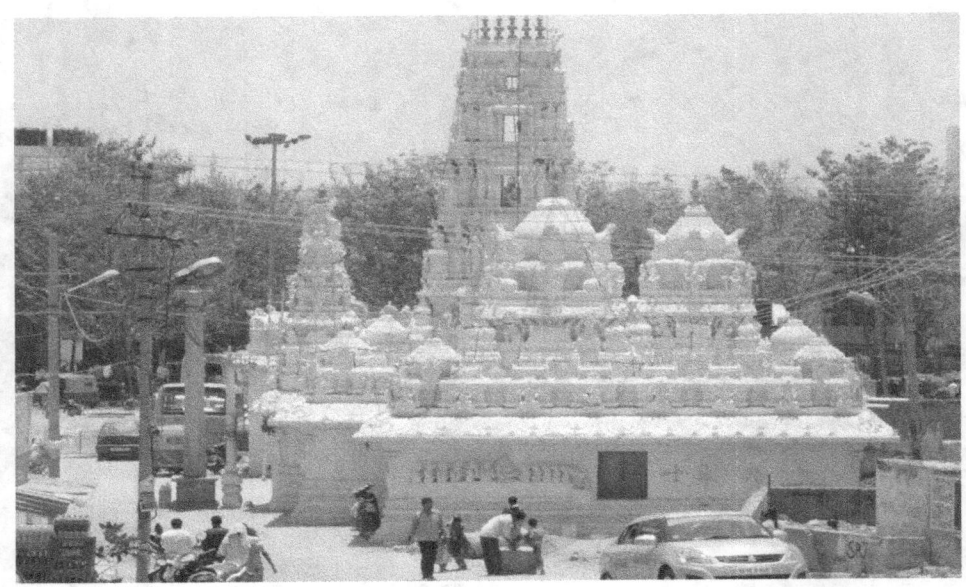

Plate 6-105: Hulimavu Temple

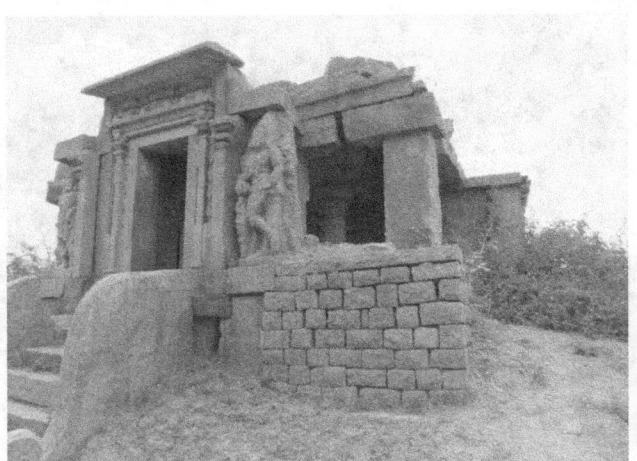
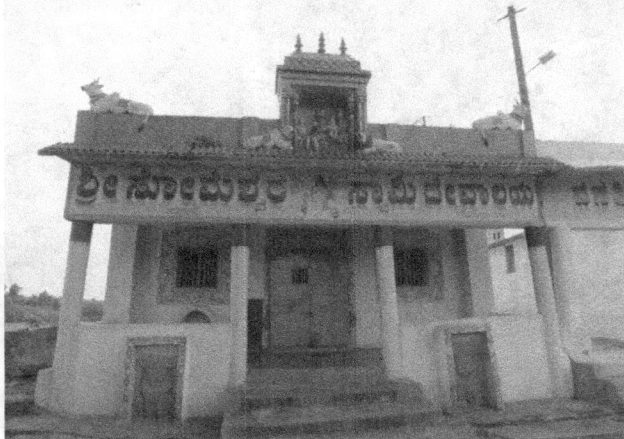

Plate 6-106: Kapileswara and Someswara Temples, Manne

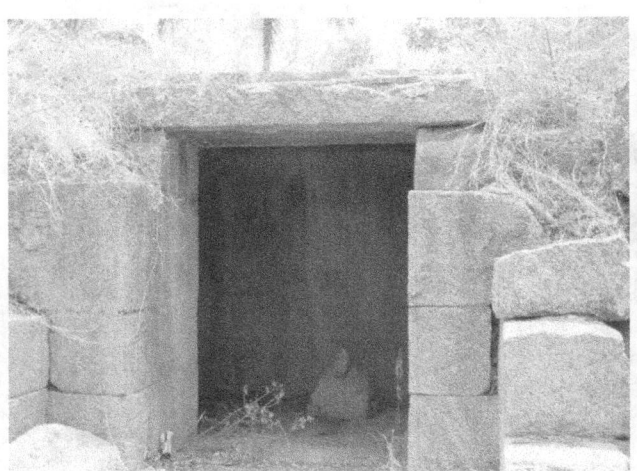
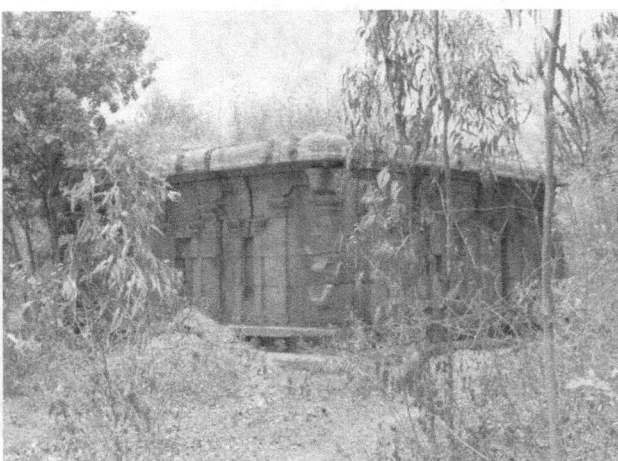

Plate 6-107: Akka Tangi Temple Manne

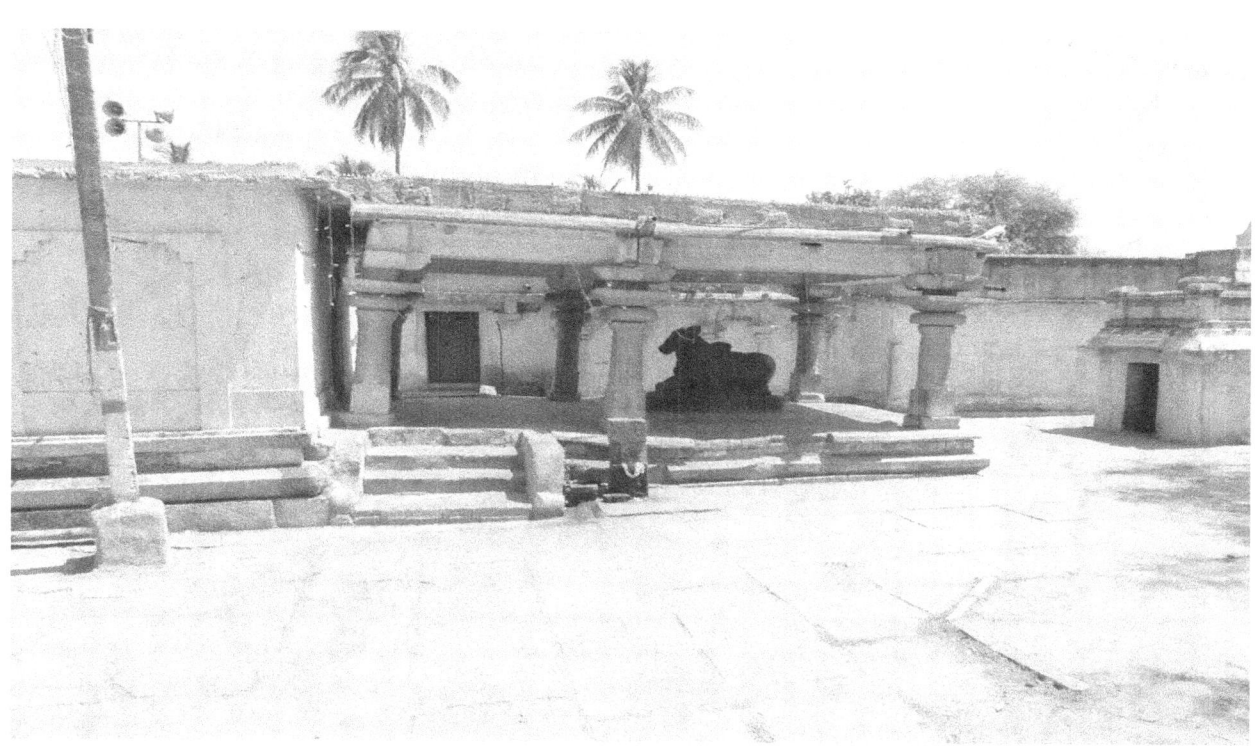

Plate 6-108: Nagareswara Temple Begur

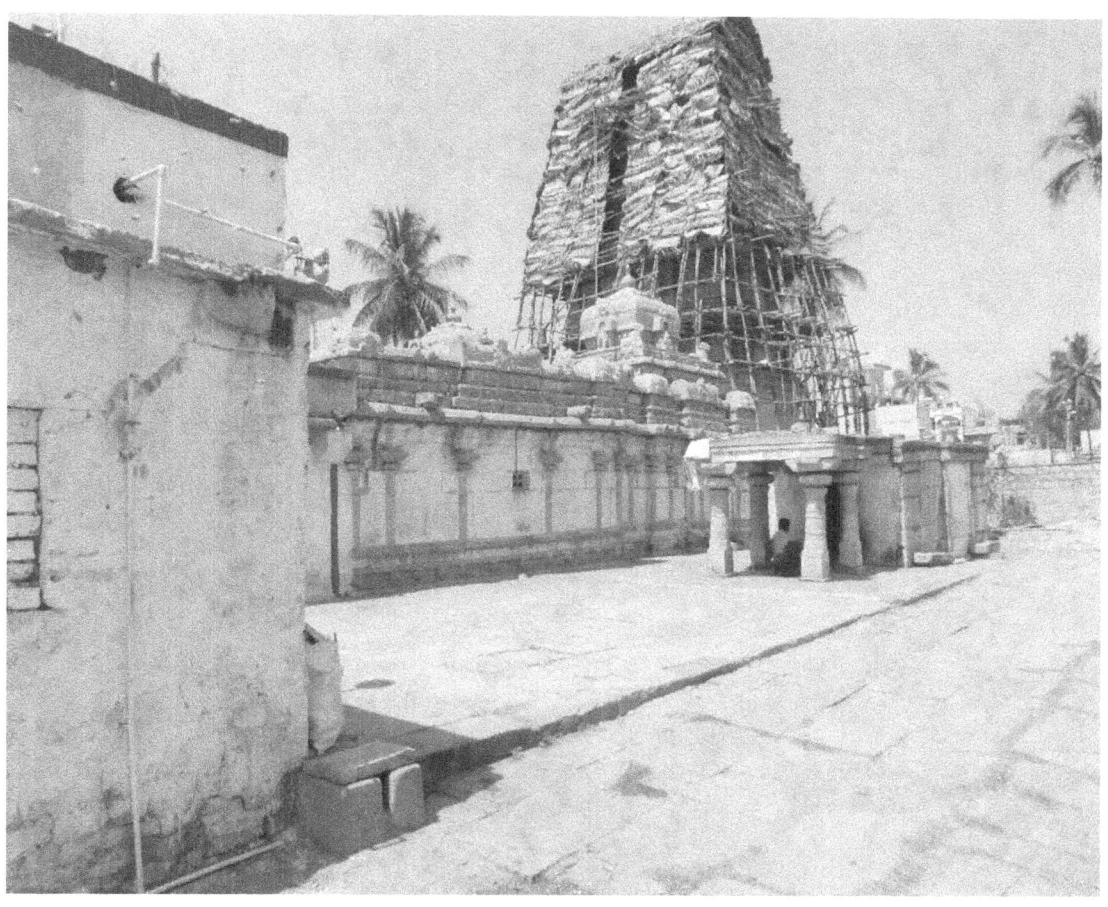

Plate 6-109: Nageswara Temple Begur

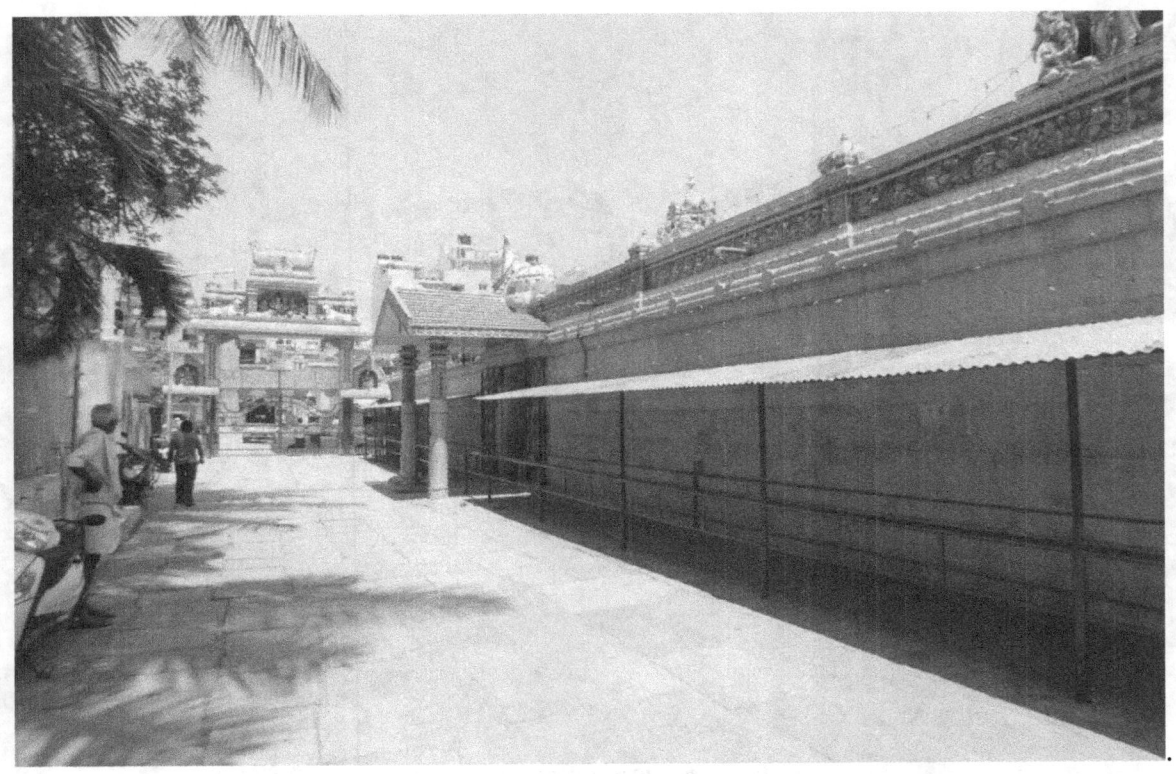

Plate 6-110: Someswara Temple Madivala Bengaluru

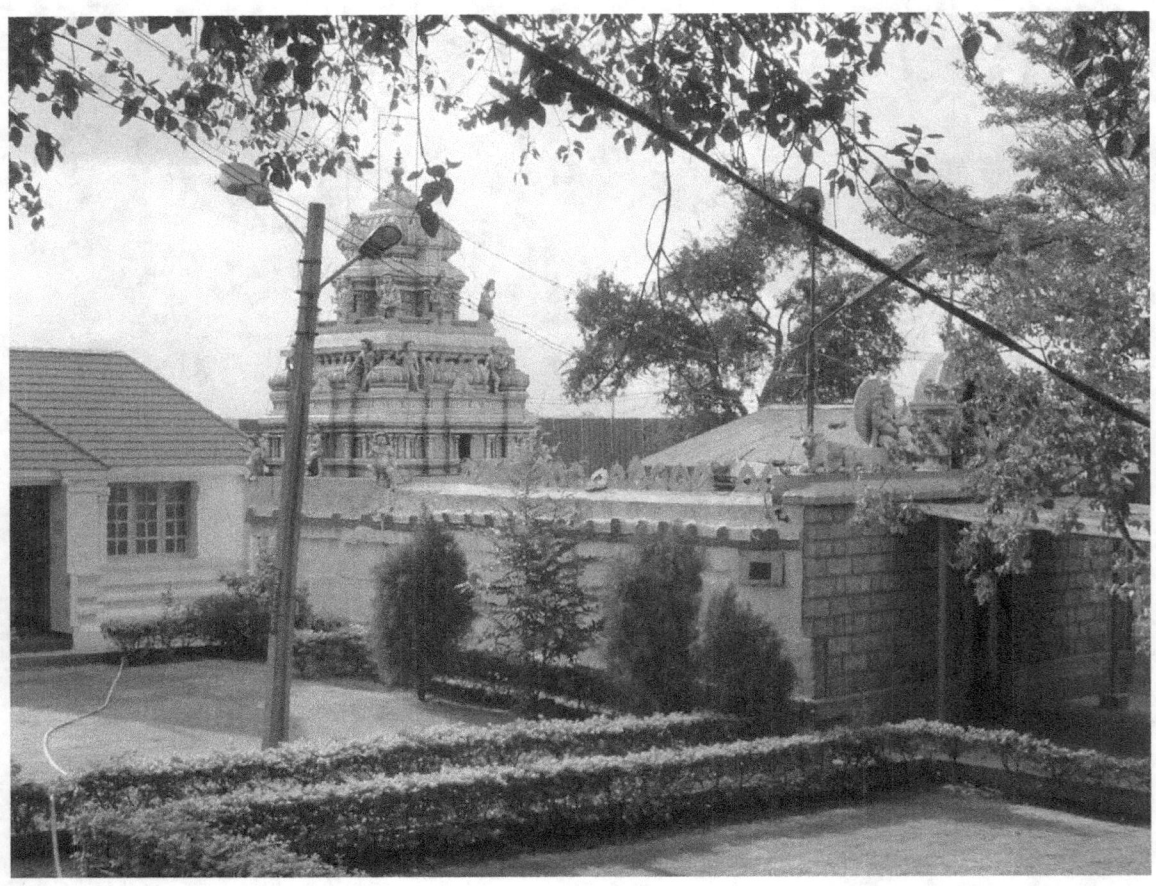

Plate 6-111: Someswara Temple Agara Bengaluru

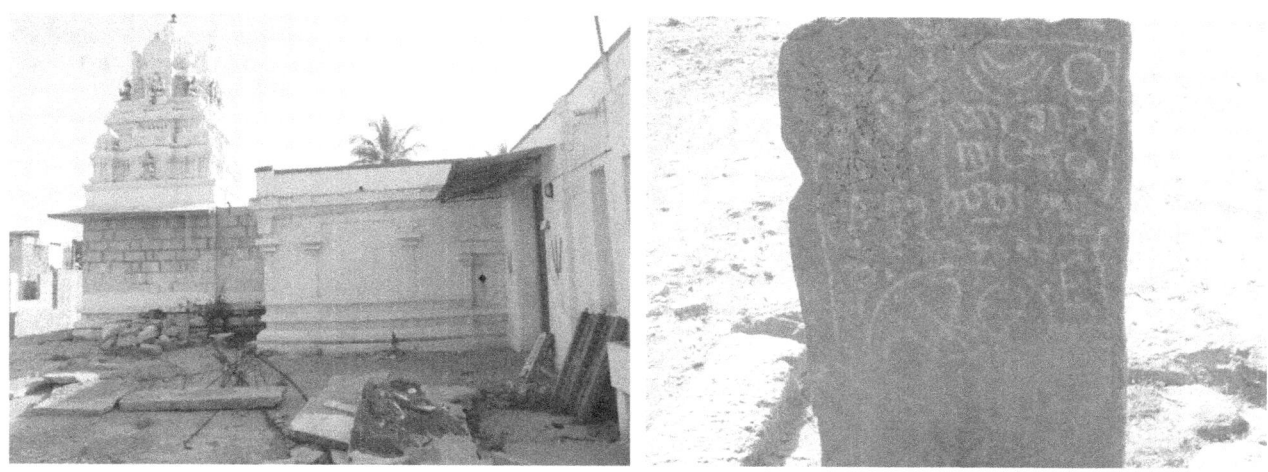

Plate 6-112: Varadaraja Temple Vagata and Inscriptions Outside Temple

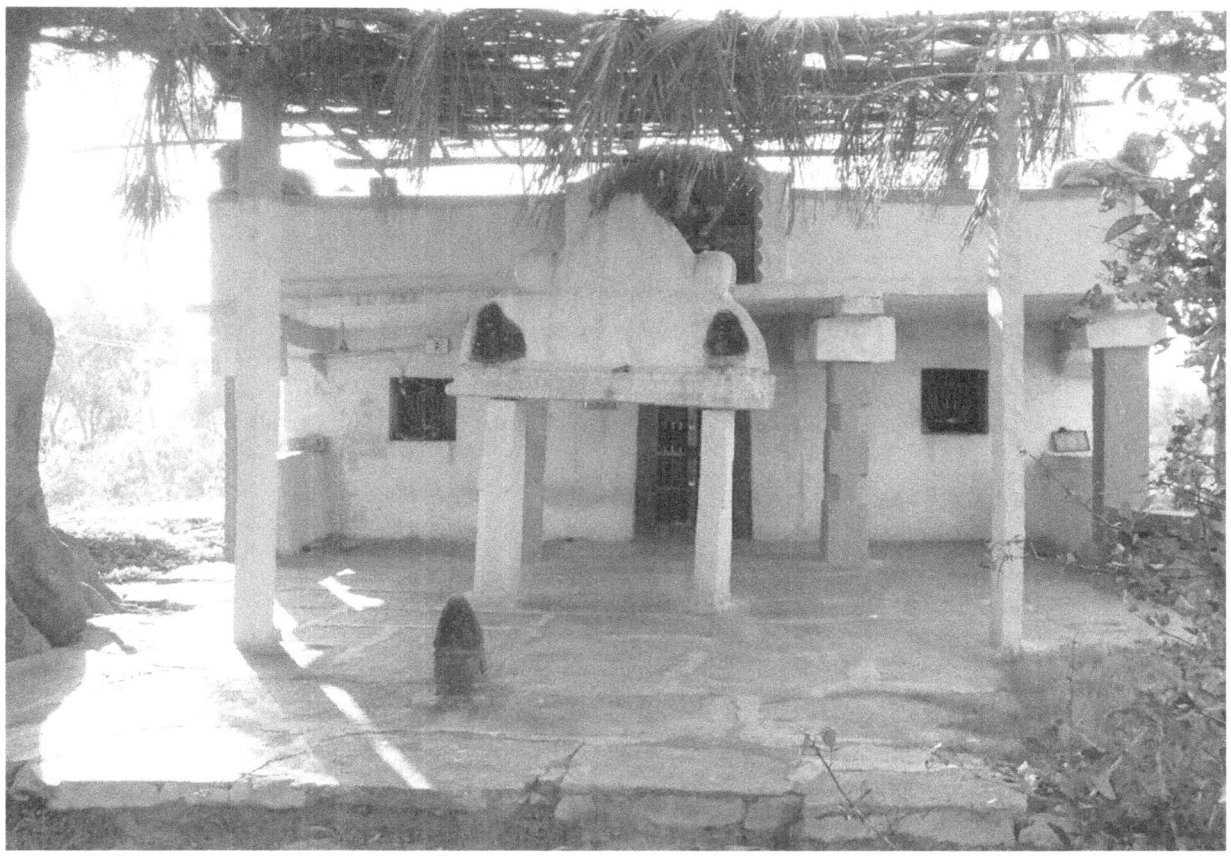

Plate 6-113: Chowdeswari Temple Vagata

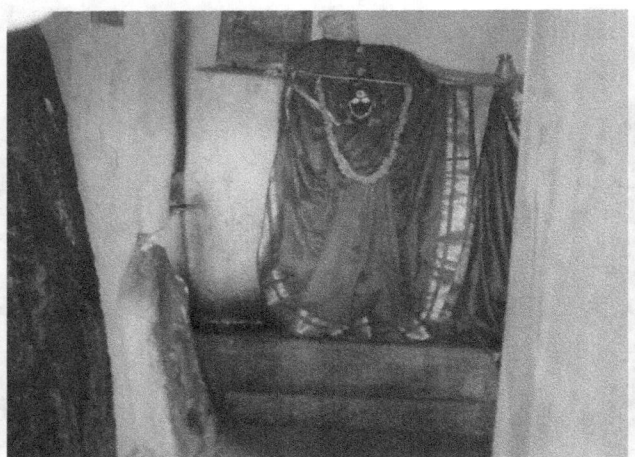 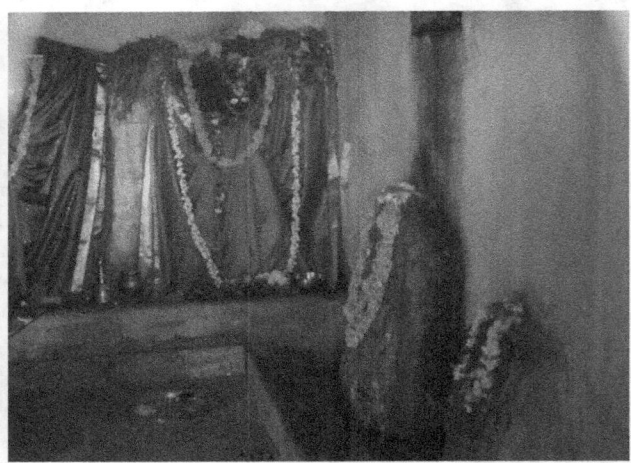

Plate 6-114: Images of Saptamatrikas in the Garbhagriha Chowdeswari Temple Vagata